Discovering Christ

Day By Day

Discovering Christ

Day By Day

Donald S. Fortner

Go *publications*

Go Publications

The Cairn, Hill Top, Eggleston, Co. Durham, DL12 0AU, ENGLAND

© Go Publications 2014

First Published 2014

British Library Cataloguing in Publication Data available

ISBN 978-1-908475-02-2

Printed and bound in Great Britain By Lightning Source UK Ltd.

Dedicated to:

The Saints of God at Danville, Kentucky

Grace Baptist Church of Danville

Reading the Word of God

Open thou mine eyes, that I may behold wondrous things out of thy law
(Psalm 119:18)

Many true believers, I fear, read the Word of God very little. As a result of their neglect of the Holy Scriptures they get little comfort from the Word when they need it, they are never really established in the truth of God, and their lives are a long, sad history of mistakes made because of their ignorance of God's revelation. This neglect of God's Word is as shameful as it is costly. If you have been negligent in this area, repent of your negligence at once and begin reading the Word of God this very day with regularity, seeking to know and worship him of whom the Book speaks.

Are you willing to read the Word of God? Do you want to profit from it? Here are seven suggestions which I picked up from J. C. Ryle several years ago that will help you to profit by the reading of the Word of God.

1. Read the Bible with an earnest desire to understand it. Do not be content to just read the words of Scripture. Seek to grasp the message they contain.

2. Read the Scriptures with a simple, childlike faith and humility. Believe what God reveals. Our reason must bow to God's revelation.

3. Read the Word with a spirit of obedience and self-application. Apply what God says to yourself and obey his will in all things.

4. Read the Holy Scriptures every day. We quickly lose the nourishment and strength of yesterday's bread. We must feed our souls daily upon the manna God has given us.

5. Read the whole Bible and read it in an orderly way. "All Scripture is given by inspiration of God and is profitable." I know of no better way to read the Bible than to start at the beginning and read straight through to the end, a portion every day, comparing Scripture with Scripture.

6. Read the Word of God fairly and honestly. As a general rule, any passage of Scripture means what it appears to mean. Interpret every passage in this simple manner, in its context.

7. Read the Bible with Christ constantly in view. The whole Book is about him. Look for him on every page. He is there. If you fail to see him there, you need to read that page again.

A Bible Reading Calendar

This Bible reading calendar was designed for our Church family in Danville to assist our congregation in reading through the Scriptures together on a daily basis each year.

Pastor Don Fortner
Grace Baptist Church of Danville
Danville, Kentucky

JANUARY

1 Genesis 1-3
2 Genesis 4-8
3 Genesis 9-11
4 Genesis 12-16
5 Genesis 17-19
6 Genesis 20-23
7 Genesis 24, 25
8 Genesis 26, 27
9 Genesis 28-30
10 Genesis 31, 32
11 Genesis 33-35
12 Genesis 36, 37
13 Genesis 38-40
14 Genesis 41, 42
15 Genesis 43, 44
16 Genesis 45-47
17 Genesis 48-50
18 Exodus 1-3
19 Exodus 4-6
20 Exodus 7-9
21 Exodus 10-12
22 Exodus 13, 14
23 Exodus 15-17
24 Exodus 18-21
25 Exodus 22-24
26 Exodus 25-27
27 Exodus 28, 29
28 Exodus 30-32

29 Exodus 33, 34
30 Exodus 35-37
31 Exodus 38-40

FEBRUARY

1 Leviticus 1-4
2 Leviticus 5-7
3 Leviticus 8-11
4 Leviticus 12, 13
5 Leviticus 14, 15
6 Leviticus 16-18
7 Leviticus 19-21
8 Leviticus 22, 23
9 Leviticus 24, 25
10 Leviticus 26, 27
11 Numbers 1, 2
12 Numbers 3, 4
13 Numbers 5-7
14 Numbers 8-10
15 Numbers 11-14
16 Numbers 15, 16
17 Numbers 17-19
18 Numbers 20-22
19 Numbers 23-26
20 Numbers 27-29
21 Numbers 30-32
22 Numbers 33-35
23 Numbers 36-Deuteronomy 1
24 Deuteronomy 2-4

FOREWORD

Our Almighty God has always honoured His promise to give to His church "pastors according to mine heart, which shall feed you with knowledge and understanding" of the "whole counsel of God". Every heaven-born child of God will be drawn to hear the Shepherd's voice and for them this voice is spirit and life.

Pastor Don Fortner's daily readings are encouragements to look to the Lord Jesus Christ as our Daily Bread and a spur to read through the whole Bible in a year, not as a yoke that binds, but as the revelation of life in Him.

The studies reveal the sinner's desperate need for salvation and God's gracious provision of His Son, the only Saviour. They illuminate the gospel of Jesus Christ clearly and distinctively, positively extolling its glorious truth and also exposing the many false "gospels" proliferating today.

In these devotions it will be seen each day that Christ is *the* message of all the scriptures; "they are they which testify of me". The gospel of Jesus Christ and Him crucified is vital both for the salvation of sinners and the life sustaining feeding of the saints, to the glory of God. "For thou art my lamp O LORD; and the LORD will lighten my darkness" (2 Samuel 22:29).

Look for the Lord Jesus in the Scriptures and you will find Him and find Him delightfully and graciously meeting the needs of your particular time and circumstances. You will find His Sovereign grace, His covenantal grace, His immutable grace, His saving grace, His triumphant grace; the glorious grace of Christ who is the Alpha and Omega of all blessings in time and eternity.

That I write this in Australia is testament to the fact that the Lord has used the gospel proclamations of Don Fortner to bless His scattered sheep throughout this world, well beyond the immediate responsibilities of the flock at Danville to whom we are thankful for the shared labours of their pastor.

May these devotions lead His people to see the Lord Jesus Christ more clearly in all the Scriptures and may our loving God cause His grace to live and grow in redeemed souls that they might "show forth thy lovingkindness in the morning, and thy faithfulness every night" (Psalm 92:2).

Angus Fisher
Shoalhaven Gospel Church,
Nowra, Australia

A personal note ...

More than thirty years ago, I put together a daily Bible reading schedule for our congregation, reading directly through the Word of God each year. We have followed the reading schedule as a congregation for many years. At the time I made the reading schedule, I thought to myself, "It might be very beneficial to have a book of devotional readings summarizing the chapters read each day, or focusing on some portion of each day's Scripture portion."

On January 1, 2013, I began the work you now have in your hands. The Lord graciously enabled me to finish it on December 31. I am very thankful to Go Publications for agreeing to publish it months before the readings were finished. A special word of thanks must be given to my wife, Shelby, who labours with me in everything I do. Along with her countless hours of unseen work every week in our offices, she proof reads and corrects misspelled words, grammatical errors, and incorrect punctuation. I thank God continually for that dear lady. She truly is, as she often says, her husband's third hand.

It is my prayer and hers that our God will be pleased to make each of these daily readings profitable to your soul by the blessing of his Spirit. If Christ is honoured and his people helped, my ambition in producing this volume will be fully accomplished. May you truly be found *Discovering Christ Day By Day*, as you read the Scriptures, using this volume as a companion to your daily readings.

Donald S. Fortner, Pastor
Grace Baptist Church of Danville,
Danville, Kentucky, USA

Discovering Christ Day By Day

January 1
Today's Reading: Genesis 1-3
"In the beginning God"
Genesis 1:1

In the opening chapters of the Inspired Volume we are given the seed of all divine truth. The opening words of the Book of God declare that which is essential to the understanding of all things: "In the beginning God". All things have their origin in the Lord God himself, the Triune Jehovah.

In the beginning God created all things. When he was done, he rested from his works, keeping the first sabbath and showing us the meaning of the sabbath of faith. We rest from our works, trusting Christ alone as our Saviour.

In the creation, ruin, and restoration of the natural creation, we are given a picture of grace and salvation. As the earth was created, became a ruin, and was restored by the moving of God's Spirit upon the face of the deep, so we (originally created in the image of God and then ruined by the sin and fall of our father Adam) are restored in Christ and made new by the sovereign operations of God the Holy Spirit.

In the creation of Adam we have a picture and type of Christ, the second Adam (Romans 5:14).

In the creation of Eve, we are shown the purpose for and origin of God's church. As Eve was taken out of Adam and made for him, so the church of God was born from Christ the second Adam, and was made for him.

In the fall, we see a picture of Christ's love for his church. Adam, because of his love for Eve, plunged himself into sin, death, and condemnation, so Christ, because of his love for us, plunged himself into sin, death, and condemnation as our Substitute, under the wrath of God.

In Genesis 3:9, the offended God seeks the offending sinner to show him mercy. In Genesis 3:15, God himself preached the first gospel sermon to needy sinners. In the kids slain to make a covering for Adam and Eve we see redemption and righteousness by the sacrifice of Christ the Lamb of God.

As we begin a new year, let us carry through the day, through the year, and through all the days of our lives the comfort of this blessed fact: "All things are of God". As all things have their beginning with the will, purpose, and decree of our heavenly Father, so all things are brought to pass by the wise, unerring hand of his good providence, and shall ultimately bring forth everlasting praise to him. "Of him, through him, and to him are all things."

Yet, there is more. "All things work together for good to them that love God, to them who are the called according to his purpose." All that has been, is and shall hereafter be is brought to pass by our God for the everlasting good of his elect. Let us find in this blessed truth comfort for every sorrow, strength to endure every trial, courage to face every foe, and joy to lighten the load of our daily pilgrimage through this world. Let these things inspire our hearts to heed the admonition of 1 Thessalonians 5:18, "In everything give thanks: for this is the will of God in Christ Jesus concerning you."

January 2
Today's Reading: Genesis 4-8
Distinguishing Grace
Genesis 6:8

What sad consequences there are to sin! That horrible heart-hatred of God which resides in the hearts of Adam's sons and daughters works havoc in the earth and will bring us all down to hell in the end unless God steps in to save. The only hope there is for fallen, depraved, helpless sinners is the omnipotent intervention of God's irresistible grace.

Blessed be his name, God does intervene to save! He does not have to save. No mortal will ever seek salvation from him until first he is sought of him. But God has, in indescribable, infinite mercy, chosen to save a people for his own name's sake; and save them he will.

Cain And Abel
Beginning with its opening chapters and throughout the pages of Inspiration, the Book of God is filled with pictures of our heavenly Father's free, sovereign, saving grace. Adam had two sons: Cain and Abel. God passed by Cain and chose Abel. Abel is the one to whom God revealed himself in Christ, evident by the fact that Abel brought God a blood sacrifice, which God provided, and thereby Abel found acceptance with the holy Lord God. The only way sinful man can approach the holy Lord God is through the merits of Christ, the sin-atoning Substitute, who is both God and the substitutionary sacrifice God has provided.

The only difference there is between the fallen sons of Adam is the difference God makes (1 Corinthians 4:7). The only thing that made Abel to differ from Cain was the fact that God chose Abel, revealed himself to Abel, and called Abel.

Enoch
We see the distinction of grace in Enoch, too. "Enoch walked with God", when few men did. He pleased God. And he escaped death because God took him. How did he walk with God? He walked with God the only way any sinner can walk with God, by

20

faith in Christ. How did he please God? He pleased God the only way any sinner can please God, by faith in Christ. Walk with God by faith in Christ, and you, too, shall escape death (John 11:26; Revelation 20:6).

Noah
"Noah found grace in the eyes of the Lord." The whole world was lost. The whole world was corrupt. The whole of Adam's race was degenerate and walked in wickedness, provoking the wrath of God. But God, in great pity, mercy, and compassion, showed himself gracious to one man. "Noah found grace in the eyes of the Lord." God spared Noah. God saved Noah. Through him, God preserved his family, preserved our race, and thus preserved his elect for all generations to come!

> Grace! 'Tis a charming sound!
> Harmonious to the ear.
> Heaven with the echo shall resound,
> And all the earth shall hear!

January 3
Today's Reading: Genesis 9-11
"I will remember my covenant"
Genesis 9:15

How wondrously our God displays himself in grace. From among a race of rebels who deserve his wrath, he has chosen to save a people for the praise of the glory of his grace! He chose to save his own, loved by him with an everlasting love in Christ. And from the very beginning, he has shown us the blessed good news of the gospel (grace to sinners through a Substitute) in type, picture, and prophecy.

The Ark
When God was about to destroy the whole human race (except for eight chosen souls), he provided an ark for the saving of his chosen. What a blessed picture of Christ our Saviour and of our salvation in him! It was an ark of God's providing. God called Noah and his family into the ark, an ark built specifically for him. God shut them in! Then God poured out the fury of his wrath upon all the earth. All the wrath of the Almighty fell upon the ark. Yet, not one drop of the water of God's terror fell upon Noah, his wife, his sons or their wives. The ark absorbed it all.

That is what Christ, the Ark of our salvation, did for us. The holy Lord God prepared him and sent him specifically for the saving of his people (Matthew 1:21, Hebrews 10:10-14). He put us in Christ in electing grace before the world began

(Ephesians 1:3-6). At Calvary, when he sacrificed his darling Son for us, the holy Lord God poured out all the fury of his wrath and justice upon all his chosen to the full satisfaction of his justice,. But Christ bore all the hell of God's wrath alone. Not so much as an angry look falls upon us, his redeemed.

The Rainbow
When Noah came out of the ark, God put a rainbow in the clouds of the sky and promised never to destroy the earth by water again. God told Noah the bow would be a token of his covenant, and promised to remember his "everlasting covenant". As it was God's covenant with Noah that preserved the world from another flood, so it is God's everlasting covenant (the bow encircling his throne in Revelation chapter 4) that preserves the world for the salvation of his elect, because he is not willing that any chosen sinner for whom Christ died should perish (2 Peter 3:9).

God's Promise
How we ought to rejoice in covenant love! Let us ever give thanks to our great God for his purpose of grace, his performance of grace, and his perseverance in grace toward his covenant people! Here is our comfort, encouragement, joy, and confidence in this world. God says, "I will remember my covenant". Noah's drunkenness would not make him forget his covenant. Ham's exposure of his father's sin would not alter God's purpose of grace toward that man who "found grace in the eyes of the Lord". Nimrod's mighty rebellion and man's proud attempt to build a fortress to protect himself from God's wrath at Babel changed nothing. So it is to this day, God remembers his covenant and saves his own for the glory of his own great name.

January 4
Today's Reading: Genesis 12-16
Christ Our Priest And Our Sacrifice
Genesis 14:18-20

The Book of God often reveals the sinful deeds of righteous people, teaching us plainly and repeatedly that God's elect in this world, though washed in the blood of Christ, though robed in his righteousness, though forgiven of all sin, though born of his Spirit, are all sinners still (1 John 1:8-10). Abram, called of God and brought out of Ur, in time of trial went down to Egypt for help. There he shamed himself greatly. No sooner did he come back to Bethel and worship God for his goodness than a strife arose between his herdsmen and Lot's. It was a strife between brethren, a strife about cattle! Righteous Lot "pitched his tent toward Sodom".

Discovering Christ Day By Day

Our Melchizedek

In Genesis 14 we see Melchizedek coming to Abram. This man, Melchizedek, was the king of Salem and "the priest of the most high God". This Melchizedek is, at least typically, the Lord Jesus Christ, our great High Priest (Hebrews 6:20). Let us, this day, meditate upon this blessed, glorious, soul-cheering fact. The Lord Jesus Christ, the Son of God, is our great High Priest. He is the sinner's Advocate in heaven (1 John 2:1, 2).

> Arise, my soul, arise!
> Shake off thy guilty fears!
> The bleeding sacrifice
> In thy behalf appears!

The bread and wine Melchizedek brought to Abram speak of the body and blood of our dear Saviour. His body (his humanity) was especially prepared of God so that he could come into this world to obey God for us and die in our stead at Calvary. His righteousness (his obedience to the law), and his blood (his satisfaction of justice), our great Melchizedek pleads for us in heaven. "Thanks be unto God for his unspeakable gift".

Justified By Faith

In Genesis 15 we see Abram, a man to whom God revealed himself, to whom God promised a Saviour, believing God. Standing in the midst of the sacrifice (looking to Christ), God made a covenant with him. "He believed in the LORD; and he counted it to him for righteousness". Abram was justified, justified from eternity in the Lamb slain from the foundation of the world, and now justified in his own conscience by faith in Christ, declared righteous before God by God himself. The righteousness of Christ was imputed to him.

So it is with all God's elect. Our only righteousness before God is that which God himself gives to all who believe on the Lord Jesus Christ. We are made the righteousness of God in Christ. It is righteousness, without works, received by faith. Let us ever give thanks to God for his grace. Believing sinners are "justified freely by his grace through the redemption that is in Christ".

January 5
Today's Reading: Genesis 17-19
"Is anything too hard for the Lord?"
Genesis 18:14

We should endeavour, with the reading of Holy Scripture each day, to remember what we have read so that we can meditate upon it throughout the day. As we read the Word of God and meditate upon it, let us pray that God the Holy Spirit will graciously apply it to our hearts and lives and inspire us by his Word to consecrate ourselves to the Lord Jesus Christ. To that end, let us meditate today upon seven specific things in the passage we have read.

1. God's Promise
The Lord God promised Abraham a Seed with whom he would establish his covenant in the earth and in whom a chosen multitude scattered through all the nations of the earth would be blessed. That Seed promised to Abraham is Christ our Saviour. Abraham seems to have understood clearly that God's promise extended far beyond Isaac to One coming in whom he himself would find everlasting righteousness, acceptance, and blessedness before God. He believed God could do all he promised, though God's promise was totally contrary to all appearance. May God give us grace to trust him and look to Christ for everything (1 Corinthians 1:30, 31).

2. Circumcision
What was the meaning of circumcision? Why was this painful act practised and required throughout the Old Testament? Circumcision was a token, or sign of God's covenant. It was a symbolic cleansing, by cutting away the filth of the foreskin of the flesh. Any who were not circumcised among the Jews were to be permanently severed from the people. All these things tell us (as does the New Testament in Colossians 2:11) that circumcision pointed to and portrayed the work of God the Holy Spirit in the new birth, by which all who are born of God are sealed (experimentally) into the kingdom of God and the blessedness of his covenant people.

3. A Father's Prayer
When Abraham knew God's gracious purpose for Isaac, he feared for Ishmael. He cried to God, "O that Ishmael might live before thee". Blessed are those children whose father's seek the welfare of their souls above all other things.

4. Submissive Faith
Though he loved Ishmael and sought the same grace for Ishmael as God promised to Isaac, when the Lord God made his will known to Abraham (17:21), even regarding his son Ishmael, believing God, Abraham bowed his will to God's will. May God give us such grace!

5. Hospitality
Abraham's example of hospitality is used in the book of Hebrews to urge us to graciously entertain others in our homes. Believers who open their homes, their families, and their hearts to God's pilgrims in this world often find those they entertain to be divinely sent messengers of grace, by whom they are blessed (Hebrews 13:1, 2).

6. Intercessory Prayer
The Lord God spared Lot when he destroyed Sodom because Abraham prayed for him. May God the Holy Spirit teach us this day that "the effectual, fervent prayer of a righteous man availeth much".

7. Sovereign Grace
How marvellously the deliverance of Lot from Sodom displays God's sovereign, saving grace in and by Christ Jesus. As the angels could not destroy that place until Lot was safely delivered, so the Lord God will not destroy this world until all his chosen have been saved by his grace (2 Peter 3:9). As God sent his messengers to Lot when the time for his deliverance had come, so the Lord God graciously sends his appointed messengers to chosen sinners when the "time of love" for them has come (Romans 10:17, 18). When "Lot lingered", grace snatched him from Sodom, as a brand from the burning. O Lord God, we praise you this day for the blessed violence of your grace, by which you saved us, even when we would not be saved!

January 6
Today's Reading: Genesis 20-23
"Jehovah-Jireh"
Genesis 22:14

What marvellous things we have seen today! Our great God in his infinite sovereignty withholds the wickedness of men when it pleases him to do so, as he kept Abimelech from defiling Sarah. What wickedness he allows, he overrules for the good of his people and the praise of his name (Psalm 76:10). He always fulfils his word and promise. Nothing hinders him. What men call "laws of nature" are his laws. When it pleases him, he can easily make the barren womb of an old woman fruitful. When sinners, like Hagar in the wilderness are in utter despair, God Almighty comes in grace, opens their eyes, and brings them to drink from Christ the Well of Living Water. And when God sends his saints through great trials, he does so to make himself known in great goodness.

25

Discovering Christ Day By Day

The Lord God revealed himself to Abraham in many ways; but no revelation given to that man who was the friend of God was more delightful or instructive than the name by which God revealed himself to Abraham at Mount Moriah, the name "Jehovah-Jireh".

Jehovah-Jireh might be translated by three expressions: "the Lord will see", "the Lord will provide", and "the Lord will be seen". However the name is translated, it expresses the idea of God seeing and being seen. For God, to see is to provide. By this name, Jehovah-Jireh, God our Father would have us to know that he sees our need and faithfully provides for our need, and that he will be seen in the provision he makes. Without question, this encourages our hearts to trust his daily providence. But the thing which inspired Abraham to raise up this memorial to God's honour was the substitution of the ram to die in the place of his son, Isaac, and Isaac's deliverance from death. Jehovah-Jireh is a name of our God which describes his saving grace in Christ Jesus.

The Lord Will See
Jehovah-Jireh means "the Lord will see". Our Father, from eternity, saw the need into which we would fall by the sin of Adam in the garden and by our own iniquity, transgression and sin, in time. And with the foresight of divine love, he provided his Son, the Lord Jesus Christ to be our Substitute in the covenant of grace. When the fulness of time was come, God met our need by sending Christ to die. And when God, by his Spirit, created a need in our hearts for Christ, causing us to seek him, he gave his Son to us. Today, by his free grace, God gives his Son to all who need him.

The Lord Will Provide
Jehovah-Jireh means "the Lord will provide". Jehovah-Jireh was Abraham's testimony to the goodness and grace of God in providing a ram to die in Isaac's place. And it is our testimony of praise to God for providing Christ to be our Substitute. But this name also implies that our God, who gave us his Son, will also freely give us all things in his Son (Romans 8:32).

The Lord Will Be Seen
Jehovah-Jireh means "the Lord will be seen". "In the mount of the Lord it shall be seen". God is seen in the sacrifice of his Son at Mount Calvary. And God shall be seen in the face of his Provision, Christ Jesus, upon Mount Zion in heaven. All this was included in Abraham's prophecy. All who see God in Christ, the crucified Substitute, who died in our place upon Mount Calvary, shall see God face to face in Christ Jesus, who is himself Jehovah-Jireh!

26

January 7
Today's Reading: Genesis 24, 25
Five Wells
Genesis 25:11

Isaac was pre-eminently the man of the well. His life revolved around five wells. These five wells are named for us because, typically, they represent the experiences of God's elect in this world from which all of God's people must drink.

Lahairoi
When Isaac came down from Mount Moriah he dwelt by the well Lahairoi (Genesis 25:11) in the presence of God. Lahairoi means "The Living One who sees me". At Mount Moriah Isaac had been redeemed and saved from death by Jehovah-Jireh. Now he dwelt in the presence of his great God. And every sinner redeemed by Christ shall, at God's appointed time, be brought to live in the presence of God by faith.

Esek
While he dwelt in Gerar's dry valley he dug a well that the Philistines filled with sand. Isaac called that well Esek (Genesis 26:20). Esek means "strife". As long as you and I live in this dry valley among the Philistines of this world, we will have to drink the bitter waters of Esek. "In the world ye shall have tribulation" (John 16:33).

Sitnah
Isaac left Esek and dug another well; but the Philistines were still around. Again there was strife. Isaac called that well Sitnah (Genesis 26:21). Sitnah means "hatred". Our Lord Jesus told us plainly, "Ye shall be hated of all men for my name's sake" (Matthew 10:22). It is impossible to confess Christ before his enemies and not be hated by those who hate him.

Rehoboth
Isaac left Sitnah and dug the well Rehoboth (Genesis 26:22), which means "spacious abundance". He was God's child and God made room for him, abundantly supplying his needs, according to his own riches in glory by Christ Jesus. And he will do the same for you and me (Philippians 4:19). We never have reason to fear the world or compromise with it. God our Saviour will provide for his own!

Shebah
At last, Isaac came to the place where he had worshipped God with his father Abraham, and dug again the well Shebah (Genesis 26:33), which means "fulness" or "an oath". Walking in the old paths, seeking the good way, looking to Christ, trusting Christ, obeying Christ, Isaac found all fulness in Christ and found God's oath and promise sure. So will we, as we walk with Christ (Jeremiah 6:16).

January 8
Today's Reading: Genesis 26, 27
"Behold, a ladder set up on the earth"
Genesis 28:12

The ladder Jacob saw in his dream was our Saviour, the Lord Jesus Christ (John 1:51). When the Lord God revealed his Son to Jacob, he revealed him as a ladder. What an instructive and helpful representation that is of our Saviour. The Lord Jesus Christ is made of God unto us a ladder!

Christ The Ladder
Here is a Ladder reaching from earth to heaven. Jacob saw the foot of it upon the earth, "and the top of it reached to heaven". This represents the two natures of our Redeemer. He is both God and man in one glorious Person, as fully God as though he were not man and as fully man as though he were not God. Though he stood upon the earth as a man, he never ceased to be God. He never left the bosom of the Father (John 1:18; 3:13).

The God-man
As a man, he was set up on the earth (Galatians 4:4, 5). As God, he was always in heaven, the eternally begotten Son of the Father, infinite, eternal, incomprehensible, and unchangeable (John 1:14; 3:13). The union of these two natures, God and man, in one Person is the mystery of all mysteries (1 Timothy 3:16). That the glory of Christ's Godhead did not destroy the weakness of his manhood, nor the weakness of his manhood destroy the glory of his Godhead is incomprehensibly mysterious. If Christ would redeem us, he had to have a body in which to bear our sins to suffer and die as our Substitute. He had to have a body and nature like ours. A man he must be who would redeem man, because it was man who sinned. Because man sinned, man must suffer for sin. For this reason, God the Holy Spirit prepared a body for God the Son in the womb of the virgin (Hebrews 10:5).
　　It was our Saviour's Godhood which gave infinite merit, virtue, and efficacy to the sufferings of his manhood. Christ is both God and man, because God could not suffer and man could not satisfy; but the God-man both suffered the wrath of God and satisfied the justice of God when he bled and died as the sinners' Substitute upon the cursed tree. Moreover, it was Christ's Godhood which supported and sustained his manhood in all his sufferings. Manhood could never have borne the agony of Gethsemane and the torments of Calvary had it not been that the man who suffered is also the eternal God.

Our Mediator
Our Mediator must be both God and man so that he might bring God and man together. He must be God that he might deal with God, which man as man is not fit to do. He must be man that he might deal with man, which God in his holiness could not

28

do without consuming the sinful creature. "Thanks be unto God for his unspeakable gift". This is the meaning of our Saviour's incarnation. Immanuel is God with us, God in our nature. Were he not both God and man, he could not be Jesus our Saviour (Matthew 1:21-23).

The angels of God went up and down on the ladder which Jacob saw. Even so, we are able to ascend to God in heaven only by the Lord Jesus Christ (John 14:6); and it is by and through Christ that God comes down to us. God Almighty meets with, deals with, and blesses sinners only in Christ. The Lord God stood above the ladder and made all his promises of grace to Jacob; so all the promises and blessings of God's grace come to sinners through Christ. All spiritual blessings, all the promises of eternal life, all the glory of heaven is in Christ. All things come to chosen sinners through Christ, the Mediator, our Ladder (Ephesians 1:3-14).

January 9
Today's Reading: Genesis 28-30
"The LORD is in this place"
Genesis 28:16

We read today of Jacob being in the place where God made himself known. What could be more blessed? Blessed is that place where God meets with chosen sinners. That one place where he has promised to do so is in the assembly of his saints, gathered in the name of Christ, to worship him (Matthew 18:20).

A Danger Threatened
The first and chief glory of any local church is the manifest presence of God. Without this, our preaching, our prayers, our hymns, our gifts, and our works are all vain. If our God meets with us, our meetings are truly fruitful. If he does not, they are empty rituals. When our Lord threatened the church at Ephesus with the removal of her candlestick, he was not referring to the destruction of her buildings, or even of the congregation. He was threatening the removal of his presence. No greater evil can be brought upon a congregation than for God to write Ichabod upon her and forsake her.

A Blessing Desired
The manifest presence of God is the work and gift of God the Holy Spirit. It is bestowed upon us in the house of God and effectually brought forth by him through the ordinances of public worship. By our prayers and hymns of praise, by the reading of Holy Scripture, and by the preaching of the gospel, God our Saviour visits his church in grace. By the preaching of the gospel, God saves chosen, redeemed sinners and instructs, comforts, corrects and edifies his saints. When we come to the house of God, let us come seeking his manifest presence.

Many attempt to fake the manifestation of God's presence by clapping their hands, singing repetitive choruses, calling for audible responses from the audience, playing on the emotions of people, etc.. The church service may be very active, full of entertainment, excitement, and emotion, yet not one soul will afterwards retain any serious, lasting impressions of grace.

The Temple Of God
The manifest presence of God may be found where there is no show of religion or emotionalism. The worship may be very simple by design, the preaching bold, straightforward, and dogmatic, with nothing to impress, excite, or even attract the flesh; but God is there and the sons of Jacob know it. Wherever men and women meet in the name of Christ, trusting his blood and righteousness alone, seeking the will of God and the glory of God, waiting upon the almighty work of God the Holy Spirit, there God is. In that place, the very temple of God (1 Corinthians 3:16), God shows his glory in redemption, meets with sinners in mercy, and works his works of grace in the hearts of chosen sinners. The building may be modest and the congregation small, but that truly is the house of God. Let us make it our business to be found in that place (Psalm 1:1).

"Pray for the peace of Jerusalem (the church and family of God): they shall prosper that love thee. Peace be within thy walls and prosperity within thy palaces. For my brethren and companions' sake, I will now say, Peace be within thee. Because of the house of the LORD our God I will seek thy good".

January 10
Today's Reading: Genesis 31, 32
"Jacob was left alone"
Genesis 32:24

Esau was coming to meet Jacob with four hundred men and Jacob was terrified, fearing that he was coming to kill him. Earlier in the day he kissed his wives and children good-bye and sent them across the brook Jabbok with all his earthly possessions. "And Jacob was left alone". Confused, helpless, and afraid, he sat down and waited to die by the hand of his only brother. His plotting, scheming, and manipulating was over. He was shut up to the sovereign power and will of God. Like Israel at the Red Sea and Jonah in the whale, Jacob was totally dependent upon God to deliver him, and he knew it.

Discovering Christ Day By Day

Painful Experience
"Jacob was left alone", because those whom God is pleased to save, to whom he reveals his mercy, love, and grace in Christ must be brought down and made to know their utter inability. God's grace and God's work leaves no room for boasting and glorying in the flesh.

Jacob appeared to be in a terribly miserable condition; but he was in a truly blessed condition. To be left alone with God is the only way we can gain a true knowledge of ourselves. No man will ever truly see the corruption of his nature, the depravity of his heart, and the sinfulness of his deeds until he is left alone with God. It does not matter what we think of ourselves, or what others think of us, the great question is: What does God think of us? We can never discover the answer to that question until we are "left alone". Away from the world, away from self, away from the thoughts, reasonings, imaginations, and emotions of our proud flesh, and alone with God, thus, and only thus, can we get a real understanding of who and what we are.

Blessed Isolation
Blessed is that sinner who is left alone with God! Isolation is the forerunner of revelation, grace, salvation, and blessing. Before God saves, he always separates. Before God speaks comfort to the hearts of chosen sinners, he allures them into the wilderness alone with him (Hosea 2:14). Before the Lord Jesus spoke pardon to the adulterous woman, she found herself alone with the incarnate God (John 8:9). Before Saul of Tarsus was granted God's salvation, he was separated from his companions by light from heaven and the voice of the Son of God (Acts 9:3-8). Alone with God on the Damascus road, Saul met himself and met his Saviour. And when Jacob was left alone, the God-man, his Saviour, revealed himself to him and blessed him.

> Come, Lord, Thy grace and power impart,
> Revive my cold, languishing heart!
> My heart's affection, Saviour, move,
> To Thee alone in ardent love!
>
> Unrivalled Sovereign, reign within,
> Subdue my native lusts and sin!
> O Saviour, form Thyself in me,
> And let me live alone for Thee!

31

January 11
Today's Reading: Genesis 33-35
"I have enough"
Genesis 33:9-11

Both Jacob and Esau said, "I have enough". Their words were the same; but the meaning was not even similar. Those three words displayed a great, great difference between these two brothers. What was the difference between these two men? When we understand the difference between Jacob and Esau, we will understand the difference between God's elect and the unbeliever in all ages, ties, and circumstances.

Esau's Contentment
Esau was a lost, unregenerate, reprobate man, a man who found everything he wanted in the world. I understand the teachings of Holy Scripture regarding the sovereign, eternal, unalterable purpose of our God and rejoice in it. However, Esau was a lost man, not because God would not save him, but because he chose the world and the lusts of his flesh rather than Christ. The fact is, if you perish in your sins, if you die without Christ, it will be your own fault alone, no one else's. You will not be able to blame your eternal ruin on the purpose of God. If you are saved, that will be God's work and God's work alone. If you are lost, that will be your fault and your fault alone! Esau despised Christ and the gospel of God's free, saving grace in Christ. That is what was represented in the birthright he despised (Genesis 25:30-34). God left Esau to himself. Because Esau despised God's birthright, because he despised God's Son, because he counted Christ a common worthless thing, God left him to himself. Moreover, the Lord God put the world in Esau's heart to blind him (Ecclesiastes 3:11).

Jacob's Contentment
Jacob was a man blessed of God as the object of his everlasting free grace in Christ. Remember, that all that the Scriptures say about Jacob as the object of God's grace is true of all God's elect. We are the sons of Jacob. As such, we gladly acknowledge that the only difference between Jacob and Esau is the difference that grace has made. "By the grace of God I am what am". This is the difference between Jacob and Esau. This is the difference between all who believe and those who do not believe (1 Corinthians 4:7). God loved Jacob (Romans 9:10-26). The Lord chose Jacob (Psalm 135:4; 2 Thessalonians 2:13; John 15:16). The Lord stopped Jacob in his way and revealed himself to him at Bethel. You will recall that back in Genesis 28 Jacob was running away. But he ran smack into God! He ran into God because God put himself in the way! God met Jacob at Bethel (the house of God) and revealed himself, his grace, his mercy, and his glory in Christ. God our Saviour, the Lord Jesus Christ, wrestled with Jacob, made him confess who and what he was, and gave him a new name (Genesis 32:24-31). Beloved, now are we the sons of God. In Christ all things are new. Christ has given us a new name, put us in a new family, and made us partakers of a new covenant! The Lord God led Jacob all his life. He said, "I am with thee and will keep

32

thee in all places whither thou goest, for I will not leave thee until I have done that which I have spoken to thee of"! That is precisely God's promise to us (1 Thessalonians 5:24; Philippians 1:6; Hebrews 13:5). Let us lean heavily upon it throughout the day.

January 12
Today's Reading: Genesis 36, 37
Joseph
Genesis 37:5

Today, we have been introduced to Joseph. In the next few days we will read the story of this remarkable man, as we conclude the reading of the book of beginnings. As we read the last fourteen chapters of Genesis, it is difficult to miss the spiritual lessons revealed in the life of Joseph. Here are five of those lessons. Let us lay them to heart today, and remember them, as we read of God's wondrous works in the life of Joseph in the following chapters of Genesis.

Divine Sovereignty
Our God is absolutely sovereign (Genesis 45:5; 50:20). Nothing happened to Joseph by accident. God, who is above all, ruled and overruled all the events recorded in these chapters (all creatures and all their actions, good and bad) to accomplish his will and purpose concerning Joseph and his people. All men and women, righteous and wicked, all the elements of nature, the weather, the crops, and the cattle, even the dreams of a pagan king were used of God to accomplish his purpose.

The World's Folly
The wisdom of this world is utter foolishness (1 Corinthians 1:20). In Joseph's time Egypt, the land of the Pharaohs, was the most advanced civilization in the world, the centre of learning, science, and culture. But the Egyptians were idolaters. Hence, they had no true wisdom. What light they had was darkness. All their wise men could not decipher the meaning of Pharaoh's dreams and tell him what God was about to do. Pharaoh had to turn to Joseph, the only man in the land who knew God, for instruction.

True Wisdom
All true wisdom and knowledge begin with faith (Psalm 111:10; Proverbs 9:10). "The secret of the Lord is with them that fear him" (Psalm 25:14). God makes his counsels, purposes, and truth known, not to the wise, the mighty, and the great people of this world, but to them that believe him.

Divine Providence
All things work together for good to God's elect (Romans 8:28). Joseph's life is a demonstration of the goodness of God's providence toward his elect. Too often we become so occupied with our present circumstances that we forget God's promise. That should never happen. "Judge not the Lord by feeble sense, but trust him for his grace. Behind the frowning providence he hides a smiling face". Remember, "Better is the end of a thing than the beginning thereof" (Ecclesiastes 7:8).

Great Honour
God honours those who honour him (1 Samuel 2:30). Joseph was a faithful man. In the midst of great adversity, though he had no godly companions, living in a heathen land among idolaters, even in Egypt, Joseph walked with God. And there God so honoured him that he said, "God hath made me forget all my toil" and "caused me to be fruitful in the land of my affliction" (Genesis 41:51, 52).

January 13
Today's Reading: Genesis 38-40
"Joseph was brought down to Egypt"
Genesis 39:1

We saw Joseph as a type of Christ yesterday. As Joseph was brought down to Egypt to save his people, so the Son of God, our Lord Jesus Christ, was brought down to this earth as a man to save his people. In Genesis 39 the Holy Spirit continues with the history of this eminent type of our Saviour, giving us several more typical aspects of his life.

A Servant
Joseph was made a servant (Genesis 39:1). He who was the beloved son of his father's house was brought down to Egypt as a lowly servant. Here Joseph portrays Jehovah's righteous Servant, the Lord Jesus Christ (Isaiah 42:1-4; Exodus 21:5, 6; Isaiah 50:5-7; Psalm 40:6-10; Hebrews 10:5-14; Philippians 2:5-11). The Lord Jesus Christ voluntarily became his Father's Servant to redeem and save his people (Isaiah 50:5-7). He is that One to whom the law of God referred in Exodus 21:5, 6. The bond slave who refused his freedom because he loved his master, his wife, and his children was typical of our Saviour. In the covenant of grace, before the world began, the Son of God voluntarily made himself his Father's Servant, because he loved his Father, and his chosen family.

It was in this capacity that he spoke in Psalm 40:5-10. Hebrews 10:5-14 explains that the words of our Lord in Psalm 40 referred to his obedience unto death as our Substitute, by which the Lord of glory obtained the everlasting salvation of his chosen. Our great Saviour came into the world in the fulness of time to fulfil his covenant engagements as Jehovah's Servant. And when he had fulfilled those covenant engagements, his people were redeemed, sanctified, and perfected forever by his finished work. This is the basis of our Lord's exaltation and glory, the means by which he obtained the monarchy of the universe as the God-man, our Mediator (Psalm 2:8; John 17:1-5; Romans 14:9; Philippians 2:5-11).

God With him

"The Lord was with Joseph" (Genesis 39:2). Behold, a greater than Joseph is here. Our Lord Jesus Christ is that man who is himself God Almighty, Immanuel, the incarnate God, one with the Father, full of grace and truth (John 1:1-3, 10, 11, 14, 16, 17). Not only was God with him and he with God, the incarnate Christ is God with us.

Prosperous Servant

"The Lord made all that he did to prosper in his hand" (Genesis 39:3). Again, Joseph portrayed and typified our Lord Jesus Christ. Christ, as Jehovah's Servant is that truly blessed Man, that Man who walked not in the counsel of the ungodly, that Man who stood not in the way of sinners, that Man who sat not in the seat of the scornful, that Man whose delight was in the law of the Lord. What does the Lord God tell us about that blessed Man? "Whatsoever he doeth shall prosper ... And the pleasure of the LORD shall prosper in his hand".

A Trusted Servant

Potiphar trusted Joseph with everything he had and put everything into his hands (Genesis 39:4). Our Saviour is that Servant whom the Father has trusted with everything, into whose hands he has put everything he has. The Father trusted the Son as his Servant, putting his glory, his people, the world, and all things in it into his hands (Ephesians 1:12; John 17:2).

A Blessing

"The Lord blessed the Egyptian's house for Joseph's sake" (Genesis 39:5). Egypt was altogether insignificant, except for the fact that Joseph was there, his people must sojourn there, and redemption must be accomplished there. Therefore, for Joseph's sake, God blessed the Egyptians in providence. So, too, this world, all its nations and all its people, are altogether insignificant, except for the fact that Christ has his people here. Here redemption and grace must be performed. Therefore, God blesses the world and preserves it for Christ's sake (Isaiah 65:8, 9; 2 Peter 3:9); but his object is the salvation of his people. He does not hesitate to sacrifice men and nations for the people of his love (Isaiah 43:3, 4).

A Faithful Servant

Joseph was a faithful servant. When he was tempted to sin, Joseph proved himself a faithful man, true to his master in all things (Genesis 39:6-12). The Lord Jesus Christ, our Saviour, the Son of God, was tempted in all points like as we are, yet without sin. He who was made to be sin for us, that we might be made the righteousness of God in him, knew no sin. He was holy, harmless, undefiled, and separate from sinners.

Discovering Christ Day By Day

A Slandered Servant
Joseph was falsely accused of evil (Genesis 39:16-18). Joseph was accused of crimes he did not commit. When the chief priests, elders, and all the Jewish council did their best to find some charge against our Saviour, they found none. At last, they hired two false witnesses to perjure themselves by bringing false charges against him, and accused the Lamb of God of insurrection (Matthew 26:59-61).

Numbered With Transgressors
Joseph was numbered with transgressors (Genesis 39:19-23). It is obvious that Potiphar did not believe his wife's accusations. Had he believed her, he would probably have had Joseph executed for attempting to rape his wife. Yet, to save face before men, he delivered Joseph to prison. That is exactly what happened in the case of our Lord Jesus Christ. Pilate knew that our Master was totally innocent of the charges trumped up against him. He knew that the Jews wanted him crucified simply because of their spiteful envy. Yet, to save face with men, he delivered the Son of God over to the hands of the soldiers to crucify him as a common criminal. Not only was our Lord Jesus Christ numbered with transgressors, he died in the transgressors' place, as our Substitute (Isaiah 53:7-12).

Our reading today has been more lengthy than normal. I trust every word has been blessed of God, to set our hearts upon our great Saviour, to love, adore, and praise him. In all these things, Joseph was a type of our Saviour, the Man whom the Lord God sent to save us, whom he has made Lord of his house and Ruler of all his Substance. "He sent a man before them, even Joseph, who was sold for a servant: Whose feet they hurt with fetters: he was laid in iron: Until the time that his word came: the word of the LORD tried him. The king sent and loosed him; even the ruler of the people, and let him go free. He made him lord of his house, and ruler of all his substance" (Psalm 105:17-21).

January 14
Today's Reading: Genesis 41, 42
Joseph opening the storehouses
Genesis 41:56

Joseph opened the storehouses in Egypt by royal authority (Genesis 41:41, 44, 45). Pharaoh gave all things into Joseph's hands, all food, all authority, all power. When the people came to Pharaoh for anything, he said, "Go to Joseph". Behold! A greater than Joseph is here! By God's royal design and decree, all things pertaining to life and godliness (all grace, all mercy, all salvation, all life, and all heaven) have been given into the hands of the Lord Jesus Christ. God the Father has put all things in Christ

36

(John 3:35, 36). All power and authority belong to him (John 17:3). All the fulness of the Godhead is in Christ (Colossians 2:9, 10). All the fulness of grace and glory are in Christ (John 1:16; Colossians 1:19). The only way any sinner can get anything from God is to go to Christ. He has everything (Ephesians 1:3, 4). Why? "For it pleased God". God is determined "that in all things Christ might have the preeminence".

A Worthy Man
Joseph was the only fit person to open the storehouses (Genesis 41:53-55). He was the only one who knew what was going on and what must be done. Joseph had prophesied that the famine would come. No one else knew about it. Joseph planned the crops and built the storehouses, and had them filled before the famine came (Genesis 41:35, 36, 49). Even so, our blessed Saviour is the only fit Person to open the storehouse of God's mercy, love, and grace to needy sinners. As Joseph built the storehouses and filled them in anticipation of the famine, so Christ in the covenant of grace provided for the needs of his people before the world began. The storehouse of grace is God's covenant (Ephesians 1:3; 2 Timothy 1:9). The provision is Christ, the Lamb slain from the foundation of the world (Revelation 13:8).

A Filled Storehouse
Christ filled the storehouse, too. In the fulness of time the Son of God came to this earth in human flesh. He obeyed the law in order that his people might have perfect righteousness before God. He died on the cross that we might be justified through his blood. The storehouse is full. Let all who are hungry come. Sinners find grace abundant and free in Christ. He alone has the capacity to contain all fulness. He alone has the wisdom to distribute all fulness. He alone has all fulness forever, immutable and undiminished, though all his people draw upon it continually (2 Timothy 1:12; Philippians 3:20, 21).

An Opened Storehouse
We are specifically told that Joseph opened the storehouses "when the people cried for bread" (Genesis 41:55-56). When hungry sinners cry for bread, Christ opens the storehouse of grace and feeds them (Matthew 7:9-11; Luke 11:5-13). Lost sinners who cry to him will be heard (Romans 10:13). Needy believers who cry to him will be heard (Hebrews 4:16). As often as we cry to him for the bread of his grace, he gives it. Joseph opened the storehouses to all who came (41:57). And our Lord Jesus Christ opens the storehouse of grace to all who come to him. "Whosoever will, let him come, and take of the water of life freely".

Discovering Christ Day By Day

January 15
Today's Reading: Genesis 43, 44
"I will be surety for him"
Genesis 43:8, 9

We read in chapter 42 that Reuben volunteered to be surety for Benjamin; but Jacob did not trust his Benjamin to Reuben's hands. There is good reason for that. Our great Surety, the Lord Jesus Christ, is the Lion of Judah's tribe. Therefore, in God's providence, as a type of our covenant Surety, the Lord Jesus Christ, to whom God the Father trusted his elect (Ephesians 1:12), Jacob trusted Benjamin to Judah's hand, when he said, "I will be surety for him".

The Spirit's Work
God the Holy Spirit is anxious for every believer to enjoy the comforting assurance of salvation in Christ. He is our Comforter. That is the work he was sent to perform. His method of comfort is to take the things of Christ and show them to us (John 16:7-14). He knows that the more fully we know Christ, and the more clearly we see him, the more we shall enjoy the comfort and assurance of our salvation in him.

Therefore, the Spirit of God always points us to Christ, especially in the inspired volume of Holy Scripture. He not only tells us who Christ is, what he has done, and what he is doing for us, he also uses metaphor after metaphor to show us pictures of our great Saviour, pictures designed to assure God's believing people that all is well between us and our God.

Types In Genesis
We see this repeatedly throughout the Book of Genesis. When Adam and Eve were naked, God provided them with the skins of an innocent victim and clothed them (3:21), portraying Christ as our Righteousness, Redemption, and Salvation. When the flood came, God saved Noah by an ark (7:15, 16), portraying Christ as our Ark of Refuge from the wrath of God, and our salvation by his substitutionary sacrifice. As the ark bore all the wrath of God so that Noah and his family bore none, so Christ bore all the wrath of God for his people and we bear none (Romans 8:1). As Noah and his family suffered all the wrath of God in the ark, so God's elect have suffered all the wrath of God in Christ (Galatians 3:13). When Isaac was bound to the altar on Mount Moriah, God provided himself a lamb for a burnt offering (Genesis 22:8, 13), typifying Christ as our Substitute (John 1:29; 2 Corinthians 5:21). When Jacob was alone, helpless, and afraid, God showed him a ladder, by which he could ascend to God (28:12, 13), picturing the Lord Jesus Christ as our Mediator.

Christ Our Surety
Here (Genesis 43:8, 9), the Spirit of God gives us another beautiful and instructive picture of the Lord Jesus Christ and of the grace of God in him. As Judah became surety for Benjamin, assuming all responsibility for him, so the Lord Jesus Christ, who sprang from the tribe of Judah, became Surety for God's elect before the worlds

were made in the covenant of grace, assuming total, absolute responsibility for the salvation of his people (Hebrews 7:22). In his hands, all is well. What a thought for meditation this is for the day before us!

January 16
Today's Reading: Genesis 45-47
"Fear not"
Genesis 46:3

The Lord appeared to Jacob "in the visions of the night" to say to him "fear not". Jacob's fear had to be removed. It is both displeasing and dishonouring to God for us, "the sons of Jacob", to walk in carnal fear (Matthew 6:19-33).

Afraid To Obey
Fear is an indication of a quarrel with God's will. Jacob must go down to Egypt by God's command; but he was afraid. He was afraid to obey God's command. We must not judge him too harshly. Who has not been guilty of the same offence? God will never send us where he will not go with us. God will not require us to do anything he will not enable us to do. No believer will ever meet a trial or temptation in the path of obedience through which God will not sustain him (1 Corinthians 10:13; 1 Thessalonians 5:24). His word to his servant is, "Fear not".

Peaceful Assurance
The Lord removed Jacob's fear in the most tender and gracious manner imaginable. Our God always deals with his children in grace. What a picture we have here of God's grace dealing with poor, fearful Jacob, and with us. He removed Jacob's fear by letting him know that he knew him. "God spake unto Israel in the visions of the night, and said, Jacob, Jacob". In essence, he said, "I know you, I know what you are going through, and I know what lies before you".

Then he caused Jacob to know by experience that he was in communion with God. When the Lord spoke to Jacob, Jacob spoke to God and said, "Here am I". That is the language of a submissive heart in communion with God (Genesis 22:1; 1 Samuel 3:10; Isaiah 6:8). Next, the Lord assured Jacob of his covenant faithfulness. He said, "I am God, the God of thy father". That means, "I am the God of the covenant. The blessing I have promised I will perform. I am the God who is for you" (Romans 8:28-32). Then the Lord promised Jacob that he would bless him in Egypt. "I will there make of thee a great nation".

These things should ease us of fear, as we face the trials through which our heavenly Father is pleased to send us. Where God brings us, God will bless us. Peter, James, and John "feared as they entered into the cloud" (Luke 9:34). But they were blessed of God in that place. And we shall be blessed of God in whatever place or circumstance we find ourselves by following his direction.

Divine Promises
The Lord also assured Jacob of his presence, saying, "I will go down with thee". He further promised his servant that, no matter what happened in Egypt, his inheritance in Canaan was sure. He said, "I will also surely bring thee up again". This is precisely what he says to us to assure, comfort, and strengthen our hearts in the face of trial. Our inheritance in Christ is sure (Romans 8:33-39).

The Lord gave Jacob one more word of promise, by which he removed his fear. God told Jacob that he would die in peace with Joseph by his side. "Joseph shall put his hand upon thine eyes". He has done the same for every believer. For the child of God, death is a covenant blessing. "So he giveth his beloved sleep". At God's appointed time, the Lord Jesus shall put his hand upon your eyes. It is written, "Blessed are the dead which die in the Lord". Therefore, the sons of Jacob are told to cease from fear (Isaiah 43:1-5). For the believer, there is no cause for fear.

January 17
Today's Reading: Genesis 48-50
"God meant it unto good"
Genesis 50:20

Joseph's brothers were uneasy. Their former transgressions made them fearful. Their guilt caused them to be suspicious of Joseph's goodness. In spite of all the kindness they had experienced at his hand, they were not assured of their acceptance with him. They feared that they might yet be made to suffer for what they had done to him. Therefore, they sued for mercy in the name of their father Jacob, whom they knew Joseph loved dearly.

They sent a messenger to Joseph with a message from Jacob (Genesis 50:15-17). When Joseph heard their request, his tender heart broke and he wept, because of his love for Jacob and because of his love for his brothers; but probably their suspicions of him, more than anything else, broke his heart. What an evil thing it is for sinners saved by the grace of God in Christ to be suspicious of his great goodness. Yet, it is an evil of which we are all, far too often, guilty.

Then Joseph's brothers themselves came before him (Genesis 50:17, 18). They confessed their sin. They sought forgiveness in Jacob's name, upon his word. And they bowed before Joseph as his servants. This was the thing they had refused to do before. It was this very thing that had before been the cause of their hatred. When they heard that they must bow as servants to Joseph, they said, "Shalt thou indeed reign over us?" (Genesis 37:8). Then they sold him into bondage. But now they are humbled. Now, they bow and say, "We be thy servants".

This is the issue that must be settled in the hearts of men. We must bow to Christ (Luke 14:25-33). He must be owned and acknowledged as our rightful Lord (Romans 10:9, 10). There is no salvation without the voluntary surrender of our hearts and lives to Christ's dominion as our Lord. When they bowed before Joseph as their rightful lord and master, he assured them of his good intentions toward them and comforted them (vv. 19-21). What a tender picture we have before us. It is a scene that needs no explanation. It is full of spiritual instruction for our souls. It clearly sets forth three lessons we should each lay to heart. As we close the Book of Genesis today, let us seek grace from God to learn and live in accordance with these three great, spiritual lessons.

God's grace is abundant and free in Christ. We have great reason to give thanks to him. As Joseph freely forgave his brothers, so God freely forgives believing sinners for Christ's sake.

God's providence is always good for his people. We should always be content with what our heavenly Father brings to pass. Joseph endured great trials, heart-breaking betrayal, and long imprisonment at the hands of his brothers. Yet, he said, "God meant it unto good ... I am in the place of God". "We know that all things work together for good" to God's elect.

The love of God in Christ, when experienced, teaches saved sinners to love and forgive one another. As Joseph loved his brothers because they were his brothers, so let us love our brethren for Christ's sake (Ephesians 4:32-5:2).

January 18
Today's Reading: Exodus 1-3
The Exodus
Luke 9:31

Knowing God's promises that "all things work together for good to them that love God, to them that are called, according to his purpose", that "no evil shall happen to the just", that "no weapon that is formed against thee shall prosper", how often have you looked at your circumstances and thought, "I know those promises are true, but everything I see, everything I am experiencing, everything I feel appears to me to be evil, and is telling me that all things are against me, every weapon formed against me is prospering"?

I am sure that is exactly how the Children of Israel felt when they found themselves bondmen in Egypt, serving as slave labourers under cruel taskmasters who made their lives bitter according to the whims of Egypt's reprobate king, Pharaoh. God had promised that he would be with them, bless them in all things and at all times, that he would make them a great nation. He had promised to give them all the spoils of the land of Egypt. But Pharaoh ordered that the nation be destroyed, that every male child born to the Children of Israel be drowned as soon as it was born. They must have thought the same thing their father Jacob thought, when Joseph was secretly arranging to bring them down into Egypt. "All these things are against me".

May God the Holy Spirit give us grace ever to trust him and rest in his blessed and sure purpose of grace in Christ Jesus. Here are three matters of great importance that we should always keep in mind as we read the book of Exodus and the rest of the Old Testament Scriptures.

God's True Israel
First, we should always remember that the nation of Israel was chosen of God, used of God, and blessed of God for spiritual, not carnal reasons. It was never God's intention that Christ would come to the earth to reign as a physical king over Abraham's physical descendents. Rather, God used Abraham's physical descendents (the nation of Israel) to accomplish his purpose of grace to his elect, the spiritual seed of Abraham, his church, called in the New Testament, "the Israel of God". Israel was, throughout the Old Testament, typical of God's church. All God's dealings with Israel as a nation have a spiritual meaning and must be interpreted in a spiritual way as applying to all God's elect, the church of the living God. By preserving the nation of Israel, the Lord God graciously preserved Abraham's seed, through whom Christ, the woman's Seed, came into this world. As God fulfilled all his promises to the nation of Israel when he brought them into the land of Canaan, so he will fulfil all the promises he has made to his elect, Abraham's spiritual seed, in Christ (Joshua 21:43-45; Romans 11:25-27).

For Us
Second, the Holy Spirit tells us that everything that happened in the book of Exodus, indeed, everything that happened in the history of the Old Testament, was not only written for our instruction, but also happened for our instruction. Everything that came to pass was brought to pass by our God for our instruction, comfort, and edification in the knowledge of Christ (Romans 15:4; 1 Corinthians 10:1-6, 11).

The Exodus
Third, everything in the history of Israel is directly related to the redemption of our souls by Christ. In Luke 9:31, while on the mount of transfiguration, Moses and Elijah appeared with our Saviour and spoke to him about "his decease which he would accomplish at Jerusalem". Our Saviour's substitutionary death at Jerusalem was not something that happened to him. It was something accomplished by him. It was the accomplishment of God's eternal purpose, all the prophecies, pictures and types of the Old Testament, God's covenant promises, and our eternal redemption. The word "decease" in Luke 9:31 is particularly instructive. It is the word "exodus". It means "departing". And the departing, the exodus, that our Saviour accomplished in his death was typically portrayed throughout the Book of Exodus.

January 19
Today's Reading: Exodus 4-6
How important is obedience to the will of God?
Exodus 4:24-26

How important is obedience to the will of God? Here is an illustration from the life of Moses that should answer that question. While Moses and his family were on their way to Egypt, they stopped in an inn for rest. There the Lord met Moses and sought to kill him, because he had refused to obey that which he knew God required of him.

Moses' Disobedience
The Lord God required Moses to circumcise his son, but he had not done so. Moses knew what God required of him. It should have been done eight days after the boy was born. But Moses had not obeyed God's will. Maybe he was waiting until the boy was older. Maybe he had neglected his responsibility in deference to his wife Zipporah, choosing to please her rather than obey God. Maybe he just looked upon God's command as a trivial, unimportant matter and neglected it. We are not told why he was disobedient, only that he was.

God's Response
Because of Moses disobedience, God sought to kill him. God crossed Moses' path in the inn and demanded obedience. How he confronted him we are not told. But these things are clear: First, God made it known to Moses and his wife that he was determined that either Moses would obey him or he would kill him. Second, the specific matter of disobedience was the circumcision of his son. Third, Moses had to make a choice on the spot between his will and God's will. In other words, God said to Moses, you are going to make a decision right now. You will either surrender everything to My rule, even your wife and son, or you will die.
Once Zipporah had circumcised their son, the Lord let Moses go. God will never accept partial surrender, or partial obedience. He requires absolute and universal surrender. Moses was willing to face Pharaoh at God's command; but he was not willing to circumcise his son! The Lord would not tolerate such an attitude. Moses had to be broken at his point of rebellion.

Your Point Of Rebellion
What is your point of rebellion? Whatever you know to be God's will to which you are yet disobedient is your point of rebellion; and that is the point at which you must surrender to Christ. You will never find peace with God until you surrender to Christ. Whatever the issue is between you and God, settle it quickly. If you refuse to do so, the Lord will slay you!

43

January 20
Today's Reading: Exodus 7-9
God's work and God's means
Exodus 8:20

Ten times God sent Moses to Pharaoh with this message. Why do you suppose the Lord did not speak to Pharaoh himself? Why did he send Moses to declare his message? He made the work all the more glorious and all the more glorifying to him by using a man to do it. And in the salvation of his elect, in calling chosen, redeemed sinners from death to life in Christ by his Spirit, God has chosen to make his wondrous work of grace all the more glorifying to himself by using men to preach the Word of life to them (1 Corinthians 1:18-31).

Why doesn't God speak to every sinner directly and save his chosen without the use of men? Certainly, he could do so. But when he condescends to use poor mortals, who have tasted his grace, he uses weak things to confound the mighty and foolish things to confound the wise, making his wonders of grace all the more admirable.

God's Work
Every believer recognizes and rejoices in the fact that "Salvation is of the LORD". It is God's work and God's work alone. It is in no way dependent upon, conditioned upon, or determined by anything in man or done by man. We contribute nothing to the salvation of our souls; and we contribute nothing to the salvation of others. It is entirely God's work. "Salvation is of the LORD". That cannot be stated too strongly, too often, or too fully. None "can by any means redeem his brother, nor give to God a ransom for him" (Psalm 49:7). And "none can keep alive his own soul" (Psalm 22:29). Salvation is God's work (John 1:12, 13; Romans 9:16).

God's Means
Every believer understands that salvation is God's work alone, but many fail to realize that, in his infinite sovereignty, the God of heaven condescends to use saved sinners to save lost sinners, to use the preaching of the Gospel as the instrument by which he saves his elect, though this is clearly taught in Holy Scripture (Romans 1:14-17; 10:13-17; 1 Peter 1:23-25). "It pleased God, by the foolishness of preaching, to save them that believe" (1 Corinthians 1:21).

All the works of God redound to his glory; but when the instruments he uses appear to be totally inadequate to do the work he performs by them, our reverence is excited, while our reason is awed, and we marvel at the power we cannot understand. It was by Moses alone that God brought Israel out of Egypt. It was by Moses alone that God led and instructed Israel.

Every time they imagined that God spoke to them by another, they got into trouble. When they thought God spoke to them by Aaron, they found themselves dancing naked around a golden calf, while pretending to worship Jehovah! When many of them looked upon Korah as God's prophet, the Lord killed them and their self-appointed prophet!

Gospel Preachers
So it is today. God saves his people, instructs them, guides them, edifies them, and feeds them by his Spirit by the preaching of the Gospel. He puts the treasure of his grace in earthen vessels of flesh, to make the treasure shine more gloriously (Ephesians 4:7-16; 1 Thessalonians 5:12, 13; Hebrews 13:7, 17).

Once Moses was convinced that he was sent of God, sent to carry God's Word to men, he was fearless before Pharaoh, Egypt, and Israel. Insignificant as he was in and of himself, the very fact that God sent him to speak for him silenced his fears. Being sent of God, he was absolutely assured of success. "Then the LORD said unto Moses, Now shalt thou see what I will do to Pharaoh: for with a strong hand shall he let them go, and with a strong hand shall he drive them out of his land" (Exodus 6:1).

With that sweet assurance, Moses steadily kept at his work, until he saw God's salvation accomplished. He persevered with diligence in the work God sent him to perform, until his work was done. And in the end, he led the people of God out of Egypt and across the Red Sea, triumphing over Pharaoh and Egypt.

January 21
Today's Reading: Exodus 10-12
Three felt things
Exodus 10:21

True Christianity is primarily a religion of the heart. It is inward and spiritual. A man believes with his heart. He repents in his heart. Prayer is found in and comes from the heart. And those things that are found in the heart are felt things. It is "Christ in you", whom the Spirit of God calls, "the hope of glory" (Colossians 1:27). Those who seek and worship him "feel after him". The Book of God speaks of three distinct things that are "felt" in the experience of every heaven born soul.

Felt Darkness
When the Lord God brought his ninth plague upon the land of Egypt, by which he destroyed the land, that is to say, by which he destroyed the strength and confidence of the Egyptians, it was a plague "of thick darkness ... even darkness which may be felt". And when God the Holy Spirit comes in the mighty operations of his grace to save a sinner, his first task is to destroy all creature strength in the sinner. He does so by bringing into the soul of the chosen sinner the thick darkness of guilt. When he comes to convince a sinner of his sin, he brings into the land of man's soul "thick darkness ... even darkness which may be felt". Darkness is often used in Scripture in this symbolic way (Isaiah 9:2; 29:18; 42:5-7; 50:10; Matthew 4:16; 2 Corinthians 4:6; Ephesians 5:8; Colossians 1:12-14). The conviction of sin is something felt in the soul. "I am the man that hath seen affliction by the rod of his wrath. He hath led me, and brought me into darkness, but not into light" (Lamentations 3:1, 2).

Discovering Christ Day By Day

Felt Healing
The first thing the Holy Spirit does in the sinner in the experience of grace is to bring felt darkness into his soul by the conviction of sin. Then, he brings felt healing by the conviction of righteousness. He convinces the sinner of righteousness, because Christ has returned to the Father, having accomplished what he came into the world to accomplish. He brought in everlasting righteousness. The bringing in of righteousness involved two things: obedience and satisfaction (2 Corinthians 5:21; Galatians 3:13; 1 Peter 2:24; 3:18). If ever God gives a poor sinner faith to touch Christ's clothes, his righteousness, "the garments of salvation" (Isaiah 61:10), he will feel the healing of grace in his soul when he discovers that Christ has made him whole, righteous before God. We see this beautifully illustrated in Mark 5:25-29.

Felt No Harm
In Acts 28 we see a third felt thing. When Paul was bitten by a viper, "he shook off the beast into the fire, and felt no harm". Like Paul, you and I have been bitten by a viper, the viper of hell, that old serpent, the devil. What pain the viper's bite has caused us and is causing us! But as soon as the poor, perishing sinner is convinced by God the Holy Spirit (John 16:11) that judgment has been forever removed from him by the sacrifice of Christ, because justice has been satisfied on his behalf by the death of God's dear Son, he looks to Christ in faith, shakes off the serpent, and soon feels no harm in his soul (Romans 8:1-4, 31-35). I cannot imagine a more glorious felt thing than "no harm". Can you? Yet, this is something that cannot be fully felt until that great day (And it can't be too soon!), when we shall at last shake off the beast of hell, that old serpent, the devil, into the fire of hell, and so completely and thoroughly triumph over him that we shall feel no harm! It is written, "And God shall wipe away all tears from their eyes; and there shall be no more death, neither sorrow, nor crying, neither shall there be any more pain: for the former things are passed away" (Revelation 21:4). We shall forever feel "no harm" from the serpent's bite and the sin caused by it!

January 22
Today's Reading: Exodus 13, 14
A lamb for an ass
Exodus 13:13

Throughout the Mosaic dispensation, every day in the Jewish nation opened and closed with the sacrifice of a lamb. A lamb was offered upon God's altar, at the door of the tabernacle every morning to begin the day; and another lamb was sacrificed every evening to conclude it. The Lord God said, "I will meet you to speak there unto thee" (Exodus 29:42). The lamb sacrificed was the place of meeting. God came to his

46

Discovering Christ Day By Day

people and his people came to him by a sacrificed lamb. There was no other way for the two to come together. If God came to man, it was by a lamb sacrificed. If man came to God, it was by a lamb sacrificed. That lamb sacrificed was given to the Children of Israel for a token, a sign, upon the hand that made the sacrifice and in the eyes that beheld it. And this is what the token promised, this is what the Lord God said by the sign, This is how I will dwell among you and be your God, this is how you "shall be sanctified by my glory" (Exodus 29:38-46).

The Lamb God's Glory

According to the typical revelation of the law given in Exodus 29, sanctification was by the sacrifice of a lamb; and in verse 43 we are told that it is by God's glory. Does the Lord God mean for us to understand that all our salvation and all his glory is in that Lamb, to whom these typical lambs pointed, the Lamb of God, Christ our Passover, the Lamb of God sacrificed for us? Indeed, he does! Both our salvation and God's glory are in the Lamb of God slain for sinners.

Unclean Made Clean

In verse two of Exodus 13 the Lord God commands, "Sanctify unto me all the firstborn, whatsoever openeth the womb among the children of Israel, both of man and of beast: it is mine". What about the unclean animals? The Lord God gave a very specific command, forbidding that any unclean beast be offered to him (Leviticus 27:11). He makes two commandments that seem to contradict one another. If one is fulfilled, it would appear that the other cannot be. He demands that all the firstborn of man and beast be sanctified unto him. Yet, he also forbids offering anything that is unclean to him. How can such a law (the law is one) be fulfilled? How can all the firstborn be sanctified to the Lord, and no unclean thing be offered to him? The Lord God himself answers that question in verse 13. The ass was redeemed, made clean, and accepted by God by the sacrifice of a lamb.

The Wonder Of Grace

The Lord God met the difficulty by providing a substitute for the unclean ass. Though the ass must be God's, it could not be, except by substitution. The Lord God says concerning the unclean ass, "Every firstling of an ass thou shalt redeem with a lamb". What a sweet, beautiful picture this is of the glorious gospel of Christ! The Lord God often compares man to an ass. It is written, vain man is born "like a wild ass's colt" (Job 11:12). You and I are all born by nature "like a wild ass's colt", foolish, senseless, and stubborn, given to lust and debauchery, and wild. As the wild ass will not bear the yoke, so none will ever bow to the yoke of Christ, except the Son of God break him. Man by nature is like "a wild ass used to the wilderness, that snuffeth up wind at her pleasure" (Jeremiah 2:24; Job 39:5).

Yet, the holy Lord God said, I will take the wild ass, the unclean thing, make it clean, use it for my service, and show my glory in redeeming it by a Substitute, by the blood of the Lamb. He said, they "shall be sanctified by my glory"! He spared not his own Son, but delivered him up to die in our stead, as the Lamb of God, our Substitute; and that is his glory, the glory that sanctifies us (Romans 5:6-8; 2 Corinthians 4:4-6; 5:17-21). This is the great wonder of grace. Being redeemed by the precious blood of

47

Christ, we are the sheep of God, the lambs of Christ's flock, made fit to sit far above principalities and powers in the heavenly places with Christ Jesus! Lost by sin through the fall, and utterly unclean, God's super-abounding grace has made us utterly clean, without spot and without blame, through the sin-atoning blood of his dear Son!

January 23
Today's Reading: Exodus 15-17
Israel at Marah
Exodus 15:22-27

After God had so graciously delivered the Children of Israel across the Red Sea, miraculously opening a path for them in the sea and then drowning Pharaoh and the armies of Egypt in the depths of the sea, he brought Israel into the wilderness of Shur. There, for three days, they wandered without water. The scorching sun beat down upon them. The desert sands scalded their feet. Their cattle were perishing. Their children's tongues were swollen. Their lips were parched. They had roamed for three days in the barren wilderness without water. Then, at last, they came to the plentiful fountains of Marah. When they saw the waters of Marah, how their hearts must have rejoiced in hope and expectation. They could almost taste the water. They could almost feel the cool, refreshing water in their mouths. But when they got there, the waters were so bitter that they could not drink them! Can you imagine the frustration and disappointment these men and women must have felt?

Immediately, they turned upon Moses and began to murmur and complain. Actually, they turned upon the Lord God who had brought them to this place! Though the Lord had led them by the fiery and cloudy pillar, though he was with them, though he had miraculously and graciously delivered them from the bondage of Egypt and promised to do them good, they could not see him! All they could see, all they could think about were the bitter waters before them and the thirst within them. Because they saw nothing good in God's providence, they despised God's providence.

Do you know anyone like that? I blush to tell you I do. When these chosen, redeemed people should have remembered God's goodness, they thought only of their troubles. When they should have looked to their merciful Deliverer, they looked only upon Marah's bitter waters. When they should have prayed, they murmured. When they should have believed, they grumbled. "But God, being full of compassion, forgave their iniquity, and destroyed them not ... For he remembered that they were but flesh" (Psalm 78:38, 39).

They had just before sung the song of salvation on the borders of the Red Sea. They had that great sight fresh in their minds. They had been redeemed and all their enemies were swallowed up in the sea. They were now on the march toward the Promised Land. Three days they had travelled into the wilderness and found no water.

48

When they came to Marah, though water was there in abundance, it was bitter and they could not drink it. They murmured against Moses; and Moses cried unto the Lord. When he did, the Lord showed him a tree, which, when cast into the waters, made them sweet. Let every ransomed soul personally apply these things to himself. The Lord my God has brought me out of spiritual Egypt. He has led me through a new and living way, through the red sea of Christ's blood. He has put a new song in my heart, the Song of Moses and the Lamb. He has made himself my Strength, my Salvation, and my Redemption.

Yet, as he brought Israel through the wilderness of Shur, so he is bringing you and me through the wilderness. And in this wilderness we ought to expect such experiences as one is likely to find in a wilderness. This is not the Land of Promise. This is the wilderness! Though we often do, we should never call into question the wisdom and goodness of our God for leading us through the wilderness. Though we blush to acknowledge that we do, we should never question our God's faithfulness, mercy, love, and grace because he sends us some bitter thing, by which he has purposed to sweeten our souls and to sweeten himself to our souls!

O Lord God, as often as you bring us to the waters of Marah, show us the tree you showed Moses that day, Jesus Christ our crucified Saviour, cast him into our souls' experience, and make every bitter thing sweet!

January 24
Today's Reading: Exodus 18-21
Moses' great mistake
Exodus 18:24

The work with which the Lord God had trusted Moses was a great, demanding work, involving the highest honour any man can have upon the earth. Moses was God's spokesman to his people (Exodus 18:15, 16; Ephesians 3:8). It was a work for which the Lord had graciously equipped his servant.

Jethro's Counsel

But when his father-in-law, Jethro, saw what Moses was doing, he said, "The thing that thou doest is not good. Thou wilt surely wear away, both thou, and this people that is with thee: for this thing is too heavy for thee; thou art not able to perform it thyself alone ... Hearken now unto my voice, I will give thee counsel ... Appoint judges to help you ... God will be with you ... So shall it be easier for thyself ... They shall bear the burden with thee ... Thou shalt be able to endure" (Exodus 18:17-23). Jethro's counsel probably arose from loving concern for Moses' health. It was in a fleshly sense wise and prudent counsel. But Moses did wrong in obeying Jethro's

49

counsel. He made a great mistake, from which there was no recovery. That will be obvious to anyone who reads in Numbers 10 and 11 what happened after "Moses hearkened to the voice of his father in law".

Remember, Jethro was an unbeliever, a heathen priest. He had no spiritual discernment. The servant of God must never allow himself to be guided by natural principles. He must not confer with flesh and blood (Galatians 1:15). He must not ask himself, "What is best for me? What is best for my family? What would family and friends have me to do?" That man who is engaged in the service of God must never heed the counsel of carnal wisdom. He must take his orders only from his Master. "Whatsoever he saith unto you, do it"! (John 2:5). If we would obey our God, if we would serve him in any area of life, our actions must be determined only by the Word of God, the will of God, and the glory of God.

A Great Burden

That which had been Moses' highest honour and greatest privilege became a great burden to him once he began to consider himself. When he began to consider himself rather than the will of God, the glory of God and the people of God, he began to look upon his service as a great burden and greatly resented it (Number 11:11-15). He sighed, "I am not able to bear all this people alone, because it is too heavy for me" (Numbers 11:14). God never called him to bear the burden of his people alone. And God had never left him alone.

Perhaps Moses' relinquishing of his burden had the appearance of humility; but it was only an appearance of humility. With his lips, he said, "I am not sufficient". But he was really saying, "Lord, you are not sufficient". Let no man thrust himself into any work. But to shrink from any work or responsibility God has put upon us is both cowardice and unbelief. "Is anything too hard for the Lord?" No work is too great. No burden is too heavy for God! Someone once said, "With him the weight of a mountain is nothing; without him, the weight of a feather is overwhelming." The Apostle Paul asserted, "I can do all things through Christ which strengtheneth me" (Philippians 4:13). That is the proper attitude. Any place where God puts me is a place of honour. Any work God puts in my hands is honourable work (1 Corinthians 1:26-29). It is never an act of humility or faith to depart from any divinely appointed post, or any divinely appointed work for any reason. Difficulties are nothing to God. He who divided the Red Sea can open the way before you. Needs are nothing to God. He who owns all the deep mines of the earth can supply our needs. Our inabilities are nothing to God. "When I am weak, then am I strong"! God can draw a straight line with a crooked stick. He can conquer a nation by an old man. And he can speak to the hearts of sinners by a stuttering, stammering tongue. God can speak as easily by a jackass as by a man. The power by which we do his work is not ours, but his!

The Burden Removed

When Moses complained of the burden God had imposed upon him, the Lord quickly took it away (Numbers 11:16, 17). God will never force us to serve him. If I don't want to speak for him, he can raise up stones to do so. If I don't want to wash and kiss the Master's feet, someone will. If I don't want to break my alabaster box of ointment and anoint him, someone will. If I don't want to be bothered by serving Christ, he will not force me to do so. He doesn't need me; and he doesn't need you! If the honour and privilege God has given us in his service becomes a burden to us, and we want to lay it down, he will let us. We can step down from the place of dignity if we want to, and sink into the place where base unbelief is sure to put us. Thus God took the burden away! And when the Lord relieved Moses of his burden, he also relieved him of his honour, the blessing of the burden, and Moses withered (Numbers 11:21-23).

January 25
Today's Reading: Exodus 22-24
"Behold the blood"
Exodus 24:4-8

These days, people do not like to talk about blood atonement, blood redemption, and blood-bought salvation. Some churches and denominations have even gone through their literature and hymnbooks and carefully removed every mention of the precious blood of Christ, lest they offend the tastes of cultured reprobates. But God Almighty still demands blood. You cannot be saved without the blood of Christ. That by which the Lord Jesus Christ redeemed his people from their sins was his own precious blood. The Son of God entered into heaven and obtained our eternal redemption "with his own blood" (Hebrews 9:12). Our redemption was accomplished, wrought out, and obtained by the precious blood of Christ by the sacrifice of his life which was represented and present in that blood which was shed so freely for the remission of our sins and the ransom of our souls. How I thank God for the blood, the precious blood of Christ! Read about it and rejoice (Exodus 12:13; Ephesians 1:7; 1 Peter 1:18-20; Revelation 5:9). Let me remind you of just three things about the precious, sin-atoning blood of our Lord Jesus Christ.

Deliberately Shed
Our Saviour's blood was deliberately shed. Had it been possible for his blood to have been spilt involuntarily, by accident, or by some outside force against his will, it would not have been a proper redemption price. It could not have answered for us as a payment to the justice of God. But it was purposely and voluntarily shed with our Master's full consent. Christ had the full control and disposal of his own life. He freely gave his life a ransom price for many. "I lay down my life for the sheep", he said, as a ransom price for them; "I lay it down of myself".

Human Blood
The blood shed for our sins at Calvary was human blood, the blood of a man. That blood which was so freely shed for us was the same as the blood which flows in our veins today. This, too, was necessary. We could not be redeemed with the blood of

bulls and goats, which could never be an adequate price of redemption. Human blood must be shed for the atonement of sin. Christ partook of the same flesh and blood with the children for whom he died. The only difference was this: his blood was not tainted with sin as ours is.

This was another requirement for our redemption. The ransom price had to be the blood of an innocent, perfectly righteous man. Much notice is given in Scripture to the innocence, holiness, and righteousness of the Redeemer. He was holy in his nature and blameless in life. He knew no sin. He never committed any evil. He is the just and Holy One. He suffered the Just for the unjust. Great emphasis is laid upon this fact. The price with which men are redeemed is "the precious blood of Christ, as of a Lamb without blemish and without spot" (1 Peter 1:18, 19). If he had had any sin in him, he could not have been a redeemer from sin. His blood could not be the price of redemption. Yet, there is more.

Divine Blood
It was divine blood, the blood of a man who is God. It was necessary, if atonement was to be made and redemption accomplished for God's elect, that the blood shed must also be the blood of One who is himself God as well as man. None but Christ ever made such a claim; and none but Christ meets this requirement! Therefore, we are told that God, who is Christ, "purchased the church with his own blood" (Acts 20:28). It is the blood of Jesus Christ, God's Son, which cleanses us from all sin (1 John 1:7).

January 26
Today's Reading: Exodus 25-27
The mercy-seat
Exodus 25:22

If we could go behind the veil with the High Priest on the Day of Atonement into the holy of holies, the very first thing that would strike our eyes would be "the cherubim of glory shadowing the mercy-seat;" but we would not look long at the cherubim. Their eyes, their faces, their wings direct our attention away from themselves to the mercy-seat.

Christ Our Propitiation
The mercy-seat represented Christ, God's propitiation, the propitiation for our sins (Exodus 25:17, 21, 22; 1 John 2:1, 2; 4:9, 10; Romans 3:24-26). In fact, the word translated "propitiation" elsewhere in the New Testament is the same word that is translated "mercy-seat" in Hebrews 9:5.

The Day Of Atonement

In the Old Testament on the Day of Atonement, Aaron took the blood of the paschal lamb behind the veil, into the holy of holies, and sprinkled the blood on the mercy-seat, making ceremonial atonement for the sins of the people of Israel. And the holy Lord God promised to meet his people there upon the blood-sprinkled mercy-seat, in peace, forgiveness, and reconciliation.

That ceremonial service was a beautiful, instructive picture of the obtaining of eternal redemption for God's elect by Christ, our great High Priest. "By his own blood (by the merit of his blood) he entered in once into the holy place, having obtained eternal redemption for us". The mercy-seat of the Old Testament was typically what Christ is in reality: the place of substitution, sacrifice, satisfaction, atonement, reconciliation, forgiveness, peace and worship.

The Publican

The Publican in Luke 18 cried, "God, be merciful to me, a sinner." He understood exactly what was portrayed in the Old Testament mercy-seat. It is reflected in his prayer. He prayed, "God, look on the blood upon the mercy-seat, the blood covering your holy law, which I have broken, and be propitious to me, the sinner, forgiving my sin for Christ's sake".

God's Presence

Standing in the holiest of all with Christ, our Aaron, our great High Priest, suddenly we realize that we are standing before the mercy-seat, the symbol of God's presence. With blood upon the mercy-seat covering the broken tables of the law, there we see the glory of God in the pardon of sin by the sacrifice of Christ (Leviticus 9:23, 24). This is exactly what Isaiah saw when he saw the Lord Jesus in his glory (Isaiah 6:1-6). And this is what the heaven born soul is made to see when he sees "the glory of God in the face of Jesus Christ" (2 Corinthians 4:6; Psalm 85:9-11). The holy Lord God not only meets us upon the mercy-seat, there in Christ, he abides with us. No matter where we are if we are in Christ, the name of the place is Jehovah-Shammah, "The LORD is there". Our lives are hid with Christ in God (Isaiah 43:1-5).

January 27
Today's Reading: Exodus 28, 29
"The Urim and the Thummim"
Exodus 28:30

We are never told what the Urim and Thummim were. All we know is that these were worn upon Aaron's breastplate of judgment (discernment), upon his heart continually before the Lord, along with the names of the twelve tribes of Israel. Though we do not know what they were, through grace and the teaching of God the Holy Spirit, we do have a very clear knowledge of what they represented and what they meant.

Lights And Perfections
The words "Urim" and "Thummim" mean "Lights" and "Perfections". As Aaron, the high priest, was a clear, instructive type of Christ, our great High Priest, so, by bearing on his breast-plate "the Urim and the Thummim", it is obvious that the Lord Jesus Christ is represented by these emblems as the light and perfection of his people. As Aaron bore all the names of the tribes of Israel upon his heart, where "the Urim and Thummim" were worn, so the Lord Jesus Christ bears all his elect, all his redeemed, upon his holy heart and in his own light and perfection before God. Sweet and precious thought! Contemplate its majesty and its comfort. As Christ is Light, so are we in him. As Christ is Perfection, so are we in him! As Christ is accepted, so are we in him!

With God's Holy One
This is a matter of such great magnitude and importance that just before the Lord took him out of this world, as he was giving his final words to the Children of Israel, Moses expressly commanded of Levi, "Let thy Thummim and thy Urim be with thy holy one" (Deuteronomy 33:8). He who is Jehovah's Holy One can be none other than the Lord Jesus Christ. With him, "the Urim (Lights) and the Thummim (Perfections)" eminently remained, and with him only. During the time of the Babylonian Captivity, the physical "Urim and Thummim" were lost with the destruction of the temple, and were never again restored. But it continues on everlastingly, unmarred, and unchanged with Christ Jesus in his everlasting and unchangeable priesthood. Like Christ himself, it is "the same yesterday, and today, and forever". It is our blessed Lord Jesus who is "the Urim and the Thummim" to our souls. He, and he alone, who is Jehovah's Holy One, is the Light and Perfection of his people in grace here, and glory forever.

Christ The Urim
All light and perfection are found in Christ and only in Christ. Apart from Christ there is no light of any kind; and apart from him there is no perfection (Colossians 1:19; 2:3). Christ is the Urim, the Light (John 1:9), the Light in whom all light is found and from whom all light comes. As the Lord God dispelled the darkness of the old creation by commanding light to appear on the first day, in the new creation of grace he commands light to shine out of darkness by the revelation of Christ, giving us the light of the knowledge of the glory of God in the face of Christ. As sun was made to be the light of the world by day on the fourth day, so the light of the new creation is Christ, the Sun of Righteousness. As the light of the earth is but the reflected light of the sun, so the light that is in us is but the reflection of Christ, who is the Sun of our souls and the Light of the world. All the light of grace is found in and comes from Christ. The light of grace is that light which comes upon poor sinners, sinners born in darkness, raised in darkness, living in darkness, walking in darkness, and loving darkness, causing them to be made "light in the Lord". And sinners enlightened by Christ, enlightened with the enlightenment of grace, testify with the man in John 9:25,

Discovering Christ Day By Day

"One thing I know, that whereas I was blind, now I see". God's saints are called "children of light" because they have been called, by the almighty, irresistible power and grace of the Holy Spirit, out of darkness into light, out of the darkness of depravity, death, and sin into the marvelous light of life, grace, and righteousness in Christ. If anyone receives this light, it is by the gift and grace of Christ our God (Ephesians 5:14). If any are called to light, it is by Christ. If any walk in the light, they walk in Christ. He is given of God the Father, "A Light to lighten the Gentiles".

Christ The Thummim
Our Lord Jesus Christ is the true Thummim, too. All perfections are found in him fully, completely, and everlastingly. Whenever we think about perfections, let us only think of Christ. He comprehends them all and possesses them all. All the perfections of the Triune God are in him (Colossians 2:9). All the perfection of the gifts of the Holy Spirit is in him, and flow to us from him (Psalm 68:17-20). All the perfection of grace is in Christ and comes to chosen, redeemed sinners through Christ and for Christ's sake (1 Corinthians 1:30; Ephesians 1:3-6). All the perfection of the blessings and promises of God to sinners in the covenant of grace are in Christ. He is our Joseph. He owns and holds the key to all the storehouse of God's grace (2 Corinthians 1:20). All the perfection of life is Christ our Lord. He is our Life; and he is the Fountain of Life (John 17:2). And Christ is our Perfection before God, our Holiness and our Righteousness, in whom we are made whole and in whom we are complete (Colossians 2:10).

January 28
Today's Reading: Exodus 30-32
Five pictures of redemption
Exodus 30:11-16

The only hope for fallen, guilty, depraved sinners is redemption, a redemption which includes atonement for sin, satisfaction for justice, and effectual deliverance from the guilt, power, dominion, and consequences of sin. Such redemption could be accomplished by only one Person, the Lord Jesus Christ, the Son of God our Saviour. Not only could he alone do it, he has done it; and he has done it alone (Isaiah 63:5). Every statement in the Word of God about Christ's death at Calvary declares that he who is God our Saviour effectually accomplished the eternal redemption of his people by the sacrifice of himself. The Lord Jesus Christ bought his elect from among the fallen sons of Adam out of the hands of God's offended justice, and delivered us from our sins by the shedding of his precious blood. That is what redemption is; anything less than that is not redemption. This is the work of redemption pictured for us in the Old Testament Scriptures.

55

The Redemption Of Israel Out Of Egypt
The deliverance of the people of Israel out of Egypt was a very special and remarkable type of our redemption by Christ out of a far worse state of bondage than that of Egypt (Psalm 106:6-12). Israel was brought into Egyptian bondage by an act of sin, when Joseph's brothers sold him into slavery. Israel was redeemed by the hand of a man God raised up, Moses the deliverer-prophet who typified Christ (Acts 7:35). The price of redemption was the blood of the paschal lamb (Exodus 12:13). The power of their redemption was the omnipotent hand of God, a picture of regeneration and conversion by God's omnipotent grace (Exodus 14:13, 14; 15:1, 2, 16). This was a blood redemption, redemption of a particular people, and an effectual redemption.

The Atonement Money Paid By Israel
Exodus 30:11-16 describes redemption by atonement money. This numbering of the Children of Israel and the atonement money they paid so that no plague come upon them was typical of our ransom by Christ. None but Israelites were ransomed. A specific, number were ransomed. The ransom price was the same for all. And all who were ransomed were preserved from any plague (Proverbs 12:21; Psalm 91:10).

The Kinsman Redeemer
The buying again, by one of his near kinsman, of an Israelite who by reason of poverty had sold himself to another, is a beautiful picture of our redemption by Christ (Leviticus 25:47-49). We have sold ourselves into bondage. We cannot redeem ourselves. No friend is able, or has the right to redeem us; but there is a near Kinsman, who is both able and willing to redeem, the Lord Jesus Christ (Hebrews 7:25). Like Boaz, Ruth's kinsman-redeemer, our Lord Jesus Christ as a man is our Near Kinsman. He is able to pay our debt. He willingly laid down his life to ransom us!

The Deliverance Of A Debtor From Prison
In ancient times a man in debt was liable to be arrested and cast into prison. There he would have to remain in bondage until his debt was paid, either by himself or another. That is what the Lord Jesus Christ has done for God's elect (Isaiah 49:8-10; 61:1-3; Philemon 1:18). Our sins are debts. They are debts which we can never pay. We are all shut up in debtor's prison by nature. But Christ has paid our debt and set us free!

The Ransom Of A Slave
In the days of the Old Testament, godless men often took their slaves and threw them into deep pits at night. They would take them out of their pits only to perform slavish labour, or if a ransom price was paid for their deliverance. Christ has ransomed us and delivered us from the pit of slavery and corruption (Job 33:24; Zechariah 9:11).We are all slaves to sin and Satan by nature. Our old master, the devil, kept us ever in the deep, dark pit of darkness and night, until Christ came to deliver us. The Lord Jesus Christ delivered us from the slavery of Satan and the pit of darkness, corruption, and sin by the power of his omnipotent grace. The price he paid for the deliverance of our souls was his own precious blood.

Discovering Christ Day By Day

January 29
Today's Reading: Exodus 33, 34
How did the Lord God show Moses his glory?
Exodus 33:18-23

Moses asked the Lord God to show him his glory (v. 18). In response to that great request, the Triune Jehovah declared, "I will make all my goodness pass before thee, and I will proclaim the name of the LORD before thee; and will be gracious to whom I will be gracious, and will shew mercy on whom I will shew mercy" (v. 19). Then he told his servant exactly how he would reveal his glory to him and how he reveals his glory to his chosen in all ages. "And the Lord said, Behold, there is a place by me, and thou shalt stand upon a rock; and it shall come to pass, while my glory passeth by, that I will put thee in a cleft of the rock, and will cover thee with my hand while I pass by; and I will take away mine hand, and thou shalt see my back parts: but my face shall not be seen".

The Place
Before any sinful man can behold the perfections of the infinitely glorious, righteous, and holy God, he must be put into a place of security and peace. Moses had to be put into a cleft of the rock before he could see God. That Rock was Christ. He is the Rock, the Rock of Israel, the Rock of Ages, the Rock of Refuge, Salvation, and Strength. Blessed be his name forever! Our God has provided us a place of shelter in the cleft of the Rock.

> Rock of Ages, cleft for me, grace has hid me safe in Thee!
> Let the water and the blood from Thy wounded side which flowed,
> Be of sin the double cure, cleanse me from its guilt and power.

It is only in the cleft of the Rock that you can behold the glory of God. In North Carolina there is a mountain called "Grandfather Mountain". As you drive along the highway, you can look at that mountain from many different places, and wonder where it got such a name. But, if you drive on until you get to the north side of it, you can look up from its base and see clearly and distinctly the image of a man with a flowing beard. And so it is with us. Come with me under the shadow of the cross. Come there as a penitent sinner. Look there upon that visage more marred than any man. Realize that the Sufferer hangs as the guiltless Substitute, dying for your sins. And you will see in him the glory of God's goodness. His beauty will ravish your soul. But the only place to behold that glory is in the cleft of the Rock. Until you see God's glorious goodness in Christ, any sight of the thrice holy Jehovah will terrify you.

Till God in human flesh I see, my thoughts no comfort find;
The holy, just, and sacred Three, are terrors to my mind!

Blessed Security
Look at the beautiful picture that we have here of the believer's absolute security in Christ. "Thou shalt stand upon a Rock". We stand before God today and for all eternity upon this blessed Foundation; and we shall not be confounded.

Jesus, Thy blood and righteousness, my beauty are, my glorious dress;
Midst flaming worlds in these arrayed, with joy shall I lift up my head.

The Lord God said, "I will put thee in a cleft of the rock", because no sinner can put himself into Christ. We were chosen in him, redeemed in him, accepted in him. And we were "created in Christ Jesus". Then, God said, "I will cover thee with my hand". Not only is the believer in Christ. He is protected by the Father's hand. "My Father, which gave them me, is greater than all, and no man shall pluck them out of my Father's hand". (John 10:29). "He that dwelleth in the secret place of the Most High shall abide under the shadow of the Almighty" (Psalm 91:1).

Great Superiority
Here is the great superiority of the Gospel over the law. The law had only a shadow of good things to come, and not the very image of those things. But look at the blessed fulness of the Gospel "God who commanded light to shine out of darkness, hath shined in our hearts, to give the light of the knowledge of the glory of God in the face of Jesus Christ" (2 Corinthians 4:6).

January 30
Today's Reading: Exodus 35-37
Rest to service
Exodus 35:2, 3

Exodus 35 is all about serving God. In the previous chapters we are told about the pattern God gave Moses in the Mount. Here the work is actually begun; and it is begun with another declaration of God's command that the Children of Israel must keep the sabbath. In this chapter we see the Children of Israel serving God with willing hearts. Here are God's chosen people making sacrifices with joy and labouring with gladness; but the chapter begins with a commandment to keep the sabbath day holy.

Rest First

So the first thing evident in this chapter is the fact that service begins with rest. We cannot do anything for God until we quit trying to do something to appease God. We cannot serve the Lord until we rest in Christ, our blessed Sabbath Rest. We cannot bring anything to God until we find rest in Christ.

Remember the Tabernacle was designed of God and given by God to portray and typify our Lord Jesus Christ and the full accomplishment of salvation by him and in him. So, before the work of erecting the Tabernacle is begun, the Lord God gives this commandment again. "Six days shall work be done, but on the seventh day there shall be to you an holy day, a sabbath of rest to the LORD: whosoever doeth work therein shall be put to death". Before we are fit to serve the holy Lord God, we must rest in Christ. Before we can bring anything to him, we must receive grace from him.

This is the seventh and last mention of the sabbath in the Book of Exodus, the Book of Redemption and Deliverance. It was Solomon, "a man of rest" (1 Chronicles 22), who alone could build a house to Jehovah's name. Both the sabbath days of the Old Testament and Solomon, the man of rest, typified our Lord Jesus Christ, our blessed Sabbath, in whom and by whom we rest.

No Fire Kindled

In verse 3 an additional feature is added to the observance of the sabbath. Even the lighting of a fire on the sabbath day is prohibited! "Ye shall kindle no fire throughout your habitations upon the sabbath day". The Lord never mentioned that before. Why is it added here? There may be other reasons for this additional requirement; but I am sure that this is intended to show us at least these two things. First, faith in Christ is a complete cessation of works, a total dependence upon the Son of God for our entire salvation. And second, faith in Christ is the means by which God the Holy Spirit purges our consciences of guilt, and imputes to the believing sinner the righteousness of Christ, as he did to Abraham. Once the conscience is purged, once guilt is removed from the conscience, having faith in the Son of God, trusting Christ alone as our Saviour, resting in him, every believer calls the Sabbath a delight (Isaiah 58:13, 14).

Great Honour

In the rest of the chapter we see the high honour God puts upon his people. He so honoured the Children of Israel that he allowed everyone in the nation to contribute to making the Tabernacle. God did not need Israel's assistance. Everything the Children of Israel brought to him, he had given them. Yet, the Lord God condescended to use the people he brought out of Egypt to establish his place of worship and all the things connected with his worship while they were in the wilderness.

Great as that privilege was, high as that honour was, it pales into insignificance when compared to the great, high honour and extraordinary privilege the Lord God has placed upon you and me, upon every believing sinner in this world. God Almighty has chosen us as his witnesses and his servants in this world (Isaiah 43:10-12; 44:8; Acts 1:8; John 20:20, 21; 2 Corinthians 5:17-6:1). This is the great, high honour the Lord God has put upon us in this Gospel Day (1 Corinthians 1:26-29).

January 31
Today's Reading: Exodus 38-40
"Cloths of service"
Exodus 39:1

As the Mosaic record of the Tabernacle's construction ends, Moses was inspired of God to give us a description of "the holy garments" made for Aaron. Aaron was required to wear them whenever he went into the Tabernacle doing service before the Lord God as Israel's high priest. They are called "cloths of service". These "cloths of service" were highly symbolical. They are listed three times by Moses (Exodus 28, Exodus 39 and Leviticus 8). Aaron was not allowed to appear before the Lord God as Israel's priest to do service in the holy place without these "holy garments", without these "cloths of service". They were vital to his priestly work; and we are specifically told they were "garments of consecration", "for glory and for beauty".

Aaron's Garments
These garments were made specifically for Aaron, to show forth the glory and beauty of his work as Israel's high priest. But they show more than that. These garments were made for and put upon Aaron to show forth the glory and beauty of our Lord Jesus Christ, our great High Priest, of whom Aaron was but a type.

Actually, Aaron had two sets of priestly garments. This glorious apparel which he wore before Israel and before the Lord in his common, daily functions in the tabernacle, and those holy linen garments mentioned in Exodus 39:28, and more fully described in Leviticus 16:4, which he wore once a year, on the Day of Atonement. On that great Day of Atonement, when he went in with the blood of the paschal lamb before the Lord God into the holy of holies, Aaron was robed only in spotless white, portraying the infinitely meritorious obedience and holiness of the Lord Jesus Christ, by which he was worthy and able to undertake and accomplish the work of putting away the sins of his people by the sacrifice of his own blood.

Our Beauty
The garments described in Exodus 39 were specifically ordained of God to show Aaron's glory and beauty to the people he represented and served as a priest. These garments are described in great detail for us, so that we might see and be assured of the glory and beauty of our Lord Jesus Christ, our great High Priest. Try to picture the Lord Jesus in his glory in heaven. Try to picture our Saviour's great beauty before God as your Mediator and High Priest in heaven. All his glory and beauty he has put upon us and made ours! Every sinner who trusts the Son of God is made exceedingly beautiful before the thrice holy Jehovah in the beauty of God's own Son (Ezekiel 16:6-8; Psalm 149:4; Isaiah 61:1-3). In the perfect beauty of Christ, being one with Christ, every saved sinner is holy, blameless and the perfection of beauty before God!

February 1
Today's Reading: Leviticus 1-4
"Offering of turtledoves"
Leviticus 1:14-17

From the very beginning, the Lord God has promised that he will forgive sin; but he has also declared that he will forgive sin only by blood atonement. It is written, "without shedding of blood is no remission" (Hebrews 9:22). The holy Lord God demands blood atonement; and he provides what he demands in Christ. This is what is taught in the typical sacrifices he demanded of Israel under the Mosaic law, as they are described in the book of Leviticus.

The sacrifices of burnt offering could be a sacrifice chosen from the herd, or from the flock, or from the fowls. If it was a sacrifice from the herd, or from among the sheep, or the goats, it must be a male without blemish. However, if the sacrifice offered was from the fowls, it might either be male or female; and there was no requirement even that it must be without blemish. That was not by accident, but by divine design and decree, because the holy Lamb of God must be made to be sin for us if he would redeem us from our sins (2 Corinthians 5:21).

Believing God, Adam, Abel, Noah, Abraham, and Moses believed the promise made in Genesis 3:15, and offered typical sacrifices, which by divine institution represented the Lord Jesus Christ, the Lamb of God. They did not trust the sacrifices that typified Christ, but could never take away sin. They trusted Christ. If we would find atonement and righteousness, if we would find acceptance with God, we must, like those ancient believers, look to Christ. We must believe on the Son of God (Romans 3:19-26; 8:1-4).

For The Poor
Turtledoves and pigeons were distinctly the sacrifices of the poor (Leviticus 14:21, 22). As such, they were eminently typical of our blessed Saviour. The Lord Jesus always identified himself with the poor and needy, because he came here to redeem and save poor, needy, helpless, destitute, bankrupt sinners (Luke 2:21-30). As the dove was slain by the priest, with one violent stroke, so the Lord Jesus Christ, our all-glorious Saviour, was slain by the violent stroke of God's holy wrath when he bore our sins in his own body on the cursed tree (v. 15; Isaiah 53:10, 11).

Symbol Of Peace
The dove is not only the epitome of humility, meekness, devotion, purity, and chastity; it is also the constant emblem of peace and reconciliation. It is held before us in Holy Scripture as the type, picture, and symbol of peace, and of Christ who is our peace. It was a dove that brought the olive branch back to Noah, declaring that the storm of God's wrath was over. After our Lord Jesus Christ had, by the sacrifice of himself, completely and forever exhausted the wrath of God for his people, he sent the Holy Spirit (The Dove of Heaven!) to his church, declaring reconciliation by blood

61

atonement (Acts 2). This is exactly what was symbolized in our Lord's baptism (Matthew 3:13-17). And when the time of love comes for the calling of Christ's redeemed ones, he sends the Dove of heaven with the olive branch of peace, declaring that justice is satisfied, wrath is gone, judgment is over, and reconciliation is accomplished.

February 2
Today's Reading: Leviticus 5-7
Restitution made and God glorified
Leviticus 5:16 and 6:5

Blessed is that enlightened soul who, by the grace of God, is able to see Christ in the Old Testament as well as in the New. Blessed are those eyes that behold the Lord Jesus Christ in all the promises, precepts, and prophecies of the Old Testament as well as in the proclamations of the New. Blessed are those hearts that can see the beauty and glory of Christ in the ordinances, types, and shadows of the law, as well as in the shining light of the Gospel.

It is a sad fact, but a fact it is, that most who read the Bible and most who preach and teach from it see nothing in the Old Testament but historic facts, legal precepts, carnal ceremonies, and moral ethics. To the vast majority of the religious people I know the Old Testament is a sealed Book, without meaning or message. They simply cannot unlock it, because they don't have the key. They are like those whom Isaiah describes in Isaiah 6. Seeing they see not, hearing they hear not, understanding, they understand not the things written in the Old Testament Scripture.

The Key to the Old Testament is Christ. What a great blessing it is to have the Key! Yet, there is no room for boasting here. If we see, hear, and understand the Scriptures, it is because God has graciously caused the light of his glory and grace to shine in our hearts by his Spirit. It is because we have been taught of God. It is because the Lord God has opened our understanding that we might understand the Scriptures (Luke 24:45). It is written, "Blessed are your eyes, for they see: and your ears, for they hear" (Matthew 13:16).

Nowhere is man's spiritual blindness more evident than in the things written about the Mosaic law and the Levitical sacrifices. The law of God requiring restitution for any wrong done by one person to another and the sacrifices requiring restitution for atonement were not intended merely to teach a moral precept of restitution. Rather, these things were written to teach by precept and by picture that the Lord Jesus Christ would, by his great work of redemption, turn the tables and make a full restitution of all things to the everlasting praise and glory of the Triune God. They all testify of that which is written of him in Psalm 69:4 "Then I restored that which I took not away".

The long list of laws of restitution given in Exodus 21-23 is introduced by the law of the bond slave. The Lord God has made us holy by the obedience unto death of the Lord Jesus Christ, his voluntary bond slave, Jehovah's Righteous Servant. Our blessed Lord Jesus, because of his love for his Father and his love to us, his captive wife and children, cheerfully bowed to be Jehovah's Servant to have his ears opened and would not go out free, until he had accomplished all the work to which he was called and had graciously undertaken. He would not quit his service until he had, by the sacrifice of himself, "obtained eternal redemption for us".

February 3
Today's Reading: Leviticus 8-11
The efficacy of the blood
Leviticus 8:14, 15

Read Leviticus 8:14, 15 and then read Leviticus 8:30 and you will see that in the typical, ceremonial law God gave to Israel all were anointed with the anointing oil for whom the blood of the sin-offering was shed. So, too, in the fulfilment of the type, all are born of God for whom blood atonement has been made by the Lord Jesus Christ.

The Prominence Of The Blood
Christ's sin-atoning blood is set before us prominently throughout the Scriptures. It is typically unfolded in great detail in the eighth chapter of Leviticus. Throughout this chapter the thing constantly set before us is the necessity and the efficacy of our Saviour's blood for atonement, acceptance, and reconciliation with God. On that great day, when Aaron and his sons were consecrated as priests unto God, it was the blood of the sacrifice that was constantly before the eyes of the people.

What are these typical blood sacrifices intended of God to teach us? They teach us plainly that sinners are accepted of God only by and because of Christ's shed blood (Ephesians 1:7; 1 Peter 1:18-21). We cannot approach, worship, or find acceptance with the holy Lord God except by the sin-atoning blood of our Lord Jesus Christ. Only a bloodstained ear can hear God's Word. Only a bloodstained hand can do God's work. Only a bloodstained foot can walk in the courts of the Lord's house. We cannot come to God except by the blood of Christ; but blessed be his holy name, we can come to God by that blood (Hebrews 10:19-21).

The Efficacy Of The Blood
As the blood of Christ was prominent in all the sacrifices and services of the typical Levitical priesthood, so too, was the efficacy of our Saviour's blood. Effectual redemption by Christ (also called limited atonement) is the point of Satan's most persistent opposition to the Gospel. This is the point at which self-serving prophets of

deceit most quickly compromise the Gospel. When I speak of the efficacy of Christ's blood I mean just this: the blood of Christ has effectually accomplished all that our Saviour intended to accomplish by shedding it. He put away our sins, all the sins of all God's elect. He obtained eternal redemption for all his chosen. Every sinner for whom Christ shed his blood at Calvary shall, at God's appointed time of love, be given the blessed anointing of the Holy Spirit. Every chosen, redeemed sinner shall, at God's appointed time, be born again by the almighty, irresistible power and grace of God the Holy Spirit. All for whom Christ died shall be saved by the power and grace of God the Holy Spirit. The efficacy of Christ's blood is seen in the anointing that follows it. All for whom blood was shed were anointed with the anointing oil. That is the thing typically set before us in Leviticus 8.

February 4
Today's Reading: Leviticus 12, 13
The Lord and the leper
Leviticus 13:17

In Leviticus 13 and 14 the Lord God gives us ceremonial laws regarding uncleanness. Chapter 13 is all about the ceremonial uncleanness and ceremonial cleansing of the leper. The unclean leper represents fallen man in his uncleanness before God. The leprosy of the body represents the uncleanness of the soul. The cleansing of the leper represents the salvation of God's elect and our cleansing from sin in and by Christ, our Saviour. As leprosy in ancient times was considered incurable by any human means, the sin and uncleanness, the ruin of fallen man is an evil from which there is no cure and no deliverance but by God. Who but God can forgive sin?

Aaron, as the great high priest to whom the leper was to show himself, typified Christ, our great High Priest. Everyone infected by the filth of leprosy was to show himself to the priest. And the sinner who would obtain God's forgiveness must show himself to the Saviour (1 John 1:7, 9). Everything written in this chapter indicates the spiritual disease of the soul. It is an old disease. It is a corruption of the heart, and is not merely skin deep. The sinner is full "of wounds, and bruises, and putrefying sores" (Isaiah 1:5). And none but the Priest of priests, even the Lord Jesus Christ, that great High Priest of our profession, can cleanse from sin.

The spots which appear without may differ, but the leprosy is the same within. Sin breaks out in many ways, but the polluted fountain of our fallen nature is the source of all the outward evil. Out of the heart proceed all evil thoughts and wicked deeds (Matthew 15:18-20). The only remedy for our evil is Christ. It is the blood of Christ alone which cleanses us from all sin.

How gracious it is of God the Holy Spirit to show us by these shadows of the law the leprous state in which we stood before God by reason of sin. How very precious is the Lord Jesus, our great High Priest, as he is brought to us here as that One appointed by God our Father to whom the convinced sinner must show himself, the only one who can pronounce the leper clean. He alone can show us our leprosy. He alone can cure the leprosy. And he alone can pronounce us clean.

Teach me, O Spirit of God, the horrid leprous state of my fallen nature, in which I was born. Give me grace to plunge continually into that Fountain opened for sin and for uncleanness in the Saviour's precious blood. Ever lead me to him by thy sweet, irresistible mercy. When I am enabled to draw nigh and show myself naked before him that he may search me and try me, when under the deepest conviction of misery, give me grace to trust him. Cleanse me, O Lord, from my soul's deep, deep leprosy. Wash me, and I shall be clean! Clothe me with the garments of salvation. Give me daily grace and hourly strength to "put off, concerning the former conversation, the old man which is corrupt according to the deceitful lusts, and be renewed in the Spirit of my mind: and to put on the new man which after God is created in righteousness and true holiness".

February 5
Today's Reading: Leviticus 14, 15
"A running issue"
Leviticus 15:1, 2

The "running issue" described so graphically in Leviticus 15:1-33, is a sickening, revolting type and picture of something far more sickening and revolting in us. The sin that is in us by nature, the corruption of our vile, base, depraved hearts, is a foul, obnoxious pus constantly oozing from our hearts, by which we are defiled and which defiles everything we touch. This is something worse than the leprosy seen in the flesh. This is the secret, hidden corruption and uncleanness of our hearts.

Our hearts are overflowing fountains of corruption, constantly oozing foulness, impurity, and uncleanness. If I could be more graphic in describing the corruption of our hearts, I would be. But the Holy Spirit here uses three very graphic pictures by which we are compelled to cry before God, "I know that in me, that is in my flesh, dwelleth no good thing" (Romans 7:18).

First, the corruption of our heart is portrayed under the picture of a man with a running issue out of his flesh (vv. 1-15). This running issue is the equivalent of what we call gonorrhoea. What a proper picture that is of our hearts' corruption! Gonorrhoea is a vile plague contracted by illicit behaviour. It is something you get from someone else. But it becomes a part of you. It is something you try to hide. But the corruption from deep within oozes foulness from your body. That pretty well describes the evil that is in us. We became sinners by the illicit, criminal, adulterous behaviour of our father, Adam. The sin of our father is now ours, so much ours that sin is what we are. Oh, how we try to hide it from ourselves, from other people, and from God, but it is what we really are! The corruption constantly oozes uncleanness from within.

Second, the foulness and corruption of our nature is pictured by the spilling of a man's seed (vv. 16-18). We are not told whether the seed spilt is spilt in some profane act, or in the conjugal privileges of a husband and wife, or nocturnally. But this entire chapter is describing things of the most private nature. I am therefore inclined to think that this particular text is dealing with that which occurs nocturnally. It speaks of something that is unavoidable. Because it is unavoidable, the natural outflow of a man's body, we commonly associate nothing evil with it. But the Lord God declares a person unclean who is in anyway touched by a man's seed. Why? The reason is clear. Everything that comes out of a man, everything is corrupt and unclean.

The third uncleanness presented in this chapter is the uncleanness of a woman with an issue of blood (vv. 19-24). Isaiah declares that all our righteousnesses are as filthy rags, discarded menstrual cloths. Here our very nature is described as the uncleanness of a woman's discharge during her monthly cycle.

This is the doctrine taught by these three repulsive examples of foulness, examples so disgusting that we simply do not discuss them in public unless the matters are absolutely unavoidable. We are corrupt and everything that comes out of us is corrupt and corrupts everything it touches (Romans 7:18; Matthew 15:18, 19). But our great, infinitely holy Lord God has made a way for us to be separated from our pollution and be clean before him. Oh, bless his holy name and rejoice! God himself, he who cannot look upon iniquity, has made a way for unclean sinners to be made clean (vv. 13-15). "By the washing of regeneration and renewing of the Holy Ghost" the sin-atoning blood of Christ separates chosen redeemed sinners from their uncleanness and makes the heaven-born soul clean before God.

February 6
Today's Reading: Leviticus 16-18
"It is the blood that maketh an atonement"
Leviticus 17:11

The seventeenth chapter of Leviticus has nothing to do with the imaginary sanctity of animal life. It has nothing to do with the health risks involved in eating red meat, or even with eating red meat rare. Leviticus 17, like all the rest of this Inspired Volume, is all about the gospel. It is all about Christ. There are two principal things revealed in this chapter. They are lessons of tremendous importance. We must learn them. Without the knowledge of these two things, we will never understand the Book of God, the Gospel of God, or the work of God. These two lessons are vital.

Discovering Christ Day By Day

Christ The Way

All worship except the worship of God through the blood atonement of the Lord Jesus Christ is idolatry; and all idolatry is the worship of devils (Leviticus 17:1-10). Christ is the Way. There is no other. Christ is the Truth. There is no other. Christ is the Life. There is no other. Will we ever learn this? Christ is the Door. There is no other. All who attempt to come in some other way are thieves and robbers, thieves who would rob God of his glory. God will not tolerate them. After giving the law regarding the Day of Atonement, the Lord God gave commandment to the Children of Israel requiring that they bring their sacrifices to him at the door of the Tabernacle, that they offer sacrifices nowhere else except at his altar. It was a commandment which he required every Israelite to observe, and a commandment he required every stranger who sojourned among them to obey. Any who refused to do so were to be cut off from among the people of God, put out of the camp, banished from the Church. Remember the context. The Lord had just finished declaring to Israel that they were to observe the Day of Atonement every year on the tenth day of the seventh month. This was made as an everlasting statute (Leviticus 16:29-34). Of course, everything required in this statute portrayed our Lord Jesus Christ in his great work of redemption. The high priest made atonement for the holy sanctuary, the tabernacle of the congregation, the altar, himself, the priests, and for all the people of the congregation of the Lord. That is a picture of particular redemption. By the sin-atoning blood of Christ, God's Israel has been cleansed, made clean from all sin before the Lord (1 John 3:5). That great and glorious day, when Israel saw redemption ceremonially accomplished and sin put away by God's sacrifice, was "a sabbath of rest ... by a statute forever". That is a picture of the blessed rest of faith. Not only do we cease from our works, we rest in him who has done all for us.

Blood Atonement

The Lord God says, "I have given the blood to you upon the altar to make atonement for your souls" (Leviticus 17:11). The blood of our Lord Jesus Christ was shed at Calvary for one specific purpose: "To make atonement for your souls". Will it do the job? Is it enough? What does God say? "for it is the blood that maketh an atonement for the soul". Yes, the blood of Christ poured out upon the cursed tree accomplished precisely what God intended. His blood made atonement for his people! Just as the blood of the paschal lamb made atonement for the whole congregation of Israel, so the blood of Christ our Passover, who was sacrificed for us, made atonement for all God's Israel (Romans 5:6-11). It is not the blood and something else. The word is most explicit. It attributes atonement exclusively to the blood. "Without shedding of blood there is no remission" (Hebrews 9: 22). Only in this way can God be both "a just God and a Saviour". Only by the blood can he be both just and the justifier of all who believe.

February 7
Today's Reading: Leviticus 19-21
"Ye shall be holy"
Leviticus 19:2

This is God's word to us today. "Ye shall be holy: for I the Lord your God am holy". Because the Lord our God is holy, he requires that we also be holy.

A Promise
First and foremost this is a promise and declaration of grace. The Lord God is here declaring to his chosen, covenant people that they shall be a holy people, not partially holy, not mostly holy, but entirely holy. This is not a recommendation, but a declaration. It is a declaration of grace made to a specific people.

The word "holy" has two distinct meanings. Both definitions of the word must be understood and applied here. First, to be holy is to be separate, distinct, peculiar, set apart, and severed from all others. Second, to be holy is to be pure or purified. The Lord God here declares to his Israel, to all who stand before him as his covenant people, "You shall be separate, distinct, peculiar, set apart, and severed from all others, pure and purified before me". We know that this is the intended meaning of this statement by comparing scripture with scripture (Exodus 19:6; Leviticus 11:44; 20:7, 26; 1 Thessalonians 4:7). The Lord God Almighty, by the work of his sovereign, free, distinguishing grace, takes such things as we are, such things as he finds in the dung heap of fallen humanity and makes them holy. He does this by the precious blood of Christ in free justification (Titus 2:11-14). He does it by divine regeneration, the new birth, making the chosen, redeemed sinner partaker of the divine nature, a new creature in Christ, "created in righteousness and true holiness" (1 Corinthians 6:9-11; 1 Peter 2:7-10). And he will bring this great work of grace to its final consummation in resurrection glory (Ephesians 5:26, 27; Jude 24, 25).

A Call
This is also a call to holiness that we must heed. "Ye shall be holy: for I the Lord your God am holy." The Lord God here calls you and me to holiness, godliness, and righteous behaviour in our daily lives. He here calls us to be separate, distinct, peculiar, set apart, and severed from all others, pure and purified before men in our conduct (Leviticus 19:37). We know also that this too is the intended meaning of these words because they are so used for this purpose by the Spirit of God in the inspired writings of both the apostle Paul and the apostle Peter (1 Thessalonians 4:1-7; 1 Peter 1:13-16).

Here in Leviticus 19 the holy Lord God calls for you and me to be holy as we live in this world; and he does not leave it for us to decide what he means. He tells us specifically how we are to live in this world as his holy people in these thirty-seven verses. I can hear some say, "But, Pastor, these verses are found in Old Testament law, and we are not under the law." You are right on both counts. But the fact that we are free from the law in Christ does not mean that we are without law, not at all. The believer's law, the believer's rule of life is the whole revelation of God in Holy Scripture. That which is here written is addressed to you and me and is just as authoritative as Ephesians 1 or Romans 9. True, it must be understood and applied in Gospel terms; but it must be both understood and applied. Here the Lord God tells us specifically how we are to live in this world in a way that honours God. We please God by faith in Christ. Without faith it is impossible to please him (Hebrews 11:6). But we must never imagine that if we believe in Christ it does not matter how we live. It is written in 1 Thessalonians 4:1 that we must take care as to how we "ought to walk and to please God". "Whether therefore ye eat, or drink, or whatsoever ye do, do all to the glory of God" (1 Corinthians 10:31).

February 8
Today's Reading: Leviticus 22, 23
"It shall be perfect to be accepted"
Leviticus 22:21

How good does a person have to be to get to heaven? He has to be perfectly good, as good as God himself. That which man looks upon as his "personal righteousness" he calls good but it is of absolutely no value in the sight of God. God calls all your thoughts and deeds of righteousness, and mine, "filthy rags". They are an abomination to him (Isaiah 64:6). Man's definition of righteousness depends entirely upon his definition and understanding of God. The problem is most have never seen God in his glorious holiness. Once a sinner sees God in his holiness, he will cease forever to speak of his own goodness, personal holiness and self-righteousness. With Isaiah, he will cry, "Woe is me! I am undone" (Isaiah 6:1-6). Who can stand in the presence of the holy Lord God?

No son of Adam can ever stand in the presence of the holy Lord God, because we are all cursed (Galatians 3:10). God is so infinitely holy that he charges the angels with folly, so holy that the heavens are not clean in his sight, so holy that when he found sin upon his own dear Son, he forsook him and killed him! Are we better than the angels? Are we purer than the heavens? Dare we imagine that God will accept us with our polluted works, when he killed his own Son for sin? Only one who is himself equal to God can stand in the presence of God and please him (Psalm 24:3-5; Matthew 17:5). That righteousness which God requires, only God can give. Yet, it must be the work of a man, or it is of no value to men. Blessed be God! There is a Man who is himself God, who has magnified the law and made it honourable. He has brought in an everlasting righteousness by his perfect obedience to the law as a man, even the very righteousness of God. He has satisfied the law's justice, by dying under its curse. And he lives forever to give righteousness and eternal life to sinners. That Man-God is Jesus Christ the Lord.

The Word of God plainly declares that no one shall enter into the glory of heaven who is not worthy to do so (Revelation 21:27; 22:11; 1 Corinthians 6:9). And all are by nature unrighteous (Ecclesiastes 7:20). We are all sinners. We all deserve the wrath of God. Yet God the Holy Spirit tells us that there are some who have been made worthy to be partakers of the inheritance of the saints (Colossians 1:12). How can that be? How can a sinner be made worthy of heaven? Only God can do it! Grace alone can make us worthy of heaven's glory. Every believer, every sinner saved by grace, everyone who trusts Christ alone as his Saviour and Lord has been made worthy of heaven by three mighty works of God.

First, the believer's sins have been fully paid for through blood atonement by the Lord Jesus Christ, so justice cannot require further payment. Second, the righteous obedience of Christ has been imputed to all who trust him, so that the believer stands before God as one who is perfectly righteous, having fulfilled all his holy law in the Person of Christ, our Substitute. Third, in the new birth God the Holy Spirit gives every chosen, ransomed sinner a holy nature. By these three works of grace, sinners are transformed into saints and made worthy of heaven, "perfect in Christ Jesus"!

February 9
Today's Reading: Leviticus 24, 25
The Day of Atonement
Leviticus 25:9

The most important and instructive of all the typical ceremonies of the Old Testament was the Day of Atonement. The Day of Atonement pictured, foreshadowed, and typified the sin-atoning work of our Lord Jesus Christ. He is our great High Priest, our substitutionary Sacrifice for sin, our Scapegoat, our Altar, and our Mercy-Seat. Only through him do sinners have access to and acceptance with the Holy Lord God.

In order for the holy Lord God to deal with sinful men in mercy, grace, and peace, without compromising his character and violating his justice, there had to be a Day of Atonement. A holy, just, and true God could never allow fallen, sinful man to live before him, unless a suitable atonement is made for man's sin. Justice must be vindicated. Sin must be punished or else God and man can never come together in peace. Therefore God ordained that a Day of Atonement be observed in Israel once a year, as a picture and pledge of the great Day of Atonement to be accomplished at Calvary by the slaying of the Lamb of God for the redemption of God's elect.

The Lord God gave Moses meticulous, detailed instructions about how the Day of Atonement was to be observed in the sixteenth chapter of Leviticus. The Day of Atonement was ordained and initiated by God himself. It was not a human invention in time, but a Divine ordinance reflecting God's eternal purpose of grace to redeem and save his elect (Job 33:24).

The Day of Atonement was set for a specific time each year (16:29; 23:27). "The seventh month, on the tenth day of the month". God's great Day of Atonement was set, fixed, appointed, and determined by God himself. "When the fulness of the time was come God sent forth his Son" (Galatians 4:4). "In due time Christ died for the ungodly" (Romans 5:8).

There was only one Day of Atonement each year, because our Lord Jesus Christ was to make only one offering for sin. "Now once in the end of the world hath he appeared to put away sin by the sacrifice of himself ... Christ was once offered to bear the sins of many" (Hebrews 9:26, 28).

The sacrifices offered on the Day of Atonement were only typical. They could never put away sin and could never remove the curse of the law (Hebrews 10:1-4); but our blessed Christ has both put away all the sins of his chosen and removed the curse of the law from us (Galatians 3:13, 14) by the sacrifice of himself as our Substitute.

All the typical, ceremonial sacrifices were fulfilled by Christ and have ceased because Christ fulfilled them (Hebrews 10:11-14, 18). God requires no sacrifice but Christ. God will accept no sacrifice but Christ. And all who offer something for forgiveness with Christ trample the blood of Christ under their feet and deny the merit of his atoning sacrifice altogether.

All was done for a specific, chosen people and resulted in God's ceremonial blessing upon those people. So too, all that Christ did as the God-man Mediator he did for his elect alone; and that which he did for us effectually fetches all the blessings of the Triune God upon his chosen (Galatians 3:14).

February 10
Today's Reading: Leviticus 26, 27
"I will give you ..."
Leviticus 26:1-13

The first thirteen verses of Leviticus 26 hang heavy with rich clusters of unimaginable temporal good. What a dazzling catalogue of goodness the Holy Spirit sets before us in this passage! The Lord God promises to rid the land of his chosen people of assailing armies, ravenous beasts, hunger, thirst, and uneasiness of any kind.

Faith In Christ
These bounties are spoken of in the language of external, carnal things; but earthly language is used here to convey spiritual blessedness, spiritual delights for our souls, bounties of grace scattered by God's infinite hand. These bounties are promised to all who walk in his statues and keep his commandments; that is to say, to all who believe on his Son. That is not a fanciful stretch. That is exactly what God says obedience to his law is (Romans 3:31; 10:1-4; Galatians 3:19, 24; 1 John 3:23; 5:1-3).

The promise of God to all who trust his dear Son is, "For I will have respect unto you, and make you fruitful, and multiply you, and establish my covenant with you" (v. 9). He says I will look upon you with delight and pleasure. My eye will be upon you to care for you, watching over you to do you good and protect you from all evil. I will turn myself from all others to you, having a distinct and particular regard for you. Cast all you care on me and I will care for you.

Constant Grace
Then, in verse 10, he says, "And ye shall eat old store, and bring forth the old because of the new". With those words, the God of all grace promises every believing sinner a constant supply of grace, an unbroken continuity of grace to our souls forever, grace sufficient to meet our spiritual needs without fail.

His supplies of wisdom, love, joy, peace, and power to our souls are always enough and more than enough for our needs. Even when we complain of languishing in our hearts, of hunger and thirst in our souls, the flow of his grace is uninterrupted. Our great God and Father, the God of all grace, the God and Father of our Lord Jesus Christ, is ever pouring forth grace for his elect, all grace and all-sufficient grace in Christ Jesus. He sometimes appears to withhold his grace. He sometimes appears to be angry. But, insofar as his chosen are concerned, that is never the case. Believing sinners are accepted in the Beloved, because of the Beloved, and as the Beloved, as one with Christ himself.

That means that the Niagara of God's goodness in Christ, the infinite flood of his grace toward his chosen people can never be stopped, paused, or even diminished. May God the Holy Spirit sweetly constrain us to keep our poor, empty vessels beneath the downpour of his goodness at the throne of grace. In our Father's house there is bread enough and to spare (Psalm 31:19). The gift of Christ leaves no gift withheld. "He who spared not his own Son, but delivered him up for us all, how shall he not with him also freely give us all things".

February 11
Today's Reading: Numbers 1, 2
"I will set my face against you"
Leviticus 26:14-20

Faith finds abundance in the Land of Grace. For every sin there is a Fountain opened. For all unrighteousness there is a white robe. "In the Lord have I righteousness and strength." For every burden there is help at hand. "Casting all your care upon him, for he careth for you." Light to guide and peace to consol shine brightly in the Gospel of God. When Satan terrifies, the cross of Christ gives calm. When conscience trembles, the crucified Saviour shows his hands and side. When the law thunders, Calvary spreads its sheltering wings. When heart corruptions vex, the Spirit comes with renewed grace.

How blessed is God's Israel! Zion's King, the Lord Jesus, floods his Land of Grace with his goodness. We live every day at heaven's gate. All the past has been one wide flood of mercy, the present a stream of joy. And all the future an ocean of glory! But when the end comes and our freed spirits wing their upward flight, what will that glory be? When our all-glorious Christ is revealed, if faith finds him so dear, what will be the realizing sight! "We shall be like him; for we shall see him as he is".

Then, when the grave restores its prey, when this poor body puts on immortality's attire and shines more brightly than a thousand suns, like Christ himself forever; what then? The Triune God, our almighty Jehovah, Father, Son, and Holy Ghost, shall be fully known and fully loved, fully adored and fully praised, while the endless ages reveal the splendour of his glory. Eternal love planned all this blessedness. The blood of Christ purchased it. The Holy Spirit seals it to us and fits us for it as partakers of the Divine nature. Soon grace shall be crowned with glory! But not for all!

The first 13 verses of Leviticus 26 speak only of grace, promises of grace and God's performance of grace. Then, the scene changes. Beginning in verse 14, we have a scene of woe, wrath, and terror; terror to you who will not believe on the Son of God. God's word is as fixed as heaven's high throne. You have madly scorned his rule. You have rashly followed your own heart's desire. Except you repent, nothing but judgment awaits you. The gospel cherished is all this everlasting joy. The gospel scorned is all this everlasting woe (John 3:36).

> How will your heart endure, the terrors of that day;
> When earth and heaven, before his face, astonished shrink away?
> Ye sinners, seek his grace, whose wrath ye cannot bear,
> Fly to the shelter of his cross, and find salvation there!

February 12
Today's Reading: Numbers 3, 4
The Levites and the service of the sanctuary
Numbers 3:12

As we read in Numbers 3 and 4 about the separation of the Levites to the service of the sanctuary, let us lift our hearts heavenward and behold our Saviour, the Lord Jesus, who was consecrated and set apart to our heavenly Father's service from everlasting for the salvation of our souls! He undertook the work of redemption for us, as our Surety and Jehovah's righteous Servant, with holy earnestness before the worlds were made. With utter, unrelenting zeal, faithfulness, and devotion he performed all the work.

In love for our souls, he who is Lord of all, who thought it not robbery to be equal with God, took upon himself the form of a servant. The Word was made flesh! God became one of us that he might make us the sons of God! Living as a man, as the God-man Mediator, our dear Saviour magnified the whole law and made it honourable. His labour of love continued until, at last our Saviour could say to his Father and our Father, "I have glorified thee on the earth, I have finished the work thou gavest me to do".

Unlike Aaron, his sons, and the Levites, our Lord Jesus Christ did not merely offer sacrifice for sin; he made himself the sacrifice for us! He is our Priest but he is also our Altar and our Sacrifice. To make us the righteousness of God, he was made sin for us. He who knew no sin was made a curse for us. To give us life, he died under the wrath of God in our place. With his own blood, our Saviour entered in once into the holy place, having obtained eternal redemption for us! With his blood, he opened a new and living way for us, a way by which sinners may draw near to God "in full assurance of faith". By his blood and righteousness, every sinner who comes to God may have "the full assurance of hope" with "the full assurance of understanding". That is to say, trusting Christ we understand that God is just in justifying us and accepting us through the merits of our Saviour, without our works. Christ has opened heaven for us; and none can shut that which he has opened.

Now, by grace, all who believe are made "a royal priesthood" and are numbered among the sons of Levi for the service of the sanctuary. As we behold our God and Saviour, the Lord Jesus Christ, as he who was set apart and willingly made Jehovah's Servant for us, may God the Holy Spirit give us grace to be wholly devoted to our Redeemer's glory in the service of his church and kingdom, so that we may truthfully say, with God's servant of old, "Truly, I am thy servant, I am thy servant and the son of thine handmaid; thou hast loosed my bonds" (Psalm 116:16).

What glory, what inconceivable weight of glory will break upon our souls, when this earthly tabernacle of ours shall be taken down, and the pins and the sockets, with their silver cords and instruments, are broken at the cistern, when Christ Jesus shall again raise it up a glorified body, without spot, or wrinkle, or any such thing, when our vile bodies shall be made like unto his glorious body. Then all that was typified in the tabernacle, its services, and its priesthood, shall be fully accomplished and known.

February 13
Today's Reading: Numbers 5-7
"He shall be called a Nazarene"
Matthew 2:23

When God gave his law to Israel by the hand of Moses, one of the most thoroughly expanded laws given was "the law of the Nazarite" in Numbers 6. There are many things in the law of the Nazarite that cannot be applied to our Saviour. He both touched dead bodies and drank wine, though he was never made unclean by doing so. Yet, strictly speaking, as that one who was wholly devoted and separated to the Lord God, our Saviour is the Nazarene typically referred to in this Old Testament law. He is the one and the only one man who perfectly fulfilled it. This is evident from the fact that the law is never mentioned again until we see it mentioned in connection with Samson (another type of our Redeemer) in Judges 13.

Our Lord Jesus Christ was set apart and sanctified to the Father to do his will from eternity. "And for their sakes I sanctify myself, that they also might be sanctified through the truth" (John 17:19). Our Saviour fulfils the type gloriously. The church is described as having hair like a flock of goats (Song of Solomon 4:1). Like the hairs of his head, a vast multitude grow up in Christ and upon him. No razor shall ever separate us from our Lord. Like the hair on our heads, we live upon Christ, depend on him, and draw life and strength from him, because we are a part of him and can never be separated from him. As Samson's strength and glory was his hair, so we are Christ's glory. But our mighty Samson shall never lose his glory. The hair is the last part of the body to die; and we shall never perish, because Christ our Saviour lives forever! Therefore it may be said of every member of Christ's Church, as we read in Lamentations 4:7, "Her Nazarites were purer than snow, they were whiter than milk, they were more ruddy in body than rubies, their polishing was of sapphire".

We must not overlook the fact that in all these offerings for sin shadowed forth the one great, all-sufficient sacrifice of Christ, our great Nazarite, by which our sins were put away. Waving the offering before the Lord was both an acknowledgement of sin before the holy Lord God and a celebration of sin's pardon and removal by the blood of Christ. In Mark 14:24, 25 our Saviour spoke of his work as the Nazarene being fulfilled when he said, "This is the blood of the new testament, which is shed for many. Verily I say unto you, I will drink no more of the fruit of the vine, until that day that I drink it new in the kingdom of God".

We have the clearest possible evidence that all that is seen in this Nazarite law refers to Christ and his great work of redemption in the last verses of Numbers 6. In verses 22-27, upon the basis of the Nazarite's obedience and sacrifice, God commands his blessing upon his people. Then Nazarite is mentioned is in Judges 13:5. Here it is used to describe Samson as a Nazarite (Judges 13:5), another great type of our Saviour in his consecration to God from his mother's womb. Isaiah also used this very word when he prophesied of Christ coming to save us by the sacrifice of himself. "And there shall come forth a rod out of the stem of Jesse, and a Branch (netzar - Nazarite) shall grow out of his roots" (Isaiah 11:1).

The fact that our Saviour was born at Bethlehem in fulfilment of Micah 5:2 tells us that he was, at the time of his conception in the virgin's womb, "a Nazarene" (Luke 1:26-33). "That Holy thing", Christ our Mediator, was the Nazarite from the womb, brought forth in the city of Nazareth by the power of the Holy Spirit, just as Isaiah told us he would be (Isaiah 7:14; 9:6). In all these things, we see that Christ the Nazarene is "the end of the law for righteousness to every one that believeth", having fulfilled it entirely as our Substitute and Saviour.

———

February 14
Today's Reading: Numbers 8-10
"A shadow of good things to come"
Hebrews 10:1

All the law of the Old Testament, with all the ceremonies and sacrifices of the Mosaic age, formed "a shadow of good things to come", portraying our Lord Jesus Christ, his obedience and death as our Substitute, and the blessings of God's salvation and grace in him. We have read in Numbers 8, 9, and 10 about the seven lamps on the candlestick in the tabernacle, the Levites who served in the tabernacle, the passover sacrifice, the pillar of cloud and of fire over the tabernacle, and the sounding of silver trumpets to gather Israel to God's altar. As we walk through the tabernacle sanctuary, may God the Holy Spirit give us grace always to look for and see our Lord Jesus Christ, the true Tabernacle, and see him everywhere.

The Lights
First, we read about the lights in the tabernacle, seven lamps on the golden candlestick. It is true that our Lord Jesus declares God's church and each believer in it to be the light of the world. The seven lamps, no doubt, represent the seven churches (the churches of God in this world) as seen and described by John in Revelation 1-3. But the golden candlestick holding forth the lights represents our Lord Jesus Christ, the Light of the world. Whatever light we may have, whatever light we may give forth to others, we have and we give forth by his Spirit; but Christ is the Light. Shine, precious Saviour, into my heart, give light to my dark mind, enliven my lifeless soul, warm my frozen affections!

The Levites
We have also read today about the Levites given to God's high priest Aaron to minister in the tabernacle, to serve in the holy things. No Levite was allowed to enter into this great service until he was twenty-five years old. Ripeness of age was required for this sacred employment. The Spirit of God gives us similar instruction concerning those who are set apart for the ministry of the gospel (1 Timothy 3:1-7). These were men chosen of God, cleansed, and consecrated to the Lord. So it is with all whom God puts into the blessed work of the gospel ministry. Chosen to salvation and chosen to be gospel preachers, they are first cleansed by blood atonement and by "the washing of water by the Word", the regenerating (sanctifying) work of God the Holy Spirit. Then being called of God, they are consecrated to him and to the blessed work of the gospel in the totality of their lives. He who chose them and called them gives them gifts and qualifies them for their work. Gospel preachers are but earthen vessels carrying the treasure of the gospel through this world. Pause and pray for them, those men who are ministers of God to your soul, particularly your own pastor. Ask God to uphold them, teach them, strengthen them, open doors of utterance before them, and use them to gather his elect to himself.

Discovering Christ Day By Day

The Passover
Numbers 9 speaks of the passover service in the Old Testament tabernacle. We rejoice to know that "Christ our Passover is sacrificed for us" (1 Corinthians 5:7). How our hearts ought to dance when we read the word of God to Moses in verse ten. "Speak unto the children of Israel, saying, If any man of you or of your posterity shall be unclean by reason of a dead body, or be in a journey afar off, yet he shall keep the passover unto the LORD". Yes, the unclean are welcome at God's Altar, being made clean by the precious blood of Christ our Passover! Coming to God by faith in Christ Jesus, the Lord God gives us his Holy Spirit, as he gave Israel the pillar of cloud by day and the pillar of fire by night, to guide us through the hostile enemy territory of this world unto our glorious rest above. Blessed Saviour, send your Spirit before me to guide me in your will and your way. Let me never run unsent or uncalled; and give me grace to follow you, O Lamb of God, whithersoever you go until my appointed time on earth is finished and I am brought at last into the glory of heaven with you.

The Trumpets
The silver trumpets in Numbers 10 represent the gospel's joyful sound, the sound of Christ's blood and righteousness, by which God the Holy Spirit gathers chosen, redeemed sinners to the Saviour, the sound by which he calls, comforts, corrects, and cheers his people. "Blessed is the people that know the joyful sound: they shall walk, O LORD, in the light of thy countenance" (Psalm 89:15).

Let us this day, like God's servant Moses, urge others to partake of the grace which is in Christ Jesus. Well satisfied with the inexhaustible fulness that there is in Christ for all the countless seed of Israel, let us urge the unregenerate around us to come to the Saviour, to taste and see how good and gracious the Lord is.

February 15
Today's Reading: Numbers 11-14
Jehoshua: Jehovah is salvation
Numbers 13:16

When Moses changed the name of Oshea, the son of Nun, to Jehoshua, he was making a declaration. The name Jehoshua means, "Jehovah is salvation". And that is the essence of all that is taught in the Book of God. I cannot find any other doctrine taught in Holy Scripture.

When Moses stood before the unbelieving Children of Israel at the Red Sea, he cried, "Stand still and see the salvation of the Lord". The entire Book of Jonah is a declaration of what he said while he was yet in the whale's belly: "Salvation is of the Lord". David, in his psalms of praise, declares this over and over again. He sang, "The salvation of the righteous is of the Lord". "In God is my salvation and glory: the rock of my strength, and my refuge, is in God". These were his last words, "Although my house be not so with God; yet he hath made with me an everlasting covenant, ordered in all things and sure: for this is all my salvation, and all my desire".

As this was the message of the Prophets in the Old Testament, it is the message of the Apostles in the New. "By grace are ye saved through faith; and that not of yourselves: it is the gift of God: not of works, lest any man should boast". "Not by works of righteousness which we have done, but according to his mercy he saved us".

If this is the message of all the Prophets and all the Apostles who spoke for God in the past, it is the message of every preacher who speaks for God today. Any doctrine that departs from this message departs from the Scriptures, departs from the Gospel, and is heresy. All heresy has its beginning with the addition of something man does to the work of Christ. All heresy either adds to or in some way diminishes this fact: "Jehovah is salvation".

This is my doctrine. This is my hope. This is my message. "Jehovah is salvation". The whole of the work whereby a son of Adam is delivered from the power of sin, the kingdom of darkness, the guilt of transgression, the curse of the law, and the bondage of iniquity into the glorious liberty of the sons of God is of the Lord. Salvation is God's work alone!

February 16
Today's Reading: Numbers 15, 16
"Thus shall it be done"
Numbers 15:11

If we would worship the God of heaven, we must do so in the way he has prescribed in his Word. He will not be worshipped in any other way and will not be served in any other way. He says, "Thus shall it be done". And it shall not be done another way.

Due Order

Read 1 Chronicles chapters 13 and 15 and learn the importance of worshipping God "after the due order". We must learn to worship and serve the Lord our God after the due order. That which is done in the name of God must be done according to the Word of God and for the glory of God, or it will never be accepted before God. In our worship of God, everything must be done after the due order. Our hearts must be right, trusting Christ, motivated by the love of Christ and the glory of God.

And our doctrine must be right. We must be careful that we form our doctrine by "Thus saith the Lord". If our doctrine is not the pure doctrine of the gospel of Christ, our worship cannot be accepted before the Lord (Isaiah 8:20). That which is plainly revealed in the Word of God must be plainly declared from the pulpit. God never has blessed compromise and never will.

Discovering Christ Day By Day

There are some things plainly revealed in the Scriptures. God is God. That means he is sovereign, absolutely sovereign in all things (Psalm 135:6). All men are guilty, helpless, ruined, totally depraved sinners (Ephesians 2:1-4). God has a people whom he has chosen, a people who must and shall be saved (2 Thessalonians 2:13, 14). The Lord Jesus Christ effectually redeemed those people chosen of God (Isaiah 53:8-12). Salvation is accomplished by the irresistible, effectual power of God the Holy Spirit (John 6:63). All who believe on Christ are saved forever (John 3:36). Christ is Lord of all. He has ascended up on high and led captivity captive (John 17:2; Romans 14:9). Christ is coming again in the fulness of his glory to judge the world (Revelation 1:7).

Our worship must be right. All that is done in worship, particularly in public worship, must be according to the Word of God. We must omit nothing which the Word of God requires; and we must add nothing which the Word of God does not require. The honour of God and reverence for him must be first and foremost. Our ordinances must arise from the Word of God and be observed according to the Word of God. One innovation leads inevitably to another. One compromise will bring another compromise. Hear and heed God's warning. "Seek not after your own heart and your own eyes" (Numbers 15:39). If we follow our own hearts and our own eyes, they will cause us to "go a whoring" after other gods.

Trust Christ
God's command requiring all the congregation to stone the man to death who dared to pick up sticks on the sabbath day (Numbers 15:32-36) was a visible demonstration of the fact that anyone who attempts to do anything to make himself righteous and holy before God will perish under the wrath of God. Christ is our Sabbath. We find rest in him. We dare not even pick up a stick to give ourselves rest and peace! The Lord killed Uzza for putting out his hand to steady the ark, because that ark, like the sabbath, represented Christ's finished work (1 Chronicles 13:12). And the holy Lord God will send all to hell forever who put their hands to Christ's work, who attempt to make themselves righteous and holy before him. And when he does, all Israel (all God's elect) will say, "Amen. The Judge of all the earth has done right".

February 17
Today's Reading: Numbers 17-19
God sees no sin in his people
Numbers 23:21

These words do not suggest that there was no sin or perverseness in Israel. There was an abundance of perverseness among them; but the Lord God did not mark the sins of his people against them. He did not impute sin to his chosen. He did not look upon their sins with the eye of his justice, but hid his face from them and forgave them.

79

That which God did for his elect among the Children of Israel, he has done for all his elect in Christ, his true Israel, "the Israel of God".

Though there is much sin in us and done by us, as every true believer readily acknowledges and confesses (1 John 1:8, 10), yet God sees no sin in his people. The Lord Jesus Christ came into the world to destroy, purge, remove, and take away the sins of his people; and he has done it (John 1:29; Hebrews 1:3; 9:26; 1 John 3:5). All the sins of God's elect were laid upon Christ. He bore them in his own body on the tree, endured and satisfied the wrath of God for them, and bore them away. The Son of God redeemed us from the curse of the law, made an end of our sins, and justified and sanctified us by his blood. God Almighty has, through the effectual atonement of Christ, so thoroughly blotted out our sins that he does not behold them. He has cast our sins into the blessed, deep sea of Divine forgetfulness. He has cast our sins behind his back. He has removed them from us as far as the east is from the west, and remembers them no more. Therefore God sees no sin in his people!

I am fully aware that this doctrine is commonly rejected and despised by men. It has been described by some as "a freak doctrine of perverted minds that leads to licentiousness and sin". Why? I simply do not know. I cannot imagine anyone, who has tasted the bitterness of his own depravity and sin and has experienced the blessed forgiveness of sin by the grace of God through the blood of Christ, objecting to the fact that God "hath not beheld iniquity in Jacob, neither hath he seen perverseness in Israel". The fact that God sees no sin in his people is a most glorious, comforting doctrine of the Gospel, "without which", John Gill appropriately declared, "the gospel must cease to be good news and glad tidings to the sons of men".

Would you have this forgiveness? What would you give to go to bed tonight knowing that God Almighty does not behold sin in you and will never charge sin to you, to lay your head upon your pillow tonight with these words ringing in your heart: "Blessed is the man to whom the Lord will not impute sin"? If you are a sinner in need of such forgiveness, come now to the Son of God. Confess your sin to God, trusting Christ, and go your way, like the publican of old, justified. It is written in the Scriptures, "If we confess our sins, he is faithful and just to forgive us our sins, and to cleanse us from all unrighteousness" (1 John 1:9). Both God's faithfulness and his justice demand the forgiveness of all who believe on the Lord Jesus Christ.

February 18
Today's Reading: Numbers 20-22
How is it that God sees no sin in his people?
Numbers 23:21

The sweet and blessed fact that God sees no sin in us does not in any way imply that we do not sin or that God's omniscience fails to observe it. This is a matter of Divine justice. The record books of heaven record no iniquity, no transgression, and no sin against God's elect. God will not impute sin to his saints, or require satisfaction from us, because our sins were made Christ's and were justly imputed to him when he was made sin for us. He paid for them. Our sins have been forever expunged from the book of God's offended justice by our Saviour's precious blood. Read the testimony of Holy Scripture and rejoice (Romans 4:8; 8:1, 33, 34; 2 Corinthians 5:19-21). Let all who trust Christ get hold of this blessed, glorious fact: "he hath not beheld iniquity in Jacob, neither hath he seen perverseness in Israel". Rejoice in it. Give praise to God for it. And walk in the blessed comfort and assurance of it all the days of your life.

The Lord Jesus Christ has, by the sacrifice of himself, put away all our sins past, present, and future. They were imputed to him, laid upon him, punished in him, and put away by him (Isaiah 53:4-6). He made an end of our sins (Daniel 9:24). He took all the iniquity of his people in one day, by one sacrifice (Zechariah 3:9). In him we are fully justified from all things, so much so that in the eyes of God's holy law and justice we have no sin (Acts 13:38, 39; 1 John 3:5). By his one great sacrifice for sin the Son of God has made all God's elect perfect in his sight (Hebrews 10:11-14).

God the Father has freely and fully forgiven the sins of his people. Christ's blood, like the blood on the mercy-seat, covers our sins. They are not visible to the eyes of God's justice. The blood of Christ has blotted them from the ledger book of heaven, so that justice cannot see sin in us. For Christ's sake, the holy Lord God has cast our sins behind his back and into the depth of the sea, so that they are not only forgotten, but insofar as his law and justice are concerned, completely gone (Jeremiah 50:20).

In God's esteem, all believers are the very perfection of beauty and holiness in Christ. God looks upon us in Christ, washed in his blood, robed in righteousness; beautiful, perfect, holy, unblameable, unreproveable. Read what he says about the matter (Ezekiel 16:14; Song of Solomon 4:7, 9; Ephesians 5:25-27; Jude 24, 25). The fact that God sees no sin in his people is says John Gill, "the glory of the Bible and the marrow of the Gospel". It is this which most fully displays the riches of God's grace, the efficacy of Christ's blood, the completeness of his righteousness, and the fulness of his satisfaction. This fact is the foundation of all solid, biblical hope of future happiness, the foundation of our confidence and faith before God, the abiding comfort of our souls, and will be the ground of our triumph in the hour of death.

February 19
Today's Reading: Numbers 23-26
The omniscient God sees no sin in his people
Numbers 23:21

We know that God Almighty is omniscient. He knows all people and all things. Nothing is or can be hidden from his all-seeing eye. All the actions of all men, whether bad or good, are seen and known by God. He sees not only what we do, but why we do it. He sees the secret, inward, hidden things of our hearts, the fountain from which all our evil deeds flow like an open, overflowing sewer. His omniscient eye sees all the sins of his own people as well as the sins of the reprobate. There can be no debate about the fact that the omniscient God sees everything about everyone and everything (Job 34:21, 22; Psalm 11:4, 5; 139:1-7; Hebrews 4:12, 13).

When Scripture declares, "he hath not beheld iniquity in Jacob, neither hath he seen perverseness in Israel", the reference is to God's justice not his omniscience. The meaning is this, insofar as God's law and justice are concerned, he sees no sin in his people. Debts paid and cancelled are debts the law cannot see. What is not written against us in the book of God's law cannot be seen by the eye of God's justice. He sees no sin in his people because justice has been fully satisfied by the blood of Christ sacrificed for our sins (Isaiah 43:25; 44:22).

As our heavenly Father, the Lord God certainly takes notice of our sins and is displeased with them (2 Samuel 11:27). Yet, I rejoice to declare to every believing sinner that God will never punish you for your sins, nor hold you accountable, nor withhold any blessing of grace or glory from you because of your sins. For him to do so he must violate his own justice and overturn the satisfaction made by his own Son. Either Christ bore the wrath of God for us or he did not. Either he satisfied the justice of God as our Substitute or he did not. Either he put away our sins or he did not. If he has not done this for us perfectly, completely, and permanently, then we must bear the wrath of God for our own sins, pay for our own crimes, and perish in hell.

But if the Son of God has satisfied the law, wrath, and justice of God for our sins, we shall never be punished for them. Justice will not allow it. God will not, in justice he cannot, punish sin twice. Still, we must never imagine that God does not take notice of, or is not displeased with our sins as our heavenly Father. It is plainly written in the Scriptures that "the thing that David had done displeased the Lord". Only a very foolish father fails to see the faults, weaknesses, and offences of his child. Though his justice forbids and prevents his wrath, our Father's love will not allow him to let his children live in rebellion to him. In great mercy and lovingkindness, he chastises us for our sins, not to punish us, but to correct us (Psalm 89:30-33; Hebrews 12:5-11).

<hr />

February 20
Today's Reading: Numbers 27-29
"A day of blowing the trumpets"
Numbers 29:1

This blessed Gospel Day is "a day of blowing the trumpets". The feast of trumpets was held at the time of ancient Israel's New Year. The spiritual significance of the feast is very plain. It represents the gospel call, as the prophet Isaiah specifically tells us. "It shall come to pass in that day, that the great trumpet shall be blown, and they shall come which were ready to perish ... and shall worship the LORD" (Isaiah 27:13). Have you heard this joyful sound, and do you keep this spiritual feast? "Blessed is the people that know the joyful sound: they shall walk, O LORD, in the light of thy countenance" (Psalm 89:15). What instructive shadows of the "joyful sound" of gospel grace we have set before us in the commandments, institutions, and ceremonies of the law.

Zelophehad's Daughters
Zelophehad's daughters, five sisters, daughters of a sinful man, believed God and sought an inheritance among the sanctified (Numbers 27:1-4). Moses was commanded of God to number the people; and God promised that those which were numbered would be the possessors of Canaan (Numbers 26:53). But the daughters of Zelophehad were not numbered. Consequently, they had no claim in that promise. Yet, when Moses sought God's mind in the matter, Zelophehad's daughters obtained inheritance with God's Israel in the land of promise.

These five sisters give us a picture of God's grace bestowed upon his elect among the Gentiles. The earthly Canaan was but a type of the everlasting inheritance earned and purchased for God's elect by the obedience and blood of our Lord Jesus Christ. It is an inheritance given to none but the numbered of Israel, God's elect. Yet, those who inherit heaven's glory with Christ are a multitude no man can number, Jews and Gentiles out of every nation, kindred, tribe, and tongue (Isaiah 49:18-23; Revelation 7:4-10; Romans 11:26). "In Christ Jesus ye who sometimes were far off are made nigh by the blood of Christ" (Ephesians 2:13).

May God grant that we might be as anxious to obtain an inheritance among them that are sanctified as these daughters of Israel were for an inheritance among their brethren. Let this be the highest ambition of our souls (Matthew 6:33; Colossians 3:1-6). Oh, for grace to mind heavenly things rather than earthly things and to set our affection on eternal things rather than upon temporal things!

Canaan In Sight
As the Lord told Moses to go up on Mount Abarim to see Canaan, the land of promise, so let us stand upon the tiptoe of expectation with our heavenly Canaan ever before our eyes. It is appointed unto all men once to die, but the death of each of God's saints is precious in his sight. Moses was given a view of the Promised Land to strengthen his faith in God's promises. Surely we are to see in this the sweet assurance of an everlasting inheritance in heaven for all God's elect by the merits of him whom Moses beheld in the bush. Though he was not allowed to enjoy the privileges of the earthly Canaan because of his own sin, he was assured of an eternal inheritance in the heavenly Canaan because Christ, his sin-atoning Sacrifice, gave him perfect righteousness and immutable, everlasting acceptance with the holy Lord God. With that assurance, Moses resigned himself to the will of God and walked into the grave fully aware of his great sin and fully confident that Christ had put away all his sin. O Holy Spirit, give me such grace!

Burnt Offering
Throughout the typical, legal, Mosaic era God's people were required to keep at his altar "an offering made by fire unto the LORD ... a continual burnt offering" (Numbers 28:3-6), to keep in the minds of every worshipper a sense of sin, constantly reminding all that "without shedding of blood is no remission" (Hebrews 9:22). Behold, my soul, the Lord Jesus Christ in this continual burnt offering, and be assured of his precious fulness and of the infinite all-sufficiency of his great salvation, who by the one offering of himself has forever perfected them that are sanctified (Hebrews 10:10-14).

February 21
Today's Reading: Numbers 30-32
"Wherefore discourage ye the heart of the children of Israel"
Numbers 32:7

We ought always to look each one upon the things of others, ever seeking to help, protect, provide for, and encourage our brothers and sisters in Christ. Our pilgrimage through this world is full of pain and heartache, temptations and trials, sorrow and weeping. Let it be our determination to make one another's lives sweeter, brighter, and more pleasant. May God the Holy Spirit give us grace to enrich the lives of his people and keep us from discouraging one another.

Our Vows And Our Husband
Our Lord Jesus is both the Everlasting Father of his elect and the Husband of his saints. As such he will both confirm and strengthen our souls by his all-sufficient grace to perform all that he directs us to do for his cause, his people, and his honour. And all the rash vows we make, to which we might foolishly and sinfully obligate ourselves, he will rescind and undo by his sovereign power and right of dominion over us. He has by his Holy Spirit begotten us again to new life. We are children by adoption and grace. Moreover, he has betrothed us to himself forever in his marvellous loving kindness. My Maker is my Husband; the LORD of Hosts is his name. In believer's baptism we publicly dedicated ourselves to him and his service forever. May he give us grace to perform our vow of dedication to him. "I will pay my vows unto the LORD now in the presence of all his people, in the courts of the Lord's house" (Psalm 116:18, 19).

Our Warfare
In the contemplation of this holy war of Israel with Midian we have the figure and similitude of that war in which our souls are constantly engaged. Pray for grace from God in the strength of his Spirit to make war with our souls' enemies (the world, the flesh and the devil) and never to seek terms of peace. Do not spare any of those lusts

in our corrupt members which war against our souls. May Christ Jesus, as the great Captain of our salvation, go before us and, by the precious influences of his Holy Spirit, prevail against them daily, until at last he drives them out, and they are utterly consumed in resurrection glory. Then we shall sing the song of Moses and the Lamb, giving glory to God for his great salvation. In that great day it shall be said of all the redeemed in the holy army of the Lord, "They overcame by the blood of the Lamb, and by the word of their testimony; and they loved not their lives unto the death" (Revelation 12:11).

Reuben And Gad
The children of Reuben and Gad were terribly injurious to their brethren in the pursuit of Canaan. They rose up as the "increase of sinful men", loving the world, seeking ease and pleasure, rather than the will of God, the glory of God, and the benefit of God's Israel. Let them stand as beacons to warn us of such evil. We are strangers and pilgrims upon earth, seeking a better country. What have we to do with the perishing things of time? Blessed Saviour, so endear yourself to our hearts that we may esteem it our great happiness to endure affliction, if need be, with the people of God, rather than enjoy the pleasures of sin for a season. Like your servant of old, enable us to esteem the reproach of Christ greater riches than all the treasures of Egypt on this side Jordan.

February 22
Today's Reading: Numbers 33-35
"Cities of refuge"
Numbers 35:11

When the Children of Israel were settled in the land of Canaan, God ordained that six cities of refuge be set aside, to which a man might flee for security, if he had unintentionally killed another man. Those cities of refuge were located strategically throughout the land, so that any one of them could be easily reached within a day's journey from any place in the land of Canaan. If the guilty man could get into the gates of the city before the avenger of blood caught him, he would be secure. These cities of refuge together form a picture of the Lord Jesus Christ. They typically represent him to whom we have "fled for refuge to lay hold upon the hope set before us" (Hebrews 6:18).

We are informed by the ancient Jewish rabbis, that at least once every year, the magistrates of each city were responsible to survey the road to their city, making certain that the road was clear of all debris and easily passable. There must be no obstacles in the way that would hinder any who might flee to the cities of refuge. The magistrates would send out work crews to remove all large rocks and fallen trees from the road, taking the greatest care to remove every stumbling block. Any low places in the road would be filled. High places would be levelled. Along the road they placed markers with the word "REFUGE" written in bold letters. When the fugitive came to a crossroad, he need not hesitate for a moment. Seeing that blessed word, "REFUGE", he kept on his breathless pace, with relentless determination, until he reached the merciful place of safety. Once he entered the gates of the city, he was safe and secure.

The Lord Jesus Christ is the refuge for sinners. All who come to him are saved from the wrath of God. The way to Christ is plainly revealed. "Believe on the Lord Jesus Christ, and thou shalt be saved." By his obedience and blood, he has removed every obstacle that might keep the sinner who seeks him from finding him. He even sends his Spirit to reveal the way, lead us, and bring us safely to our souls' Refuge.

Those six cities of refuge, which Joshua appointed in the land of Canaan, are beautiful types of Christ and salvation by him. Men who would be lawfully slain anywhere else found salvation in the cities of refuge. Not only were those cities typical of Christ in providing salvation for all who entered them, the very names of the cities represented our blessed Saviour.

Kadesh means "holy". Christ is the Holy One, both as God and man. Being the holy God-man, he is abundantly qualified to be our Mediator, Saviour, and Redeemer. Christ is the Fountain of Holiness to his people. He is made of God unto us righteousness and holiness, justification, and sanctification (Psalm 16:10; Hebrews 7:26; 1 Corinthians 1:30).

Shechem means "the shoulder". Christ is our broad-shouldered Redeemer. He carried the enormous load of our sin upon the cross and put it away (Isaiah 53:6). The government of the world in general and of his church in particular is upon his shoulder (Isaiah 9:6). And in conversion he finds his lost sheep, lays it upon his shoulder, and carries it home (Luke 15:4).

Hebron means "fellowship". "Truly our fellowship is with the Father and with his Son Jesus Christ" (1 John 1:3). In Christ we have access to and fellowship with the eternal God, and shall have uninterrupted communion with him in heaven's eternal glory (1 Corinthians 1:9; Ephesians 2:18; John 17:24).

Bezer means "a fortified place". "I will say of the Lord, he is my refuge and my fortress: my God; in him will I trust" (Psalm 91:2). "The name of the Lord is a strong tower: the righteous runneth into it and is safe" (Proverbs 18:10). Christ is the fortress and defence of his people, the stronghold in which the prisoners of hope are secured.

Ramoth means "exalted". Christ is our exalted Saviour. "God hath highly exalted him" (Philippians 2:9). Christ is the One by whom we have been exalted from our low estate to sit among princes and to inherit the throne of glory (Ephesians 2:4-7). Christ is the One we exalt, honour, and magnify as God our Saviour (Revelation 5:9, 10).

Golan means "revealed or manifested". Christ is God manifest in the flesh (1 Timothy 3:16). He is the One revealed to us, to whom we are called, and by whom we are saved (Galatians 1:15, 16). In Christ the glory of God is revealed (2 Corinthians 4:6). And that revelation of the glory of God in the face of Christ is salvation. Meditate upon Christ today, and use him as the Refuge for your soul.

February 23
Today's Reading: Numbers 36-Deuteronomy 1
Marry in the tribe
2 Corinthians 6:14-17

God's commandment concerning the marriage of the daughters of Zelophehad, requiring them to marry within the tribe of their father, thereby preserving "their inheritance in the tribe" (Numbers 36), was obviously given in the prospect of gospel mercies. Our Lord Jesus is the head of the tribe of his people. With him and his people, our alliances must be made. Let each child of God marry whom he or she will, but only in the Lord (1 Corinthians 7:39). "Be ye not unequally yoked together with unbelievers".

Tender Care
How graciously our dear Saviour watches over his people in all their affairs! How dear we must be to him who has numbered the very hairs of our heads and tenderly watches over us for good, to guide us in all our ways, and to keep us from harming ourselves, or being injured by others! It was for the good of those five sisters, each individually and all five collectively, good for all Israel, and best for the glory of God that they be required by law to marry only in the tribe of their father. So it is with all that God our Saviour requires of us in his Word. Let us seek grace to follow its precepts as well as its doctrine in all things, carefully governing our lives by God's Holy Word.

Let all the sons and daughters of Israel be united only to their own tribe. In every near and tender relationship of life we will be wise to choose for friends and companions only those who worship and serve our God.

Self-Righteous Separation
There is a self-righteous separation, which we should avoid. Our Lord never taught his disciples to isolate themselves from sinful men. We cannot preach the gospel to people to whom we will not speak. Nor did our Lord teach his disciples to refrain from the enjoyment of entertainment, amusement or recreation, so long as we do not overly indulge in them. Many denounce all sports, music, recreation, television and movies as sinful and evil things; but those things are not necessarily evil. Neither did our Lord forbid his disciples the use of anything he had created. "Let no man therefore judge you in meat, or in drink". Use all things, but abuse none.

Righteous Separation
Yet, the Bible does require separation in the people of God. Believers and unbelievers really have nothing in common. Light and darkness, righteousness and unrighteousness, Christ and Satan have no agreement. Children of God, seek your companions among God's children. "How can two walk together, except they be agreed?" Those who love Christ, love the gospel, seek God's will, and seek God's glory strengthen one another's hands. Nothing can be more detrimental to a believer's

life on this earth than to be married to an unbeliever. Your desires, motives, ambitions, and principles will be exact opposites. An unbelieving husband or wife would be like a millstone around your neck. I urge you for Christ's sake, for the gospel's sake, and for the sake of your own happiness to avoid such an intolerable burden. If Christ cements the union between souls, blessed is that union, for they that are in the Lord, being joined to the Lord, are one spirit.

As God's children, we are to live by a principle of separation. The principle by which the people of this world live is self-interest. They are seeking wealth, security, fame, property, and power. The children of God live by another principle; the glory of Christ. Live in this world for Christ's glory. Make the glory of Christ paramount in all your decisions. Who will I marry? Where will I live? Where will I work? If we will seek Christ's glory in our everyday lives we will not go far astray.

———

February 24
Today's Reading: Deuteronomy 2-4
"That goodly mountain"
Deuteronomy 3:25

The happiest, most pleasant memories of my childhood are memories of times spent in the mountains of North Carolina. There I had grandparents, aunts and uncles who spoiled me; cousins and friends and family laughed with me. In the mountains I was never in trouble. Everything, even the air was better in the mountains. How often we find ourselves, as we read the Book of God, at the foot of a mountain, or on a mountain, a "goodly mountain". Here is Moses, God's faithful servant, praying "Let me go over, and see the good land that is beyond Jordan, that goodly mountain". What is "that goodly mountain" Moses desired to see?

Calvary's Mount
Surely there is more here than the mere desire to see the good land of Canaan. Canaan was, at its best, but a type and shadow of heaven, but in no way equal to it. Yet, Moses here expresses an intense desire and prayed for grace to "see the good land that is beyond Jordan, that goodly mountain". He knew, because God had told him, that he would not be allowed to enter Canaan. He would not have the type; but the substance he was assured of having. He was barred from Canaan; but he was going to heaven! There must have been something else that caused Moses to long for the sight of it. "Let me go over, and see the good land that is beyond Jordan, that goodly mountain". This seems to have been the one hallowed spot Moses longed to see and to feast his eyes upon. He who had seen and spoken with God in the bush wanted to behold, and with sacred meditation by faith, converse with him on the very spot, which in after ages he knew the Lord Jesus would be crucified.

Moses wanted to see and hear the Saviour he trusted, loved, and served in his redeeming glory on Mount Calvary. I am not guessing about this. In verse 24 the Holy Spirit tells us that the Lord God had begun to show his servant his greatness and glory; but Moses wanted to see and know more. He wanted to see it all and know it all in all its infinite fulness. Tell me, poor sinner saved by grace and redeemed by blood, is that not the case with you? This man Moses would be privileged to talk with his Redeemer, on the Mount of Transfiguration in days to come, about the death he would accomplish at Jerusalem (Luke 9:31); but he wanted to know all he could of his Redeemer's greatness and glory while he lived in this world.

Good Will
Moses knew "the good will of him that dwelt in the bush" (Deuteronomy 33:16) was the redemption and everlasting salvation of God's Israel by his own precious blood. He who walked with Christ by faith in Egypt, esteeming the reproach of Christ greater riches than all its treasures, wanted to know the presence of his Lord in sweet communion in "that goodly mountain". Moses kept the passover and the sprinkling of blood in the ordinance of the paschal lamb throughout his wilderness journey, anticipating the day when "Christ our Passover" would be sacrificed for us. Who can imagine what this man of God must have felt as he traversed the sacred "goodly mountain"? As he beheld the day of Christ afar off, "Here", he must have thought, "he who dwelt in the bush will accomplish his good will and reveal his greatness and glory by making his soul an offering for sin. Here, that One who knows no sin shall be made sin that God may be just and justify me! Here, that one great Sacrifice will be offered to God, which is typified in all the services and ceremonies of the tabernacle, that one Sacrifice by which the Lord Jesus will forever perfect them that are sanctified! Here, the Son of God will forever put away my sin by the sacrifice of himself".

Our Mediation
O Holy Spirit of God, make our daily meditation be about "that goodly mountain", and make that meditation sweet to our souls! "Let" us this day, throughout the day, and throughout all the remaining days of our pilgrimage here "go over and see that goodly mountain". There we would bless and praise God and the Lamb for the wonders of redemption. And when our appointed days are finished and our appointed work is done, graciously carry us across the swelling Jordan into "the good land that is beyond Jordan, the goodly mountain, and Lebanon". There "I will behold thy face in righteousness: I shall be satisfied, when I awake, with thy likeness"!

February 25
Today's Reading: Deuteronomy 5-7
"Because the LORD loved you ..."
Deuteronomy 7:8

How delightful our lives would be if only we could remind ourselves that all that we experience in this world, if we are Christ's, we experience "because the Lord loved you", because he loved us with an everlasting love. Let every rising sun awaken our souls with anticipation. Today I shall experience that which my heavenly Father has ordained for my soul's good, because the Lord loved me. Let every setting sun remind us of the same. Throughout the day today, carry in your soul, my blood bought brother and my chosen, redeemed sister, the sweet remembrance of what we have read in these three chapters.

Ascension Gifts
First, Deuteronomy 5 gives us a blessed representation of the ascension gifts of our Lord Jesus Christ to his church. "He gave some, apostles; and some, prophets; and some, evangelists; and some, pastors and teachers" (Ephesians 4:11).

Moses was a faithful prophet and pastor to Israel, labouring for God's people, even in his old age, to the very close of life, seeking God's message for his people and faithfully delivering his Word. God's servants are men who labour in the Word and doctrine, praying for God's people, and caring for their souls day and night. Faithful pastors devote their entire lives and the entirety of their lives to you, showing you, again and again, all the great things the Lord has done, is doing, and has promised to do for you, "because the Lord loved you".

"Because the Lord loved you", he gave you his holy law, showing you what God requires of man. He gave us his law to show us our need of a mediator and substitute who could keep the law for us and satisfy its last demand. "Because the Lord loved you", he gave us that Mediator, the Lord Jesus Christ, his darling Son, who was typified in Moses himself.

Triune Jehovah
In Deuteronomy 6:4 we are given the revelation of our great God in the trinity of his sacred Persons. "Hear, O Israel: The Lord our God is one Lord". Three times in this one very short verse God's name is given. Three times to convey the glorious truth of a threefold character of Persons in the divine unity. Though he exists in three Persons, he is one Jehovah. As we read in 1 John 5:7, "For there are three that bear record in heaven, the Father, the Word, and the Holy Ghost: and these three are one."

All three Persons in the Godhead are constantly engaged from everlasting for the salvation of our souls. The Father's everlasting love, the Son's atoning blood, and the Spirit's mighty operations of grace are bestowed upon us "because the Lord loved you".

Sovereign Election
"Because the Lord loved you", he chose you to be a special people unto himself, a peculiar people, under his special care, as the apple of his eye, before the worlds were made. "Because the Lord loved you", he redeemed you with the precious blood of Christ. "Because the Lord loved you", he brought you out of the bondage of sin and death in his saving grace by the mighty, irresistible hand of grace. "Know therefore that the Lord thy God, he is God, the faithful God, which keepeth covenant and mercy with them that love him and keep his commandments to a thousand generations." Teach these things "diligently unto thy children, and shalt talk of them when thou sittest in thine house, and when thou walkest by the way, and when thou liest down, and when thou risest up".

February 26
Today's Reading: Deuteronomy 8-11
I never could do enough
Deuteronomy 10:12, 13

The Lord God calls for us to remember all the way in which he has led us all the days of our sojourn through this world in Deuteronomy 8. Oh, let us never forget our God and the goodness of him who "performeth all things for us". Chapter 9 describes our sin, the breaking of God's law. But blessed be his name, God himself repaired the law we broke by the work of a man, the God-man our Saviour, typified by Moses (Deuteronomy 10:4; Romans 10:4); and we fulfil the law by faith in our Substitute. That faith in Christ is portrayed in Deuteronomy 10. Then in the eleventh chapter we are taught to utterly consecrate ourselves to God our Saviour because of his great grace bestowed upon us in Christ. What could be more reasonable (Romans 12:1, 2)?

A Son's Guilt
I spent the first seventeen years of my life making life miserable for myself and everyone around me. Everyone who loved me and cared for me was injured and abused by me. My wanton rebellion and ungodliness caused embarrassment, pain, and heartache to all my family. None were more hurt by my actions than my mother.

After God graciously stopped me in my mad rush to hell and saved me by his grace, one great goal of my life was to make up to my mother for all the heartache and misery I brought into her life.

I spent thirty-two years trying to atone, trying to make up for the things I had done to her and against her. I failed miserably! She would have disagreed with that statement. In fact, she did disagree on the many occasions she heard it. But my conscience is not satisfied. My conscience tells me incessantly, "You have not done enough". I have to live with the pain of that fact until I leave this world.

I have written these things and made this acknowledgement to you for a reason. I want you to consider this: if one sinner cannot make up and atone for his offences against another sinner to the satisfaction of his own conscience, how can any of us hope to make up and atone for our sins and crimes against the thrice holy Lord God?

God's Requirement
What does God require of us? He requires, upon penalty of eternal death, that we walk before him in reverence, obey his Word, and keep his statutes perfectly, without the least deviation, from the cradle to the grave, and serve him in absolute holiness, with all our hearts, souls, minds, and beings, all the days of our lives. God requires from us, as sinners, perfect righteousness, that is perfect obedience (Matthew 5:20), and complete satisfaction for all our sins (Ezekiel 18:20).

Not only does God require these things from us, he has put his voice in our inmost beings demanding the same things. Our consciences can never be satisfied with less than perfect righteousness and perfect satisfaction. That is the reason no man can truly find peace before God until he is brought by grace to rest in Christ alone as that all-sufficient Saviour, who alone is our righteousness and redemption.

Christ Is Enough
I could never make up to my mother, because I could never do enough, give enough, or make myself good enough to satisfy my own conscience. And no sinner can ever do enough, give enough, or make himself good enough to satisfy even his own conscience, much less God himself. But, blessed be his name, the Lord Jesus Christ is enough! Trusting Christ alone as my only atonement for sin, my only righteousness before God, my conscience speaks peace to my heart saying, "Christ is enough", because God himself says, "Christ is enough".. His obedience is enough (Romans 5:19). His blood is enough (Romans 3:24-26). Christ is enough. He is the propitiation for our sins.

February 27
Today's Reading: Deuteronomy 12-14
"Be not snared"
Deuteronomy 12:30

How instructive, wise, and needful is the counsel of God in these three chapters! May God the Holy Spirit graciously write his statutes and judgments upon our hearts and minds that we may live unto Christ and for Christ, in the enjoyment of his statutes and judgments, all the days of our lives.

Discovering Christ Day By Day

Worship
First, we are taught to worship God, the Triune Jehovah, alone. If we would worship God, we must worship him at his altar, Christ Jesus. In this gospel day, we worship God in the Spirit. We call no earthly place or thing, holy. We have no carnal altars of worship. Christ is our Altar. "We have an altar, whereof they have no right to eat which serve the tabernacle" (Hebrews 13:10). We bring our gifts to God by him and our gifts (whatever they may be) are "acceptable to God by Jesus Christ" (1 Peter 2:5; Ecclesiastes 9:7).

Our Lord Jesus Christ was the Law-giver; and he alone is the Law-fulfiller! Our acceptance with God is in him. He is the end of the law for righteousness to every believer (Romans 10:4).

Levites
We are specifically commanded, "forsake not the Levite" (Deuteronomy 8:19). The Levites were given to Aaron to minister to him in the tabernacle. Each Levite was given a specific task. As such, they give us a fair representation of gospel preachers, those men who are pastors according to God's own heart (Jeremiah 3:15), who serve Christ by serving his people in the house of God. If you would worship God, "forsake not the Levite", forsake not the assembly of God's saints and the ministry of the gospel.

Idolatry Despised
If God is worshipped, every false prophet and all false religion, everything connected with idolatry is to be despised and cast from us. I do not suggest that we are to be mean to will-worshippers and works-mongers. Just as we send missionaries to Africa and New Guinea to preach the gospel to the heathen, so we must and should preach the gospel to the religious heathen next door and in our own houses. Just as the missionary in New Guinea or Africa lives peaceably with his heathen neighbour, we are to live peaceably with our Arminian, will-worshipping neighbour. But we are not to embrace them as brethren, worship at their altars, or give credibility to their false prophets. That is the message of Deuteronomy 13. Let us heed it! If, by the grace of God, I live a life of faith in Christ, I am here taught that I should have a holy jealousy to throw down all idolatry and count it dung, for Christ's sake.

Belong To God
Deuteronomy 14 reminds us that we belong to God our Saviour. May God give me grace to see that he has chosen me to be one of his own, that he has adopted me into his family, that he has sanctified me by his grace, and that I am his property, his peculiar treasure, in marriage union to the Lord Jesus Christ by an everlasting covenant which cannot be broken. Spirit of God, enable me, day by day and hour by hour through the day, to live for the glory of God. God teach me to learn, from the precepts in this chapter, how to live as one of thine own in purity and holiness unto God. May it be my meat and my drink to do thy will!

February 28
Today's Reading: Deuteronomy 15-18
"Remember"
Deuteronomy 15:15

Today, in this portion of Holy Scripture, the Lord our God calls us to remember. Has God saved you by his almighty grace? Are you now numbered among his saints? If so, this is God's word to you: "Thou shalt remember that thou was a bondman in the land of Egypt, and the LORD thy God redeemed thee".

Bondage
The bondage of sin, from which we have been redeemed, was typified by the bondage that the Jews experienced in Egypt. We were all "children of wrath" by nature. We were all the servants, the slaves of our lusts and of Satan by nature. Paul states it plainly, "Ye were the servants of sin" (Romans 6:17, 20). Before God saved us by his grace, we were enslaved by a power against which we were without strength. I do not suggest that we all behaved as wickedly as we could. I am simply declaring that we all walked in the path of sin and rebellion against God. Some were highhanded, openly profligate rebels. Others were sneaky, hypocritical rebels. Some were very immoral. Others were very moral, after the judgment of men. But all were the servants of sin. We had no will to righteousness.

Yet, even if we had had the will to escape the power of Satan and the slavery of our lusts, we were without strength to do so. Have you forgotten that time "when we were yet without strength"? We were without strength to keep God's law, resist Satan's temptations, or obey the gospel. We were perfectly content in our bondage. Our bondage was such that we had no heart, desire, or even inclination to escape it.

I am a Southerner. I am so much a Southerner, that if I were not a Southerner, I would be ashamed. But the greatest blight upon our Southern heritage is that terrible inhumanity called slavery. I wish it had never happened, or could somehow be erased from memory, but that cannot be. Slavery is an ugly scar that will forever mar the beauty of the South. One aspect of slavery is that it so degraded men that they often became content to be slaves. Such contentment is a moral castration of manhood. He is not truly a man who is content to be a slave. Yet, such was our spiritual condition by nature that we were content to be in bondage and slavery to sin and Satan. We hugged our chains and kissed our manacles, as if they were ornaments of beauty!

Redemption
The redemption of our souls by Christ was pictured in the Jews' deliverance out of Egypt. As the Jews were redeemed from Egypt by the blood of the paschal lamb and by the blood of the Egyptians themselves, so too, we have been redeemed by blood, by the price of Christ's precious, sin-atoning blood. Having sacrificed his darling Son to save us, the Lord God will not hesitate to sacrifice anything or anyone, even as he did the firstborn in Egypt, Pharaoh, and his armies, to save his elect (Isaiah 43:1-4).

At God's set time, we were redeemed by the power of his irresistible grace in effectual calling. In Bible terms "redemption" means deliverance as well as ransom. The word "redemption" implies far more than merely the paying of a ransom price. All for whom the ransom price was paid at Calvary shall be delivered by grace!

Remember
In the Word of God we are constantly told to remember what we are by nature and what the Lord God has done for us in Christ. The reason for this is simple and clear. Everything in the kingdom of God is motivated by grace and redemption. That which governs the lives of God's saints is their remembrance of redemption and grace

Great care was taken by God that the Jews never forgot what he did for them in bringing them up out of the house of bondage. He intended for them to be reminded of it everywhere they turned and commanded them to remember it forever. The month of their deliverance was made the first month of the year to them (Exodus 12:2). A special ordinance was established to be kept by the Children of Israel perpetually, throughout their generations, until the coming of Christ (Exodus 12:3-14). Even in the giving of their law, they were commanded to remember their redemption from Egyptian bondage by the hand of God (Exodus 20:1-3). The Jews were also required to instruct their children in the matter of redemption. The gospel was to be handed down orally, from father to son, generation after generation (Deuteronomy 6:20, 21).

If this was the responsibility of parents in those days, how much more is it our responsibility to instruct our sons and daughters in the gospel of Christ. Seize every opportunity to do so. Explain to your sons and daughters why you worship where you do, the way you do, and why the cause of Christ's glory and truth are so important to you. We remember that we were bondmen in the land of Egypt, and the LORD our God redeemed us. Repeatedly, the Jews were commanded by God, "Thou shalt remember that thou wast a bondman in the land of Egypt, and the LORD thy God redeemed thee".

Something Far Greater
They were carefully instructed to do so and how to do so. Yet, their deliverance and redemption was only typical. How much more shall we heed this word from our God! Our redemption by Christ and our experience of grace in him must always be held in the forefront, never cast into the background. In all our worship, in all our preaching, in all our teaching, in all our singing, in all our praying, in all our witnessing, in all our living, in all our thoughts, redemption must always be the primary matter of consideration. Redemption and grace by Jesus Christ is not the primary thing in gospel doctrine. It is everything!

When Paul wishes to promote peace between Jew and Gentile he reminds us of our redemption (Ephesians 2:11-14). When he challenges us to holiness and devotion, he reminds us of our redemption (Romans 6:17, 18). When he seeks to promote mercy, love, kindness, and forgiveness among saints, he motivates us by our experience of grace in Christ (Ephesians 4:32-5:1). "Thou shalt remember that thou wast a bondman in the land of Egypt, and the LORD thy God redeemed thee."

March 1
Today's Reading: Deuteronomy 19-21
"A double portion"
Deuteronomy 21:17

Deuteronomy 19 reminds us that Christ alone is the Refuge for our poor souls. What a blessed refuge he is, our sure Hiding Place from the broken law of God, all the accusations of our own consciences, and all the malice of Satan! Oh, may God the Holy Spirit speed our flight to our mighty Refuge day by day! What a complete and satisfying refuge our Saviour is! No plague shall come nigh our Dwelling, if Christ is our dwelling. In the twentieth chapter we are reminded Christ, the Captain of our salvation, our mighty Man of War, has gone before us and conquered our foes. And what a blessed thing it is to be reminded of our portion as the Lord's firstborn.

The Spirit of God describes God's elect as "the church of the firstborn, which are written in heaven" (Hebrews 12:23), and calls his chosen "my firstborn" (Exodus 4:2; Jeremiah 31:9), identifying his own as a people who are one with Christ, his Firstborn. And by the precept of God's law the firstborn must be given "a double portion".

Double For Our Sins
Twice in Holy Scripture the Lord God woos and entices poor, needy, empty, bankrupt sinners to Christ by proclaiming that all who trust his darling Son shall receive in him the heritage of the Firstborn. This is the message he sends his servants to proclaim. "Comfort ye, comfort ye my people, saith your God. Speak ye comfortably to Jerusalem, and cry unto her, that her warfare is accomplished, that her iniquity is pardoned: for she hath received of the Lord's hand double for all her sins" (Isaiah 40:1, 2). "Turn you to the strong hold, ye prisoners of hope: even today do I declare that I will render double unto thee" (Zechariah 9:12).

He who has put an end to our warfare, finished our transgressions, and put away our sins by the sacrifice of himself has given us a double portion of grace. He has both pardoned our iniquity and made us the very righteousness of God. And he says to all who turn to the Stronghold, to Christ our Refuge and High Tower, "even today do I declare that I will render double unto thee".

Double For Our Troubles
He will give us double for all our troubles, just as he gave Job twice as much as he had lost. He will give us double for all our shame. "For your shame ye shall have double; and for confusion they shall rejoice in their portion: therefore in their land they shall possess the double: everlasting joy shall be unto them" (Isaiah 61:7). He will give us double, "grace for grace", for all our need (John 1:16). And he will give us double for all our expectation. "Now unto him that is able to do exceeding abundantly above all that we ask or think, according to the power that worketh in us" (Ephesians 3:20).

God's Declaration

All who turn to the Stronghold, Christ Jesus, may do so confidently expecting to enjoy all fulness of grace, all the blessings of his salvation, all the promises of God for this life and that which is to come, and all the glory of heaven, as "heirs of God and joint-heirs with Christ" (Romans 8:17).

The word "double" is to be connected with the word "declare", and should be read, "This day, at this present time, no matter how distressing the day may be, or how uncomfortable and distressed you may be in it, I declare double to you. Double grace! Double blessedness! Double joy! Double satisfaction". He is saying, where sin abounds and sorrow abounds, grace does much more abound!

March 2
Today's Reading: Deuteronomy 22-24
"Keep thee from every wicked thing"
Deuteronomy 23:9

In these three chapters the Lord God teaches us by repeated commands to walk before him in this world as sinners saved by his grace, ever adorning the doctrine of God our Saviour, as a blood-bought people who belong wholly to Christ. May he give us grace to do so throughout this day, and day by day, until our days on earth are done.

Deuteronomy 22

"Thou shalt not sow thy vineyard with divers seeds ... Thou shalt not plow with an ox and an ass together. Thou shalt not wear a garment of divers sorts, as of woollen and linen together. Thou shalt make thee fringes upon the four quarters of thy vesture, wherewith thou coverest thyself."

Understand these commands as the Spirit of God intends them to be understood. We must distinguish between things that differ. There can be no mixture of works and grace, of merit and mercy in doctrine. Our hearts and minds must not be sown with diverse doctrines. The gospel preacher, that man who ploughs spiritually, must not mingle anything idolatrous with the true worship of the God of Israel. We must never attempt to wear the woollen garment of our own righteousness with the white linen robe of the righteousness of God in Christ. We must never mingle anything of our own with the perfect and complete robe of Christ's salvation. Like the garment that covered our Redeemer's sacred body in the days of his flesh was without seam, woven from the top throughout (John 19:23), his righteousness bestowed upon us is a perfect, seamless garment of his making, bestowed upon us by his free grace alone. Let us take care that we make no fringes to the garment he has given us, as if we might add something to his finished work.

Deuteronomy 23
While we behold the many disqualifications by which men were kept away from the congregation of Israel, think of the privileges that are ours in and by Christ.

"Wherefore remember, that ye being in time past Gentiles in the flesh, who are called Uncircumcision by that which is called the Circumcision in the flesh made by hands; That at that time ye were without Christ, being aliens from the commonwealth of Israel, and strangers from the covenants of promise, having no hope, and without God in the world: But now in Christ Jesus ye who sometimes were far off are made nigh by the blood of Christ" (Ephesians 2:11-13).

Deuteronomy 24
How I bless God my Saviour, my Husband, who wed himself to me from eternity and graciously caused me to be married to him by faith, he will never behold anything in me that displeases him and will never allow me to lose favour in his sight! He will never give any poor soul he has married a bill of divorcement! He has not only given us his name, he has given us his righteousness in free justification and his very nature in sanctification. He says of his beloved, "My love, my dove, my undefiled, there is no spot in thee". Though I am altogether unworthy of his love, because "he hateth putting away", and because he has said he will be mine and I will be his forever, so it shall be! He has done what he promised. He has betrothed me unto him forever. Yea, he has betrothed me unto him in righteousness, and in judgment, and in lovingkindness, and in mercies. He has even betrothed me unto him in faithfulness, not mine, but his, forever (Hosea 2:19, 20).

March 3
Today's Reading: Deuteronomy 25-27
"I profess this day"
Deuteronomy 26:3

What blessed thoughts with which to open the day! Thank you, blessed Spirit of God, divine Comforter and Teacher of chosen, redeemed sinners, called by grace and taught of God, for this portion of Holy Scripture! Thank you for reminding me of all that I have professed and am still enabled with joy to "profess this day"!

The Saviour's Stripes
How sweet it is today to look up to heaven with the eye of faith and behold him with whose stripes I have been healed. Blessed Lord Jesus, you were wounded for my transgressions, you were bruised for my iniquities, the chastisement of my peace was

upon you, when you were made to be sin for me upon the cursed tree. How I praise you for your great mercy, love, and grace!

Yes, by the sin-atoning death of God's darling Son, when he was made sin and was justly condemned in the place of the wicked, all for whom he bled and died were made the righteousness of God in him and are therefore justified by God himself in complete accordance with his holy law. Sin could not be imputed to our Substitute until he was made sin for us. Justice could not touch him until he "bare our sins in his own body on the tree". Nor could we be justified by God's law and have righteousness imputed to us until we were made the righteousness of God in him. But now, since Christ was made sin and was punished for our sin made to be his, God is both "a just God and a Saviour" to his redeemed.

Ox Not Muzzled

"Thou shalt not muzzle the ox when he treadeth out the corn" (Deuteronomy 25:4). Why did the Lord God put this commandment in his law? "Doth God take care for oxen?" Take care, child of God, that you highly esteem and generously provide for that man (those men, faithful gospel preachers, pastors, missionaries, evangelists) who cares for and labours for your soul. Compared to the strong, labouring ox (Ezekiel 1:10), God's servants labour in the Word and doctrine of Christ. As such, they are worthy of and should always have from you both love and honour. As faithful labourers for your soul, all their needs are to be provided for and supplied by you generously (1 Corinthians 9:9, 10; 1 Timothy 5:17, 18).

Perfect Balance

My Father, give me grace day by day to honour you, to honour the gospel of your grace, and to bring no reproach upon your name, your gospel, or your church. Compel me, by the sweet, irresistible constraint of your Spirit, to "have a perfect balance and just weight, a perfect and just measure" in all my dealings with men in this world.

Firstfruits

Christ is the firstfruits, the first and the last. He is the offering of our souls to God by which we are perpetually, as from eternity, "accepted in the Beloved". Early let us bring him to God, the first of every year, the first of every day, and the first at the close of every day, rejoicing in him whose name is "The Lord our Righteousness".

Avouched

"Thou hast avouched the Lord this day to be thy God ... And the Lord hath avouched thee this day to be his peculiar people". How honoured we are to avouch that the Triune Jehovah is our God, declaring by our baptism and our confessed faith that we are his, chosen, redeemed, called, and devoted by faith to him. But how indescribably blessed it is to have the Triune Jehovah avouch that we are his! As soon as the sinner looks to Christ in faith, trusting him as his Wisdom, Righteousness, Sanctification, and Redemption, he has within him God's own avouched assurance that he is God's! The blood of Christ sprinkled on the heart, the love of God shed abroad in our hearts by the Holy Ghost gives assurance that "I am my Beloved's, and my Beloved is mine" (Song of Solomon 6:3). It is this avouchment, that we are God's property, that was confessed in the tithes of the law and is confessed in the free, voluntary gifts of God's saints in the house of God week by week.

March 4
Today's Reading: Deuteronomy 28, 29
Fear God
Deuteronomy 28:58

If God, in his great mercy, has caused this volume to meet the eye of a poor, trembling soul, under a sense of his just wrath, may he cause the reading of Deuteronomy 28 to sound as an alarm in your soul. "That thou mayest fear this glorious and fearful name, THE LORD THY GOD". God's judgments are as sure as they are righteous. Yet, God, the faithful God, as he has sworn that he will perform his wrath, has also promised mercy to every sinner who seeks his mercy by faith in Christ. May God the Holy Spirit open your eye, convince your heart, awaken your soul, and cause you now to flee from the wrath to come. Flee to Christ! Look to him, and live!

> Poor sinner, seek his grace,
> Whose wrath you cannot bear;
> Fly to the shelter of his cross,
> And find salvation there!

Fury Gone
Reading today about God's great, righteous, and just judgments upon disobedient Israel, my heart swells with increasing love, adoration, gratitude, and praise to God who, punishing his own dear Son in my stead, now says to every believing sinner, "Fury is not in me". O Blessed Redeemer, my dear Saviour, thank you for redeeming me with your blood, saving me by your grace, clothing me with your righteousness, and forgiving me of all my sin! Eternal praises are your due!

Behold, my soul, God in Christ reconciling the world unto himself, not imputing our trespasses unto them. Every blessing of God, for time and to all eternity, flows freely to sinners through Immanuel's precious blood. "Thanks be unto God for his unspeakable gift".

Secret And Revealed
Happy we are to know that "the secret things belong unto the Lord our God". Those things he has not revealed in his Word, in his Son, and by his Spirit to our souls, we gladly leave to him. We will not attempt to pry into secret things. But never allow

anyone to make you think eternal election, covenant grace, and sovereign predestination are secret things! These are things clearly revealed in the Book of God (Romans 8:28-20; 9:13-23; Ephesians 1:3-14; 2 Timothy 1:9, 10). In these things every believer rejoices! Loved with an everlasting love, we live day by day in the comfortable assurance that he who loved us freely from everlasting will love us freely unto the end and to everlasting!

March 5
Today's Reading: Deuteronomy 30-32
"As an eagle"
Deuteronomy 32:11, 12

Like other creatures of our God, the eagle not only appears to show great affection for her young but manifests tremendous superiority over other winged creatures in taking care of her brood. She provides for them and protects them, as other birds of the air do. But, in training them, she constantly shelters them from danger, far more than other birds do their young. The Lord our God seems to have created her with such excellence that she might be illustrative of his affection for, tender care towards, and protection over his children.

John Gill wrote, "Of all animals the eagle is most affectionate to its young, and most studiously careful of them. When it sees anyone coming to them, it will not suffer them to go away unpunished, but will beat them with its wings and tear them with its nails."

Stirs Up
"She stirreth up her nest". Though they might be naturally inclined to do so, the eagle will not allow her young to be lethargic. She stirs her nest, calling them to life and excitement. As she stirs her nest, she "fluttereth over them", over her young. The eagle does not go into her nest suddenly. She first makes a noise and awakens her chicks with her wings, striking them against a tree or its branches. Being awakened, they receive her gladly, without fear.

On Her Wings
She "spreadeth abroad her wings, taketh them, beareth them on her wings". In this way she both teaches them to fly and protects them. Other birds carry their young in their talons. Held in their claws, the young might be easily snatched away and killed by some bird of prey. If someone from the ground should shoot at the bird, her young might be killed and the bird herself unharmed. But the eagle carries her young on her wings, so that no arrow from beneath can touch the young, until it has first pierced the heart of the old bird.

So The Lord

"So the Lord alone did lead them." What a precious word this is to us! What a picture this is of our God's tender mercy toward us in Christ! Our great God, "the God of all grace", by the irresistible power of his Holy Spirit, stirs up his nest. He will not allow his children; chosen, redeemed sinners, to remain as they are born into this world. He would not allow us to sleep forever in the unawakened state of sin and death. He has brought us out of our unregenerate state of death.

We were at ease and had no desire to be awakened and stirred out of our death slumber. But the Lord our God, because of his great love for us, awakened us, stirred us up, and brought us out, by sending a gospel preacher in the power of his Spirit to arouse us. He sent his law into our consciences, working in us a sense of guilt, wrath, and death. By his Spirit, revealing Christ in us, he convinced us of our sin, of Christ's righteousness, and of judgment finished. Exerting the omnipotent power of his grace, he plucked us as brands out of the burning. Taking us up on his omnipotent wings of mercy, he teaches us to fly with heart aspirations after him, setting our hearts upon Christ and things above.

He has led us and fed us all the days of our lives. He has, as it were, hovered over us, though we knew it not, from our mother's wombs. Even now, he causes us to "mount up with wings as eagles", to soar aloft in the exercise of faith, hope, and love, entering within into the veil, into the holiest of all by the blood of Christ, living in the constant and comfortable expectation of "the mercy of our Lord Jesus Christ unto eternal life". He lifts us up from our low estate and raises us in sweet communion with himself, bearing us on his heart, in his hands, and on his arm, supporting us in all our temptations and afflictions and carrying us through all our troubles and difficulties, safe to eternal glory and happiness.

One Chosen

The eagle will usually lay three eggs, but normally only hatches and rears one, devoting everything to its chosen. So the Lord our God has chosen One, even our Lord Jesus Christ, as his Elect; and, blessed be his name, he has chosen us in him and as one with him. Though all the rest of Adam's fallen race are left to themselves, as the unhatched eggs in the eagle's nest, our great God and Father devotes himself entirely to his chosen!

Let every ransomed sinner rejoice and give thanks for this sweet, comforting word of grace from our God. "As an eagle stirreth up her nest, fluttereth over her young, spreadeth abroad her wings, taketh them, beareth them on her wings; so the Lord alone did lead him". Christ, our God and Saviour, has born and still bears us upon eagles' wings. He stirred us up and brought us to himself. He will not allow any of his little ones to perish. It is written, "he that toucheth you toucheth the apple of his eye". While on his omnipotent wings of mercy, nothing can touch us until it first touches him. Nothing can harm us, until it first harms him. Nothing can destroy us, until it first destroys him! How safe, how secure we are on his wings!

After commenting on this portion of Scripture, Robert Hawker made the following supplication to our God. Blessed are those, whose hearts echo his prayer. "Oh Lord, give me grace rightly to enjoy and use such marvellous blessings. And since, to the wisdom and strength of the eagle, thou hast now added the tenderness and solicitude of the hen, do thou, Lord, gather me under thy wings, and nourish me with thy love and favour, that I may be thine forever, and live here by faith, as hereafter I hope to live with thee in glory".

March 6
Today's Reading: Deuteronomy 33-Joshua 1
Pisgah's sight and Moses' death
Deuteronomy 34:1-9

In Deuteronomy 34 we read about Moses' vision of the Promised Land from the "top of Pisgah" and his death and burial by the hand of God on Mount Nebo. Moses' death upon this mountain was by the express purpose of God to teach us very important spiritual lessons.

Divine Revelation
We are told that when Moses stood on Mount Pisgah and looked over Canaan's Promised Land, he surveyed the whole land (Deuteronomy 34:1-4). We are expressly told that he saw all the land of Gilead unto Dan, and all the land of Naphtali and Ephraim and Manasseh, and all the land of Judah unto the uttermost sea, together with the south and the plain of the valley of Jericho, the city of palm trees, unto Zoar. That was some vision!

If you care to take some measurements by an atlas, you will find that with one view, from one spot, Moses clearly saw at least 60 miles in one direction and 120 miles in the other, taking in all the Land of Promise. That would be impossible for any man, except by supernatural, divine assistance. Therefore, we read, "I have caused thee to see it with thine eyes".

That is the way it is with all spiritual things and all spiritual sight. Everything we know and see by faith we know and see by divine revelation, with eyes of faith that see eternal things. Our dear Saviour is to the eye of faith precious and lovely, gracious and glorious; but to the carnal eye, "there is no beauty that we should desire him".

Law's Death
Then, after taking in all the Land of Promise, after surveying the fulfilment of all God's covenant promises, Moses died (Deuteronomy 34:8, 9). Moses could not bring Israel into the possession of God's covenant promises. Here is a picture of the law's death. Yes, I meant to say the law's death. If we are "dead to the law", as God in his Word declares we are (Romans 7:4; Galatians 2:19), the law is dead to us. Moses died on Mount Nebo, but Joshua lived. So it is spiritually: Moses is dead; but the Lord Jesus Christ, our great Joshua, lives!

Five things are stated in Deuteronomy 34:8, 9 by which God the Holy Spirit gives us a picture of our complete freedom from the law of Moses in Christ our Saviour, who "is the end of the law for righteousness to everyone that believeth".

1. Moses (the law) died, having fulfilled his appointed service. Moses was 120 years old, as full of health and strength when he died, as he was when he was twenty-five years old. And the law, retaining all its strength, being fulfilled by Christ, was nailed to the tree and slain by our Saviour (Colossians 2:14). As God buried Moses in Mount Nebo and all hell cannot dig up his body, so Christ nailed the law to his cross, taking it out of the way forever, and though Satan constantly seeks to raise it up, Michael the Archangel (our blessed Lord Jesus) stands by his finished work and pours out his grace and righteousness in the full forgiveness of sin upon his chosen (Jude 9; Zechariah 3:1-9).

2. The Children of Israel wept for Moses and mourned. So the natural man weeps and mourns for the dead letter of the law, ever clinging to it, always desiring to make himself righteous by the vain delusion of law obedience. All lost men and women seek to make themselves righteous. And all who seek to make themselves righteous by their works are lost. While boasting of their obedience to the law, their religion makes them miserable.

3. Joshua was full of the Spirit and wisdom of God. And Christ Jesus, our Joshua, is full of the Spirit of God and is made unto us Wisdom, Righteousness, Sanctification, and Redemption. All the fulness of grace and all the promises of God are in him and are ours in him.

4. Moses laid his hands on Joshua, fully approving of him. So the holy law of God approves of, is fulfilled, and is fully satisfied with Christ. He magnified the law and made it honourable by his obedience in life and his obedience in death as our God-man Mediator and covenant Surety.

5. With Joshua as their head, the Children of Israel did as the Lord commanded Moses. If you read the book of Joshua, you will see that Israel no more obeyed Joshua than they did Moses. In fact, Joshua said to them, "Ye cannot serve the LORD: for he is an holy God; he is a jealous God; he will not forgive your transgressions nor your sins" (Joshua 24:19). Yet, we are told by God the Holy Spirit that "the Children of Israel hearkened unto Joshua, and did as the Lord commanded Moses" (Deuteronomy 34:9). Obviously, there was a sense in which they did obey God. Under Joshua's lead, with Joshua at their head, they entered into, conquered, and possessed all the Land of Promise; and the Lord God fulfilled to them all the covenant promises he made to Abraham (Joshua 23:24).

What a picture of grace! In Christ our Head, our Mediator, our Representative, our covenant Surety, all God's elect have fulfilled all God commanded by the law. Our Saviour's obedience to the law all the days of his life was our obedience. His death under the penalty of the law was our death. And now, in him, by the merit of his blood and righteousness, every believer is made an heir of God and joint-heir with Christ himself. All the blessings of God's covenant are sealed to every chosen, redeemed sinner by God the Holy Spirit with the gift of faith in Christ. Thus grace reigns through righteousness unto eternal life by Jesus Christ our Lord.

March 7
Today's Reading: Joshua 2-5
"The waters of Jordan"
Joshua 4:23

How often God the Holy Spirit inspired holy prophets and apostles to remind us of "the waters of Jordan". Surely he intends for us to associate "the waters of Jordan" with our God and his great salvation wrought out for us, purchased for us, and bestowed upon us by our Lord Jesus Christ, that One of whom Joshua was a type.

Joshua
In his name and in his work Joshua was an eminent type of our almighty Joshua, the Lord Jesus Christ. As we read this portion of Holy Scripture, covering a period of just a little more than twenty years, let us always read it with this in mind. Joshua typified our Lord Jesus, who saves his people from their sins. The conquest of Canaan and the division of the land to Israel by the order of God portrays the accomplishment of our salvation by the grace of God and the ultimate gift of heavenly glory awaiting every chosen, redeemed sinner.

Baptism
When the Lord God dried up "the waters of Jordan" and Israel crossed over on dry land, "On that day the Lord magnified Joshua in the sight of all Israel". So it was with our mighty Joshua, the Lord Jesus. It was at his baptism in "the waters of Jordan" that the Triune Jehovah first began to magnify our great Joshua on the earth. Coming up from the watery grave, by which he symbolized the fulfilling of all righteousness in his death and resurrection, God the Father spoke from heaven saying, "This is my beloved Son, in whom I am well pleased". At that very time, the Holy Spirit descended from heaven.
    Thus began the public ministry of our Saviour, as Joshua began his by the crossing of the Jordan. In exactly the same way every believer should commence his new life in Christ, confessing the Lord Jesus in believer's baptism. By our burial with Christ in the waters of baptism, we confess our death with him upon the cursed tree. Rising up from the watery grave, we confess that we are his, henceforth, to walk with him in the newness of life.

Death
There is a double view of our Lord's ministry in "the waters of Jordan". Not only do they speak of our baptism in Christ, introducing us into the wilderness-state of temptation, warring with the world, the flesh, and the devil, "the waters of Jordan" also speak of the close of this wilderness journey. In the Jordan of death our Joshua, Jehovah-Jesus, will lead us through to our immortal possessions, prepared for us from the foundation of the world, for which he fits us by his blood atonement and his

saving grace. Soon, very soon, our great Saviour will graciously cause each of his own to fully inherit and possess the heavenly Canaan.

In this river, in "the waters of Jordan", the ark of the covenant of the Lord of the whole earth once rested. Here the Lord Jesus Christ, whom the ark represented, was baptized. Here Israel passed over; and here you and I must pass over in the hour of death. How sweet and blessed in the swellings of Jordan to behold the Lord Jesus and hear his well-known voice, "Fear not; for I have redeemed thee; I have called thee by thy name: thou art mine. When thou passest through the waters, I will be with thee; and through the rivers, they shall not overflow thee".

March 8
Today's Reading: Joshua 6-8
"Joshua saved Rahab the harlot"
Joshua 6:25

When the Lord God sent Joshua and the Children of Israel across the Jordan River and into the land of Canaan to take possession of the land, the first order of business was to destroy the city of Jericho. Jericho was one of the largest, most prosperous, and most thoroughly fortified cities in the land. But the city was cursed of God and marked for destruction. The sentence of death had been passed upon it forty years earlier (Exodus 23:27, 28).

Damned, Yet Alive
Though the inhabitants of Jericho prospered in the world, though they worked and played, laboured by day and partied by night, though they filled their lives with every amusement, comfort, and pleasure they could find, though they were utterly ignorant of it, they were a people cursed of God, a people whose numbered days were up, and a people about to be forever damned!

They were as sure for hell as if they were already there when Joshua and the Children of Israel crossed over the river Jordan; but they were oblivious to the fact of it! Though they were full of life, the inhabitants of Jericho were already damned, and would soon be in hell. How that fact ought to make every lost sinner tremble with fear and flee to Christ! But none will, except God the Holy Spirit give them life and faith in Christ.

Jericho's Fall
The Scriptures tell us that the Children of Israel marched around Jericho carrying the ark of the covenant everyday for seven days. On the seventh day, they marched around the city seven times, blew their trumpets, and shouted. When they did, the walls of Jericho came tumbling down and fell flat to the ground. The whole city was

completely destroyed at once, except for one house. There was one small section of the wall that did not fall, because there was a house on that section of the wall that could not fall.

A Harlot Saved

Why? Why was that house preserved? The answer is found in Hebrews 11:31. There was a woman in that house who believed God. There was a woman in that house who was sheltered by a scarlet cord, which represented the precious blood of Christ.

Though all of Jericho was destroyed under the wrath of God, Rahab and her father's house were saved; the house of the town's most notorious harlot could not fall.

When I read that, being the kind of curious, inquisitive person I am, I want to know why? Why was this one house left standing, while all the other houses were destroyed? Why, when the entire wall surrounding the city collapsed under the weight of God's wrath, was this harlot's house left standing? The Book of God shows us clearly that there are five reasons why Rahab's house did not and could not fall when the judgment of God fell on Jericho.

1. Rahab was the object of God's sovereign, electing love.
2. Rahab's house was under the blood.
3. Rahab believed God.
4. Rahab had the promise of God for her security and that of her house.
5. Rahab stayed in the house.

Believing God, she obeyed his Word given by his messengers. Hiding behind the scarlet cord, she would not be moved. Let us follow Rahab's example. Taking refuge under the blood of Christ, so let us ever abide in the house of grace, walking with God by faith in Christ (Colossians 2:6).

March 9
Today's Reading: Joshua 9, 10
The day the Son stood still
Matthew 20:32

Joshua, that man by whom the walls of Jericho fell, commanded the sun to stand still in the midst of heaven. And at the command of a man, "the sun stood still". We are told, "There was no day like that before it or after it, that the Lord hearkened unto the voice of a man". But here is a thing even more remarkable. The Lord Jesus Christ, "the Sun of Righteousness", as he was coming up out of Jericho on his way to

Jerusalem to redeem his people, heard two blind beggars crying to him for mercy. At the sound of their cry, we are told, "Jesus stood still"!

God Stopped

What a wonderful, amazing picture is here drawn by the pen of inspiration! Here is the omnipotent God stopped in his tracks, held fast by the cry of two needy souls seeking his mercy. The Lord Jesus was on his way to Jerusalem to accomplish the redemption of his people, to fulfil the will of God, to finish the work set before him for the glory of God. Nothing had been able to stop him, deter him from his work, or even cause him to pause. But two blind beggars crying for mercy, two helpless souls looking to him for grace and help, believing him, crying out to him, stopped the Son of God in his tracks. "Jesus stood still". There are lessons to be learned here that are of more value than gold.

Unexpected Believers

Faith is frequently found where it is least expected. Multitudes followed the Lord Jesus as he walked along and taught the people. Some for loaves and some for love. Some for greed and some for grace. Some out of curiosity and some out of conviction. But there were very few in the crowd who believed on Christ. Many who saw his mighty miracles did not believe on him. But these two blind men never saw any of the Lord's miracles. They knew of him only by the hear-say testimony of others. Yet, "when they heard", they believed.

In The Way

If we hope for mercy, we must avail ourselves of every means of good to our souls. When they heard that "Jesus passed by", these two men were found "sitting in the way". They said to themselves, "he who healed the blind man on the other side of town is going to be passing by here. He may never pass this way again. If we are to be healed, it must be now. Let us sit down 'in the way'. Perhaps he will heal us too". If you care for your soul, do not despise God's appointed means of grace (Romans 10:17; 2 Timothy 3:15). Put yourself "in the way" of blessing, in the place where mercy is most likely to be found (Matthew 18:20; Hebrews 10:25). And seek the Lord in earnest prayer (Jeremiah 29:12, 13).

Full Of Mercy

How compassionate the Son of God is to needy sinners! "Jesus passed by". He visited these men in prevenient grace, giving them blindness, so that in "the time of love" they would be found "in the way" as he passed by in saving mercy. Blessed blindness! When he heard their prayer, "Jesus stood still". He called them to himself. And he touched them! What condescending grace. "Immediately their eyes received sight and they followed him." Faith always obtains mercy. Faith never goes away from Jesus Christ empty-handed!

March 10
Today's Reading: Joshua 11-14
"He left nothing undone"
Joshua 11:15

Blessed be his holy name forever, our great Joshua, Jehovah-Jesus, shall leave nothing undone, which he covenanted to do for us as our Surety before the world began!

War's End
The eleventh chapter of Joshua concludes the inspired account of the holy war and the conquest of Canaan. Joshua conquered all and took possession of the land, as God commanded by Moses. Even so, our Lord Jesus has conquered all our foes (Colossians 2:14, 15) and has taken possession of all things as our Surety and Forerunner (Hebrews 6:20), having accomplished for our souls all that God demands from us; perfect righteousness and complete satisfaction! "He left nothing undone".

If we read about these wars merely as historical facts, they profit us nothing. The Word of God is not to be read as a book of historic, religious, or even supernatural facts. It is to be read with a spiritual eye of spiritual discernment, given by God the Holy Spirit. When read with the spiritual eye of faith, we discover much instruction couched under those commands of our God requiring the complete destruction of every foe. As Joshua destroyed every enemy in the land, so our dear Saviour shall at last destroy sin in us. Oh, what blessed hope this is! Soon, when we have dropped these robes of flesh, we will drop sin in the grave and it shall never rise again. When our Lord Jesus comes again, when he raises our bodies from the grave and makes all things new in resurrection glory, all the evil consequences of sin shall be gone.

Hard as it is for me to believe that, here is something even more profoundly honouring to the wisdom and grace of God our Saviour. When he has made all things new, just as Israel was enriched by the wealth of the Canaanites, our dear Saviour shall make us rich beyond imagination by delivering us from sin, indescribably richer than we could have been had we not fallen in Adam (Psalm 76:10). Neither the devil, nor sin, nor all the foes of our souls shall rob God's elect of anything, only enrich us; and they shall gain nothing, but shall be utterly destroyed! As God turned Balaam's curse into a blessing and then killed Balaam, so he shall make all things blessings to our souls forever (Numbers 13:2; 22:23, 24; 31:8; Joshua 13:22; Romans 8:28).

Immutable Saviour
We read of Joshua's old age and weakness, even at this distance, almost with a tearful eye. It is painful to see a faithful servant of God, one so useful for so much good, to the benefit of so many, weaken with the infirmity of age, knowing that there is so much yet to be done. Yet, how sweetly we are reminded that our great Saviour, our Joshua, is the immutable God, that he changes not, that he is "the same yesterday, and today, and forever".

Caleb

Today's reading concludes with Caleb's petition before Joshua, seeking the land Moses promised him. Here is Caleb, the oldest man in the nation, an eighty-five year old zealot, ready to go to war for God! From his youth, throughout his life, even in his old age, Caleb's zeal never diminished; his devotion never cooled; his consecration never failed. Caleb "wholly followed the Lord God of Israel".

Read what God says about this man in Numbers 14:24, "But my servant Caleb, because he had another spirit with him, and hath followed me fully, him will I bring into the land whereunto he went; and his seed shall possess it".

The name Caleb, I am told, has two meanings. First, it means "a dog". Though commonly, when a man is referred to as a dog, it is a great offence; that is not the case here. A dog has one admirable feature, one virtue that no other animal possesses. A dog always follows his master. He is the most loyal, faithful animal on the earth. In that sense Caleb was indeed a dog; a loyal, faithful dog. He followed his Master from the day that he left Egypt until the day that he was called home to glory. God, make me such a dog!

The name Caleb also means "all heart". What a name for a man! But it perfectly suited this man. Caleb was all heart. There was nothing half-hearted, lukewarm, or insincere about him. Caleb was all heart. I have known many who had a head to understand, but no heart, a hand to work, but no heart, and feet to go, but no heart. Not Caleb! His head was clear. But he was all heart. His hands were strong and his feet were both steady and ready. But he was all heart. Whatsoever he did in word or in deed he did with all his heart!

Caleb means "a dog" and Caleb means "all heart". Put the two together and you have the character of this man. He was faithful to his Master in all things, following the Lord fully with all his heart. "He had another Spirit" (Ezekiel 36:24-30). God the Spirit was in him. The Spirit of God in a person makes that person Christ's faithful dog to the end. Oh, blessed Saviour, evermore give me your Spirit and make me your faithful dog to my last breath!

March 11
Today's Reading: Joshua 15-17
"Could not drive them out"
Joshua 15:63

How the heaven-born soul agonizes due to indwelling sin! When I was but a babe in grace, I foolishly thought I would quickly get the victory over sin. I did not imagine it would be totally eradicated from me before the Lord took me to glory but I did think I would be able to control my vile lusts. After forty-six years in this pilgrimage, I must confess what we are told four times in Joshua 15-17. As the children of Judah could not drive their enemies out of the land, so with my sins I "could not drive them out".

Discovering Christ Day By Day

The Jebusites
That the Jebusites dwelt in Israel's dominions, even in the royal and holy city of Jerusalem, where Jehovah pitched his tent and established the temple of Zion, teaches us that everything here below is far from perfect. Jebusites dwell even to this day in Jerusalem. Much corruption remains in that heart where grace dwells: and while our bodies are the temple of the Holy Ghost, the best of God's saints find cause to cry out with the apostle, "Who shall deliver me from the body of this death?" What a joyful relief is it to the soul groaning under a sense of sin that soon the God of peace shall bruise Satan under our feet and the Canaanite shall be no more in the house of the Lord of Hosts (Zechariah 14:20, 21; Romans 16:20).

Enemies Within
Again we read, "And they drave not out the Canaanites that dwelt in Gezer: but the Canaanites dwell among the Ephraimites unto this day, and serve under tribute". So it shall be so long as we live in this body of flesh. When Rebekah found two nations struggling in her womb she asked, in Genesis 25:22, the question every believer often asks. "Why am I thus? And she went to enquire of the Lord" This is exactly what Paul experienced (Romans 7:18-21). We are reminded "the children of Manasseh could not drive out the inhabitants of those cities; but the Canaanites would dwell in that land". So it shall be until we drop this robe of flesh. To every soul struggling with indwelling sin, the Lord Jesus, our mighty Joshua, says, "My grace is sufficient for thee".

Victory Sure
Joseph's narrow boundaries serve to teach us that even in Canaan here below there is much to displease the heaven-born soul. There is no place of satisfaction here. In the Canaan above there are many spacious mansions perfectly suited to the highest and most holy desires of God's people. Wisely and graciously our Father sends his people painful and trying providences to make us thirst the more for heaven. He takes away those pillows we make ourselves of earthly things, making us long to return to him in whom we find rest for our souls (Psalm 116:7), assuring us that we shall at last "drive out the Canaanites, though they have iron chariots, and though they be strong".

March 12
Today's Reading: Joshua 18-20
"Your refuge"
Joshua 20:3

We should not fail to remember that all the land of Canaan was divided to God's Israel by lot, not by chance or caprice, but by lot, that is by God's appointment. It is God who fixes the bounds of our habitation (Deuteronomy 32:8). He fixes the bounds

111

of the habitation of each of his elect in time according to his own gracious and wise designs from eternity. How content, how joyful, how thankful we ought to be every day for the lot our God has given us in this world, by which he is pleased both to bless us and use us, and by which he sweetly prepares us for our eternal habitation above!

Our Sanctuary
When the Lord God gave Israel their possession in the land of Canaan, he appointed six Cities of Refuge where men who were guilty of manslaughter might flee for sanctuary. These Cities of Refuge, he called "your refuge", because they were typical of our Lord Jesus Christ, the one and only Refuge and Sanctuary for our souls. Isaiah wrote of him, "He shall be for a sanctuary" (Isaiah 8:14). The Lord Jesus Christ is the place of refuge for guilty sinners. He is a hiding-place, an ark of safety, a sanctuary from the wrath of God.

We frequently use the word "sanctuary" this way. Many cities are bird sanctuaries. It is against the law to kill certain birds within their limits. Certain places have been set aside as game sanctuaries. You dare not, under penalty of law, hunt wild game in those places. Within the city of refuge, the divinely appointed sanctuary, the avenger of blood could not touch the person who might be lawfully executed outside the city. There the guilty one was under the protection of God's own law.

Like those cities of refuge, our Saviour is a place of secure refuge and sanctuary for sinners who flees to him. The moment a sinner believes on Christ, he is safe; safe in life, safe in death, safe in judgment, safe in eternity. The wrath of God cannot touch any sinner who takes refuge in Christ by faith (Hebrews 6:18, 19).

Faith
Faith in Christ gives sinners refuge and sanctuary in Christ. If you believe on Christ, if you trust his blood and righteousness for your acceptance with God, if you forsake all confidence in yourself and put your confidence in Christ alone, your immortal soul is secure, saved, and safe forever. Nothing can destroy you or even harm you (Romans 8:32-39). No sin can be laid to your charge. No condemnation can be executed upon you. Nothing shall ever separate you from the love of Christ.

March 13
Today's Reading: Joshua 21, 22
"Shiloh, which is in the land of Canaan"
Joshua 22:9

Shiloh was the place of Israel's government. It was centrally located. Joshua made his headquarters in Shiloh. There God set the tabernacle of worship. And there Joshua cast lots for the people, dividing the land of Canaan to the chosen people by the decree of God. Shiloh means "place of rest". Canaan was the place of Israel's rest. Yet, even in "Shiloh, which is the land of Canaan", things were far from perfect. So it has been, so it is, and so it shall be. So long as God's church is in this world, there is much that troubles us and much that delights us.

The Levites

For Israel's good and for the service of his own worship God provided his people with the priestly tribe to do all the service of the tabernacle, "to keep the charge of the tabernacle of testimony", for the glory of God. Those Levites who served God's church in the Old Testament were in many ways representatives of faithful gospel preachers, the ascension gifts of Christ to his church in the New Testament (Ephesians 4:8-16). They are truly blessed to whom the Lord God gives pastors according to his own heart, to feed their souls with knowledge and understanding (Jeremiah 3:15).

By divine appointment the Levites (Joshua 21) were scattered through the land in four groups. God set them in the houses of Aaron, Kohath, Gershon and Merari. As the Lord God dispersed the Levites in the land of Canaan, so he sends his servants out to preach the gospel to every creature, to needy sinners everywhere, because his elect are found in and must be gathered out of all nations by the power and grace of his Spirit. Those Levites who ministered about holy things had no portion, no lot of inheritance in Israel. They lived on the holy things given by the people. So let God's servants devote themselves to the work of the gospel. And let God's people, whose souls they serve, generously provide for the carnal, material needs of his servants.

God's Faithfulness

What a magnificent picture we have of God's faithfulness to his covenant people in Joshua 21:43-45! Jehovah accomplished all that he promised to Abraham. "There failed not ought of any good thing which the Lord had spoken unto the house of Israel; all came to pass." The Lord gave Israel all of Canaan, brought them to his holy mountain, divided to each tribe its portion, and drove out all their enemies before them. As the Lord God called for Israel to glorify him for his faithfulness to them (Deuteronomy 7:9), let all the Israel of God give praise, honour, and glory to him for his great faithfulness. Thank you, our great God, for this sweet consolation to our souls. "He abideth faithful". Knowing my own unfaithfulness and unbelief, I give relentless thanks to God for his faithfulness (1 Corinthians 1:9; 2 Timothy 2:13).

Brethren Misjudged

Israel's misjudging of the Reubenites, Gadites, and the half tribe of Manasseh concerning the altar they erected ought to remind us of that horrible tendency of our depraved hearts to misjudge the behaviour of others. How quick we are to judge and condemn as evil what another says, or does! Thinking we know their intentions we presume they are evil! What a veil of ignorance the fall of Adam has thrown over our minds! What evil folly! Spirit of God, teach me to view the actions and words of my brothers and sisters in Christ in the best light possible, thinking no evil of those you have caused me to love (1 Corinthians 13:4).

March 14
Today's Reading: Joshua 23-Judges 1
Buried in Shechem
Joshua 24:32

The Children of Israel kept Joseph's bones for two hundred years, carrying them through all their journeys, even in the midst of battle after battle. They brought Joseph's bones out of Egypt, across the Red Sea, through the forty years of their wilderness wanderings, through the Jordan, and buried his bones in Shechem. What a funeral service that must have been! They did this to honour Joseph, burying him in the earth in anticipation of the resurrection, just as Joseph had charged them to do before his death (Genesis 50:25; Exodus 13:19). "The memory of the just is blessed" (Psalm 10:7).

Just as believers are buried with Christ in the watery grave of baptism in anticipation of the resurrection, we bury the bodies of our brothers and sisters in the earth in hope of the resurrection (1 Corinthians 15:51-58; 1 Thessalonians 4:13-18). By this means, we honour the memory of the righteous.

Burial Or Cremation
I am often asked, "Should a believer be cremated, or buried?" While the Scriptures do not give any commandment, they do, in my opinion, clearly indicate that the burial of our bodies is most consistent with the faith of the gospel. Our Lord was buried in the earth; and we confess our Saviour and our faith in him by a burial in believer's baptism. Clearly, there is a connection between burial and our faith in Christ.

God the Holy Spirit tells us in Hebrews 11 that Joseph made his brethren swear to carry his bones out of Egypt by faith. Moses carried his bones out of Egypt by faith and Joshua buried his bones in Canaan by faith. Was this not an indication of the way believers ought to honour the dead bodies of those the Lord has taken to glory?

Moses And Joseph's Bones
Why does the Spirit of God tell us that Moses carried Joseph's bones out of Egypt? It is certain that Moses did not personally, physically carry that coffin containing Joseph's bones out of Egypt. Yet, God declares that the carrying of Joseph's bones out of Egypt was specifically the work of Moses. Why? Moses represented the law of God. Joseph was typical of our Lord Jesus Christ who was raised from the dead because, the law being satisfied, death had no more claim upon him. Joseph also represented God's elect who have been brought out of the bondage of sin and death, because God's holy law has no claim upon us, since Christ has put away our sin by the sacrifice of himself (1 Peter 4:1, 2).

Joshua And Joseph's Bones
But Moses, the law, could never give Joseph and Israel the possession of the land of Canaan. That was a work that had to be done by Joshua. Joseph's bones were buried in Canaan with Joshua's, after the Lord God fulfilled every promise he had made to

Abraham and the nation of Israel concerning that land (Joshua 24:29-32). So it shall be with you and me. As Joshua brought Joseph's bones into Canaan and laid him to rest with himself in the land of promise, so the Lord Jesus Christ, our great Joshua, shall give us rest in the land of God's promise (Hebrews 4:1-1). When I leave this body of flesh, it shall be buried in the earth with my Redeemer to await the resurrection, testifying to all who see my corpse lowered into the earth, "This man believed in the Son of God, who is the Resurrection and the Life, and the sure resurrection of the dead at his glorious advent".

March 15
Today's Reading: Judges 2-4
"Nevertheless the LORD raised up judges"
Judges 2:16

The book of Judges covers a period of about three hundred years, three hundred years of great turbulence in Israel's history. Yet, there were periods of great revival in God's church during those years. The object of God the Holy Spirit in giving us the book of Judges appears to be threefold.

These twenty one chapters were written by divine inspiration to show us the unbelief, failure, and sin of God's people, even in the midst of great privileges and blessings. So it is with us! Yet, in the midst of their unworthiness, how graciously the Lord God dealt with them. So it is with us! All the judges he raised up to deliver his people, he raised up as so many types and pictures of our great Redeemer, the Lord Jesus. By them the Spirit of God here glorifies him.

Our Conflicts

We see in this little portion of Israel's history what conflicts await God's elect after his work of grace is begun in the heart. "Let not him that girdeth on his harness boast himself as he that putteth it off" (1 Kings 20:11). Never, until we drop this body of flesh in the grave, can Zion's soldiers be done with battle. "The last enemy that shall be destroyed is death" (1 Corinthians 15:26). But what a sweet relief it is to our souls to know that triumph is sure! Though countless Canaanites are still in the land, the promise is that they shall not always be. "There remaineth a rest to the people of God" (Hebrews 4:9). Child of God, walk in the comfort of this sweet assurance today. Until the day of deliverance comes, let us be found fighting the lusts of our flesh under the banner and in the strength of him who is the Lord our Righteousness.

God's Purpose

Our heavenly Father has wise and gracious reasons for leaving us in our present state throughout our sojourn here, daily struggling with the world, the flesh, and the devil.

Discovering Christ Day By Day

The history of Israel presented in the book of Judges shows us that God's church is the same in all ages. Here the Lord God, our heavenly Father, leaves his people in the midst of their enemies to try us and prove us, preparing his chosen as polished stones for his temple. His intent is to make us ever aware that "salvation is of the Lord", and cause our hearts to yearn the more for our home above.

As often as Israel behaved perversely and forsook the Lord their God, he sent their enemies to afflict them. So it is with God's Israel today. He has promised (not threatened), "I will chasten him with the rod of men, and with the stripes of the children of men" (2 Samuel 7:14). He has promised (not threatened), "Then will I visit their transgression with the rod, and their iniquity with stripes" (Psalm 89:32). Let us never forget that though it be a rod, it is the rod of the covenant, the rod of our ever-gracious, ever-wise, loving heavenly Father, not the rod of our enemy, but of our dearest, most loving Friend. Though he raises up enemies to correct us, those enemies are his instruments of good for us. They can do nothing but that which he commands them. My Father, give me grace to remember this. Do, my gracious God, whatever is needful to hedge up my way with thorns, that I may not find my path, when my way is perverse before you.

The Judges
How very precious is it to see in Israel's history how everything pointed to the Lord Jesus! Brought, as the people were, by sin and rebellion, into a state of repeated slavery, God raised up the judges as their deliverers. But what are Othniel, Ehud, and Shamgar compared to our Lord Jesus Christ, who has delivered us with an everlasting salvation from the wrath to come! Look up, my soul, to your Saviour when the corruptions from within and foes from without would bring you again into bondage. Out of all distress and bondage and sorrow let your mighty Advocate hear your cry. He was sent and sealed of the Father to drive out our enemies from before us; and he yet will do it. He who loved us and gave himself for us has made us more than conquers by his mighty conquests; and soon we shall wear the crown he has won for us!

March 16
Today's Reading: Judges 5-7
"The LORD sent a prophet"
Judges 6:8

As we read these chapters and reflect upon Israel's repeated departures from the Lord their God, the Father of all mercy, may God the Holy Spirit allow us to behold ourselves and our God. How often, how very often, our adorable Redeemer saves us from our enemies. Yet, how prone we are to forget him. How soon we forget the gracious hand that wrought our salvation, the hand that daily brings fresh supplies of grace! While we are here reminded again of our unworthiness, we are again reminded of our dear Saviour's compassions that fail not and his mercies that are new every morning.

Deborah And Barak

"I will cry unto God most high; unto God that performeth all things for me" (Psalm 57:2). The resources of our God, by which he faithfully cares for, protects, and benefits his elect throughout our pilgrimage here, are without limit. What has he not wrought? What is he not able to accomplish? And although Israel merited nothing but wrath and judgment, yet, for his own names' sake, the Lord wrought salvation for them, that he might make his mighty power known in the earth (Psalm 108:6). As it was with Israel of old, so it is with the Israel of God today. How unfaithful I am! How faithful you are, O God, my Saviour!

As Deborah and Barak had their day of triumph by the arm of the Lord, so have we, my brother, my sister in Christ, in the day the Lord Jesus made bare his holy arm and rescued our souls from the arrows of the enemy and graciously caused us to draw water from the wells of salvation. Our long night of captivity ended when the Lord Jesus arose and led captivity captive. When he went forth out of Seir and marched out of the field of Edom, then the mountains of sin in our nature melted before the Sun of Righteousness at his rising, and Sinai, with all its terrors, gave way at the presence of Jehovah-Tsidkenu! The Lord our Righteousness won the victory for us! Oh, Holy Spirit, give us grace and awaken in our hearts a song of praise to him who is our song and our salvation!

Prophets Sent

What mercy it is that God sends his prophets to his people! Countless have been the times my God has, when I was in great need, sent one of his prophets to my soul with precisely the message I needed at the time. How blessed are those people to whom God sends his faithful servants to instruct their souls!

But God has other messengers by which he speaks to our souls, messengers we should seek wisdom and grace to hear. His daily visitations in the common providences of life, in sickness, trouble, and adversity are voices like the voice of this prophet, by which the Lord God speaks. When these messengers of correction are accompanied with his grace and cause our hearts to weep before God, the Lord Jesus flies to our aid, like Gideon, his type, and delivers our souls from the oppressor. In repeated tokens of mercy, love, and grace our great Redeemer shows himself as God who is for us! With the unalterable assurances of his Word and his grace, we should never seek either the moistened nor the dry fleece as signs to tell us that he who is our God is "the faithful God", who keeps his covenant and his mercy for his chosen (Deuteronomy 7:9). Amid all the departures of our unworthy hearts, let us still stedfastly believe the record God has given of his dear Son.

Gideon's Three Hundred

By the instrumentality of three hundred scared men carrying earthen pitchers and blowing trumpets, God conquered the mighty armies of Midian and delivered Israel out of their hands! As it was then, so it is now, so it always has been, and so it shall be so long as time stands. "Salvation is of the Lord." "Not by might, nor by power, but by my Spirit saith the LORD of hosts."

Again we are reminded that the resources God uses in the salvation of his people are without limit. Trumpets and earthen pitchers are effectual weapons when the Lord God sends them to conquer mighty armies! He who used hornets to drive out the Hivites of Canaan used things considerably less fearful to conquer Midian. And he uses things even more useless than trumpets and earthen pitchers to save his elect. He condescends to use sinful men to preach the gospel to sinful men, because "it pleased God by the foolishness of preaching to save them that believe". And the men he uses are not those mighty men skilled in war, but those who lap water like a dog, those who know they are less than useless, except God make them useful. God still uses "things which are not to bring to nought things that are: that no flesh should glory in his presence" (1 Corinthians 1:28, 29). "We have this treasure in earthen vessels, that the excellency of the power may be of God, and not of us" (2 Corinthians 4:7)

March 17
Today's Reading: Judges 8, 9
"Faint, yet pursuing"
Judges 8:4

These words describing Gideon's little army well describe me. Do they not describe you, my fellow pilgrim? I know that in and by Christ Jesus victory is sure. Yet, it is equally sure that we shall have battles all the days of our lives. Our pilgrimage is a relentless warfare. From the moment that God called me out of darkness into his marvellous light, my whole life has been a state of constant warfare. I feel what Paul felt and groan as he groaned in this body of sin and death, sorrowful though rejoicing, dying though I live, in turmoil though kept in perfect peace! Yes, my Lord, I am faint, faint under the many heavy assaults of the world and the devil, and more than anything else the assaults of my own sinful flesh! Still, sustained by your grace, "I press toward the mark for the prize of the high calling of God in Christ Jesus". As it was with Gideon and his army, so it is with God's saints in all ages in this world. There can be no truce in this war. May God give us grace that we may be found faithful unto death.

Grace Sufficient
Indeed, our dear Saviour has promised, "My grace is sufficient for thee". His strength is made perfect in our weakness. That is to say, he displays the perfection of his strength in saving and sustaining such weak and sinful things as we are! While the world, the flesh, and the devil assault us relentlessly, though without are foes and

118

within fears, still "in the Lord we have strength". Though we have nothing, though we are nothing, our Saviour promises, "in me is thy help". He promises, "the righteous shall hold on his way; and he that hath clean hands shall wax stronger and stronger". And so it shall be! The worm Jacob will thresh the mountains. "He giveth power to the faint; and to them that have no might he increaseth strength. Even the youths shall faint and be weary, and the young men shall utterly fall: But they that wait upon the LORD shall renew their strength; they shall mount up with wings as eagles; they shall run, and not be weary; and they shall walk, and not faint" (Isaiah 40:29-31).

Jotham's Curse
Jotham's curse upon Abimelech and his ultimate, shameful death as he and Shechem mutually destroyed one another reminds us that our God shall at last bring every thought into captivity to the obedience of Christ. Whatever it takes, my God, to do that in me, do it I pray, according to your own wisdom and grace.

How very sad it is to see that all this strife, all this misery, all this trouble, all this destruction came upon Gideon's house and upon Israel because Gideon made an ephod of gold and all Israel went a whoring after it (Judges 8:27). Aaron fell into a similar transgression with the same results (Exodus 32:1-4). Take care, take great care, O my soul, to influence others for good and not for evil. God make me a blessing to those I influence and not a curse, for Christ's sake!

March 18
Today's Reading: Judges 10-12
"I have opened my mouth unto the LORD,
and I cannot go back"
Judges 11:35

Gideon was a farmer. Barak was a soldier. Samson was a Nazarite. David was the youngest of Jesse's sons and was despised by his brothers. Samuel was the first person used by God in his service while he was still a child. Our great God delights to use weak, insignificant, despised instruments to accomplish his greatest works in this world (1 Corinthians 1:26-29).

God's Chosen Instrument
This fact is never more demonstrably illustrated than in the case of Jephthah. Jephthah was born in shame, the bastard son of a harlot (Judges 11:1, 2). As such, he bore all his life the pain and shame of his mother's base, bestial immorality. He was by law excluded from the congregation of Israel (Deuteronomy 23:2). But Jephthah was beloved of God, chosen in Christ, and ordained as an instrument by whose hand he would save his people.

Discovering Christ Day By Day

The Lord God poured out his Spirit upon Jephthah and exalted him to the highest dignity and usefulness among his people. Jephthah was one of God's elect. As such, he was prospered by God in all that he did. No outward condition, be it ever so base, can hinder God's purpose, or thwart his grace.

God Honouring Faith

Jephthah feared God (Judges 11:9, 10) and believed his Word (Judges 11:14-27). His faith was evident in ascribing Israel's conquests to the Lord (Judges 11: 21, 23). He called on the God of all truth to judge between Israel and Ammon (Judges 11 27).

The Lord God honoured the faith that honoured him by delivering the Ammonites into Jephthah's hand. Jephthah's fidelity and perseverance in the faith is seen in the keeping of his vow (Judges 11:30-32). He had no idea that the one who would come out of his house and be the first to meet him would be his only child. But when he saw her, though his vow caused him great pain, he kept it. He said, "I have opened my mouth unto the Lord, and I cannot go back". In accordance with his oath, he offered his only child as a burnt-offering to God, banning her to continual virginity.

Believer's Baptism

Let us follow noble Jephthah's example of faith. In our baptism we publicly avowed ourselves God's forever, willing burnt-offerings to our God (Romans 6:4-6). Let us live as those who are God's. When we united with God's people in church membership, we publicly wed ourselves to God's saints in that local assembly. Let us live for the good of and serve the interests and needs of that local assembly into which God has placed us. Brothers and sisters in the household of faith serve one another in love. They seek not to be served, but to serve.

Persevering Faith

What a great example God the Holy Spirit sets before us in the man Jephthah! I know that all of God's elect are preserved by the grace of God in Christ. Not one of the chosen shall ever be lost. Not one of the redeemed shall ever be damned. Not one of the called shall ever perish. Not one true believer shall come short of eternal glory. But I also know that true believers never quit. They never stop following Christ. They never cease to seek the way of God, the will of God, and the glory of God. They will be tried. They will be tempted. Satan will roar against them, but he cannot devour them. The world will press them and caress them, calling them away from Christ. But the believer, like Jephthah of old, has opened his mouth to the Lord and cannot go back. He will persevere. Those who forsake Christ never knew Christ, for if they had known him, they could not have forsaken him.

March 19
Today's Reading: Judges 13-15
The angel of the LORD did wondrously
Judges 13:19

How precious such views of our dear Saviour's one grand and all-sufficient offering for sin in the sacrifice of himself for our souls! Truly, the sight Manoah and his wife beheld could not have been more wondrous. This man and his wife did nothing but look on. Faith can go no further. To lift a tool upon the altar is to pollute it (Exodus 20:25). Christ is the sacrifice, the altar (rock) on which the sacrifice is offered, the High Priest who offers the sacrifice, and God who accepts it. Well might they look on when the Lord did things so wondrously. Oh, may God give you and me eyes of faith ever to look on this great sight, Jesus Christ crucified!

The Nazarite
The promised child, Samson, was to be a Nazarite from the womb (Judges 13:4). As such, Samson was a great type of our Lord Jesus, who was not only separated from the very shadow of guilt and utterly devoted to his Father's service, but was miraculously conceived by the overshadowing power of the Holy Ghost. Samson, though set apart from his mother's womb a Nazarite by birth, was born in sin and shapen in iniquity. But the almighty Samson of our salvation was holy, harmless, undefiled, separate from sinners, and made higher than the heavens. The earthly Samson was raised up by God to deliver his brethren from temporary affliction. But our almighty Samson, the Lord Jesus, was raised up to deliver his people from everlasting ruin and to save us from the wrath to come.

Samson's Riddle
In the men of Timnath we see the baseness, treachery, and unprovoked hatred of humanity toward Christ our King. Fallen man, like these base creatures, returns for his goodness nothing but treachery! But there is set before us in Samson's riddle a beautiful allusion to the honey of the gospel. How unexpected honey from a lion's carcase? What a riddle it is to the wisdom of this world that God should choose weak things to confound the mighty. Oh, give me to eat of this honey! Make it food to my soul to heal the wounds of sin and the plague of my heart!

No Danger
When he was "sore athirst", Samson cried, "Shall I die for thirst?" What a sweet thought that question suggests. The Lord had wrought a great deliverance for Samson. Now, on a renewed pressing occasion, that deliverance already accomplished is made an argument of prayer for deliverance again. It is as if he had said, "Can I not expect God to do the same as he has done?" Let every saved sinner reason like Samson. He who has saved us will save us! He who has delivered will deliver!

Has the Lord Jesus Christ, the Son of God, redeemed us, brought us out of the hands of offended justice, given us this great deliverance from both the guilt and dominion of sin, taken us into covenant relation with himself, opened a new and living way for us in his blood; and does he ever live to keep it open by his intercession? Has the Lord Jesus saved you, loved you, blessed you, given himself for you, and treasured up for you all fulness of grace? Has he gone before us to prepare an everlasting fulness of glory for our enjoyment with himself to all eternity? Indeed, he has done all these great things for us; and the fact that he has ought to fill our souls with constant assurance that we shall never perish. He who promised it will perform it. "I give unto them eternal life; and they shall never perish, neither shall any man pluck them out of my hand" (John 10:26-28).

March 20
Today's Reading: Judges 16-18
"Let me die with the Philistines"
Judges 16:30

As Samson cried unto the Lord God, "Let me die with the Philistines", and bowed himself into death with all his might, our Lord Jesus Christ died for his enemies and with his enemies, bowing himself into death under the wrath of God with all his might. As one of Israel's judges, one of those raised up by God to save Israel from her enemies, Samson is set before us in these three chapters of Inspiration as a vivid type and picture of our Lord Jesus Christ. His name, "Samson", means "sunshine", or "shining sun", and our Lord Jesus Christ is "the Sun of Righteousness". Samson loved a woman "in the valley of Sorek". "Sorek" means, "a vine" or "redness", as in red wine. And our dear Saviour loved a woman, the Church of God's elect, he calls his vine, his fruitful vine, in the red earth, a woman washed in the fountain of his red blood. The woman's name was "Delilah". She is a vivid representation of us. Her name means, "languishing, feeble, oppressed, low, emptied, failing, impoverished, thin, wasted". Well might I be called "Delilah".

His Coming
Everything about Samson's birth, his life, and his death was intimately connected with three things: a promise, a sacrifice, and a name.

First, Samson was born, lived, and died according to the merciful promise and purpose of God to save his people (Judges 13:5). So it was with our Lord Jesus Christ. He came into this world on an errand of mercy to save his people, because God promised eternal life to his elect before the world began (2 Timothy 1:1; Titus 1:2).

Second, everything about this man was related to and for the glory of the name Wonderful, by which the Angel of the Lord revealed himself to Manoah and his wife (Judges 13:18). Everything is designed to bring honour and glory to the Lord Jesus Christ, our Samson, whose name is Wonderful. Most particularly, the work of redemption and salvation is to the praise, honour, and glory of his wonderful name (Revelation 4 and 5).

Third, everything Samson was and did for Israel was connected with, arose from, and pointed to, a sacrifice (Judges 13:19-21). The offering Manoah made, the slain lamb, is a picture of Christ the Lamb of God who was sacrificed for us. Once the sacrifice was made to the Lord, "the Angel did wondrously". Once justice was satisfied by the precious blood of the Son of God, our crucified Saviour did a wondrous thing. He was resurrected from the grave. Next, we are told that the Angel of the Lord "ascended in the flame of the altar". Even so, our great Saviour ascended up into heaven, obtained eternal redemption for us, and took his seat at the right hand of the Majesty on high by the merit of his sacrifice "in the flame of the altar".

His Commission
When the Angel of the Lord announced Samson's birth, he declared that this great deliverer would come into the world with a special commission from the Lord (Judges 13:5). In that commission, he was also typical of Christ. "He shall begin to deliver Israel out of the hand of the Philistines." Just as Samson came to deliver Israel from the Philistines, the Son of God came into this world to save his Israel from their sins (Matthew 1:21).

His Consecration
Samson was also typical of the Lord Jesus in his consecration to God from his mother's womb as a Nazarite (Judges 13:5-7). As such, he was typical of him of whom all Nazarites and the law of the Nazarite (Numbers 6) spoke: "Jesus the Nazarene". Samson's strength, like our Saviour's strength as a man, was his consecration to God. What a lesson there is for us in this. Children of God, here is your strength in this world, consecration to God our Saviour. Let us be true Nazarites to God.

His Choices
Samson was also a beautiful, clear, blessed picture of our dear Saviour in his choices, particularly his choices in the women he loved. This otherwise great man seemed to have an insatiable love for harlots. In Samson's case, his choice of harlots was a terrible evil, just as was his choice of a Philistine (Gentile) woman. Both were forbidden by God's holy law. Yet, even in this, perhaps most in this, he was a type of our blessed Saviour. I do not see why anyone who knows the grace of God would object to that, but many do. The Scriptures tell us plainly that this, too, was of the Lord (Judges 14:1-4). When the Lord Jesus Christ came into this world to get a bride for himself, he chose publicans, Gentiles, harlots, and sinners as the objects of his love and grace.

His Conquests
As Samson rent a lion as a young kid, with nothing but his bare hands, so the Lord Jesus has crushed the serpent's head and destroyed forever our accuser, who is as a roaring lion, seeking whom he may devour. When he comes again to take his bride home, our mighty Samson will eat honey out of this lion's carcass, and will give

honey to his Father as well! Like Samson, our great Redeemer voluntarily laid down his life for us and thereby destroyed forever all those who would destroy us: sin, Satan, death, hell, and the grave.

O Lord Jesus, may your sovereign word be like Samson's mighty arms, pulling down all the strong holds of sin and Satan. Let that cursed foe be beheld by your people, falling as lightning from heaven. Let every false god and every false way be cast down and the ruin of antichrist be brought to pass. "Thy kingdom come. Thy will be done in earth, as it is in heaven."

March 21
Today's Reading: Judges 19, 20
No king, no deliverer
Judges 19:1

In Judges 18:28 we are told there was "no deliverer". Here we read "there was no king in Israel". Be reminded, where Christ is Saviour, Christ is King (Matthew 10:37-39, Mark 8:34-38, Luke 14:26, 27). He will not be my Saviour if he is not my Lord. Spirit of God, give me grace to bow to my Lord in all things. Graciously force me to bow! If you do not, I will not and cannot bow.

Chronological Order
The last five chapters of the Book of Judges are placed after the death of Samson; but these chapters record a terribly evil period in the history of Israel sometime between the death of Joshua and the first of Israel's judges (Othniel). Chronologically, what we have recorded in these chapters probably occurred at the period of time described in Judges 2:10-13. It should not surprise us that these events are not revealed in chronological order.

No King
All that is recorded in the last five chapters of the book of Judges took place at a time when there was no king in Israel, and every man did that which was right in his own eyes (Judges 17:6; 18:1; 19:1; 21:25). Nothing is more dangerous, nothing is more certain to ruin our souls than doing that which is right in our own eyes. "He that trusteth in his own heart is a fool" (Proverbs 28:26). Of this you can be sure, Everything that is right in our own eyes is wrong. And that is most especially true when it comes to spiritual and religious matters (Proverbs 12:15; 14:12; 16:25).

Actually, there was a King in Israel. They had no physical, visible king as other nations had. But we are told in 1 Samuel 12:12 that the Lord God was their King. The problem was not that there was no king, but that they did not know their King and refused to acknowledge and serve God as their King. Anytime men and women refuse to bow to, obey, and worship the Lord Jesus Christ as their King, the result is what we have described in these chapters. Everyone does that which is right in his own eyes.

These people got into the mess they were in, not by every man doing what was wrong in his own eyes, but by every man doing what was right in his own eyes. And when people do what is right in their own eyes, the results are exactly the same as the things recorded in these chapters; idolatry, pragmatism, hedonism, humanism.

Christ Our King
Remember, the Lord Jesus Christ is our God and King. That means that he is our Ruler, our Lord, our Saviour, our Defender, our Provider, our Protector, our Judge, and our Deliverer. Oh, for grace ever to acknowledge, worship, and bow to him as our great King! The very first principle of saving faith is the surrender of our souls to Christ our King (Luke 14:25-33). To believe on Christ is ceasing to do what is right in our eyes and bowing to his will as our Lord and King. Faith in Christ is the surrender of myself to him, trusting him alone as the Lord my Righteousness.

The Right Place
The events of these chapters are out of order chronologically; but they are in exactly the right order of Divine Revelation. Moses (the law) was dead. He died in the wilderness because the law of God can never bring Salvation. Joshua had brought Israel into the land of Canaan. He portrayed Christ bringing salvation. God had given Israel 12 judges (deliverers, Saviours, and kings) who typified Christ and his continual deliverance of our souls by his grace. The last judge was Samson. As Samson brought deliverance by his death, so our great Samson obtained eternal redemption for us by his death. In these last chapters of Judges we see the corruption and depravity, idolatry, and debauchery that possesses all men by nature. Yes, before they are converted by God's omnipotent grace, before Christ is revealed in them, God's elect are just like all other men, "children of wrath even as others". Then, when we get to the next page in the Book of God, we see our great Samson revealed again in the Person of Boaz. Blessed be his holy name, Christ our Kinsman Redeemer will yet do all that is required for our souls.

March 22
Today's Reading: Judges 21-Ruth 3
Naomi's decision
Ruth 1:6

Naomi was a woman of remarkable faith. We do not know much about her husband, or her sons, but Naomi was a believer. She left Bethlehem with her husband. And she stayed in Moab after Elimelech died. Yet, her heart was never in Moab. As Lot's wife looked back to Sodom with regret, so Elimelech's wife looked back to Bethlehem with regret; but hers was the regret of a believing heart. It appears that by one means or another, all the time she was in Moab she kept up with what was going on in Bethlehem (v. 6). She maintained correspondence with Bethlehem.

Providence

Here is a work of providence for Naomi. The Lord God always deals with his children as a wise and loving father (Hebrews 12:5-12). Because he loved Naomi, the Lord would not allow Naomi to stay in Moab. He would not permit her to continue there, away from Bethlehem, away from his people, away from his worship. But to get her back he had to deal with her in a very trying way. First, the Lord killed her husband. Then, he killed both of her sons. He made Moab bitter to her. Thank God for those painful thorn hedges that force us to return to him, when we would forsake him (Hosea 2:6, 7).

The Word

Here is a work of the Word. The Lord caused this chosen one to hear the good report of his grace toward his people. Naomi "heard in Moab how that the Lord had visited his people in giving them bread". When Naomi heard what God had done for his people, she believed the message and arose to return to Bethlehem.

"Faith cometh by hearing." By some means or another, God got the good news to Naomi that he had visited his people and given them bread. This is the way God saves sinners. He sends a preacher to proclaim the good news of his rich, free, abundant grace. The Lord has visited and redeemed his people. The Bread of Life has come down from heaven. Whenever God brings deliverance to his chosen, he causes them to hear the good news of his accomplishments of grace (Romans 10:17). He never by-passes the use of means, the means he has ordained for the salvation of his people.

Faith

Here is a believer's work of faith. "Wherefore she went forth out of the place." There can never be reconciliation with God without separation from the world. Those who eat at the Father's table have to leave the hog troughs of the world. You cannot serve God and mammon. A choice must be made. "Choose you this day whom ye will serve." Naomi had made her choice, and so must we (2 Corinthians 6:17; 1 John 2:15). She was determined to leave Moab and return to Israel. She was willing to leave her dearest and nearest relatives. Naomi was a true believer. She knew from whence she had fallen. She knew what she had lost. She remembered how blessed things had been in Bethlehem. And she was determined to return. She counted no cost too great.

Those who truly believe the gospel of God are controlled in their lives by things not seen (2 Corinthians 4:18-5:1; Hebrews 11:13-16). Spirit of God, control my heart, my thoughts, my life, all the days of my life in this world. Give me grace to live, hour by hour and day by day, by faith in Christ my Lord, to the glory of God.

March 23
Today's Reading: Ruth 4-1 Samuel 2
"I am thy near kinsman"
Ruth 3:12

How sweet, how wonderfully sweet it is to hear our dear Saviour, the Lord Jesus, the Son of God, say to our souls, "I am thy near Kinsman". That is the message of the book of Ruth. Our Lord Jesus Christ, having assumed our humanity, became one of us that he might be made sin, pay the price of our ransom with his blood, and redeem our poor souls from all our loss and poverty by the sin and fall of our father, Adam.

Kinsman-Redeemer
The subject of this book of Ruth is redemption. The whole book is a picture of our redemption by Christ, our Kinsman-Redeemer. The kinsman is the one who has the right to redeem. The prophetic law of the kinsman given in Leviticus 25:25 was given to be a picture of Christ and was fulfilled by him. The word translated "kinsman" in Ruth 3:9, 12, 13, 4:1, 3, 6, 8, and 14 is translated "redeemer" in the margin of our Bible. And it is translated "Redeemer" elsewhere in the Word of God, as in Job 19:25, where Job says, "I know that my Redeemer liveth". In Isaiah 45:6, this is the name by which our dear Saviour identifies himself "Redeemer". Our father Adam sold us into bondage and sin; but Christ, our Kinsman-Redeemer, bought us and brought us into liberty, righteousness, and life (Romans 5:19).
The Book of Ruth is a beautiful picture of the work of our Lord Jesus Christ as our Kinsman-Redeemer. It shows us both our need of a Kinsman-Redeemer and the way we may obtain the blessings of redemption.

Redeemer's Call
There are many things in the book of Ruth by which we see our Saviour's great work of redemption. We see God's sovereign election and distinguishing grace in the choice of Ruth as the object of his mercy. His special providence is displayed in the "handfuls of purpose" Boaz commanded his servants to leave for Ruth. Certainly Ruth's coming to Boaz in chapter three portrays true faith in Christ, bowing at his feet and surrendering all to him. In the fourth chapter, Boaz's redemption of Ruth according to the law of God is a type of Christ Jesus, our Kinsman-Redeemer, redeeming us from the curse of the law. But none of this could be known without a special, effectual, irresistible call of grace.
"Ho, such an one" (Ruth 4:1). How blessed we were when a general call in the gospel became a personal call to our souls! If we are called, how blessed we are because we have been called of God to life and faith in Christ! The general invitation is, "Ho, every one that thirsteth, come ye to the waters". The personal call is, "Ho, such an one". Jesus calls his own sheep by name. How is this done? Any time the

Lord speaks by the preaching of the gospel to their particular state and circumstances, he says, "Ho, such an one".

When he says, "I came not to call the righteous, but sinners to repentance". Faith answers, "That call is for me, for I am a sinner". In the gospel we are told, "God commendeth his love to us, in that while we were yet sinners Christ died for us". Faith replies, "That love must be for me, for I am both by nature and by practice a sinner before God". We are told that Christ Jesus ascended up on high and received gifts for men, yea, for the rebellious, that the Lord God might dwell among them. The believing sinner says, "I have been a rebel all my life. This gift must be for me".

When the word of salvation is sent to the soul by the effectual power of God the Holy Spirit, the poor, needy, bankrupt sinner sees Christ as a suitable Redeemer for such a wretch and sees himself a sinner suitable for such a Kinsman-Redeemer! Then, as with Boaz's kinsman, the call becomes personal, changing the appellation from everyone, to "such an one;" and the believing soul comes at the call, turns aside, and sits down, as the very one with whom the business at hand is to be transacted.

Faith is a precious gift of grace. It can never be satisfied until it possesses all that the soul needs; and that all is found in Christ, our mighty Boaz. Faith is a personal enjoyment of all grace and salvation in Christ. Salvation is proclaimed from heaven for sinners. God the Father gives it. God the Son purchased it. God the Spirit sends it to the heart with an, "Ho, such an one, turn aside, sit down here." And God-given faith sits at the Saviour's feet, having Christ himself formed in the heart the hope of glory.

March 24
Today's Reading: 1 Samuel 3-6
"Samuel was established to be a prophet of the LORD"
1 Samuel 3:20

Yesterday, in the second chapter of 1 Samuel we read Hannah's prayer of praise to God for his great goodness. She did not speak of her son's excellence or the promising features she thought he possessed. Her soul was absorbed in adoring the Lord God who had given her Samuel. The holiness, faithfulness, goodness, and wisdom of her prayer-hearing and prayer-answering God consumed her heart, as she brought her darling Samuel as a burnt-offering to God, as Jephthah did with his daughter, his only child. Having God for her Rock and as the horn of her salvation, Hannah was full of praise and fully confident that her son Samuel was in good hands, for she had put him in the hands of her God. Now, we read that "Samuel was established to be a prophet of the Lord". Hannah honoured God in believing him, trusting him to give her a son. She honoured God in giving her son to the Lord. And God honoured Hannah in making her son his prophet.

Discovering Christ Day By Day

Manifestations Of Grace
The third chapter of 1 Samuel shows us how the Lord God graciously made himself known to Samuel. Though at first Samuel was utterly ignorant of God's grace, that grace is manifest in all God's dealings with him, both outwardly in providence and inwardly by the impressions of his Spirit upon the young boy's soul.

Are you, my reader, a young man, or a young woman? Be wise. Pray to the God of all grace, as Eli instructed Samuel, "Speak, Lord, for thy servant heareth". Ask the Lord God continually to manifest his grace to you and in you, as he did to Samuel, that you may be a partaker of that grace which is in Christ Jesus!

Are you an aged believer like God's servant Eli? Bow your heart to God and give him praise and heartfelt thanks for all his goodness and grace bestowed upon you these many years; and beg of him that he will yet speak to you by his prophet. Then, beg for grace, like Eli, to bow to the revealed will of God in all things. O my God, give me grace to bow to you, surrendering my will to your will, especially when your will opposes the lusts of my flesh!

Trembling For The Ark
Eli trembled for the ark of God. He was a faithful man whose sons were rebels. The fault of his sons was in great measure his own, because "he restrained them not". Yet, this man faithfully judged Israel for forty years. And when his rebel sons were slain by God and the ark of God was taken, his greater concern was for the ark of God. The ark of God was the symbol and token of the divine presence and of the covenant engagements of our God in the person of his dear Son for his people. It symbolized God's salvation in and by Christ our Lord. God's glory, God's salvation, and the honour of God's name were things of greater concern to this old man than his dearest earthly kin. My Father, give me such grace, for Christ's sake.

Dagon's Ups And Downs
When the Philistines had beaten the Israelites in battle and captured the ark, they boasted and gloried as though they had defeated God himself! They set the ark, like a trophy, in the temple of their god, Dagon, to show that he was mightier than Jehovah. Thus, they thought to mock God. But Dagon fell before the ark of God night after night, until there was nothing left of him but the stump on which the ignorant idolaters placed their helpless, useless god!

Jehovah's answer to his foes was Dagon broken to shivers before his ark and the Philistines plagued with tumours, until in their desperate pain and dire disgrace, they gladly sent the ark back to Israel loaded with gold. So it shall yet be! Though antichrist, freewill-works religion seems to triumph on every hand, our God will defend his honour. Dagon must and shall fall before our all-glorious Christ. He will make bare his holy arm and cast the beast and the false prophet down before his Son and his church. And when he is done, all the gold of Babylon shall be brought into the New Jerusalem!

March 25
Today's Reading: 1 Samuel 7-9
Christ our Ark
1 Samuel 7:1

"The men of Kirjathjearim came and fetched up the ark of the Lord." We have reason to thank God that no one has ever found that ark! If anyone were to find it, foolish men and women would make an idol of it, make pagan pilgrimages to the "holy land" to see it, and worship it. But in its day, under the ceremonial, typical religious service of the Old Testament, the Ark of the Covenant was one of those "ordinances of divine service", which beautifully typified and pictured the Lord Jesus Christ and our redemption by him.

The Ark
We can never understand the Old Testament Scriptures until we see that everything in the Old Testament Scriptures represents, points to, and pictures Christ our Substitute (Luke. 24:27; 44, 45). And the Ark of the Covenant was one of the most beautiful and instructive types of Christ in the Old Testament. It was made out of shittim wood, overlaid on the inside and the outside with pure gold, representing both the incorruptible humanity and glorious deity of our Saviour. The ark was the symbol of God's holiness, power, and glory. It was carried about from place to place upon the shoulders of the priests by staves fitted into rings attached to the ark. Even so, Christ is carried throughout the world upon the shoulders of chosen men, through the preaching of the gospel.

Inside The Ark
Never, like the men of Bethshemesh, would I presumptuously look into the secret things which belong unto the Lord our God. But with an eye of faith, let us look today inside the Ark, asking God the Holy Spirit to show us our Saviour.

Come into "the Holiest of all", by the "golden censer" of our Saviour's merits, asking God to show you Christ, our Ark, as he was portrayed in that Old Testament type. What can be found in the ark? Let us do by faith what no mortal man could ever do in those days of types and shadows. Let us lift up the mercy-seat and look inside the ark. Remember, the Ark was but a picture of the Lord Jesus Christ. What do we see in the ark? We see the two tables of the law of God, which we have broken. The broken law, our sins, is under the mercy-seat, under the blood.

God's Purpose
Those broken tables of the law, under the blood, represent God's purpose of grace. The law was written upon tables of stone, representing both the hardness of our hearts and the inflexibility of God's law. The law represents our curse and condemnation by reason of sin. The tables of God's broken law were always kept in the Ark, under the

mercy-seat (Exodus 25:16, 21), representing perfect redemption by Christ. That perfect redemption of his elect is the purpose of God (Romans 8:28-31). The law of God, being perfectly satisfied by Christ, cries as strongly for our salvation as the grace of God. We are, in Christ, free from the law, because the law's demands have been fully met for us by Christ's obedience and blood

God's Power
Look again. There is something else inside the ark. There is Aaron's rod that budded. That rod represents God's power. Aaron's rod that budded portrayed the gospel of Christ, the Man whom God has chosen (Numbers 17:10). Christ, the Rock of our salvation, was smitten by Moses' rod, which represented God's holy law. The water of life flows out to sinners by Aaron's rod, the gospel, which is the power of God before which Dagon must fall, the power of God unto salvation (Romans 1:16, 17)

God's Provision
There is one more thing inside the ark, the golden pot that had manna. That is a picture of Christ, God's Provision (Exodus 16:33, 34). It was a golden pot, portraying the richness of God's free grace in Christ. It was a big pot, holding an omer of manna; and Christ is a great Saviour, a bounteous store of mercy and grace! This golden pot had manna, the bread of heaven, portraying Christ the Bread of Life. All God's provision for sinners is in Christ Jesus. His name is Jehovah-Jireh, the Lord will provide (Ephesians 1:3). All the provisions of grace, of providence, and of eternity are in Christ! Come to the Ark, Christ Jesus. The way is open. All who come to God by Christ are forever saved. All we need, all God requires, all that heaven can bestow is in Christ, the Ark. Come to the Ark!

March 26
Today's Reading: 1 Samuel 10-12
"Great things he hath done for you"
1 Samuel 12:24

"Only fear the Lord, and serve him in truth, with all your heart; for consider how great things he hath done for you". After assuring the Children of Israel of God's abiding faithfulness, of the Lord's sovereign electing love, and of his own unceasing intercessions for them at the throne of grace, God's prophet gave his people this wise, affectionate word of pastoral counsel. He had just recapitulated Israel's history in the manifestations of God's love for his chosen people. May God the Holy Spirit give us grace this day to remember his great mercies and our unworthiness before him! Let us refer all our blessings, as we review them, to the mercy, love, and grace of our God in

Christ Jesus. Remembering past mercies, let us find strength for today, and seek confident faith in Christ for tomorrow.

Beyond Calculation

When we begin to consider what great things the Lord God has done for us and how he has done them, we are at a loss to know where to start and where to end. Shall we consider God's mercies in creation, in providence, or in grace? How can we calculate those great mercies even in one of these spheres? Will you open with the consideration of God's mercies towards you in nature, or providence, or grace? "It is of the Lord's mercies that we are not consumed, because his compassions fail not. They are new every morning: great is thy faithfulness". The riches of his grace in Christ Jesus are "unsearchable riches". Who can count them? We do not know; we cannot even imagine the countless mercies performed for us and bestowed upon us during the long season of our unregenerate state. Even since faith came, we are more ignorant of God's mercies than we are knowing. That is to say, his mercies are unimaginably more than those of which we are aware. Truly, when I consider "how great things he hath done for" me, I am compelled to first acknowledge that they are beyond calculation, too great for me to number.

Eternal Mercies

How can we begin to consider the great things the Lord has done for us if we do not begin before time began, considering his eternal mercies given to us in Christ Jesus, our Surety and Covenant Head before the world began? "Blessed be the God and Father of our Lord Jesus Christ, who hath blessed us with all spiritual blessings in heavenly places in Christ: According as he hath chosen us in him before the foundation of the world, that we should be holy and without blame before him in love: Having predestinated us unto the adoption of children by Jesus Christ to himself, according to the good pleasure of his will, To the praise of the glory of his grace, wherein he hath made us accepted in the beloved". "Who hath saved us, and called us with an holy calling, not according to our works, but according to his own purpose and grace, which was given us in Christ Jesus before the world began". The mercies of God are eternal mercies. All the works he performs for us in time were finished from eternity!

Providential Mercies

What a huge volume might be written if we could write down only the Lord's providential mercies performed for us! His constant watchfulness over us, his secret and manifest provisions for us, and his unfailing faithfulness in graciously and wisely making all things minister to and become subservient to our souls' welfare are amazing things to consider. Oh, what great things the Lord has done for us! He performs all things for us. Imagine that! While we mark the footsteps of his love and remember our wanderings from him, we are both bowed with shame and lifted with hope. He who has spared us, saved us, and sanctified us, in spite of ourselves, will yet keep us in perfect security in spite of ourselves. "Bless the Lord, O my soul, and forget not all his benefits."

Since Conversion

Moving from the outer court of nature and providence and entering into the inner court of grace, consider what great things the Lord has done for us since the day of our Lord's effectual call and the conversion of our souls. It would tire the arm of an angel to write them down. Precious Lord Jesus, in you, and by you, and from you, all our mercies flow! You, dear Saviour, are the Alpha and the Omega, the Beginning and the End, the First, the Last, and the Best of all! Christ is the comprehensive gift of God. He is the channel of all blessings temporal, spiritual, and eternal. He is the River of Life flowing from the throne of God, through whom all mercies come and praise returns. He purchased them. He gives them. And he sustains them. All the covenant mercies of God in Christ are "the sure mercies of David" to his elect.

Fear And Serve

These things should inspire our souls with joyful confidence to fear the Lord, and serve him in spirit and in truth with all our hearts. "He is thy praise, and he is thy God, that hath done for thee these great and terrible things, which thine eyes have seen." "I beseech you therefore, by the mercies of God, that ye present your bodies a living sacrifice, holy, acceptable unto God, which is your reasonable service." Blessed Spirit of God, give me grace to do so, for Christ's sake.

March 27
Today's Reading: 1 Samuel 13, 14
"Is Saul also among the prophets?"
1 Samuel 10:12

We read in 1 Samuel 10:9 that God gave Saul "another heart". Samuel had told him that the Spirit of the Lord would come upon him, that he would prophesy, and that he would be turned into another man. Obviously, a great change was wrought upon him. Saul was given "another heart", and was made "another man". He no longer sought asses, but a kingdom. Instead of being employed in his father's service, he was now "another man", pursuing his own grandeur. But these changes are not to be regarded as the special work of God the Holy Spirit on the heart. Saul was found among the prophets; but was not born of God. He was made "another man", but not a new man. He was given "another heart", but not a new heart. There is not a word in the inspired record to indicate that Saul was a regenerate man.

New Creature

If we are saved by the grace of God, we must be born again, we must be made new creatures in Christ, we must have Christ formed in us, being made partakers of the divine nature, having in us "that new man, which after God is created in righteousness and true holiness". No outward situation, no providential changes, however prosperous in themselves, no elevation in social rank or religious order, no increase in power and position, no change of behaviour, no improvement of knowledge is to be looked upon as a work of grace in the heart. All those things combined avail nothing without faith in Christ, faith wrought in the heart by the new creation of grace.

Profaned Sacrifice
When Saul profaned the priest's office, like Uzzah after him, he put his hand to God's work, put his hand to God's Sacrifice, attempted to supplant Christ and his blood atonement, expecting God to accept him and his sacrifice instead. This is a matter of indescribable importance. God always sends people to hell for putting their hand to his Ark, for lifting up their tool upon his Altar, for mixing their works with his grace. Christ alone must be the Offering by which we draw near to God. Christ alone must be the Sacrifice by which we seek acceptance with the Almighty. Christ alone must be our Priest, our Sacrifice, our Righteousness, our Sanctification, and our Atonement. God's Precious Jesus!

Ever remember Saul. Let me never, like him, bring my poor offerings, or fancied peace offerings, my imaginary good works to God, seeking acceptance with the Holy One by my abominations. Christ alone has made peace by the blood of the cross. To seek acceptance with God in any other way, though with the most costly rites and ceremonies and sacrifices, as Saul did, is to show contempt to his person, his blood, and his finished righteousness. Such profanation calls down the vengeance of heaven upon the person who vainly imagines the he or she is righteous.

But as we, by the gracious influence of the Holy Spirit, are enabled to look stedfastly to Christ and rely on his precious, sin-atoning blood and sacrifice for acceptance with God, we have testimony from God himself that we are made the righteousness of God in him. Trusting the Lord Jesus Christ, sinners, like you and me, are urged to "come boldly to the throne of grace, that we may obtain mercy and find grace to help in time of need".

Sin's Consequences
We are compelled by our reading of God's Word this day to remember the consequences of rebellion and sin. In the history of this man Saul we see the sure consequences of rebellion against God. The word of the Lord assures us, that, "when a man's ways please the Lord, he maketh, even his enemies to be at peace with him". But when sinners neglect and despise the Lord God, he turns even their comforts into crosses. And though God gave Saul a crown, he filled it with thorns.

Great Difference
How different things are with God's elect! How gracious the Lord is, notwithstanding all our multiplied transgressions. By some insignificant instrument like Jonathan, he works out deliverance for his people and turns our crosses into comforts. In the midst of all manifold transgressions, let us never lose sight of God's mercy, love, and grace flowing to our souls by Christ Jesus. When trials and afflictions are brought to us by our Father's hand to prove our faith, may God the Holy Spirit give us a steady eye,

"looking unto Jesus", that we might be revived and enlightened with the droppings of his grace, as Jonathan was by the honey he received.

Depend upon it, child of God, in the strength of the Lord Jesus you will find all difficulties as nothing. He can and will make you more than conqueror, through the sovereignty of his power. All obstacles in the way to the accomplishment of his holy purpose will be as nothing, for "there is no restraint to the Lord, to save by many or by few". And, "as the Lord liveth, there shall not one hair of your head fall to the ground", if you are in Christ.

March 28
Today's Reading: 1 Samuel 15-17
"This is he"
1 Samuel 16:12

"And the Lord said, Arise, anoint him; for this is he. Then Samuel took the horn of oil, and anointed him in the midst of his brethren".

Behold, a greater than David is here! As David was singled out from and chosen above his brothers to be the Lord's anointed, the king of Israel, so the Lord Jesus, of whom David was such a vivid type, is God's Anointed, his Chosen One, the King of Israel. "Then thou spakest in vision to thy holy one, and saidst, I have laid help upon one that is mighty; I have exalted one chosen out of the people. I have found Jesus my servant; with my holy oil have I anointed him: With whom my hand shall be established: mine arm also shall strengthen him" (Psalm 89:19-21). "Behold my Servant, whom I uphold; mine Elect, in whom my soul delighteth; I have put my spirit upon him: he shall bring forth judgment to the Gentiles" (Isaiah 42:1).

Typified in David, we see our dear Saviour, the Lord Jesus Christ, the Lord our Righteousness. And let my soul make this sweet subject the meditation and song of my heart. He who is both David's son and David's Lord is the chiefest among ten thousand and altogether lovely.

From Everlasting
"Art thou not from everlasting, O Lord my God, mine Holy One?" his "goings forth have been from of old, from everlasting". Behold our dear Emanuel with the eye of faith as coming up from everlasting. He stood forth as our Surety, this glorious One, to be the God-man Mediator, the Christ, for the salvation of his people, whom (even then) he did not disdain to call his brethren. Yonder, in eternity, before ever the worlds were called into existence by his word, our Mediator stood forth, pre-eminent above his fellows, and was appointed to be the Head and King of his church, that vast multitude chosen to be the recipients and beneficiaries of all God's abounding grace in him. In him, from him, and through him, the Triune Jehovah predestined that they

become a glorious church, not having spot or wrinkle, or any such thing, but that he might present it to himself in love.

Our Chosen

As our Lord Jesus Christ is God's Chosen One, so he is the Chosen One of all who are chosen in him, redeemed by him, and called to him. As all the sons of Jesse passed in review before Samuel, had all his redeemed been present to have chosen one to be their head and king, none but Christ could have been chosen. All voices would have echoed Jehovah's proclamation: "Arise, anoint him; for this is he". Truly, Lord Jesus, "thou art he whom thy brethren shall praise: thy hand shall be in the neck of thine enemies; thy father's children shall bow down before thee". He is the heir of all things, the chiefest and first, born in the womb of mercy. "His name shall endure for ever: his name shall be continued as long as the sun: and men shall be blessed in him: all nations shall call him blessed."

Delight unceasingly in this contemplation of our Saviour. God the Father has chosen him. He has anointed him with the holy oil for salvation; and the Spirit was given unto him without measure. Is God's Chosen your Chosen? Is the Father's Anointed your Anointed? Is there any in heaven, or upon earth to whom you look for help, or strength, or comfort, or salvation, but to the Lord Jesus Christ? Who but Christ, would you have for a Saviour? What object is so desirable as he to claim our love? Witness for me children of light, witness for me angels who see his face and do his pleasure, Jesus Christ, the Son of God is my only beloved, my hope, my portion. Soon, I shall join your assembly, and with you bless and adore him in endless song, the fairest and chiefest among ten thousand!

March 29
Today's Reading: 1 Samuel 18-20
"Seemeth it to you a light thing?"
1 Samuel 18:23

"David said, Seemeth it to you a light thing to be a king's son in law, seeing that I am a poor man, and lightly esteemed?" David considered it his high honour to be allied to the family of King Saul, an earthly king. What then must be the dignity to which believers are called as the sons of God? Being the sons and daughters of God, we have been made heirs of God and joint-heirs with Christ, by his almighty, free grace.

The apostle John was utterly lost in the contemplation of this unspeakable mercy. He cried out with holy rapture, "Behold, what manner of love the Father hath bestowed upon us, that we should be called the sons of God". And am I begotten to this immense privilege? Amazing love! Amazing grace!

Sons we are through God's election,
Who in Jesus Christ believe;
By eternal destination,
Sovereign grace we have received!

Our Rich Inheritance

Ponder well the vast inheritance we have bestowed on us by divine predestination and God's sovereign, distinguishing grace in Christ as "the sons of God". This is not a barren title or an empty name. "Beloved, now are we the sons of God". This relationship brings with it a rich revenue of all temporal, spiritual, and eternal blessings. Believers are born to an inheritance incorruptible and undefiled, and that fades not away. We have the Spirit of adoption and of grace. "Because ye are sons, God hath sent forth the Spirit of his Son into your hearts, crying, Abba, Father."

Though they may be poor in outward circumstances, bread shall be given and water shall be sure. And your defence shall be the munitions of rocks. God's sons and daughters may be afflicted in body or in mind, their back shall be made as strong as the burden their heavenly Father lays upon it, and as their days demand so shall their strength be. Every child shall have his own portion, the Father's blessing sanctifying all. Even death itself is a part of the inheritance of God's dear children, for by that means the Lord God brings his chosen home to himself.

Our Greatest Privilege

It is the greatest privilege of grace heaven can bestow upon sinners here below. "Beloved, now are we the sons of God". "This is a privilege", wrote John Gill, "that exceeds all others. It is better to be a son than to be a saint. Angels are saints, but not sons. They are servants. It is better to be a child of God than to be redeemed, pardoned, and justified. It is great grace to redeem from slavery, to pardon criminals, and justify the ungodly; but it is another and a higher act of grace to make them sons; and which makes them infinitely more honourable, than to be the sons and daughters of the greatest potentate upon earth; yea, gives them an honour which Adam had not in innocence, nor the angels in heaven, who though sons by creation, yet not by adoption".

To be called a son of God is the most noble title in heaven or earth. If we are sons, we should not live like slaves in bondage, under the terror of the law. Let every sinner who believes on the Son of God constantly enjoy all the privileges of full-grown sons in the family of God. Soon, we shall know fully and perfectly what Paul meant when he spoke of "the glorious liberty of the children of God".

What shall we say regarding these things? "I am", as David, "a poor man and lightly esteemed".

But I've been adopted, my name's written down,
An heir to a mansion, a robe, and a crown!

March 30
Today's Reading: 1 Samuel 21-24
David's men
1 Samuel 22:2

"And every one that was in distress, and every one that was in debt, and every one that was discontented, gathered themselves unto him; and he became a captain over them." These were David's men, those who gathered themselves to David, those over whom David was captain. In this, too, we see David as a great type of our dear Saviour, the Lord Jesus, David's son and David's Lord.

My Experience
I see myself in these men. When first I came to the Lord Jesus by the sweet, irresistible force of his grace, I was a poor, guilty sinner, in distress, in debt, and discontented; bitter in soul, in the pain of great poverty and need of soul, pressed sore and heavy laden, disconsolate and troubled. Misery filled my heart. My soul was empty. And "no man cared for my soul".

Oh, what a precious thought it was that God the Holy Spirit put in my heart. "Go to Christ." And when I came to him, I found him able and willing to save to the uttermost! He graciously condescended to be my Captain, my mighty Saviour. My insolvency he took away. Coming to him, I discovered that he had fully paid all my debt. Trusting him, I found that all the demands of God's holy law and infinite justice had been fully satisfied for this poor sinner. For me he had already magnified the law and made it honourable! All my distress under the apprehension of divine justice he removed. My quaking, screaming conscience was immediately silent and at ease; for God's justice, by Christ, is not only satisfied, but glorified! All that once disquieted my soul is now forever gone. My soul shall never again be discontent; for in Christ, my God richly supplies all my needs "according to his riches in glory by Christ Jesus". All grace is mine here and all glory hereafter!

All praise, honour, and glory to Christ, the great and glorious Captain of my salvation! In him I see that Leader and Commander which Jehovah, the Father, promised to give to the people. He is that Holy One commissioned by the Father to this very purpose, that every one that is in soul distress by reason of sin, and are debtors to the broken law of God, may come to him, bow to him, and find in him their Captain.

Christ's men, his army, like David's, is composed of none but distressed souls. None will ever take him for their Captain whose spiritual circumstances are not desperate. None but those whose hearts are distressed by reason of sin, and are sinking under the heavy load of guilt will come under his banner.

Condescending Grace
Oh, but what condescending mercy, love, and grace there is in Christ. He condescends to receive such sinners and be gracious to them. Indeed, they are the very people he has chosen as the objects of his grace. Only to these poor, impoverished, empty,

needy souls can he be all. But to such, he is all, all our Wisdom, all our Righteousness, all our Sanctification, and all our Redemption (1 Corinthians 1:26-30). I say to every poor sinner, to every insolvent debtor, to every needy soul who feels and knows the plague of his heart, come to Christ, the Captain of my salvation. He is the Near Kinsman, able to redeem and recover all you have lost. He is Jehovah the Healer, able to recover you from all your sorrow. Go to him, my brother, as I have done. He will take away your distress by taking away your sin. He will liberate you from all your debt, having paid it himself. He will banish all discontent from the mind, giving you peace with God by his blood.

Captain Over
And this almighty Captain, the Lord Jesus, is Captain over his people, as well as Captain to his people. He is Lord of all and over all in the hearts of his own. By the sword of his Spirit, which is the Word of God, he works conviction in our hearts, makes all our enemies fall under him, leads all his people on to victory, and makes us more than conquerors by his omnipotent grace! Christ's men shall be triumphant! Blessed Captain of my soul, put the military garments of salvation on my soul, the whole armour of God, that under your banner I may be found in life, in death, and for evermore!

March 31
Today's Reading: 1 Samuel 25-27
"The LORD'S anointed"
1 Samuel 26:11

David was chosen and anointed of God to be king over Israel. But Saul, according to God's providence, was still upon the throne. Saul was a wicked man. God had rejected him. But God had not yet taken him off the throne. And David was not about to attempt an overthrow of God's providence. Painful as it may have been to endure Saul's evil deeds, David was content for Saul to reign as long as God would have him reign. He said, "The Lord forbid that I should stretch forth mine hand against the Lord's anointed".

It seems obvious to me that God the Holy Spirit has given us this portion of Holy Scripture to teach us how we are to treat "the Lord's anointed". No less than four times in 1 Samuel 26 David referred to Saul, that wicked man, as "the Lord's anointed", giving that as the reason he would do him no harm.

God's Servants
How does this apply to God's church today? We have no king, but Christ. Yet, Christ our King, our risen Lord, has given his church pastors according to his own heart to

feed his people with knowledge and understanding. These men are God's anointed messengers to his church. They are the angels of the churches.

But few men today have David's wisdom in their treatment of God's servant. Today, it is common for men to take it upon themselves to seat and unseat men in the kingdom of God. I refer specifically to the pastoral office. One of the most lamentable evils of our day is the utter disdain and contempt with which most people treat faithful gospel preachers. Such disdain and contempt we expect from the world. But I think the angels must blush when they see it in the church. True pastors are not hirelings to be seated and unseated by men. Those who treat God's ambassadors as hired hands, do so at their own peril. God will not allow any man to wrong his servants with impunity. He will reprove kings for their sakes. He says, "Touch not mine anointed, and do my prophets no harm" (1 Chronicles 16:21, 22).

God's Ambassador

When a congregation seeks a pastor, it should be by the direction of the Holy Spirit. When a church calls a man to be its pastor, that congregation has voluntarily placed itself under the pastoral rule of that man (Hebrews 13:7, 17). He is God's ambassador, God's spokesman, and God's representative to that congregation. As such, he is to be treated with respect, obedience, and love.

He is to be esteemed very highly in love for his works sake (1 Thessalonians 5:12, 13). He deserves such treatment, if for no other reason, because of the God he represents and the gospel he preaches.

See that you treat God's servants as the servants of the most high God. The peace of the church depends upon it. "And we beseech you, brethren, to know them which labour among you, and are over you in the Lord, and admonish you; And to esteem them very highly in love for their work's sake. And be at peace among yourselves. Now we exhort you, brethren, warn them that are unruly, comfort the feebleminded, support the weak, be patient toward all men" (1 Thessalonians 5:12-14).

April 1
Today's Reading: 1 Samuel 28-31
"David's spoil"
1 Samuel 30:18-20

"And David recovered all that the Amalekites had carried away: and David rescued his two wives. And there was nothing lacking to them, neither small nor great, neither sons nor daughters, neither spoil, nor any thing that they had taken to them: David recovered all. And David took all the flocks and the herds, which they drave before those other cattle, and said, This is David's spoil".

Here David is a type of Christ. In his conquest over the Amalekites, in his recovery of that which had been lost, and in the spoils he gathered, David represents our Saviour. When Christ accomplished redemption for us by his death on the cross, he recovered all that we lost in the fall and gathered great spoil for us (Isaiah 53:12).

Enriched By The Fall

The spoils David brought back to Israel were things they could never have possessed had the Amalekites not first taken them away. Captivity was painful to experience but it proved to be a most blessed thing in the end. Israel lost nothing by captivity, but gained much in recovery. And God's elect really lose nothing by our fall in Adam.

It is a painful, sorrowful thing to experience. But in the end it will prove to have been a great act of mercy on God's part that he ordained the fall of our race in Adam, that we might be redeemed by Christ. I say with Martin Luther, "O happy fall". In the end God's elect will find great reason to praise and give thanks to God for their fall in Adam, because it paved the way for our redemption by Christ. Had there been no fall, there could be no song of redemption to the glory of the Lamb (Revelation 5:9-14). Yes, even the fall is among those "all things" that work together for the everlasting good of God's elect. So great, so magnanimous, so good is God our Saviour that he used and uses even the devil and the fall to enrich our souls in Christ!

The Spoils

Here are a few of the spoils Christ has won for us, treasures we could never possess had God not ordained the fall and redeemed us by our great David, the Lord Jesus Christ. Manhood is lifted to the highest possible glory and honour, because we are now one with Christ our God (Ephesians 5:30). We shall be creatures in heaven who have known the glory, grace, love, and goodness of God in redeeming us from sin by Christ (Revelation 7:14). In redeemed sinners God shall show the riches of his glory to wondering worlds, as they could never have been known apart from the fall (Ephesians 2:7, 3:10). We shall be conformed to the image of Christ in glorious resurrection bodies, which we could never have possessed had there been no fall.

As David turned Israel's loss to gain, our Deliverer turns our fall to blessing. In him the promise is sure, "They that spoil thee shall be a spoil" (Jeremiah 30:16, 17).

141

April 2
Today's Reading: 2 Samuel 1-3
David's lamentation
2 Samuel 1:17

The book of 2 Samuel covers a period of about forty years, covering the entire reign of David as king over God's chosen nation. David was, throughout his life, an eminent type of our dear Saviour, the Lord Jesus Christ. Here God the Holy Spirit gives us the details of David's life, his character, and his rule over Israel, because he would have us to see our Saviour in this man. It is the office and pleasure of God the Holy Spirit to take the things of Christ and show them to his people. So as we read David's history, let us look for David's Lord. May God give us "the Spirit of wisdom and revelation in the knowledge of him", giving us a seeing eye, a hearing ear, and an understanding heart, that this portion of God's Holy Word may come to our hearts in power and in much assurance of faith, by the blessing of his Holy Spirit.

Grace Manifest
When we read David's lamentation over Saul, we are given a marvellous display of God's grace manifest in a believer. Grace enables the believer to overcome natural enmity and even to reward evil with good. O Holy Spirit of God, give me such grace! For the glory of Christ and the good of your church and kingdom, I ask, my God, for grace to forgive any wrong done to me and to do good to those who injure me, or would injure me. Give me grace never to avenge myself.

This I know: nothing but the grace of God can accomplish this in us. Nothing but the grace of God can enable us to cast aside the jealousies of life.

Anticipating Death
As Saul and Jonathan died, so too must you and I. Are you prepared to die? Can you this day look death in the face with comfort? Until we know Christ, until we are truly and savingly united to the Son of God by faith, we cannot think of death with comfort or meet it with fortitude. It is the death of Christ that overcame death for his people. His blood has removed its sting. His victory over death, hell, and the grave is the everlasting consolation of his people. By his death as our Substitute, the Son of God has destroyed him that had the power of death, that is the devil. He is able to "deliver them who through fear of death were all their lifetime subject to bondage" (Hebrews 2:14-16). What a blessing of God and his rich grace in Christ it is to think of dying with peace and joy! With my iniquity pardoned, with my transgressions forgiven, with my sin put away by my Redeemer, death has no terror for my soul, and the grave causes no alarm.

Saul And Ishbosheth
In the second chapter we see that Saul was dead; but Ishbosheth his son was alive to harass and oppose David. So it ever is with God's saints in this world of sin and

sorrow. When we are delivered from one trial another follows. We must through much tribulation enter into the kingdom of God. Though David was chosen by God himself to be king, he must go through many conflicts and much sorrow before obtaining the kingdom. So it shall and must be for you and for me, child of God. Our Saviour has told us plainly, "If ye were of the world, the world would love his own; but because ye are not of the world, but I have chosen ye out of the world, therefore the world hateth you". So it shall be because God our Father has so ordained it in infinite wisdom and goodness to our souls. But soon all our Ishbosheths shall also perish. And our light afflictions, which are but for a moment, shall make heaven more glorious than it could otherwise be!

I cannot fail to call our attention to another thing in this regard. When David went up to Hebron, he brought everything with him. He left nothing behind. O my soul, rejoice! Our great David, the Lord Jesus Christ, our King, who has gone up to the Hebron of Hebrons, the heaven of heavens, will leave nothing of his household here below! He has declared, "there shall not an hoof be left behind" (Exodus 10:26).

Depravity And Grace
The third chapter of 2 Samuel is all treachery, deceit, and evil. It shows us what the heart of man is. Your heart and mine is, by nature, nothing but a mass of treachery! How sad the state of man is since the fall of our father Adam! How I thank God for the one word of grace, the one glimmer of hope in this chapter. We read in verse one that "David waxed stronger and stronger". Blessed Saviour, in the light of our iniquity, transgression, and sin, you and your work of redemption and grace to remove our sin and guilt and undo our ruin is prized by our ransomed souls. Our great David shall manifestly wax stronger and stronger, until he has at last put all his enemies and ours beneath his feet!

April 3
Today's Reading: 2 Samuel 4-6
Praise inspired by election
2 Samuel 6:21

"And David said unto Michal, It was before the LORD, which chose me before thy father, and before all his house, to appoint me ruler over the people of the LORD, over Israel: therefore will I play before the LORD."

Multitudes are perishing, being deceived by the strong delusion of Arminianism, free-willism, easy-believism, and decisionism. God has sent "them strong delusion, that they should believe a lie: that they all might be damned who believed not the truth, but had pleasure in unrighteousness. But we are bound to give thanks always to

God for you, brethren beloved of the Lord, because God hath from the beginning chosen you to salvation" (2 Thessalonians 2:11-13).

Yes, my brother, my sister, we also would be damned in false religion had it not been for God's eternal election of us to salvation by the Lord Jesus Christ. Had God left us to the choice of our sinful free will, we would be eternally lost. This fact humbles us before God and inspires our hearts to sing his praise with David of old, saying, "Blessed is the man whom thou choosest, and causest to approach unto thee, that he may dwell in thy courts: we shall be satisfied with the goodness of thy house, even of thy holy temple" (Psalm 65:4).

Here are three reasons for which every believer should continually offer praise and thanksgiving to God.

We Were Chosen By God In Eternal Love

Before the world was made, the eternal God set his heart upon us. He loves us with an everlasting love. In his great love, God chose us and determined to save us by the substitutionary sacrifice of his own dear Son, the Lord Jesus Christ. "Blessed is the man whom thou choosest", O Lord.

We Have Been Called By Divine Irresistible Grace

At the time appointed, God sent his Spirit to us, revealing Christ in the gospel, and gently, tenderly, effectually, irresistibly caused us to come to him in faith. Are not you thankful God would not let you perish in unbelief? "Blessed is the man whom thou causest to approach unto thee".

We Shall Be Satisfied With The Goodness Of God's House

We are satisfied with all the needs of our souls here by the goodness of God's grace and providence. And we shall be satisfied with all the goodness of God in eternal glory. "As for me, I will behold thy face in righteousness: I shall be satisfied, when I awake, with thy likeness" (Psalm 17:15).

April 4
Today's Reading: 2 Samuel 7-10
Prayer found in the heart
2 Samuel 7:27

"For thou, O LORD of hosts, God of Israel, hast revealed to thy servant, saying, I will build thee an house: therefore hath thy servant found in his heart to pray this prayer unto thee".

Prayer is one of those holy, spiritual activities that is better practised than written about or discussed. It is an intensely personal activity, an activity that modesty always keeps hidden away in the closet, out of public view. I do not pretend to know much about prayer. But I do know that prayer is a subject about which there is much confusion. Because there is so much confusion about prayer, it might be wise for us to meditate for a brief while today on three simple facts revealed in this verse of Holy Scripture about prayer. May God the Holy Spirit, the Inspirer and Creator of all true prayer, stamp these three things upon our hearts and minds.

Heart Work

First, true prayer arises from the heart. It is a heart work. David did not find a prayer in his books, or in his memory, or even in his mouth, but in his heart. Far too often, I fear, my prayers arise from my lusts, my personal desires, rather than from a heart of faith that seeks the will and glory of God (James 4:2-4). God listens only to what the heart speaks in prayer. He has no regard for the sounds of our mouths, or the thoughtless, selfish, self-centred desires of our flesh.

Therefore, we should carefully weigh our words before God, and prepare our hearts to pray. Robert Murray M'Cheyne once wrote, "A great part of my time is spent getting my heart in tune for prayer".

Yet, we ought to approach God with the simplicity of a child speaking to his father, with absolute confidence and sincerity. John Trapp wrote, "God respecteth not the arithmetic of our prayers, how many they are; nor the rhetoric of our prayers, how long they are; nor the music of our prayers, how methodical they are, but the divinity of our prayers, how heart sprung they are. Not gifts, but graces prevail in prayer."

Divinely Inspired

Secondly, if prayer is found in the heart, God put it there. Prayer is the communication of a believer's spirit with God who is Spirit, by the power and grace of God the Holy Spirit. He teaches us to pray by showing us what the will of God is. He does this by his Word, by his providence, and by putting a burden upon our hearts that will not go away. Then he graciously inclines our hearts to pray, to seek what God has purposed to do. He has many ways of doing that (Psalm 107:1-31).

God's Promise

Thirdly, God will perform the thing that he puts in our hearts to seek by earnest prayer. True prayer is seeking the will of God by the Spirit of God, through faith in the Son of God. And whatever we ask according to his will, he will do (1 John 5:14, 15). Prayer is not an attempt by man to conform God to his will, but the cry of a heart conformed by grace to God's will. It is breathing out to God what God has breathed into our souls. "Lord, teach us to pray."

April 5
Today's Reading: 2 Samuel 11, 12
"The thing that David had done displeased the LORD"
2 Samuel 11:27

We have read today of that horrible sin committed by God's child, David, in the matter of Uriah. We are told plainly that "the thing that David had done displeased the Lord". Nothing is omitted. Nothing is held back. No excuses are offered to mitigate David's crime. Everything is given to display the enormous infamy of this righteous man's wicked conduct. His lust, his adultery, his betrayal, his plotting, his murder of his faithful servant, everything is set before us. Nothing is held back. Why? Why did God the Hoy Spirit set these things down in the inspired record? The answer is given by God the Holy Spirit himself. "All these things happened unto them for ensamples: and they are written for our admonition, upon whom the ends of the world are come." "For whatsoever things were written aforetime were written for our learning, that we through patience and comfort of the scriptures might have hope." Spirit of God, be our Teacher, and write the lessons of these two chapters upon our hearts this day.

Sinners Still
Learn, child of God, from this sad part of David's history that God's saints in this world are sinners still. The best of men are but men and are as liable to fall into the worst of sins as the unrenewed and unawakened. Our old Adamic nature of corruption is unchanged. Though we have been made partakers of the divine nature, though Christ is formed in us, our old nature of flesh is still just flesh, ever lusting against the spirit, so that we cannot do the things we would. If the lusts of our flesh do not break out and show themselves as vilely in us as in the reprobate, it is not because our flesh is more pure than theirs, but because of the blessed grace of God that restrains us from evil.

Restraining Grace
Oh, how we ought to thank God for that restraining grace by which he keeps us from the evil that is in us! "Keep back thy servant also from presumptuous sins; let them not have dominion over me: then shall I be upright, and I shall be innocent from the great transgression." "Take not thy Holy Spirit from me." My gracious Father, my dear Saviour, if you keep me not from evil by the unfailing restraint of your grace by your Spirit, what falls are they by which I would dishonour your name! Hear my daily prayer for these many years, my God, and in my aging days make it the constant cry of my heart, "Keep me, my God, from the evil that is in me, for the glory of your own great name".

Blood Atonement
Surely, these things are written to teach us the blessedness of blood atonement, of perfect, full redemption by Christ Jesus, and to remind us that there is salvation in no other; for there is no other name under heaven given among men whereby we must be

146

saved. How sweet it is to be reminded that Christ is our redeemer and that we are redeemed by his precious blood, so fully and completely redeemed that God himself will not, and in justice cannot, charge us with sin! It was this man, David, who taught us to sing, "Blessed is the man to whom the Lord will not impute sin".

April 6
Today's Reading: 2 Samuel 13, 14
What will it take for God to get your attention?
2 Samuel 14:29-31

"Therefore Absalom sent for Joab, to have sent him to the king; but he would not come to him: and when he sent again the second time, he would not come. Therefore he said unto his servants, See, Joab's field is near mine, and he hath barley there; go and set it on fire. And Absalom's servants set the field on fire. Then Joab arose, and came to Absalom unto his house, and said unto him, Wherefore have thy servants set my field on fire?"

Today, I ask God to speak to you by his Word. The application of these two chapters and, particularly, of these verses to my own heart, by God the Holy Spirit, I will for now keep to myself for just one reason. Today, I want each one who reads what I believe God has directed me to write as a personal word to you. May God the Holy Spirit make these thoughts effectual to your soul's good for Christ's sake.

Absalom tried in vain to get Joab's attention. He sent for him and sent for him again; but Joab had no regard for or interest in Absalom. Finally, Absalom sent his servants out to set Joab's fields on fire while they were full of barley. That got Joab's attention.

Wicked as that deed was, it is a picture of God's gracious actions toward chosen sinners. Knowing our obstinacy, that we will not come to his gracious throne until he forces us and makes us willing to come, he sets our barley fields on fire. While judgment will never produce repentance by itself, God often sends his grace to us by means of providential judgments (Psalm 107).

As I write this article, I pray for you who will be caused by God the Holy Spirit to read it; the burden of your immortal soul is heavy upon my heart. It is no accident that you are now reading these lines. By what means has God brought you to read them? What will it take for God to get your attention?

Unbeliever
Are you yet without Christ, unconverted, lost, under the wrath of God? I pray that God will not let you die in that condition. Has God the Holy Spirit spoken to you by his Word? Is your heart moved by the preaching of the gospel? Certainly, you have had providential warnings enough to make you tremble, if you had sense enough to hear them. Yet, you harden your heart. If God has chosen you, he will get you. I know

that. Yet, I cannot help wondering, "What will it take for God to get your attention?" What will it take for God to bring you to Christ, to bring you to yourself, and bring you to himself? Eventually, every poor, lost prodigal must and shall be brought home to the Father's house of grace. But what will it take for God to get your attention?

Believer
I wonder the same thing about you who are saved by the grace of God, you who trust the Lord Jesus, you who are heirs of salvation, who have entangled yourselves too much with the cares of this world. Your business has just about choked out the Word of God. You willingly absent yourself from the worship of God and the fellowship of his saints. You neglect the regular reading of God's Word and prayer. The world and the things of the world, "the care of this world" consume your life. At present, you think your neglect is necessary. If truly you are the Lord's, he will not lose you. If he must set your barley fields on fire, if he must destroy your business, your health, your wife, your child, or anything else, he considers that a small thing for the salvation of your soul. For that he sacrificed his own dear Son! Your barley fields are nothing in comparison! What will it take for God to get your attention? I believe I would think about that, if I were you.

April 7
Today's Reading: 2 Samuel 15-17
"Where he worshipped God"
2 Samuel 15:32

In the midst of his great trial, a great trial brought upon him by his own sin, David worshipped God. How very gracious the Lord is in condescending to correct his people, in order to bring his fallen children home to himself. Without those loving, fatherly corrections, we would wander from him forever.

Our Deliverer
Precious Saviour, what great lovingkindness is displayed in our recoveries from our falls by your mercy! How very sweet and blessed are your countless deliverances! Our Lord Jesus redeemed us to God by his precious blood; and there is in his blood an everlasting efficacy, which again and again effectually pleads for us in heaven.

Though he brings us down by affliction, he will not cast us off. Though we are chastened, we are not destroyed. Though in us there is nothing but weakness and sin, in our Saviour is omnipotent strength and perpetual merit. He ever lives to make intercession for us; and his blood perpetually cleanses us from all sin. Our Deliverer is our Advocate with our Father; and "He is the Propitiation for our sins".

Our Afflictions Our Gain
As we see David fleeing from Absalom, the son he cherished, and shamefully and publicly cursed by Shimei, may God the Holy Spirit remind us again that "all things work together for good to them that love God, to them who are the called according to his purpose".

David's frame of mind under very heavy and painful afflictions displays great grace in his heart, planted there by God the Holy Spirit in the gift and operation of faith. He said concerning Shimei's vile cursing, "Let him alone, and let him curse; for the LORD hath bidden him. It may be that the LORD will look on mine affliction, and that the LORD will requite me good for his cursing this day."

Spirit of God, give me grace to live upon the perfections, promises, and covenant engagements of my covenant-keeping God, when it appears that his mercy is clean gone forever! "Although the fig tree shall not blossom, neither shall fruit be in the vines; the labour of the olive shall fail, and the fields shall yield no meat; the flock shall be cut off from the fold, and there shall be no herd in the stalls: Yet I will rejoice in the LORD, I will joy in the God of my salvation. The LORD God is my strength, and he will make my feet like hinds' feet, and he will make me to walk upon mine high places. To the chief singer on my stringed instruments."

Ahithophel's Counsel
As God turned Ahithophel's counsel into foolishness for the destruction of Absalom and David's enemies led by his rebel son, so it is that by his special providence, our enemies are prevented from destroying us or even harming us. It is the bridle of divine providence which our God puts into their jaws that he overrules the designs of hell and wicked men against his chosen. Christ our Redeemer holds the reins of the universe in his hands, controlling all things, even all evil, and says to the proud waves that would swallow up our souls, "Hitherto shalt thou come and no further". It is our mighty Sovereign who causes the world that hates us to help us, even as it tries to destroy us (Revelation 12:16). Blessed Lord Jesus, how we thank you for your absolute rule of all things for our souls' everlasting good! Give us grace to honour you by faith, trusting you, even in the midst of our most painful sorrows.

April 8
Today's Reading: 2 Samuel 18, 19
"While the child was yet alive"
2 Samuel 12:22

Today we have read of David's great sorrow and grief because of Absalom's death under the judgment of God. What mother or father, knowing the grace of God, living in union with Christ by the grace of God, cannot enter into David's great pain? What unknown, inexpressible agony must have crushed his heart! I cannot imagine what it would be like to live to see a rebel son or daughter perish under the wrath of God, knowing that as I lower the dead body of one so dear to my heart into the earth his or her soul justly suffers the unquenchable fire of God's wrath in hell. To you, who have or shall endure such pain, I can only say, flee away to Christ your Saviour and cast your soul on him, finding the solace you need in your God's wisdom, goodness, grace, and covenant faithfulness (2 Samuel 23:5). Our God is too wise to err, too good to do wrong, and too strong to fail.

Another Dead Son

But David had another son who died, not as a grown rebel, but as an infant. What a great mercy it was for him to bury that infant son, killed by God because of his father's sin. I can well imagine David thinking, as he cried "O Absalom, my son, my son", would God you had died from the womb!

Let us think today of that better day in David's life, when God took his infant son in death. When David's son died, he arose, washed, and anointed himself, put on his dress clothes, went to the house of God, and worshipped. When he came home, he asked his servants to prepare dinner for him. The servants who had watched him weep, mourn, and pray for his dying son were astonished. They could not understand David's change of behaviour. While his son was alive, but dying, David was full of sorrow. We have no way of knowing everything that was going through his mind. But this much we do know:

Though David's heart was broken over his sin, he was assured of his own forgiveness and acceptance with God (2 Samuel 12:13).

David knew that his child's sickness unto death was by the hand and will of the God he worshipped, loved, and served (2 Samuel 12:14, 15). "The Lord struck the child."

David was prepared to and did submit to the will of God, even when it meant the death of his son (2 Samuel 12:22, 23; Psalm 51:4).

David was fully convinced that upon his son's death he would depart and be with the Lord (2 Samuel 12:23), yet he did not want his son to die (2 Samuel 12:16, 22).

Was David bitter: Probably. Was he downcast? Of course. Was he in great pain? Yes. His heart was crushed. He withdrew from all others, refused the ordinary joys and necessities of life, and "besought God for the child". Though it was evident that the child was to die, both by its appearance and by the fact that God had told him it must, David still hoped that God might be gracious to him and heal his son.

Comfort Refused

Any who saw him during this time (any who did not know David, or had never experienced what David was experiencing) might have thought David had lost his faith. Nothing could have been further from the truth. Though his behaviour changed radically during those days of horrible, indescribable sorrow, David believed God and he poured out his soul to him, when he could express his feelings to no one else. When his closest friends tried, in their helplessness, to help him, David refused to be comforted, or even to eat bread with them (2 Samuel 12:17). He was in such a state of sorrow, agony, and devastation that he simply could not bring himself to discuss his grief with anyone but God. He refused to put on a good religious front. Yet, he would not let go of his God.

Blessed Prospect
What faith this man exemplified when others may have thought he had none! And when the Lord took his son, God's servant David both bowed to the will of God and found comfort in it. He lived in hope of a day when he would be reunited with his son in a world where there is no more sickness, no more pain, no more sorrow, and no more death, because there shall be no more sin (2 Samuel 12:23). He lived in hope of God's fulfilment of his covenant (2 Samuel 23:5). Now, David, Bathsheba, and their son, united around the throne of God, understand the necessity for all that sorrow; and they thank God for it. Thus it shall be for every grieving, sorrowing believer in the world to come. We will soon understand the necessity for every sorrow experienced here and give thanks to God our Saviour, who through great sorrow, brings his chosen to everlasting joy with him!

April 9
Today's Reading: 2 Samuel 20, 21
A wise woman of Bethmaachah
2 Samuel 20:16

Solomon speaks of a poor man who by his wisdom saves a city (Ecclesiastes 9:14, 15). That man is our dear Saviour, the Lord Jesus Christ, who saves the church of his elect, the City of God, by his blood and by his grace. He who is Wisdom is made of God unto us Wisdom, and Righteousness, and Sanctification, and Redemption as our Saviour. But here is a wise woman, who saved the city of Bethmaachah by her wisdom. Interceding for her people and saving them, she stands in the Book of God with a few women like Deborah who were typical of our Saviour.

Christ Our Saviour
It is delightful to see this mother in Israel saving the city by her intercession. How thankful we ought to be for every reminder of our great Saviour, the Lord Jesus Christ, saving the world of his elect by the effectual exercise of his glorious office as our Mediator. He accomplished peace and reconciliation by the gift and sacrifice of himself.

God the Son stood forth as our Surety in the covenant of grace, before ever the worlds were made, pledged himself to the work of our salvation for the glory of God, and the Triune God trusted him to perform the great work (Ephesians 1:12).

Christ Trusted

Three times in the first fourteen verses of the book of Ephesians God the Holy Spirit tells us that the purpose of the Triune God in our salvation is that we should be to the praise of his glory. One reason given why we should desire his glory is "that we should be to the praise of his glory, who first trusted in Christ".

Our heavenly Father entered into a covenant with his Son on our behalf before the world began for the saving of our souls. In Hebrews 13:20, it is called the everlasting covenant. Frequently it is called the new covenant. This covenant was made in eternity between God the Father and God the Son; but it was made for us. Insofar as the benefits and blessings of it to us are concerned, it is an unconditional covenant. The Lord God said, "I will love them freely? I will be their God; and they shall be my people". This everlasting covenant of grace is a sure covenant, a covenant which infallibly secured and guaranteed to God's elect all the blessings of salvation and eternal life in Christ (Jeremiah 31:3, 31-34; 32:38-40 2 Samuel 23:5).

Trust Accomplished

Blessed be his name forever, our Lord Jesus accomplished all he was trusted to accomplish as our Mediator! The only condition to the covenant and the blessings of grace and salvation promised in it was the obedience of the Son of God as our Substitute unto death (Hebrews 13:20). And there never was a danger of that condition not being met by the Son of God! There was never the slightest possibility of failure on his part. He was willing to obey. He was able to obey. And he did obey his Father's will even unto death, even unto the shedding of his blood, the blood of the everlasting covenant!

Having found a ransom for our souls in the Person of his own Son, our heavenly Father gave his chosen into the hands of his Son, as sheep into the hands of a shepherd, and trusted him with the salvation of our souls and the glory of his own great name (John 6:39). If God the Father has trusted his glory to his dear Son as our Substitute and Saviour and trusted the salvation of our souls to his hands, how we ought to trust him with our immortal souls and with all that concerns us. If the Father trusted him, he is a trustworthy Saviour!

Saved From Eternity

Upon the basis of this covenant, our heavenly Father accepted us in Christ from eternity (Ephesians 1:4-6). Be sure you do not fail to grasp the teaching of Holy Scripture regarding the matter of our acceptance before God. Our acceptance is in Christ. Our acceptance is from everlasting to everlasting. Our acceptance is absolute and unconditional. Our acceptance means that God the Father, our heavenly Father, looks upon us in Christ as perfect in him, and has done so from eternity. He declares, "It must be perfect to be accepted". Being "accepted in the Beloved", our heavenly Father has blessed us with all spiritual blessings in Christ from eternity, and has promised to bless us forever for Christ's sake (Ephesians 1:3; 2 Timothy 1:9). The Lord God commanded Aaron, his high priest, to bless his people symbolically (Number 6:23), because he had sworn from eternity, for Christ's sake, saying, "I will bless them" (Numbers 6:27).

Let Jesus Christ our Mediator be eternally praised, eternally loved, eternally adored for this great interposition of grace!

Goliath's Sons
In 2 Samuel 21 we are reminded by God the Spirit that David's first exercise in the field of battle was with the giant Goliath; and his last was with the same enemy. In our spiritual warfare it is the same. The great champion we contend with, the devil, began the war; and he, with the hordes of hell, seeks our destruction to the end. By David's final slaughter of Goliath's sons, I am reminded of the precious thought that, "the God of peace shall bruise Satan under your feet shortly" (Romans 16:20).

How these two things ought to cheer our hearts this day and inspire in our souls a holy expectancy of everlasting glory!

April 10
Today's Reading: 2 Samuel 22, 23
God's covenant our comfort
2 Samuel 23:5

Can you and I say, as David sang in the twenty second chapter we have just read, the Lord is my Rock, my Shield, my Tower, my Refuge, my Saviour. Blessed are they who have a well grounded assurance of their covenant interest in Christ. This is, indeed, the comfort of our souls.

As David lay dying, he found no comfort for his heart in himself, his family, or his kingdom. Though he was the richest, most powerful king in the world, though he was used of God for much good, for the comfort of his soul and the sustenance of his heart he looked to nothing but the covenant made between the Persons of the Holy Trinity on his behalf before the world began. Read again the last words of David and learn the comfort of the covenant.

"Although"
"Although my house be not so with God". It matters not whether we take the words "my house" to refer to David's kingdom, his family, or his earthly life, the lessons are clear.

So long as we live in this world, in this body of flesh, things are never altogether right with God's saints. Nothing here is really as we desire.

Grace does not run in blood lines, only sin (John 1:12, 13; Romans 9:11-16). The afflictions of God's people, both personal and domestic, are fruits of covenant grace (Psalm 89:30-34; 2 Corinthians 4:17-5:1).

The sins of a faithful man's family are not an indication of evil in him, or a bar to his usefulness in the kingdom of God. David was God's anointed king, prophet, and hymn writer, a preacher and a psalmist in Israel in spite of the fact that he had a wife like Michal and sons like Amnon and Absalom.

"Yet"
"Yet the Lord hath made with me an everlasting covenant ordered in all things and sure". This is not the covenant of works that the Lord God made with Adam, which he broke and we broke in him (Romans 5:12-18). It is not the covenant of circumcision, which God made with Abraham (Genesis 17). That was a Jewish covenant and has been forever abolished by God's own word (Galatians 5:4). Certainly, it is not the legal Sinai covenant that God made with Israel through his servant Moses, for that legal covenant has passed away (Hebrews 8:6, 7). The law of God found its end in Christ (Romans 10:4). The covenant, curse, and constraint of the law have been abolished for God's elect. The covenant in which David found his comfort was the covenant of grace, and life, and peace made with him in the Person of Christ, the covenant Surety (Hebrews 7:22), before the world began.

"Everlasting"
It is an everlasting covenant, both ways. It was established in eternity and shall stand throughout eternity (Proverbs 8:23-31). It is an unconditional covenant of grace (Psalm 89:19-35; Jeremiah 31:31-34).

"Ordered" And "Sure"
"Ordered in all things and sure". It is an ordered covenant. Whatever the covenant required, it also gave (Ephesians 1:3-14; 2 Timothy 1:9). It is a sure covenant. Its mercies are "the sure mercies of David". They are sure to all who are heirs of the covenant, sure to all the elect, all the redeemed, all the called, all who believe. This covenant by which all God's elect are saved is an immutable covenant (Psalm 89:30-37). No matter what is done to or done by God's elect, the covenant stands firm.

"All My Salvation"
"This is all my salvation". Christ, the Surety of the covenant, Christ who is the covenant (Isaiah 49:8) is all our salvation (1 Corinthians 1:30). In a very real sense, all of God's elect were completely saved in eternity, when the covenant of grace was made. All who dispute that fact must argue against the very words of Holy Scripture. Read Romans 8:29, 30 and 2 Timothy 1:9. This is not a point of logic. It is plainly declared in these two texts that God's elect were saved in eternity. We rejoice to declare with David that our salvation springs from, depends upon, and is determined by God's covenant (Jeremiah 32:38-40).

"All My Desire"
"And all my desire, although he make it not to grow". "It is the desire of every believer who knows anything of the covenant of grace and the scheme of salvation by it, to be saved this way, by and through the covenant of grace, and not of works" says John Gill. "Let me have an interest in this covenant and the promises of it, and I have enough. I desire no more" agrees Matthew Henry. To be an heir of this covenant is to be elected by grace, loved of God, adopted as his Son, redeemed by Christ, forgiven

of all sin, accepted in the Beloved, an heir of God, sealed by the Spirit, and forever one with Christ, "the fulness of him that filleth all in all".

Here is the comfort of God's covenant: Our sins cannot destroy our hope. They should not haunt us with fear in the hour of death. And they cannot rob us of our everlasting inheritance in Christ (Psalm 32:1-5; Ephesians 1:11). In the very teeth of his sins David trusted Christ. Believing God, he was confident that God would not impute his sin to him. He had his covenant to assure him of it. How sweet to my soul is covenant grace this day!

April 11
Today's Reading: 2 Samuel 24-1 Kings 1
"I have sinned, and I have done wickedly"
2 Samuel 24:17

"And David spake unto the Lord when he saw the angel that smote the people, and said, lo! I have sinned, and I have done wickedly; but these sheep, what have they done?"

God the Holy Spirit tells us that for man's sin the whole creation groans and travails in pain. The slaughter of every beast, the sacrifice of every lamb proclaims with a louder voice than words can declare the horrid evil of our transgressions. When David saw the destroying angel brandishing his dreadful sword over Jerusalem, he remembered his own sin with great grief, knowing that it was his sin that brought the judgment of God upon the guiltless sheep of Israel. The people were not guilty, but David, of numbering Israel. Yet, they suffered for David's transgression. The thought of that fact crushed David's heart.

Just For The Unjust

Oh, how our sins ought to crush our hearts before our crucified Redeemer, the Lord Jesus Christ, before him who "died the just for the unjust, to bring us to God". May God the Holy Spirit cause our hearts and minds to think always, throughout every day, of the sufferings of the holy Lamb of God for our sins, that we may constantly bow before him in repentance and lift our hearts to him in praise, gratitude, and love.

Sin's Great Evil

We get some idea of the evil of sin when we behold the apostate spirits cast out of heaven. We see something of the terrible evil of sin when we think of the curse of God upon the earth and upon all the sons and daughters of Adam sinning in him. The destruction of the old world by water, the burning of Sodom and Gomorrah by fire, and the everlasting torments of the damned in hell, all give us some sense of sin's enormous evil in the sight of the holy Lord God.

But if we would see sin in all its exceeding sinfulness and tremendous evil, we must go to Calvary. There we behold the Lamb of God, taking away our sin by the sacrifice of himself. Here, at the foot of the cross, let us take up the words of David and ask our own hearts, while confessing that we have sinned and done wickedly, "What had this Lamb of God done?"

He who knew no sin became sin. He who "was holy, harmless, undefiled, separate from sinners, and made higher than the heaven", became both sin and a curse for his redeemed, "that we might be made the righteousness of God in him".

Devotion Desired
Oh, blessed, Holy Spirit, give me ever to set my heart upon the Lord Jesus, my almighty Surety, and to remember that in all he did, in all he sustained, and all he suffered, he bore my sins in his own body on the tree, and that not a single sin of omission or commission was left out! All my iniquities, all my transgressions, and all my sins, the Lord Jehovah laid on his darling Son, as Aaron laid the sins of Israel on the paschal lamb on the great day of atonement (Leviticus 16:21). Help me, Holy Spirit, with increasing confidence of faith, with holy hope, with ardent joy, and with ever-increasing consecration, to look upon Christ my Surety and glory in him, unceasingly in him, who of God is made unto me Wisdom, and Righteousness, and Sanctification, and Redemption.

April 12
Today's Reading: 1 Kings 2, 3
"David drew nigh that he should die"
1 Kings 2:1

There is something very moving about the dying moments of men and women, those moments when immortal souls are about to leave their earthly tabernacles and enter into eternity. As our lives draw near their end, we see things differently than we have in the past. These things are true of all dying men and women. But when God's saints are about to die, their dying moments are both instructive and comforting. I love to be in the company of dying saints. I am always anxious to know what they will say, as they step into Jordan's chilly waters. Here we are brought again to David's deathbed. What shall we learn from this man? What does God the Holy Spirit teach us in the life and death of this man of faith, this man after God's own heart? There is much more to be learned than that to which I will direct our hearts and minds today; but if God the Holy Spirit will set these things in our hearts, they will serve us well.

Discovering Christ Day By Day

A Concerned Pastor
As he lay dying, David the King of Israel was very concerned to provide God's people with a man to succeed him who would be an even better pastor to the Lord's sheep than he had been. Faithful men, who have served the people of God faithfully all their lives, are always very concerned for the well-being of God's church they are leaving behind.

Of all the thoughts pressing upon the heart of a faithful pastor, this must be one of his heaviest concerns: who will the Lord set over this household? Who will God send to go in and out before his people? Who will the Lord God raise up to feed his people with knowledge and understanding? Nothing is of greater concern to a faithful gospel preacher than the souls of those to whom he devotes his life. And when he comes to die, no weight is heavier. David's determination to thrust out Adonijah and establish Solomon in the kingdom vividly portrays a dying, faithful pastor in his concern, desire, and earnest prayer that the Lord would cast out all the Adonijah's who serve their own bellies and send the people a pastor after his own heart!

Knowing that concern as a pastor, I find comfort here. Our Lord Christ still has the keys. He still walks in the midst of his churches. He is still King upon his throne. When David died, Solomon reigned. When the Lord God puts out one light, he can easily cause another to shine. He has the stars in his right hand!

A Forgiven Sinner
Great as this man David was, he was a sinner, just like you and me. David was a man found in obscurity, brought into royalty, and elevated to the highest possible dignity by the hand of God. How God blessed him! How God honoured him! How God used him! Then David fell by horrible transgression, giving the enemies of God occasion to blaspheme. And David was recovered by that same, divine, omnipotent hand of grace that had lifted him up on high. David died as a sinner chosen in eternal love, redeemed by precious blood, saved by sovereign mercy, and preserved by immutable grace, a forgiven sinner! What mercy! Well might we pray this day, "Let me die the death of the righteous, and let my last end be like his".

A Type Of Christ
And as David was the man after God's own heart, we see in him a very obvious type of the Lord Jesus Christ, Jehovah's elect, our Saviour, of whom God says, "This is my beloved Son, in whom I am well-pleased."

As David fought the battles of the Lord, as he slew Goliath, the armies of the uncircumcised Philistines, and all Goliath's sons, it was Christ, our mighty David, who alone obtained the victory over all our foes and won our everlasting salvation.

As David was anointed king over Israel and Judah contrary to the wishes of Saul and contrary to all the expectations of men, our blessed Redeemer was crowned king in Zion in direct defiance of Herod and of the Jews who declared that they would not have this man to reign over them.

As David made his way to the throne, by a relentless series of persecutions, afflictions, and distresses, so our Saviour purchased our redemption and won his crown by all the sorrows he endured in his body, in his heart, and in his soul, in his life, and in his death. Go again and again, my soul, to Gethsemane, Gabbatha, and

Golgotha, go a thousand times a day to the cursed tree and see the glory of our great David voluntarily made sin for us that we might be made the righteousness of God in him!

April 13
Today's Reading: 1 Kings 4-6
None that can hew timber like the Sidonians
1 Kings 5:6

It takes a lot of scaffolding to erect a large building. The scaffolding is useful in many ways, but is never a part of the building. And when the building is finished, the scaffolding is hauled away. So it is in the building of the church and temple of our God. He uses much scaffolding that has no part with the building.

That is the thing that struck me as I read these three chapters of Holy Scripture. Hiram's servants were skilled workmen, wisely employed by Solomon, for the building of God's temple in Jerusalem. They were like many in every age, and particularly in our day, to whom God has given great talents and abilities, but no grace.

No Foundation
What multitudes there are to whom the Lord God gives great natural abilities of a carnal nature, but to whom no grace is given! Many possess such gifts who know nothing of the gracious work of God the Holy Spirit upon the heart. Many minister in holy things, who are not partakers of holy things. Hear the Word of God ...

Many will say to me in that day, Lord, Lord, have we not prophesied in thy name? and in thy name have cast out devils? and in thy name done many wonderful works? And then will I profess unto them, I never knew you: depart from me, ye that work iniquity (Matthew 7:22, 23).

No declaration ever fell from our Saviour's lips that is more fearful than this. "Many will say unto me in that day, Lord, Lord, have we not prophesied (preached) in thy name? And in thy name have cast out devils?" How many, like Judas, Demas, and Diotrephes, have been instruments in the hands of God, by which God the Holy Spirit delivered the word of salvation to others, by which our omnipotent Saviour has bound the strong man and cast him out of the soul in the name of Christ, who never knew him or the grace of God in him! A more wonderful work cannot be done. What a wonderful thing it is for poor, lost sinners to be born of God and given faith in Christ, converted by God's almighty grace, through the instrumentality of gospel preaching!

Discovering Christ Day By Day

But how very fearful it is to know that too many such preachers, teachers, and religious workers, the Son of God will speak these dreadful words: "I never knew you: depart from me, ye that work iniquity". They do not know him; and he does not know them. They do not own him as Lord; and he does not own them as his people. They have no part with him; and he has no part with them. All that they think they do that is good and in the service of God, the Lord Jesus calls works of iniquity, for which they are to be forever damned! How tormenting it will be to their souls to know that, though they were helpful instruments in the hands of God for the salvation of his elect, daily serving in the house of God, because they themselves believed not on Christ, they are forever damned! They pointed others to the Foundation-Stone, Christ Jesus, but they were not built upon the Foundation-Stone themselves. They had a refuge; but it was "a refuge of lies". They were nothing but pieces of scaffolding by which God builds his house!

Solid Rock
Are we built upon the Rock Christ Jesus? Am I built upon the same Foundation as the apostles and prophets, which is the Lord Jesus Christ himself, the Chief Corner-Stone? Are you? If so, we are inexpressibly happy and blessed of God in our souls, looking up to our God and Father in Christ Jesus, with a humble hope that he is our Portion.

Yes, blessed Saviour, you alone are the Foundation of my soul, the Foundation of all my hopes, all my desires, all my wishes, all my joys, and all my salvation! God, our Father, in his infinite mercy, love, and grace laid this Foundation. The whole structure of his house, his temple, his church rests upon Christ Jesus. His precious blood and perfect righteousness is the cement which unites and keeps the living stones of this holy temple eternally together; and each stone in the building is "fitly framed together" by the effectual, irresistible work of God the Holy Ghost, who has built our souls upon the sure Foundation, Christ Jesus.

Blessed Lord God, carry on, complete, adorn, and finish the work in my soul. May your mercy be built up forever. Then, when your work of grace is finished in me and with me, bring forth the top stone of your spiritual building "with shoutings of grace, grace unto it" for the everlasting glory of your great name.

April 14
Today's Reading: 1 Kings 7, 8
"Will God indeed dwell on the earth?"
1 Kings 8:27

493 years after the Children of Israel came out of the land of Egypt, and seventeen years after his father David had gone to glory, Solomon finished building the temple

159

in Zion. It took him seven years to build it. Then, when the temple was finished and the Ark of the Covenant had been brought into the most holy place, the Lord God condescended to come into the temple Solomon had built. And the glory of the Lord filled the house of the Lord!

God Extolled

Then Solomon extolled the Lord God as the only true and living God (1 Kings 8:22, 23). He declared that there is no God but our God, none beside him, none like him, none to be compared to him in his nature or in his works. He is the supreme sovereign of the universe, the covenant-keeping God of his people, merciful, gracious and good, faithful and true, fulfilling all his promises to all his people!

God Came Down

Yet, this great and glorious God, who inhabits eternity, condescended to come into the temple and to dwell in the midst of his people upon the earth! To Solomon this was a matter of utter astonishment (vv. 26, 27). Solomon was utterly astonished at the goodness of God in coming to dwell upon the earth. "Will God indeed dwell on the earth?" This is not an expression of doubt or unbelief, but an expression of utter amazement!

God Incarnate

Will God, who dwells on high, who humbles himself to look upon things in heaven and stoops to consider things upon the earth, will this great and glorious God condescend to dwell with men upon the earth? That is astonishing! But this display of our God's great condescending grace foreshadowed something indescribably greater. It foreshadowed and typified the incarnation of God the Son for the accomplishment of our redemption and everlasting salvation.

"Will God" the Son, our Lord Jesus Christ, "dwell on the earth?" Indeed, he has and he does. This is marvellous in our eyes! This is astonishing indeed (2 Corinthians 8:9). Jesus Christ is God; yet, he tabernacled upon the earth in our nature (John 1:1, 14). Moses' tabernacle was a type of Christ's human nature. His humanity is "the true tabernacle which the Lord pitched, and not man" (Hebrews 8:2). The temple which Solomon built, into which God came and dwelt, was also a type of our Saviour's human nature. He said, "Destroy this temple (referring to his body) and in three days I will raise it up" (John 2:19). Christ came into this world to fulfil the covenant he made with the Father on our behalf before the world began (Hebrews 10:5-17).

Indwelling God

The wonder of the incarnation only increases as we contemplate it. Once the Lord Jesus obtained eternal redemption for us, he entered into heaven in our flesh. And now, though he has gone to heaven to make intercession for us, our Lord still dwells upon the earth. He who is God our Saviour is the infinite God, the incarnate God, and the indwelling God. Particularly, the Lord God, in the person of and by the Spirit of Christ, dwells in the hearts of all true believers (John 14:18). The Father comes and makes his abode with us (2 Corinthians 6:16). The Spirit comes and dwells as our Comforter (John 14:26). The Son dwells in our hearts by faith (Ephesians 3:17).

Imagine that! What an astonishing fact this is: The Lord Jesus Christ dwells and lives in his saints upon the earth! He dwells not in our heads only, not in our lips only, but in our hearts. He dwells where sin dwells, in our hearts! He dwells where he is often slighted, in our hearts (Song of Solomon 5). He dwells where his Holy Spirit is often grieved, in our hearts! Our God, the Lord Jesus Christ, dwells in us permanently! No wonder Solomon spoke with such astonishment. "Will God indeed dwell on the earth?" Child of God, take this thought with you throughout the day, God's saints are the dwelling place of God's Son.

April 15
Today's Reading: 1 Kings 9, 10
"It was a true report that I heard"
1 Kings 10:6

If the queen of Sheba was so astonished in the view she had of Solomon's wisdom and riches, how much more ought we to be unceasingly astonished in the contemplation of our dear Saviour, in whom are hid all the treasures of wisdom and knowledge!

When first you heard of the Lord Jesus, when first you were constrained by the irresistible, effectual call of his Spirit to come to him for mercy, how little you knew, either of yourself or of him. You knew you were but a poor blind ignorant sinner. You knew that he was God your Saviour. And that is wonderful, wonderful beyond the expression of words! Then ...

His Revelation
The Lord Jesus told you all that was in your heart. He made your spirit, like this queen of Sheba's before Solomon, to faint within you, when he showed the depth and hideousness of your sin and the great fulness of his salvation. Since that day, with every fresh discovery of your emptiness and his fulness, of your sinfulness and his holiness, of your debt and his forgiveness, of your filth and his cleansing, you are constrained to say of Christ what this woman said of Solomon. "It was a true report that I heard in mine own land of thy acts and of thy wisdom. Howbeit I believed not the words, until I came, and mine eyes had seen it: and, behold, the half was not told me: thy wisdom and prosperity exceedeth the fame which I heard."

His Love
"Behold, a greater than Solomon is here". Though we heard of Christ's love, mercy, grace, and glory, it was not until we came to him ourselves, it was not until we trusted him for ourselves that we saw and experienced in him the wisdom and power and glory of God (Job 42:1-6; Isaiah 6:1-4; John 1:1-4). We stand amazed (is it not so?) in

the presence of our all-glorious Lord and Saviour, realizing that it is impossible to put into words the riches of his grace and glory (2 Corinthians 12:2-4).

His Bounty
Truly, all who belong to Christ are blessed! O Blessed Son of God, "Happy are thy men, happy are these thy servants, which stand continually before thee, and that hear thy wisdom". Then the queen of Sheba blessed the Lord God who delighted in Solomon, who put him on the throne of Israel to exercise judgment and mercy.

His Glory
"Behold, a greater than Solomon is here". The Father loves the Son and has given "all things" into his hands (John 3:35). The Father delights in the Son and gave him preeminence in all things and over all things (Proverbs 8:23-30; Matthew 3:17; Colossians 1:18). The Father made Christ the Surety, Prophet, Priest, and King of his Israel because he loved us in Christ with an everlasting love. Christ came to the earth to honour God's law, satisfy God's justice, to do judgment and justice in the earth that God may be just and the Justifier of all who believe on him (Romans 3:25, 26).

"And king Solomon gave unto the queen of Sheba all her desire, whatsoever she asked, beside that which Solomon gave her of his royal bounty". "Behold, a greater than Solomon is here". Our great King, the Lord Jesus Christ, receives every sinner who comes to him for grace. He gives us, not of his royal bounty, but all his royal bounty (John 17:22). He gives us all that our souls desire! Forgiveness! Righteousness! Grace! Eternal Life!

April 16
Today's Reading: 1 Kings 11, 12
"The cause was from the LORD"
1 Kings 12:15

What a light this one statement throws upon the things we have read today! "The cause was from the Lord". Solomon was a truly great man. After reading 1 Kings 11, we must not forget what God the Holy Spirit told us of this man's God-given wisdom. Let us not forget his building of the temple at Jerusalem and his exemplary prayer at its dedication. Let us not forget the wonderful revelation of the most intimate spiritual things given to us in the Song of Solomon, the wisdom of his gospel doctrine in Proverbs, or the majesty of his instructions as the preacher in Ecclesiastes.

Yet, here he is, brought down in his old age by the gratification of his most base lust into something even more base: idolatry. What a sad display of human depravity closed this great man's life. Still, even in this, we who know God know that he makes even the wrath of man to praise him and works "all things together for good" to his elect (Psalm 76:10; Romans 8:28). "For the cause was from the Lord".

Take Heed

The cause is this: "Let him that thinketh he standeth, take heed lest he fall". By nature, all men are the same. All are equally prone to evil. But for the blessed influences of God's preventing and restraining grace, we would all do the very things we are shocked to read of Solomon doing. May God the Holy Spirit, by a deep sense and conviction of this fact, ever cause us to cling to the Lord Jesus Christ and keep us from such presumptuous sin!

As all have sinned and come short of thy glory; so nothing but the precious blood of Christ and his perfect righteousness can be our refuge and our salvation. It is Christ and Christ alone who has made reconciliation for iniquity and brought in an everlasting righteousness by his finished work of redemption. It is only by the merit of his blood and the riches of his grace that we are accepted of God in him, and only by the sweet, effectual, irresistible influence of his Spirit that we are kept from any evil deed.

God's Dominion

When we are told that King Rehoboam hearkened to the counsel of fools and despised the wise counsel of wise men, a thing obviously incredible, we are told, "the cause was from the Lord". By Rehoboam's folly, our all-wise God was bringing about the sacred purposes of his holy will.

What a great blessing it is to see God's hand in all things. Let us ever remember that "our God is in the heavens: he hath done whatsoever he hath pleased". Spirit of God, write these words upon our hearts. Remind us of this fact when public troubles arise, when war breaks out, when pestilence comes; and graciously remind us that our God rules in heaven, earth, and hell when personal woes fall upon us.

When the gracious, wise, and good providential appointments of our God cause us pain, God of all grace, make this our soul's comfort, "The cause is from the Lord". Thus "the man after God's own heart" was cursed by Shimei, while he was fleeing from his own son! Yet, David found solace and strength here. "The cause was from the Lord". He said, "Let him curse, for the Lord hath bidden him. It may be that the Lord will look on mine affliction, and that the Lord will requite me good for his cursing this day".

May God teach us, day by day, to trust him in all circumstances. He has said, "I know the thoughts I think toward you, thoughts of peace and not of evil, to give you an expected end".

163

April 17
Today's Reading: 1 Kings 13, 14
"The man of God who was disobedient"
1 Kings 13:26

May God the Holy Spirit inscribe upon our hearts a portion of that for which he has caused these two chapters to be written in the Book of god for our learning, our admonition, our comfort, and our hope.

Jeroboam
King Jeroboam reminds us of a fact that is commonly forgotten. Judgment never brings repentance. Providential judgments often alarm the wicked and cause the unbeliever to cry out to God, but that which is born in the storm dies in the calm. Jeroboam's hand was miraculously withered by God and miraculously healed by God, but his heart was unchanged. "Let favour be shewed to the wicked, yet will he not learn righteousness: in the land of uprightness will he deal unjustly, and will not behold the majesty of the Lord" (Isaiah 26:10).

The Lying Prophet
In the character of the lying prophet we are given an alarming reminder of the fact that men may minister in holy things and never partake of the things themselves. Here is an old man who had been a prophet for many years. How often he spoke to others in the name of God and spoke the Word of God in truth. Yet, he was a lost, unbelieving man. He never knew the very things he preached, was never influenced in his heart by the Word of God, and never experienced the life-giving power and grace of God the Holy Spirit in his soul.

The Disobedient Prophet
The disobedient man of God was a truly faithful man, a bold prophet who spoke for God to the rebuke of the king and did so face to face with the king. Few men of such boldness and faithfulness exist in any age or any society. Yet, even such a bold man is but a weak sinner saved by grace alone. The power of the king could not persuade this prophet to disobey God, but the subtle deception of a deceiving prophet of smooth words brought him down to the grave. Let us learn again from this man that there is in every child of God in this world two distinct, mutually warring natures, flesh and spirit. There is in every child of God this side of eternity a mixture of faith and unbelief.

God's Work
These things are written here in the Book of God to remind us that salvation is God's work alone. The only thing that distinguishes the elect from the reprobate is God's grace. The only righteousness we have is Christ our Righteousness. The only holiness we have is Christ our Holiness. The only sanctification we have is Christ our

Sanctification. The only redemption we have is Christ our Redemption. The only safety we have is Christ our Saviour. "Thanks be unto God for his unspeakable Gift".

Ahijah

While we see the sad consequences of our fallen nature in a man so dreadfully wicked as Jeroboam, let us seek grace to put our faces in the dust and lay low in self-abasement before the throne of our God, the God of all grace, knowing and acknowledging that if we differ from him it is grace alone that makes us to differ. As we do, as we bow before the throne of grace, knowing that it is grace alone that makes us to differ from the reprobate, let us give thanks to our God for that grace and for faithful prophets like Ahijah, by whom the Lord God brings us the gospel of his grace.

Let our hearts be lifted as one, asking God to raise in his church many Ahijahs in this dark, dark day. Ask the Lord, with importunate pleading to send forth faithful prophets who will neither fear the frowns, nor court the smiles, of any man. Ask for men who will proclaim the whole truth of God as it set forth in Holy Scripture, and keep back nothing that may be profitable to the salvation of chosen, redeemed sinners, the comfort of believers, the edification of God's saints in the faith of the gospel, and the reviving of God's church, for Christ's sake.

April 18
Today's Reading: 1 Kings 15-17
"The ravens brought him bread"
1 Kings 17:6

1 Kings 15 brings to our memory good king Asa. His reign was long and prosperous. God the Holy Spirit tells us that his heart was perfect with the Lord all his days, "and Asa did that which was right in the eyes of the Lord".

A Good King

When Asa was seated as king over Judah, he expelled the sodomites from the land and destroyed the idols his father had made. He even removed his mother from being queen and destroyed her god, because she was an idolater.

What an evident token of divine judgment it is that the Lord God has given us sodomites, idolatrous will-worshipping Arminians, and religious infidels to be our political rulers today! What a blessing it would be if our God would raise up rulers in this day like good king Asa!

Wages Paid

1 Kings 16 should cause us to remember that all workers of iniquity shall come to a shameful and terrible end under the wrath of God. The history of the ungodly is

always the same, no matter their rank or station in life. They are captives and slaves, the servants of sin, people who cannot cease from sin. That describes all Adam's fallen race. And the wages they have earned shall be given them, death and after death the second death in hell. How sad!

Such we all are by nature; sinners, captives, slaves to every lust obscene, a people who cannot cease from sin. But we are washed, we are sanctified, we are justified by the Spirit of God and the precious, sin-atoning blood of Christ. When he died in our stead upon the cursed tree, justice paid us our wages, for we died with our blessed Substitute. And, now, since we died in Christ and with Christ at Calvary, we shall never die! Being made the righteousness of God in him, we shall have our just reward, eternal life!

Elijah
In 1 Kings 17 we are introduced to God's prophet Elijah. His name means "Jehovah My God", and Jehovah showed himself to be God in the life of this man Elijah. "Declaring the end from the beginning, and from ancient times the things that are not yet done, saying, My counsel shall stand, and I will do all my pleasure: Calling a ravenous bird from the east, the man that executeth my counsel from a far country: yea, I have spoken it, I will also bring it to pass; I have purposed it, I will also do it" (Isaiah 46:10, 11).

What a man of faith Elijah was. He believed God; and God proved himself faithful to his faithful servant. But where did Elijah obtain the faith by which he lived? Was it not the Spirit of Christ which was in the prophets, who showed them the sufferings of Christ and the glory that should follow? Indeed it was (1 Peter 1:11). It was the same Spirit of Christ in the prophets who gave them life and faith that gives life and faith to God's elect today. Yes, Christ is the almighty Author and Finisher of our faith. It is Christ who gives his Holy Spirit to chosen, redeemed sinners and by him gives us faith. He is the cruise of oil that shall never fail to supply our souls with his Spirit, his grace, and his gift of faith while we live in this world. He is that vessel of meal that can never be emptied by use. O my soul, use him, use him for every need! Spirit of God, give us grace to use our Saviour, trusting his blood, his righteousness, his grace, his providence, trusting him in all things and for all things!

April 19
Today's Reading: 1 Kings 18, 19
God's remnant
1 Kings 19:18

"Yet I have left me seven thousand in Israel, all the knees which have not bowed unto Baal, and every mouth which hath not kissed him".

166

Regarding Elijah's confrontation with the prophets of Baal, nothing is more remarkable than the prayer of God's prophet in 1 Kings 18:36, 37. Elijah's prayer was offered at the time of offering the evening sacrifice. That specific time was solemnly observed by the faithful throughout the Old Testament with an eye of faith looking to the one all-sufficient, effectual, sin-atoning sacrifice of the Lord Jesus on the cross. It was addressed to Jehovah in his covenant relations. And its object was the glory of God and the welfare of his people. O Holy Spirit, teach us so to pray, looking to Christ, seeking God's glory and the welfare of God's elect!

Seven Thousand
When we see Elijah in 1 Kings 19, dejected and cast down, he foolishly imagined that he alone worshipped and served God. But the Lord God assured his servant that was not the case. In this dark, degenerate, apostate age, we sometimes think like Elijah. We sometimes imagine that there are few who worship and serve God. Sometimes we even imagine that there are few, if any, elect sinners yet to be called. Let us not be so foolish.

God still has his elect in this world. Throughout the Book of God, God's people are described as a remnant "The remnant of Jacob". What is a remnant? A remnant is what is left over. A remnant is that which is useless, despised, and thrown away. A remnant is the last piece of cloth on a bolt, or roll. If it is not thrown away, it is always sold at a discount, because it not worth much. That is a pretty good description of you and me. God's elect are looked upon as being below the mark, not fit for society, as narrow, crude, crotchety, peculiar. They are a nuisance and aggravation to the world.

And God has his elect who shall be called. They are an elect remnant; but God's remnant is seven thousand. Seven speaks of completion and perfection. Seven thousand speaks of a great multitude that no man can number, who shall completely fill the house of God forever.

God's Remnant
It was true in Elijah's time, and it is true today, that the church and people of the living God are a poor, needy remnant, a remnant scattered among the nations, an elect remnant, a redeemed remnant, a protected remnant, but God's remnant. Particularly and distinctly, we are God's remnant in Christ's hands, under Christ's care, given to Christ, our Prince, Priest, Provider, and Protector (Micah 5:4).

The God of all grace deals with a remnant. He seeks a remnant. He builds his house with a remnant. His treasure is a remnant. Here are five things revealed in the Book of God about his remnant.

1. There is a remnant according to the election of grace (Romans 11:5). God has not chosen to save all men; but there is a remnant chosen from among the ruins of Adam's fallen race, who must and shall be saved (Ephesians 1:3-6; John 10:16).

2. Everything God does he does for his remnant. All men benefit from God's goodness to his remnant. His benevolence, rain, sunshine, peace and pestilence, draught, darkness, and war come upon all men alike. But they come for and belong to the remnant (1 Corinthians 3:21; Psalm 57:2).

3. God is longsuffering with all men for the sake of the remnant (2 Peter 3:9). Were it not for God's elect remnant, he would have destroyed the world in his wrath

long ago, as he did Sodom and Gomorrah. God's elect are truly the salt, the preservers, of the earth. As God spared Adam for Abel's sake and Sodom for Lot's sake, God spares the world today for his elect's sake, that they all might be saved.

4. God's remnant in this world is always small and feeble (Isaiah 16:14). In the end they will be a great multitude. But in this world God's people are always a very small minority.

5. God will save his elect remnant (Romans 9:27, 11:26). Not one of that great remnant for whom God made, rules, and disposes of this world shall be lost. God the Father loved them. God the Son redeemed them. God the Spirit calls them. And God, by his great grace, will preserve them unto life everlasting.

April 20
Today's Reading: 1 Kings 20, 21
"Thy servant was busy here and there"
1 Kings 20:40

Hugo Grotius of Holland was one of the most brilliant and influential men of the 17th century. He was a poet and a philosopher of recognition. He was a theologian, whose commentaries on the scriptures are regarded by many to be of great value. And Grotius was, perhaps, the most significant historian of his day. But when he lay dying from wounds he suffered in a shipwreck, he made this statement, "I have consumed my life in a laborious doing of nothing! I would give all my learning and honour for the plain integrity of John Urick", a poor, but godly man with whom he was acquainted. Grotius was busy here and there. But in the end he lost his soul; and everything else was vanity!

I once read of a dying nobleman who exclaimed upon his deathbed "Good God, how have I employed myself! In what delirium has my life been passed! What have I been doing while the sun in its race and the stars in their courses have lent their beams, perhaps only to light my way to perdition! I have pursued shadows, and entertained myself with dreams. I have been treasuring up dust and sporting myself with the wind. I might have grazed with the beasts of the field, or sung with the birds of the woods, to much better purposes than any for which I have lived." This man had everything a man could want, but peace with God. He was busy here and there. He had gained the whole world but he called his life a "delirium", a vain and meaningless dream. In the end he lost his soul; and everything else was vanity!

Let us not be so foolish! Do not allow the cares of this world to destroy your soul. Do not allow the providential blessings of life to keep you from Christ. Has God given you a wife? Do not allow your wife to keep you from God. Has the Lord given you children? Do not let your children keep you from worshipping Christ. Has God given you a business? Do not allow your business to interfere with worship, prayer, and obedience to your Lord.

Let us not be busy here and there with this world to the ruin of our immortal souls. We have a Saviour to honour, a kingdom to serve, a gospel to preach, and a constant sacrifice to make (Romans 12:1, 2; 1 Corinthians 6:19, 20). As wise men and women, let us redeem the time God has given us and serve him well in it for Christ's sake (1 Corinthians 7:29-31; Ephesians 5:15, 16).

April 21
Today's Reading: 1 Kings 22-2 Kings 1
"I hate him"
1 Kings 22:7, 8

"And Jehoshaphat said, Is there not here a prophet of the LORD besides, that we might enquire of him? And the king of Israel said unto Jehoshaphat, There is yet one man, Micaiah the son of Imlah, by whom we may enquire of the LORD: but I hate him; for he doth not prophesy good concerning me, but evil. And Jehoshaphat said, Let not the king say so".

What a good and faithful prophet Micaiah must have been! Ahab, the wicked, reprobate king of Israel, acknowledged that he spoke for God and that he neither courted the favour of the king, nor feared his disfavour. Here is a standard by which we may identify faithful prophets in any age or place. Faithful servants of God speak the Word of God. For that, they are commonly hated by wicked men, about whom they can never speak anything good.

Greatness And Failure
As I close the reading of 1 Kings, I am struck with the fact that Solomon was a great man with many failures. The importance of our influence upon those around us is set before us dramatically in the life and reign of Solomon, as it is described in 1 Kings. Chapters 1-11 give us a picture of Solomon's greatness and glory as the king over all Israel for forty years. Then, chapters 12-22 display the horrible consequences of Solomon's disobedience upon the kingdom. These chapters set before us the first eighty years of the divided kingdom, a kingdom divided because of the evil influence of Solomon's life. The key to understanding the last half of 1 Kings is found in God's Word to Solomon in 1 Kings 11:11. "Wherefore the Lord said unto Solomon, Forasmuch as this is done of thee, and thou hast not kept my covenant and my statutes, which I have commanded thee, I will surely rend the kingdom from thee, and will give it to thy servant."

Still, the message of 1 Kings is Christ, of whom Solomon was in many ways a type. If you read Psalm 72, which was "A Psalm for Solomon", you will immediately see that the things there spoken of Solomon could only find their fulfilment in Christ, the Prince of Peace.

God's Faithfulness
In the lives of the few faithful servants and prophets of the Lord, raised up to minister in holy things in the midst of general corruption, it is a great blessing to remember that the Lord has not and will not cast away his people whom he foreknew. The promised mercy shall come. The Seed of the woman shall crush the serpent's head. God will maintain his witnesses in every generation and sustain the light of the gospel in the darkest of times.

Blessed Saviour, "thine is the kingdom, and the power, and the glory, forever and ever". Fix our hearts and minds on you as we in our day behold that which Elijah and your elect remnant beheld in their day, idolatry practised in your name, the profaning of your holy ordinances, and the despising of your Word by the very people who are responsible to declare it and defend it.

Intervening Mercy
In the sad example of Ahaziah and his captains of fifty, I am reminded of the fact that sin hardens the heart and makes sinners ripe for punishment. How we have earned our wages! But for grace, how justly the fires of hell would forever torment my wretched soul! Had not the mercy of my God intervened, had not the God of all grace interposed himself and stopped me in my mad rush for hell, the endless torments of the damned would be mine today!

Blessed Saviour, how I thank you and adore you for your great mercy, love, and grace, for your precious blood, and perfect righteousness so richly and freely bestowed upon me, by which you have redeemed me and saved me from myself! O my God, my great Saviour, make me faithful to you!

———

April 22
Today's Reading: 2 Kings 2-4
"Here is Elisha"
2 Kings 3:11

2 Kings 2 tells us of Elijah's marvellous translation to heaven. Surely, we cannot fail to see in that a type of Elijah's God, our Saviour, the Lord Jesus Christ. After suffering and dying as our Substitute at Calvary, he arose from the dead. Then, in the presence of his disciples, he was taken up to heaven. So it shall be with all God's elect. Yes, many will lay down the tabernacle of clay, before the Lord Jesus appears the second time without sin unto salvation. But God's elect shall never die! That is the promise of our Saviour (John 11:25, 26). We shall all (that is all who trust Christ), like

Elijah, be translated into heaven, some when the body dies and all when the Lord Jesus comes again.

The fourth chapter is full of good instruction; but for the present, let us remember that it gives us a vivid picture of the tender care God's servants have for his people, and the tender care God's people have for his servants. For our souls' meditation today, I call your attention especially to 2 Kings 3.

Where Needed

God's prophet Elisha was found in a very strange place. Elisha was in the camp with the army. That would be strange indeed, but for one thing. That was where he was needed. That is precisely where we should expect to see God's preachers. Wherever the Lord God is about to work wonders of grace, there he sends his preachers.

The fact that Elisha was in the camp with the army tells us that the Lord was about to bestow some great mercy upon his people. The Lord God graciously sends his holy Word, by the mouths of his servants, to the people he has chosen to bless with his saving operations of grace. In all ages, "Faith cometh by hearing, and hearing by the Word of God". Blessed are those people in this world to whom God sends his servant with his Word in the power of his Spirit!

Poor Servant

Though God's prophet was in their midst, the king did not know it. None of the mighty or influential were aware of his presence. But there was a poor, despised, insignificant servant who knew God and his prophet. How commonly that is the case! While Christ and his gospel are hid from the wise and prudent, they are revealed to babes.

Elisha was sent of God into the camp of the army specifically for the salvation of Jehoshaphat, his army, and the people; and he chose to make himself and his prophet known to the king by an unnamed servant. So it is in every age and in every place (2 Corinthians 4:7).

The Time

The time when all that is written here of Elisha's prophecy transpired was "in the morning when the meat-offering was offered". Surely, we are informed of this specific time by these specific words because God the Holy Spirit would point our hearts to our great sin-atoning sin-offering, the Lord Jesus Christ. The daily offering of the two lambs, one in the morning and the other in the evening, with this meat-offering, points us to our Redeemer's precious sacrifice of himself for us, which he offered to God for a sweet smelling savour. The morning and evening lamb offered daily was a perpetual type of the Lamb of God, slain from the foundation of the world, who in time laid down his life for us at Calvary. The continual presentation of this sacrifice sets forth the perpetual and unfailing efficacy of Christ's precious blood shed for us. "For he hath made him to be sin for us, who knew no sin; that we might be made the righteousness of God in him" (2 Corinthians 5:21).

171

April 23
Today's Reading: 2 Kings 5-7
"Behold, now I know"
2 Kings 5:15

After reading the wonders of God's goodness, grace, and power displayed in these three chapters by the Spirit of God, if we are taught of God and experience the things these wonders are intended of God to teach, we will confess with Naaman, "Behold, now I know that there is no God in all the earth, but in Israel: now therefore, I pray thee, take a blessing of thy servant".

Naaman's Healing
We all enter into this world with the leprosy of sin. We were, as David confessed, conceived in sin, shaped in iniquity, and brought forth in transgression. Are you sensible of this fact? Do you know it? Do you believe it? Then fly now to the Prophet of God who is God the sinners' Saviour, the Lord Jesus Christ. He is able to save to the uttermost all who come to God by him. Never did a leper come to him for healing who was not healed! Never did a sinner come to him for grace who did not obtain grace!

Blessed Son of God, I come to you this day, with all the leprosy of my heart and nature. Never was there a soul so leprous as mine! If you will, you can make me clean. O God of all grace, stretch forth the hand of your omnipotent mercy, pronounce the word of your saving power, and I shall be made whole!

Healed by you, as Naaman was, this sinner is fully convinced that there is no God in all the earth, no other name under heaven given among men, whereby sinners must be saved! How sweet it is to know that we are washed, that we are sanctified, that we are justified in the name of the Lord Jesus and by the Spirit of our God! Let us live this day, and each day of our remaining appointed days, as a people redeemed by blood, bought with the price of Christ's own life, and saved by his omnipotent mercy, as a people who belong to God.

Swimming Axe Head
In the sixth chapter of 2 Kings we see God's prophet causing a lost axe head to swim that it might be recovered; but if that is all we see, we have read the passage with no profit to our souls. Spirit of God, give us eyes of faith with which to see our dear Saviour and the wonders of redemption, grace, and salvation in him in every portion of your holy Word.

Why did Elisha cut down a tree and cast it into the water to recover the axe head? He did so because the only way God can save guilty sinners is by the sin-atoning death of his darling Son, the Lord Jesus Christ, as the sinners' Substitute. Like the axe head, we were lost. The place where the axe head was lost was the Jordan River, which is ever held before us in Holy Scripture as a symbol of death. As the axe head was lost in death, we were dead in trespasses and in sin. As Elisha cut down the tree and cast it into the water to recover the axe head, we preach Christ crucified to poor, needy sinners; we cast into this river of death called "humanity" the cross of Christ. And by the blessing of God's Spirit upon the gospel, as that axe head was made to swim, dead sinners are raised from death to life by the gospel (James 1:18; 1 Peter 1:23-25). The iron did not "float" on the water. A dead corpse can float. The Book of God says, "and the iron did swim". That which was dead was raised to life!

Then, we read in verse 7, "Therefore said he, Take it up to thee. And he put out his hand, and took it". The prophet's reaching out his hand and taking it did not make the axe head swim. It was swimming already. Life was there. Yet, he was commanded to reach out his hand and take it to himself. So, too, our faith in Christ does not give us life before God. Life is given by the command of God. Yet, we are commanded of God to take hold on eternal life (1 Timothy 6:19); and the sinner born of God does just that. Believing on the Lord Jesus Christ, we take hold on eternal life, we take the life God has given us in Christ.

Four Leprous Men
I cannot conclude my thoughts on these three chapters from the Book of God without reminding myself and you who read these pages of those four leprous men (chapter 7) who found life in the most unexpected of places. What a famine there is in the City of Mansoul by reason of sin, a famine not of bread and of water, but of all spiritual comfort, ease, and satisfaction; of life, and peace, and rest! In the unexpected, surprising deliverance of these four men we have a beautiful picture of Christ and his great salvation. The believing soul, like these leprous men going from one tent to another, finds in the unceasing experience of God's great salvation such multiplied discoveries of the Saviour's love that it is hard to grasp the fact that all this salvation, all this mercy, all this grace, all this fulness of Christ made over to our souls is real. Again and again our hearts cry out with overflowing gratitude and joy, "Thanks be unto God for his unspeakable gift".

April 24
Today's Reading: 2 Kings 8, 9
"The man of God wept"
2 Kings 8:11

Well might the man of God weep, knowing the wickedness around him and the judgment of God about to be executed! We weep for ourselves and our own wickedness, but rejoice in the full and free forgiveness of sins by the blood of Christ. We weep for the wickedness around us, knowing the terror of the Lord that shall soon seize the ungodly! Many are the gospel instructions found in these chapters. May God the Holy spirit write them upon our hearts.

Inheritance Restored
The restoration of the Shunammite's land reminds of the joyful fact that our Lord Jesus has effectually secured our inheritance for us as the sons and daughters of the Almighty. Though we forfeited everything in the sin and fall of our father Adam, though there has been a seven year famine (that is to say, a complete and utter famine) and poverty in our souls, Christ our King has restored and will restore all. He has restored and will restore all that we lost in Adam, and indescribably more! Indeed, our Redeemer and God is our Inheritance!

Hazael's Wickedness
In the account of Hazael's great wickedness we should be reminded that this is the character of all the sons and daughters of Adam by nature. Sin is what we do, because sin is what we are! The fact that you and I may not actually perform such crimes as we read here is not because we are of a different character. It is not because we are better people than Hazael. The difference is altogether God's doing (1 Corinthians 4:7). We do not act out the evil that is in our hearts only because God prevents it by his restraining grace. That is true of all men. God allows none to do all they are capable of doing (Psalm 76:10). But I want grace to remember always that the only thing that keeps me from doing any evil known to man at any time is God's grace. My brother, my sister, the same is true of you. May God the Holy Spirit constantly cause that fact to burn in our hearts and keep us looking to Christ for all our righteousness and trusting him to keep us by the power of his grace.

Judah Preserved
We are told again and again in the Old Testament scriptures that the Lord God would not destroy Judah for David's sake; and we have read it again today. So it has been and so it is. Judah's Lord still lives. He still reigns. The efficacy of his blood and righteousness and the power of his grace are everlastingly effectual. He changes not! We live by and upon this covenant God in Christ. In him is all fulness; and his grace is all-sufficient! He is able to keep us; and he will keep us! He will, at last, present every chosen, redeemed sinner faultless before the presence of his glory with exceeding joy!

The House Of Ahab
How miserable was the end of Ahab's house! His family, though rich and powerful, though constantly reproved by God's faithful prophets, though constantly made aware of God's power by singular displays of his greatness and his dominion, was destroyed and cast into hell! Ahab and Jezebel brought themselves and their children down to hell!

Yet, Ahab and Jezebel stand as fair representations of reprobate men and women in every age, in every part of the world, throughout history who set themselves in opposition to Christ our God and his church and kingdom. They are especially representative of the politically powerful and influential. In the end, they shall do no harm to God's kingdom, no injury to Christ's church, and give no hindrance to the cause of the Triune Jehovah in this world. They shall all die. They shall all be brought down to hell. And the cause of Christ shall be triumphant in all ages! All the Ahabs and Jezebels of all ages shall only serve the benefit of God's people. God our Saviour shall use them and all their intended evil for our everlasting good, just as he turned Shimei's cursing of David into a blessing upon David's head!

Take that thought with you through the day this day and lay down upon that pillow tonight and be at peace, O my soul!

April 25
Today's Reading: 2 Kings 10-12
"Come ... see my zeal for the Lord"
2 Kings10:16

How instructive these three chapters are in spiritual things! 2 Kings 10 describes the utter destruction of Ahab's house, the slaughter of idolaters, and the destruction of Baal's house by Jehu, all done in the name of the Lord and in zeal for the honour of Jehovah, his name, and his worship. In the eleventh chapter we read of Athaliah's destruction of all the royal seed, except for one male child, Joash, by whom God preserved Abraham's seed. Then, in chapter 12 we have seen the good reign of Jehoash as long as he followed the instruction of God's priest Jehoiada; but in his old age the king failed miserably and was slain by a conspiracy of his servants. What are we to learn from these things? Spirit of God, what are the instructions you have given us by these three chapters of Israel's and Judah's history?

I do not pretend in these brief daily survey's to give all the instructions contained in the chapters read. Indeed, I do not pretend to know all the lessons taught in them by the Spirit of God. It is my purpose only to catch one or two primary lessons each day from each portion read. Focusing on one or two prominent lessons, clearly intended by the Spirit of God. I pray that your heart and my own will be set upon our dear Saviour, the Lord Jesus Christ, his great salvation, and the blessed anticipation of eternity with him.

Jehu's Zeal
How zealous Jehu was for the Lord and for his worship, for the name of God and the truth of God! How zealous he was to rid the land of idolatry! How proud he was of his zeal! "He said, Come with me, and see my zeal for the Lord." We should learn from Jehu that a person may be very zealous in the service of God without the grace of God, without spiritual life, and without faith in Christ. Spirit of God, give me a zeal for God that soars up from within, that springs up from the love of God shed abroad in

my heart in the saving knowledge of Christ crucified, zeal springing from and constrained by the love of Christ.

The King's Son

Even in the very worst of times our God has his servants ready to execute his gracious designs. He has a Jehosheba to hide a chosen instrument of mercy when it is needful, and a Jehoiada to bring forward his chosen according to the counsel of his own will. May the God of all grace give us grace to see his hand in all his providence. Nothing can be more comforting to our souls in times of trouble, darkness, and adversity than the remembrance that this world is under the government of our heavenly Father, the government of our blessed God and Saviour, "who performeth all things for me".

This little portion of the history of Joash ought to turn our hearts to our great King, the Lord Jesus, the lawful King of Zion, brought forth in triumph over the tyranny of sin and Satan. Behold the King's Son, the rightful heir of all things, by whom Jehovah made the worlds! Behold him in the glories of his Person, "being the brightness of the Father's glory and the express image of his person". Behold him as the great Covenant-head of his people set up from everlasting, though hidden and his name Secret through the ages,. But, when the fulness of time was come, the Triune Jehovah "brought forth the King's Son". See him standing in his temple, as Joash stood by the pillar, to confirm the covenant, of which he is himself the sum and substance for his people and to his people.

Joash's End

Joash was a great, remarkable man and an equally remarkable king. But in the end Joash died under the judgment of God (2 Chronicles 24:17-25). How is it that many who seem to begin well end ill? How is it that many who seem to follow Christ for a time turn back and walk no more with him in the end? The Holy Spirit tells us plainly that they who depart from Christ and his gospel "went out from us, but they were not of us; for if they had been of us, they would no doubt have continued with us: but they went out, that they might be made manifest that they were not all of us" (1 John 2:19).

One reason given for the apostasy of professed believers is found in the third chapter of the book of Galatians. Having begun in the Spirit, at least by profession, they seek to be made perfect by the flesh. Men and women come into the church and are baptized in the name of Christ, professing that they trust Christ alone as their Saviour. But after a time, by the constant appeals of false prophets to their proud flesh, they think they make themselves perfect by the flesh. They who professed joy, being made free from the yoke of the law, return to the law. They who confessed themselves nothing but sinners begin to think themselves righteous. Vainly they dream of sanctifying themselves and making themselves holy by works of the flesh!

Spirit of God, give me grace and give grace to those who read these lines, as we received Christ Jesus, so to walk in him all the days of our lives, renouncing all personal worth, merit, and righteousness, confessing our sin, trusting Christ alone for all wisdom, righteousness, sanctification, and redemption.

176

April 26
Today's Reading: 2 Kings 13, 14
Elisha's bones, the resurrection, and believer's baptism
2 Kings 13:21

The miracle recorded in 2 Kings 13:21 is too remarkable to pass over with little thought. By this miracle, we are made to understand that Elisha's doctrine, the gospel of Christ by which the Word of God is preached and made known to immortal souls, brings life to the dead. By miraculous, omnipotent, free grace, God the Holy Spirit gives life and faith to dead sinners by the preaching of the gospel.

The Dead Raised
Elisha was also an eminent type of Christ. As such, the revival of this dead man, when his body touched Elisha's bones, portrayed the sure and certain resurrection of God's elect in the last day. Being crucified with Christ (Galatians 2:20) at Calvary, believers publicly confess our faith in him in believer's baptism; being buried with Christ in the likeness of his death and raised up from the watery grave to walk with him in the newness of life, we attest to all our blessed hope that we shall be resurrected with him at his glorious second advent (John 11:25; Romans 6:4-6). This is the confident hope of every believer. "For I know that my redeemer liveth, and that he shall stand at the latter day upon the earth: And though after my skin worms destroy this body, yet in my flesh shall I see God" (Job 19:25, 26).

Believer's Baptism
This hope of the resurrection is a part of our confessed faith in Christ. Baptism, that is immersion, is the symbolic burial of our bodies in the watery grave and the symbolic resurrection of our bodies from the watery grave, by which we confess and portray the gospel of the grace of God.

Because baptism looks to Christ and his death upon the cross, this is how it must be performed and the reason it must be performed this way. Baptism is a burial. "We are buried with him by baptism." It is a picture of death. What do you do with a dead corpse? Sprinkle sand in its face? Pour dirt on its head? Of course not! You bury it. And when a person is baptized, he is buried in water. Immersion is not a mode of baptism. It is baptism. Without immersion, baptism cannot be performed.

Baptism is unto death. It is the believer's confession of faith in the merit, efficacy, and sufficiency of Christ's death for his eternal salvation. Baptism says to all the world, "I trust Christ for all my salvation. Looking to him, his bloody death upon the cursed tree, trusting him alone, I am justified before God".

In baptism we confess our commitment to Christ. Rising up out of the watery grave, we confess to all the world that as Christ arose from the dead by the glorious power of God the Father, "even so we also should walk in newness of life". We have been raised from spiritual death to spiritual life by the glorious power of God's almighty grace. Henceforth, we declare in baptism, we are determined, by the grace of God, to walk in newness of life. We renounce our former life, ways, hopes, and beliefs. Christ is our Life, our Way, our Hope, and our Truth. We are no longer our own. We belong to Christ. We will no longer live under the rule of sin, self, and Satan. We give ourselves to the rule and dominion of Christ our Lord, to walk with him in newness of life. Because baptism looks to Christ and his death upon the cross, this is how and why it must be performed.

April 27
Today's Reading: 2 Kings 15-17
Idolatrous Samaritans
2 Kings 17:25-34

These three chapters cover a sad period in the history of Israel and Judah. Ahaz was king in Judah. Hoshea was king in Israel. Two more wicked men are hard to find in all the pages of history. The prophets Hosea and Isaiah were faithful servants of God in those dark, dark days. As in our day, in the days of those faithful prophets, idolatry was practised everywhere, idolatry practised in the name of worshipping Jehovah!

After settling in the land of Israel, the Samaritans professed faith in the Lord God, but continued to serve their own gods. They learned "the manner" of the Lord, but not the fear of the Lord. Their religion was an insult to God, for they refused to acknowledge that he alone is God. Though practised in the name of God, it was idolatry of the worst kind, for its whole purpose was their own pleasure and satisfaction, not the glory of God. 2 Kings 17 compels a question: Is our religion idolatry? Are we Samaritans, who worship God only in pretence, or are we "Israelites indeed", who worship God in sincerity and truth? Let each one judge himself. But these things are certain ...

1. Our religion is idolatry if we worship God only one day in seven. True believers worship God continually. Their lives are lived for him (Colossians 3:1-3).

2. Our religion is idolatry if we sacrifice to God that which costs us nothing. We worship God only when we give him that which we need, only when we give him the best, the firstfruits of what we have been given by him (2 Samuel 24:24).

3. Or religion is idolatry if we are more interested in temporal, material things than we are in the kingdom of God (Matthew 6:33). Charles Simeon once observed, "God in Christ is professedly the object of our worship: but the gods whom we really worship, and by choice, are the pleasures, and riches, and honours of this vain world. On them our heart is fixed. To them our time is devoted. And, if we but obtain them to the extent of our desires, we bless ourselves as having gained the objects most worthy of our pursuit." If that is the case, our professed religion is nothing but idolatry.

4. Our religion is idolatry if we are more concerned for our own name and recognition than we are for the honour and glory of God (Psalm 115:1; Jeremiah 45:5). All who walk in the fear of God, in all things seek the glory of God (1 Corinthians 10:31).

5. Our religion is idolatry if we are more anxious to be happy and comfortable than we are to be a blessing, helpful, and useful to others by the blessing of God (Acts 20:24). Believers do not live for their own pleasure, but seek to be useful to one another and useful to the cause of Christ.

6. Our religion is idolatry if we profess to follow Christ but in reality refuse to do so (Matthew 15:8, 9). It is the believer's meat and drink to do his Father's will.

7. Our religion is idolatry if our religion is man-centred rather than Christ-centred. In true religion, the will of God, the glory of Christ, and the gospel of God's grace and glory in Christ are central and dominant (1 Corinthians 1:17-31).

"Little children, keep yourselves from idols. Amen."

April 28
Today's Reading: 2 Kings 18, 19
"He did that which was right in the sight of the LORD"
2 Kings 18:3

Hezekiah was twenty-five years old when he began to reign over Judah. He reigned for twenty-nine years in Jerusalem. "And he did that which was right in the sight of the Lord." I am interested in that. What did this servant of God do which the Holy Spirit declares "was right in the sight of the Lord"? He was an idol smasher. He not only insisted that the people under his influence worship the Lord God, this man insisted that they worship the Lord God alone, and that they worship him in the way he prescribed.

High Places Removed
"He removed the high places". The high places were temples and shrines built on the mountains for the worship of idols. The Children of Israel had mingled with and married among the heathen. The result then of such a mixture, as it is now and always must be, was compromise. To keep up their relationships with the ungodly, to maintain their unholy alliances, the Children of Israel had to forsake the worship of God, though they convinced themselves that they retained the worship of Jehovah.

They were only being conciliatory, trying to get along with others. But they had forsaken God. What a price to pay! In order to restore the worship of God in the land, Hezekiah knew that idolatry had to be rooted out completely. So "he removed the high places, and brake the images", the statues of pagan gods and the idolatrous representations of Jehovah. Then, this godly man "cut down the groves", the wooded areas where men and women had erected altars to their gods, altars that his own father had built.

The Brazen Serpent

He also "brake in pieces the brazen serpent that Moses had made". The Jews had kept that brazen serpent from the days of Moses, burning incense to it, because they imagined that it would aid them in finding favour with God. Perhaps they had only kept it as a relic up to this time. But now they worshipped it! Religious relics always become objects of worship. Therefore, Hezekiah smashed to pieces that venerated brazen serpent, calling it "Nehushtan", a worthless piece of brass!

Why?

Why was this man so bent upon the destruction of idolatry in Israel? God tells us. "He trusted in the Lord God of Israel", clave unto the Lord, followed the Lord and obeyed his Word (vv. 5, 6). What was the result of his faithful service? "The Lord was with him; and he prospered." Men despised him; but God honoured Hezekiah, the idol smasher. My heavenly Father, raise up some Hezekiahs today, men who will dare to preach your gospel boldly, to the destruction of every idol, the glory of your dear Son, and the salvation of your elect. Give me the grace you gave your servant Hezekiah, and teach me as you taught him to follow you and serve you in my generation, for Christ's sake.

April 29
Today's Reading: 2 Kings 20-22
"I have heard thy prayer"
2 Kings 20:5

Hezekiah's prayer did not cause God to alter his purpose. Rather, it was the very means by which God accomplished his purpose of grace for his elect. Wicked as he was, Hezekiah's son, Manasseh, was one of God's elect (2 Chronicles 33:12, 13); but Manasseh would never have been born had Hezekiah not prayed and been spared fifteen years. And Josiah, Manasseh's grandson, Hezekiah's great grandson, was a direct ancestor of our Lord Jesus Christ (Matthew 1:10, 11).

Never was there a king in Israel or in Judah more loyal, more godly, more thoroughly consecrated to God than Josiah. He destroyed the idols his father had built. He established the worship of God alone in Judah. More importantly, it was through Josiah's descendants that the Lord Jesus Christ came as the Messiah and held rightful title to the throne of Israel.

God never makes a mistake. Providence never makes a wrong turn. God is always accomplishing his purpose of grace toward his elect. He gave Hezekiah the fifteen years he wanted (or thought he wanted), because it was his purpose to save Manasseh, Josiah, and you (child of God), and me, through Hezekiah's distant, distant Son, the Lord Jesus Christ, the Son of God!

Hezekiah

The favourites of heaven are exposed in common with all others to the humiliation of the grave. These bodies of flesh must die. These tabernacles of clay must return to the earth. But when believers drop their robe of flesh, all that lies before us is delightful! "Blessed are the dead which die in the Lord." "Precious in the sight of the Lord is the death of his saints." With the unbelieving, it is not so. Our dear Redeemer has turned our deathbeds into beds of peace, and hope, and anticipation. By his death, he overcame death. By his finished salvation, he delivered us who through fear of death were all our lifetime subject to bondage. He who is God our Saviour, the great I AM, is the Resurrection and the Life; and believing in him we shall never die!

When we exchange by the grave the outer courts of God's house for the inner temple of his glory, we shall see our Saviour as he is. We shall awake in his likeness and be with him forever! Yes, we must and shall leave the inhabitants of the world when we drop off this earthly tabernacle. But can it be a matter of regret to exchange this world for the upper, to exchange earth for heaven, to leave the company of evil men for the company of angels and the spirits of just men made perfect, to exchange mortality for immortality? Will any blood-bought, heaven-born soul think of the everlasting bliss of perfect conformity to Christ, perfect communion with Christ, and perfect consecration to Christ with sorrow, regret, or hesitation? Let it not be so with me. Let it not be so with you.

Manasseh

Manasseh stands before us as a marvellous monument to mercy. Manasseh tells us that there is forgiveness with God that he may be feared. Yet, when we look at Amon his son, hardened in rebellion and unbelief, we are reminded that grace does not run in bloodlines. Salvation does not come by family connections. Salvation is the gift of God's free, sovereign, distinguishing grace in Christ. We have been born again, "not of blood, nor of the will of the flesh, nor of the will of man, but of God". "So then it is not of him that willeth, nor of him that runneth, but of God that sheweth mercy." "Blessed is the man whom thou choosest, and causest to approach unto thee, that he may dwell in thy courts: we shall be satisfied with the goodness of thy house, even of thy holy temple."

Josiah

When he was but a child, Josiah sought the Lord. When he was just sixteen years old, "while he was yet young, he began to seek after the God of David his father". The young king walked with God. When he was just twenty years old, he began to purge Judah and Jerusalem of idolatry. O God of all grace, give our nations such rulers again! Give your church and kingdom in this world such rulers, such faithful pastors again!

Discovering Christ Day By Day

Blessed Lord Jesus, make me such a man as this young man Josiah was! Make my heart tender before you; graciously compel me to humble myself before you, and bow down my heart in the dust before you in the acknowledgement and confession of my sin. Grant that your precious blood and perfect righteousness may be my constant and everlasting hiding place. "Be thou my strong habitation, whereunto I may continually resort: thou hast given commandment to save me; for thou art my rock and my fortress."

April 30
Today's Reading: 2 Kings 23, 24
"He read in their ear all the words"
2 Kings 23:2

Good king Josiah assembled all the people of Israel and, standing by a pillar in the house of God, "he read in their ears all the words of the Book" of God that Hilkiah the priest found in the Temple. With holy joy, he led the people in the celebration of the passover and covenanted together with all the people to walk with God, consecrating themselves to him "with all their heart and all their soul ... And all the people stood to the covenant".

Our Assemblies
How thankful and joyful we ought to be in the assembly of God's saints for the worship of God in this gospel day! What a great privilege it is to hear the gospel of the ever blessed God preached, to read his Word, to sing his praises, and to call upon his name in prayer in union with his saints in the house of God! As Josiah gathered all under his influence to the house of God, so we ought to exert all the energies at our disposal to bring all under our influence with us to the house of God, that they may come to know, trust, love, and worship God our Saviour.

If the mere celebration of the typical passover feast was so memorable, how our hearts ought to erupt with joy at the thought of keeping the feast of Christ our Passover in the Church of the living God! Truly, there never was holden such a passover as this! Christ our Passover was sacrificed for us; and we feast upon him by faith, eating his flesh and drinking his blood. Feasting on him, we have eternal life abiding in us.

Jerusalem Ruined
As we close the book of 2 Kings, we see Jerusalem ruined. Generation after generation the Children of Israel and Judah despised God's ordinances, ignored his prophets, and went a whoring after the works of their own hands. How brazenly the sons and daughters of Adam persevere in sin, shoving God out of their way (if I might

be permitted to use such language), and running madly to hell! In the destruction of Jerusalem we see the sure and inevitable consequence of sin. "The wages of sin is death."

In the light of the things we read in 2 Kings 24, I am compelled, my God, to beg your grace that I may constantly flee to Christ for refuge. Ever fleeing to Christ, let me hear your voice in my soul saying, "O Israel, thou hast destroyed thyself; but in me is thine help". O Lord God, be gracious to your land, your church. For Christ's sake, be not angry with your people. Remember our iniquities! But be jealous for your name and for your Zion. Turn us; and we shall be turned. Draw us; and we will run after you. Heal us; and we shall be healed.

———————

Discovering Christ Day By Day

May 1
Today's Reading: 2 Kings 25-1 Chronicles 2
"He spake kindly to him"
2 Kings 25:28

God's quarrel with his people because of their determined perseverance in rebellion brought Jerusalem to utter ruin. Israel and Judah were made desolate and carried away into captivity by the judgment of God and brought into total ruin. How sin reduces men to vanity! How sin reduces nations to vanity! Zedekiah rejected the counsel of God by his prophet Jeremiah (Jeremiah 37-39) to his and the nation's destruction. Be warned. All who reject the counsel of God reject it to the everlasting destruction of their souls!

Mercy Portrayed
In wrath God remembers mercy; and even in this picture of divine judgment and ruin, we have in Jehoiachin a picture of God's great mercy in Christ. After thirty-seven years of imprisonment, the king of Babylon brought him into liberty and "he spake kindly to him", changed his prison garments, gave him bread, and supplied all his life's needs to the end of his days.

Here is a picture of the wonderful changes the grace of God makes, when from the prison of death and sin, the soul is brought forth to the light and liberty of the gospel. The Lord Jesus, by the omnipotent power of his Holy Spirit, opens the prison door in conversion and calls forth his captives from the pit of condemnation, corruption, and death. By the blood of his covenant, our great Saviour sends forth his prisoners of hope from the pit in which is no water (Zechariah 9:11).

What everlasting freedom that will be when death itself shall, at the trump of God, give up its dead and all the children of God shall sit down at his banqueting table to go out no more! Precious thought! Let it cheer our hearts amid all the changeable events in the providence of our God and Saviour throughout the remaining days appointed for us on this earth. In this world everything is changing; but we live upon the unchangeable God in Christ Jesus. He is our life and peace here and will be our life and peace forever.

The Genealogies
The genealogies of Chronicles and elsewhere in the book of God are read with boredom, if they are read at all, until we are made to see the purpose for which they are given. In these genealogies we are given the earthly line of our Saviour's family, the line of the human race in which God preserved a people through whom the Seed of woman must come into the world at his appointed time. The Lord God said concerning the fallen race, "Destroy it not, for a blessing is in it. There is life in the root. There is salvation in the stock. The woman's Seed, the Lord Jesus, is in these people. In this seed is he in whom all the nations of the earth shall be blessed".

The very first line of 1 Chronicles reads, "Adam, Seth, Enosh". No mention is made of Cain or Abel, the first two sons of Adam, because neither of them is in the genealogy of Christ. Abel was one of Christ's seed, one of his elect; but he died childless. So Christ was not of Abel's seed. Cain, the reprobate son of Adam, was not in the Saviour's family tree. The woman's Seed promised in the very first gospel message (Genesis 3:15) is traced back to Adam and Eve through Seth. Of all the objections raised by the Jews against our Saviour's claims as the Messiah, they never once raised a question about his genealogy, because they knew his genealogical records were meticulously preserved and precisely accurate. What mercy, wisdom, and goodness! We have before us in these genealogical records a marvellous display of God's great wisdom and his minute providence, using ancient Jewish family records to point to Jesus of Nazareth, his darling Son, the incarnate God, and declare with irrefutable authority, "Jesus is the Christ".

May 2
Today's Reading: 1 Chronicles 3-5
The Prayer of Jabez
1 Chronicles 4:10

The story of Jabez is sandwiched between fragments of a genealogical listing of the descendants of Judah. Apparently Jabez's mother experienced greater pain than normal during the birth of her son. Following the delivery she named her son Jabez, which is a play on the Hebrew word for "pain". We know nothing about Jabez's life except what we read in 1 Chronicles 4:9, 10. We are told that "Jabez was more honourable than his brethren" (v. 9). Then God the Holy Spirit gives us the brief prayer (v. 10) of this honourable man for our learning.

1 Chronicles 3
David's family tree was meticulously preserved with an eye to our Lord Jesus. Still, it is difficult to read the genealogy of David's family without connecting with it the great sorrow his children brought upon this man after God's own heart. Surely, even this is for our comfort and edification. Where do brokenhearted mothers and fathers, who trust and worship God, find relief and strength and comfort when they think of their rebel sons and daughters who hate the God they love? They find it exactly where David found it, and only there, in God's covenant love and covenant faithfulness. "Although my house be not so with God; yet he hath made with me an everlasting covenant, ordered in all things, and sure: for this is all my salvation, and all my desire, although he make it not to grow" (2 Samuel 23:5). Troubled saint, brokenhearted mother, heavy-laden father, set your heart on Christ and have peace. God our Saviour

does all things well. Therefore, I repeat, he is too good to do wrong, too wise to make a mistake, and too strong to fail.

1 Chronicles 4

Judah was the most illustrious and the most numerous of all the tribes of Israel. It formed a separate kingdom, including Levi, Simeon, and Benjamin. When the other tribes were scattered and almost lost by the Assyrian conquests, Judah became conspicuously great and flourishing. Why was Judah preserved? Why was Judah so exalted? It was God's purpose to bring our Saviour into the world through the tribe of Judah. He who is God our Saviour is "the Lion of the tribe of Judah".

1 Chronicles 5

The genealogies of Israel in the tribe of Reuben, and also in the tribe of Gad form the principal subjects of this chapter. Reuben, Jacob's oldest son, forfeited the birthright by incest (Genesis 49:4). Therefore Joseph was given both his own portion and Reuben's. Looking to Christ, the promised Seed in faith (Hebrews 11:21), the dying patriarch gave Joseph's sons Ephraim and Manasseh their portion. But Jacob declared by the spirit of prophecy that the sceptre would not depart from Judah, nor a lawgiver from between his feet until Shiloh (Christ) come (Genesis 49:10).

How precise the prophecies and promises of God in the Old Testament were! Truly the promises of God in Christ are yea and amen. None shall fall to the ground!

Jabez

Go back in your mind to Jabez and his prayer. We read in 1 Chronicles 4:9, 10 that "Jabez was more honourable than his brethren ... And Jabez called on the God of Israel, saying, Oh that thou wouldest bless me indeed, and enlarge my coast, and that thine hand might be with me, and that thou wouldest keep me from evil, that it may not grieve me! And God granted him that which he requested". Surely Jabez is set before us here as one remarkably typical of the Lord Jesus. Our blessed Saviour, like Jabez, was more honourable than his brethren. He was and is "greatest in the kingdom of God", who became least when he was made sin for us. This he did for the enlargement of his coast that the heathen by his Father's decree might be given to him for an inheritance and the utmost part of the earth for his possession.

Jabez also represents every believing sinner seeking the mercy and grace of God in Christ. What is it to be blessed of God, but to have my sins forgiven through the precious blood of Christ? Truly, our coast is enlarged if Christ has made us free! We are assured by God's own word he will keep us from all evil, keep us from the evil one, keep us forever in the arms of his omnipotent mercy, love, and grace in Christ!

Oh Lord God, as you heard and answered the prayer of Jabez, hear me and grant my request for all these spiritual blessings in Christ Jesus! Bless me, my God, and make me truly happy indeed, by making me all that thou wouldst have me to be in Christ. Make him and him alone my Portion, my Hope, my Joy, my Life, my Salvation, my All, all the days of my life and to all eternity!

May 3
Today's Reading: 1 Chronicles 6, 7
"To make an atonement for Israel"
1 Chronicles 6:49

1 Chronicles 6 gives us the genealogy of Levi. How defective and fluctuating that legal priesthood of Israel was. "And they truly were many priests, because they were not suffered to continue by reason of death." Reading of that priesthood that is no more, that priesthood that could never put away sin by all their countless sacrifices, how we ought to rejoice and give thanks to our God for him who continues forever an unchangeable Priest over the house of God, our Lord Jesus Christ, who is able to save to the uttermost all who come to God by him (Hebrews 7:4-25).

Temple Singers
David appointed specific men to lead singing in the house of God, "after that the ark had rest"; and their singing was all about God's greatness, God's glory, and God's salvation, everything looking to the mercy-seat and the atonement blood on the mercy-seat. So it should be in all our solemn assemblies. Let us speak to one another and to our God in "psalms and hymns and spiritual songs, singing with grace in our hearts unto the Lord". And let every song be filled with Jehovah's praise, giving thanks to God for his great salvation through the blood and righteousness of his dear Son, our great Saviour, the Lord Jesus Christ.

Sons of Levi
As we behold the sons of Levi and remember their sacrifices to the Lord, Spirit of God, give us grace to remember our great Saviour, who made his soul an offering for sin that we might be made the righteousness of God in him, and lift our hearts with joy to him in songs of praise and thanksgiving. How thankful we ought to be to and for the Lord Jesus, typified by these men, who wears a vesture dipped in blood and ever lives to make intercession for us by the will of God! He is our almighty, effectual, saving Priest of a better covenant, established upon better promises. The law made men priests which had infirmities; but Christ is our perfect, holy Priest, consecrated with an oath by him that swore and will not repent, "that thou art a priest forever, after the order of Melchisedec". He takes our cause, our persons, our poor offerings, all that we have, and all that we are into his nail-pierced hands, and perpetually presents us an offering acceptable and well-pleasing to God, acceptable and well-pleasing to God by the merits of his blood and righteousness, acceptable and well-pleasing to God in union with himself!

Insignificant Man
1 Chronicles 7 continues with genealogical records. In the short span of these first seven chapters thousands of men, their lives, and their deaths are covered in a few short pages. How insignificant man is! What is your life? Nothing but a vapour that appears for a brief time and then vanishes away! Not even the memory of a man's

187

name commonly survives a generation or two. How utterly meaningless and insignificant is man! Yet, the Son of God became one of us, "the Word was made flesh and dwelt among us", that he might save poor, worthless sinners like you and me. That he might make of vanishing, sinful mists, sons of God forever!

Atonement
Carry from our reading today the words of 1 Chronicles 6:49, "to make an atonement for Israel". May God the Holy Spirit inscribe these words upon our hearts and memories. The atonement made by Aaron and his sons for Israel pointed to the death of our Lord Jesus Christ to make atonement for his elect, the Israel of God.

The Lord Jesus Christ, the Son of God, died upon the cross more than two thousand years ago. Though he was crucified by the hands of wicked men, he died according to the will and purpose of God (Acts 2:23). He died as a sin-atoning substitute for a specific people (Isaiah 53:8). By his death upon the cursed tree, the Son of God finished the work of atonement (John 19:30), brought in an everlasting righteousness (Daniel 9:24), obtained eternal redemption (Hebrews 9:12), and purchased an inheritance in heaven (Ephesians 1:11) for somebody. Without question, all for whom he died shall be saved by his blood and enter into heaven at last, because "He shall not fail". "He shall see of the travail of his soul, and shall be satisfied". His blood was not shed in vain. All for whom the Saviour died must be saved! But, for whom did he die? Did the Lord Jesus Christ die for you?

He died for his sheep (John 10:11), for God's elect. Is it not absurd to imagine that he died for those who were already in hell when he died? Christ died for those for whom he makes intercession. He makes intercession for some, but not for others (John 17:9, 20). Do you not think it ridiculous to hear men declare that the Son of God died for people for whom he refused to pray? The Lord Jesus Christ died and made atonement for all who trust him. If you believe on the Lord Jesus Christ, he died for you. Your faith in him is both the gift of his grace and the proof of his grace to you (Hebrews 11:1).

May 4
Today's Reading: 1 Chronicles 8-10
"So all Israel were reckoned"
1 Chronicles 9:1

What a succession of men and monarchies have passed through the world whose names, whose works, whose riches, whose momentary fame no one knows! Yet, scattered among those vast numbers of men spread over the face of the earth is a people, poor and despised, unknown among men, whose names are held in everlasting remembrance, because they are the Israel of God.

Discovering Christ Day By Day

Written In Heaven

Rejoice, my soul, that your name is written in heaven, written in the Lamb's book of life by the finger of God before the worlds were made! Think of that great day soon to come when the dead, both small and great, shall stand before God in judgment. "And I saw a great white throne, and him that sat on it, from whose face the earth and the heaven fled away; and there was found no place for them. And I saw the dead, small and great, stand before God; and the books were opened: and another book was opened, which is the book of life: and the dead were judged out of those things which were written in the books, according to their works. And the sea gave up the dead which were in it; and death and hell delivered up the dead which were in them: and they were judged every man according to their works. And death and hell were cast into the lake of fire. This is the second death. And whosoever was not found written in the book of life was cast into the lake of fire" (Revelation 20:11-15).

With every memory of everlastingly damned souls everlastingly forgotten, blessed Lord Jesus, give me grace to remember and give thanks to you for your great grace and your great salvation. You have delivered your chosen people from the wrath to come. For that great deliverance by your blood and righteousness, by your power and grace, by your love and mercy, I rejoice and give thanks for the pleasing, glorious hope that my name, worthless as it is, is written in heaven!

Heal Us

When the Children of Israel returned from Babylon, which is where 1 Chronicles 9:1 begins, the people returned to their beloved city, finding Jerusalem and Zion as a ploughed field. How sad the picture! Jerusalem was ruined by sin. Yet, how little we think of sin's effect! If God so punished Israel, what security does any other nation have? If God spared not the natural branches, what must the nations of the Gentiles expect?

Let us this day, for ourselves and for our nation, confess our sins to God and beg his mercy. O Lord God, visit us again in mercy! Come with grace to pardon, grace to sanctify, grace to bless, grace to deliver, grace to renew, grace to heal all our diseases. "Come, and let us return unto the Lord: for he hath torn, and he will heal us; he hath smitten, and he will bind us up" (Hosea 6:1).

Saul's Ruin

Saul, who murdered God's priests was deserted by God. Saul murdered himself in darkness and despair. He who abandoned his dearest friend was abandoned by every man and abandoned forever by God. Such shall be the end of every rebel sinner dying with his fist in God's face, eternally abandoned by every friend and eternally abandoned by God in hell! O precious, precious Lord Jesus, keep me, keep me in your hands, keep me in your grip, lest I depart from you at last!

May 5
Today's Reading: 1 Chronicles 11-13
"Understanding of the times"
1 Chronicles 12:32

It was the peculiar honour of the sons of Issachar that "they were men that had understanding of the times". Israel was passing through some troublesome, unsettling times. Critical issues had to be faced and dealt with. The Lord had now established David as king over his people. But Saul had just been slain. And some of the tribes of Israel did not know what to do. The question of the day in Palestine was, "Who should be king?" Many in Israel did not know whether to accept David as their king, or not. Some were inclined to seek a king from Saul's family, and would not commit themselves to David. Others boldly came forward and proclaimed David as their rightful king.

David's Men
From among the Benjamites were mighty men and helpers of the war. "They were armed with bows, and could use both the right hand and the left in hurling stones and shooting arrows out of a bow." From among the Gadites were men of might, men of war. Those mighty men who came to David in Ziklag were utterly devoted to the king. "Then the spirit came upon Amasai, who was chief of the captains, and he said, Thine are we, David, and on thy side, thou son of Jesse: peace, peace be unto thee, and peace be to thine helpers; for thy God helpeth thee. Then David received them, and made them captains of the band." From among Zebulon, there came to David men expert in war who could keep rank, and "they were not of double heart".

Among these bold and valiant men were the children of Issachar. And in our text the Holy Spirit singles out these men for one particular and very significant characteristic. He says of the children of Issachar that they "were men that had understanding of the times, to know what Israel ought to do".

I do not doubt that this sentence, like every sentence of Holy Scripture, was written for our learning. These men of Issachar are set before us as a pattern to be imitated and an example to be followed. If we would be useful to our generation, nothing is more important than this: we must understand the times in which we live and know what it is that these times require of us. We must seek the grace and wisdom of God to understand the times in which we live, and to know what Israel ought to do in these days.

The Demands Of The Day
The day in which we live demands men of courage, boldness, and extremity for the cause of Christ in this world. The world has never known such perilous times as these. Men today are perishing in a church pew, going to hell with a prayer on their lips, a song in their hearts, and a Bible in their hands. Surely this day demands something from us. It demands men with courageous hearts, bold spirits, and extreme dedication

to the Gospel of Christ. The souls of men and the glory of Christ compel us to be men of purpose and determination.

What does our day require of us? What must Israel do in this day? What do the times in which we live demand of the people of God? This is a day that demands a bold, uncompromising, unflinching adherence to the authority of Holy Scripture. Let all men know, by unflinching testimony from your lips, that the Holy Bible is the Word, the only written revelation of the only true and living God.

These days of darkness demand of us distinct and decided testimony to gospel doctrine. Let no one be ashamed to testify to all, in public and in private the utter depravity of the human race, God's unconditional electing love, Christ's particular and effectual atonement, the irresistible grace and power of God the Holy Spirit, and the sure perseverance of every sinner saved by the grace of God.

These dark days of self-serving false prophets, hired for a dime and a smile, demand faithfulness, dedication, and sacrifice in preaching the gospel of Christ. Let us pray daily for God to raise up Elijahs and John the Baptists in our midst, men who will boldly proclaim the gospel, with fire from heaven burning in their bellies.

These days of great need demand from every believing sinner, saved by the grace of God, a clear recognition of our most important priorities and our most weighty responsibilities. Child of God, consecrate your life to Christ. In the totality of your being worship and serve him who loved you and gave himself for you.

Once more, this dark, dark day of religious wickedness demands that each of us exercise a diligent watchfulness over our own souls. Blessed Holy Spirit, be my Teacher and Comforter every day and every hour, constantly convincing me of my sin, of Christ's finished and perfect righteousness as the Lord my Righteousness, and of judgment finished by my Redeemer's one sacrifice for sin!

May 6
Today's Reading: 1 Chronicles 14-17
"We sought him not after the due order"
1 Chronicles 15:13

The Lord God made a breach upon David and the Children of Israel and slew Uzza, because, as David rightly observed, "we sought him not after the due order". We should not fail to observe David's modesty and humility. He included himself in this neglect. He said, "We sought him not after the due order". It is a blessed mark of grace in believers when we take shame to ourselves, rather than put it upon others. Accepting the punishment of our iniquity is made a testimony by the Lord God himself of our being in the covenant (Leviticus 26:41).

Motivated By Love
David loved God intensely. During Saul's reign, the worship of God and the ordinances of his house were almost totally forgotten and neglected. When David was made King in Israel, the first order of business was to re-establish that form of worship which God had ordained. He set about to do what he could to revive the true worship of the true God. It was out of pure love and reverence for God that David called all the people together and consulted with them about bringing the ark of the Lord up to Mount Zion. It would be set in a conspicuous place, near the palace of the king. It would become the centre of worship for the entire nation. It was to be placed near that sacred spot where Abraham of old had offered up his son, Isaac.

God's Word Neglected
David's intentions were excellent. No fault can be found with his motives or his desires. However, he forgot the law of God! It is an evil day for the people of God when they do things according to their own whims and notions, and fail to yield implicit obedience to the Word of God. We serve a jealous God. Though he graciously pardons our sins and overlooks our faults, the Lord God will have his Word reverenced and his commands obeyed.

Uzza Killed
David put the ark upon a new cart, intending to bring it up to Jerusalem. The cart jolted slightly and the ark was, so far as Uzza could tell, about to fall into the mud; so he put out his hand to steady the ark; and in the moment that he touched it, the Lord killed him. Then, after three months of thoughtful consideration, David realized the cause of God's judgment. He said, "The Lord our God made a breach upon us, for that we sought him not after the due order". If we would worship God, we must worship him in the way he has prescribed, or he will not accept our worship.

That ark represented the Lord Jesus Christ and redemption and salvation through his blood. When Uzza put his hand to it, he was declaring, "Redemption, grace, and salvation must be in some way dependent upon the works of men." That is what it meant to put your hand to the ark. It meant God's work ultimately depends upon the will, work, and efforts of men!

These people brought will-worship to God, instead of that worship which he had ordained. They paid no attention to that which God had spoken. They had no regard for the rules of worship he had laid down.

What do I mean by will-worship? I mean any kind of worship which is not prescribed in the Word of God. The first commandment may be broken, not only by worshipping a false god, but also by worshipping the true God in any way other than that which he has ordained (Exodus 20:3-5, 24-26; Isaiah 66:1-4).

True Worship
If we would worship God, we must worship him in the way he has prescribed in his Word. We must worship him in spirit and in truth, by his Spirit and according to revealed Truth, ascribing all salvation to God's free and sovereign grace in Christ, our almighty, effectual Saviour, having no confidence in the flesh (Philippians 3:3). We must worship him from our hearts, by faith in Christ, holding forth the word of the

truth of the gospel. If our doctrine and ordinances of worship are not precisely as ordered by God in his Word, we only pretend to worship God, but really worship ourselves, putting our hands on God's Ark, mixing our works with his grace. For that high crime of treasonous unbelief and will-worship, God still slays proud sinners and sends them to hell. "The hour cometh, and now is, when the true worshippers shall worship the Father in spirit and in truth: for the Father seeketh such to worship him. God is a Spirit: and they that worship him must worship him in spirit and in truth."

May 7
Today's Reading: 1 Chronicles 18-21
"Let us behave ourselves valiantly"
1 Chronicles 19:13

The Ammonites had come against Israel with a very great army. Even to Joab, a man of great military skill and experience, things looked bad. But he encouraged himself and his brother, Abishai, with these words: "Be of good courage, and let us behave ourselves valiantly for our people, and for the cities of our God: and let the Lord do that which is good in his sight". In this time of great difficulty and danger, Joab set before us an example of persevering faithfulness and reverent submission, which should be followed by all who seek the glory of God and serve the interest of his kingdom in this world. May God the Holy Spirit give us grace today and throughout the days of our appointed time in this world to heed this good counsel.

Faithfulness
Our lives should be characterized by a persevering faithfulness to our God and to the work he has committed to our hands. I say to you, "Be of good courage, and let us behave ourselves valiantly for our people, and for the church of our God."

The Lord God has entrusted us with the gospel of his grace. "We have this treasure in earthen vessels, that the excellency of the power may be of God, and not of us". He has not given us this treasure to hide in a vault, but to spread through all the earth for the salvation of his elect. God has given us the means and the opportunity to proclaim the gospel to this generation; and he has commanded us to do so. We have greater means at our disposal for the preaching of the gospel than any generation in history. Let us be found faithful unto death in the employment of the means he has given us for the furtherance of the gospel of Christ. This is the point of our responsibility. We do not know what God has decreed, but we do know what he has commanded; and what he has commanded we must do. "Go ye into all the world, and preach the gospel to every creature. He that believeth and is baptized shall be saved."

Submission
Serve the Lord your God with reverent submission. "Let the Lord do that which is good in his sight." Joab was saying to Abishai, "If God saves us, we shall be saved. If we perish, we shall perish. That is up to him. But we will serve him valiantly." This is our work. We must preach the gospel to all as God gives us occasion. If he is pleased to save some, we shall rejoice and preach the gospel. If God is pleased to harden some, we shall still rejoice and preach the gospel. He is God. We are his servants. Let him do with us what he will. "Let the Lord do that which is good in his sight."

Blessed Holy Spirit, grant grace to your church and your preachers in this day, grant grace to this worthless, dirty instrument, by which you may be pleased to spread forth your Word, that I may ever be found faithful to God my Saviour and submissive to his will in all things, for the glory of Christ.

May 8
Today's Reading: 1 Chronicles 22-24
"Arise therefore, and be doing, and the LORD be with thee"
1 Chronicles 22:16

O Lord, my God, give me grace by your Spirit to begin and go through every day of my life in the service of your church and kingdom in this world, to have this charge from the very mouth of my God stirring my heart. "Arise therefore, and be doing, and the Lord be with thee."

In these three chapters of Inspiration we have read about David's preparations for the building of the temple in Jerusalem. He was not permitted to build it himself; but he was permitted to make all the preparations for it. The honour of building it would be another's; but that did not keep David from doing the lesser work with all his might. That is the way we must serve our God. Let us be pleased to have our names forgotten and left in obscurity, and the name of God our Saviour be known and exalted alone.

Having gathered all the material required for the building of God's house, David gave Solomon his son a solemn charge. Solomon was then appointed to be king in David's stead; and the Levites and officers were appointed to their specific work.

1 Chronicles 22
God's servant David prepared his silver and gold for the service of him from whom he received all and to whom he owed all. With generosity and greatness of mind, he determined to use everything at his disposal for the glory of God, and in the service of his church and kingdom. May God the Holy Spirit sweetly constrain you and me to do the same. We are not driven by law to do so. We are not motivated by fear, or by hope of reward, or by dread of loss. "The love of Christ constraineth us." There is no power

to motivate, inspire, and lay claim to all like love. Blessed Son of God, so flood my soul with the knowledge of your love for me that I have no will to keep back anything for myself; neither of talents, nor of time; neither of power, nor of purse, but to cast all at your feet. Use me, my God, for your glory and the service of your people. What an honour that would be for you to heap upon such a useless, sinful wretch! How we, your people, rejoice to know that it is your good pleasure and your glory to use just such things as we are for the salvation of your elect and the benefit of your saints (1 Corinthians 1:26-31).

Make us, blessed Saviour, pillars in your temple, built upon the same foundation as the apostles and prophets, Jesus Christ himself being the chief corner stone, in whom the whole building is fitly framed together, that we may grow up unto an holy temple in the Lord for an habitation of God through the Spirit.

1 Chronicles 23

What a great multitude of Levites there were whose lives were devoted to the service of the house of God! There were multiplied thousands of them. Yet, there was not only room enough for them, but also plenty for them all! "They shall be abundantly satisfied with the fatness of thy house; and thou shalt make them drink of the river of thy pleasures" (Psalm 36:8). Child of God, remember that promise; and remember that all God's people are spiritual Levites, "a royal priesthood". Christ has made us kings and priests unto God our Father. "Blessed are they that dwell in thy house: they will be still praising thee. Selah" (Psalm 84:4).

No doubt there is in these Levites a representation of God's faithful servants in every age. He calls them "pastors according to mine heart" (Jeremiah 3:15). As you taught us, we beg of you, O Lord of the harvest, send forth labourers into your vineyard today. Raise up and send forth men, able because they are gifted by your Spirit, and willing because they are inspired by your glory. Raise them to labour in your Word and doctrine, to devote themselves to your cause, and to be anxious to do the work of evangelists, sounding abroad the gospel of your grace among all nations!

1 Chronicles 24

Here the Levites are set apart by lot to stand before the Lord and serve him and his people according to the order of their course and according to the abilities God gave them for their specific work. So all the members of Christ's spiritual temple, the church, are each set apart to present their bodies a living sacrifice, holy and acceptable unto God in Jesus, because this is our "reasonable service".

O royal priests of God, my brothers and sisters in Christ, what vast dignity our God has put upon us! Our great High Priest has brought us nigh. He has opened for us a new and living way by his blood into the holiest of all, and bids us ever to come to him (Hebrews 4:16). God give us grace to live as his priests in this world! Let us continually draw near with true hearts, in full assurance of faith, confident of God's acceptance by the blood and righteousness of his dear Son, our Lord Jesus Christ. "Arise therefore, and be doing, and the Lord be with thee."

May 9
Today's Reading: 1 Chronicles 25-27
"Able men ... for the service"
1 Chronicles 26:8

Those men called and gifted of God for the service of his church and kingdom are gifted of God the Holy Spirit for the work to which he calls them. These are not natural gifts of intellectual ability, oratorical ability, or leadership ability; but spiritual gifts incorporating all the God-given abilities of their nature. No man is called of God to preach the gospel who is not equipped by God with such gifts.

Let every saved man desire the work of the ministry, desiring from God a double portion of Elijah's spirit. That is noble and right. But let no man thrust himself into the work. Gospel preachers are called, gifted, and sent of God. If God creates a bird to fly, he gives it wings; and if God calls a man to preach, he gives him the gifts necessary to perform the work. These men and their gifts are illustrated for us in the men David appointed to be singers, porters, and treasurers "to minister in the house of the Lord" in these three chapters of 1 Chronicles.

Singers
Songs of praise to our God were a very large and important part of temple worship in the Old Testament. The singing was not for entertainment, but for worship, to direct the minds of the worshippers toward God. David appointed 288 Levites for this service, "for song in the house of the Lord" (1 Chronicles 25:6).

"O come, let us sing unto the LORD: let us make a joyful noise to the rock of our salvation." "Sing unto the LORD, O ye saints of his, and give thanks at the remembrance of his holiness." They sang with musical accompaniment, with trumpets and cymbals representing joyful expressions of the heart, expressions of triumph and thanksgiving. So we are taught to sing with grace in the heart, "Speaking to yourselves in psalms and hymns and spiritual songs, singing and making melody in your heart to the Lord". These Levites prophesied (worshipped) "with harps, with psalteries, and with cymbals". So let us worship God in his house and in our homes with songs of praise to him. Think today of him whose praise these ancient singers celebrated, and sing your song of redemption to his praise.

Porters
Porters in the temple were the doorkeepers of God's house. The word "porter" carries with it the idea of one responsible for janitorial work. But notice that the porters held an office of high honour and great importance in the house of God. Their office was an office to be desired. But only those who were specifically fitted by God for the work were chosen for this great work. They are described in 1 Chronicles 26 as "able men for strength for the service ... strong men ... wise counsellors ... and mighty men of valour". The porters were responsible to open and shut the doors of the temple, to keep out those people and things that would defile God's house, cause disruption in the house, or take anything from the house of the Lord.

196

The spiritual porters of Christ's church have a very solemn trust to keep the doors of God's house. By their God-given wisdom and strength, they are to give out "all the counsel of God" in Holy Scripture, feeding God's family with "knowledge and understanding". As labouring janitors, they are to keep the house of God clean with the pure doctrine of Christ. By the preaching of the gospel, the Lord Jesus uses these porters to separate the wheat from the chaff, and shall at last present his church to himself a glorious church, having neither spot of sin nor wrinkle of infirmity.

Treasurers
The treasurers were responsible for the treasures stored in the house of God, all the gold, silver, and brass, especially that contained in the furnishings of the temple by which God's Israel worshipped him in that age of symbolism and type. The treasurers of God's house today guard that which is far more valuable.

Child of God, do not neglect to pray for those men set in the house of God as pastors in his church. These men are the ascension gifts of Christ to your soul. We have the treasure of the gospel committed to our trust and are responsible to bring it out to you in all our preaching, writing, and conversation for the enriching of your soul day by day.

Entrusted with the charge of his holy Word, his ordinances, and all his precious truth, the gospel preacher performs the highest, noblest, most honourable, and most demanding work in the world. From the inexhaustible storehouse of Holy Scripture, he must bring forth continually to the people of God the unsearchable riches of Christ. What a terrible, inexcusable abuse of their office do they make, who preach themselves, instead of Christ Jesus the Lord!

The instructions given in these chapters concerning these porters and treasurers show us something of the devotion and vigilance with which gospel preachers, faithful pastors, must give themselves to the work of the ministry. Blessed Lord Jesus, give the preacher who writes these words and give to all your servants in this world the wisdom and grace needed to perform their work with a single eye to your glory, to promote the cause of your church in this world for the salvation of your elect and the comfort, edification, and everlasting benefit of your people. Amen.

May 10
Today's Reading: 1 Chronicles 28-2 Chronicles 1
"The LORD magnified Solomon"
1 Chronicles 29:25

The design of God the Holy Spirit in the compilation of these Chronicles is to preserve an accurate and faithful record of David's family. The dying patriarch, Jacob, under the influence of God the Spirit, had prophesied that the sceptre would not depart from Judah, nor a law-giver from between his feet, until Shiloh had come (Genesis 49:10). These Chronicles, when compared with the other books of the Inspired Volume of Holy Scripture, show us the fulfilment of Jacob's prophecy. We are able, by these records, to trace the lineal descent of David's royal house. The Jews never lost sight of their own king; and even during times of captivity, they retained their own laws, until Christ appeared in our flesh, until Shiloh came. In him, the Lord Jesus Christ, the royal house of David emerged and that throne and kingdom appeared which shall have no end. But these inspired Chronicles are more than records of David's family. They are full of spiritual instruction for our souls. May God the Holy Spirit write their lessons upon our hearts.

Christ Set Forth
Here, and throughout the pages of Holy Scripture, our dear Saviour, the Lord Jesus Christ, is set forth. The eye of faith should always be on the lookout for him and for his great work of redemption. The Bible was written to show us our Redeemer. Indeed, creation itself, with all its magnificence, was designed for that purpose. The Lord Jehovah determined the redemption of his people from everlasting; and when he performed his works of creation, he did so in preparation for and to display his greater and more glorious works of redemption. Every event of time, from the creation of the world to the coming of the Lord Jesus Christ, was in preparation for and designed to introduce him. So, as we read the Book of God, let us ever ask God the Holy Spirit to show us our Saviour in the sacred pages of the Book.

Chequered Life
What a chequered life God's servant David had in this world! His was a life marked by grace, marked by remarkable displays of special providence, and blessed beyond measure. David was chosen of God, redeemed by Christ, regenerated by the Holy Ghost, forgiven of all sin, and accepted in the Beloved. He was a prophet of God and king in the house of God. He was the sweet singer of Israel and the giant slayer. David was, by the grace of God, a remarkable man of faith, courage, and devotion. He was loved of God; and he loved God. Yet, David was a great sinner. No effort is made to hide or excuse David's horrendously sinful deeds. And this man so greatly blessed of God, throughout his life, experienced heartache after heartache, betrayal after betrayal, and slander after slander all the days of his life. Throughout his life, David found himself at the throne of grace, begging God to show himself gracious. Trials without and troubles within kept David on his knees before God.

So it is with every saved sinner in this world. The Lord God graciously arranges all the affairs of our chequered lives to wean us from this world and to set our hearts upon Christ, heaven, and eternity.

Blessed End
Blessed Holy Spirit, Divine Comforter, graciously set our hearts upon our Saviour. Teach us to live for eternity in this world of woe. And when our appointed days on this earth have been accomplished, bring our lives to the same blessed end as that which was given to David. Let us be found unto our last days serving the interests of your church and kingdom, the cause of your glory, seeking the furtherance of the

gospel and the worship of our God in generations to come! Let us be found, like David, promoting the glory of our God unto the end. Then, give us grace to leave this world of woe with joyful confidence in our covenant God and his great salvation in Christ Jesus.

Christ Our King
Solomon, like his father, was a king typical of our Lord Jesus, the King of Zion, the Prince of Peace. By our great Solomon's ascension to his throne, he obtained eternal redemption for us with his own blood. In him, our exalted Saviour and King, are hid all the treasures of wisdom and knowledge. Like Solomon, of whom we have read today, let us ask of God for that wisdom and knowledge that he alone can give, the light of the knowledge of the glory of God in the face of Jesus Christ.

God the Father has set him as King in Zion. He has put all things in our Saviour's hands. Grace, mercy, peace, righteousness, forgiveness, and eternal life are in him, "who of God is made unto us wisdom and righteousness and sanctification and redemption". All fulness is in him for us, his people. None are more needy than we; and none are so ready to give as he. "Let us therefore come boldly unto the throne of grace, that we may obtain mercy, and find grace to help in time of need."

May 11
Today's Reading: 2 Chronicles 2-5
Solomon's Letter to Hiram and Hiram's Response
2 Chronicles 2:11

"Then Huram the king of Tyre answered in writing, which he sent to Solomon, Because the LORD hath loved his people, he hath made thee king over them".

In 2 Chronicles 2-5 we have read how Solomon built the temple at Jerusalem. That typical house of God was truly magnificent. All its furnishings, all the sacrifices and ceremonies conducted there, and the temple itself foreshadowed our great God and Saviour, the Lord Jesus Christ, and his great salvation, obtained for chosen sinners (all the Israel of God) by the shedding of his blood in the sacrifice of himself. In our reading from the Book of God today, I find the correspondence between Solomon and Hiram particularly instructive.

Solomon To Hiram
The letter, which Solomon sent to Hiram (2 Chronicles 2:3-10), is a remarkable piece of correspondence, preserved for us by God the Holy Ghost for our learning and instruction. Solomon wrote to the king of Tyre to solicit his help in building the house of God at Jerusalem. But he wrote to him as a faithful witness, seeking the everlasting benefit of this heathen king's immortal soul.

He plainly told Hiram that the Lord our God, the Triune Jehovah, is God alone, and declared his greatness as God, saying, "Great is our God above all gods". Solomon explained to Hiram how that God is and must be worshipped by the sacrifice he has ordained and accepted, Christ Jesus, who was represented in all the sacrifices he mentioned in this letter.

Solomon obviously sought to magnify God in Hiram's eyes. He wanted his friend to know God. And, judging by Hiram's response (2 Chronicles 2:11-16), it appears that Solomon's efforts were blessed of God the Holy Spirit to Hiram's conversion and everlasting salvation. I cannot speak with certainty about that; but Solomon the king bore faithful witness to Hiram of God and his greatness. Let us follow his example. Look for and seize every opportunity afforded you, child of God, to tell eternity bound sinners about God our Saviour, the Lord Jesus Christ; about his greatness and his salvation. It may be that God will use you to fetch home his banished ones.

Hiram's Response
"Then Huram the king of Tyre answered in writing, which he sent to Solomon, Because the Lord hath loved his people, he hath made thee king over them". How truly might these words be addressed to our blessed Lord! Because the Lord God loved us, he gave his only-begotten Son, his well-beloved, to be both a Prince and a Saviour. Salvation is in him alone.

God's loving appointment in making Christ our King is apparent when we are made to know and experience his greatness, his glory, and his grace. And when we contemplate how that our Lord Jesus entered into his kingdom and ascended to his throne as our King by the sacrifice of himself in our stead, our hearts are compelled to say of him, "Because the Lord hath loved his people, he hath made thee king over them."

Do you bow to Christ your King, surrendering all to him in love and faith, trusting him for all? You can never know the love of God for his elect until the Lord Jesus sets his throne in your heart and graciously bends and bows you to himself. Then, and only then, the love of God is shed abroad in our hearts by his Spirit.

> O worship the King, all glorious above,
> And gratefully sing his power and his love!
> Our Shield and Defender, the Ancient of Days,
> Pavilioned in splendour and girded with praise!

May 12
Today's Reading: 2 Chronicles 6, 7
"Will God in very deed dwell with men on the earth?"
2 Chronicles 6:18

This was not a question of doubt, or unbelief, but of astonishment. Solomon understood that the temple, the ark of the covenant, and the sacrifices offered to God in that typical age were but the reiteration of the promise God made to our fallen parents in the Garden of Eden. Solomon understood that God's own Son would come to dwell with men upon the earth, that he might redeem and save a people for the praise of his own great and glorious name. Knowing this, Solomon cried out before God in utter astonishment and praise, "Will God in very deed dwell with men on the earth?"

The Incarnation
God the Son, our Lord Jesus Christ, came into this world and has dwelt with men, as a man among men, on the earth to work out the righteousness, redemption, and salvation of his people. "Will God" the Son, our Lord Jesus Christ, "dwell on the earth?" Indeed, he has and he does. This is marvellous in our eyes! This is astonishing indeed (2 Corinthians 8:9). Jesus Christ is God yet he tabernacled upon the earth in our nature (John 1:1, 14).

He is high above all nations, great above all creatures, and exalted above all creation (Philippians 2:9-11; Hebrews 1:4-6). All the angels of God are called upon to worship him, because he is their Creator. All men, good and bad, are subject to him. He dwells, and always has dwelt, in the highest heaven. He "rideth upon the heavens of heavens" (Psalm 68:32-35). He is "over all God, blessed forever". Therefore, he is called, "the Lord from heaven" (1 Corinthians 15:47). Yet, Christ Jesus is that One who came down from heaven to do his Father's will; and he was in heaven while he was here upon the earth doing his Father's will (John 3:13).

He never ceased to be God, though he dwelt upon the earth in human flesh! This is an amazing fact. Jesus Christ, who is God, the Maker of all things, the Ruler of all things, dwelling in the highest heaven, "over all God, blessed forever", came to dwell on the earth!

Covenant Engagements
"Will God indeed dwell on the earth?" Yes! He most certainly will; and he certainly has! But why? Why did God come to dwell upon the earth in human flesh? What was the purpose of the incarnation? Christ came into this world to fulfil the covenant he made with the Father on behalf of his elect before the world began (Hebrews 10:5-17). It was proposed to him in the everlasting covenant that he should assume our nature, dwell upon earth with mortal men as a man, bring in everlasting righteousness for his chosen, and put away the sins of his elect, by the satisfaction of justice by the sacrifice of himself. He agreed to it, and said, "Lo, I come; in the volume of the book it is written of me; I delight to do thy will, O my God" (Psalm 40:7, 8). He came in

human nature, he came into the world, he came to dwell among men to do his Father's will, to obtain redemption for lost sinners.

This was proposed; and to this he agreed. Therefore, he is represented as one, from eternity, rejoicing in the habitable parts of the earth, in which he had agreed to dwell, where those people would dwell for whom he became a Surety and a Saviour. And from everlasting, his delights were with the sons of men (Proverbs 8:22-31).

Finished Work
Remember what the Son of God came into the world to do. He came to work out the salvation of his people, to seek and to save that which was lost. He came to save lost sinners, lost in Adam, so lost that they could never find their way to God. Christ came to save sinners, the worst of sinners, the chief of sinners! He came and dwelt among men upon this earth to save us! And it is written of him, "He shall not fail" (Isaiah 42:4). What did Christ come to do? Here are five things revealed in the Scriptures.

1. The Lord Jesus came to save his people from their sins (Matthew 1:21).
2. The Son of God came to redeem us from the curse of the law (Galatians 3:13; 4:4, 5), to put away sin by the sacrifice of himself!
3. Our Lord Jesus Christ came here to be made sin for us that we might be made the righteousness of God in him (2 Corinthians 5:21).
4. Christ Jesus the Lord came here to redeem unto himself a peculiar people, zealous of good works (Titus 2:14).
5. Our blessed Saviour came to bring many sons to glory (Hebrew 2:10).

When he had finished the work he came here to do, when he had laid down his life for us, "with his own blood he entered in once into the holy place, having obtained eternal redemption for us". After his resurrection from the dead, he was received up into heaven in the sight of all the Apostles. There Stephen saw him standing at the right hand of God. There every believer, by faith, beholds him crowned with glory and honour, at the right hand of the Majesty on high. There he must sit and reign until he has put all his enemies under his feet. Then, at the time of the restitution of all things, he will come again. "To them that look for him, he shall appear the second time, without sin unto salvation" (Hebrews 9:28).

May 13
Today's Reading: 2 Chronicles 8-11
"This thing is done of me"
2 Chronicles 11:4

"Thus saith the Lord ... this thing is done of me". Spirit of God, write these words upon my heart and cause me truly to "know that all things work together for good to them that love God, to them who are the called according to his purpose". Give me grace to see that every event in history and every event, circumstance, and experience of life is accomplished by the will of my God, my heavenly Father, according to his all-wise, all-good purpose of grace for my soul and for all the hosts of God's elect. As we read these inspired Chronicles, let us never fail to remember that in all that is recorded our God was accomplishing his purpose for his elect and performing his will to foreshadow his redemption accomplishments by his Son, our Saviour, the Lord Jesus Christ.

Pharaoh's Daughter

Solomon is held before us as an eminent type of our dear Saviour, the Lord Jesus. His marriage to Pharaoh's daughter was a typical picture of Christ's marriage union with his church, particularly including his elect among the Gentile, as well as his chosen among the Jews. Psalm 45 is called "A Song of Loves". It is a marriage song written by David under the Spirit of Inspiration, and speaks of this marriage of the Lord Jesus Christ to his church. It is commonly thought that the Song of Solomon was written at the time of Solomon's marriage to Pharaoh's daughter. That great song of love gives us a marvellous, instructive display of loves, the love of Christ for his church, and the love of our souls for our great Husband, the Lord Jesus.

Appointed Sacrifices

"Solomon offered burnt offerings unto the Lord on the altar of the Lord ... at a certain rate every day". Every morning and every evening, by divine appointment during the legal dispensation of types and pictures, sacrifices were offered upon God's altar. The morning lamb and the evening lamb were sacrificed daily. At three o'clock in the afternoon (the ninth hour of the day by Jewish reckoning) the evening sacrifice was offered. Why? Because that was the hour, which had been appointed before all worlds, for the offering of the body of our Lord Jesus upon the cross. At the ninth hour, our dear Redeemer cried, "It is finished". At the ninth hour, the whole of redemption was then completed. The Holy Ghost marked this hour in all the evening sacrifices with an eye to our Substitute from the beginning.

Queen Of Sheba

The Queen of Sheba coming to Solomon is a beautifully instructive picture of the chosen, redeemed sinner, taught of God and called by grace, coming to Christ. Solomon's condescension in receiving her portrays our Saviour's great condescending mercy in receiving poor sinners, like you and me, and communing with them. As Solomon told her all, so our Saviour tells us all that our hearts desire of him. How astonished was the queen of the south in that the king of Israel told her all that she desired. But how much more abundantly we are overwhelmed with astonishment when the Lord Jesus opens to us all his grace and shows us all his will, removing all those anxieties and fears that once held us in such great confusion, bondage, and dread!

What are your thoughts of our Almighty Solomon concerning these things? Have you heard, as did the queen of the south, of the fame of our Solomon? Do you come to prove him with hard questions? Have you been with him? Has he, by his Spirit, told you all that is in your heart? Then I do not need to tell you – for you can better tell me

– your astonishment. Surely, you have concluded as she did, the half of Immanuel's greatness and wisdom has not been told; and of his love you had no conception. Go then, as the queen of Sheba went to her country, and spread abroad his fame. Invite thousands and tens of thousands to come to him and prove him for themselves, that he is infinite in council and might. Let the fathers and mothers make known his praise to their sons and daughters, and to their children's children.

May 14
Today's Reading: 2 Chronicles 12-15
"A covenant of salt"
2 Chronicles 13:5

Every sacrifice was to be salted with salt (Mark 9:49). The covenant of salt was a covenant made with a sacrifice. David, speaking prophetically with an eye to Christ, describes God's saints gathered to him in faith by the Spirit of God as "those that have made a covenant with me by sacrifice" (Psalm 50:5). Abijah stood on Mount Zemaraim and declared "that the Lord God of Israel gave the kingdom to David (i.e. Christ) forever by a covenant of salt". God gave his church, his kingdom, all the hosts of his elect, to Christ by an everlasting covenant of grace. He did this through Christ's sacrifice, by which we were made his from eternity, as the Lamb of God slain from the foundation of the world. It is precious to see our Saviour and his salvation portrayed in the general circumstances of his people in the remote history recorded in these Chronicles.

Rehoboam
How many, like Rehoboam, fill up their place in history in vanity! The sum total of their lives is this: they lived, they ate, they drank, and then they died. How sad! Oh, for distinguishing grace to live all our days to the glory of God, to live for Christ, and live to Christ! What can be sweeter and more precious than living in fellowship with the Father and with his Son Jesus Christ? God, grant that this may be my portion. Let nothing take our hearts from our Saviour! In Christ we possess all things. If Christ is ours, we have all and abound, for "Christ is all". If he is ours, we shall be truly happy and blessed with all true riches in time and to all eternity.

Abijah
Abijah, Rehoboam's son, was given a name every son of Adam might covet. Abijah means, "Father Jehovah, or the Lord is my Father". Jeroboam had thrown off the worship of God. Making calves for gods and consecrating the basest of men for priests, he led Israel into rebellion and idolatry. Abijah sternly exposed and pointedly denounced Jeroboam's sin and, in particular, his idolatrous religion. Then he asserted,

"As for us, the Lord is our God, and we have not forsaken him ... God himself is with us for our Captain". In the midst of this declaration, King Abijah identified the observance of God's appointed sacrifice as the distinguishing feature of all true religion. It is faith in Christ, particularly faith in the effectual, sin-atoning sacrifice of our Lord Jesus Christ, that distinguishes true religion from idolatry.

Asa

What a great blessing it would be to any nation to have a king, or a president, or a prime minister like good king Asa, the king of Judah! As soon as he ascended to the throne, he began to abolish all the remnants of idolatry, which had crept in during the latter end of his grandfather Solomon's reign. He re-established in Judah the worship of the Lord God of Israel. He even removed his mother from being queen, "because she had made an idol". God the Holy Spirit tells us that "the heart of Asa was perfect all his days".

God give us grace to follow Asa's godly example. He preferred God's honour to his own mother's pleasure and honour. Love for Christ admits no rivals! Our Saviour said, "He that loveth father or mother more than me is not worthy of me". He who made me, redeemed me, and gives me all grace has the unquestionable right, above all others, to be loved and adhered to by me.

Azariah

Asa was the king. Asa brought about marvellous reforms in Judah. Asa was the man whose name was known everywhere. But God raised up a prophet by the name of Azariah to teach the king the ways of the Lord his God. "How beautiful upon the mountains are the feet of him that bringeth good tidings, that publisheth peace; that bringeth good tidings of good, that publisheth salvation; that saith unto Zion, Thy God reigneth". Blessed are they to whom God sends a man, called, gifted, and anointed by his Spirit, as the ambassador of Christ to his soul, proclaiming the good news of his free grace in the accomplishment of redemption by Christ Jesus the Lord (2 Corinthians 5:17-6:2).

May 15
Today's Reading: 2 Chronicles 16-19
"Asa was wroth with the seer"
2 Chronicles 16:10

What a sad end we have read today of a man whose life had been so remarkably blessed, of a man who had done so much good for the people of God, the truth of God, and the worship of God! "Asa did that which was good and right in the eyes of the Lord his God" (2 Chronicles 14:2). Asa's alliance with the heathen king of Syria,

Benhadad, shockingly displays the proneness of our fallen, corrupt nature to that which is evil. Except the Lord God keep you and me from the evil that is in us by nature, there is no evil to which we will not run. Keep me, my God, from the evil that is in me, for Christ's sake!

God Knows

The words of Hanani the prophet to Asa, if sealed to our hearts by the Spirit of God, will be words of comfort and encouragement to our souls in the face of every trial and adversity. "The eyes of the Lord run to and fro throughout the whole earth, to shew himself strong in the behalf of them whose heart is perfect toward him." How foolish of Asa to forget this great fact! How foolish of us when we forget it! Our God not only predestined all things and knows all things, his eyes run through the earth, not to get information for himself, but to convince us that he who is our God is ever by our side! He is always near at hand to deliver his saints out of all their troubles and temptations.

Prophet Imprisoned

Asa was enraged by the reproof of God's prophet and cast the man who was faithful to his soul, the man who faithfully declared to him the Word of God into prison as a traitor. Asa "was in a rage with" Hanani, because Hanani delivered God's message to him.

Rejecting God's message and his messenger, Asa hardened himself in obstinate rebellion. He oppressed the people to whom he had been such a good ruler. At last, he died, "diseased in his feet". Even in the end, though in what must have been excruciating pain, "he sought not to the Lord, but to the physicians".

The king had imprisoned God's prophet; and now the Lord God made his palace his prison. The prophet's prison was converted to a palace, for the Lord was with him. Asa's palace was turned into a dungeon, for he had not the light of God's countenance. He sought aid from the physician, forgetting that it is the Lord who kills and who makes alive, who brings down to the grave and brings up. Physicians are of no value except the Lord uses them to heal. Asa's funeral was conducted with great pomp. What that dying man might have given in his dying hour for one whisper of grace from the Lord with whom he once walked in sweet communion! All the shouts of men over his unconscious dust could not undo the evil he had performed in his end, or cause any to recall the much greater good he had done for so many years before.

Our Faithful God

We should take these things to heart and beg of God the unfailing supply of his grace that we may be found useful to the end of our days. But Asa's failures and unfaithfulness in his end remind me of something better. "If we believe not, yet he abideth faithful". Like a stubborn child being corrected by his loving father, Asa was put to bed in the dark, yet still a child beloved of his Father. His righteousness before God was not a righteousness he could mar. It was the righteousness of God in Christ Jesus.

O my ever-faithful God, make me faithful to you to the end of my days, for Christ's sake! I am a man like Asa, both flesh and spirit. Who can or will deliver me from this body of death? None, O Christ, but you! None but you, my blessed Saviour!

May 16
Today's Reading: 2 Chronicles 20-22
"Jehoshaphat ... set himself to seek the LORD"
2 Chronicles 20:3

2 Chronicles 20-22 gives us a brief history of the reigns of Jehoshaphat, Jehoram, and Ahaziah. Jehoshaphat was a great, remarkable, godly king; but his sons Jehoram and Ahaziah were reprobate men who walked in the ways of Ahab. Those wicked kings, Jehoshaphat's sons, died "without being desired", but Jehoshaphat "did that which was right in the sight of the Lord". Thus we are again reminded of the fact that grace is not a family possession. It does not run in bloodlines. Sinners obtain God's salvation only by God-given personal faith in the Lord Jesus. "As many as received him, to them gave he power to become the sons of God, even to them that believe on his name: Which were born, not of blood, nor of the will of the flesh, nor of the will of man, but of God" (John 1:12, 13).

Desiring to serve God our Saviour in our generation as Jehoshaphat did in his, let us carry the memory of this man and his conduct, as here given by the Spirit of God, through this day.

Jehoshaphat's Prayer
All Judah stood before the Lord God with their king and joined him in prayer. Men, women, and children; all the nation was led in prayer by their king, and joined him in praying to the Lord God, seeking his mercy and grace.

First, king Jehoshaphat pleaded God's sovereignty. Then he turned Jehovah's covenant relationship with Abraham, his friend, and the covenant engagements as Abraham's God into an argument for present mercies. Next, King Jehoshaphat and Israel together renewed their devotion to God as the objects of his choice, looking to the temple, the mercy-seat, and to Christ represented in those typical things, as Solomon had taught them. The looked to the merits of Christ's blood and righteousness, to the Lamb as the Substitute God had given them and by which they knew they had claim to God's favour.

After stating these things as the ground of their hope and confidence in God's protection, Jehoshaphat presented Israel's need at the time as reason for God's intervention and their deliverance. Throwing himself and his people upon the sovereign goodness of the Lord God, Jehoshaphat and his nation obtained "mercy and grace to help in time of need".

We will be wise to read this prayer as a word of instruction from God the Holy Spirit for us. Salvation in Christ Jesus is by the sovereign mercy of the Triune Jehovah. In everlasting love and infinite wisdom he predestined the salvation of elect sinners. Calling chosen, redeemed sinners like us to life and faith in Christ, the Triune God puts himself into the closest possible covenant-relationship with us. By the blessing of God upon his Word, by God-given eyes of faith, we behold gospel mercies in the finished redemption of Christ shadowed forth in that ancient time. Thank you, blessed Holy Spirit, for showing us the things of Christ in the Book of God.

Jehoshaphat's Victory
King Jehoshaphat's only weapon by which he engaged the heathen who opposed him was God-given faith. Such is ever the weapon of God's church against those who oppose God's cause and God's worship. He went forth depending upon the Lord his God. Believing God, Jehoshaphat began his preparation for battle with a song of victory. So all the soldiers of Christ should go forth against Satan and all that opposes God and our souls. The victories of God's church are not won by sword, nor by the ballot box, nor by vain philosophy, but by the Spirit of God. "Not by might, nor by power, but by my spirit, saith the Lord of hosts " (Zechariah 4:6). If it is in his strength that we fight, the outcome is sure. The battle is, in fact, already over. Christ has conquered, and his people overcome by his blood.

"The battle is not yours, but God's". Judah had no hand in the matter. Applying this piece of history to ourselves, let us rejoice to remember that the gospel of our God declares plainly and forcibly that "salvation is of the Lord". We have no hand in the matter. Our mighty Saviour's right arm has gotten himself the victory. "So then it is not of him that willeth, nor of him that runneth, but of God that sheweth mercy."

Our Refuge
Where shall souls fly for refuge in time of trouble? To our covenant God in Christ. As the children of Ammon and Moab, and the multitudes of foes beyond the sea arose as one in opposition to Jehoshaphat, the world, the flesh and the devil, all the corruptions of our own nature and all the powers of darkness come against our souls day by day. Our very existence in this world is a relentless warfare; and our greatest foes are those within our own evil hearts! Instead of trying to muster human strength, let us, like Jehoshaphat, take refuge in God our Saviour continually, looking to him alone for righteousness and strength, trusting his grace, looking altogether outside ourselves to him for all our salvation!

As God the Holy Ghost gives us grace thus to look to Christ alone for hope, making his blood, his righteousness, his grace our boast, we shall find every place the valley of Berachah, the place of blessing and praise to our God!

Discovering Christ Day By Day

May 17
Today's Reading: 2 Chronicles 23, 24
Athaliah overthrown, God's worship restored
2 Chronicles 24:7

"Babylon is fallen, is fallen; and all the graven images of her gods he hath broken unto the ground" (Isaiah 21:9). "Babylon is suddenly fallen and destroyed" (Jeremiah 51:8). "Babylon is fallen, is fallen, that great city, because she made all nations drink of the wine of the wrath of her fornication" (Revelation 14:8). "Babylon the great is fallen, is fallen, and is become the habitation of devils, and the hold of every foul spirit, and a cage of every unclean and hateful bird"(Revelation 18:2). When I read of Athaliah's overthrow, I am reminded of Babylon and her overthrow. She was called by God the Holy Spirit "that wicked woman". Her sons "broke up the house of God; and also all the dedicated things of the house of the Lord did they bestow upon Baalim". For her wickedness, she was slain with the sword. So all false religion, all the freewill-works, antichrist religion of the great whore Babylon shall be destroyed and the church and kingdom of our God shall be triumphant.

The Covenant
The first thing Jehoiada did in restoring the worship of God was to show that God graciously looks upon his people and remembers his covenant. The covenant he made was made "between him and between all the people, and between the king". It was a covenant made between Jehovah, his people, and his king by Jehoiada his priest. Behold the Lord Jesus, our glorious Head and Mediator, whom Jehoiada typified. Where we expected to find nothing but a simple narrative concerning Judah's history, God the Holy Ghost has given us another beautiful foreshadowing of the Lord Jesus Christ, our Saviour.

Baal Destroyed
Jehoiada's next task was the destruction of Baal and his images. When the hearts of men and women are turned to the Lord God in faith, the destruction of idolatry is immediate. All who love Christ hate his enemies. David declares that this hatred of all who hate our God, the hatred of every false way, is a proof of sincere love and faith (Psalm 139:21; 119:104, 128).

When Baal was destroyed, arrangements were made for the temple service. During the tyranny of that wicked woman Athaliah, idolatry was rampant. Now the Lord Jehovah was worshipped in the beauty of holiness. Then the nation's government was brought into order. The problem with our world is not the corrupt government of the nations, though it appears that all modern governments are the governments of the basest of men. The problem is the idolatry of the church, the idolatrous will-worship of men and women who profess to be worshippers of our God and his Christ. When God is honoured in his house of prayer and true religion prevails in any nation, the people are truly happy and blessed (Psalm 144:15)

209

One Greater

Let us bless God for the mercies he wrought for his Judah, and for the fact that he raised up Jehoiada for the deliverance of his people. As you do, I hope you are compelled to think of that everlasting deliverance wrought for our souls, when God our Father brought forth his dear Son, here typified in Jehoiada, and set him as his King in Zion, declaring the redemption and salvation of his elect in the risen, exalted Christ. That was the everlasting overthrow of Satan's usurpation, tyranny, and power! By our Saviour's exaltation, his kingdom of righteousness and peace was introduced, which shall flourish forever.

Behold, a greater than Jehoiada is here! Our Lord Jesus Christ made a covenant for us in his blood and righteousness. He is himself the whole of the covenant (Isaiah 49:8). He is all the Wisdom, Righteousness, Sanctification and Redemption of his chosen. In and by him, our dear Saviour, we are a people dedicated to God and accepted by God forever!

Joash And Zechariah

Joash gives us a warning. Men and women are often very religious who do not know God and have no grace. Joash was outwardly a very good king, thoroughly devoted to God, until he lost the influence of Jehoiada's good life. But there was rottenness in his soul. Though he led the way in restoring the worship of God, he never worshiped God in his heart. He was a reprobate man. Everything he did he did for Joash. He had no regard for God, his honour, or his Word.

Zechariah stands before us as an example of true faith. Faithful to the end, that good prophet spoke the word of God, and was stoned to death by the very people for whose souls' eternal good he devoted his life. Spirit of God, give me grace, like Zechariah, to be strong in the Lord and in the power of his might, utterly devoting my life to "the testimony of Jesus".

My brother, my sister in Christ, surrounded by that great cloud of witnesses who have gone before us, let us unceasingly beg of God the grace needed to run with patience the race that is set before us, "looking unto Jesus, the author and finisher of our faith".

May 18
Today's Reading: 2 Chronicles 25-27
"The LORD is able to give thee much more than this"
2 Chronicles 25:9

It is never pleasant to lose money; but when the loss comes at the expense of a matter of principle the flesh always rebels. "Why lose that which may be so usefully employed? May not the truth itself be bought too dear? What shall we do without this money? Remember the children and our small income". All these things and a thousand more tempt us to that which is evil, tempt us to compromise deeply held convictions, and tempt us even to abandon the worship of God, when doing that which we know is right involves serious loss. How many I have seen move their families away from the preaching of the gospel and the worship of God in his house for a better paying job!

God's Provision
When we are tempted by the fear of loss or hope of gain to that which we know is contrary to the revealed will of God, may God the Holy Spirit cause these words to ring in our ears. "The Lord is able to give thee much more than this". Our Father holds the purse-strings, and what we lose for his sake he can repay a thousand-fold. It is ours to obey his will. We may rest assured that he will provide for us. A grain of heart-ease is worth more than a ton of gold. God's smile and a dungeon are enough for one who has Christ. His frown and a palace would be hell to a heaven-born soul. Let worst come to worst, let all material goods be forfeited, we have not lost our Treasure. "I have been young, and now am old; yet have I not seen the righteous forsaken, nor his seed begging bread". "The Lord is able to give thee much more than this".

God's Prophets
God's prophets and preachers in all ages have a very painful work. Often their faithful preaching of God's Word brings upon them the hatred of those who hear them; but whether they are loved or hated for their work, faithful men are faithful. Whether the Amaziahs of the present day will hear, or whether they will forbear, God's servants must and will be found faithful. They abide faithful through evil report and good report. The injuries they sustain God will recompense. He that despises them despises God who sent them. In the end God will judge their cause and bring forth their integrity as the light of the noon-day sun. Knowing these things, the Apostle Paul said to the Corinthians, "with me it is a very small thing that I should be judged of you, or of man's judgment".

King Uzziah
When we read that King Uzziah did that which was right in the sight of the Lord, we are to understand it in the same sense as we did of Amaziah. Uzziah kept up a form of religion in the land in opposition to idols; but he only had a form of godliness. The sequel of his life proves he was not a regenerate man. His searching after God was nothing but research into the things of God. Thousands in all ages are like him. They fill their heads with knowledge, though their hearts remain empty and dead (Zechariah 7:5, 6).

Despising God and his Sacrifice (the Lord Jesus Christ), Uzziah invaded the priest's office to the everlasting destruction of his soul. The incense offering typified the Lord Jesus, because none but Christ can approach Jehovah to make intercession and to offer sacrifice for the sins of the people. So Uzziah's daring act, going in himself, with his own offering, displayed his contempt for the way of salvation God has appointed. Who is like Uzziah? All who, being ignorant of the righteousness of

God in Christ, refusing to submit themselves to the righteousness of Christ, presumptuously attempt to approach the holy Lord God in their own righteousness. All such will-worship idolaters are yet plagued with a dreadful leprosy of soul and live in a separate house, without God, and without Christ in the world.

Faith In Christ
Is there one like Uzziah reading these lines? What multitudes there are of lost religionists who count the blood of the covenant an unholy thing and do despite to the Spirit of grace! Having no real sense of their own state by nature, to their own filth, corruption, lusts and universal depravity, totally unconscious of the infinitely precious value of the sin-atoning blood of Christ, they are strangers to themselves, strangers to the Saviour, and strangers to God's grace and salvation in Christ. Blessed are they who, being taught of God, know the necessity of the work of God upon the soul, and the absolute expediency of being washed from the leprosy of sin in the blood of Christ!

I give you praise, my God, from the depths of my soul, for your free and sovereign grace bestowed upon my poor, wretched, sinful soul that caused me to see the preciousness of Christ's blood and your salvation in him! How I thank you for that blessed gift of faith wrought in me by the Holy Spirit that causes me to trust my dear Saviour! Being found in him, I am cleansed from the leprosy of sin and uncleanness and accepted of God by the censer of Christ's perfect righteousness!

Oh, glorious, gracious, precious Lord Jesus, you alone have brought life and immortality to light in my soul by thy gospel! Give me grace to love, trust, and adore you, consecrating my entire life to you today, tomorrow, and forever. Amen.

May 19
Today's Reading: 2 Chronicles 28, 29
"Carry forth the filthiness out of the holy place"
2 Chronicles 29:5

In these two chapters God the Holy Spirit has given us the brief histories of the reprobate idolater, Ahaz, who did everything he could to destroy the worship of God and the souls of all under his influence, and his son, the godly King Hezekiah, who did everything he could to restore and promote the worship and glory of God and the salvation of his elect.

Obed The Prophet
How good and encouraging it is to read in 2 Chronicles 28 that even in the dark days of Ahaz there was a faithful Obed to speak for God, and a faithful remnant, according to the election of grace, who had not departed with their families and their nation from

the worship of God. God never leaves himself without a witness. He always has his elect remnant scattered among the nations. And he always provides his sheep with good shepherds, pastors after his own heart, to feed them with knowledge and understanding.

Ahaz stands before us as a glaring example of the lost, depraved, hardened and wretched state of fallen humanity. How sin has reduced man! How it has robbed us! But, as we are forced here to think of fallen man's sinfulness and worthlessness, let us adore God's grace and his faithfulness. As soon as our father Adam fell and we fell in him, the Lord God promised redemption by his Son. To generation after generation the Lord God sent his faithful servants, like Obed and Isaiah, to keep alive the memory of his promised mercy, assuring his people that redemption was approaching and would appear in and be accomplished by Immanuel, a virgin's child!

King Hezekiah
As we turn the page and read about the reign of Ahaz's son, Hezekiah, we are again reminded that grace is not hereditary. Reprobate fathers sometimes have elect sons, and elect fathers often have reprobate sons. Hezekiah had it put into his heart by the Spirit of God to restore God's worship to Israel and to restore Israel to God. He "did that which was right in the sight of the Lord ... opened the doors of the house of the Lord ... and carried forth the filthiness out of the holy place".

His charge to the priests and Levites was a charge that every gospel preacher should take to himself as a charge from God. "My sons, be not now negligent: for the LORD hath chosen you to stand before him, to serve him, and that ye should minister unto him, and burn incense". As we stand in God's house preaching the gospel of Christ, let us be found faithful, knowing that as we serve his people, we "minister unto him" and "stand before him".

Temple Cleansed
Hezekiah's cleansing of the temple reminds me of the gracious work of God the Holy Ghost in cleansing the hearts of chosen sinners by "the washing of regeneration" (Titus 3:5), washing "away the filth of the daughter of Zion with the spirit of judgment and the spirit of burning" (Isaiah 4:4).

In the solemn service performed "according to the commandment of the Lord by his prophets", everything pointed to our Lord Jesus Christ and his sacrifice for us as the Lamb of God. The sin-offering represented Christ our Saviour who was made sin for us that we might be made the righteousness of God in him. The king and the people laid their hands upon the goats, ceremonially transferring their sins and their guilt to the innocent victim to be sacrificed. Blessed Spirit of God, let me never forget, not even for a moment, the thing here typified. The Lord God really made all the sins and all the guilt of his people to be our Redeemer's. "The Lord hath laid on him the iniquity of us all." "For he hath made him to be sin for us, who knew no sin; that we might be made the righteousness of God in him."

May 20
Today's Reading: 2 Chronicles 30-32
"Christ our passover is sacrificed for us"
1 Corinthians 5:7

When Hezekiah was made king in Judah, "he opened the doors of the house of the Lord and repaired them". But the time appointed by God to keep the passover was already over. Unwilling to allow that blessed service to go unobserved for another year, good King Hezekiah availed himself of permission given in the law of God (Numbers 9:10, 11) for those who could not keep it in the first month because of uncleanness to do so in the second. Remember, the Lord's passover sacrifice and the feast accompanying it typified Christ our Passover and his great sacrifice for our sins upon the cursed tree.

As the Old Testament passover anticipated our Saviour's sacrifice of himself for us, the Lord's Supper in this gospel day commemorates it. As often as we eat the bread and drink the wine of the Lord's Table we "show the Lord's death till he come". Every Lord's Day local churches in this gospel age observe this blessed ordinance. And we who are made kings and priests unto God by Christ Jesus carry in our bodies "the dying of the Lord Jesus, that the life also of Jesus might be made manifest in our body" day by day.

One Heart
Hezekiah sent word both to Judah and to Israel, calling all who named Jehovah as their God to keep the passover at Jerusalem, as God commanded. He called all who claimed to be God's to join him in the worship of God, looking with the eye of faith to "Christ our passover". Both Israel and Judah had revolted; and both were called to return to the Lord, promising that if they would return to him, they would find that "the Lord your God is gracious". Many of the people laughed the messengers to scorn and mocked them; but some "humbled themselves and came to Jerusalem" to keep the feast. And we are told that God gave them "one heart" to worship him.

What great mercy it is that the church of God; sinners saved by grace out of every nation, kindred, tribe and tongue, worships with one heart at God's Altar, Christ Jesus, keeping the gospel feast by God-given faith!

People Healed
As they worshipped God, "the Lord healed the people". They prepared their hearts to seek the Lord; and they found God's grace ready to heal their souls. Before proceeding to keep the feast, idolatry was put away. The people who would worship God must first destroy every altar to every false god. So too, if we would keep the feast of faith, the old leaven of malice and wickedness must be put away (1 Corinthians 5:7, 8). There is no perfecting of holiness in the fear of God, no faith in Christ, among the multitudes who refuse to come out of Babylon. We cannot worship at the altar of freewill and the altar of free grace (2 Corinthians 6:14-7:1).

Hezekiah asked the Lord God to pardon and to accept the people; and God heard the king's prayer, healing all who sought his face. What sweet gospel works are here displayed! How precious, how infinitely precious is the thought suggested by this. There is an infinite, perpetual sin-atoning efficacy in Christ our Passover who was sacrificed for us at Calvary! The merit and virtue of his precious blood sanctifies our poor souls perpetually, giving us acceptance with the holy Lord God and healing all our souls' diseases.

Everything Sanctified
In Christ everything is sanctified. Even the most ordinary enjoyments of life are sanctified in him. The Lord God who blessed us with all spiritual blessings in Christ Jesus has made a covenant with everything on our behalf. He blesses his people in their basket and in their store. If Christ is yours, all things are yours. The Lord Jesus promises, "he that overcometh shall inherit all things; and I will be his God; and he shall be my son".

"Go thy way, eat thy bread with joy, and drink thy wine with a merry heart, for God now accepteth thy works." The garment we wear before our God is the righteousness of Christ. It is always white. And the believing sinner lacks no ointment, because the Holy Ghost sheds abroad the love and grace of God in Christ Jesus continually (Hosea 2:18-20).

At the close of the feast, the priest blessed the people according to the commandment of God (Numbers 6:22-26), with the promise of God attending the blessing (Numbers 6:27). Let every believing sinner take this word from God to his heart; apply it to every part of your life. "I will bless them." Rejoice and give thanks, Oh, my soul!

May 21
Today's Reading: 2 Chronicles 33, 34
Manasseh and Amon
Romans 9:18

"Therefore hath he mercy on whom he will have mercy, and whom he will he hardeneth." When the Lord God showed Moses his glory, he showed him his sovereignty and his grace, declaring, "I will be gracious to whom I will be gracious, and will shew mercy on whom I will shew mercy". It is the glory of God to have mercy on whom he will have mercy. Nowhere is this fact more clearly displayed than it is in the lives of Judah's three kings: Manasseh, Amon and Josiah. May God the Holy Spirit inscribe upon our hearts the lessons he intends for us to learn from this family as their lives are set before us in 2 Chronicles 33 and 34.

Manasseh
What abundant grace there is in our God! What mercy there is flowing out to sinners from the Triune Jehovah, of whom the prophet said, "He delighteth in mercy"! What efficacy there is for poor needy sinners in the blood and righteousness of our Lord Jesus Christ! What irresistible power and grace there is in God the Holy Ghost to save sinners! It matters not how high-handed, how indescribably evil, or how brazenly obstinate sinners are; the grace of God so infinitely transcends our offences that none are beyond the reach of God's omnipotent mercy and saving grace. Never are these facts more clearly revealed than in the salvation of Judah's wicked King Manasseh. Truly, the fact of Manasseh's salvation by our God is intended to teach us that "where sin abounds grace doth much more abound"!

Manasseh was the monstrously ungodly son of a very godly man. "Manasseh made Judah and the inhabitants of Jerusalem to err, and to do worse than the heathen, whom the Lord destroyed before the children of Israel." Never was there a king upon a throne more wretched and vile than Manasseh. Yet, he obtained mercy. He is set before us in the scriptures as an instructive picture and illustration of the grace of God.

Manasseh's name means "forgetfulness". He forgot the example of his father, Hezekiah, the Word of God's prophet, his grandfather, Isaiah, and the counsel of his mother, Hephzibah. And he forgot the Lord his God. But God never forgot Manasseh! Manasseh was loved of God from eternity, chosen and ordained to be a miracle and monument of mercy, a trophy of his grace. God the Holy Spirit holds Manasseh before us as an example of what God does for sinners when he saves them by his free grace in Christ.

Amon
The short, sinful life of Amon, terminating as it did in a violent death, serves to remind us of the wretchedness and hopelessness of all men by nature. "For yet a little while, and the wicked shall not be: yea, thou shalt diligently consider his place, and it shall not be" (Psalm 37:10). Contemplating the lives of Manasseh and his son Amon, we are again reminded that grace is sovereignly dispensed according to God's will. God has mercy on whom he will have mercy; and whom he will he hardens. How thankful saved sinners ought to be for God's sovereign goodness.

Manasseh deserved God's wrath as fully as his son Amon; but God had mercy on Manasseh! Manasseh was, in great measure, the cause of his son's ruin. He spent most of his life leading his son to hell; but God had mercy on Manasseh!

By our sin, we destroy ourselves, ruin our friends, and lead those nearest and dearest to us in evil. As a rule, the wicked terminate their existence in vanity and vexation of spirit. But think, Oh, my soul, what a miracle of grace it is when any, like Manasseh, are delivered out of the snare of the devil, who were once taken captive by him at his will! O my God, I thank you for your intervening, sovereign, saving mercy, so richly and freely bestowed upon my wretched soul in Christ Jesus!

May 22
Today's Reading: 2 Chronicles 35-Ezra 1
Restoring the worship of God
2 Chronicles 34:8

What a timely reading we have before us in these chapters! Everything here speaks to us about the great need of our day. May God the Holy Spirit inscribe the message of these chapters upon our hearts. In the eighteenth year of his reign good King Josiah began "to repair the house of the Lord his God".

It was once said, "We ought to take a big, black paint brush and paint 'Ichabod' (the glory of God has departed) on the door of the church in this age". God has done just that. The most proper and fitting name for the professed church of this day is "Ichabod"! The glory of God has departed from it. That was exactly the situation in Judah in Josiah's day.

Both Israel and Judah had departed from the true worship of God. The temple was deserted and laid in ruins. Evil kings had reigned, and covetous priests and prophets had led the people into all forms of idolatry, turning the hearts of Israel and Judah away from the living God.

Josiah
Then this young man, Josiah, was made king. They crowned him king of Judah when he was just eight years old. When he was sixteen years old, he "began to seek after the God of David". And when he was twenty years old, Josiah began purging idolatry from Judah and Jerusalem, destroying the idols, the groves, the priests, and the sodomites, whose numbers are always multiplied by idolatry. By the time he was twenty-six years old, he had purged the land of idolatry and began "to repair the house of the Lord his God". Josiah was determined to follow the God of his fathers. He was determined to restore the worship of God in his day.

Josiah ordered the idols to be destroyed and the reprobate priests to be put to death. He sent word for the temple to be cleaned out and the worship of God to be restored.

Book Found
While they were cleaning out the temple, Hilkiah the priest found a Book, a most important Book. This was the Word of God written by Moses. This Book was "the Book of the law of the Lord God given by Moses". Hilkiah the priest found the Book, the Word of God, dusted it off and brought the Word of God to the young king Josiah. Hilkiah the priest and Shaphan the scribe brought this Book, the Word of God, to this young king Josiah.

He had never read the Word of God. He had never even heard anyone read it. "And it came to pass when the king heard the words of the Lord", when they read the Scriptures to him, "he rent his clothes". Then he said to the priest, "Go, enquire of the

LORD for me, and for them that are left in Israel and in Judah, concerning the words of the book that is found: for great is the wrath of the LORD that is poured out upon us, because our fathers have not kept the word of the LORD, to do after all that is written in this book."

Today's Religion
It must be acknowledged, it must be confessed, "Our fathers and our church leaders have not taught, nor preached the words of this Book". The religion of this age, I am talking about professed Christianity, no more resembles New Testament Christianity and the church of the New Testament than a brothel resembles chastity! The churches, preachers, and religious leaders of this age have neglected the Word of the Lord. What God has written has been lost and ignored in all the ceremonies of religion, in all of the customs and rituals and traditions. The entertainment and foolishness that go on in the name of religion today would make the prophets of Baal blush with shame. The most contemptible thing in this apostate religious world is its religion! You know that and I know it.

Our Lord said, "God is Spirit and they who worship him must worship him in Spirit and in truth." Will we ever return in our churches to the worship of God? Today, preaching the Gospel and preaching the Word of God has been literally pushed aside to make room for every imaginable thing. Will we ever return in our churches to the worship of God? Only if the Lord God is pleased to restore the preaching of the gospel and pour out his Spirit upon us.

False Gospel
What is more, when today's religion does get around to talking about God, the Lord Jesus, the Spirit of God, salvation, grace, or righteousness, everything taught in its freewill, works creed is contrary to the Book of God. Paul warns us in 2 Corinthians 11 and Galatians 1 that men will come preaching another Jesus. They will come preaching another spirit and another gospel. And the preachers of this day preach another god, another Jesus, another spirit, and another gospel. I have no hesitation in saying that most of what is going on today in the name of God is another gospel. It is another spirit and it is another Jesus. It is not at all the gospel of God's grace and mercy. It is not glorifying to God and it is not exalting to our Lord Jesus Christ. As a result almost everyone you know is religious, but virtually no one knows Christ!

That which passes for worship today is not the worship of God; and that which passes for the gospel is not the gospel of God. May God give us wisdom, boldness, and grace in our day such as he gave to King Josiah to repair the house of God and restore the worship of God.

May 23
Today's Reading: Ezra 2, 3
"His mercy endureth for ever"
Ezra 3:11

Though Ezra 1 was included in our reading schedule yesterday, I purposefully omitted any comment on that chapter in yesterday's meditation because I thought it better to keep our thoughts on the book of Ezra together. As we read these ten chapters and meditate upon them over the next few days, I remind you that we should be on the lookout in each chapter and verse for our Lord Jesus, of whom the whole book of Ezra and all the Book of God speaks. Only as we see Christ in the Scriptures are they profitable to our souls and able by the blessing of God the Holy Ghost to make us wise unto salvation.

This is he of whom Moses and the prophets did write. This is he whose day the patriarchs saw and in whom they rejoiced in hope. And this is he for whose sake Jehovah declared himself to Cyrus two hundred years before Cyrus was born that he had called him by name and commissioned him to deliver (Isaiah 45:14). This is he whose redemption we must have, to whom the fathers looked in faith, whose faith we follow, considering the end of their conversation, Jesus Christ, the same yesterday, and today, and forever.

Cyrus
The book of Ezra opens with the proclamation of Cyrus, king of Persia, to permit the Jews to return from their captivity in Babylon to Jerusalem. The beginning of Cyrus' reign was the end of Israel's seventieth year in Babylonian captivity; and their deliverance by Cyrus at God's appointed time both confirmed the Word of God concerning the time of Jerusalem's desolation (Jeremiah 25:11, 12), and typified the deliverance of our souls in God's salvation by our Lord Jesus Christ.

God called Cyrus his anointed (Isaiah 45:1) to call our attention to the fact this man was raised up as a special type of our Lord Jesus Christ, Jehovah's Anointed, whom he raised up from everlasting to deliver his prisoners out of prison, and them that sat in darkness out of the prison house (Isaiah 45:4-7).

Captives Returned
Ezra 2 lists the names of those captives who were returned to Jerusalem after their seventy year captivity in Babylon. Though cast down for their sins, they were not cast off by God. Jehovah was still their God; and his covenant engagements were not broken. Interpret this spiritually. It speaks of God's elect, the true children of promise in Christ. We are the children of God. Our record is on high. Our names are written in heaven, in the Lamb's book of life. As Israel was saved and brought home, because of God's covenant promises to Abraham, everlastingly certain and sure are the covenant engagements of Jehovah with his dear Son. Every chosen one purchased and forgiven by the precious blood of Christ shall be brought home to God, "because his mercy endureth forever".

219

God's Altar
Though they were poor, though they were surrounded by countless foes, though they lived in perilous times, these captives set free set up God's altar at Jerusalem, offered sacrifices according to the law, and worshipped the Lord God who had preserved them in captivity and set them free at the appointed time of love. Let us in these dark days and perilous times follow their example. "We have an altar" forever established by God himself, by whom we draw near to God. Our Altar is God's own Son, Jesus Christ our Saviour. He is the sum and substance of every altar, sacrifice and priest, the temple, its foundation and top-stone, brought forth with shoutings of grace, grace unto it. On this Altar alone we lay ourselves and our sacrifices. On this Altar alone we worship God. On this Altar alone we are accepted of God, and accepted forever, "because his mercy endureth forever".

May 24
Today's Reading: Ezra 4-6
"The LORD had made them joyful"
Ezra 6:22

Our reading today begins with the sad pause of the people in building the temple, a pause caused by their enemies, and ends with the joyful celebration of the passover in the dedication of the house of God. The adversaries of God's people spoke of them reproachfully, falsely accusing them of insurrection, rebellion, and sedition. We must not be surprised when that happens to us. Such has been and must be the lot of God's saints in this world.

The Enemy
As it is now, so it was in Ezra's day. The reproach came from people who professed to be followers of Jehovah. The slanders and reproaches cast upon them were cast upon them by people of a mongrel religion, people who professed to call upon the name of the Lord, and yet served other idol gods. In every age, and in every place the greatest enemies with which believing souls must contend are not open infidels, but those who profess to believe and worship God. Profess to worship Christ while practising will-worship, despising the gospel of God's free and sovereign grace in Christ, and effectively "denying the only Lord God and our Lord Jesus Christ".

Our Lord Jesus told us plainly that a man's foes are those of his own household (Matthew 10:36). So it is. So it has been. In a spiritual sense, we have foes even greater and nearer than these. Our own hearts, so full of sin and unbelief, and the vile corruptions of our fallen nature constantly oppose us in our walk with God and our service to his kingdom. But, blessed be our God and Saviour, he has promised that we

220

shall prevail at last. God's house shall be completed. His holy temple shall be finished. All his elect shall be saved!

Work Ceased
"Then ceased the work of the house of God". Yet, history plainly proves that the hand of the Lord was in it. How often we think the work of God in our souls has ceased; and we mourn with heaviness of heart. Then our Saviour returns, graciously grants us a little refreshing, and makes us joyful. He has his set time to favour Zion. He is everlastingly pursuing the designs of his love. As Zion's walls were continually before him, even in her most desolate circumstances, so the work of his grace in the hearts of his chosen he never ceases to perform, though it may seem to us that he does.

Work Sure
At such times, our Saviour is, by this very means, emptying us of self and working in our souls, causing us to seek him and his grace. It is by these things, so bitter in the experience, that our great God and Saviour sweetly turns our hearts heavenward. Destroying all creature confidence, he forces us to look to him for everything and causes us to "cry unto the Lord". Then, he appears again in the revelation of his goodness. Then, how sweet the experience! "When the Lord shall build up Zion, he shall appear in his glory" (Psalm 102:16). Be assured, child of God, that "He which hath begun a good work in you will perform it until the day of Jesus Christ" (Philippians 1:6).

Blessed Son of God, are these the lessons you teach us in the deadness, emptiness, and barrenness of soul that makes us groan? Oh, for grace to cease from self and have my whole heart and soul fixed upon you, in whom alone is all righteousness, grace, redemption, and fulness! Ever make me to know my weakness, my Redeemer, for when I am most weak in myself, then, I am most strong in you and in the power of your might.

May 25
Today's Reading: Ezra 7-9
Salt without measure
Ezra 7:22

Take a careful look at the great bounty heaped upon Ezra, God's priest, the ready scribe, raised up and appointed by God to lead his people in rebuilding the temple at Jerusalem. Artaxerxes, the heathen king of Persia, ordered that his treasurers supply Ezra and the people of God with everything they needed to do the work God sent them to perform (Ezra 7:21-26). Did that idolatrous heathen monarch assist the cause of God and the people of God? Surely there is bread for our souls here.

Great Wonder
John saw a wonder in heaven when he saw the earth helping the woman (Revelation 12:16). This is truly a wonder that can be explained only by the sovereign grace and distinguishing goodness of our God! Wicked men are often made the unwitting instruments by which God accomplishes his good purpose of grace in predestination for his people, causing the reprobate to accomplish the very reverse of what they intend. The sons of Jacob intended to ruin Joseph, but only exalted him. So, too, when the Jews, full of envy, malice, and barbaric cruelty, crucified the Lord of life and glory, they became the instruments to accomplish the very purpose for which God created the world, the redemption of our souls by the precious blood of his dear Son (Acts 2:23).

How we ought to admire and adore the Lord God of Abraham, Isaac, and Jacob for the wonderful change he wrought in the minds of Artaxerxes and his princes, causing them to favour the cause of God and his people so highly. Not only was Ezra given authority to take with him all who were inclined by the Spirit of God to go up to Jerusalem, he was supplied with money and materials so liberally that he was able to perform all that God required at Persia's expense! More than that. Artaxerxes imposed upon all his subjects complete obedience to Ezra, requiring them to do whatever Ezra demanded to build again the house of God! "The king's heart is in the hand of the LORD, as the rivers of water: he turneth it whithersoever he will" (Proverbs 21:1). "Surely the wrath of man shall praise thee: the remainder of wrath shalt thou restrain" (Psalm 76:1).

Salt And Grace
Salt was used in every offering made by fire unto the Lord. Because of its preserving and purifying properties, it was an emblem of divine grace in the soul. When Artaxerxes supplied Ezra the priest with everything needed to build the house of God at Jerusalem, he gave him "salt without measure". And when the King of kings distributes grace to his chosen, among his royal priesthood, he gives grace without measure. "That as sin hath reigned unto death, even so might grace reign through righteousness unto eternal life by Jesus Christ our Lord" (Romans 5:21).

He who gathers manna is free to gather all he desires. Though there is often famine in ours poor souls, there is never a famine in God's Jerusalem. God's children are never required to eat their bread by weight and drink their water by measure. Some things are measured to us; but not our blessings.

Our vinegar and gall are given us with such exactness that we never have a single drop too much, but of the salt of grace no stint is made. "Ask what ye will, and it shall be done unto you" (John 15:7). Our God is never niggardly in his gifts. Parents must hide candies and sweets from their children, lest they overindulge themselves; but salt may be left on the table. Few children will eat too much salt. And though we may get too much money or too much honour, we cannot have too much grace. When Jeshurun waxed fat in the flesh, "he forsook God and lightly esteemed the Rock of Israel" (Deuteronomy 32:15). But there is no fear of anyone becoming too full of grace. An excess of grace is impossible. More wealth brings more care; but more grace brings more joy. Increasing wisdom brings increasing sorrow; but abundance of grace is fulness of joy. Therefore, grace and peace and mercy and love are always multiplied to God's elect, never subtracted and never divided, just multiplied (1 Peter 1:2; 2 Peter 1:2; Jude 2).

Child of God, go to the throne for a large supply of heavenly salt. It will season your afflictions, lest they be unsavoury to you. It will preserve your heart, which corrupts if salt is absent. And it will drive away sin as salt drives away reptiles. We need much salt. So seek much and have much (Hebrews 4:16).

May 26
Today's Reading: Ezra 10-Nehemiah 2
"We have trespassed against our God"
Ezra 10:2

What a remarkable man of faith Ezra was! What a great leader God gave his people in this man Ezra. Believing God, he was ashamed to ask for the help of the king and the protection of the king's soldiers against the enemy. O my God give me grace to follow Ezra's example! If we believe God, we ought to be ashamed to seek, let alone crave the help of man.

My Confession
Yet, when Ezra prayed for the people, confessing the sins of the nation, he began by confessing his own sin. Have I not reason to do the same? Going astray from my mother's womb, speaking lies, I sought and formed strange alliances with anything and everything opposed to God all my life. Never would I have put away those strange wives of Babylon had not the Lord Jesus, like another Ezra, have come with grace in his lips and love in his heart, and by his Holy Spirit convinced me of sin, of righteousness, and of judgment. He, by omnipotent mercy, cut me off from everything I chose, divorced me from the wicked objects of my ardent devotion, betrothed me to himself, and made me forever his!

How I thank you, my God, my Saviour, my omnipotent, ever-merciful Bridegroom, that you would not take "no" for an answer from me; but graciously forced yourself upon me, and sweetly forced me into your arms of mercy by your all-conquering love! Yes, our Maker is our Husband. The Lord of Hosts is his name.

One Concern
As we leave Ezra and enter Nehemiah, we are again met with the brief, historic records of a small remnant left in captivity in great affliction and reproach. The men and women who make up this small remnant are, to all natural appearance, utterly

223

insignificant. Compared with other nations, Israel and Judah are nothing. Yet, the histories recorded by God upon the pages of divine Inspiration give no consideration to any other nation. In fact, the great nations of the earth, the vast empires of the world are not even mentioned in the Book of God, except as the recorded history of God's church is mixed with the truly insignificant history of the world.

Pharaoh, Artaxerxes, and Nebuchadnezzar, Egypt, Persia, and Babylon are never even mentioned in the Word of God, except in a collateral way as having some connection or interaction with the people of God. Those mighty, flourishing kingdoms, those monarchs who terrified the world, all the world's great philosophers, all the rich and mighty people of the earth are glossed over in Holy Scripture almost as though they never existed, as if they were totally insignificant. Why?

In the language of Scripture, "Behold, the nations are as a drop of a bucket, and are counted as the small dust of the balance: behold, he taketh up the isles as a very little thing" (Isaiah 40:15). Learn, Oh my soul, learn this lesson. Holy Spirit of God, write it upon my heart. The only nation of concern to God is his church, that holy nation of his redeemed, his elect, "the Israel of God". All other nations and all other people exist only to serve the interest of the nation. Ham exists only to serve Shem and Japheth. O blessed, free, distinguishing grace! "Happy art thou, O Israel; who is like unto thee, O people saved by the Lord."

May 27
Today's Reading: Nehemiah 3-5
"They fortified Jerusalem"
Nehemiah 3:8

"Eliashib the high priest rose up with his brethren the priests, and they builded the sheep gate; they sanctified it, and set up the doors of it; even unto the tower of Meah they sanctified it, unto the tower of Hananeel". The high priest was first to put his hand to the work of the Lord. Thus Eliashib shows us that God's servants must lead by example, and that faithful men are faithful labourers. God's servants labour in the Word and in the doctrine of Christ. Eliashib was also typical of our Lord Jesus, our great High Priest. His almighty hand is and must be first with all spiritual builders. "Except the LORD build the house, they labour in vain that build it" (Psalm 127:1).

God's Zion
In the repairing of the walls of Jerusalem we should look beyond the letter of the Word and remember that Jerusalem is the city of the great King. Abraham's physical seed represent God's elect, those people God has taken into covenant with himself. Jerusalem's walls were laid waste. Her enemies entered in by her gates. She was carried into captivity by her foe. By whom was this done? Why was it done? Jeremiah

tells us, "He that scattered Israel will gather him, and keep him, as a shepherd doth his flock". The Lord God always looks after Zion. He comforts her and sustains her. His word to his church in every age is, "At that time will I bring you again, even in the time that I gather you: for I will make you a name and a praise among all people of the earth, when I turn back your captivity before your eyes, saith the Lord" (Zephaniah 3:20).

Recovered By Christ
The recovery of Israel from her Babylonian captivity and the rebuilding of Jerusalem and her temple are meaningless pieces of history to our souls, until we see what these things represented, typified, and foreshadowed. The whole Babylonian captivity and the recovery of Israel and Judah from it by divine intervention speaks of our recovery by Christ from the captivity of sin and Satan. It speaks of the building of his church, and of our great Saviour bringing the redeemed of the Lord home to Zion with songs of everlasting joy upon their heads.

Looking beyond this world to the world to come, we are moved of God in reading this portion of Israel's history to contemplate that great day, appointed from everlasting, when all things are finished. When the Lord has finished building Zion, his glory will fill his house forever. In that great, eternal day, our God will make every child of grace a praise among all people; having forever turned back our captivity, the God of peace will bruise Satan under our heels to the praise of the glory of his grace!

Our Help
We are building for eternity, and there are many foes. Let us learn, as Nehemiah did, where our strength is found and from whence our help comes. If we are built upon Christ, the Sure Foundation, if God the Holy Spirit will give us rest upon this precious Corner Stone, the promise is sure; we shall never be ashamed, nor confounded, world without end.

Is Christ your foundation? Do you rest your soul on him? Do you lay the whole weight of your salvation on him? Do you live upon him? Do you live to him? These are heart-searching questions. But if the Lord God enables you to build upon Christ, depend upon it, in defiance of all opposition, he who has begun a good work in you will perform it until the top-stone is brought home and laid in its place with shoutings, and crying, "Grace, grace unto it". Let a thousand Sanballats arise, or ten thousand Tobiahs mock; he that is with us, is more and greater than all who are against us!

Go on, my brother, go on, my sister, in the strength of the Lord, crying out in the words of the prophet, "Who art thou, O great mountain? Before our Zerubbabel thou shalt become a plain" (Zechariah 4:7).

225

May 28
Today's Reading: Nehemiah 6, 7
"I am doing a great work, so that I cannot come down"
Nehemiah 6:3

Nehemiah 6 describes Sanballat's opposition to and persecution of God's servant Nehemiah and his people. It also describes God's gracious intervention on behalf of his own to deliver them from the designs and devices of their foes. Chapter 7 describes the government of Jerusalem under Nehemiah and gives us the genealogy of those who first returned from Babylon. Blessed Holy Spirit, inscribe upon our hearts the things of Christ in these chapters you would have us to learn this day.

Satan's Rage
Satan's rage against Christ and his church is manifest in all times and in all places; but it is manifest in different ways. Sanballat and Tobiah first showed their contempt for Nehemiah and his cause with ridicule and laughter. They laughed and said the work was so meaningless and worthless that a little fox could easily undo it. When ridicule failed, under pretence of kindness, they invited Nehemiah to a conference, intending to do him some mischief. Then Nehemiah had to endure slander. He, and with him God's church, was accused of things he concocted from his own depraved heart. Nehemiah said, "thou feignest them out of thine own heart". Such are Satan's devices against the spiritual building of God's house. Satan is a subtle foe. By private fraud, and by open opposition, as best suits his hellish policy, he attacks God's people. Let us ever be aware of his devices! As the Lord God intervened for Nehemiah and his people then, so he intervenes for us today to deliver the godly out of the snare of the devil. One of the sweetest, most pleasant experiences of life for a child of God is to watch God's deliverances. No doubt, we are unaware of most of our Lord's interventions on our behalf; but those that are known to us are more precious than gold.

Jerusalem's Safety
Jerusalem's safety and the means Nehemiah zealously adopted to preserve her from the foe ought to remind us of our almighty Governor, the Lord Jesus. When he returned to the court of heaven, having finished salvation for us by his own blood and righteousness, he set watchmen upon the walls of his Zion, poured out his Spirit, and gave his church pastors according to his own heart, a perpetually standing ministry to maintain the safety and security of his redeemed ones. By the direction and power of God the Holy Ghost, those divinely appointed watchmen keep the doors of his house night and day. Those faithful men of God will give the Lord Jehovah neither rest nor peace, until he has made Jerusalem a praise in the earth.

Too Important
When Sanballat, Tobiah, Geshem, and the Jews' enemies heard that Nehemiah was being used of God to build the walls of Jerusalem, that there was no breach left in the

wall, they were determined to undermine the work, destroy Nehemiah's usefulness, and destroy the work God raised him up to perform. Sanballat and Geshem sent word to God's servant, calling him to come down from the work Jehovah had entrusted to his hands and meet with them.

These men were not interested in Nehemiah, his work, the glory of God, the people of God, or the house of God. They had no interest except themselves. Therefore, they tried to do Nehemiah mischief by getting him to come down to them. Nehemiah was not taken by their snare. He refused to stoop to the level of his foes. He would not come down to them. His reasoning was magnificent. "I am doing a great work, so that I cannot come down: why should the work cease, whilst I leave it, and come down to you?"

Every servant of God in every age would be wise to follow Nehemiah's example. I say to every man called of God to preach the gospel, let no one turn you aside from the work to which God has called you. There is no work on this earth so great, so needful, so magnificent as the preaching of the gospel of Christ. It is ours to seek the Lord's sheep, to bring Christ to sinners and bring sinners to Christ, to serve God's elect, to build his church and his kingdom. We must devote ourselves entirely to this great work, and renew that devotion with every rising sun, for there are many devices by which Satan would call us down from the wall; and he makes them all appear to be both legitimate and needful.

Controversies arise, and we feel compelled to put them down. Why? We try to convince ourselves and others that it is for the glory of God. But if nothing is to be gained for the good of men's souls, if nothing is brought forward to comfort and edify God's saints, if nothing is done for the salvation of poor, lost sinners, how is God glorified? Leave the controversies alone and preach the gospel.

Another ploy of the devil is slander. When wicked men, like Sanballat, feign out of their own wicked hearts (Nehemiah 6:9) slanderous accusations against you, ignore them. Do not attempt to defend the honour of your name. Our business is the honour of God's name. You can never defend yourself from the assaults of men without leaving the work God has entrusted to your hands, without laying aside the work of the gospel, prayer and study to do so.

How many Satan has pulled off the wall of service in the cause of Christ by "the cares of this world, and the deceitfulness of riches, and the lusts of other things" (Mark 4:19). The children need more things, your wife needs more attention or you crave property, financial security, or a little ease of life, those legitimate things other men pursue. All those things you can have, if you want them; but not without coming down and leaving the work God has given you.

May 29
Today's Reading: Nehemiah 8-10
"So they read in the book in the law of God distinctly,
and gave the sense, and caused them to understand the reading"
Nehemiah 8:8

Nehemiah 8 is an inspired record of the Word of God being read, interpreted, and preached. There is much to be learned from it. While chapters 9 and 10 are full of instruction for our souls, in our day nothing is more contemptible than the flippant, casual way people interpret Holy Scripture and that which is called preaching. So I call your attention and my own to this great work, this work upon which God himself has ordained that the salvation of his elect, the building of his church, and the edification of his saints, depends.

Interpreting Scripture
It is not necessary to know the ancient languages to accurately interpret the Bible. God has given us his Word in our own language. Only two things are necessary for an accurate interpretation of Holy Scripture: faith and honesty. We must believe what God says, subjecting our reason, opinions, and emotions to the revelation of God in the Scriptures. And we must interpret the Word of God with honesty. An honest interpretation of God's Word is a contextual interpretation. Three things are involved in an honest, contextual interpretation of the scriptures.

1. Context. Everything revealed in the Scriptures must be interpreted by the context in which it is given. It is dishonest to take a man's words out of context, much more so to take God's words out of context. Every word, phrase, verse, and chapter of the Bible must be interpreted in the light of its context. I mean it must be interpreted in the light of its immediate context, and in the light of the whole Book of Divine Revelation, "Knowing this first, that no prophecy of the scripture is of any private interpretation" (2 Peter 1:20).

2. Plain Statements. We must build our doctrine upon the plain statements of Holy Scripture and upon the whole Volume of Inspiration. We must not form our doctrine by logic or tradition, and then seek to find "proof texts" for the doctrine we have built. And we must not build our doctrine upon isolated portions of scripture. We build our doctrine upon the whole testimony of God.

3. Place Explained. If we would know the truth of God concerning any subject, we must go to that place in the Scriptures where that specific subject is explained by an inspired writer. If you want to know what the Bible says about baptism, you must not go to Acts 2:38, but to Romans 6. If you want to know what the Bible teaches about marriage and divorce, you must not go to Romans 7:1-4, but to 1 Corinthians 7. If you want to know what God has to say about his purpose of grace, you do not go to John 3:16, but to Ephesians 1, Romans 8, 9, and 10. Honesty compels a man who seeks to know the truth of God to find that place in the Bible where a subject is taught and explained and to build from there his doctrine upon God's revelation. Honesty and faith will keep us from error.

Preaching God's Definition

You will not find a clearer, more direct definition of preaching than is here given by God the Holy Spirit. "Ezra the scribe stood upon a pulpit of wood, which they had made for the purpose." Standing upon this elevated pulpit above the people, so that he could be seen and heard by all, Ezra lifted up praises to the Lord God and led the people of God in the reverent worship of Jehovah our Saviour. Then we are told that Ezra and those who preached with him on this great day did three things, three things that every preacher must do every time he stands to speak to eternity bound sinners in the name of God.

1. "They read in the Book in the law of God distinctly". If we would preach to immortal souls in the name of God, let us preach the Book of God. If we would preach the Book of God, we must read the Word of God in our assemblies. The public reading of Holy Scripture is as important as congregational singing and prayer. Notice that Ezra and his assistants in worship read the Word of God "distinctly". Let us do the same. Before reading a portion of Scripture in public, the man reading should go over that portion in private, reading it many times in preparation for the public worship service, so that he may read it "distinctly". When we read the Word of God in public worship (or lead the congregation in prayer), we should do so "distinctly", carefully pronouncing each word with clarity and speaking with sufficient volume to be heard.

2. "And gave the sense". How blessed we are when God sends a man to speak to our hearts by his Word who gives us the meaning of his Word! To give the sense of any portion of Scripture is to expound the text, giving out the meaning of the text as it stands in the Book of God. Preaching is not telling people what you think about a passage, or what a passage reminds you of, or how you think a passage applies to modern life! To preach the Word of God is to faithfully give the message of God the Holy Spirit in the text. The only way a preacher can do that is by diligent preparation, prayer, and study.

3. "And caused them to understand the reading". If the people to whom we preach do not understand what we preach, if they are not by our preaching caused to understand the Word of God, then our preaching is utterly meaningless. The man called and sent of God to preach the gospel is "apt to teach", gifted of God to cause those who hear him to understand the Word of God. He preaches with such simplicity and boldness that no one can misunderstand what he preaches.

May 30
Today's Reading: Nehemiah 11, 12
"The joy of Jerusalem"
Nehemiah 12:43

When the temple was built again at Jerusalem, and the people of God crowded the streets going up to the house of God, as they offered sacrifices, gave thanks, and sang praise to God, "the joy of Jerusalem was heard even afar off". Truly, God's Jerusalem, the church of the living God, has reason to rejoice in the Lord always and to make her joy known through all the earth.

Abraham's Seed
We are Abraham's seed. We have every reason to rejoice. When the Levites in Nehemiah's day offered praise to God as the sons of Abraham and sought his blessings upon them, they gave God praise for five things in particular which he had done for Abraham. Now, remember, if you are a believer, you are one of Abraham's spiritual children. And what God has done for our father Abraham, he has done for us in Christ. The blessing of Abraham has come upon us through the blood of Christ (Galatians 3:13, 14). (1.) "Thou art the Lord God who didst choose Abram". Abraham was sovereignly chosen by God to be the object of his grace. He passed by many but the Lord chose Abraham. Had God not chosen him, he would never have chosen God (John 15:16). (2.) "And broughtest him forth out of Ur of the Chaldees". Abraham was effectually called by irresistible grace to a life of faith in and obedience to Christ (Psalm 65:4). (3.) "And gavest him the name Abraham". God changed his name because he was a converted man, converted by grace (1 Thessalonians 1:9). (4.) "And foundest his heart faithful". Abraham was a new creature in Christ. Grace imparted to him made him a faithful man. He was preserved by grace and he persevered in faith (Philippians 1:6). (5.) "And madest a covenant with him". All that God did for Abraham, he did by covenant promise. His blessings were all sure, covenant blessings, sealed to him by God's immutability (Ephesians 1:3; 2 Timothy 1:9).

God Ready To Pardon
After confessing the sins of the people, the Levites offered prayer to God for Israel and said, "But thou art a God ready to pardon". Here is good news for sinners who are ready to perish! The God whom we have offended, against whom we have sinned, whose wrath we deserve is "a God ready to pardon". "Unto thee, O LORD, do I lift up my soul; for thou, Lord, art good, and ready to forgive; and plenteous in mercy unto all them that call upon thee" (Psalm 86:4, 5).

A God ready to pardon is a God prepared to pardon. Everything is prepared by which God can forgive sin. The road used to be blocked up. But Christ has, by the blood of his cross, tunnelled every mountain, filled every valley, bridged every gulf and cleared away every obstacle. Now all things are ready. God, for Christ's sake, is "a God ready to pardon".

A God ready to pardon is a God who can easily pardon. Though he could never pardon sin without the satisfaction of his justice, now that justice has been satisfied by the death of Christ as the sinner's Substitute, God can easily pardon us for Christ's sake. It takes nothing but his word. "Thy sins are forgiven thee."

A God ready to pardon is a God who quickly pardons. There is no need for any sinner to wait, even for a moment, for pardon. The pardon of sin is an instantaneous work (1 John 1:9). In a moment, in the twinkling of an eye, God gives pardon to the believing sinner.

> The moment a sinner believes,
> And trusts in his crucified God,
> His pardon at once he receives,
> Redemption in full through his blood.

A God ready to pardon is a God who cheerfully pardons. Can you grasp this? "He delighteth in mercy." As God loves a cheerful giver, he is a God who cheerfully pardons guilty sinners for Christ's sake. It is more the nature of God to forgive sin than it is the nature of man to commit sin. His forgiveness is infinite! "The LORD thy God in the midst of thee is mighty; he will save; he will rejoice over thee with joy; he will rest in his love; he will joy over thee with singing" (Zephaniah 3:17). Can you imagine that? The Triune God singing because of us whom he has pardoned! What a thought! As God pardons sinners, he bursts into a song! This is "a God ready to pardon". And he is our God!

May 31
Today's Reading: Nehemiah 13-Esther 1
"Remember me, O my God, for good"
Nehemiah 13:31

We have now reached the end of Nehemiah. What zeal for God we have seen in this man! He served God and his generation with wisdom and grace. Yet, as he finished his work, this man was still a mercy beggar at the throne of grace. His prayer, O my God, is my prayer. Give me grace to make it my prayer throughout my appointed days. "Remember me, O my God, for good."

They Read
"They read in the book of Moses in the audience of the people." When they heard God's holy will read, that the stranger should be separated from Israel, the people obeyed. How very important it is that we read the Word of God in our churches, in

our homes, and in our closets. O blessed Book of God! The merciful epistle sent down from heaven ought to be our meditation all the day and through the night. O blessed Lord Jesus, holy Lamb of God, alone worthy to open the book and loose the seals, open to my soul all the wondrous things of your law. And open my heart to the right understanding of it, that I may separate all that is mixed and corrupt in my heart, and cast it out.

God's people have always been taught, as here, to keep separate from all others, never to mingle with them, much less to form alliances with them, and learn their ways, and the ways of their gods. See then that you come out from among them and touch not the unclean thing.

Ahasuerus' Feast

The royalty and liberality of this Persian monarch immediately directs my mind to the Lord Jesus in his royalty and grace. The extent of the bounty and great majesty of this earthly potentate sinks to nothing before our great King. Ahasuerus' kingdom included 127 provinces, stretching from India to Ethiopia. Our Saviour's dominion is "from sea to sea, and from the river even unto the ends of the earth". He has "all power in heaven and in earth" and "the keys of hell and the grave".

Ahasuerus' feast lasted 140 days. When it was over, nothing followed but sickness and sorrow. Not so with our King! The eternal and everlasting day to which he invites poor sinners and in which he entertains all who come to him, whom he has made "kings and priests unto God and the Father", knows no end! Not only does our Saviour King cause us to feast with him, and he with us, he graciously causes us to sit down with him on his throne, as he has overcome and is seated with his Father on his throne!

And in this one eternal, never-ending feast of grace, from which the guests shall go out no more, there is nothing to nauseate, nothing unpleasant, nothing unhealthy for our souls. All is light, and joy, and peace, and unspeakable blessedness! Here our incomparable Saviour King openly shows the riches of his glorious kingdom and the honour of his excellent majesty! Here he brings his redeemed into a perfect acquaintance with himself, and opens to our unceasing astonishment and delight the wonders of his person and the wonders of his love, and fills our ravished souls "with joy unspeakable and full of glory", in the knowledge of "the mystery of God, and of the Father, and of Christ".

June 1
Today's Reading: Esther 2-4
"Esther was brought also unto the king's house"
Esther 2:8

We must never overlook the goodness, wisdom, and minute detail of God's providence. It is magnificently displayed in the way the Lord God arranged for Esther to be made queen of Persia at precisely the time she was needed, and in the way King Ahasuerus was inclined to grant her desire for the deliverance of Israel, and the destruction of those who sought to destroy them.

Corruption And Grace
The vile things that transpired during and as the result of the feast Ahasuerus held for his revelling friends are but a small display of the depravity of our fallen race, and the vile corruptions of our hearts by nature. Let us, by every remembrance of sin, be inspired to give thanks to our God for the pure gospel of his free grace in Christ. The angels call it "glad tidings of great joy". Truly it is that! The gospel of Christ is good news to poor sinners, who feel a body of sin and death, uncleanness, inordinate affections, and obscene lusts within. It tells poor, needy, dirty sinners that there is a fountain open for sin and uncleanness, grace for the guilty, and mercy for the most vile in Christ Jesus! It is the proclamation of liberty to poor captives. The Lord Jesus Christ, the Son of God, proclaims deliverance in the gospel by his great salvation. Deliverance from sin! Deliverance from death! Deliverance from the law! Deliverance from the wrath to come! Deliverance by his blood, his grace, and his power!

Overruling Providence
How sweet, comforting, and joyful it is to see God's overruling providence in the book of Esther! We see here how he makes even the corrupt passions and deeds of wicked men serve his purpose, the good of his people, and his everlasting praise. Never does the Lord God more strikingly display his sovereignty and grace than when he compels the wicked to promote the purposes of his sovereign will. God's people were about to be brought into great danger. How shall the Lord deliver them? Wicked King Ahasuerus divorces his Queen Vashti to gratify his anger. He marries Esther, and makes her, a Jewess, queen of Persia! This young Queen Esther shall be the Lord's instrument by which he shall preserve his people in captivity.

There is more to the story. Mordecai is made aware of a plot against the king's life. A record is made of his loyalty in the chronicles of the kingdom. Mordecai is forgotten until one night when Ahasuerus cannot sleep. A servant reads from the chronicles; and Mordecai is brought forward to be rewarded. The man Haman hated, and planned to hang, is now exalted to Haman's place; and Haman, the Jews' enemy, is hanged on the gallows he built to hang Mordecai. Sweet it is to my soul to watch the ways and works of our wondrous God! "Thy way is in the sea, and thy path in the great waters, and thy footsteps are not known." "The eyes of the Lord run to and fro throughout the whole earth, to shew himself strong in the behalf" of his elect!

No Harm, Only Good

Never was there a more deadly plot devised by any wretch than that which Haman devised against the Jews. But all his devices fell upon his own head. So shall it be with all the devices of the devil. Satan's schemes and assaults upon our God and his Christ and his church shall fall upon his own head (Romans 16:20).

It is not enough merely to say that Satan and his devices shall do no harm. The Book of God reveals much more than that. The Word of God tells us plainly that they shall all do good. "For all things work together for good to them that love God". Does Satan plan my soul's destruction? Does he want to get me in his snare? Does he desire to have me, that he may sift me as wheat? Without question, all these things are so.

At times, I feel his power utterly overwhelming! He joins with my corruptions to cast me down. He raises Moses up to accuse and condemn me. But when he does, I am then forced to cry to the Lord for help. I am compelled to fly out of myself and take refuge in my High Tower, Christ Jesus!

How sweetly, how graciously the Lord our God overrules even the devices of the devil for our souls' welfare and good. Therefore God the Holy Ghost, by his servant James, teaches us to rejoice when we fall into divers temptations. Blessed Lord Jesus, let me rest my soul always on you, on your finished work of salvation, and on your everlasting purpose of grace, worked out every day, every hour, in all the minute details of your sovereign, universal providence for my good!

June 2
Today's Reading: Esther 5-8
"If I perish, I perish"
Esther 4:16

As we read this history of Esther going in before the king, full of fear, doubt, and a thousand misgivings, we call to mind the state in which many of God's elect go in before King Jesus seeking mercy. And as we behold the kindness and complacency with which Ahasuerus received Esther, our hearts must surely be moved to contemplate the everlasting mercy, love, and grace the Lord Jesus shows to all mercy beggars at the throne of grace. Coming to Christ in faith, we now blush with shame to remember that we once feared coming to him.

Contrast

Esther went in before the king uncalled and contrary to the law. Yet she found favour. But every poor sinner who knows his need of Christ is called, invited, even commanded to come. The golden sceptre of our great Sovereign is always held out in mercy. Our God is God who waits to be gracious and delights in mercy! Sinners have no uncertainty, no "ifs" or "maybes" respecting our reception at the throne of grace.

We have no Hamans to oppose us. Satan the adversary, who stands to resist God's Joshuas, is rebuked and silenced by our mighty Michael, the Lord Jesus! We have a sure Advocate with the Father, who pleads our cause and secures our acceptance.

Holy Boldness
Oh, for grace always to come to the throne of grace with holy boldness, not in slavish fear and chains of bondage! The redeemed of the Lord ought always to come to God as those whom the Son of God has made free, as the sons of God. If we draw near by the blood of the cross, we may draw near with joyful confidence. If we come to God in Christ's name, trusting his blood and righteousness, his merit and his person as our only access to the thrice holy God, we have every reason to come, not as Esther, saying, "If I perish, I perish", but with confident assurance.

Mordecai's Honour
King Ahasuerus asked Haman, "What shall be done unto the man whom the king delighteth to honour?" Shall we not ask the same concerning our dear Saviour, the Lord Jesus? "What shall be done unto him whom God delighteth to honour?" God has made him both Prince and Saviour. All principalities and powers have been made subject unto him. Why? Because the Lord Jehovah is delighted with him and delighted to honour him. He has not only given him a name which is above every name, but it has pleased the Father that in him should all fulness dwell.

How shall you and I honour him whom the Father delights to honour? There is but one way. The Father honoured the Son by putting all things in his hands, by trusting him (Ephesians 1:12). That is how we must honour our Lord Jesus, by faith in him, by trusting him, by putting all things in his hands. Oh, for grace so to trust my Saviour! As the Lord God commits all his purpose, people, will, and glory to the God-man Mediator, Christ Jesus, so I commit all my salvation, all my life, all things to him.

As all the evil intent of Haman was overruled, and all the mischief he caused was overturned, soon our great God and Saviour shall overturn all the mischief our adversary the devil has caused in his creation, and overrule his intended harm for our everlasting benefit and joy. O Spirit of God, give us grace to honour our Saviour by trusting him with all things, in all things, for all things, and at all times!

June 3
Today's Reading: Esther 9-Job 2
"A day of feasting and gladness"
Esther 9:17

Three times in chapter 9 of Esther we are told that the Jews kept a day of rest and made it "a day of feasting and gladness", in celebration of God's great deliverance.

An annual festival was established by which they would remind themselves of God's great goodness in delivering them from their cruel enemies.

Gospel Feast

Let us get away to "the mountain of holiness" which is God's church, as often as she gathers to worship the God of all grace, giving thanks for his great salvation in Christ Jesus and his constant, unfailing deliverances of our souls. And let us daily celebrate the same, keeping the blessed gospel feast. "And in this mountain shall the Lord of hosts make unto all people a feast of fat things, a feast of wines on the lees, of fat things full of marrow, of wines on the lees well refined" (Isaiah 25:6).

That great deliverance from the wrath to come, which the Son of God accomplished for us by his obedience and blood and bestows upon poor sinners by his almighty grace, is a thing never to be forgotten, not for a moment. Here is cause for everlasting festivity! May God the Holy Spirit cause the living waters of grace to bubble in our souls unceasingly and inspire in our hearts the joyful remembrance and celebration of God's great goodness to us! Then we shall experience the thing he declares in Romans 14:17, "the kingdom of God is not meat and drink, but righteousness, and peace, and joy in the Holy Ghost".

Oh, for grace from God to celebrate in a constant jubilee deliverance from the curse of God's law, the terrors of a guilty conscience, and the everlasting damnation of hell!

Blessed be his name forever! The King's decree has been published and sent through all the earth. There is mercy, grace, and peace, free forgiveness of sin, and full salvation in Christ Jesus! God so loved the world that he sent his only begotten Son to be the Saviour of the world, so that all who believe in him should not perish, but have everlasting life! God the Holy Ghost confirms the glorious truth by giving sinners grace to believe the record God has given of his Son in his Word. This is the greatest reason in all the world for men and women to celebrate. "Let all those that seek thee rejoice and be glad in thee: and let such as love thy salvation say continually, Let God be magnified."

Mordecai

What a great man Mordecai must have been! Highly exalted, he "waxed greater and greater". And he used all his greatness to promote the happiness, peace, and prosperity of his people, God's Israel. But Mordecai fades before him of whom he was a type, our Lord Jesus Christ. Infinitely higher, infinitely greater, infinitely surpassing every other in love and grace and mercy, in power and wisdom and goodness is our dear Saviour and King, the Lord Jesus Christ. And he uses all, all that he is and all that he possesses to promote the happiness, peace, and prosperity of his people, the Israel of God, his church!

A Perfect Man

Moving from Esther to the book of Job, we meet with one of whom God says, "There is none like him in the earth, a perfect and an upright man, one that feareth God, and escheweth evil." I cannot question these facts. Job was God's servant. He feared God and hated evil. He was a perfect and upright man.

We know that Job was a perfect man, because God says he was. But we also know that he was not a sinless man in the flesh, because he confessed, "I have sinned" (Job 7:20). He said, "If I justify myself, mine own mouth shall condemn me: if I say, I am perfect, it shall also prove me perverse" (Job 9:20). The doctrine of sinless perfection in the flesh, and those who claim to be without sin claim perfection, is contrary to everything revealed in the Word of God. Those who boast of possessing such perfection expose both their ignorance and their corruption. Those who suppose they are equal to the demands of the law of God are ignorant of the law. And those who claim to be perfect, without sin, are vile, wicked, perverse men. They are liars, claiming what they know is false to be the truth, and declaring that God himself is a liar (1 John 1:8-10). What can be more wicked?

What does God mean when he uses the word "perfect" to describe this man Job? Is it possible for a sinful man to be perfect? Can I be both perfect and sinful? Indeed, that is exactly the truth with regard to all who are born of God. In ourselves, in our flesh, by nature, we are nothing but sin. In Christ, we are perfect. In him we are "meet to be partakers of the inheritance of the saints in light". All who trust Christ, all who are born again are, to use the language of Holy Scripture, "perfect in Christ". He has brought in everlasting righteousness for us by his obedience to Jehovah as our Representative. He has put away our sin by the sacrifice of himself as our Surety. And he has made us "partakers of the divine nature", taking up residence in us.

Rejoice, my brother! Rejoice, my sister! God says of you as he did of Job, "PERFECT". As Christ was made sin for us, he has made us the righteousness of God in him. That is what it is to be perfect before God.

June 4
Today's Reading: Job 3-7
"Job ... cursed his day"
Job 3:1

This portion of Holy Scripture begins with that perfect and upright man, Job, who feared God and eschewed evil, cursing the day of his birth, and ends with that same man confessing to the Lord God, apparently in the hearing of Eliphaz, his great sin. "I have sinned; what shall I do unto thee, O thou preserver of men? Why hast thou set me as a mark against thee, so that I am a burden to myself?"

Eliphaz obviously misjudged God's servant Job, and was a miserable comforter (Job 16:2). Though this Temanite of the seed of Esau accused Job as did Satan (Job 2:5) of hypocrisy, he had many good, instructive words we would be wise to observe. God the Holy Spirit can and does make use of men with evil designs to serve the interest of his glory and the good of his elect. "Hear instruction, and be wise, and refuse it not" (Proverbs 8:33).

237

Sinners Still

This account of Job is one of the most important things revealed in this inspired record of his life. It shows us, even in this earliest book of Holy Scripture, that God's saints in this world are sinners still. In the examples of great and good men, the Spirit of God graciously and wisely shows us their frailties, imperfections, and sins. While we are called upon to behold the patience of Job (James 5:11), we are to be taught that he was a man of like passions with ourselves.

The same was true of Noah, Lot, David, Peter, Paul, and others. Jeremiah behaved just like Job when he was severely afflicted (Jeremiah 20:14-18). No excuses are given for the faults, failures, and sins of these men in the Book of God. They are recorded as facts. Nothing more is said about them than the facts themselves.

Why are these things written out in bold letters in the Sacred Volume? They are written to teach us that though chosen, redeemed, justified, and sanctified by the grace of God, as long as we live in this world, all saved sinners are people with two warring natures: flesh and spirit, the old man and the new. Our only righteousness is Christ our Saviour. Knowing these things, let us ever look to Christ, begging him to keep us from the evil that is in us. And let us ask of God grace to be gracious to our fallen brothers and sisters, restoring the fallen in the spirit of meekness and bearing one another's burdens, in the fulfilling of the law of Christ (Galatians 6:1-3).

Birth And Death

What Job said about the day of a man's birth, as it concerns our being born in sin, is certainly true. And in this spiritual sense, the day of our death, when we die to sin and are new born unto a life of righteousness in Christ Jesus, by the regenerating work of God the Holy Ghost, is far better (Ecclesiastes 7:1).

If in his infinite mercy the Lord God has given you and me a new life in Christ, we should ever remember and give thanks to him for his great blessings of grace upon us, both in our old creation and in our new. Many have cursed the day of their birth in nature, including me, I confess to my shame. Oh, how I now bless God for the day of my new birth in Christ!

The Grave

What Job says of the grave for those dying in the Lord is true indeed and most blessed. For the believer, death is entering into rest and the ceasing of all trouble. But without Christ, death like that of an infant, who never saw the light of day, would be indescribably more desirable. If the damned in hell could speak to men upon earth, all would say, "Amen".

No Hypocrisy

Though Job complained bitterly in his pain of body and soul, God graciously restrained him and kept him from Satan's designs against him. Though he was provoked by the adversary to curse the day of his birth, we do not hear a word of him cursing God. That was Satan's accusation. He had said that if the Lord God touched all he had, Job would curse God to his face; but that never happened. God prevented it by his grace working mightily in and upon the object of his love. God permitted the devil to afflict Job severely, because he had accused Job of hypocrisy, and said that he had no real love of God in his heart. But the accuser was cast down! Job never forsook his Redeemer, or gave up his hope in Christ. Under all his great and long trials, this man of exemplary faith never spoke a word against God, though in honesty he so loathed himself that he said to the God he loved and trusted, "So that my soul chooseth strangling, and death rather than my life" (Job 7:15). Spirit of God, give me grace so to loathe myself, and trust my God, while I await my appointed deliverance into heavenly glory, and freedom from my sin, the source of all my sorrows here.

June 5
Today's Reading: Job 8-11
"My soul is weary of my life"
Job 10:1

Poor Job! What mere mortal has known such trials as those wherewith he was afflicted? The Lord God had, by the instrumentality of Satan's hellish cruelty, taken away all his family, all his wealth, his health and his reputation of high esteem. Added to that are these three friends who became his tormenters. Both Eliphaz and Bildad groundlessly accused God's servant of hypocrisy. Satan used Job's friends to try to expose Job as the hypocrite he accused him of being.

Then Zophar spoke. Of Job's three friends, he seems to have been the most cruel. Eliphaz and Bildad had, in some measure, softened their speech. Zophar called Job a hypocrite and a liar, and accused him of mocking God. Let us ever be aware of this fact. When other devices fail, Satan makes even our friends a snare for our souls. Our Lord Jesus tells us plainly that a man's foes are those of his own house (Matthew 10:26); and here we see that friends are sometimes our foes.

Just God
Again, Bildad gives words of instruction that declare the truth of God as clearly as any inspired apostle, though he spoke for the purpose of condemning one who was just. He asked, "Doth God pervert judgment? Or doth the Almighty pervert justice?" Then he declared, "Behold, God will not cast away a perfect man".

Truly, he who is God is both "a just God and a Saviour". Nowhere is this seen so clearly as it is seen in the sacrifice of his darling Son as our Substitute. God will not save at the expense of his justice. Therefore he sent his own dear Son to Calvary to die in the place of his elect, to declare his righteousness, that he might be both just and the Justifier of his people (Romans 3:24-26). Because the Almighty cannot and will not pervert judgment and justice, because he will not cast away a perfect man, before he could impute sin to the holy Lord Jesus, the Lord God "made him sin for us who knew no sin, that we might be made the righteousness of God in him".

What grace, what wondrous mystery these words contain! "He", God the Father, "hath", in holy justice and infinite mercy, "made", to become, created, "him", the Lord Jesus Christ, his infinite, well-beloved, only begotten, immaculate Son, "sin", an awful mass of iniquity, "for us", helpless, condemned, sinful rebels! Should any ask, "Why was the Holy One made sin? Why did Christ die? The answer is this, God is just. "Thanks be unto God for his unspeakable gift". Job asked, "How can a man be just with God?" No other answer can be given, but this. "For he hath made him to be sin for us, who knew no sin; that we might be made the righteousness of God in him".

Comfort For The Weary
Job was but a man, like you and me, a man struggling with his flesh, tormented by his miserable comforters, tempted by Satan, and afflicted by his heavenly Father. Much weakness may be seen in this poor, weary soul. His sins are not hidden from us. Yet, Job was God's. He believed God and loved him. He knew, contrary to his friend's accusations, that he was a sinful man, and frankly confessed that fact. "If I justify myself, mine own mouth shall condemn me: if I say, I am perfect, it shall also prove me perverse." Those are not the words of a self-righteous man, but the words of a humbled, broken sinner whose only hope is Christ.

Yet, Job was weary with his trials, weary with the woes heaped upon him by God's providence, so he turned to the Lord and pleaded for comfort (Job 10:20). Though full of confusion (Job 10:15), he knew that he was the object of divine favour. Though greatly afflicted, he found comfort in the fact that God who tried him was God his Preserver. He said, "Thou hast granted me life and favour, and thy visitation hath preserved my spirit" (Job 10:12).

How sweet it is for God's elect to know that in the midst of a thousand afflictions there is no curse! Our dear Saviour, the Lord Jesus Christ, the Lamb of God, our Beloved, took all the curse away when he was made a curse for us! What a sweet, soul-reviving, soul-comforting thought for God's weary ones! Blessed Redeemer, you took the cup of trembling and drank it that your people might drink the cup of salvation. Receive our thanks and give us grace, though we may at times be weary in this world, never to forget you. "Thou hast granted me life and favour, and thy visitation hath preserved my spirit." Amen.

June 6
Today's Reading: Job 12-15
"I know that I shall be justified"
Job 13:18

In chapters 12-14, Job replies to Zophar's continued accusations. He and his companions in cruelty mocked God's servant Job, and laughed the just and upright man to scorn. In chapter 15, Eliphaz again accuses Job of hypocrisy. Job, remember, is speaking specifically to these "miserable comforters" as he asserts his uprightness. In chapter 12, he declares God's glorious sovereignty in all things, acknowledging that it was his God who had brought all his woes upon him.

In the face of all his troubles, he clings still to his God and Saviour in resolute faith and devotion, saying, "Though he slay me, yet will I trust in him: but I will maintain mine own ways before him ... Behold now, I have ordered my cause; I know that I shall be justified" (Job 13:15, 18). Should you, my God, be pleased to try me as you did your servant Job, give me the grace you gave Job to trust you as he did, for Christ's sake.

In the fourteenth chapter of this instructive book describing the experiences of one of God's saints, that faithful man who was so greatly tried teaches us by the Spirit of God what we must expect while we live in this world. Here is a saint in trouble, pouring his heart out to God, seeking comfort and instruction for his afflicted soul. Job came boldly to the throne of grace to obtain mercy and find grace to help in his time of need. In the opening verses of this chapter he declares four facts about life in this world which he had learned. The sooner we learn these things, the better.

Short
Life in this world is short. "Man that is born of woman is of few days." Our days on earth are short. What is your life? It is a momentary vapour, a passing ship, a fleeing shadow, a fading flower, a weak blade of withering grass. The strongest man is feeble, frail, and fragile. May God "so teach us to number our days, that we may apply our hearts unto wisdom" (Psalm 90:12). May God give us grace ever to set our hearts on Christ our Wisdom.

Sorrowful
Life in this world is sorrowful. "Man that is born of woman is of few days, and (those few days are) full of trouble." The days of man upon the earth are short lived and sad lived. Every day is filled with labour and sorrow, toil and trouble, fretting and fearing, hurting and grieving. Is it not so with you? Life in this world is filled with trouble. "In the world ye shall have tribulation." There are no exceptions. Anyone who always appears to be happy is either a liar or insane. You cannot escape trouble in this world. You simply have to face it and learn to live with it. Where there is sin, there is sorrow. We will never escape sorrow until we escape sin. And that will not happen in this world.

Sinful
Life in this world is sinful. "Who can bring a clean thing out of an unclean?" Here Job traces all the sorrows of our race to sin, and all the sin of our race to its original source. Our lives are unclean, because we are all unclean by nature. Our lives are short and sorrowful, because we are sinful. We are all born in a state of sin (Psalm 51:5; Romans 5:12). We will never be able to understand and deal with the problems of life until we understand and deal with original sin.

Set Time
Life in this world is for a set time. Man's "days are determined, the number of his months are with thee. Thou hast appointed his bounds that he cannot pass." Yes, you and I must die. And the time of our death has been appointed by God from eternity. No amount of care, diligent exercise, strict diet, or medicine can add one second to your life. At God's appointed time, he will call, and you will answer.

For the believer, the death of the body is the freeing of the soul. It is a welcome relief (Philippians 1:21-23; Revelation 14:13). While living in this world, we seek to be content with God's wise and good providence. We want to glorify our great God by living before him in faith, resigning all things to his will. We would not change our lot in life, even if we could. Our heavenly Father knows and always does what is best.

Life A Burden
Yet, life in this world, at best, is a burden to the heaven-born soul. In this tabernacle we groan (2 Corinthians 5:1-4). We groan for life! Our hearts cry, "O wretched man that I am! Who shall deliver me from this body of death". In this body we struggle with sin. In heaven we shall be free from sin. In this body we are tempted and often fall. In heaven we shall never be tempted and shall never fall. In this body we weep much. In heaven we shall weep no more. In this body we long to be like Christ. In heaven we shall be like Christ. In this body we long for Christ's presence. In heaven we shall forever be with Christ.

We have many friends in heaven whom we dearly love. We miss them. But we do not sorrow for them. We envy them! The believer, as long as he is in this world, is like an eagle I saw once while visiting a zoo. He sat on an iron perch, with a chain holding him to the earth, gazing into heaven. It appeared that he longed to soar away into the distant clouds; but the chain held him fast to the earth. When an eagle is happy in an iron cage or chained to an iron perch, when a sheep is happy in a pack of wolves, when a fish is happy on dry land, then, and not until then, will the renewed soul be happy in this body of flesh. Death for God's saints will be a welcome relief (Psalm 17:15). "O that thou wouldest hide me in the grave, that thou wouldest keep me secret, until thy wrath be past, that thou wouldest appoint me a set time, and remember me! If a man die, shall he live again? All the days of my appointed time will I wait, till my change come. Thou shalt call, and I will answer thee: thou wilt have a desire to the work of thine hands."

June 7
Today's Reading: Job 16-21
"I know that my redeemer liveth"
Job 19:25

At last, Job had had enough! I imagine he was boiling with indignation. Even the patience of Job had its limits! His heart was heavy. His soul was troubled. Under the afflictions of his Father's rod, he simply could not bear the insults of his pretentious friends any longer. Therefore, he plainly informed them of that which he knew by experience in his soul, which they could never take from him. Even in his poverty, pain, and perplexity, Job knew more and possessed more than his "friends" could imagine.

Job's Sure Knowledge
Job had one true Friend in the midst of many cruel friends. All earthly friends are conditional friends. The very best of them will, in time, bring sorrow to our souls. But "there is a Friend that sticketh closer than a brother". And that Friend is Jesus Christ. Blessed is the man who has Christ for his friend, who can lift his heart to heaven, seeing Christ by faith, and say, "This is my Beloved, and this is my Friend" (Song of Solomon 5:16).

Job found real property in the presence of absolute poverty. He uses the word "my" to speak of his personal interest and property in the Son of God. Blessed is the man who can, with honesty and confidence, call Christ, "my Redeemer".

Job had a living Kinsman in the presence of a dying family. His statement, "I know that my redeemer liveth", may be translated three ways.

First, "I know that my kinsman liveth". Christ is our nearest kinsman; and he is our kinsman by his own gracious choice. If the Son of God is my Kinsman, then all is well! In order to be our Redeemer, Christ must be our Kinsman. And Christ Jesus is never ashamed to own his brethren. Even when they had all forsaken him, he called his disciples "my brethren".

Second, "I know that my vindicator liveth". At the appointed time, God will vindicate his own. He will set all crooked things straight. Oh, for grace to trust Christ to be our Vindicator! The saddest passages in the Book of Job are those in which Job attempted to vindicate himself. Job's foolish attempts at self-vindication have led many to conclude, erroneously, that Job was a lost man, because this is out of character for a man of faith. Like you and me, Job did not always think, behave, and speak like a believer; but he was a man of God-given faith in Christ. He trusted Christ to vindicate him of Satan's accusations spewed from the mouths of Eliphaz, Bildad, and Zophar, just as Paul trusted Christ to vindicate him from the charges of false brethren (1 Corinthians 4:3-5). Spirit of God, give me grace to do the same.

Third, "I know that my redeemer liveth". Christ, who is our God, is our Redeemer. He has redeemed us from the curse of the law by his blood. He has redeemed for us all that we lost in the fall. He has redeemed us from the bondage of sin by the power of his grace. And he shall redeem us from the grave at last. If I know that my Redeemer lives, I have peace!

Job possessed absolute knowledge in the face of great uncertainty. "I know", he said. His faith made him certain. Invisible things, revealed by God, are certainly known by those who believe him (Hebrews 11:1-3). Faith is not speculative knowledge, but certain knowledge.

Job had a sure hope in the face of utter hopelessness. He lived, even then, in the hope of Christ's Second Advent. He had hope of eternal acceptance with God. And he hoped for the resurrection of his body. The basis of his hope was the finished work of our dear Saviour, the Lord Jesus Christ, his Redeemer. His redemption was finished, even before the world began, for his living Redeemer is Jesus Christ, the Lamb of God, slain from the foundation of the world!

Job's Comfort
The Lord God had taken every comfort of life, every source of earthly joy, and every form of temporal good away from his servant Job. His property, his health, his riches, his influence, his children, and his friends were all gone! And his wife was as good as gone. Job was completely alone in this world, alone with his boils, his pains, and his troubles. But in the midst of his troubles, Job found an argument for peace and sweet comfort for his soul. "I know that my Redeemer liveth." He was driven by the precious trial of faith to look to God, his Redeemer, alone for comfort. His trials drove him away from every earthly good into the arms of his Redeemer. Blessed is the man whose trials cause him to flee to Christ! In the midst of sorrow, Job found great joy. In the midst of trouble, he found great peace. In the midst of darkness, he discovered great light. In the midst of uncertainty, he possessed a sure knowledge, by which his soul was possessed with peace, "looking unto Jesus the author and finisher of our faith".

June 8
Today's Reading: Job 22-27
"Can man be profitable unto God?"
Job 22:2

Eliphaz raised the question, "Can a man be profitable unto God?" The answer is a resounding, "No". How can puny, finite man be, or do, anything that is profitable to the infinite, all-sufficient God? Sufficiency is an attribute of God's Being that needs to be understood and universally proclaimed. All-sufficiency implies self-sufficiency and independence. This attribute of the great and glorious God teaches us three things.

Discovering Christ Day By Day

No Need
First, let us ever remember that God needs nothing from anyone. The self-existent God is the self-subsistent God. He is perfect, complete, happy, and satisfied in himself. We can add nothing to him. And we can take nothing from him (Romans 11:35, 36). We stand in need of God. He alone supplies our every need and supports us in life. By him we consist. In him we live and move and have our being. He upholds us by the word of his power. But God needs nothing from us (Psalm 50:7-15). Our worship, services, acts of obedience and faith, and greatest sacrifices, add nothing to God (Job 22:2, 3; Luke17:10).They only benefit us (Titus3:8). And our sins, though they are against him, take nothing from God (Job 35:6-8). God is so infinitely great, so thoroughly self-sufficient that no creature can add anything to him, take anything from him, hinder his work, impede his purpose, or in any way alter him.

Able To Supply
Second, the Lord God is able to supply all the needs of all his people (Philippians 4:19). He is able to do whatever he pleases. He is able to fulfil all his promises. He is able to accomplish all his decrees. And he is able to do exceedingly, abundantly above all that we ask or think. Nothing is too hard for our God! He who sent manna from heaven to feed a hungry nation everyday for forty years can feed you and me with ease. He who caused water to gush out of a Rock in the desert can refresh us. He who caused a pair of shoes to last a man forty years and remain new, and caused a coat to last for forty years without the least evidence of wear, can clothe us. He who caused an axe to swim for the benefit of a labouring man can keep you and me afloat. The name of our God is El Shaddai, God All-Sufficient! And he is the God of all grace. He gave his Son to be the all-sufficient Mediator of an all sufficient covenant to bestow upon us his all-sufficient grace. He makes all grace to abound toward us according to his riches in glory by Christ Jesus.

Self-Righteousness A Delusion
Third, God's infinite self-sufficiency teaches us that every thought of self-righteousness in man is a delusion. How can man be profitable to God? That is a question which never can be sounded too often, nor too loudly through the chambers of every self-righteous man's heart. Indeed, it is astonishing that any man's heart could ever be snared by this delusion. Yet, all men by nature choose to embrace it and delude themselves with it. The glories of God in creation, in redemption, and in the salvation of innumerable souls, by his wondrous mercy, love, and grace in his dear Son, all manifest God's greatness, graciousness, and goodness.

But what profit is brought to my God in the salvation of such a sinner as I am? Oh, precious Lord Jesus, give me grace to rightly value your everlasting love and infinite grace. Cause me ever to lay low in the dust before you, and be content to be nothing. I am worse than nothing! I am ruined, lost, and undone in myself. That I would forever be were it not for your righteousness, by which I am made the righteousness of God in you! It is in and by your complete and free salvation that I am now, and from eternity, and forever accepted. Yes, you, my dear Redeemer and Lord, are my All! "Of him are ye in Christ Jesus, who of God is made unto us wisdom, and righteousness, and sanctification, and redemption: that, according as it is written, he that glorieth, let him glory in the Lord." Amen.

June 9
Today's Reading: Job 28-31
"The words of Job are ended"
Job 31:40

In the chapters we have read Job continued to defend himself from the false accusations of his pretended friends, justifying himself against their unjust charges. Many fault Job for this, as though he justified himself before God. That was not the case. Job appealed to the Lord his God to plead his cause. He did not attempt to justify himself before God. That is evident from the words of his own mouth. "If I justify myself, mine own mouth shall condemn me: if I say, I am perfect, it shall also prove me perverse" (Job 9:20). It is one thing to justify our conduct against the unfounded reproaches of men, and another thing altogether to deny our sins against the sovereign majesty of our God. At that throne of God's justice, Job always pleaded guilty. He repeatedly confessed himself a sinner before God, and never attempted to cover his sin before God. Before God, he had nothing to say to justify himself. He confessed, "I have sinned, what shall I do unto thee, O thou Preserver of men?" (Job 7:20).

Confession And Forgiveness
How blessed a thing it is to sinners in need of mercy to hear the testimony of God the Holy Ghost by his servant John, "If we confess our sins, he is faithful and just to forgive us our sins, and to cleanse us from all unrighteousness" (1 John 1:9). How delightful it is to know, when we know ourselves sinners, that "we have an advocate with the Father, Jesus Christ the righteous: And he is the propitiation for our sins" (1 John 2:1, 2).

All our righteousness and justification before God is in the righteousness and blood of his dear Son. We claim no righteousness before God but Christ, the Son of God, who justifies all who believe on him. The patriarch Job was born of God and taught of God. He trusted Christ, his kinsman Redeemer. He knew that Christ alone was his Saviour. Being taught of God the Holy Spirit, he looked to Christ alone for all his salvation.

Our Defender
Let us ever look to Christ to be our Defender, not only from the assaults and accusations of men, but also from the assaults and accusations of Satan. Precious Lord Jesus, when Satan raises Moses up against me, stand by my side and be my defence, as you were Joshua's defence and stood by his side. Make your righteousness, as my

glorious Mediator and Surety, to be the everlasting comfort, confidence, and joy of my heart. Then shall I be enabled to stand against all the accusations of Satan, of false friends, and of open foes, and cry in the holy triumph of the faith you have given me, "Who shall lay anything to the charge of God's elect? It is God that justifieth. Who is he that condemneth? It is Christ that died, yea rather, that is risen again, who is even at the right hand of God, who also maketh intercession for us" (Romans 8:33, 34).

June 10
Today's Reading: Job 32-36
"I have found a ransom"
Job 33:24

There is much to be learned from Elihu, but nothing more precious than this. In Christ our Surety God found a ransom for our souls. In the person of his Son, the Lord Jesus Christ, he found a ransom for his chosen people. By the substitutionary sacrifice of his own well-beloved Son in the place of his people, the Lord God found a way to punish sin to the satisfaction of his divine Justice, and to be gracious in saving every believer. By this one mighty, all-sufficient, sin-atoning ransom, he would be perfectly just, while at the same time justifying every believer.

Satisfaction Demanded
God's purpose of grace in predestination, and his execution of that purpose in providence is according to his sovereign choice of his people unto salvation in Christ before the world began in eternal election (Ephesians 1:4; 2 Thessalonians 2:13, 14; 1 Peter 1:2). Not only did the Lord God choose to save us, our heavenly Father found a way to save us that is altogether consistent with and honouring to his own glorious holiness, justice, and truth.

Love chose us; but justice demanded satisfaction. Mercy resolved to spare us; but truth said, "The soul that sinneth, it shall die". Grace cried, "Forgive". But holiness insisted, "Without holiness, no man shall see the Lord. It must be perfect to be accepted".

Our heavenly Father looked on his darling Son as he stepped forward as our Surety. The eternal Son of God was willing to become a man, to live the full age of a man for the fulfilment of all righteousness, and to die as a Substitute for us for the satisfaction of divine justice. Then the Father, willing to sacrifice his dear Son for us, looked upon the whole, innumerable multitude of his elect as one in Christ, and graciously cried, "Deliver him from going down to the pit: I have found a ransom."

247

A Divine Work
This ransom was the invention of divine wisdom. Only the infinite mind of the eternal God could or would have devised such a gracious and just plan to save fallen man. Truly, the cross of Christ gloriously displays the manifold wisdom of God. Only by this mighty, sin-atoning ransom could the prophecy be fulfilled "Mercy and truth are met together; righteousness and peace have kissed each other. Truth shall spring out of the earth; and righteousness shall look down from heaven ... Righteousness shall go before him; and shall set us in the way of his steps."

Infinite Love
This ransom was the gift of infinite love. "For God so loved the world that he gave his only begotten Son, that whosoever believeth in him should not perish, but have everlasting life." "God commendeth his love toward us, in that while we were yet sinners, Christ died for us." "Herein is love, not that we loved God, but that he loved us, and sent his Son to be the propitiation for our sins." The price of our ransom was the precious blood of Christ. Justice could demand no more, and love could give no more than the precious blood of Christ. "Thanks be unto God for his unspeakable gift."

This ransom has been fully paid. Just before he breathed out his spirit, our Lord Jesus cried triumphantly, "It is finished." Those words simply mean, "The ransom is paid, redemption is complete." By his mighty atoning sacrifice, our Lord Jesus Christ has satisfied the law of God, honoured the justice of God, brought in everlasting righteousness, and put away all the sins of all who will ever trust him. God neither requires, nor will he accept anything from the sinner to complete the work. Christ has done it all.

And this ransom is gloriously effectual. Every soul that was purchased from the hands of divine justice by the blood of Christ must be saved by divine power. The very justice of God demands it. In the fulness of time the Lord will "Deliver him from going down to the pit", saying, "I have found a ransom".

> Love found a way to redeem my soul,
> Love found a way that could make me whole;
> Love sent my Lord to the cross of shame,
> Love found a away – O praise his name!

The gospel of God has the stamp of Divinity upon it. No form of religion in the world, except that which is found in the Book of God, sets forth salvation by God himself sacrificing his own darling Son in the place of sinners. No man ever invented such a thing. Substitutionary atonement for chosen sinners by the incarnate God could never have been conceived, except in the mind of God's infinite wisdom. The gospel sprang from the heart of that God whose name is "Love". Again, I say, "Thanks be unto God for his unspeakable gift."

June 11
Today's Reading: Job 37-40
"Behold, I am vile"
Job 40:4

Elihu declared the goodness, rectitude, wisdom, and mercy of our God. Then he asserted that God's ways and works are unsearchable. His message (Job 32-38) to Job was noble and as full of instruction for us as it was for Job. "Then the Lord answered Job out of the whirlwind." Showing Job his glorious, universal sovereignty, he made Job to understand his nothingness before God. Then, in the opening of Job 40, the Lord God demands an answer from Job.

A Fearful Thing
It seems to me that there must have been a long pause between God demanding an answer from Job, and Job answering him. Job understood that, "It is a fearful thing to fall into the hands of the living God" (Hebrews 10:31). He had asked God to answer him; but when he did, I can almost see the patriarch trembling before the holy, Lord God.
     David tells us that he trembled when he thought of God's judgments. David, the man after God's own heart, a man trusting Christ, looking to the Lord Jesus alone for acceptance with the Almighty, trembled when he thought of God's judgments (Psalm 119:120). Oh, what horrors must instantly seize that soul that meets God after death without blood to cleanse from all sin, without righteousness to justify, without a Mediator to intercede, without the God-man to redeem, without Christ to present him before the presence of God's glory!

Job's Answer
How does Job answer God? "Then Job answered the LORD, and said, Behold, I am vile; what shall I answer thee? I will lay mine hand upon my mouth." This is where we must be brought. Every awakened sinner is sweetly forced to see this fact about himself and confess it to God. Grace triumphs, and the sinner casts himself wholly upon God's sovereign mercy in Christ.
     O sweet grace! O wondrous mercy! O magnificent love! When God comes to a sinner in the saving operations of his grace, he graciously convinces the object of his mercy of sin. That is the beginning of the Spirit's work in us as our Divine Comforter. He who is convinced of his own sin is convinced of righteousness in Christ and of judgment finished forever by the sacrifice of God's dear Son.

> Boasting excluded, pride I abase,
> I'm only a sinner saved by grace!

249

June 12
Today's Reading: Job 41-Psalm 5
"Job answered the LORD"
Job 42:1

Having shown Job his sovereignty and power over all creation, the Lord God convinced Job both of his nothingness and of the greatness of Jehovah. "Then Job answered the Lord, and said, I know that thou canst do everything, and that no thought can be withholden from thee ... I have heard of thee by the hearing of the ear: but now mine eye seeth thee. Wherefore I abhor myself, and repent in dust and ashes."

Being taught by God the Holy Spirit, Job abhorred himself. What a difference there is between the teaching of men and the teaching of God! All that men can say, all the preaching of men, without God the Holy Spirit ends just where it began, in the hearing of the ear. But when God speaks, the Word of the Lord brings conviction to the heart. When God speaks, those who hear his voice are brought low and Christ is exalted. Blessed Spirit of God speak to me and I shall hear!

Job A Type
There is much we should learn in the history of Job about the way God deals with his elect in mercy, love, and grace. But it might be profitable to our souls, if God will be pleased to make it so, for us to remember God's servant Job as a very instructive type and picture of our Lord Jesus Christ.

Job was the greatest man of the East. Christ, the Wisdom-man, whose goings forth have been from everlasting, is the greatest of all. In all things he has pre-eminence.

Job was perfect and upright, fearing God and eschewing evil. Our dear Saviour, the Lord Jesus, was the perfect God-man: holy, harmless, undefiled, and separate from sinners.

Job was suddenly brought from great riches to great poverty. "Ye know the grace of our Lord Jesus Christ, that, though he was rich, yet for your sakes he became poor, that ye through his poverty might be rich" (2 Corinthians 8:9).

Job was assaulted by Satan. But what were the sufferings of Job compared to the sufferings of our Lord Jesus for the salvation of our souls? Satan was the instrument that brought sorrow to Job; but all his adversities came by the will, decree, and hand of God; and he knew it. So it was with our dear Saviour (Lamentations 1:12).

Job made an effectual sacrifice and effectual intercession for his friends by the will of God. How our hearts rejoice to know that our Lord Jesus Christ made an effectual sacrifice for us and effectually intercedes for us.

Because Lord God accepted Job he accepted those for whom Job made intercession. Because our great God accepts his Son for us he accepts us in him.

Job was laid low that he might be exalted very high. Our Lord Jesus was made least in the kingdom of heaven that he might be the greatest (Philippians 2:5-11).

Discovering Christ Day By Day

The Psalms

As we have begun to read the inspired Psalms, let us look for our dear Saviour in each holy song, knowing by the very Word of God the Holy Spirit that the Psalms, like all other portions of Holy Scripture, speak of him (Luke 24:25-27; 44; Acts 10:43).

Psalm 1 is a song of praise to Christ the perfect Man. How we ought to thank God for that one perfect Man who is God, for that one Man who fulfilled all righteousness, for that one Man who is God, whose righteousness is of infinite merit and efficacy for his people! Christ, the Mediator-man, earned for himself as a Man, and for us as our Surety, all the everlasting blessedness God himself can bestow upon men!

Psalm 2 declares the exaltation and glory of Christ our King, the glory he earned as our Covenant Head by his obedience unto death.

Psalm 3 describes the things David suffered under the chastening hand of God; but David was a type of the Lord Jesus. Here is a description of our dear Saviour's suffering. He was throughout the days of his humiliation "a man of sorrows and acquainted with grief".

Psalm 4 is the first psalm with the title, "To the Chief Musician". All the psalms with this title should be read as psalms addressed to the Lord Jesus. We have in this fourth Psalm a holy cry to God in the name of Christ, pleading the merits of the Lord our righteousness, "Christ Jesus, who of God is made unto us wisdom, and righteousness, and sanctification, and redemption".

Psalm 5 takes us with David into his closet. But who can read the words of David's petitions in these sacred verses without hearing the Lord Jesus interceding for his people? Thank you, Spirit of God, for taking the things of Christ revealed in Holy Scripture and showing them to us! O Holy Spirit, give us hearts to trust and cherish him who loved us and gave himself for us! Amen.

June 13
Today's Reading: Psalm 6-16
"I will praise thee, O LORD, with my whole heart"
Psalm 9:1

Oh, that God would give me grace at every day's beginning and every night's end, and throughout every hour between, to praise him with my whole heart, Father, Son, and Holy Ghost for all he is and all he does, has done, and shall hereafter do!

As we read through the psalms, we are distinctly taught and led by God the Spirit to give praise to God, the Triune Jehovah, for his name. The Psalmist David declares of God our Saviour, "They that know thy name will put their trust in thee". God's name is the revelation of his character. Here are ten names by which the Lord Jesus Christ, our God and Saviour, reveals his character to us. May God the Holy Spirit cause us to know his name and put our trust in him.

Jehovah-Hoseenu "The LORD Our Maker" (Psalm 95:6). He who is the Lord our Maker, not only made us, he has made us his people (1 Samuel 2:22).

Jehovah-Jireh "The LORD Will Provide" (Genesis 22:13, 14). Having provided a substitute for Isaac on Mount Moriah, the Lord provides all things for his elect in Christ our Substitute. This is the message of the gospel. Jehovah-Jireh is the constant object of our faith in both salvation and providence.

Jehovah-Rapha "The LORD That Healeth Thee" (Exodus 15:26). Our lives were bitter until the cross of Christ made them sweet by his grace.

Jehovah-Nissi "The LORD Our Banner" (Exodus 17:8-15). As Moses and the Children of Israel fought with the Amalekites and won the victory through the strength of Christ, we too prevail only by Christ.

Jehovah-M'kaddesh "The LORD Who Sanctifies You" (Exodus 31:13, 14). Sabbath observance declared the sanctification, or salvation of a sinner and is the work of God (Leviticus 20:7, 8). It is our salvation by God's grace that inspires our obedience to him, and causes us to set ourselves apart to his service, will, and glory.

Jehovah-Shalom "The LORD Our Peace" (Judges 6:24, 25). When Gideon saw the Angel of the Lord, he feared that he would die. But "the Lord said unto him, Peace be unto thee; fear not: thou shalt not die". Christ is our Peace.

Jehovah-Raah "The LORD My Shepherd" (Psalm 23:1). Christ is our Shepherd. We are his sheep. He sustains us by his provision. We live under his protection.

Jehovah-Tsidkenu "The LORD Our Righteousness" (Jeremiah 23:6). The Lord Jesus Christ is made of God unto us righteousness. He is our righteousness; and we are the righteousness of God in him (Jeremiah 33:16).

Jehovah-Shammah "The LORD Is There" (Ezekiel 48:35). Find a believer, the Lord is there! Find a gospel church, the Lord is there! Find heaven, the Lord is there!

Jehovah-Jesus "The LORD Will Save" (Matthew 1:21). He who is the incarnate God has a people in this world. They were his people long before he came into the world. These people were given to him in eternity by his Father. He came here specifically to save his people; and save them he shall. Everyone of them!

These are the names of our God and Saviour, as he reveals himself in Holy Scripture. Call upon the Name of the Lord, and you shall be saved (Romans 10:9-13). The Name of the Lord is a strong tower; run to it for refuge (Proverbs 18:10).

June 14
Today's Reading: Psalm 17-21
"Hear the right, O LORD"
Psalm 17:1

No one could ever make such a prayer as this before God and be accepted except the Perfect-man, the God-man, our Mediator. Only he can appeal to the justice of his cause and the rightness of his deeds as a reason for God to hear him. So, when we read expressions like this in David's psalms, it is obvious that God the Holy Spirit would have us see our Saviour in the psalmist's expressions.

In Him
Child of God, you and I approach God with boldness, and obtain the things we desire of him in Christ's name. In his righteousness we look to God, who is just and the Justifier of all who trust his dear Son, for mercy and grace. It is in union with Christ, by the merits of his blood and righteousness, that we are accepted at the Throne of Grace. To the Throne of Grace we may come, to the Throne of Grace we are commanded to come with boldness. At the Throne of Grace, the sentence of our justification in Christ comes forth with sweet assurance, because the Holy Spirit gives us faith to look up to God in heaven and cry, "Abba, Father."

God has found no iniquity in our glorious Surety. Therefore, when we come boldly to the Throne of Grace in Christ's name, we are telling our heavenly Father that the life of his darling Son was perfect, that his blood is our only and our effectual cleansing from sin, that his righteousness is all our righteousness, and that he is all our acceptance with the holy Lord God. How sweetly the Father hears such acclamations given to the Son of his love. He turns away none coming to him in the Saviour's name.

Precious Lamb of God! What unanswerable arguments may the souls of thy redeemed find in this holiness of thine as our Surety! And what can a sinner tell Jehovah so pleasing to him as when he follows up the gracious voice and proclamation from heaven, in which the Father said, "This is my beloved Son, in whom I am well pleased;" and saith, Lord! I am well pleased, too, in Jesus and his justifying righteousness, and am now come for acceptance in the beloved!

Christ Our Victor
Psalm 18 speaks of David's deliverance from Saul and all his enemies, and of his mighty conquests. Behold, my soul, a greater than David is here. Christ is our mighty Victor. Here he declares his love to God for all his promised help and strength as our Mediator in this world. Our Divine Representative was the only man of perfect faith ever to live. Then, having accomplished our redemption, having conquered death and hell, sin and Satan for us, he sat down in heaven as our mighty Victor in whom we triumph and glory for the everlasting glory of God and salvation of our souls.

God's Books
Our great and gracious God has written three great books by which he declares himself to men upon the earth, so that all are without excuse. These books his chosen, redeemed, called, children delight to read. These three books of God are set before us in Psalm 19. Enlightened minds hear God's voice in his word of creation by which he shows his eternal power and godhead, his word of providence by which he accomplishes his will and warns of judgment to come, and his word of inspiration, the Bible, by which he reveals the gospel of his grace and everlasting salvation in Christ, showing sinners the way of life.

Christ's Glory

Psalm 20 is a prayer for the prosperity of Christ as the King of Zion, the Head of his Church, a prayer for his conquest over all his foes. Soon this prayer shall be answered! Soon every knee shall be bowed before him and every tongue made to confess him as Lord, either in mercy or in grace. O gracious God, every day, every hour, and forevermore bow my heart to Jesus Christ as my rightful and only Lord!

Psalm 21 declares that our dear Saviour's glory shall be great in God's salvation. In the accomplishment of that salvation, the salvation the Triune God devised for our souls from everlasting, Christ obtained his glory as the God-man our Saviour (John 17:5). That glory he has given us (John 17:20; Romans 8:17). And it is great glory!

June 15
Today's Reading: Psalm 22-30
"One thing have I desired of the LORD"
Psalm 27:4

The Psalms we have read today are full of our Saviour. How good it is to be reminded of our redemption by Christ, of our great Substitute's sufferings, and the glory that followed in Psalm 22. In Psalm 23 our hearts are cheered by the knowledge of Christ our good Shepherd, who watches over, provides for, and protects us. Psalm 24 tells us of our mighty Sovereign, the King of Glory, who rules the universe for our everlasting benefit.

Let us lift up our souls to God, the Triune Jehovah, and ask him to show us his ways and lead us in his paths (Psalm 25), as we seek to know, follow, and serve our Lord Jesus Christ, of whom David spoke prophetically in Psalm 26. He alone could declare to God his integrity as the basis upon which he would be judged of God. This he pleads effectually as our Representative.

Psalms 27 and 28 are songs of faith, offering prayer and praise to the Lord. They are songs of sweet communion with our God. These precede the celebration of God's great sovereignty in Psalm 29 and his great goodness in the salvation he has bestowed upon us in Christ. He has turned our mourning into dancing and girded us with gladness.

Like David, let us set our hearts upon "one thing", seek that to the exclusion of all other things; and let the "One Thing" we seek be the Lord Jesus Christ himself. Give me Christ, O God, and I will ask no more.

One Object

If I understand the aim and purpose of the gospel, it is just this: it is to cause all the capacities, powers, talents, ambitions, and affections of our hearts to be concentrated upon one object and to beat with one pulse for that object. And that one object upon which our hearts must be fixed is the Son of God, our blessed Redeemer, the Lord Jesus Christ. Oh, that God would graciously cause you and me to have one solitary object possessing our beings! Oh, that God the Holy Ghost would cause our hearts to burn with desire for nothing but Christ! This is my prayer, "Lord, compel me by whatever means necessary, by the irresistible power and grace of your Spirit, to set my heart upon Christ alone."

A Choice

I know this: you and I must choose what we will seek and what we will serve. It will either be Christ and the cause of his glory in this world, or it will be the world and the lusts of our own flesh. We cannot serve both. And we cannot have both. "Ye cannot serve God and mammon" (Matthew 6:24). "Choose you this day whom ye will serve" (Joshua 24:15).

Will I serve Christ or self? Will I seek Christ, or the lusts of my flesh? This is a choice that is made at the beginning of the walk of faith. But it is also a choice that is made day by day in every believer's experience. And the older we get, the longer we live in this world, the more difficult it is to renounce the world, say no to the flesh, take up our crosses daily, and follow Christ. But it must be done! "Seek ye first", above all else, to the exclusion of all else, "the kingdom of God", the rule of Christ in your heart, "and his righteousness", the righteousness of Christ by faith; and all other things will be supplied by your heavenly Father (Matthew 6:33). "Lay not up for yourselves treasures upon earth" (Matthew 6:19). Earthly treasures of every kind are vanity. Do not set your heart upon vanity! Set your heart upon Christ.

One Thing Desired

The man after God's own heart desired and sought but "one thing" from the Lord. "That I may dwell in the house of the Lord all the days of my life." David desired to dwell in the conscious awareness of Christ's manifest presence, in sweet communion on earth and perfect communion in heaven. "To behold the beauty of the Lord", by faith here, and face to face hereafter. "And to inquire in his temple", to be taught and directed by his Spirit, and to be taught perfectly in his glorious presence.

One Thing Needful

In Luke 10:42 our Lord said to Martha, "One thing is needful". It is true; we live in this world with many cares and responsibilities, which we must not neglect. Yet, even in this world, only one thing is needful. And that one thing is Christ. "Martha was cumbered about much serving". Martha was "careful and troubled about many things". How sad! Mary chose one thing. Mary sought one thing. The one thing Mary sought is the one thing needful, Christ Jesus. Mary "sat at Jesus' feet, and heard his word". How blessed!

One Thing Known

In John 9:25 the blind man, whose sight had been restored by the power of God, said, "One thing I know". He knew that once he was blind; and he knew who caused him to see. That was enough. If you see the things of God, you know who caused you to see.

Like the blind man, you lay all praise at the feet of Christ. If you know this one thing, you know enough.

One Thing Done
In Philippians 3:13 the Apostle Paul said, "One thing I do". We have not yet attained perfection, or even come close. We have not yet won the prize we seek, perfect conformity to Christ. But this one thing we must do, "Forgetting those things which are behind, and reaching forth unto those things which are before", we must "press toward the mark for the prize of the high calling of God in Christ Jesus". We must persevere, expending every effort, using every means, seeking the Lord Jesus Christ, until at last we are found in him, righteous, perfectly holy, perfectly conformed to our blessed Saviour in body, soul, and spirit by the grace of God. Then "shall I be satisfied, when I awake in thy likeness" (Psalm 17:15).

June 16
Today's Reading: Psalm 31-36
"Oh, how great is thy goodness"
Psalm 31:19

Psalm 31 contains some of the very words our Saviour spoke as he hung upon the cursed tree. He who was made sin for us sighed in agony of soul, "My strength faileth because of mine iniquity". Yet, he is our mighty Saviour, our great Victor. When he had finished his work of redeeming our souls, he cried, "Into thine hand I commit my spirit: thou hast redeemed me, O Lord God of truth." Well might we sing, "Oh how great is thy goodness, which thou hast laid up for them that fear thee; which thou hast wrought for them that trust in thee before the sons of men."

Neither tongue nor pen can ever tell the great goodness of our God. The best we can do is to observe and declare that which is upon the surface of experience and the marrow of Revelation. But to declare the essence of God's goodness would be to declare the essence of God himself; and that cannot be done. Yet, I know this, goodness is that which God laid up for his people in eternity in the purpose of his grace, and that which he has wrought, is working, and shall work for his people before the sons of men.

Goodness Prepared
God has laid up goodness for his elect in Christ in his eternal purpose of grace (Ephesians 1:3). Before the worlds were made, God bestowed every blessing of his grace upon every sinner who shall ever trust his Son. Name something good, truly good, whatever it is, it is the property of every believer. Election, redemption, adoption, forgiveness, justification, preservation, eternal life, these and all other good

things have been given to God's elect in Christ from eternity. And in eternal predestination God mapped the course by which all the goodness of his grace must come to his elect.

Goodness Provided
The Lord has wrought goodness for us throughout the days of our lives (Romans 8:28). Many of our friends are suffering great, heavy trials: sickness, bereavement, wayward children, unfaithful companions, slander, etc.. How can we say that these afflictions of God's providence are works of goodness?
We believe God! We interpret the events of our lives by the Word of God. We never interpret the Word of God by the events of our lives. We read the Book of Divine Providence through the light of the Book of Divine Revelation. And we know that "all things are of God". If all things are of God, they must be good in their ultimate end, because God is good. Looking back over the pages of our lives, God's people are made to realize that in all things the Lord has wrought goodness for us.

Goodness Performed
Our great God shall work his goodness in us before the sons of men. I do not know how he will do it; but in the last day, when God spreads the trophies of his grace before wondering worlds, throughout eternity the Lord God will cause his enemies and ours to see the works of his goodness upon us. The rich man in hell will never cease to behold the works of God's great goodness upon Lazarus in glory. "Oh, how great is thy goodness."

June 17
Today's Reading: Psalm 37-43
"Mine iniquities have taken hold upon me"
Psalm 40:12

Be astonished, O my soul! Adore the mystery of substitution and the great mercy, grace, and love of the Lord Jesus Christ, the sinner's Substitute! That these are the words of our Saviour, when he was made sin for us, we cannot doubt. (Hebrews 10:5). His love for us was and is so great that in verse 7 he declares his readiness to assume a body and to accomplish his Father's will in the salvation of his chosen, agreeably to the ancient settlements written in the Volume of the Book, saying, "Lo! I come, I delight to do thy will, O my God". Then in verses 11 and 12, he prays for deliverance from his deep distresses.

Why?

Why was the Son of God brought to such sorrow and grief? Here is the answer. "He hath made him sin for us, who knew no sin, that we might be made the righteousness of God in him." Indeed, he could never have suffered the painful, shameful, ignominious death of the cross as our Substitute had he not been made sin for us. Justice would never have allowed it. The Lord God declares, "He that justifieth the wicked, and he that condemneth the just, even they both are abomination to the Lord" (Proverbs 17:15; Exodus 23:7).

Real Substitution

Hear the Saviour's words in Psalm 40:12, and worship him. "For innumerable evils have compassed me about." The Blessed One of God, who knew no sin and did no sin, was made sin! He cried, "Mine iniquities have taken hold upon me, so that I am not able to look up." He had no sin, but sin was laid on him; and he took it as his own. He was made sin for us. The transfer of sin to our dear Saviour was real, so real that it produced in him such horror he could not look up, such horror of guilt that he could not look into the face of God, bowing him down with crushing anguish and woe intolerable!

My soul, what would our sins have done to us eternally if the Friend of sinners had not condescended to take them all upon himself? Oh, blessed Scripture! "He hath made him sin for us." Oh, marvellous depth of love, that made the perfectly immaculate Lamb of God to stand in the sinner's place, and bear the horror of great trembling which sin must bring upon those who are forever keenly conscious of it in hell!

Conscious Guilt

"They are more than the hairs of mine head: therefore my heart faileth me." The pains of God's holy fury against sin, his unbending justice and unmitigated wrath were beyond calculation; and the Saviour's soul was so crushed with them, that he was sore amazed with the load of guilt. Imagine that. The Holy One of God oppressed with an agonizing load of guilt that no other man could ever know, the guilt of all the sins of his people! His heaviness of heart caused by the anticipation of this guilt caused him to break out in a sweat of blood in dark Gethsemane. His strength was gone, his spirit sank, he was in great anguish of heart (Psalm 22:14, 15). It was the thought and anticipation of being made sin for us, not of simply paying the debt due unto our sins, but of being made sin, that caused his bloody sweat in Gethsemane. It was this fact, the fact that he was made sin for us, that caused him to be forsaken of his Father as he hung upon the cursed tree on Golgotha's hill (Psalm 22:1-3).

O Spirit of God, let me never cease to be overwhelmed by the love of God in Christ which constrained my all-glorious Redeemer to be made sin for me!

Discovering Christ Day By Day

June 18
Today's Reading: Psalm 44-50
"The redemption of their soul is precious"
Psalm 49:8

No sinner can redeem himself, and none can redeem his brother, because we have nothing with which to pay the ransom price. "For the redemption of their soul is precious." The only ransom price by which the souls of men could be redeemed is "the precious blood of Christ".

Precious Redemption
"For the redemption of their soul is precious, and it ceaseth forever." Dear and precious is the redemption of the soul. It cannot be bought with corruptible things like silver and gold. But the precious blood of Christ is a ransom price of infinite worth. Sinners ransomed by the sacrifice of Christ are dearly purchased, so dearly purchased that once the ransom price was paid redemption ceased forever. Those purchased cannot be lost.

Particular Redemption
How we rejoice in the sweet gospel doctrine of limited atonement! God's elect, being redeemed by the precious blood of Christ, are effectually redeemed forever! What mercy is here! Oh, precious Lamb of God, all thanks and praise we give to you for your great, tender compassion toward us, "for thou wast slain, and hast redeemed us to God by thy blood out of every kindred, and tongue, and people, and nation".

Just Redemption
Redemption is as much an act of divine justice as it is a matter of divine mercy. It is God's greatest act of love and mercy that he gave his Son to die in the place of sinners. But it is also the clearest display of his justice. The precious blood of Christ was shed as a ransom price, paid into the hands of justice. It was the price required by the law. It is now clear that God is inflexibly just, for when his own darling Son was made sin for us he was slain according to the strict requirement of the law. And now that the law has been fully satisfied justice will not allow one soul to perish for whom Christ died.

Payment God cannot twice demand,
First at my bleeding Surety's hand,
And then again at mine.

Justice will not allow a double payment for sin. The justice of God pleads as strongly as his mercy for the eternal salvation of his elect. The price of redemption for them was paid at Calvary. At the cross, "Mercy and truth are met together; righteousness and peace have kissed each other". Because Christ died and rose again,

259

"He shall see of the travail of his soul and shall be satisfied". Sovereign mercy purposed it. And satisfied justice demands it.

Effectual Redemption
A just redemption is and must be a particular and effectual redemption. The foolish notion of universal redemption, the doctrine that Christ died for everyone, is as blasphemous as it is foolish. We rejoice to hear God say of our Redeemer, "He shall not fail". The cross of our Lord Jesus Christ shall never be discovered a miscarriage. Every sinner for whom the Lord Jesus died shall live forever with him. Each ransomed soul shall be born again at God's appointed time by the omnipotent operations of his grace. Because the redemption of our souls was accomplished by the precious blood of Christ, the Lord God declares, regarding every redeemed sinner, "He shall live forever, and not see corruption" (Psalm 49:9).

Thanks, eternal thanks and praise, everlasting praise, we give to you, O God, our Saviour, for the redemption of our souls!

June 19
Today's Reading: Psalm 51-59
"The God of my mercy shall prevent me"
Psalm 59:10

What a sweet, comforting, instructive declaration this is! "The God of my mercy shall prevent me." The word "prevent" means "precede" or "go before". Prevenient mercy is that mercy and grace that precedes and prepares the way for God's saving grace. God's goodness and mercy toward his elect secretly go out to them and pursue them, even before God the Spirit comes to them in the saving operations of his grace. Preventing mercies are mercies that go before hand. They are mercies that come to our souls before they are known, sought, or even thought of by us. God is always first. His mercy pursues its object from everlasting, and never gives up its pursuit until the chosen sinner is landed safe with Christ in heavenly glory in the house of God. What a sweet subject for meditation!

Preserving Grace
In the opening verse of Jude, it is declared as that grace by which we are preserved in Jesus Christ. All who are God's, because we are from eternity "sanctified by God the Father", are "preserved in Jesus Christ". The word "preserved" means "watched over", "guarded", "kept from loss or injury". It is a passive verb. So the sweet message of God to our hearts in these words is this. Because God has set us apart unto himself in Christ in eternal election, we are absolutely kept from any harm coming to us, because we are in Christ made the objects of his unceasing care. Throughout the

days of our rebellion, ignorance, and unbelief, we were preserved in Christ unto the time of our calling by the Holy Spirit at the appointed time of love.

We were preserved from condemnation and the second death. We were not preserved from falling with the rest of mankind in the sin and fall of our father Adam. We were not preserved from the depravity and corruption of human nature, which all men have by birth from Adam. And we are not preserved from iniquity, transgression, and sin. We are all, by nature, "children of wrath".

Yet, even in those days gone by, though fallen, depraved, hell-bent "children of wrath", Jude tells us, and all of Scripture teaches us, that we who now believe on the Lord Jesus Christ, and all who shall yet believe on him were so completely and absolutely preserved, watched over, guarded, and protected by our God, by virtue of our union with Christ, that it was not possible for us to suffer any real loss or injury by all that we experience in time! We were, even in our wrathful state of unbelief, so preserved that the law could not execute the sentence of condemnation on us, sin could not damn us, and Satan could not destroy us.

"Preserved in Jesus Christ." What blessed words! What unspeakable blessedness! What unknown wonders are here described! Only in eternity will we be able to see them. Yet, there are some things plainly revealed in the Book of God about the meaning of these words; "preserved in Jesus Christ."

Providential Grace
Prevenient grace is providential grace, the secret operations of grace that precede and prepare the way for God's saving grace. According to his purpose of grace, God ordered all the affairs of our lives, forming us as he would, moulding our personalities, to prepare us for his mercy (Galatians 1:15; Jeremiah 1:5). In marvellous restraining mercy, he kept us from those things that would have destroyed us, saying, "Hitherto shalt thou go and no further". Oh, how sweetly "the God of my mercy" went before me, overruling evil for good on my behalf! He sends his angels to watch over and protect his elect unto the time of their calling!

Read Psalm 107 and see how providence obeys God's command for the salvation of his elect. "Oh that men would praise the Lord for his goodness, and for his wonderful works to the children of men."

Preparatory Grace
Prevenient grace is preparatory grace. It is that grace that prepares the chosen, redeemed sinner to receive God's saving grace (Matthew 13:3-9). Sweet, indescribably sweet is that work of God's providence and purpose that precedes his grace, prepares the way for his grace, and brings his grace! Just ask any who have experienced it!

"The God of my mercy shall prevent me." As he has gone before me, he shall go before me all the days of my life. Therefore, let every heaven-born soul sing to his everlasting praise, "Surely goodness and mercy shall follow me all the days of my life: and I will dwell in the house of the Lord forever."

261

June 20
Today's Reading: Psalm 60-68
"Blessed is the man whom thou choosest"
Psalm 65:4

O God of my salvation, how I praise you for your sovereign election! How I praise you for choosing me in Christ before the world was, and for causing me, by irresistible, omnipotent mercy, to come to my Saviour!

God's choice and election of his people is not the result of something we do, but the cause of everything he does for us in Christ. Because this great work of grace is known and experienced in time, in Psalm 65:4 election is spoken of as being in the present tense, though it was done before the world began. No one knows his election until he has been effectually called by the Holy Spirit to life and faith in Christ.

Choosest
Notice the progression of grace running through this verse of Scripture. "Blessed is the man whom thou choosest". That is election. God chose to save some in eternity; and those whom he chose to save in eternity he graciously cuts out from the rest of mankind in time, like a rancher at round-up time cuts his own cattle out of the many roaming the open range. They were his cattle before. He simply rounds them up at the appointed time.

Causest
"And causest to approach unto thee". What a sweet word that is! "Causest". This refers to irresistible, saving grace, the effectual call of God the Holy Spirit. Election both precedes and is the source and cause of this call. Look at the next line. Thanks be unto God, he causes chosen sinners to come to Christ. I never would have come and never could have come had God the Holy Ghost not caused me to come.

Courts
"That he may dwell in thy courts". Sinners chosen and called by grace are caused to dwell, not to visit, but to dwell in the courts of divine worship. Those who are chosen and called by the grace of God to life and faith in Christ are kept and preserved by that same grace unto eternal glory.

Satisfied
"We shall be satisfied with the goodness of thy house, even of thy holy temple". Election is the source and cause of the everlasting happiness and satisfaction of God's saints in heaven. The house and temple of God in the Old Testament were typical of and representations of Christ and heaven, of God's salvation and our everlasting nearness to and worship of him. This is true blessedness; and this blessedness,

according to Holy Scripture, arises from and is effectually caused by God's election of his people unto salvation in Christ before the world began.

Praise
No wonder David sang, "O the blessedness of the man whom thou choosest and causest to approach unto thee". No wonder God's election was so much on his mind and heart. It was the thought of God's election that made him leap and dance before the ark of God (2 Samuel 6:21). It was the fact of his election by God unto salvation and eternal life in Christ that sustained his heart and rejoiced his soul as he lay upon his deathbed. Indeed, this is a doctrine full of joy and comfort to every child of God. Let us bless and praise him for his free, electing love in Christ, the fountain of all past blessedness and the guarantee of all future blessedness for his people. God does everything in accordance with his electing love toward us (Romans 8:28-30).

June 21
Today's Reading: Psalm 69-73
"I was as a beast before thee"
Psalm 73:22

How beastly we are by nature! How often God's saints in this world are compelled, like Newton of old, to sigh ...

If I love, why am I thus?
Why this dull and lifeless frame?
Hardly sure can they be worse,
Who have never heard his name.

Many of the doubts and fears God's people experience in this world, regarding their saving interest in Christ, arise from a failure to realize that every heaven-born soul lives in this world with two natures. In Scripture these two natures are referred to as "the old man, which is corrupt according to the deceitful lusts" and "the new man, which after God is created in righteousness and true holiness" (Ephesians 4:22-24), "flesh" and "spirit" (Galatians 5:16, 17). These two natures are constantly at war, the flesh lusting against the spirit and the spirit against the flesh.

Re-generation Not Re-formation
It is commonly assumed that in the new birth man, i.e. the natural, carnal man, is changed. That the old man is sanctified, that he who once loved sin is made to love holiness, that the enmity of the heart is slain, and that the old man renewed by grace

grows more and more holy in progressive sanctification, until he is ripe for glory, and the Lord takes him home.

That fanciful dream deludes multitudes, until, after being born again, they suddenly discover that the old lusts are still there. The discovery is sometimes shocking, simply because we have been taught that those old devils within us would vanish. How many there are who live in constant turmoil, knowing the abiding evil of their nature, but never daring to acknowledge it, lest they be scorned by others who pretend to be holy.

The new birth is not a re-formation, but a re-generation. The new birth is not reforming the old nature of fallen man, but a re-creation of life in man by the Spirit of God. The new birth is not transforming that which is sinful into that which is righteous, but the imparting of a new, righteous nature. In the new birth Christ is formed in us, and we are made new in him (Colossians 1:27; 2 Corinthians 5:17). In the new birth chosen, redeemed sinners are made "partakers of the divine nature" (2 Peter 1:4).

Two Natures
In every believer there are two natures (sin and righteousness), two men (the old man Adam and the new man Christ), two principles (sin and holiness); and these two constantly oppose one another. This fact is plainly declared in Scripture (Romans 7:14-24; Galatians 5:16-22; Colossians 3:9, 10; Ephesians 4:22-24). The old man, Adam, can never be sanctified; and the new man created in righteousness and true holiness, "Christ in you the hope of glory", cannot sin (1 John 3:9).

Adam lives in us by birth. By natural generation, we are made partakers of Adam's nature. Christ lives in us by the new birth. By regeneration, we are made "partakers of the divine nature" (2 Peter 1:4).

Creation And New Creation
God created man in his own image and after his own likeness (Genesis 1:26, 27). When the Lord God had formed a body for Adam from the dust of the ground, he then "breathed into his nostrils the breath of life and man became a living soul" (Genesis 2:7). Genesis 5:2 tells us that all men were created at one time in the creation of Adam. That is to say, every living soul descends by natural generation from Adam, partaking of his nature. All his sons and daughters are begotten in the image of their father, generation after generation (Genesis 5:3; Psalm 51:5; 58:3; Romans 5:12).

Every living soul was created in and simultaneously with "the first man Adam". Being born of Adam, we are all partakers of his nature; and we are called by his name, "Adam" (Genesis 5:1, 2).

As it was in the original creation, so it is in the new creation. Adam, we are told by the Spirit of God, was a figure (a type) of our Lord Jesus Christ. As all the human race had being in Adam when Adam was created, so all God's elect have had their being in Christ from everlasting when he stood forth as our Surety. As all human beings have their being from Adam, all God's elect have their being from Christ. As all in the old creation are born with the nature of Adam, all God's saints in the new creation of grace are born with the nature of Christ and are "made partakers of the divine nature" (2 Peter 1:4).

Having two natures, one completely sinful and one perfectly righteous, war breaks out in the soul, a warfare from which there will be no release until the God of peace bruises Satan under our heels when we drop the robe of flesh in the death of this body of flesh. "Blessed hope."

June 22
Today's Reading: Psalm 74-78
The problem of evil
Psalm 76:10

"Surely the wrath of man shall praise thee: the remainder of wrath shalt thou restrain."

The question is often raised, "How did sin and evil arise in God's creation?" If God is absolutely sovereign, absolutely holy, and absolutely good, if he created all things good, how is it that pride was found in Lucifer's heart? How were the fallen angels led to rebel against his throne? How was Adam seduced to sin?

Augustus Toplady wrote, "The origin of evil, whether among angels (with whom evil seems, strictly, to have originated), or among men, is the most difficult question, perhaps, and the most mysterious part of the divine conduct that ever presented itself to human investigation. Clouds and darkness are the seat of its residence; though wisdom, goodness, and justice, were certainly (in a manner unknown to us) the motives to its permission."

Submissive Faith

Yet, the existence of evil is a problem which vexes our minds continually. We must, whenever considering such a subject, at once, as Toplady put it, "clip the wings of curiosity". Knowing that God is not the author of sin, and that he never tempts any to evil (James 1:13-17), knowing that nothing comes to pass without his all-wise decree, the matter cannot be resolved in a more God honouring way than to use the words of our Lord Jesus as the expression of submissive faith, "Even so, Father, for so it seemed good in thy sight".

We bow before God in reverent submission, and confess, "O Lord God, we are darkness. You alone are Light. We bow to you, to your infinite wisdom and perfect goodness." Before him of whom are all things, we acknowledge our utter ignorance. We must be content to wait until our souls are freed from the influence of evil in the world above to know the mind and purpose of God in ordaining and permitting the evil which yet engulfs our minds. Still, two things we know by divine revelation.

God's Glory

Everything God does, or permits others to do is to show forth the greatness of his glory (Romans 11:33-36; Ephesians 1:11, 12; Revelation 5:13). It appears, then, that the perfections of God could not have been so gloriously revealed, as they now are in Christ, had evil never been permitted to enter the universe. God all-wise ordained and permits sin and evil that he may use it and overrule it to his own praise. Clearly that is the declaration of God the Spirit in Psalm 76:10. Had sin never been permitted, how could the justice of God be known in punishing it? Had evil never existed, how could the wisdom of God be seen overruling it? Had sin never entered the world, how could the goodness of God be made manifest in pardoning and forgiving it? Had there never been any wickedness in God's creation, how could the power of God be revealed in subduing it?

Our Good
Without question, all evil in the world is included in the "all things" which work together for the everlasting good of God's elect (Romans 8:28-30). The fall of our father Adam, and the entrance of sin into the world by him, was one of the countless links of providence essential to Christ's incarnation and crucifixion for the redemption of his people. To suggest, as many ignorantly do, that the fall was not purposed by God is to assert that the incarnation, birth, life, death, resurrection, and glory of Christ, and the salvation of his people by virtue of his obedience as our Substitute is all, from beginning to end, the result of chance, luck, or blind fate.

We know better. All who are taught of God know that God's purpose is always accomplished, his will is always done. We rejoice to bow before you, our great God, and rejoice to know, our heavenly Father, that of you, through you, and to you are all things. To you, O great God, our God, be all honour and glory forever and ever! "Surely the wrath of man shall praise thee: the remainder of wrath shalt thou restrain." Amen.

June 23
Today's Reading: Psalm 79-86
"Grace and glory"
Psalm 84:11

"The Lord God is a sun and shield: the Lord will give grace and glory: no good thing will he withhold from them that walk uprightly." What a great, blessed promise of God to his people this is! Grace and glory are inseparable gifts of God to his elect. Indeed, they are the same thing, given in different degrees. Grace is glory in the seed. Glory is grace in full bloom. Glory begins with grace. And grace is completed with glory. Both are free gifts of God. Neither grace nor glory can be earned, merited, or purchased by man. God cannot be obliged to bestow either grace or glory. He freely gives both to his elect in Christ.

"The Lord Will Give Grace"
How we love that word, "grace". Grace is *God's riches at Christ's expense.* Grace is the unmerited favour of God to sinners who deserve his wrath. To whom will the Lord give grace? He will give grace to all his elect (Romans 9:15, 16), to all who have been redeemed by Christ (2 Corinthians 5:21), to every sinner who believes on the Lord Jesus Christ (Romans 10:9-13).

What is this grace God promises to give? It is regenerating grace (Ephesians 2:1-5), convincing, convicting, converting grace (John 16:7-11), justifying grace (Romans 3:24), sanctifying grace (Hebrews 10:10-14), preserving grace (Philippians1:6), instructing grace (John 16:13), directing grace (Proverbs 3:5, 6), comforting grace (John 14:18), reviving grace (Isaiah 57:15), and sufficient grace (2 Corinthians 12:9).

How does God give grace? Mediatorially through Christ (Ephesians 1:3) and by the use of his appointed means (Jeremiah 29:13, 14), by prayer, the ministry of the Word, and the ordinances of public worship. God gives grace through faith. I know no one can believe unless he has grace and none can have grace unless he believes.

Read the promise as broadly as your needs require. It is addressed to every child of God. "The Lord will give grace" to serve him, to walk with him, to suffer for him, to live for him, and to die in him. And ...

"The Lord Will Give Glory"
If we have grace, we shall have glory, too. God will not give one without the other. Grace is the bud. Glory is the flower. Grace is the fountain. Glory is the overflowing river. Grace is the firstfruits. Glory is the full harvest. The Lord will give his elect all the fulness of glory freely, all the glory of heaven and eternity, all the glory of perfect holiness, the glory of total victory, the glory of complete conformity to Christ, yea, all the glory of Christ himself, with whom we are one (John 17:22; Romans 8:17)!

Nothing Withheld
"No good thing will he withhold from them that walk uprightly". Our God withholds no good thing from his chosen. Those who walk uprightly are those who "walk in the Spirit", living in union with Christ by faith. "He that spared not his own Son, but delivered him up for us all, how shall he not with him also freely give us all things?"

June 24
Today's Reading: Psalm 87-92
"One that is mighty"
Psalm 89:19

Is the Lord Jesus Christ qualified to be our Redeemer? To believers that question is redundant. Yet, it will do our hearts good to meditate once more upon our Saviour's glorious fitness to be our Redeemer. What a fit Redeemer he is! There are none fit to redeem our souls, but him. No animal sacrifices could redeem us. No mere man could redeem us. No angel could redeem us. Not even God in his strict character as God could redeem us. The incarnate Son of God alone is a fit Redeemer for sinners.

God And Man

Christ's fitness for the work of redemption lies in the fact that he is both God and man in one glorious person. It was God the Son who was sent to redeem us. He is of the same nature, and possesses the same perfections and attributes as his Father. He is the brightness of his Father's glory and the express image of his person. This man was and is in the form of God. Therefore, he thought it not robbery to be equal with God. Jesus Christ is God the Son, the second Person of the holy Trinity. He is the great and true God. Therefore, he is fit to be the Redeemer and Saviour of men. What a mighty Redeemer he must be! He is Jehovah, the Lord of hosts; therefore equal to such a great work as this (Galatians 4:4; 1 John 5:20; Titus 2:13; Jeremiah 50:34).

Our great Saviour and Redeemer is both God and man (Isaiah 9:6). He is the child born as man, and the son given as a divine person. He is Immanuel, God with us, God in our nature, God manifest in the flesh. As such, as the God-man, the man who is God, Christ is fit to be a Mediator between God and man; an Umpire, a Daysman to lay hands on both, and to do the work required of a Redeemer of men, to make reconciliation for our sins, and to take care of things pertaining to the glory of God, honouring his law, his justice, and his holiness.

As Man

As man, he could be made, as he was made, under the law, and, so, capable of yielding obedience to it and of bearing the penalty of it. It was necessary that he do so, if he would be the Surety and Redeemer of God's elect. As man, he had blood to shed. It was with this most precious blood he redeemed us unto God. As a man, he had a life to lay down, a sufficient ransom price for his people. As a man, the Son of God was capable of suffering all the wrath of God and dying in our room and stead, thereby making full satisfaction to divine justice for us!

As God

As God, he was zealously concerned for the glory of God in all the perfections of his nature. He secured the honour of all the divine attributes in that redemption which he wrought out and accomplished as our Substitute. As God, he put an infinite virtue into his blood. Divinity united to humanity in one person made his sacrifice of himself a full and adequate ransom price for the purchase of his church and the redemption of our souls. Our great Saviour's divinity gave support to his human nature under the load of sin as he suffered the wrath of God for us. His divinity was able to carry his humanity through the work, enabling him to endure the horrendous ordeal. Otherwise, he could never have endured the cup of God's wrath, and could never have stood before his indignation until his indignation and wrath were satisfied.

Right To Redeem
As both God and man, he had a right to redeem. As Lord of all, he had a right, as well as power, to redeem them that were his. The right of redemption belongs to him as a man as our near kinsman. Therefore, he wears the names "Kinsman" and "Redeemer". And a near Kinsman and precious Redeemer he is (Leviticus 25:47-49). No one could be so fit a Redeemer of the Church as Christ, our near Kinsman. He is our Head and our Husband. Jesus Christ, the Son of God, the Son of Man, is our Boaz!

June 25
Today's Reading: Psalm 93-102
"The set time, is come"
Psalm 102:13

The title given by our translators to Psalm 102 is, "A Prayer of the afflicted, when he is overwhelmed, and poureth out his complaint before the Lord." The cause of the affliction and trouble of which the psalmist complains was the low estate of God's church and kingdom. The children of light were in a time of great darkness. The children of the free woman were in terrible bondage. Because of their sin and unbelief, the Lord had hidden his face from the people of his favour, causing them to "eat ashes like bread" and mingle their drink with weeping (v. 9). Israel was reproached by her enemies (v. 8). Yet, the psalmist watched, "as a sparrow alone upon the house top", in expectant faith for mercy, anticipating a time of refreshing and revival (v. 7). He cried, "Thou shalt arise, and have mercy upon Zion: for the time to favour her, yea, the set time, is come".
Perhaps "the set time" has come for our God to again favour Zion. Oh, may God be pleased to pour out his Spirit upon us and send us "times of refreshing from the presence of the Lord" (Acts 3:19).

A Confident Expectation
"Thou shalt arise, and have mercy upon Zion". This is an assured, confident expectation. The psalmist "speaketh with as much confidence", John Trapp wrote, "as if he had been in God's bosom." He firmly believed and boldly prophesied that the Lord's apparent inaction would cease, that he would "arise and have mercy upon Zion" again. God will surely stir himself and work effectually for and in Zion, the church of God's elect, which he has chosen for himself. She is highly favoured, gloriously inhabited, and wondrously preserved. The memory of her past mercies assures us of future mercy. Though he may have hidden his face from us for a season, to chasten us in love and sweetly force us to seek his face, our God has sworn, "With great mercies will I gather thee ... With everlasting kindness will I have mercy upon thee, saith the Lord thy Redeemer ... My kindness shall not depart from thee, neither

shall the covenant of my peace be removed, saith the Lord that hath mercy on thee" (Isaiah 54:7-10). Our God will not leave us in such a low condition. He may, for a while, hide himself from us to make us see our nakedness and poverty; but he will arise in his great love to our defence, and pour out his mercy upon us.

The Set Time
"For the time to favour her, yea, the set time, is come". By his own decree, our heavenly Father has appointed a season for the blessing of his church. When "the set time, is come" she shall be blessed. Just as there was an appointed time for the Jews in Babylon, so there is an appointed time for our adversity. But, when the time was fulfilled, no bolts and bars could hold the ransomed of the Lord in Babylonian bondage. When the time came for the walls of Zion to be built, Israel was delivered from her bondage. So it shall be again. When the Lord God rises to deliver, none can hinder him.

And we have every reason to expect him to arise if we can honestly say, "For thy servants take pleasure in her stones, and favour the dust thereof" (v. 14). If we pity God's church, if we earnestly seek her good, how much more God must pity us and seek our good! If the dust of Zion's spiritual ruins moves us to compassion, how much more must it move our God! He has let the powers of darkness have their hour, only that "the set time" of his hour may be sought by us, and that it may be more glorious when it comes.

Is Come
Do not fail to see the joyful blessedness in these two words, "is come". "Yea, the set time, is come". Can those words be understood by us as a word of promise? Perhaps they can. This much I know: God's set time to favour Zion "is come" when Zion is humbled before him, acknowledging her great need of Christ, his cleansing, his righteousness, his grace, his power, and his presence. God's set time to favour Zion "is come" when he inspires his people with faith and expectation, "looking for the mercy of our Lord Jesus Christ" (Jude 21). God's set time to favour Zion "is come" when our hearts are enflamed by his Spirit with love for Christ, our God and Saviour, for his glory, and for his people. God's set time to favour Zion "is come" when he strips from us all pretence and hypocrisy, making us honest and sincere before him.

Those times of extremity and adversity, by which we are overwhelmed, are designed and brought to pass by our God to strip us that he may clothe us, to wound us that he may heal us, to make us know our need of him that we might be compelled to seek him earnestly. "Now therefore, O our God, hear the prayer of thy servant, and his supplications, and cause thy face to shine upon thy sanctuary that is desolate, for the Lord's sake" (Daniel 9:17). "Turn us again, O LORD God of hosts, cause thy face to shine; and we shall be saved" (Psalm 80:19).

June 26
Today's Reading: Psalm 103-106
"Bless the LORD, O my soul"
Psalm 103:1

"Bless the Lord, O my soul; and all that is within me, bless his holy name". How beautifully this psalm begins! Here the psalmist calls the soul to sweet, pleasant service of praising God! It is with the "Heart man believeth unto righteousness", while with the mouth "confession is made unto salvation". Unless the heart is engaged in any service, there is nothing truly valuable in the service. Therefore at the opening of our worship services in the house of God, we call upon ourselves and God's saints gathered for worship to "Lift up our hearts unto the Lord". Let us now lift up our hearts to our God, and bless him.

God's Name
"Bless his holy name". God's name represents who he is, embracing every attribute of his Being. Someone suggested, "Before we can thank God for his blessings, we must thank him for his Being". This is what David stirs up his soul and ours to do. We must bless God for who he is: The Lord God Almighty, full of grace and truth (Psalm 113:1-6; 115:1, 3; 117:1, 2; 118:1; 136:1-3; 139:1-24). It is the Lord God himself who is to be well spoken of, eulogized, and blessed with sincere thanksgiving and praise (Ephesians 1:3).

His Benefits
"Forget not all his benefits". There is no better way to stir up our hearts to bless the Lord our God than to recall all the benefits and blessings of grace we have personally experienced from him. Here are five things God has done, and is doing for us in Christ, for which we should ever bless his holy name.

Forgiveness
"Who forgiveth all thine iniquities". Our God is a God of forgiveness! He forgives all our sins; and God's forgiveness of our sins is a constant, perpetual act of grace through the blood of Christ (1 John 1:9). My soul, how I have sinned this day! Weep with joy, my God forgives all my sins!

Healing
"Who healeth all thy diseases". The corruption of nature is the sickness of the soul. It is its disorder, and threatens death. It is healed in sanctification. By the new birth, the disease of the heart is cured. Am I diseased in body and soul by reason of sin? God in Christ heals all my diseases.

Redemption
"Who redeemeth thy life from destruction". We were ruined and undone by reason of the fall. Christ redeemed us when he died upon the cursed tree (Galatians 3:13). He

271

obtained eternal redemption for us when he entered in once into the holy place with his own precious blood as our Representative (Hebrews 9:12). This redemption is applied to our hearts by God the Holy Spirit in the new birth (Hebrews 9:14). The power of redemption is experienced continually in our deliverances of grace (Psalm 130:1, 8).

Lovingkindness

"Who crowneth thee with lovingkindness and tender mercy". Christ has made us kings and priests unto God; and he has crowned us with God's constant favour. God in Christ crowns our lives with all that is needful here in grace, and all that is good in glory. What lovingkindness, what tender mercies he heaps upon us in Christ Jesus day by day and forever!

Satisfaction

"Who satisfieth thy mouth with good things, so that thy youth is renewed like the eagle's". Nothing can satisfy the soul but Christ! Christ, who satisfies our souls, promises to continually renew and revive us by his grace. As God replenishes the eagle's feathers every year, so he recovers his saints from their falls and decays, filling them with new life and joy as their days demand.

Precious, precious salvation; eternally secured for us and sealed to us by our God in Christ Jesus!

June 27
Today's Reading: Psalm 107-113
"Thy people shall be willing"
Psalm 110:3

This is a coronation Psalm. It describes the coronation of the Lord Jesus Christ as our King. Having accomplished our redemption by the sacrifice of himself, having finished the work which his Father gave him to do as our Mediator, having fulfilled all the Father's will as our Surety, "The Lord said unto my Lord, Sit thou at my right hand, until I make thine enemies thy footstool."

Earned Dominion

This coronation of Christ as King of kings and Lord of lords has nothing to do with his divinity. As God, he always has been and always will be Lord and King of the universe by divine right. This coronation is the exaltation and dominion which our Saviour earned as our Mediator and Surety. This is the reward of his faithful obedience and finished work as the God-man (John 17:2; Romans 14:9; Philippians 2:8-11; Hebrews 1:1-3; 10:10-14).

Discovering Christ Day By Day

Once our Lord Jesus was crowned as the omnipotent Prince and King of the universe, the sceptre of righteousness was put in his hands; he was given power, dominion, and authority over all flesh for the saving of his people, with this blessed promise, "The Lord shall send the rod of thy strength out of Zion: rule thou in the midst of thine enemies". The Triune God has turned over the dominion of the universe to the man Christ Jesus. He who died to redeem his people at Calvary now reigns over all things, even in the midst of his enemies, to save those sinners purchased with his blood.

His People
But where are his people? A king without subjects is no king at all. The title of "King" is a mockery if there are no people, no subjects to the king. Where, then, shall the Christ of God find subjects who shall at last fill up "the fulness of him that filleth all in all"? The Scripture promises, "A seed shall serve him" (Psalm 22:30). But who are they? Where are they?

Sometimes we fear that God is saving no one, that our labour is in vain. We preach the gospel to hard-hearted, obstinate sinners, to proud, dead, self-righteous religionists, to a valley full of dead, dry bones. Frequently, we almost despair, wondering, "Where shall we find subjects for this great Potentate, our God and Saviour and King? Where shall we find men and women willing to bow to the Son of God?" Then, when we read Psalm 110:3, our fears are silenced and laid to rest. "Thy people shall be willing in the day of thy power, in the beauties of holiness from the womb of the morning: thou hast the dew of thy youth".

Blessed be the name of our great God! Nothing is in jeopardy. There is no danger of failure with him. There is a people in this world who belong to the Lord Jesus Christ. They are God's elect, a people given to him, put into his hands as the Surety of the covenant before the world was made. They were his people before he came to save them, and shall be his people forever. As surely as the Father gave them to him in eternity, the Spirit shall give them to him in time by his almighty, effectual, irresistible, saving grace (Matthew 1:21; John 6:37-40). His people are safe and secure in his hands from eternity (John 10:27-30). They shall never perish! Be sure you get the meaning of this promise. It is this: our all glorious Christ, our great King shall never lack for a people to serve him, because all his people are made willing in the day of his power to be his subjects forever.

Make me, O my Saviour, your willing servant with every breath of my lungs and every beat of my heart, knowing that I am not my own, but yours, the purchase of your blood!

273

June 28
Today's Reading: Psalm 114-118
"This is the day"
Psalm 118:24

"This is the day which the Lord hath made; we will rejoice and be glad in it". Without question the day specifically spoken of in this sweet psalm of praise was prophetic, referring to the day of our Saviour's resurrection, the day when "the stone which the builders refused" became "the head stone of the corner". The day spoken of here is this great gospel day of grace in which we live. "This is the day which the Lord hath made".

The Lord God, our Saviour, made this glorious gospel day by obtaining eternal redemption for us. "We will rejoice and be glad in it". If those saints of old rejoiced in the confident prospect of this day, how much more joyful we ought to be in it! This is the day of grace our God made for us. The first man, Adam, brought in a day of sadness; but Christ, the last Adam, has brought in an everlasting day of gladness for his elect.

Christ Our Sabbath
We delight in the fact that our Saviour was raised from the dead on the first day of the week, and rejoice to gather with his people in his house on "the Lord's Day" (every Sunday) to worship the risen Christ. But those who suggest that this verse of Scripture speaks of establishing a Sunday sabbath in this gospel age both greatly constrict the meaning of the psalmist's words and teach a doctrine nowhere taught in Holy Scripture. Christ is our Sabbath of rest. Resting in him, we call the Sabbath a delight (Isaiah 58:13).

As the rising of the sun in the eastern sky brings day upon the dark earth, so the rising of Christ, the Sun of Righteousness, in our souls with healing in his wings brings into our sin-darkened souls the never-ending day of life and grace, a never-ending Sabbath of rest and delight.

Every Day
Let us, therefore, look upon every day in which we live and walk in his grace as "the day which the Lord hath made", understanding that he made it specifically for us. I often hear God's saints speak of days gone by, as though they were better days, almost complaining that they did not live in another day. In doing so, they make themselves and others miserable.

Child of God, this day, this very day is "the day which the Lord hath made" for you and me; and he made us for this day. There never was and never can be a better day in which you and I could live and serve our God. You know, I am sure that it is our God, our heavenly Father, who made this day. Be sure you understand this, too. He made, rules, and disposes of everything in this day according to his own everlasting love for us.

Rejoice

Knowing these things, Paul, the prisoner of the Lord, says to you and me, "Rejoice in the Lord alway: and again I say, Rejoice". We always have cause for joy, because we are Christ's and Christ is ours! Yes, we all must endure trials, hardships, sorrows, and pains. Yes, we are all constrained, as long as we live in this body of flesh, to be at war with our vile lusts. But in our saddest conditions, in our most painful circumstances, we are living in the day, including all that is experienced in it, which the Lord has made. We sometimes have banner, red-letter days of gladness, and sometimes disappointing days of grief; but every day we live was ordered from eternity for us; and each is preparing us for a better day still, the day of eternal bliss and glory. So sing, my brother, sing, my sister. Sing, O my soul, today, "This is the day which the Lord hath made; we will rejoice and be glad in it".

June 29
Today's Reading: Psalm 119
"Thou hast dealt well with thy servant, O LORD"
Psalm 119:65

I could never find better words to sum up my life's experience than these. God my Saviour has dealt well with me. What an awesome thought! All the days of my life, my God has dealt well with me. All the days of my life, the Angel of the Lord has pitched his tent around me and dealt well with me (Psalm 34:7). The word David uses for "well" is one of those magnificent little words that is bursting with meaning. It means "most favourably, most kindly, most graciously, most lovingly, most pleasurably, most sweetly, most prosperously, most finely, most joyfully, and most merrily". Particularly, since he saved me by his grace, my God has dealt well with me as his servant. Of course, he has dealt with me as his son, as his spouse, and as his friend. But, like David, I take particular delight in saying he has dealt well with me as his servant, in appointing me to be his servant, in calling me into his service, in providing every need of his servant, in protecting his servant, and in rewarding the labour of his servant. He has dealt well with me all the days of my life according to his Word: according to his word of predestination, his word of promise, his word of grace, and according to Christ his Word.

In Eternity

"Thou hast dealt well with thy servant, O Lord", from eternity. When we think of all that our Saviour did for us as our Surety in eternity, before the world was, our hearts gladly confess, "Thou hast dealt well with thy servant, O Lord". In the covenant of grace, when he took upon himself all responsibility for our souls, and espoused our cause as our great Surety, he dealt well with us. He drew nigh to God on our behalf.

His delights were with us. His heart upon us. He pledged to redeem and save us. He gave himself as the Lamb of God to redeem us. The Father accepted us, blessed us with all spiritual blessings in him, trusting him as our Surety (Ephesians 1:3-7).

In Grace
Pause once more to reflect upon this fact, too. "Thou hast dealt well with thy servant, O Lord", in the mighty operations of your saving grace. You have forgiven all my sin and made me the very righteousness of God (Psalm 32:1-5; 2 Corinthians 5:21). You have preserved me in grace and kept me in faith in the midst of countless temptations and countless falls (Psalm 34:1-6; 116:1-7). Your love for my soul has proved and is continually proving itself immeasurable, infinite, and immutable (Ephesians 3:17-19; 1 John 3:1; 4:19). Truly, he loves this sinner "freely".

In Providence
What a good God and Saviour we have! "I will sing unto the Lord, because he hath dealt bountifully with me". The Lord has dealt bountifully with us. He who gave us his darling Son has with him freely given us all things. He has given us his Spirit; and he conveys to us all spiritual blessings in Christ. Our God deals with us like a God. He lays open all his infinite fulness to us. "And of his fulness have all we received, and grace for grace." Is not your life a verification of this fact? Mine is. Truly, in all the affairs of providence, "Thou hast dealt well with thy servant, O Lord". And that which he has done, he is doing, and shall forever continue to do, until he has finished doing all that he purposed to do in eternity.

Then, we shall look back upon all things and say, "Thou hast dealt well with thy servant, O Lord". In that great day, when our mansions are prepared, our bodies raised from the dead, and we are perfectly conformed to his image in resurrection glory, when we hear him say, "Come, inherit the kingdom prepared for you from the foundation of the world", oh, with what rapture, gratitude, rejoicing, and love shall we shout, "Thou hast dealt well with thy servant, O Lord". In the light of these facts, can you imagine what must be awaiting us on the other side, in that land where there is no darkness, no weeping, no sorrow, no pain, and no sin in that blessed place called "Heaven", where "former things are passed away"?

June 30
Today's Reading: Psalm 120-135
"Plenteous redemption"
Psalm 130:7

The only hope for fallen, sinful men is redemption, a redemption which includes atonement for sin, satisfaction for justice, and effectual deliverance from the guilt, power, dominion, and consequences of sin. Such redemption could be accomplished by only one Person, the Lord Jesus Christ, the Son of God, our Saviour. Not only could he alone do it, he has done it; and he has done it alone. He declares, "I looked, and there was none to help; and I wondered that there was none to uphold: therefore mine own arm brought salvation unto me; and my fury, it upheld me" (Isaiah 63:5).

Most Important
Redemption by the precious blood of Christ is the most important of all gospel truths. In our day men more quickly attack the doctrine of the cross than any other. They more vehemently deny the glorious efficacy of Christ's sin-atoning blood than any other doctrine. Multitudes who sing the words of Cowper's hymn ...

> Dear dying Lamb, Thy precious blood
> Shall never lose its power,
> 'Til all the ransomed Church of God
> Be saved to sin no more.

... assert, with absolute dogmatism, that there is no real saving power and efficacy in Christ's blood; for they declare that multitudes are in hell today for whom Christ died; thus demonstrating that they know nothing of that Saviour revealed in Holy Scripture, of whom the hymn was written.

Because the doctrine of redemption by the precious blood of Christ is so very important, let us study the Scriptures for ourselves, comparing scripture with scripture, asking God the Holy Spirit to give us a clear understanding in the teachings of Holy Scripture about redemption.

Old Testament Pictures
The Holy Spirit declares in Hebrews 10:1, "For the law having a shadow of good things to come, and not the very image of the things, can never with those sacrifices which they offered year by year continually make the comers thereunto perfect". In the Old Testament, under the types and shadows of the law, the Lord God gave many pictures and prophecies of what he would do for and give to his people through his Son, the Lord Jesus Christ.

Obvious Facts
The sacrifices offered to God in the Old Testament could never take away one sin. However, the law did have many instructive pictures, types, and shadows of our redemption by the precious blood of Christ. In each of those types, pictures, and prophecies setting forth the redemptive work of Christ several things are obvious. Here are three very obvious facts revealed in the Word of God about our redemption by Christ. These three revealed facts teach us much about the subject of redemption.

The redemption portrayed and promised in the Old Testament was revealed only to a chosen people. Only the nation of Israel had the passover sacrifice and the promise of a redeemer, because only the Israel of God, God's elect, are the people for whom Christ the true Passover was sacrificed.

277

The redemption sacrifice was made by the command of God, offered to God, and accepted by God for a specifically chosen people, named by God himself. Even so, our Lord Jesus Christ died for those people given to him by the Father in the covenant of grace before the world began. He said, "I lay down my life for the sheep". The good Shepherd died for his sheep, not for the goats of the world.

The redemption portrayed the effectual deliverance of all those for whom it was accomplished. Every soul for whom the passover lamb was slain walked out of Egypt by the power of God. Even so, every sinner for whom the Son of God made atonement by his substitutionary death at Calvary, shall be delivered from the curse of God's holy law and saved from sin, death, and hell by the merit and power of his precious blood. Not one of those for whom Christ died under the wrath of God shall perish in hell. They all must and shall be saved, because Christ, the Son of God, died to save them; and "He shall not fail".

Discovering Christ Day By Day

July 1
Today's Reading: Psalm 136-144
"I am fearfully and wonderfully made"
Psalm 139:14

Psalm 139 clearly displays the omniscience, omnipresence, and omnipotence of our great God as our Creator, Ruler, and Judge. David speaks by divine inspiration, declaring his astonishment in the consideration of his own creation and sustenance as a man, God's knowledge of him, and the Lord's care in providing for and protecting him. But who can read this psalm and not see clearly that David, writing by inspiration of the Holy Spirit, spoke prophetically of the Lord Jesus Christ, our Saviour?

Behold a greater than David is here! This blessed psalm will be full of comfort to our souls, if we see our dear Saviour in the things written here. This psalm was written by God the Holy Ghost that we might know him whom truly to know is life eternal (John 17:3).

Covered In The Womb
Our Saviour declares that the Lord covered him in his mother's womb. Then he says, "I am fearfully, and wonderfully made". With those words, our God-man Mediator asserts that he was no ordinary man. The creation of his manhood was something more than an ordinary work of creation. Our Saviour's humanity, his body of flesh and bones, was "fearfully and wonderfully made". The word "wonderfully" means "differently, distinctly, in a unique way". So it was with our Saviour's incarnation. "The Word was made flesh, and dwelt among us, (and we beheld his glory, the glory as of the only begotten of the Father,) full of grace and truth" (John 1:14).

Body Prepared
The apostle Paul, commenting upon the prophecy of David concerning Christ as set forth in Psalm 40, wrote, "Wherefore, when he cometh into the world he saith, Sacrifice and offering thou wouldest not, but a body hast thou prepared me" (Hebrews 10:5). How was his body prepared? The angel who announced the miraculous conception to Mary declared, "The Holy Ghost shall come upon thee, and the power of the Highest shall overshadow thee" (Luke 1:35). Truly, his holy humanity was "fearfully and wonderfully made". The Lord God created a new thing in the earth. A woman compassed a man, just as the Prophet of God said (Jeremiah 31:22). Our Saviour was conceived in Mary's virgin womb, without the use of a man, by God the Holy Ghost. He had no earthly father.

But this work is even more wonderful in our eyes when we remember that Mary had no part in the creation of our Saviour's body in her womb either. She was altogether passive in it. The Lord Jesus was not begotten of a woman, but was made

279

of a woman. Being conceived in the virgin womb by the work of God alone, without the aid of a man or the aid of a woman, our dear Saviour is the man from heaven (1 Corinthians 15:47). Because God the Holy Ghost formed Christ's body in Mary's womb, our Redeemer said, "I am fearfully and wonderfully made". He was indeed made secret, and curiously wrought in the dark place of the virgin's womb, called the lowest parts of the earth. "My substance was not hid from thee, when I was made in secret, and curiously wrought in the lowest parts of the earth.

Mystical Body
Then, the Saviour says, "Thine eyes did see my substance yet being imperfect; and in thy book all my members were written" (Psalm 139:16). The members of his mystical body, the church, were written in the Lamb's book of life from eternity (Philippians 4:3; Revelation 13:8; 17:8; 21:27). When the Lord God said, "Let us make man" (Genesis 1:26), he made Adam and all the human race in him. But we never read of a book in which all the members of the human race were written before their creation. Obviously, the psalmist's words cannot refer to men in general. Rather, these words refer to our Lord Jesus Christ, our God-man Surety and Representative, and all his members, God's elect, the members of his mystical body, the church. "For we are members of his body, of his flesh, and of his bones" (Ephesians 5:30).

July 2
Today's Reading: Psalm 145-Proverbs 2
God's ice, God's cold, and God's thaw
Psalm 147:16-18

Everything in God's creation is designed by infinite wisdom to portray something about the new creation of grace.

"He Giveth Snow Like Wool"
What a strange way to speak of snow! Can cold snow be compared to warm wool? Though the snow is cold, freezing cold, it forms a blanket like wool to protect the unseen vegetation beneath the earth. In fact, the freezing snow is necessary to protect the life and health of the vegetation hidden within the earth that it may revive and thrive at God's appointed time.

How often have you asked, "Lord, Why do I find such coldness in my soul? Why do such times of lukewarmness engulf my heart? Why am I so often hardened, frozen like the ground covered with snow in the winter?" This, too, is according to the wise design and decree of our God. It is necessary to preserve the life he has planted within, to keep us clinging to Christ as our only Life and our only Salvation. God our heavenly Father gives the snow like wool!

"He Scattereth The Hoarfrost Like Ashes"
There is a black frost that brings death. We look out at the late spring frost with sadness, because every plant in the garden and every bud in the tree is black with death. The black frost has killed the tender life springing out of the earth. But the hoarfrost, though it burns, it makes everything sparkling white. So it is with our times of spiritual adversity. The more we are compelled to abandon all hope in self and trust our blessed Saviour, the more we acknowledge and confess our sin and hope in his righteousness, the more beautifully we sparkle in his whiteness!

"He Casteth Forth His Ice Like Morsels"
What ice is this? Is it the light snow that is like a blanket of wool to the earth? Is it the driving sleet that is so painful to feel on your face that you are forced to seek refuge from it? Is it the beating hail that destroys every crop of human planting? Or is this ice the hard freeze of gradual accumulation that breaks weak limbs from the mighty oaks and dead branches from living trees? The ice here refers to every form of ice. Our Father casts it out of the windows of heaven, not as an instrument of destruction, but as morsels of bread for our souls. By hard freezing, breaking trials, inward and outward, he feeds and nourishes our souls.

"Who Can Stand Before His Cold?"
When God withdraws his light, nothing is left but darkness; and when the Lord God withdraws the heat of the Sun of Righteousness, nothing is left but a coldness that cannot be thawed by any activity, a coldness that we cannot resist! But blessed be his name forever, that is not the last word about the matter!

"He Sendeth Out His Word, And Melteth Them"
"He causeth his wind to blow, and the waters flow." At the time appointed, as surely as he sent the cold, our faithful God and Saviour will send his Word to melt our hearts again before him. He will cause his wind (his Spirit) to blow upon his garden and make it spring forth with life, that the spices may flow out, that he may eat his pleasant fruits! "Awake, O north wind; and come, thou south; blow upon my garden, that the spices thereof may flow out. Let my beloved come into his garden, and eat his pleasant fruits" (Song of Songs 4:16).

281

July 3
Today's Reading: Proverbs 3-7
"Honour the LORD with thy substance"
Proverbs 3:9

To honour the Lord with our substance is to use that which God has given us in his providence for his glory, the benefit of his people, and the cause of his kingdom in this world. Particularly, it is to give a portion of your substance to God again.

Not A Tithe
The Lord does not tell us how much to give. Under the law, a tithe of all was required; but we are not under the law. Therefore, legal precepts have no authority over us. And, certainly, those who know the grace of God in Christ Jesus are not so niggardly as to think they honour God by allotting only a tithe of their income for gifts!

God's people are not miserly tithers, but generous, cheerful givers. They give as much of their substance as prudence will allow, in proportion as the Lord has prospered them. And they give in faith, for they give of "the firstfruits of all (their) increase". Week by week, they allot a portion of their income to be given for the honour of God first. Some can give much more than others, because their needs are less and their income more. But all who honour God in their hearts honour God in their substance.

No Loss
And though we never give for the purpose of gaining more (God's saints are not mercenaries!), none who honour God with their substance will ever be impoverished by doing so. Solomon says, "So shall thy barns be filled with plenty, and thy presses shall burst out with new wine" (v. 10). And he who is greater than Solomon said, "Give, and it shall be given unto you; good measure, pressed down, and shaken together, and running over, shall men give into your bosom. For with the same measure that ye mete withal shall it be measured to you again" (Luke 6:38).

Because the Philippians, from their great poverty, gave so generously to one of God's own, the Apostle Paul assured them that God would supply all their need "according to his riches in glory by Christ Jesus" (Philippians 4:14-19). Because they had honoured God with their substance, Paul assured them that God would honour them by supplying all that they needed, both to live in this world and to continue honouring God with their substance.

As Prospered
Let every believer give generously of his substance, "as God has prospered him", for the honour of the Lord our God. As we do, every need will be supplied for every work and every ministry the Lord would have performed in every generation. Every pastor, every missionary, every labourer in God's vineyard in every part of the world will have all that is needed to do the work trusted to his hands.

Faith
How can anyone be expected to obey this precept? How can anyone be expected to "honour the Lord" with their substance, using what God puts in their hands for God's honour, instead of their own comfort? Such giving, such use of our time, talents, money, and property is inspired and motivated by faith in Christ. There is an obvious reference to Christ in Solomon's wise admonition. He said, "Honour the Lord with thy substance, and with the firstfruits of all thine increase". The "firstfruits" were offered in faith. "Abel brought the firstlings of his flock" (Genesis 4:4). All the firstfruits had reference to Christ. "Trust in the Lord with all thine heart; and lean not unto thine own understanding, In all thy ways acknowledge him, and he shall direct thy paths" (Proverbs 3:5, 6). Blessed Spirit of God, give me grace and faith day by day, as only you can, to honour God my Saviour with all my substance.

July 4
Today's Reading: Proverbs 8-11
Christ Our Wisdom
"I wisdom dwell with prudence ... I am understanding"
Proverbs 8:12-14

Christ is Wisdom. Christ is Understanding. He gives wisdom and understanding; but here the Holy Ghost tells us much more than that. He tells us that the Mediator-man Christ Jesus is Wisdom and is Understanding. If Christ is Wisdom and Understanding, as he here asserts, then there is no wisdom and no understanding anywhere except in him. Furthermore, if Christ is Wisdom and Understanding, then all who are in him and have him possess wisdom and understanding.

In Christ Jesus
All who are born of God are "in Christ Jesus, who of God is made unto us wisdom" (1 Corinthians 1:30). We are in Christ by the rich, free grace and goodness of God the Father, who put us in him in sovereign election before the world began. In him we were and are preserved and blessed from everlasting. That secret, everlasting union with Christ was made manifest in time, when God the Holy Spirit gave us life and faith in Christ, by the operation of his mighty grace; but the union is from everlasting.

God's Work
Our being in Christ is altogether God's work. Our conversion, our saving union with Christ is not the result of something we have done. We are not in Christ because we are wiser, or better, or have made a better choice than others. We are in Christ because God put us in Christ. "Salvation is of the Lord." It is the purpose of God to make this apparent, and to force all men to acknowledge it. He dispenses his grace in such a way

that he makes men see with regard to others, and to acknowledge with regard to themselves, that salvation is his work alone.

Our Wisdom
Though we are foolish creatures by nature, by virtue of our union with him, Christ is made of God unto us wisdom. He is the one who gives us wisdom and understanding in all things spiritual. He is the shining light that dispels darkness in our souls. Christ is our wisdom objectively, too. I mean by that that our highest wisdom is knowing him. Under the personification of Wisdom, our Saviour says, "He that findeth me findeth life, and shall obtain the favour of the Lord" (Proverbs 8:35).

Christ is the Head of his body the church; and as all the wisdom of the body is in its head, so all our wisdom is in him. The Lord Jesus acted for us as our Wisdom representatively, speaking for us in the everlasting covenant of grace and peace; and he is our Advocate with the Father, still pleading our cause and interceding for us in heaven.

It is by Christ Jesus that the Triune God is made known and revealed to man. He is the embodiment of God, the embodiment of Wisdom, the Word, the Revealer of God. As all the fulness of the Godhead dwells in him, so all the treasures of wisdom and knowledge are his. By him alone they are made known to men. "No man knoweth who the Son is, but the Father; and who the Father is, but the Son, and he to whom the Son will reveal him" (Luke 10:22).

Truly Wise
This union with Christ makes the heaven-born soul truly wise, because when Christ is formed within, we are given the mind of Christ and know all things (1 Corinthians 2:14-16). All true spiritual knowledge is derived from Christ; and it is only those who are taught of him who are made wise unto salvation. Christ is our Wisdom within to direct our paths, guide us in his way, and order our steps day by day.

July 5
Today's Reading: Proverbs 12-15
Folly and wisdom
Proverbs 15:21

"Folly is joy to him that is destitute of wisdom: but a man of understanding walketh uprightly" (Proverbs 15:21).

A Multitude Of Counsellors
Solomon declares, "Without counsel purposes are disappointed: but in the multitude of counsellors they are established" (Proverbs 15:22). Anytime people seek advice

from many counsellors, their real purpose is obvious. It is their intention to take the advice of none, but either to find one who will tell them what they want to hear, or to pick and choose what they want from each, and then say, "This is what these counsellors recommend". Thereby, they establish their own purposes without assuming responsibility for their own actions. Yet, "Where there is no counsel the people fall". What we must do, especially those who are responsible to lead others, is seek "wise counsel" from Christ our Wisdom and our Counsellor, and follow it, rather than seeking safety for ourselves in a "multitude of counsellors".

Slander
Slander is the attempt of one to defame another, to make another person look bad, by whispering gossip and innuendoes. It really does not matter whether the report is true or false. When the spies cast a slander upon the land (Numbers 14:36), what they reported was factually true, but their intent was evil. That made their report a slander. Slander is simply an act of abhorrent evil. It is always an act of hatred. "A lying tongue hateth those that are afflicted by it" (Proverbs 26:28). By it multitudes suffer great pain needlessly. "He that hideth hatred with lying lips, and he that uttereth a slander, is a fool" (Proverbs 10:18). As we keep ourselves from engaging in such evil, we keep ourselves from trouble (Proverbs 21:23), and avoid hurting others.

Leave it to wicked men to search out evil matters. Swine love wallowing in the mire. Sheep prefer to avoid it. As it is the glory of God to conceal the evil of his children (Proverbs 25:2), it is both our honour and the kindness of brotherly love for us to do the same. "Hatred stirreth up strifes: but love covereth all sins" (Proverbs 10:12). "He that pursueth evil pursueth his own death" (Proverbs 11:19).

To Answer Or Answer Not
"Answer not a fool according to his folly, lest thou also be like unto him. Answer a fool according to his folly, lest he be wise in his own conceit" (Proverbs 26:4, 5). Usually, it is best never to respond to a fool, a slanderer. If he must be answered, make certain that he is not answered according to his folly, with his same evil intent, to make yourself look good, or to make him look bad. If his folly must be answered, it must be answered for the glory of God, the truth of God, and the good of his church, lest the fool "be wise in his own conceit", lest it appear that his folly is true because unanswered. Our Lord's example is the example to follow. He never once responded to the foolish, hateful slanders of men against himself. He only answered fools (religious Pharisees, Sadducees, and hypocrites) when the glory of God, the truth of God, and the people of God might be injured by them. May God the Holy Spirit give us grace to "walk circumspectly, not as fools, but as wise" (Ephesians 5:15).

July 6
Today's Reading: Proverbs 16-19
"The LORD hath made all things for himself"
Proverbs 16:4

Nothing is more delightful and nothing more comforting to God's saints in this world than the realization that all things are under the absolute control of our great and glorious God. And nothing inspires us to bear our trials and troubles, sicknesses, sorrows, and bereavements here with patience like the fact that all things are for the glory of our God.

Making Himself A Name

"The LORD hath made all things for himself: yea, even the wicked for the day of evil". I do not presently see what God is doing in all things; but I am assured that in all things the Lord is making for himself an everlasting and a glorious name. Isaiah tells us that the Lord God led Israel "by the right hand of Moses with his glorious arm, dividing the water before them" and he did so "to make himself an everlasting name". He "led them through the deep, as an horse in the wilderness, that they should not stumble, as a beast goeth down into the valley, the Spirit of the LORD caused him to rest: so didst thou lead thy people, to make thyself a glorious name" (Isaiah 63:12-14).

All Things

In everything that is, has been, or shall hereafter be the Lord our God is making himself an everlasting and glorious name. He who raised up Pharaoh and cast him down in the Red Sea, for the glory of his own great name, brings all things to pass exactly as he has purposed for the everlasting praise and glory of his great name. All things are for God.

Frequently, people point to specific things and say, "How can that bring glory to God?" Unbelieving people point to sickness, war, famine, pestilence, crimes, and other evils, and say, "If there is a God in heaven, how can these things be?" Once, I even heard a preacher say, after considering a great disaster, "God has a lot of things to answer for". What a horrible statement! The very thought of man calling God Almighty to the bar of human judgment is incredibly blasphemous!

I readily acknowledge that I do not see and cannot explain how isolated events, considered by themselves will bring glory to God. But I do understand what God says in his Word; and I rejoice to believe him. Somehow, when everything that must be has been, when all the purpose of our great God has been perfectly fulfilled, everything will render praise and honour to him. "For of him, and through him, and to him, are all things: to whom be glory forever. Amen" (Romans 11:36).

Divine Providence

In Ephesians 1:10, 11 the Holy Spirit informs us that all things are disposed of by God in time according to his own purpose of grace in eternity in divine predestination. Everything that comes to pass in time was predestinated by God in eternity, and is brought to pass according to God's eternal purpose of grace for the salvation of his elect and the glory of his own great name. Happy is that soul which has learned to trust and rest in the purpose and providence of God. All things come to pass exactly according to the eternal purpose of our God for the glory of our God.

July 7
Today's Reading: Proverbs 20-22
"He that is abhorred of the LORD"
Proverbs 22:14

"Abhorred of the Lord." What an alarming, sobering thought! Pause, O my soul, and give praise and thanks to the God of all grace "who hath from the beginning chosen you" in everlasting love, redeemed you because he loved you, and called you for that same reason! Here God the Holy Ghost speaks of one man who stands as the representative of many who are "abhorred of the Lord" but (blessed be his name forever!) there is a vast multitude no man can number, of whom the Lord God says, "I will love them freely", because he loved them with an everlasting love in Christ Jesus.

Jacob And Esau
In Romans 9:13 God the Holy Spirit uses Jacob to represent all God's elect, and his brother Esau to represent all the reprobate sons of Adam. He tells us plainly that God loved Jacob and hated Esau from eternity, without any consideration of their works. His purpose is to show us that the purpose of God according to election stands not upon the footing of human works, but upon the footing of his sovereign grace alone (Romans 9:11).

The amazing, wonderful thing in Romans 9:13 is God's statement, "Jacob have I loved". God owed nothing to Jacob. Jacob had no claim upon God. God knew what kind of person Jacob would be. A sinful wretch! Yet, God loved Jacob, all his Jacobs, with an everlasting, free, sovereign love. That love is God's eternal benevolence. "His everlasting will, purpose, and determination to deliver, bless, and save his people" said Augustus Toplady. Wonder of wonders that God should love such wretches as he knew we would be, and determine to save us!

Then, the Lord God declares, "Esau have I hated". God said it; and we dare not try to alter it. "Esau have I hated". What does that mean? The word "hated", as it is used in this text, does not imply a positive hatred, which involves contempt, anger, and wrath. That cannot be the meaning of the word in Romans 9:13, because God's anger and wrath against men is always a judicial response to man's sin. And Paul plainly tells us that Esau's works were not under consideration when God said, "Esau have I hated". The hatred there spoken of is, as John Gill rightly observed, a "negative hatred, which is God's will not to give eternal life to some persons ... a neglect of them, taking no notice of them, passing them by when he chose others. So the word 'hate' is used for neglect, taking no notice".

This is the way our Lord Jesus used the word "hate" in Luke 14:26. We are not commanded to treat our families or ourselves with contempt, anger, and wrath. But we must, as we seek to follow Christ, give no consideration to our earthly relationships. We must pass them by and choose Christ. That is what the word "hated" means in Romans 9:13. God passed by Esau, giving him no consideration. His only consideration was for Jacob, his elect. God loved Jacob. God considered Jacob. God chose Jacob. Let Jacob rejoice!

The Abhorred
In Proverbs 22:14 the word "abhorred" is similar to the word "hated", only stronger. It comes from a word that means "to foam at the mouth". The abhorred person is one against whom the Triune Jehovah is enraged with anger. This abhorrence is a matter of divine justice. Because the sinner chooses to rebel, the Lord God gives him over to his reprobate mind in judgment. God in judgment sends a strong delusion to sinners who will not receive the love of the truth. By that delusion, the reprobate, drinking iniquity like water, runs to the house of the "strange woman" of Babylon. Intoxicated by the strong wine of freewill and the narcotic of works religion, they perish forever.

Everlasting Praise
Let all who have been delivered from the "strange woman" give everlasting praise to God for his free, sovereign, saving, electing love in Christ Jesus. "We are bound to give thanks always to God for you, brethren beloved of the Lord, because God hath from the beginning chosen you to salvation through sanctification of the Spirit and belief of the truth: Whereunto he called you by our gospel, to the obtaining of the glory of our Lord Jesus Christ ... and hath given us everlasting consolation and good hope through grace" (2 Thessalonians 2:13-16).

July 8
Today's Reading: Proverbs 23-26
"Good news"
Proverbs 25:25

"As cold waters to a thirsty soul, so is good news from a far country." Try to imagine what it was like 200 years ago for a person to receive a letter from a wife, husband, or child they had not seen or heard from in six months, a year, or, perhaps, two or three years.

When we are separated from our families for a long time, nothing is more refreshing than good news from them. When Jacob's sons came back from Egypt, they brought their father gold, silver, and corn in great abundance; but nothing could compare with the good news by which the old man's heart was revived. "Joseph is yet alive" (Genesis 45:26).

Good news, like water to a thirsty soul, is refreshing, comforting, and invigorating. May God the Holy Spirit make me a messenger of good news to you today.

Good News For Sinners

Here is good news for helpless sinners from the almighty God of sovereign grace. The God against whom we have sinned is a gracious, almighty God. It is true. God is holy, righteous, and just. He must and will punish sin. But it is the glory of God to forgive iniquity, transgression, and sin. His goodness is his glory (Exodus 33:18, 19; 34:5-7). This great God has found a way to save sinners without compromising his holy character. He gave his Son, Jesus Christ, to be a propitiation for our sins. The Lord Jesus Christ has obtained eternal redemption for every sinner who comes to God by him.

Good News For Pilgrims

Here is good news for weary, heavy-hearted pilgrims from our homeland in heaven. Do you have heartaches and troubles too numerous to count? It will do you good to receive some good news from home.

The Lord our God is still on his throne. Our Saviour is still in heaven, preparing a place for you, representing you, interceding for you. There are many already in heaven just like you and me. There is a fallen David there, a doubting Thomas, an angry Moses, a feeble Philip, an impetuous Peter, and a righteous Lot. All are there by grace alone, through the merits of Christ's blood and righteousness.

And you and I are wanted there! God the Father, the Son, and the Holy Ghost want us there. The angels of God want us there. Our glorified brethren want us there. Very soon, the Lord Jesus Christ will come again to take us there (John 14:1-3).

Good News For The Church

We have good news for the church above from the church here below. Our brothers and sisters in heaven are interested in God's church on earth. They rejoice to hear that sinners are repenting. God's saints are running the race with patience. Gospel churches are being established. The gospel is spreading again through America, Mexico, Africa, Europe, Asia, Canada, Australia, and the islands of the seas. God's saints are growing in grace. Some are growing old gracefully. Some are growing feeble, but growing strong in the Lord. And some will be going home soon. Rejoice! There is good news all around!

———

July 9
Today's Reading: Proverbs 27-31
"They that seek the LORD understand all things"
Proverbs 28:5

Other people are vexed and confused by the Word of God, the ways of God, and the works of God; but God's saints understand all things. This is not a matter of supposition, but the plainest possible declaration of inspiration. "They that seek the Lord understand all things." The wise man tells us that, "Evil men understand not judgment". Then he asserts, "but they that seek the Lord understand all things". I do not suggest that religious people understand all things, not by a long shot; but the Lord God himself asserts that his people, all who know him by the saving operations of his grace, all who are born of God and taught of God, understand all things.

Believers understand that the origin of all things is God. We understand that the end of all things is the salvation of God's elect and the glory of his great name. God's people understand that the nature of all things here is temporal. Everything here in this sin-cursed earth is temporal and vanishing. Every relationship in this world is just temporal. Most importantly, those who are taught of God understand all things spiritual. This is what the Apostle John tells us. "But ye have an unction from the Holy One, and ye know all things" (1 John 2:20). All who are born of God and taught of God have the mind of Christ and understand all things vital and necessary to the saving of their souls.

Thanks For All Things
We understand that it is both the responsibility and the joy of believers to give thanks to God for all things. We are taught to give "thanks always for all things unto God and the Father in the name of our Lord Jesus Christ" (Ephesians 5:20). In the context Paul is talking about walking in the Spirit and being filled with the Spirit. The Spirit-filled life is the life of a believer giving thanks to God. "In everything give thanks: for this is the will of God in Christ Jesus concerning you" (1 Thessalonians 5:18). It is both our duty and our great privilege to give thanks to God always and for all things. It glorifies God for us to praise him and give thanks to him. It breeds joy and peace in our own hearts and among our brethren for us to ever give thanks to God for all things.

Restitution Of All Things
We also understand that there is a day coming called "the restitution of all things" (Acts 3:21). It is written, "Repent ye therefore, and be converted, that your sins may be blotted out, when the times of refreshing shall come from the presence of the Lord; And he shall send Jesus Christ, which before was preached unto you: Whom the heaven must receive until the times of restitution of all things, which God hath spoken by the mouth of all his holy prophets since the world began". In that great and glorious day, when all things are brought to their final end, when time shall be no more, all things will glorify our God! Everything that has been, is now, or shall

hereafter be, all things, all events, all creatures, and all the actions of all creatures, whether good or evil, will praise him and will prove to have been good! Everything, even you and I, will glorify the Triune God one way or another. We will either glorify his grace in Christ in our everlasting salvation; or, like Pharaoh, we will glorify his power and wrath in our everlasting destruction; but we will all glorify God!

Inherit All Things
In Revelation 21:7 we read, "He that overcometh shall inherit all things; and I will be his God, and he shall be my son". All true believers may rightfully sing, "We shall overcome some day". We shall at last, by the grace of God, completely overcome sin and all its consequences. We shall in the end overcome this world, all its lusts and all its charms, by the power and grace of our God. By God's free grace in Christ, we shall overcome Satan, too.

Many years ago, when my doctors thought I was about to die, and I was fairly certain that they were right, I got a card from a friend that lifted my spirit to heaven itself. It was totally blank, except for a Scripture reference. On the inside, my friend simply wrote the reference Romans 16:20. When I turned to it and read the text, my soul melted within me and leaped with joy in the realization of the promise contained in that text. Listen to this word from God to all his people. If you are a believer, this is God's word to you. "And the God of peace shall bruise Satan under your feet shortly." Then, we shall inherit all things, by the grace of God. We shall inherit all things with Christ, in Christ, and for Christ's sake!

End Of All Things
We who are taught of God also understand that "the end of all things is at hand" (1 Peter 4:7). "Behold, he cometh." When our great and glorious Christ appears the second time without sin, unto salvation, then the end of all things will come. The end of all our troubles. The end of all our struggles. The end of all our toils. The end of all our trials. The end of all our temptations. The end of all our sins. The end of all our sorrows.

All Things Done Well
God's saints all understand this, too. The Lord our God has done all things well! When the end of my days on this earth comes, when I look over my life's finished story, I am confident, this will be my final word then. And when the end of all things has come, this will be the final word of all "his-story", and of all rational creatures: "He hath done all things well" (Mark 7:37). This I declare now; and this I will declare in that great day, when time shall be no more. "He hath done all things well" with me and mine. "He hath done all things well" with his church. "He hath done all things well" with his world. "He hath done all things well" with you and yours.

———

July 10
Today's Reading: Ecclesiastes 1-4
"It shall be forever"
Ecclesiastes 3:14

When God saves a sinner, "it shall be forever". If salvation is the work of God and the work of God alone, as it most surely is, then it is an everlasting, eternal salvation. It can never be lost or destroyed. As Solomon asserts, "I know that whatsoever God doeth, it shall be forever: nothing can be put to it, nor anything taken from it: and God doeth it, that men should fear before him."

Union With Christ
Salvation is a real union with the Lord Jesus Christ, our Mediator. "We are members of his body, of his flesh, and of his bones" (Ephesians 5:30). All who believe on the Son of God are members of that mystical, spiritual body, the Church, of which Christ is the Head. Eternal life is a life of real oneness with the Son of God. He says, "Because I live, ye shall live also" (John 14:19). Can you imagine Christ with a maimed body? Perish the thought! His body must be perfect and complete. And if so much as one member of his body is lost, his body cannot be complete. Children of God, we are so really and truly one with Christ that not so much as one member of his body can perish, unless he also perishes. So long as our Head is safe, his members are all safe.

Performed By Grace
Our salvation must be eternally secure, because it is both performed and preserved by the omnipotent grace and effectual power of God the Holy Spirit. Salvation is not in any way to be attributed to man. We were dead in sin. But the Holy Spirit graciously regenerated us, giving us life and faith in Christ. And he preserves us in life by the influence of his almighty grace. That is one part of the office and work of the Holy Spirit. He keeps God's elect, preserving us in faith, in grace, and in life. By him, all the blessings of covenant grace, bestowed upon us in eternity in Christ, are sealed to our souls, as he gives us faith in Christ (Ephesians 1:13, 14). And, by him, we are sealed in Christ until the resurrection (Ephesians 4:30).

Completed By Grace
We know that every true believer's salvation is safe and secure in Christ, because the work of grace which God has begun, he will carry on to perfection. The apostle Paul assures us of this. "Being confident of this very thing, that he which hath begun a good work in you will perform it until the day of Jesus Christ" (Philippians 1:6).

It will never be said of our God that he began a work which he was not able to complete. Every man considers it his shame to undertake a work and be compelled to give it up before completion, because he lacked the ability, the skill, the wisdom, the power, or the dedication necessary to get the job done. But it is not possible for the

292

Lord God to be confronted with such shame. He has never known failure, and he never shall.

He began with us in eternal election. Though thousands of years rolled by, his purpose never changed. According to his wise and holy will, in the fulness of time he redeemed us by substitutionary atonement, atonement made by the sacrifice of his own dear Son. And though we went astray from him as soon as we were born, speaking lies, and spent our days and nights in rebellion, yet, he stood by his purpose of grace. He graciously preserved us until the time appointed when he would save us. Then, at the appointed time, in the time of his love, he gave us life and faith in Christ.

Since that day, our sins have been many. Our faithfulness at best has been feeble. Our service has been insignificant. But he who called us has been faithful. He has kept us by the power of his grace. He has never failed us yet, and he never will. He will not give up that work to which he has been faithful for so long. Our God will perform that which he has begun, until he brings us safe into eternal glory. He is willing to complete his work in us. He is wise enough to complete his work in us. And he is powerful enough to complete his work in us. Many ask, "Can a saved man ever be lost?" I reply, "Not until God ceases to be God". If the Lord God has saved us, "It shall be forever".

July 11
Today's Reading: Ecclesiastes 5-9
"God now accepteth thy works"
Ecclesiastes 9:7

"Go thy way, eat thy bread with joy, and drink thy wine with a merry heart; for God now accepteth thy works". These words are not addressed to everyone. They are specifically addressed to the righteous and the wise, those whose works are in God's hand, those who, being the objects of God's mercy, love, and grace, have been made righteous and wise in Christ (Ecclesiastes 9:1; Matthew 10:16).

"Go Thy Way"
How often we are brought low and downcast by distressing providences, outward temptations, and inward sins! Here we are urged to set our hearts on our God and his grace and march through this world with triumphant joy. The word translated "go thy way" has many shades of meaning. It might be translated "pursue your way", or "march your way", or "vanish in your way". The admonition carries with it a sense of joy and victory. That is how we are to live in this world. That is how we ought to walk through the earth, joyful, triumphant, and confident in faith. If Christ is our Way, we have no reason to live with fear. Though our way is the way of the cross, "the way of the cross leads home". So let us walk with joy. "The way of the righteous is made

plain" (Proverbs 15:19). "For the Lord knoweth the way of the righteous: but the way of the ungodly shall perish" (Psalm 1:6). Our way is the way appointed by our blessed God and Saviour. He is with us in the way, holds us in the way, and carries us all the way. Our way is the Highway of Holiness, by which the ransomed of the Lord return to Zion, "with songs and everlasting joy upon their heads" (Isaiah 35:8-10).

"Eat Thy Bread"
Next, the wise man urges us, by the Spirit of inspiration, to eat our bread with joy. That admonition certainly refers to the bread of daily providence. "I commended mirth, because a man hath no better thing under the sun, than to eat, and to drink, and to be merry: for that shall abide with him of his labour the days of his life, which God giveth him under the sun" (Ecclesiastes 8:15). Believing men and women ought to be the happiest, most cheerful people in the world. Everything we possess is blessed to us by Christ; and our God has promised that we shall be blessed in basket and in store, blessed in lying down and blessed in rising up, blessed in going out and blessed in coming home, blessed in time and blessed to all eternity! But we have other Bread to eat; and we are ever to eat that Bread with joy. Christ is our Bread. He is Manna for our souls. He is the source of all our blessedness. Let us go our way and eat our bread with joy, for Christ is our Way and he is our Bread.

"Drink Thy Wine"
"And drink thy wine with a merry heart". How kind, how gracious, how good our God must be if he commands his children to be merry! Like bread, wine is here set before us as a part of our daily diet. Bread represents that which is necessary. Wine represents that which is pleasurable. Both are to be used freely and enjoyed by us. But Solomon's admonition reaches far beyond eating bread and drinking wine. Solomon urges us to enjoy the bounty of God's providence and grace in this world. Christ is our Way; so let us go our Way. Christ is our Bread; so let us eat our Bread with joy. Christ's love is better than wine; so let us drink our wine with a merry heart.

"Accepteth Thy Works"
"For God now accepteth thy works". As we make our pilgrimage through this world of woe, we ought to eat our bread with joy and drink our wine with a merry heart, because God accepts our works. God accepted us in his dear Son before the worlds were made; and here the Spirit of God assures us that the Lord our God accepts our works. Imagine that. "God now accepteth thy works". Mark that word "now". "God now accepteth thy works". This is much more than an assurance that God will accept our works in eternity, or that God accepts some of our works. Rather, it is an assurance from God himself that he presently accepts and perpetually accepts our works, just as he accepts us in his dear Son. Because God my Father accepts me in Christ, I should "rejoice in the Lord always". May he teach me and give me grace to joy in what I have; joy in what I expect, joy in even what I want, for those very wants will bring me to my Saviour. Do I have fears? Yes, just as you do; but even our fears should not destroy our joy. Our fears keep us clinging to our Saviour, depending upon him for everything. When we suffer, our light afflictions are sweetly blessed to our

souls' good, and become occasions for the Lord Jesus to come to us and soothe our hearts with love. In his time he will deliver us from our troubles.

If we suffer loss, let us still eat our bread with joy and drink our wine with a merry heart, for lose what we may, we cannot lose Christ. We cannot lose his love, his favour, his grace, his Spirit, the efficacy of his blood, and the merits of his righteousness. Oh precious security, precious salvation in the Lord our Righteousness! "Say ye to the righteous, that it shall be well with him: for they shall eat the fruit of their doings" (Isaiah 3:10).

As God now accepts our works (1 Peter 2:5), because the works of our Surety are our works, and we have been washed in his precious blood, in the Day of Judgment God will accept our works (John 5:29; Revelation 20:12); and our works shall follow us to glory (Revelation 14:13). In free justification the righteous works of Christ as our Surety have been imputed to us. And because the death of Christ demands for us the non-imputation of sin, God now accepts our works, all because we are "accepted in the Beloved".

July 12
Today's Reading: Ecclesiastes 10-Song of Solomon 4
"I am sick of love"
Song of Solomon 2:5

The Lord Jesus Christ has been most gracious to me. He has brought me into his church and family, and made me to be one of his own. He has made me, at various times, to sit down in blessed fellowship with him, feasting upon the rich truths of the gospel. His banner over me is love. My heart rejoices in his eternal, special, electing, immutable love for my soul. Still, my soul is weary. A heavenly love-sickness has come over me, because my blessed Lord and Redeemer, the great Lover of my soul, does not openly and clearly manifest himself as he has in days gone by.

> How tedious and tasteless the hours,
> When Jesus no longer I see;
> Sweet prospects, sweet birds, and sweet flowers
> Have all lost their sweetness to me.

His Presence
"I am sick of love", because I long for his presence. I know Christ is always present with his church. Wherever two or three gather in his name, he is in their midst. I know that he is ever with me, that I am the apple of his eye. But, O my soul, how I long for his manifest presence, for him to make his presence known! My heart and soul yearns

for a fresh and constant sense of his love. When he reveals himself, all is well. When he hides his face, everything seems empty and vain.

His Return

"I am sick of love", because I long for his return. No man has a richer, fuller life than I. How gracious my God and Saviour is and has been to his unworthy servant. But, oh, how I long for his return! The thought fills my soul with gladness, that one day the Lord Jesus Christ will return to this earth. He will rid the world of his enemies. He will create all things new. In that blessed day, the knowledge of the Lord will cover the earth as the waters cover the sea. Every person living upon the newly created earth shall worship, serve, and praise Christ; and all will walk in the perfection of righteousness. Oh, may it please the King to return in his glory very soon. We long for him. "Come quickly, Lord Jesus".

With him

"I am sick of love", because I long to be with him. Is it not reasonable for the Lord's people to long to be with him where he is? To be with him is to be free from sin. To be with him is to enter into rest. To be with him is to come into the glorious liberty of the sons of God. I will be content to remain here so long as he sees fit. But my heart has already departed. "I am sick of love". "To be absent from the body is to be present with the Lord". "For we know that if our earthly house of this tabernacle were dissolved, we have a building of God, an house not made with hands, eternal in the heavens ... We are confident, I say, and willing rather to be absent from the body, and to be present with the Lord. Wherefore we labour, that, whether present or absent, we may be accepted of him."

While I am here, I can be content, if he will give me the comfort of his grace. "Stay me with flagons, comfort me with apples." Though at times the Lord is pleased to withdraw his manifest presence, he has left behind the wine of his grace and the fruits of his labours to sustain my heart. These are the pillows of my soul. I rejoice in them. Yet, I long for my well Beloved. "I am sick of love." Child of God, is it not so with you?

July 13
Today's Reading: Song of Solomon 5 - Isaiah 1
"Leaning upon her beloved"
Song of Solomon 8:5

This is a picture of the church universal and of every believing soul. We are coming up out of the dark wilderness of this world, leaning upon Christ, the beloved One of our hearts. While faith in Christ has nothing whatsoever to do with physical acts, physical posture, or physical movement, faith is described symbolically in Holy Scripture by many actions of the body.

Looking
Faith is looking to Christ and seeing him. He says, "Behold me, behold me ... Look unto me and be ye saved all the ends of the earth, for I am God and there is none else". Our Lord declares, "This is the will of him that sent me, that everyone which seeth the Son, and believeth on him may have everlasting life". Saving faith is looking to Christ alone for salvation, just like the perishing Israelites looked to the brazen serpent and were healed.

Coming
Faith is coming to Christ. "He that cometh to me shall never hunger; and he that believeth on me shall never thirst." "Come unto me, all ye that labour and are heavy-laden, and I will give you rest." "All that the Father giveth me shall come to me; and him that cometh unto me, I will in no wise cast out." Saving faith is coming to Christ, acknowledging him as Lord and trusting him as Saviour. We come to you, our Saviour, for pardon, for righteousness, for redemption, for life, and for acceptance with God. We have come to him. We are coming to him. And we shall come to him.

Fleeing
Faith is fleeing to Christ. We "have fled for refuge to lay hold on the hope set before us". Christ "the Lord is a strong tower; the righteous runneth into it and is safe". Realizing that we were by nature children of wrath even as others, and knowing that the Lord Jesus Christ is God's only appointed place of refuge for guilty sinners, we have fled, and ever flee to him! We venture our souls upon him, upon the merits of his blood and righteousness. We cast ourselves into his arms of power and grace, trusting Christ alone to save us. Saving faith is fleeing to Christ in hope of mercy.

Laying Hold
Faith is laying hold of Christ. Like a drowning man lays hold of the line thrown to him, we lay hold of Christ and cling to him.

Receiving
Faith is receiving Christ. "As many as received him, to them gave he power to become the sons of God, even to them that believe on his name." It is not receiving Christ into the head that brings salvation, but receiving him into the heart. It is not receiving the doctrine of Christ that saves us, but receiving Christ himself. True faith receives the whole Christ, as he is revealed in Holy Scripture. We receive him in all of his offices: Prophet, Priest, and King. We receive Christ as our only acceptance with God. We receive him in preference to all others. And ...

Leaning
Faith is leaning upon Christ. This is a richer, fuller, more intimate description of faith than we have seen before. When the believing soul is described as "leaning upon her Beloved", faith is set forth as a loving, admiring, adoring confidence in Christ. Like a

297

timid, frightened woman, passing through some strange and dangerous forest at night, would lean upon the strong arm of her faithful husband, the believer leans upon his beloved Redeemer. We lean upon Christ, because he has proven his love and faithfulness to us. We lean upon him, because he is mighty, able to save us and to preserve us from all harm. We lean upon him, because we are utterly helpless in ourselves.

Faith leans upon the Person of Christ for acceptance with God. Faith leans upon the righteousness of Christ for justification. Faith leans upon the blood of Christ for pardon and cleansing. We lean upon the fulness of Christ to supply all our needs. Every act of faith is, in its essence, just leaning upon Christ. In prayer, in worship, in praise, in service, we are simply leaning on our Beloved. All our hope before God, at all times and for all things, is the Lord Jesus Christ; so we lean upon him. Oh, may we evermore learn to lean heavily upon the Son of God. Go ahead, lean upon him. He can bear the weight.

> Every hour of every day,
> And every moment and in every way,
> I'm leaning on Jesus; He's the rock of my soul;
> I'm singing his praises wherever I go.

July 14
Today's Reading: Isaiah 2-5
"Let us walk in the light of the LORD"
Isaiah 2:5

What a very important admonition this must be for our souls! It is given to us by God the Holy Ghost repeatedly in the Book of God (Matthew 5:14-16; John 8:12; Ephesians 5:5-16; 1 John 1:5-9).

The Light
What is "the light of the Lord"? Without question, all men by nature have the light of conscience, for which they are responsible (John 1:9; Romans 1:19, 20; 2:14, 15). But "the light of the Lord" is the light of special grace given to the "house of Jacob" in regeneration and conversion. "The light of the Lord" is Christ himself, by whom the Triune God is revealed to us and in us (John 1:14, 18), the gospel of God's free grace in Christ (2 Corinthians 4:5, 6), the Holy Scriptures (Psalm 119:105), the revealed will of God (Proverbs 3:5, 6), the Spirit of God (1 Corinthians 2:11), and the example of Christ (1 Peter 2:21). This is the light God has given us. These many rays of light all shine from Christ, the Sun of Righteousness. They never contradict one another, or

shine apart from one another. It is our responsibility to walk in the light God has given. But ...

The Walk
How can we "walk in the light of the Lord"? I do not have all the answers. But I do know these things: if we would walk in the light of the Lord, we must own and acknowledge that Christ is our Lord. We must believe the light he gives. We must obey our Lord, following the direction of his light. We must pattern our lives after his example. And we must persevere to the end, walking in the light of the Lord. Christ is the Light of the world; and all who live by faith in him "walk in the light of the Lord". "The path of the just is as the shining light, that shineth more and more unto the perfect day" (Proverbs 4:18). "If we walk in the light, as he is in the light, we have fellowship one with another, and the blood of Jesus Christ his Son cleanseth us from all sin" (1 John 1:7).

The Reason
Why must we "walk in the light of the Lord"? He is the only true light. Reason makes guesses. Feelings are deceiving. Customs change. Only the light of the Lord is absolute. In his light our hearts find rest and peace. The light of the Lord gives our minds wisdom, direction, and discernment. In his light our souls find satisfaction. What can be so satisfying to the soul as the light of God's purpose, providence, propitiation, and promise? It is by walking in the light of the Lord that the sons of Jacob; chosen, redeemed sinners, have fellowship with God and one another. God has given us light. "Let us walk in the light of the Lord." May God the Holy Spirit give us grace to do so for the glory of him who loved us and gave himself for us.

July 15
Today's Reading: Isaiah 6-9
"I saw also the LORD sitting upon a throne"
Isaiah 6:1

God the Holy Spirit tells us in John 12:41 that the revelation given to Isaiah and recorded in this sixth chapter of his prophecy was a revelation of the glory of our Saviour, the Lord Jesus Christ. But what is that? What did Isaiah see, when he saw Christ's glory?

He saw God in his true character, as he really is, in his glorious sovereignty and infinite holiness (vv. 1-4). Then he saw himself as a guilty, helpless, doomed, damned, lost sinner before the holy Lord God, "a man of unclean lips" (v. 5).

Seeing God as he really is and himself as he really was, Isaiah saw the complete depravity of all Adam's fallen race, "a people of unclean lips" (v. 5). By the goodness

299

and grace of God, Isaiah saw and experienced the complete forgiveness of sin by blood atonement (vv. 6, 7).

Then, when he saw the Lord's glory, Isaiah saw the purpose of the Triune God perfectly fulfilled by Christ, Jehovah's righteous Servant (vv. 8-13). Blessed are those to whom God has given such grace! Never forget, O my soul, if I see these things, it is because God the Holy Ghost has given me eyes to see.

Gospel Preachers
The closing verses of Isaiah 6 may have reference to Isaiah and his calling as God's prophet. God's servants are all called of God, and all are volunteers in the service of Christ, being constrained by his call and his grace (v. 8). God's servants are all sent men, sent of God to preach the gospel (v. 9). God's servants are to some a savour of death unto death (vv. 10-12), and to others a savour of life unto life (v. 13).

Christ Our Surety
But Isaiah 8:6 begins with the words, "Also I heard", as if to indicate a change. It seems to me that this last section of the chapter refers not to God's servants, the gospel preachers, but to God's righteous Servant, our Lord Jesus Christ.

In the first seven verses of the chapter Isaiah tells us what he had seen and heard in a special revelation to himself. Here he tells us what he was witness to regarding the accomplishments of our blessed Saviour as the Surety of the covenant and the fulfilment of God's everlasting purpose of grace in him. The Lord God favoured his prophet with a clear revelation of his covenant mercy and "the covenant of peace" held between the Persons of the eternal God (Zechariah 6:13; Psalm 40:7-10; Isaiah 50:6-9), before the world began.

The terms and conditions of redemption were proposed: Mercy and truth must meet. Righteousness and peace must kiss each other. Righteousness must be established for the chosen by the obedience of a man of infinite worth. Justice must be satisfied by a man who is God being made sin and punished for all the sins of God's elect, fully punished, that the holy Lord God might be "a just God and a Saviour" (Isaiah 8:20). When those terms and conditions of redemption were proposed, Isaiah heard the Triune God say, "Whom shall I send, and who will go for us?" Then he saw our Divine Surety, the Son of God, step forward for us and say, "Here am I, send me".

Question Answered
In verses 9-12, Isaiah, as if struck with what he had seen and heard, raises a question: "How long shall Satan, the enemy of our souls triumph? How long shall fallen man remain under the influence of that wicked one? How long shall Satan work havoc in God's creation?" Hear what the Lord's answer is in verse 13.

"But yet in it shall be a tenth, and it shall return, and shall be eaten: as a teil tree, and as an oak, whose substance is in them, when they cast their leaves: so the holy seed shall be the substance thereof."

Oh, for grace to bless the eternal Spirit for such a revelation! Now we see why it is that God preserves fallen humanity. There is one that stands by and looks on, and while to our eye there is nothing to be seen. As we see things, the whole race is like the withered, blighted branch of the vine; everything is hopeless, and dead, and lifeless. Yet, there is in it "a tenth", "the holy seed", God's elect, who must and shall be saved. Therefore, the Lord Jesus says, "Destroy it not, for a blessing is in it" (Isaiah 65:8). Because he is longsuffering toward his chosen, an elect remnant, "the holy seed", who must be saved, the Lord God spares the world (2 Peter 3:9). The purpose of God shall be accomplished. Christ will save his people (Romans 8:28-30). That is what Isaiah saw when he saw Christ's glory.

July 16
Today's Reading: Isaiah 10-13
"Behold, God is my salvation"
Isaiah 12:2

My theology professors used to insist, "We must not confuse the teachings of the Bible." I have often heard and read warnings urging the need to view election, redemption, justification, sanctification, and regeneration as distinct and separate things. But the Word of God never makes such distinctions. The Revelation of God is one; and God's salvation is one.

"Behold, God is my salvation; I will trust, and not be afraid: for the LORD JEHOVAH is my strength and my song; he also is become my salvation. Therefore with joy shall ye draw water out of the wells of salvation" (Isaiah 12:2, 3).

God's Work For Us
Election was finished in eternity; and God's elect are spoken of as being saved (in the fullest possible sense of that word) from eternity (Romans 8:30; Ephesians 1:3; 2 Timothy 1:9). But the sovereign, eternal purpose of God the Father is not enough to save anyone. Blood must be shed. Christ had to die, for "without shedding of blood is no remission". We were redeemed, justified, and sanctified when Christ died in our place at Calvary. When he cried, "It is finished", redemption's work was done. Sin was put away. Righteousness was brought in. Atonement was made. The redemption of our souls was accomplished.

God's Work In Us
Still, something else is required. The precious blood of Christ is not enough to make us "meet to be partakers of the inheritance of the saints in light". If we are saved, if we are to enter into heaven's eternal glory, something else is necessary, just as necessary as the work of the Father and the work of the Son. We must be saved by the blessed work of God the Holy Spirit in the experience of grace (Titus 3:5-7).

It is the experience of grace that gives the sinner hope before God. God's purpose made the salvation of his elect sure, but gives hope to no one. Christ's death upon the cross is the singular basis of the sinner's hope, but gives hope to none. It is not Christ dying in your place that gives hope, but "Christ in you", formed in you by God the Holy Spirit in the experience of grace, that God says "is the hope of glory".

In the new birth we are made new creatures in Christ, made "partakers of the divine nature". God the Holy Spirit creates in us a new life. He gives chosen, redeemed sinners an entirely new nature, forms Christ in us, puts righteousness in us, makes us righteous, pure, and holy, puts in us a spirit in which there is no guile, and makes us "meet to be partakers of the inheritance of the saints in light". This new man is "Christ in you, the hope of glory". This is that "holiness" we must have, "without which no man shall see the Lord". It is written, "There shall in no wise enter into it anything that defileth, neither whatsoever worketh abomination, or maketh a lie: but they which are written in the Lamb's book of life."

The Triune God
It takes all the gracious operations of the Triune God to save us. God's salvation is one thing. None of its parts are more or less important. Take away redemption and election is meaningless. Take away regeneration and redemption is meaningless. We are saved by the work of God for us and in us, the work of God the Father, God the Son, and God the Holy Ghost (Ephesians 1:3-14). "Behold, God is my Salvation."

July 17
Today's Reading: Isaiah 14-18
Four stages of grace
Isaiah 14:2

"They shall take them captives, whose captives they were; and they shall rule over their oppressors".

In the Scriptures the work of God in the salvation of our souls is set before us as the deliverance of captives by God's omnipotent grace into "the glorious liberty of the sons of God".

State Of Captivity
Grace finds us in a state of bondage and captivity. All men like to boast of their freedom. They like to flatter themselves with the idea that they are morally, spiritually, and intellectually free. But the fact is every man by nature is in a state of bondage and captivity. If you are without Christ, you are a bondman, a slave, held in captivity to the world, the flesh, and the devil. You are a slave to sin and a slave to Satan, taken captive by him at his will. And you are a prisoner, shut up under the curse of God's holy law, a captive awaiting execution (Ezekiel 18:20). Grace finds us in a state of bondage and captivity; lost, helpless, ruined, and justly condemned. This is the condition of all men by nature.

State Of Deliverance
Grace brings us into a state of deliverance (Isaiah 61:1-3). We are by nature the house of a strong man armed. But when Christ comes in, by the power of his omnipotent grace, he binds the strong man, casts him out, and takes the spoils of victory (Isaiah 49:24-26).

This deliverance is the work of God alone. As soon as a person is born of God, as soon as Christ is revealed in the heart, as soon as you believe on the Lord Jesus Christ by the irresistible grace and power of God the Holy Spirit, you are saved. Deliverance is accomplished (Isaiah 40:1, 2).

State Of War
We are saved, if we trust Christ, saved forever. But our deliverance is not yet complete. Like the Children of Israel, after they had crossed the Red Sea, we have many enemies to face, many conflicts to endure, and many battles to fight in this wilderness, before we can enter the promised land of rest. But I want you to know that grace sustains us in a state of war.

The believer in this world is not in the land of peace. We are at war with the world, the flesh, and the devil. The world allures us, the flesh opposes us, and the devil tempts us. But, blessed be God, grace sustains us (Philippians 1:6; 2 Corinthians 12:9).

If you trust Christ, God does not promise you a life of ease, peace, and tranquillity. He promises us nothing in this world but pain, conflict, tribulation, and war. But in the midst of that warfare, he promises us peace with God and the assurance of victory at last.

In this world we have trials and tribulations to endure. We must through much tribulation enter into the kingdom of God. Yet, whatever the trial may be, however severe the tribulation, the Lord will sustain us. Indeed, the very trials themselves are means by which the Lord God works our salvation (Isaiah 43:1-7).

In this world we must endure manifold and sometimes great temptations. As our Lord was tempted in all points, so must we be. Satan will not leave us alone. When it appears that he has, we are in real trouble. But when we are tempted, our God will not forsake us (1 Corinthians 10:13). He will hold us up. When we fall, he will raise us up again. When we sin, he will forgive us (1 John 1:9; 2:1, 2).

More, while we live in this world, we must endure a constant inner warfare with sin (Romans 7:22-24; Galatians 5:17). The flesh and the spirit are at war with one another in my soul. I know that as long as I live in this body of flesh, this warfare will continue. But God will sustain me by his grace. And I think I know, at least in part, why these things are so. God will not let us trust in ourselves. He will ever make us aware that we are saved by grace alone. He will make his own to be tender with one another. He will make his own to know that Christ is all.

State Of Victory
Soon, grace shall deliver us into a state of victory and dominion. Look at Isaiah's prophecy again (Isaiah 14:2, 3, 24-27). Soon we shall be free! The God of peace will bruise Satan under our feet shortly! In the end we will rule over our oppressors. "And it shall come to pass in that day that the Lord shall give thee rest" (Revelation 7:14-

16; 21:1-5; 22:1-6). He will give you victory over all your sorrows, all your fears, all your sins, and all your hard bondage forever!

July 18
Today's Reading: Isaiah 19-23
"A nail in a sure place"
Isaiah 22:23

Our all-glorious Saviour, the Lord Jesus Christ, is the Nail fastened in a sure place, the Nail upon which we hang our souls. The Lord God declared, by his prophet Isaiah, "I will fasten him as a nail in a sure place; and he shall be for a glorious throne to his father's house. And they shall hang upon him all the glory of his father's house, the offspring and the issue, all vessels of small quantity, from the vessels of cups, even to all the vessels of flagons."

Nail Fastened
The Triune God fastened "him as a nail in a sure place" in his eternal covenant (Ephesians 1:3-6), as "the Lamb slain from the foundation of the world". This is the Nail fastened by God in the sure place in his Word (Ecclesiastes 12:11). This Nail is fastened forever in Heaven itself. The Triune God hung on him all his purpose of grace, trusting him with the salvation of his people and the glory of his own great name (Ephesians 1:12).

We hang our souls and all our hope upon this Nail, trusting Christ alone as our Saviour (1 Corinthians 1:30, 31). As the Builder of his temple, Christ the Nail bears all the glory of it (Zechariah 6:13). In a word, everything hangs on the Nail, Christ Jesus, the Nail God has fastened in a sure place.

Two Kinds Of Nails
The word "nail" is used to refer to two kinds of nails. One was a tent stake, like those used to hold the tabernacle in place. The church of God's elect is the tent and Christ is the nail to which its cords are fastened. He alone is the stability and security of his church. He alone is the stability and security of our souls.

The "nail" also refers to a peg driven into the centre pole of a tent or the wall of a house. Utensils and valuables were hung on it. As we hang works of art on our walls, in ancient times men would hang jewels and other emblems of wealth on a nail in some conspicuous place in their dwellings, to be admired by all who came in. That is what the Triune God has done. He has hung everything on Christ, to let us see and admire the exceeding riches of his grace and glory in him! All the vessels of the Father's house hang upon this one nail Christ Jesus. On him hangs all the glory of his Father's house! The Triune God has hung on Christ all his mercy, all the covenant of

304

grace, all his promises, and all his blessings. God has hung on him all our salvation. All the glory of his Father's house hangs on him!

Hang All
Has God enabled me, by his matchless free grace, to hang all the concerns of my soul for eternity upon the Lord Jesus? Indeed, he has, and I do. I have no other hope. "Christ is all" to me, because he has made himself all to me. How eternally firm and secure I rest upon him! "The Nail" upon which I hang all is "Jesus Christ, the same yesterday, and today, and forever."

He is the source, origin, fountain, and support of all my salvation. Indeed, he is "all my salvation". Every purpose of God is founded on Christ. Every promise of God is made, confirmed, and fulfilled in Christ. Every dispensation of God's providence in all the realms of nature, grace, and glory comes from Christ (Romans 11:36).

All things hang on Christ, "the Nail" God has fixed in a sure place. Are we blessed with the graces of his Spirit in life? It is from him that we derive all our spiritual strength, gifts, and graces. We depend upon him and him alone for life, ability, power, and every inclination and disposition to believe him, worship him, and serve him. Every inclination and disposition to honour him comes from him. Everything in the house of God and everything in our regenerate souls hangs upon "the Nail". The whole glory is his! Let us return to him an endless revenue of praise.

Evermore will I hang my soul, and body, and spirit, with all I have, and all I am or hope to be, in time and to all eternity, on this Nail. It is impossible to hang too much on Christ. It is impossible to hang too completely on this Nail. None can perish, nothing can be lost that hangs upon God's Christ!

July 19
Today's Reading: Isaiah 24-27
"Perfect peace"
Isaiah 26:3

The words "perfect peace" might be better translated "peace, peace", or "peace upon peace". They are intended to express peace in the most emphatic way possible. The peace that God gives his people in Christ is certain peace, real peace, increasing peace, extensive peace, and everlasting peace.

Absence Of Danger
Peace is the absence of war and danger (Isaiah 40:1, 2). There was a time when God appeared to be at war with us. But as soon as a sinner trusts Christ, his warfare is over and the danger of war is gone.

Discovering Christ Day By Day

Life Of Peace
Peace reigns over all things within the circle of the believer's life. All our sins have been forgiven, once for all, never to be charged against us. Christ has taken possession of us, never to lose us. Our heavenly Father rules the universe, never neglecting us. There is nothing we cannot safely commit to him. Cast "all your care upon him; for he careth for you".

Rest In The Soul
The peace that God gives is rest in the soul (Psalm 42:5, 11; 43:5). As the body lying upon a bed finds rest for all its members, so the soul stretching upon Christ finds rest and peace for every faculty. The heart finds rest in God's love. Judgment finds rest in his wisdom. Desire finds rest in the Lord's goodness. Hope rests in his Word. And expectation finds rest in the promises of God. Peace in the soul is resignation to the will of God, confidence in his goodness, and contentment with the providence of God.

A Matter Of Faith
"Thou wilt keep him in perfect peace, whose mind is stayed on thee: because he trusteth in thee." This peace is a matter of faith. If I do not enjoy this peace, the blame must be laid at my door alone. We make ourselves restless by unbelief. God gives us peace as he works faith in us and sustains our souls by the operations of his grace.

Look upward, my brother. There is no sword of justice against you, no cup of wrath for you to bear, no angry God against you. Look downward, dear sister. There is no condemnation, no death, no judgment, no second death, no hell for you to endure. Look backward, believing sinner. All your past sins are blotted out, forgiven, taken away, and remembered no more. Look outward, my heart. God has made all the beasts of the field, all the stones of the earth, all the trees of the forest, and even your enemies to be at peace with you. Look inward, child of God. God has set up a guard in your heart to keep your heart. His name is Peace. The Peace of God that "passeth understanding" is God's gift to faith. Look forward, O my soul. Heavenly glory awaits you. All that the Man Christ Jesus is and has done is yours! All that he has soon shall be yours! O Holy Spirit, give me faith to trust my God, ever set my heart and mind upon my most precious Christ, and keep me in perfect peace.

July 20
Today's Reading: Isaiah 28-30
"Wonderful in counsel and excellent in working"
Isaiah 28:29

When Isaiah says the Lord God is "wonderful in counsel and excellent in working", he means for us to understand and bless God for these three, indisputable facts.

Discovering Christ Day By Day

1. God Almighty has a plan by which he always works, from which he never deviates. All men look upon a person who works without a plan as a fool. Haphazard work is folly. Yet, when we insist that God Almighty in all his works is fulfilling his own great plan, men and women get angry. Let wicked men rebel as they dare against it, the truth still stands; and we rejoice in it. God always works by a plan. Nothing in this world is left to chance. God has determined the end from the beginning. He has not left a single loose screw in the machinery of providence. Whatever happens in time happens according to God's sovereign, unalterable, eternal purpose (Isaiah 14:24-27; 46:9-11; Romans 8:28-30; 2 Corinthians 5:18; Ephesians 1:11).

Man is free to do whatever he wills. And, in as much as he is able, he always does exactly what he wants to do. Every person is entirely responsible for what he does. Yet, the great, eternal God sovereignly works out his purpose and accomplishes his will as perfectly as though men and devils were machines, programmed to carry out his designs. Yes, our God is "wonderful in counsel".

2. God is "excellent in working", in the execution of his plan. As he is "wonderful in counsel", his works, which are but the execution of his counsel, the fulfilment of his plan, are excellent. Creation (Psalm 104), providence (Psalm 107), redemption (Ephesians 1:3-14), and grace (Ephesians 2:1-7) are God's excellent works. Examine them closely. Behold their beauty and perfection. Glorify God, who is "wonderful in counsel and excellent in working". Everything in time is accomplished "according to the good pleasure of his will" (Ephesians 1:5).

3. God's wonderful counsel shall be perfectly fulfilled by the excellent works of his hands (1 Corinthians 15:24-28). There is a day coming when time shall be no more. In that day, all that God purposed from eternity shall be done, perfectly and completely. Nothing shall have been done but what God purposed to be done. Nothing shall be left undone which God purposed from eternity to do, for the Lord God, our God, is "wonderful in counsel and excellent in working". "His ways are everlasting" (Habakkuk 3:6); and his purpose is sure. He always has done, is doing, and forever will do all his pleasure everywhere and in all things.

July 21
Today's Reading: Isaiah 31-34
"Thine eyes shall see the king in his beauty"
Isaiah 33:17

When Sennacherib, with his immense Assyrian army, was about to attack Jerusalem, he sent Rabshakeh with a railing, blasphemous message to Hezekiah and his people (2 Kings 18).When Hezekiah heard the threats and blasphemies of the proud idolater, "he rent his clothes, covered himself with sackcloth, and went into the house of God" (2 Kings 19:1).Then he called for the priests and sent them covered with sackcloth to the prophet of God (2 Kings 19:2-5). The people of Jerusalem had seen their king in humiliation, arrayed in sackcloth. But Isaiah, speaking by divine inspiration, sent a message to the people to cheer their hearts. His message was, "Thine eyes shall see the king in his beauty." They did (2 Chronicles 32:27-30).

Another King

There is in Isaiah's words a message to cheer our hearts today. There is a nobler King here than Hezekiah. Hezekiah was the historical figure Isaiah had in mind. But the King spoken of here by the Spirit of God is the Lord Jesus Christ, the King of kings and Lord of lords, the Prince and Monarch of the universe.

In Humiliation

We have seen our beloved King in utter humiliation. In the days of his flesh, he was "despised and rejected of men, a man of sorrows, and acquainted with grief" (Isaiah 53:3). While he lived in this world, sorrow was his robe, reproach was his coat, and adversity was his bread. None was more afflicted than the Son of man. When he died, he died the painful, shameful, ignominious death of the cross. Reproach broke his heart. He was beaten, mocked, nailed to the cross, hung up naked before a mob of drunks and cruel Pharisees, who, as they watched him die, spit in his face, beat him with their fists, plucked out his beard, and sang taunting, jeering songs of scorn.

But, who can imagine the humiliation that was his when our adorable and adored Saviour was made sin for us and forsaken of his Father that we might be made the righteousness of God in him, and never be forsaken of God!

His Beauty

Now we see our Lord Jesus triumphant over all his enemies! Now faith beholds the King in his beauty, returning with the dyed garments of Edom, robed in the splendour of victory. He no longer wears the purple robe of mockery. He is clothed with royal garments head to foot. He no longer wears a crown of thorns. A crown of glory now adorns the mighty Victor's brow. Around his waist there is the golden belt of conquest. From his side swing the keys of death, hell, and the grave. He sits upon the throne of majesty, glory, and universal dominion. His beauty is his glorious, unrivalled, incontestable sovereignty and dominion as King of the universe, King by right of his conquests as our crucified, risen Redeemer!

Altogether Lovely

All God's church sings of her Bridegroom, "He is altogether lovely" (Song of Solomon 5:16). Christ is lovely. Christ is very lovely. Christ is most lovely. Christ is always lovely. Christ is altogether lovely! On his head are many crowns (Revelation 19:12). Christ Jesus wears the crown of a Conqueror who has vanquished every foe, a Prince who can never be defeated or overthrown, a Master who has the heart allegiance of all his servants, an Intercessor who can never fail, a Brother who is full of love, a Forerunner who for us is entered into glory, and a God whose purpose is sure, whose dominion is unfailing!

July 22
Today's Reading: Isaiah 35-38
"This day is a day of trouble"
Isaiah 37:3

When Sennacherib and the Assyrian army surrounded Jerusalem and threatened to destroy it, Hezekiah the king sent this message to the prophet Isaiah: "This day is a day of trouble". Without question, those words describe the day in which we live. We are living in those perilous times Paul warned us of in 2 Timothy 3:1-9. Apostate religion holds the world in darkness; and apostate religion always brings with it lawlessness, moral perversity, and brazen wickedness.

In addition to these things, God's saints in this world of woe have personal trials, which often come one upon the heels of another, trials which bring us personal days of trouble. What are we to do in the day of trouble? Where can we find help? How can we glorify God in the day of trouble? Read Isaiah 37 carefully. In this chapter Hezekiah teaches us some valuable lessons for the day of trouble.

First, in the day of trouble, do not neglect the house of God. Broken and humbled by his circumstances, with a heavy, needy heart, Hezekiah "went into the house of the Lord" (v. 1). You will not find any help for your soul anywhere else; but just "attending church" will not help you. "Bodily exercise", the mere performance of outward religious ceremonies, "profiteth little". We need more than religious ceremony to comfort and guide our hearts in the day of trouble.

Second, in the day of trouble, seek a word from God. Hezekiah went to the house of God seeking a word from the prophet of God (v. 2). Come to the house of God praying for God to give his servant a word for your own heart, to encourage, comfort, strengthen, and direct you in faith. When Hezekiah sought a word from God, he found it (vv. 6, 7). So will you.

Third, in the day of trouble, spread your trouble before the Lord in prayer. Read Hezekiah's prayer (vv. 14-20) carefully, and learn how to pray. He simply told God what his trouble was, praised God for his greatness and goodness, and asked God to do what he had promised. Then he offered an argument God could not resist. "That all the kingdoms of the earth may know that thou art the Lord, even thou only."

Fourth, in the day of trouble, wait upon the Lord. Hezekiah left the house of God with God's word in his heart (vv. 21-38). His circumstances had not changed. Sennacherib and his army were still there; but Hezekiah had God's word; and he believed God! At God's appointed time, the day of trouble was over. In patience possess your soul and wait for God to perform his Word. Though the promise "tarry, wait for it; because it will surely come, it will not tarry".

309

July 23
Today's Reading: Isaiah 39-41
"Fear thou not; for I am with thee"
Isaiah 41:10

The purpose and object of God in the last chapters of Isaiah is to silence the fears of his people and encourage us to confidently trust him in the teeth of trouble and adversity. It is contrary to the will and glory of our God for his people to be a timid, fearful, anxious people. In order to suppress our fears the Lord God graciously assures us of his constant presence, power, and provision.

Cease From Fear
How many times our great and gracious God says to our poor, trembling hearts, "fear not". How dishonouring to him it is for his people to be fearful! Our doubting, fearful hearts dishonour our God and Saviour. O Holy Spirit, give me grace to trust my God in all things and cease from fear!

Child of God, join me in that prayer. O my brother, O my sister, O my soul, cease from fear and believe God! Though your enemies are many and mighty, "fear not". God is greater than your enemies. Though your afflictions are painful and protracted, "fear not". The Lord will deliver you. Though your path of duty is demanding and dangerous, "fear not". Your God will uphold you and help you. Though the fulfilment of God's promises cannot be seen, "fear not". Not one promise of God shall fall to the ground.

Five Promises
Anticipating all the fears that we would encounter in this world, the Lord our God here gives us five great promises, by which he says to every believer faced with danger and trouble, "Fear not ... be not dismayed".

1. "I am with thee". Were we left to ourselves to face our enemies (the world, the flesh, and the devil), we might well fear; but God says to our trembling souls, "I am with thee". Shall we not take refuge in him and be comforted? Take time to read Psalm 46:1-3, 5-8, 10, 11.

2. "I am thy God". The almighty, Triune Jehovah is ours, as truly ours as we are his! If God is my property, who or what shall I fear? A stranger might see a person injured and pass by indifferently. But a husband cannot be indifferent to the pains of his wife. A father cannot be indifferent to the troubles of his child. And our God is never indifferent to the troubles of his children (Zephaniah 2:8; 2 Chronicles 16:9).

3. "I will strengthen thee". We are told that the Lord will "put strength into his people" (Psalm 29:11). He will strengthen you with might in the inward man. Can he be in danger whose hands are made strong "by the hands of the mighty God of Jacob"? Your God will strengthen you to bear your troubles (2 Corinthians 12:5-9), endure temptation (1 Corinthians 10:13), and do his will (1 Thessalonians 5:24).

4. "Yea, I will help thee". He "helpeth our infirmities" (Romans 8:26). That means when our burden is so heavy and cumbersome that we cannot with all our exertions support it, our God will take hold of it at the opposite end and bear it together with us. In other words, to imagine that any burden is too great for us to bear is to say that it is too great for God to bear! "Is anything too hard for the Lord?" No! And nothing is too hard for those to whom God says, "I will help thee".

5. "Yea, I will uphold thee with the right hand of my righteousness". What more can we want? The eternal God is our Refuge! Beneath you are the everlasting arms (Deuteronomy 33:27-29; Isaiah 51:12, 13). If God be for us, not all the powers of earth and hell combined can, with any effect, exert themselves against us (Romans 8:31-39). With such a God and Saviour as we have in Christ Jesus, we have every reason to be comforted and fearless, even in the face of great trouble and in the midst of great enemies. Our safety is our God! "Fear not, thou worm Jacob, and ye men of Israel; I will help thee, saith the LORD, and thy redeemer, the Holy One of Israel."

July 24
Today's Reading: Isaiah 42-44
"I have loved thee"
Isaiah 43:4

It is utter nonsense to talk about God loving all men. Sometimes men who are fearful of denying God's total sovereignty and equally fearful of teaching it, try to soft peddle the issue by assuring people that there is a sense in which God loves all men with a love of benevolence, though not with a love of complacency and delight. Referring to Psalm 145:8, 9, they say, "God loves all men as his creatures", just as he loves trees and toads. If men can get any comfort from the idea that God loves them like he "loves" a frog, maybe that should not be taken away from them; but that simply is not the teaching of Holy Scripture. Psalm 145 is a psalm about the mercy of God, not the love of God. Mercy is anything other than hell. Love is something far better.

Distinctive Love
God loves his elect distinctively. He does not love all men. I would not emphasize this issue were it not for the fact that those who teach that God's love is universal are guilty of three horrible crimes. First, they make the love of God changeable. Second, they make the love of God meaningless. Third, they destroy the greatest motive there is for godliness and devotion (2 Corinthians 5:14). Let a man try telling his wife that he loves all women alike. See if that inspires her devotion to him!

The Word of God tells us in the plainest terms possible that God's love for his elect is a special, sovereign, distinctive, and distinguishing love (Isaiah 43:1-5; Romans 8:29; 9:11-24). The fact that God has sacrificed men and nations for the salvation of his people throughout the ages, and that he continues to do so should convince any reasonable person of the distinctiveness of his love for his elect.

Delightful Love
God loves his people delightfully, too. I mean by that that God delights, takes pleasure in, and is complacent with his elect, because of his love for them. God so loves us that he smiles on us perpetually, even when he appears to be frowning upon us. It is high time that all attempts to divide the love of God into categories, stages, and degrees be laid aside. They do nothing to help men, and only obscure the glory and grandeur of our God. If God loves me, he delights in me. If he does not delight in me, he does not love me. Again I say, try telling your wife, "Honey, I really do love you. I wish you well. I want nothing but the very best for you, and am willing to do anything I can for you; but you do not please me. You are offensive to me. I do not enjoy your company. In fact, I really do not want to look at you." Nonsense!

Our God loves us as he loves his darling Son. That means he is well-pleased with us (Matthew 17:5). The Father and the Son are one; and the Son of God tells us that his "delights" were with us from eternity (Proverbs 8:31). He could not have used a stronger word than this to express his love for us. The word "delights" expresses the most intimate, sweet, ravishing pleasure. Can you get hold of this? Our God so delights in us that he says, "Thou hast ravished my heart, my sister, my spouse: thou hast ravished my heart with one of thine eyes."

July 25
Today's Reading: Isaiah 45-48
"A just God and a Saviour"
Isaiah 45:21

The Lord our God, the one true and living God of heaven and earth, is a God who freely and abundantly forgives sin through the blood of his Son, the Lord Jesus Christ. This is what God himself says, "I, even I, am he that blotteth out thy transgressions for mine own sake, and will not remember thy sins."

The People Forgiven
Who are the people to whom God will be merciful? They are not good, righteous, and morally upright men and women. So long as a man thinks that he is good and righteous, he will never obtain mercy from God. The characters to whom God says he will be merciful are sinners. The grace and lovingkindness of Jehovah is reserved for sinners. Until you see that your supposed righteousness is an abomination to God, you will never obtain the righteousness of God in Christ (Romans 10:1-4). Every promise of the gospel is made to sinners. "The Son of man came not to call the righteous, but

sinners to repentance" (Matthew 11:28-30; Isaiah 1:4-6, 18; 55:6, 7). The grace and mercy of God is for sinners. Christ died for sinners. The gospel is sent to sinners. God saves sinners. God forgives sinners. I rejoice to tell you that our God is a God of mercy (Psalm 103:8-14). There is mercy in Christ and forgiveness for sinners.

Mercy's Deed
Mercy's great deed is the blessed forgiveness of sin. It is the glory of grace to forgive sin. It is the majesty of mercy to forgive sin. It is the character of God to forgive iniquity and transgression, and sin (Exodus 34:5-7). God is the only one who can forgive sin. God's forgiveness is the only forgiveness we need, desire, and must have for salvation for our souls and peace for our troubled consciences (Psalm 130:3, 4).

Just Forgiveness
How does God forgive sin? There is only one way for a holy and just God to forgive sin. God can only forgive sin through the obedience and sacrifice of an all-sufficient Substitute. God's forgiveness must be a just forgiveness. Justice must be satisfied, or sin cannot be forgiven. The Lord Jesus Christ is that Substitute by whom divine justice has been satisfied! In him, and only in him, is there forgiveness with God (Romans 3:23-26; 1 John 1:9). In Christ he who is our God is both "a just God and a Saviour".

The Reason
Why does God forgive sin? He says, "for mine own sake". The greatest honour and glory of God is his mercy, his holy, righteous, and just mercy in forgiving sin (Psalm 106:8; Ezekiel 16:62-63).

Never Remembered
What is the promise which God makes to sinners whose sins are forgiven by him? What a promise this is! "I, even I, am he that blotteth out thy transgressions, and will not remember thy sins." There are some things God himself cannot do. He cannot lie. He cannot break his covenant. He cannot forsake his people. He cannot be unjust. He cannot remember the sins of his people. I do not mean that God is not aware of the fact that we have sinned. I mean that insofar as his law and justice are concerned, our sins do not exist; therefore, God cannot remember them. He will never remember our sins so as to treat us any the less graciously because of them. He will never remember our sins so as to bring them up and require payment for them while we live. God will not remember our sins when we stand before him in judgment (Jeremiah 50:20). God will not remember our sins in the distribution of his heavenly crowns and gifts.

Would you be forgiven of all your sins? Then confess your sin, and put God in remembrance of this promise. "I, even I, am he that blotteth out thy transgressions for mine own sake, and will not remember thy sins. Put me in remembrance: let us plead together: declare thou, that thou mayest be justified" (Isaiah 43:25, 26).

July 26
Today's Reading: Isaiah 49-53
"Thy Saviour and thy Redeemer"
Isaiah 49:26

The Lord God our Saviour, the Lord Jesus Christ, declares himself to be our God, our Saviour, and our Redeemer. He also declares that it is his intention and purpose to make himself known to his chosen, redeemed people as their God, Saviour, and Redeemer, and to ultimately cause all the world to behold him as our God, our Saviour, and our Redeemer.

Saviour And Redeemer
We see in the Scriptures of the Old Testament pictures of redemption, the efficacy of Christ's atonement, the freeness and voluntariness of his obedience unto death as our Redeemer, and the causes of our redemption by the Son of God. Here it is our all glorious Redeemer himself speaking to us about himself. Child of God, try to get hold of this. The great and glorious God who created, rules, and disposes of all things exactly as he pleases, according to the good pleasure of his will, declares himself to be "Thy Saviour and thy Redeemer". If he who is our Redeemer is indeed the Lord God omnipotent, then it must be concluded that he will also be our Saviour.

The blessed comfort and consolation of the gospel is that he who shed his blood at Calvary as our Redeemer will also be the Saviour of all the redeemed. Redemption would mean nothing if it did not carry with it the assurance of everlasting salvation. However, since redemption, in its very essence, carries the assurance of deliverance and salvation, when the Lord God would send a word of hope, comfort, and good cheer in the gospel, he declares himself to be our Redeemer (Isaiah 41:14; 44:24; 48:17; 54:8).

God's Work
How did the Son of God, the Lord Jesus Christ, become our Redeemer? He was appointed to the work of redemption by his Father; and he assented to it as our Surety in the covenant of grace before the world began. It was prophesied in the Old Testament that he would come to redeem his people from their sins; and numerous pictures and types of our redemption by him were given in the Old Testament Scriptures. In the fulness of time he was made of a woman, made under the law, and sent to redeem them that were under the law. He did, by his own blood, enter in once into the holy place, having obtained eternal redemption for us. In Christ all who believe have complete, eternal redemption through his blood. He is made of God unto us Redemption. So, when it is asked how Christ came to be our Redeemer, we must, according to the Scriptures, find the answer in God himself. This is the work of the Triune Jehovah.

Salvation Sure
Because of his great love for us, the Son of God voluntarily put himself in bondage as our Surety to redeem and save us. He is the Surety of that better covenant, established upon better promises, made on our behalf before the world began (Hebrews 7:22).

Having entered into covenant engagements with the Father from everlasting, our Saviour considered himself to be, and in fact became, Jehovah's bond slave. He put himself under obligation to his Father to accomplish the great work of redemption. Therefore, he often spoke of it as something he must do (Matthew 16:21; 26:53-54; Mark 8:31; 9:12; Luke 22:37; 24:7; John 3:14; 12:34; 20:9).

Because he volunteered to be our Surety, pledged himself to redeem and save us, and the Father trusted his elect into the hands of his darling Son, now our Saviour declares that he must save his people (John 10:16; Ephesians 1:12). And that which he must do, being bound by his own honour and his own word, the Son of God will assuredly do!

Thank you, O blessed Son of God, for making yourself my Saviour and my Redeemer. "Be thou exalted, O God, above the heavens, and thy glory above all the earth."

July 27
Today's Reading: Isaiah 54-58
"The righteous perisheth"
Isaiah 57:1

The chapters we have read today are so full of both comfort and instruction that it is difficult for me to either summarize the messages of these chapters or select a single passage for our souls' meditation. In chapter 54 the Lord God graciously comforts his church, assuring us of the riches of his grace that are ours in Christ, our Lord, our Maker, our Husband. In chapter 55 Isaiah pursues the same joyful subject, assuring us that he will save his chosen, making his Word preached by the gospel effectual according to his purpose. Then, in chapter 56, the prophet warns us of those false prophets who creep into our assemblies, men who are described by God the Holy Ghost as greedy, self-serving dogs. Chapter 57 issues stern reproofs against all idolatry (all will-worship), by which men debase themselves "even unto hell", but closes with still greater displays of our great Saviour's greatness and grace. Chapter 58 denounces all creature righteousness, calls for us to look to Christ alone for righteousness, and assures every believing sinner of sure and everlasting salvation in Christ Jesus.

With such great assurances of grace and glory in and by Christ Jesus, let us joyfully meditate for a brief few moments on the deaths of God's saints. As the death of his saints is precious to our God, we who are Christ's ought to anticipate the appointed hour of our departure from this world with joy. "The righteous perisheth, and no man layeth it to heart: and merciful men are taken away, none considering that the righteous is taken away from the evil to come".

All who have even the slightest understanding of spiritual things recognize that unregenerate, unbelieving men understand nothing concerning the things of God (1 Corinthians 2:14). The unbeliever can never understand the believer. God's saints are as much a mystery to the world as is God himself (1 John 3:1). Never is this fact more evident than at that time when God's elect are taken out of this world.

Unbeliever's Death
When the unbeliever dies, he dies under the wrath of God, because of the wrath of God, and to suffer the wrath of God forever. Trying to find comfort and peace in the good he has done, his conscience is tormenting. Trying to convince himself that he is good enough to meet God, his soul is, understandably, terrified. His family and friends are distraught. They have no more hope for him than he has for himself.

Believer's Death
When the believer leaves this world, his body dies; but he enters into life. He leaves this world of woe in peace. Denouncing all personal merit, acknowledging that his most righteous works are filthy rags before God, no more worthy of God's approval than his most vile imaginations, confessing that he is (in himself) no more worthy of God's approval than the very devil himself, the believer leaves the earth in peace and hope, leaning upon Christ, trusting Christ alone as his Saviour, trusting Christ alone for acceptance with God. His family and friends, rather than behaving as hysterical pagans, weep with peace and hope, because they understand the heavenly words, "Blessed are the dead which die in the Lord." Do you ask, "How can that be?" Those who die in the Lord are eternally and indescribably blessed and happy, because:

1. They have not died! God's elect never die (John 11:25, 26). Yes, these bodies, these tabernacles of clay, must be dissolved. But these bodies are just the pup tents in which we dwell for a short time. While these bodies sleep in their bed, awaiting the resurrection, we will walk with Christ in glory in the perfection of uprightness.

2. They rest from their labour! That does not mean that the saints in heaven are floating around on clouds, strumming harps. We will continue to serve God our Saviour forever. Our labour is not with work, but with sin. Soon, we shall enter that phase of spiritual life which Christ has purchased for us, in which there shall be no more curse, no more sorrow, no more pain, and no more crying, because there shall be no more sin!

3. They are taken away from the evil to come! So long as we live in this world, we experience evil because of sin. Once we leave here, we leave all evil behind forever! Yes, it is true, "Blessed are the dead which die in the Lord."

July 28
Today's Reading: Isaiah 59-63
"Glorious in his apparel"
Isaiah 63:1

Our dear Saviour, the Lord Jesus Christ, declares, "I have trodden the winepress alone; and of the people there was none with me." The whole work of redemption and grace is the work of Christ alone. In God's great work of grace, in the salvation of our souls, no assistance is wanted, needed, required, or allowed. It is altogether the work of our Lord Jesus Christ, "travelling in the greatness of his strength, mighty to save".

A Mighty Saviour
That is exactly what Isaiah tells us in the opening verse of Isaiah 63. Our Lord Jesus Christ is "mighty to save". Reading the last two verses of chapter 62, it is obvious that the Holy Spirit is here giving us a prophetic description of our Lord Jesus Christ, and our salvation in and by him seven hundred years before his incarnation. In those two verses the prophet of God declared Christ's coming to redeem and save his people. Here in chapter 63 the prophet describes how he would accomplish that salvation.

He seems to have in his mind's eye a vision of the incarnate God, our Saviour, as he was performing the work. When he saw him covered with blood, as one coming up out of a great battle, yet full of great strength, he cried, as though he was astonished by what he saw, "Who is this that cometh from Edom, with dyed garments from Bozrah?"

Edom and Bozrah are, I think, an allusion to the ancient enmity of Esau, the head of the house of Edom, against Jacob, his brother. They are set before us here, and throughout the Scriptures, as the unrelenting enemies of God's elect. Edom and Bozrah are all those who are born after the flesh, the persecutors of those who are born after the Spirit (Galatians 4:29).

"Who is this that cometh from Edom, with dyed garments from Bozrah?" Do you see him, as he comes "in the greatness of his strength"? Behold, the Man of God's right hand, coming up as the Captain of our Salvation, returning from war; but he appears not as one who is tired, weary with battle. He comes forth to his redeemed "in the greatness of his strength". That is how Christ always comes to his people, "in the greatness of his strength" (see John 17:2).

Glorious In Apparel
And he is "glorious in his apparel". He comes in the apparel of a servant; but he is "glorious in his apparel". His garments are the garments of one who is a lowly servant. Yet, he is glorious in his garments. They are "dyed garments", drenched in blood, drenched in his own blood, yes; but here Isaiah sees him coming forth as one "glorious in his apparel", because his garments are drenched in the blood of his enemies and ours, and drenched in the blood of his redeemed! Oh, what a gallant man our Lord Jesus Christ is as he goes forth "conquering and to conqueror". He is Jehovah's Servant, that righteous Servant who was sent to deliver his people from the

hands of their enemies. He is "glorious in his apparel", because he has delivered us, having conquered all our enemies.

Speaks In Righteousness
The astonished prophet asked, "Who is this?" Immediately, the Man who is both Jehovah and Jehovah's Servant answered in great grace, "I that speak in righteousness, mighty to save." It is as though he said, "Fear not, little flock, I come not to hurt but to heal. I come not to do battle, but from battle. I come to you as he who is mighty to save."

He speaks in righteousness by the gospel (Romans 3:24-26). He speaks in righteousness as our Advocate and Mediator in heaven (1 John 2:1, 2). He speaks in righteousness when he speaks peace to believing sinners. He will speak in righteousness when he says, "Well done, thou good and faithful servant. Enter thou into the joy of thy lord."

Mighty To Save
Our Lord Jesus Christ is a mighty Saviour; and because he speaks in righteousness, our all-glorious Christ is "mighty to save" (Psalm 89:19; Hebrews 7:25). An impotent Saviour is no Saviour at all. Those who cry up a god who cannot save without the consent of man's free-will or the assistance of man's works, cry up a god who is nothing but the useless figment of man's perverted imagination. An impotent god is no God at all. An impotent god is as useless as a bucket without a bottom. If your god wants to save everyone, if your Jesus died to redeem everyone, if your divine spirit tries to save everyone, and some people go to hell in spite of all that your god has done to keep them out, you need another God, a God who is God, a God who is "mighty to save".

We worship, trust, and preach an almighty, all-sufficient, effectual Saviour. Our Saviour is the Lord Jesus Christ, the Son of the living God. And he is "mighty to save". He does not merely provide salvation, offer salvation, or try to get sinners to be saved. He saves his people from their sins by his almighty, irresistible grace (Matthew 1:21; 11:27; John 17:2; Romans 9:15, 16). He cannot fail to do so (Isaiah 42:4).

July 29
Today's Reading: Isaiah 64-66
"Destroy it not; for a blessing is in it"
Isaiah 65:8

A gardener was about to cut down a dried up vine, when the owner of the vineyard passed by and noticed a cluster of new grapes on it. He cried out to the vinedresser, "Destroy it not; for a blessing is in it." The vine looked worthless. It appeared to be needlessly occupying space. Ugly and dried up, the gardener would have cut it down, thinking that was the only thing to be done with it. Nothing in the field is uglier than a dried up vine. But the owner saw a blessing in that which appeared to be worthless. Then the Lord says, "So will I do for my servants' sakes, that I may not destroy them all." The blessing of God is often found in that which appears to be good for nothing.

God's elect

God's elect in this world are the blessing hidden among the nations of the world, for which he preserves them. The only reason why God does not destroy this world right now is the fact that there is yet a remnant according to the election of grace who must be saved (2 Peter 3:9). Everything God does in this world is for the elect's sake. Every benefit of providential mercy that reprobate men enjoy in time is because there lives among them God's elect, of whom he says, "Destroy it not; for a blessing is in it." This is not my opinion. This is what God says. "So will I do for my servants' sakes." Once Noah (the blessing) was safely in the ark, God destroyed the rest of the world. Once Lot (the blessing) was delivered unto Zoar, God destroyed Sodom. Joshua and Caleb (the blessings) entered into the land of promise, though all those who came out of Egypt with them perished under the wrath of God. The rest of the world exists and is used by God for his elect, the blessing that is in it (Isaiah 43:1-5). God's elect are always a remnant, few among many (Matthew 22:14).

God's Grace

This is also a declaration that wherever the blessing of God's grace is found in a sinner's heart it shall not be destroyed. Like new wine in the grape, grace is a new thing in the heart of man. Like new wine, grace is delightful both to God who gives it, and to man who profits by it. Like new wine in the cluster must be pressed out, so all grace must be tried. But the grace of God, once bestowed and wrought in a sinner's heart, cannot be destroyed (Ecclesiastes 3:14; Romans 11:29).

Destroy It Not

Frequently, the object of God's grace, the blessing of God in the earth, is found in that which we consider worthless. God often gathers jewels for his crown among those who are counted the off-scouring of the earth (1 Corinthians 1:26-30). These chosen ones scattered throughout the earth are a people concerning whom and for whom the Lord God says, "Destroy it not". God the Father says, "Destroy it not", for he has loved them, chosen them, and found a ransom for them. God the Son says, "Destroy it not", for he has redeemed them by his blood. God the Holy Spirit says, "Destroy it not", for he has pledged to regenerate them and make them the willing servants of the Most High. Chosen, redeemed sinners are preserved and kept by the grace of God until the appointed time of their calling by God the Holy Spirit; and God preserves the world to preserve them. Oh how magnificent your grace is, our great God!

———

July 30
Today's Reading: Jeremiah 1-3
"Pastors according to mine heart"
Jeremiah 3:15

God's prophet Isaiah warned us (Isaiah 56:9-12), as we are repeatedly warned throughout the Book of God, to "beware of dogs", false prophets. They are called dogs, because they are vile and unclean, and because, like male prostitutes (Deuteronomy 23:18), they hire themselves out to the service of the flesh. Isaiah told us that all false prophets are "beasts" who devour and blind ignorant, dumb, sleeping, greedy dogs, whose only concern is the gratification of their own lusts.

Here the Lord God, our heavenly Father, promises that he will give his church pastors according to his own heart. That means he will give his church pastors as he sees fit, and pastors who will serve the good of those people he so dearly loves. Those men God gives to his church as pastors, according to his own heart, "Shall feed you with knowledge and understanding." Here are three things that characterize every God called, Spirit anointed, heavenly ordained pastor.

A Faithful Man

Every true pastor is a faithful man. Without question, if a man is called of God to the work of the gospel ministry, he will be faithful in the work. His life and conduct will reflect his steadfastness, commitment, and faithfulness to Christ. He will faithfully seek the glory of God, faithfully study and prepare to preach the Word of God, faithfully seek the welfare of God's people, and faithfully preach the gospel of Christ. He will be faithful to Christ, to the Word, to the church, and to his own conscience. No man should be set apart for the gospel, until he has proven himself to be a faithful man (2 Timothy 2:2; 1 Corinthians 4:2).

A Fallible Man

Every true, faithful servant of God is also a fallible, sinful man. The apostles and prophets of old were themselves only frail, fallible, sinful men. They were infallible in the writing of Holy Scripture, as they were carried along by God the Holy Spirit. But they were not perfect men. Moses smote the Rock in anger. Peter took a cussing fit and denied the Lord. All the apostles forsook Christ for a while. Paul and Barnabas had a terrible fight over John Mark. And you can be sure every pastor will have many faults. Those who want to find fault with any can easily do so.

God's Ambassador

Yet, every true pastor is God's ambassador, God's servant, God's messenger. He is to be loved, cared for, respected, and obeyed as God's representative in his church. I often hear people say, "I do not follow any man". If you follow God, you will follow that man who speaks for God. You will not err by following a faithful pastor. God commands you to do so!

320

Blessed heavenly Father, how I thank you for sending me a faithful pastor, a pastor according to your heart to feed me with knowledge and understanding by the gospel of your dear Son. O my God, make me such a pastor! And we beg of you in this dark hour, God of all grace, raise up and give to your church many pastors according to your heart for the furtherance of your gospel, the salvation and edification of your elect, and the glory of your dear Son. Amen.

July 31
Today's Reading: Jeremiah 4, 5
"If ye can find a man"
Jeremiah 5:1

The two chapters brought before our eyes today reveal two things, two things we need to be reminded of unceasingly, two things set before us throughout the Book of God: the greatness of our sin and the greatness of God's grace. Here the Lord God shows his people their iniquity, and graciously calls his fallen ones to return to him. The God of all grace calls poor, degenerate sinners, sinners who repeatedly refuse to hear him, to return to him, promising mercy and grace, pardon and forgiveness. But all God's promises of mercy and grace depend upon one thing. A man must be found through whom the holy Lord God may be both just and the Justifier of poor, needy sinners.

"Run ye to and fro through the streets of Jerusalem, and see now, and know, and seek in the broad places thereof, if ye can find a man, if there be any that executeth judgment, that seeketh the truth; and I will pardon it." Blessed be the God of all grace, there is a man who has executed righteousness and judgment in the earth, the man Christ Jesus! In this world, in this sin-cursed earth, in this our spiritual Sodom, there is a man to stand in the gap and turn away the wrath of heaven, the God-man our Mediator.

Found Of God
The Triune Jehovah, our great God, found in our Surety a man on whom he laid our help, "one who is mighty", and "exalted one chosen out of the people" (Psalm 89:19). Before the world began, God found in his own darling Son a man to magnify his law and make it honourable, a man to be our ransom. He pours out his grace upon us in, by, and through that man, the Lord Jesus, our ever-blessed Christ, saying, "Deliver them from going down to the pit: I have found a ransom" (Job 33:24).

Christ Came
In due time Christ came to accomplish the work. "When the fulness of the time was come, God sent forth his Son, made of a woman, made under the law, To redeem them that were under the law, that we might receive the adoption of sons" (Galatians

4:4, 5). "In due time, Christ died for the ungodly" (Romans 5:6). Our dear Saviour came here to seek and to save lost sinners, to save his people from their sins (Matthew 1:21). And, let his name be praised forever, he accomplished what he came here to accomplish! By his obedience to the will and law of God as a man, our divine Mediator brought in everlasting righteousness for us. By his sin-atoning death upon the cursed tree, he satisfied all the fury of God's just wrath as our Substitute.

By his great work of redemption, our Lord Jesus perfectly executed judgment (the just sentence of God's holy law) by himself and upon himself. And, by mercy and truth, he purged iniquity from his chosen (Proverbs 16:6).

———

August 1
Today's Reading: Jeremiah 6-8
"Ask for the old paths, where is the good way,
and walk therein, and ye shall find rest for your souls"
Jeremiah 6:16

Christ is both the new and the living way. And being the Lamb slain from the foundation of the world, he is the old path in which we must ever dwell, if we would find rest for our souls. He is the same yesterday, and today, and forever. (Hebrews 13:8). We find rest and peace for heart and soul when we walk in the old paths of the faith. This is what God says to his people through the prophet Jeremiah: "Stand ye in the ways, and see, and ask for the old paths, where is the good way, and walk therein, and ye shall find rest for your souls." O Holy Spirit, give us grace, day by day, that we may seek and walk in the old paths of gospel truth.

If we will walk in these paths which are plainly laid before us in the Word of God, our hearts and souls shall find rest and peace. These are the things that give us peace in this world of strife and woe.

Divine Sovereignty
Here is an old, well-beaten path, upon which the saints of all ages have walked and found rest: "I am God, and there is none like me, declaring the end from the beginning, and from ancient times the things that are not yet done, saying, My counsel shall stand, and I will do all my pleasure" (Isaiah 46:9, 10).

Nothing is more comforting to our hearts than the fact that the God we trust is totally sovereign. There is nothing in this universe which is not governed and controlled by our heavenly Father. All that is in heaven above, in the earth beneath, and in all deep places is under the sovereign rule of the eternal God in whom we trust. What shall we therefore fear?

If I did not know that my God is gloriously sovereign in all things, I would soon lose all sanity. I will walk in this old path of divine sovereignty, because it gives me peace.

Electing Love
Throughout the ages, God's people have found his electing love to be a path of comfort and peace to their hearts. It is written, "The Lord did not set his love upon you, nor choose you, because ye were more in number than any people; for ye were the fewest of all people: but because the Lord loved you ... hath the Lord brought you out with a mighty hand, and redeemed you out of the house of bondmen" (Deuteronomy. 7:7, 8).

God's eternal love gives rest to our souls. From all eternity, God's heart of love has been set upon his people. Child of God, does not your heart rejoice in the peace of God's eternal, immutable love, by which he chose you to be an object of his grace in eternity?

Redeeming Blood
The old paths of the gospel are blood-stained paths. They are marked by the crimson of Immanuel's precious blood. It is written, "The blood of Jesus Christ his Son cleanseth us from all sin" (1 John 1:7). Do you walk in the blood-stained way? This is the sweet comfort of my soul; I am washed in the blood of the Lamb. To be washed in the blood is to be cleansed, pardoned, justified, and accepted with God. God said, "When I see the blood, I will pass over you" (Exodus 12:13). The eye of divine justice is on the blood of my Substitute, Jesus Christ; and there it is satisfied. So God's justice passes over and refuses to punish me.

Gospel Security
And certainly an old path of peace for the Lord's people is the promised security of God's elect. My heart rejoices to believe the Word of Christ himself, "My sheep hear my voice, and I know them, and they follow me: and I give unto them eternal life; and they shall never perish" (John 10:27, 28). What do those words mean? They mean exactly what men say they do not mean. They mean that no true believer in the Lord Jesus Christ shall ever perish!

A Warning
Beware of any preacher who continually redefines his doctrine. "Buy the truth and sell it not" is the command of God (Proverbs 23:23). Those who are not content to walk in "the old paths" are ever looking for something new, and are continually revising their doctrine. They do so only for evil reasons. They can never find rest for themselves, nor minister rest to others. Wherever they are, turbulence surrounds them.

Come, my brother, my sister in Christ, let no one turn you from the old paths. "Thus saith the Lord, Stand ye in the ways, and see, and ask for the old paths, where is the good way, and walk therein, and ye shall find rest for your souls."

August 2
Today's Reading: Jeremiah 9-11
"In these things I delight"
Jeremiah 9:24

Nothing gives me more pleasure and satisfaction than bringing delight to someone else. There is something delightful about giving delight. But, think about this: What do you suppose will give delight to the holy Lord God? There are three things specifically mentioned in the Bible as things that give delight to the Lord our God. Two of them will not surprise you, but the third one might.

God's Character

First, the Lord God, being perfect and complete, delights in his own glorious character. For any man to delight in himself (as most do) is utmost arrogance and pride. But for God to do so is right, because he is God. Perfection has reason to delight in itself. And God plainly asserts that he delights in his own character (Jeremiah 9:23, 24). The Triune God delights in lovingkindness. What words can describe the compassion and lovingkindness of our God? His lovingkindness. Oh, how free! How great! How strong! How good!

Our great God delights in judgment. Judgment is the exercise of justice. And he delights in that as fully as he does in lovingkindness. He does not delight or take pleasure in the judgment of sin upon the wicked (Ezekiel 33:11). That is his strange work (Isaiah 28:21). God will judge the wicked, because "the righteous Lord loveth righteousness". But God does not delight in the judgment of the wicked. However, he does delight in the judgment of his people's sins in Christ, by whose sin-atoning death justice was satisfied on their behalf (Isaiah 53:10).

God delights in righteousness, too, not in the self-righteous works of men, but in the perfect righteousness of Christ, which is imputed and imparted to us, by which we are now made "meet to be partakers of the inheritance of the saints in light" (Colossians 1:12).

The prophet Micah tells us, "He delighteth in mercy" (7:18). How I love those words! God Almighty, against whom I have sinned, whose law I have broken, whose holiness I have violated, "delighteth in mercy". Our God delights in these attributes of his character revealed in the work of his Son, it is by these very attributes that he saves us (Hosea 2:19).

God's Son

Secondly, the God of all grace delights in his Son (Isaiah 42:1). Obviously, the Father delights in the Son as his co-equal in the Holy Trinity. But Isaiah 42:1 is describing the Father's delight in the Son as his Servant in all his covenant engagements as our Mediator and Surety (Matthew 3:15; 17:5; John 10:15-18). The holy Lord God is delighted with the obedience of his Son unto death. It is this obedience by which his people are saved and his name is glorified in the earth (Hebrews 10:5-14).

God's Saints

Thirdly, the Lord our God delights in his people (Isaiah 62:4, 5). Imagine that. God delights in us! Be astonished, O my soul! He does not, indeed, he cannot delight in us personally. Neither can he delight in anything we do. But he does accept us, delight in us, and rejoice over us in Christ (Zephaniah 3:15-17; Ephesians 1:6). Though we are by nature, through the sin and fall of our father Adam, cast off, forsaken, and desolate, yet in Christ every saved sinner is married to and has become the delight of the living God! "Go thy way, eat thy bread with joy, and drink thy wine with a merry heart; for God now accepteth thy works" (Ecclesiastes 9:7). God delights in his saints and accepts us in the totality of our lives for Christ's sake (1 Peter 2:5).

August 3
Today's Reading: Jeremiah 12-14
"Behold, I will pluck them out"
Jeremiah 12:14

The chapters we have read today are full of judgment, setting before us God's providential judgments upon the ungodly. But in the midst of great and terrible judgment, the Lord God assures us that he will save his people. His promise is "Behold, I will pluck them out". Let us ever be mindful of this fact. In all the perplexing troubles we endure in this world, in all his judgments upon the wicked, the Lord God is saving his elect and working all things together for our good and his glory. In wrath he remembers mercy! How graciously he intersperses his promises by his prophet throughout these chapters so full of woe!

Divine Providence
Let us learn from these chapters to form one sure and unerring maxim concerning the providences of God. However puzzling they may appear to be to us, all the events of divine providence shall result in the glory of our great God and the everlasting welfare of his elect. Understanding this, our souls are strengthened and comforted, as we trust our God in darkness as well as light. Who would ever have dreamed that the cruelty of Joseph's brothers would be, by divine arrangement, the very means of his exaltation and Israel's salvation? Who would ever have conceived that the crucifixion of our Lord Jesus was, by the determinate counsel and foreknowledge of God, the very means of his exaltation and our everlasting salvation? Let us, therefore, suspend our judgment concerning all the ways and works of God, until he sets all things in their true light in the last day, showing us, to our everlasting delight, all his wonderful works in the earth.

Infinite Wisdom
In silent and humble adoration, let us observe the ways and works of the Lord our God. Our Lord Jesus has the government upon his shoulder. He is the King of nations as well as King of saints. His way is in the sea, and his paths in the great waters, and his footsteps are not known. But the end is sure. Think what infinite wisdom that must be which comprehends, accomplishes, and uses all things for his own glory, and the salvation of our souls!

God's Work
"Salvation is of the Lord." It is God's work alone, and not man's. "Can the Ethiopian change his skin, or the leopard his spots? then may ye also do good, that are accustomed to do evil" (Jeremiah 13:23).
    With those words, God's prophet reminds us of the utter impossibility of the sinner's recovery by any efforts of his own. Here again the redeemed of the Lord

rejoice to know that what the law could not do, in that it was weak through the flesh, God sending his own Son in the flesh has accomplished for us (Romans 8:3). O my soul, would I be made clean? It must be by looking to Christ alone, that I may be made whole by him.

O Spirit of God, ever give me grace to be found looking unto Jesus! Precious Lord Jesus, grant us grace to be always looking up to you, seeking your wisdom to guide, your power to protect, and your love to bless all things to our souls! "What shall we then say to these things? If God be for us, who can be against us? He that spared not his own Son, but delivered him up for us all, how shall he not with him also freely give us all things?" (Romans 8:31, 32). "Thou, O Lord, art in the midst of us, and we are called by thy name; leave us not" (Jeremiah 14:9).

August 4
Today's Reading: Jeremiah 15-17
"Thy word was unto me the joy and rejoicing of mine heart"
Jeremiah 15:16

Jeremiah 15 pronounces judgment well deserved upon a people who have forsaken Jehovah and gone "a whoring after their idols" and "with their own inventions", worshipping "the works of their hands". Yet, our ever gracious God promises, "Verily, it shall be well with thy remnant". Blessed be his name, it is always well with his elect remnant! His promise is, "I will deliver thee ... and I will redeem thee."

At the end of chapter 16, the Lord God promises to work a deliverance even greater than his deliverance of Israel out of Egypt. He will deliver all his chosen, the whole "Israel of God", "from all the lands whither he had driven them". "And so all Israel shall be saved".

In chapter 17 the folly and sin of carnal confidence, and the blessedness and security of all who trust Christ are beautifully set forth. And the Lord's knowledge of the heart is strikingly insisted upon as an evidence of his sovereignty.

Our Mediator
"Thy words were found, and I did eat them; and thy word was unto me the joy and rejoicing of mine heart: for I am called by thy name, O Lord God of hosts." In the midst of judgment, let us see and remember the blessedness pointing us to our Lord Jesus in these chapters, and feast upon him. Though Samuel and Moses are not intercessors for our souls, though Abraham be ignorant of us, and though Israel acknowledgeth us not, yet our blessed Saviour, the Lord Jesus, has stood and forever stands in the gap, having obtained eternal redemption for us.

Here then, amidst all the calamities of life, whether in private or public, nationally or individually, here would I rest and make my plea, my only plea, for I need no other. Looking to God my Father in Christ, I would say, both for myself and God's elect, "Behold, O God our shield, and look upon the face of thine anointed" (Psalm 84:9). Will you not, O Lord Jesus, take up the cause of your people?

Though our iniquities testify against us, and our sins are inexcusable, such is the everlasting and eternal efficacy of your blood and righteousness; such their infinite merit, that they plead more for us than all our sins can plead against us.

God's Word
Oh, how I treasure your word, O my God, your Word concerning your dear Son, wherein you have caused me to hope. "Thy words were found, and I did eat them; and thy word was unto me the joy and rejoicing of mine heart: for I am called by thy name, O Lord God of hosts."

Blessed Holy Ghost, by your grace, by your teaching, by your revelation, I have found Christ my Saviour, the uncreated Word. Blessed Lord Jesus, Divine Word, dwell evermore in my heart. Give me faith ever to feast upon you, O Bread of Life! Make me, as you did your prophet, as a fenced brazen wall, strong in your grace all-sufficient, and strong in faith that is in Christ Jesus. Ever be with me to save me and to deliver me, O Lord. Give me grace ever to cease from my works, and, trusting Christ alone, to hallow Christ my Sabbath, resting in him.

August 5
Today's Reading: Jeremiah 18-21
"Go down to the potter's house"
Jeremiah 18:2

God sent his prophet to the potter's house so that, by observation and inspiration, he might receive God's message to deliver to God's people. The potter had a lump of moist clay on his wheels, which he shaped, quickly and with great ease, according to his own will. "And the vessel that he made of clay was marred in the hand of the potter; so he made it another vessel, as seemed good to the potter to make it" (v. 4). Once Jeremiah saw this, the Lord God gave his message to his prophet (vv. 5-10).

Ruin And Regeneration
Without question, this vision has reference to our sin and fall in our father Adam and to the new creation of grace, to the ruin of our race in the fall and the regeneration of chosen, redeemed sinners in Christ Jesus. Adam's race, like clay in the hands of the potter, was marred by sin. But did the Potter throw it away? No! The clay was marred in the Potter's hand that he might make from it both vessels of wrath and vessels of

mercy, that he might make the vessels of mercy new creatures of grace in the Lord Jesus.

Yes, God's elect are made new creatures in Christ (2 Corinthians 5:17). Not only are we made new creatures in Christ, by virtue of our union with the Lord Jesus, we are both holy and secure.

In The Potter's Hand

The potter did not drop the vessel. The vessel was not marred by accident. It was marred according to the wisdom, will, and purpose of the potter. It was "marred in the hand of the potter". If the clay is not used for one purpose, it will be used for another. If it is not to be moulded into a vessel of honour, it will be moulded into a vessel of dishonour, according to the will of the potter. So it is with us.

Divine Sovereignty

What can be more comforting to our souls in the midst of dangers, difficulties, and discouragements, especially with regard to the work of the Gospel, than the assurance of our God's absolute sovereignty? Nothing in all the world is so comforting and satisfying as this: our God rules!

If we give way to carnal reason and unbelief, we are quickly baffled. How we need to learn the lesson God taught Jeremiah in the potter's house! As the potter has an absolute right and absolute power to do with the clay what he will, so the Lord our God has the absolute right and power to do what he will with his own (Matthew 20:15; Isaiah 45:9; Romans 9:20, 21; Isaiah 64:8). The sooner we learn this, the better.

Nothing but the pride and unbelief of our own hearts keeps us from the realization of this fact, and prevents us from finding perfect, complete satisfaction in it.

Men have countless schemes of theology and philosophy, which have been formed specifically to deny the free grace of God, darken the counsel of God, turn men away from the righteousness of God in Christ to their own righteousness, and to limit the power of the Almighty. Mortal, sinful man dares lift his defiant fists to the sovereign Lord God and say, "Hitherto shalt thou go and no further." But the throne of God is unmoved!

Universal And Unlimited

Our great God appoints, rules, and overrules all things in glorious, absolute, universal, and unlimited sovereignty, according to the purpose of his own will, and declares to all men everywhere, as he did to the house of Israel, "Behold, as the clay is in the potter's hand, so are ye in mine hand." This is our security for the present and the future, for time and eternity.

Here is the solace of our souls in this present world. "Behold, as the clay is in the potter's hand, so are ye in mine hand". This we know, "the Judge of all the earth will do right". Our God is too wise to err, too good to do wrong, and too strong to fail. If anything appears to contradict that fact, it is because of the darkness, ignorance, and unbelief of our hearts. God does not give an account of his works to men. Therefore, we cannot fully comprehend them. He alone declares the end from the beginning, because he alone knows the end from the beginning. Though what we see may seem to totally contradict it, let us never doubt for a moment that our God always does right. The time will come when he will make known to the wonder of all creatures, for the praise of his own glory and the everlasting joy of his elect, that everything that is, has been, or shall hereafter be has been done in exact agreement with infinite wisdom, justice, and truth.

Here is our solace regarding all things future, too. "Behold, as the clay is in the potter's hand, so are ye in mine hand". Our great and glorious Lord God has appointed a day when he will show all the universe that he has done right in all things; and all things shall praise him forever! We shall then see clearly what is now our great comfort to see by faith, that our God does all things well. In that great day, all God's people will forever admire his wisdom and goodness, and praise him for all that he has done; and all hell will forever confess his justice and truth.

August 6
Today's Reading: Jeremiah 22-24
"This is the name whereby he shall be called"
Jeremiah 23:6

Here is a glorious, distinct character by which Christ is revealed in the gospel. His gospel name is "The Lord Our Righteousness". May God the Holy Spirit give us wisdom and grace always to call our most glorious Saviour by this name, and find constant, unceasing satisfaction in the fact that he, who alone is righteousness, is made of God unto us righteousness. This One, who is "The Lord Our Righteousness", is himself the Lord Jehovah and the Lord our Mediator. Yet, his righteousness could never be ours were he not the infinite God. It is as our God-man Mediator that he is called, "The Lord Our Righteousness".

The Righteousness Of God
The righteousness we possess in him, have a right and title to in him is called "the righteousness of God" (2 Corinthians 5:21), because it is a righteousness required by God, wrought by God, accepted by God, given by God, and rewarded by God. Therefore, it is a righteousness that can never be lost or taken away.

The prophet says, "This is the name whereby he shall be called, The Lord Our Righteousness". By whom? He shall be, and is called, "The Lord Our Righteousness", by every sinner who is made to know by Holy Spirit conviction that he is a sinner without one shred of righteousness of his own, a wretch who is nothing but sin, and can do nothing but sin.

Blessed Assurance
We rejoice to call our Lord Jesus Christ, "The Lord Our Righteousness" when we speak to God. God is holy, righteous, perfect, and pure. It would be impossible for us ever to approach him, except through the infinite merits of Christ's blood and righteousness. However, as we enter into the holy place, waving this censer, "The Lord Our Righteousness", we "draw near with a true heart in full assurance of faith, having our hearts sprinkled from an evil conscience" (Hebrew 10:22).

We delight to call the Son of God, "The Lord Our Righteousness" when we speak to our own hearts. When Satan assails us and harasses us with our many sins, our lack of faith, our lack of love to Christ, and unfaithfulness (which is easy enough for him to observe!), we speak peace to our souls with these sweet words, "In the Lord have I righteousness and strength" (Isaiah 45:24). Only a hypocrite finds peace in his own righteousness, for his righteousness is only the imaginary righteousness of a deluded Pharisee. Believers speak peace to their souls by calling Christ, "The Lord Our Righteousness".

Saved sinners love to call the Son of God by this name when they speak to one another as well. In baptism, we confess him to be "The Lord Our Righteousness". At the Lord's Table, we remember him as "The Lord Our Righteousness". In all our songs of praise, in all our public prayers, in all our preaching, all who truly know and worship God call his Son, "The Lord Our Righteousness". We call our blessed Saviour by this name with confidence, because God the Father himself calls his Son, "The Lord Our Righteousness" (1 Corinthians 1:30).

August 7
Today's Reading: Jeremiah 25-27
"Nebuchadnezzar the king of Babylon, my servant"
Jeremiah 25:9

O my soul, take comfort in this, Nebuchadnezzar, the king of Babylon, though a mighty and a pagan king, was but the servant of the Lord of hosts, my God and Saviour! Yes, Nebuchadnezzar was Jehovah's servant, an instrument in his hand to chastise his people. Though he knew him not, like Cyrus, he was unwittingly the servant of God. So it is with all his creatures. "Surely the wrath of man shall praise thee: the remainder of wrath shalt thou restrain" (Psalm 76:10). All things, all creatures, all events, all men, all angels, all demons, everything in heaven, earth, and hell is ordered by my God, and serves him, exactly according to his purpose of grace toward his elect.

A Remnant
In Jeremiah 25 we are again reminded of the fact that God's prophets are always despised by men who hate God. Prophets of deceit the world adores. Faithful men the

world despises, especially faithful men. As it was in Jeremiah's day, so it was when the Lord Jesus Christ, the great Prophet of God, our Redeemer and Saviour, the Lord of life and glory, "came unto his own, and his own received him not". Jerusalem, the holy city, killed God's prophets and despised his Word, when he would have gathered her people, as the hen gathers her chickens under her wings, they would not be gathered to him. Self-righteous, devoted to the worship of their own works, they would not have the Christ of God. Going about to establish their own righteousness, they would not submit to the righteousness of God. Instead of embracing him, they crucified him!

Yet, God's patience was not exhausted. His love was not quenched. There was among the very men whose hands dripped with the Saviour's blood "a remnant according to the election of grace". In the very moment of his death the Lord Jesus prayed for those chosen, eternally loved ones, saying, "Father, forgive them; for they know not what they do." Oh, for grace always to keep in remembrance that love of Christ which passes knowledge! As God had his remnant in Jeremiah's day, and in the days of our Saviour's humiliation, there is still "a remnant according to the election of grace", a remnant which must be saved.

Babylon
Though Babylon appears to triumph, Babylon shall surely fall; and all shall fall with her who are made drunk by the wine of her fornications, by the wine of freewill-works religion (Revelation 18:4-10). And in the end, like Nebuchadnezzar of old, it shall be demonstrated to all that Babylon was but the servant of the very God she despised, and of his people (1 Corinthians 11:19).

Let us ever remember God's grace to his chosen during the seventy years of Babylonian captivity. Remember, too, his fulfilment of his covenant promise in bringing his people out of Babylon. All his promises, like the great Author and Finisher of salvation himself, remain eternally and unchangeably the same, yesterday, and today, and forever! Let the Lord our God be blessed and adored in all his faithfulness and truth made to a thousand generations. Let him be forever blessed by his redeemed in the enjoyment of his mercy, love, and grace in Christ Jesus!

Gospel Preachers
Let every gospel preacher learn from Jeremiah 26 the blessedness of being found faithful. Solemnly enlisted under the banner of Christ, let us devote ourselves to our Saviour's cause, and earnestly contend for the faith of the gospel. Child of God, pray for those pastors and preachers God has given to his church, pastors according to his own heart, who feed you with knowledge and understanding.

Almighty God, stand by your servants, and give each one grace to stand by you, serving your people, your gospel, and your glory faithfully, for Christ's sake. Make them a sweet savour of Christ unto you. Though a gazing stock and a proverb of derision to the world, own and bless their labours to the conversion of sinners and the comfort and edification of saints, for the glory of your great name.

False Prophets
The wretched state of false prophets is held before us in Jeremiah 27, that we might the more cherish faithful men, and highly esteem them in love for their works sake (1 Thessalonians 5:12, 13). False prophets serve their own bellies. Faithful men serve your soul. False prophets seek to please men. Faithful men seek to please God. False prophets prophesy lies, the lies of freewill-works religion. Faithful men always proclaim truth, the Truth, Jesus Christ crucified, and the gospel of God's free, sovereign, saving grace in Christ Jesus. False prophets are hirelings who care not for the sheep. Faithful men are true shepherds who care not for themselves.

August 8
Today's Reading: Jeremiah 28-30
"A man doth travail with child"
Jeremiah 30:6

In order to take away our sins, the Lord Jesus had to fully experience and fully endure all the curses of God that fell upon our fallen parents in the Garden; he had to suffer the curses of the Triune God upon Adam, and the curses of the Triune God upon Eve. The curse could not be removed except it be exhausted. Review the curses the Lord God pronounced upon the fallen pair in the Garden. In Genesis 3:15, the Lord God promised redemption by the woman's Seed; but redemption could not come without the curse being removed (Genesis 3:15-19; Galatians 3:13, 14).

Curse Removed
The Lord Jesus, in his own sacred person, literally and truly bore every curse of God against our father Adam, and his sin. In sorrow he ate his bread all the days of his earthly pilgrimage. He, and he alone, by way of emphasis, is peculiarly called, "The man of sorrows, and acquainted with grief." He alone sweat a bloody sweat as a man in the Garden of Gethsemane. He it was who was crowned with thorns from the cursed earth. He said to the Father, "Thou hast brought me into the dust of death" (Psalm 22:15).
But how shall the curse be removed from the woman, the distinct curse God placed upon the woman? How shall the curse of conception, child bearing, and subjection be removed from the woman? Isaiah tells us, "He shall see of the travail of his soul, and shall be satisfied" (Isaiah 53:11).

Delightful Shock
Thus, by the travail of his soul in death, the Lord Jesus gave birth to and brings all his children to glory. "Ask ye now, and see whether a man doth travail with child? Wherefore do I see every man with his hands on his loins, as a woman in travail, and

all faces, are turned into paleness? Alas! for that day is great, so that none is like it; it is even the time of Jacob's trouble: but he shall be saved out of it" (Jeremiah 30:6, 7).

What a delightful shock! Our all-glorious Christ is that Man, the God-man, our mighty Jacob, who supplanted death and hell for us, and won for us the birthright! He travailed for his children. And while all faces are turned into paleness by reason of sin, Christ, our glorious Jacob, our Israel, Jehovah's Servant, in the great day of his soul's travail, was saved out of it. Now, being saved out of his great travail and trouble, the Spirit of God declares, "He shall see of the travail of his soul, and shall be satisfied." He remembers no more his travail and trouble and anguish, for joy of that multitude to whom he gives birth, as innumerable as the stars of heaven and the sand upon the shore!

Christ's Travail

Did the Lord Jesus really sustain in soul a travail like those throes of nature with which a woman is panged in giving birth? Did he travail in birth for his redeemed? Pause, O my soul, and very solemnly consider this astonishing thing. The travail of the God-man! He cried, "The sorrows of hell compassed me about: the snares of death prevented me" (Psalm 18:5). We read the same thing again in Psalm 116:3. "The sorrows of death compassed me, and the pains of hell gat hold upon me: I found trouble and sorrow." Stronger expressions of agony and sorrow, of suffering and torment are not found anywhere.

"He shall see of the travail of his soul, and shall be satisfied." Isaiah 53 contains the whole of the Gospel; and this expression in Isaiah 53:11 gives us the very essence of the wondrous mystery of redemption. Here the prophet of God declares both the sufferings of Christ and the glory that should follow. If "the angels desire to look into these things", how much more should we desire to look into them? Everything stated here is true, and wonderful, and sublime, everything stated infinitely important, and absolutely necessary!

The allusion is obvious. "A woman when she is in travail hath sorrow, because her hour is come: but as soon as she is delivered of the child, she remembereth no more the anguish, for joy that a man is born into the world" (John 16:21). Both Isaiah and Jeremiah were inspired by God the Holy Spirit to use very strong and striking words to compare the risen Saviour to a woman who has delivered a child. In each case there is suffering. In each case the suffering is followed by pleasure. And in each case the pleasure is looked upon as a complete recompense of the suffering. The birth of the child repays the travail of the mother; and the salvation of God's elect satisfies the Saviour. "He shall see of the travail of his soul, and be satisfied."

Discovering Christ Day By Day

August 9
Today's Reading: Jeremiah 31, 32
"I have loved thee with an everlasting love"
Jeremiah 31:3

Meditate today upon God's everlasting love for his elect. John Gill rightly observed, "God's everlasting, unchangeable, and invariable love to his elect, through every state and condition into which they come, is written as with a sun-beam in the sacred writings".

The Eternality Of It
God's love for us did not begin yesterday. It is not something born in time. His love for us does not begin with our love for him. "We love him because he first loved us" (1 John 4:19). God's love for us springs up from eternity, and is the ground of Divine predestination, of our election and redemption by Christ, and our calling by God the Holy Spirit (Jeremiah 31:3; Ephesians 1:4-6; Ezekiel 16:8). All God's acts and works of grace performed for us before the world began arise from and are demonstrations of his everlasting love for us. Election was an act of God's eternal love (Ephesians 1:4).

The Immutability Of It
There is no possibility of change in our God (Malachi 3:6; James 1:17). God's love does not change. It cannot be taken from us; and it cannot be destroyed, neither by us nor by hell itself (Romans 8:35-39). God's love, like all his gifts bestowed upon men, is without repentance. He will never cease his own to cherish. Those who are loved of God have been loved of God from everlasting and shall be loved of God to everlasting. His love is eternal both ways. He will not depart from the objects of his love nor cease to do them good, for he cannot change (Jeremiah 32:40; Malachi 3:6; James 1:17).

The salvation of our souls does not stand upon a precarious foundation of time, but upon the immutable foundation of God's everlasting love. We change often, but there are no changes in his love.

The Gifts Of It
The gifts of God's free and everlasting love are too many for us to calculate; but here are three gifts of God's everlasting love to his elect. In comparison with these three, all others, great as they are, must be considered to be far, far less.

1. The Lord God has given us himself because of his great, everlasting love for us (Ezekiel 37:27). "I will be their God, and they shall be my people."

2. The gift of his Son, the Lord Jesus Christ, to suffer and die as our Substitute was and is the great commendation of his love to us (John 3:16; Romans 5:6-10; 1 John 3:16; 4:10). "Thanks be unto God for his unspeakable gift" (2 Corinthians 9:15).

3. The gift of his Spirit to regenerate, call, and seal us in his grace in "the time of love" is the gift of God's everlasting love to us (Ezekiel 16:8; Titus 3:3-6). Indeed, all

that God does in time, or will do to all eternity is only telling his people how much he loved them from everlasting.

The Distinctiveness Of It
God loves his elect distinctively. The Word of God tells us in the plainest terms possible that God's love for his elect is a special, sovereign, distinctive, and distinguishing love (Isaiah 43:1-5; Romans 8:29; Romans 9:11-24).

The Efficacy Of It
God's love is more than a wish or desire in his heart to save sinners. God's love for us is an effectual love. That means that those who are the objects of God's love shall be saved simply because they are the objects of his love. Otherwise the love of God is an utterly useless thing.

"We Love Him"
Knowing that God loved us when we hated him, that he loved us before the world began, that he loves us as he loves our Saviour, that his love for us will never cease, never change, and never vary, these thoughts compel us to love him, and lay us under the greatest obligations possible to reverence him, worship him, devote ourselves to his glory and his will, and serve his interests while we live in this world (1 John 4:19; 2 Corinthians 5:14; Titus 3:5-8). O Spirit of God, ever constrain us to these things by the sweet revelation and knowledge of God's everlasting love for our souls!

August 10
Today's Reading: Jeremiah 33-35
"The name wherewith she shall be called"
Jeremiah 33:16

This is a fact so indescribably glorious that it could not be believed by anyone were it not written upon the pages of Holy Scripture. The Son of God is "The Lord Our Righteousness", and we are "the righteousness of God in him". We know, by constant, bitter experience that all our righteousnesses are dross, and dung, and filthy rags. Our most righteous deeds are no more acceptable to the holy Lord God than utter blasphemy. Nothing can be found more precious to sinners, who know themselves sinners, than the fact that Christ is made of God unto us righteousness. He is so thoroughly made the righteousness of God unto us that we are "the righteousness of God in him".

How far can that thought be carried biblically? Is there danger of excess here? Must we be careful, lest someone carry this too far? Oh, no! That is impossible! Believing sinners are so thoroughly made the righteousness of God in Christ that God himself declares of his Church, "This is the name wherewith she shall be called, The Lord our righteousness". Roll that over in your heart until it overwhelms you.

Only Reasonable
If Christ is "The Lord Our Righteousness", as the Word of God declares he is, it is only reasonable and right that his Bride be called by his name. A loving, faithful wife always takes her husband's name. She is not fit to be called a wife who refuses to do so. So, too, a good husband delights to give his wife his name, and he is honoured for her to wear it and use it, because all that he is and has is hers. Yet, no earthly marriage comes close to fully portraying the union between Christ and his Church. Married to Christ, we have all that he has as our Mediator. Indeed, as his body and bride, we are "the fulness of him that filleth all in all" (Ephesians 1:23). It is written in the Book of God, "He that is joined to the Lord is one spirit" (1 Corinthians 6:17). Ours is a marriage union that transcends all marriage unions. Others shall be dissolved at death. Ours is forever (Hosea 2:19).

Meet To Be Partakers
"Christ loved the church and gave himself for it" (Ephesians 5:25). He not only died for his Bride, he gave himself for his Bride and to his Bride. He came into this world for us, lived in obedience to God for us, was made to be sin for us, died for us, arose for us, was exalted for us, intercedes for us, and reigns upon his throne for us. Everything he is as the God-man Mediator, he is for us. Everything he does, he does for us. Everything he possesses, he possesses for us and gives to us (John 17:22; Romans 8:17; Ephesians 1:3). Among all the things our all glorious Christ has wrought for us and given to us, none is more glorious, delightful, and satisfying than this: "He is made of God unto us Righteousness", and we are made "the righteousness of God in him". His righteousness is our righteousness; presently and permanently. Therefore, we are, as the Word of God declares, "meet (worthy) to be partakers of the inheritance of the saints in light" (Colossians 1:12). As in a true marriage, a husband is everything to his wife and a wife is everything to her husband, so in this: Christ is everything to his Bride and she is everything to him; and the name of this holy couple is "The Lord Our Righteousness".

August 11
Today's Reading: Jeremiah 36-38
Three black men
Jeremiah 38:7-9

The Lord God raises the question, "Can the Ethiopian change his skin?" (Jeremiah 13:23) to show us the utter futility of all human efforts by fallen man to save himself and make himself a new creature. How unspeakably blessed it is to every redeemed sinner to know what we could never do has done for us by Christ! He has made us clean by his blood's cleansing power and his omnipotent mercy, by the washing of regeneration by the Word and the renewing of the Holy Ghost.

Reading the book of Jeremiah, we run across the name of "Ebedmelech the Ethiopian", who helped God's prophet Jeremiah. There are three black men held before us in Holy Scripture, by whom God the Spirit teaches us much. May he give us grace to learn from the things here recorded about these three Ethiopians.

Ebedmelech The Ethiopian
Like Cyrus, this man, "Ebedmelech the Ethiopian", reminds us of the Lord's goodness and grace in raising instruments, from the most unexpected places and among the most unexpected people, for the deliverance of his people. Here was a stranger, a Gentile, an Ethiopian raised up by God to rescue one of his faithful prophets when all others sought his death.

Precious Lord Jesus, how can I read about this man, without being led instantly to you, blessed Redeemer and Saviour? Coming to us in our own nature, as the Divine Samaritan, the Son of God delivered us from thieves, when neither the religious priest nor the legal Levite would look upon us with mercy.

Simon The Cyrenian
Three times in the Word of God we are told that Simon the Cyrenian was compelled to take up the cross of our Lord Jesus Christ and follow him (Matthew 27:32; Mark 15:21; Luke 23:26). How I thank God for that sweet, omnipotent, irresistible, effectual grace of his Spirit by which he graciously compels sinners to take up the cross of Christ and follow him! Did he not compel us to do so, none would ever come to Christ. Did he not sweetly force us to do so, none would follow his dear Son. But by omnipotent mercy, God the Holy Spirit makes all Christ's chosen, blood-bought people willing in the day of his power

The Ethiopian Eunuch
The Ethiopian Eunuch to whom Philip was sent of God to preach the Gospel (Acts 8) is held before us in Holy Scripture as an example to teach us the necessity and blessedness of Gospel preaching and Gospel preachers. The Eunuch was reading Isaiah 53, reading what God caused his prophet Isaiah to write about the sin-atoning, substitutionary sacrifice of the Lord Jesus Christ. When Philip heard him reading that magnificent chapter, he asked, "Understandest thou what thou readest? And he said, How can I, except some man show me?"

Let us never forget the great goodness of God in sending a faithful man to our souls to tell us about our blessed Saviour and the redemption he accomplished at Calvary on our behalf. "How beautiful upon the mountains are the feet of him that bringeth good tidings, that publisheth peace; that bringeth good tidings of good, that publisheth salvation; that saith unto Zion, Thy God reigneth."

Discovering Christ Day By Day

August 12
Today's Reading: Jeremiah 39-41
"Because ye have sinned against the LORD"
Jeremiah 40:3

What volumes are spoken by these few words! "Because ye have sinned against the Lord". May God the Holy Spirit give us grace to hear them.

Nebuchadnezzar and the Babylonians took Zedekiah and Judah into captivity; the city of Jerusalem was burned to the ground; and the temple of God was destroyed because the people, the kings, the priests, and the prophets of Israel and Judah sinned against the Lord.

Sin
What evil sin has wrought in God's creation! It was sin that plunged our race into death and drove our fallen parents from the Garden of God. It was sin that caused the destruction of the old world by a flood. It was sin that caused the overthrow of Sodom and Gomorrah by fire. It is sin that causes all sickness and death, and ultimately destroys fallen man, because all have sinned.

There is an indescribably greater display of the effects of sin than the everlasting destruction of rebellious men and angels in hell. Behold the crucified Son of God! When he who knows no sin became sin and a curse for us, that we might be made the righteousness of God in him, God poured out at once upon him all the fury of his infinite wrath and justice! Our dear Saviour's death as our Substitute, when he was made sin for us, dying the just for the unjust that he might bring us to God, reveals more about the horrid evil of sin than the overthrow and everlasting destruction of all the damned in hell.

Pause, my soul, to give consideration to these things. Behold God's judgments against sin going on throughout the earth! Look at the effects of sin in the sorrows, and wars, and miseries of mankind! When these very solemn things are felt in my heart, let me look to Christ, the only Refuge and Consolation for my own sinful soul. Oh! for grace to know him, who by death has destroyed him that had the power of death, and delivered them who through fear of death are all their life time subject to bondage!

Judgment
Learn from these chapters of Jeremiah that Divine judgment never produces a gracious change in fallen man. No change is ever made in man, except grace makes the change. After Zedekiah was taken captive, after his sons and all his nobles were slain, and his eyes were put out by the king of Babylon, still rebellion sprung up among the residue of the people. Should the damned in hell be released and allowed to return to the earth, they would remain the same. The sin and malignity of their nature would remain unchanged. Except the Lord Jesus give man a new nature by

339

regeneration of the Spirit, none will ever change. Without that new birth, none can ever see and enter into the kingdom of God.

Righteousness
Reading in the Word of God, as we have today, about the sin and depravity of our race, how very sweet it is to behold the Lamb of God who was manifested to take away our sin! How blessed is the assurance of grace that we who believe are in him in whom is no sin! Nothing can comfort the soul that is conscious of man's one common nature of evil, but the consciousness that all who believe on the Son of God have one common righteousness. As by one man's disobedience, many were made sinners; so by the obedience of one, many were made righteous. In Zedekiah, Ishmael, and all the residue of the people, we see nothing but sin. In ourselves, we see and feel the same. But in Christ, we behold a fulness of grace and righteousness abounding and super-abounding to our souls. From him, we receive all and have all. "Thanks be unto God for his unspeakable gift."

August 13
Today's Reading: Jeremiah 42-45
"Johanan said ... pray for us"
Jeremiah 42:1-3; 43:2, 7

"Johanan said ... pray for us ... that the Lord thy God may shew us the way wherein we may walk, and the thing that we may do ... Then spake Johanan, saying unto Jeremiah, Thou speakest falsely ... So ... they obeyed not the voice of the Lord" (Jeremiah 42:1-3; 43:2, 7)

Until we come to Jeremiah 42, this man Johanan appears to have been a man of faith, sincerely seeking God's will and the good of God's people. Zealously, he opposed Ishmael and recovered the captives. Then, he asked Jeremiah to pray for him and the people, that they might know the will of God and do it. But there was no sincerity in him. Johanan is here held before us as a glaring example of and warning against hypocrisy and pretence before God.

How many there are in every age like Johanan. "They come unto thee as the people cometh, and they sit before thee as my people, and they hear thy words, but they will not do them: for with their mouth they shew much love, but their heart goeth after their covetousness" (Ezekiel 33:31).

Grace Needed
"Let him that thinketh he standeth take heed lest he fall." I cannot help pausing to remind myself that I am, by nature, exactly like Johanan and his friends, full of hypocrisy, ever seeking to serve myself and use others at any expense to them to serve

myself. So, too, are you. That is the nature of fallen humanity. So let us lift our hearts to the God of all grace, begging him for the constant supply of grace we need, the continual leading of his Spirit, and his unfailing mercy to restrain us from the evil that is in us.

Blessed God, my Father, keep me from the evil that is in me, for Christ's sake. Give me grace to walk before you with sincerity of heart. Make me a servant to your people; and never allow me to serve my own lusts by your people. Oh, how I need your grace!

Astonishing Hardness
Who can read about the astonishing hardness of the human heart, as set forth in the treachery and rebellion of Johanan and his followers, without trembling? Who would ever have thought it possible that when a nation had been given up by God because of its wickedness, that the remnant would be all the more outrageous in its rebellion against God? Yet, that is man, at his very best, when he is abandoned and left to himself by God! Have we not proved it so throughout our history? The best of men are but men; and all are equally capable of the same crimes as others. Corruption is the same in all men by nature. That is true of you; and it is true of me.

Grace Alone
In the light of these things, let me never forget, no, not for a moment, if there is indeed any difference between me and this vile Johanan, it is a difference made only by the free grace, distinguishing mercy, and tender lovingkindness of God heaped upon me in Christ Jesus! "For who maketh thee to differ from another? and what hast thou that thou didst not receive? now if thou didst receive it, why dost thou glory, as if thou hadst not received it?" (1 Corinthians 4:7).

Oh, for grace to seek grace, ever looking for the sweet visits of our Redeemer and daily tokens of his love. It is Christ alone who keeps us from falling, and will present us faultless before his throne with exceeding great joy. Blessed Saviour, keep me, and I shall be kept. Let me not grieve the Holy Spirit of God, whereby I am (with all your chosen) sealed unto the day of redemption. Let me never seek great things for myself, but only great good for your people, and great glory for God my Saviour. Amen.

August 14
Today's Reading: Jeremiah 46-48
"Fear not thou, O my servant Jacob, and be not dismayed, O Israel"
Jeremiah 46:27

These three chapters of Holy Scripture pronounce God's judgments upon the enemies of his ancient people. Read them, my soul, as they are intended by God the Holy Ghost, as a promise from the Triune Jehovah to his church as a whole, and to every one of his elect scattered throughout the world and the ages of time. "Fear thou not, O Jacob my servant, saith the LORD: for I am with thee; for I will make a full end of all the nations whither I have driven thee" (Jeremiah 46:28).

Salvation Sure
The promises here set before us belong to the Israel of God in all ages. The salvation of God's elect is sure. None shall perish. At the appointed time of love, each one shall be called to life and faith in Christ. Each one shall be "preserved blameless unto the coming of Christ" (1 Thessalonians 5:23) and presented "faultless before the presence of his glory with exceeding joy" (Jude 24).

God's Jacob shall not finally be lost, nor his Israel forsaken. Cast down his children may be, when their sins and rebellions make chastisements necessary; but cast off they never can be. Though we are worthy of being cast off forever, though our sins are such that everlasting abandonment is what we know we deserve, we are in Christ, in him precious to God, and altogether holy, unblameable, and unreproveable! He has taken away our sins and made us the very righteousness of God.

Moab
God's judgment shall fall upon the wicked in every nation. All the nations of the earth shall, at last, be destroyed because of sin and rebellion. God's word to Moab must be rightly applied to all nations. "Moab shall be destroyed from being a people, because he hath magnified himself against the Lord" (Jeremiah 48:42). But even in Moab there is a remnant according to the election of grace who must be saved. "Yet will I bring again the captivity of Moab in the latter days, saith the Lord" (Jeremiah 49:47).

Scattered among all the nations of the earth, God has his chosen; and he will save them. Let us, therefore, devote ourselves to preaching the Gospel throughout the world, using every means at our disposal to do so. It is by this means that God calls out and saves his elect. "For it pleased God by the foolishness of preaching to save them that believe" (1 Corinthians 1:21).

O, blessed sin-bearing Lamb of God, what everlasting love and praises the ages of eternity will bring in to you in an endless revenue of glory, when you have finally brought all your redeemed home and forever secured them beyond the reach of all possibility of danger in your own eternal righteousness in heavenly glory!

342

Discovering Christ Day By Day

August 15
Today's Reading: Jeremiah 49, 50
"Their Redeemer is strong; the LORD of hosts
is his name: he shall throughly plead their cause"
Jeremiah 50:34

Behold the gracious covenant promises of God in Christ held forth to the full assurance of faith. The final destruction of all our adversaries is sure. Every child of God by promise, as Isaac was, may well join that hymn of old, and say, "So let all thine enemies perish, O Lord: but let them that love him be as the sun when he goeth forth in his might" (Judges 5:31). Remember, child of God, the issue of the holy war is not doubtful. Christ Jesus has conquered all in our name and nature; and he will subdue for us and in us all that oppose us.

He that is for us is more than all that are against us. He will rebuke all nations for his people's sake. He will subdue the enemy and bring all their power to nothing for his own righteousness' sake. His covenant promise is sure.

God's Promise
Throughout the Book of God, Babylon represents all false religion, every form of free will, works idolatry. And throughout the Book of God we are assured that Babylon shall fall and that God's elect shall be saved.

God's Salvation
Rejoice, my soul, in God's sweet promise to save his chosen. "In those days, and in that time, saith the Lord, the children of Israel shall come, they and the children of Judah together, going and weeping: they shall go, and seek the Lord their God. They shall ask the way to Zion with their faces thitherward, saying, Come, and let us join ourselves to the Lord in a perpetual covenant that shall not be forgotten" (Jeremiah 50:4, 5).

There are tears of joy, as well as tears of sorrow. Holy mourners coming to Christ come to him with both (Zechariah 12:10; Matthew 5:4). Observe the beautiful order in the people's return. They are said first to seek the Lord their God; God in covenant. This is the first work of grace. The second is they shall ask the way to God's church, to Zion, desiring that they never forget God's covenant, his mercy, and his grace.

Was there ever a more accurate description than this of the heart of every poor returning prodigal, who by sin has run away from God and is brought back by sovereign grace, to seek the Lord's face with broken heart? Let us ever extol the grace of our God, who gives such grace, such repentance, such returning to poor sinners. Without it we would never have come to ourselves and come again to God our Saviour.

What marvellous, magnificent, matchless grace we have found in God and experienced in the reception of our souls as poor returning prodigals, when we had

343

nothing to bring and nothing to offer. Yet, in great mercy, our heavenly Father ran to, fell on our necks, and kissed us as the darlings of his heart!

———

August 16
Today's Reading: Jeremiah 51, 52
"Flee out of the midst of Babylon"
Jeremiah 51:6

Throughout the Word of God Babylon represents false religion. It does not matter what name the religion wears, every religion that declares salvation by the will, works, and worth of the sinner, in whole or in part, is the religion of Babylon. It is antichrist. It engulfs the whole world in darkness. God's command to his people concerning Babylon is not, "Reform her", "Rebuild her", or "Restore her". God's command is crystal clear and forcibly repeated throughout the Scriptures (Isaiah 48:20; 52:11; Jeremiah 50:8; 51:6, 45; 1 Corinthians 6:17; Revelation 18:4). No less than seven times he says, "Come out of her, my people, that ye be not partaker of her sins, (her religious doctrines, ceremonies and blasphemies), and that ye receive not of her plagues". We are to totally abandon all false religion, touching not the unclean thing, and align ourselves with Christ, his Gospel and his people.

Unity To Keep
We should always endeavour "to keep the unity of the Spirit in the bond of peace". Bend over backwards to get along with God's saints. Make allowances for one another's faults, failures, and offences. Never be guilty of alienating a brother, or refusing to graciously embrace one who is a child of God. But this brotherly kindness is not to be extended to those who are "the enemies of the cross of Christ". "Shouldest thou help the ungodly, and love them that hate the Lord?" (2 Chronicles 19:2; Psalm 139:21, 22; Galatians 1:6-9).

Separation To Make
With regard to all false religion, the commandment of God is as plain as the nose on your face. Our Lord Jesus says to all who are in apostate, Babylonian, free-will, works religion, "Come out of her, my people, that ye be not partakers of her sins, and that ye receive not of her plagues".
Let me be crystal clear. All freewill, works religion, Arminianism in any and every form, under any denominational name, is false religion. It may call itself Christian but it is not Christian at all. Such religion is utter paganism! It is a total denial of God's free and sovereign grace in Jesus Christ (Galatians 5:2, 4). Any mixture of works with grace is a total denial of grace (Romans 11:6). To assert that

salvation is by the will of man is to deny that "Salvation is of the Lord" (Jonah 2:9; Romans 9:16).

The Triune Jehovah calls for all who worship him to clearly separate themselves from every form of idolatry and false religion (2 Corinthians 6:14; Revelation 18:4). Yes, that means we are not to attend, support, or promote those synagogues of Satan where "will worshippers" meet.

We must never forsake the assembly of the saints (Hebrews 10:25). But we are specifically commanded to forsake the religious assemblies of those who do not worship our God and "have no fellowship with the unfruitful works of darkness".

God never once says, "Stay in Babylon, try to reform her, teach in her Sunday School, and maybe you can do a little good". Compromise will never benefit the souls of men. The only thing to do with Babylon is to "Come out of her, that ye be not partakers of her sins (her religious activities), and that ye receive not of her plagues". "Go ye out of the midst of her and deliver ye every man his soul" (Jeremiah 51:45).

Perfecting Holiness
Some who read these lines are still clinging to Babylon. You are trying to walk on both sides of the fence. You claim to believe the Gospel of God's free and sovereign grace in Christ; but you attend synagogues of Satan and support false prophets with your money, your presence, and your influence. If you do, you are as guilty of crimes against God and the souls of men as the false prophet you support. You are taking everyone under your influence by the hand (husbands, wives, children, neighbours, everyone under your influence), and leading them to hell. And you are as lost as they are. This is what the Master says; and he says it specifically to you, "Come out of her, my people, that ye be not partakers of her sins, and that ye receive not of her plagues".

This separation from Babylon, this abandonment of all attempts to make yourself righteous by your own works, this abandonment of all free will, works religion is one essential aspect of faith in Christ. You cannot trust yourself and trust Christ. You cannot trust your works and trust Christ. You cannot try to make yourself holy and trust Christ. We must forever abandon Babylon, the works of our hands, for Christ. This is what God the Holy Ghost calls "perfecting holiness in the fear of God" (2 Corinthians 6:14-7:1).

August 17
Today's Reading: Lamentations 1, 2
"Is it nothing to you?"
Lamentations 1:12

The death of our Lord Jesus Christ is the most wonderful, astounding, magnificent event in the history of the universe. Nothing that is, has been, or shall hereafter be, can be compared to it. Yet, as he was suffering the wrath of God, bearing the sins of his people, dying as the voluntary Substitute for guilty, hell-deserving, hell-bent sinners, such as we are, we hear the Son of God expressing the most woeful, unexplainable lamentation imaginable. He cried, "Is it nothing to you, all ye that pass by? behold, and see if there be any sorrow like unto my sorrow, which is done unto me, wherewith the LORD hath afflicted me in the day of his fierce anger."

Astonishing

When I hear those words falling from the lips of the Son of God, as he hangs upon the cursed tree, I simply cannot avoid asking a question. Of whom does the bleeding Lamb of God speak these words? To whom is the death of Christ meaningless and insignificant? Nothing in all the universe is more wonderful and magnificent in the eyes of God the Father than the death of his dear Son. The Saviour himself declares, "Therefore doth my Father love me, because I lay down my life". The angels of heaven ever look into the mystery and wonder of redemption by the blood of Christ with astonishment. God's servants, faithful Gospel preachers, are so overwhelmed with the wonders of redemption and the glory of the Redeemer that they never cease to study, glory in, and preach the cross of our Lord Jesus Christ (Isaiah 6:1-6; 1 Corinthians 2:2; Galatians 6:14). Redeemed sinners on the earth cherish nothing, delight in nothing, marvel at nothing like we do the death of our Lord Jesus Christ for us (Galatians 2:20; 1 John 3:16; 4:10). The ransomed in glory appear to think of nothing and speak of nothing except the dying love of the Lamb in the midst of the throne (Revelation 5:9-12). Hell itself looks upon the death of Christ as a wonderful, victorious, mysterious thing. I am certain that this is one thing that Satan himself did not understand: that Christ would triumph over him and crush his head by his death upon the cross, else he would never have put it into the heart of Judas to betray the Master.

Nothing

Yet, there are some to whom our darling Saviour speaks, as it were with astonishment, to whom his death is meaningless, insignificant, nothing! Who are these people to whom the death of Christ is nothing? Who is it that thinks little of the sin-atoning death of the Lord Jesus Christ?

Our Lord is here addressing himself to everyone who passes him by, passes by his sacrifice, passes by his death as the sinners' Substitute in unbelief, to everyone who hears and refuses to believe the Gospel. O unbelieving, Christless soul, it is you to whom the Son of God speaks! O cold, calculating, heartless preacher, you who pass by the crucified Christ and take to your lips the meaningless, insignificant trifles of politics, social corruptions, moralisms, denominationalism, historical religion, creeds, and debates about nothing, it is you to whom the Master speaks! Christ crucified is mundane, meaningless, and insignificant only to unregenerate, unbelieving souls.

Prayer

It is my heart's prayer that you and I will hear these words echoing in our soul ("Is it nothing to you, all ye that pass by? behold, and see if there be any sorrow like unto my sorrow, which is done unto me, wherewith the LORD hath afflicted me in the day of his fierce anger"), until the death of our Lord Jesus Christ is made to be the most important thing in all the world to us. I pray that you and I may become totally consumed with the crucified Christ, that our hearts, our lives, every fibre of our souls may be constantly dominated by the death of God's darling Son as our sin-atoning Saviour. Let us meditate upon and study the great, sin-atoning sacrifice of our Lord Jesus Christ until it consumes our every thought!

August 18
Today's Reading: Lamentations 3-5
"Great is thy faithfulness"
Lamentations 3:23

There was a time when I talked about God's faithfulness merely as an article of Divine truth revealed in the Scriptures. That was the best I could do, because I had not experienced (to my knowledge) much of his faithfulness. But now, it has been more than 47 years since God revealed himself to me in Christ. I have seen some trials, some temptations, and some sorrows. In them all, I must confess, my weakness in the flesh and my sin have been mournfully manifest. But this one thing I can tell you about God my Father, he is faithful! From the depths of my soul, I rejoice to acknowledge it. "Great is thy faithfulness."

God The Son
God the Son, our Lord Jesus Christ, has been faithful in his obedience to the Father as our Surety and Covenant Head (Psalm 40:6-8; Isaiah 50:5-7). In order for the holy Lord God to save his elect people, certain requirements and stipulations had to be met for us. We could not meet them. But Christ met them for us, as our Representative; and by his obedience unto death, we are saved. God required perfect obedience to his law for righteousness to be brought in, the complete satisfaction for his justice for the atonement of our sins, and the restoration of manhood to perfect holiness. Christ agreed to do it, became responsible to do it, and has done it. That is what Paul means when he says, "Christ hath redeemed us". That is what our Saviour meant when he said, "It is finished".

God The Father
God the Father has faithfully given our Mediator the reward of his obedience (Philippians 2:9-11). He has been exalted and glorified as a man (John 17:2-4). He has been given a seed to serve him forever (Psalm 2:8; John 17:9, 20, 24). God the Father gave him pre-eminence in all things and over all things as our Mediator and Surety (Colossians 1:18; Hebrews 1:1-3).

347

God The Holy Spirit

God the Holy Spirit faithfully fulfils his work in the covenant, in the fulness of time, by bringing every elect, redeemed sinner in the world into the kingdom of grace, graciously causing each one to receive the adoption of sons to which they were predestined from eternity (Galatians 4:4-7; Ephesians 1:5; 1 John 3:1-3). The salvation of sinners is a matter of Divine faithfulness, the faithfulness of the Triune God to his own purpose of grace in Christ. Every blessing of the covenant of grace we have received and shall yet receive is a matter of God's immutable faithfulness to his covenant (Psalm 89:19-37). There is not one blessing in the covenant that shall not be bestowed upon God's elect (Ephesians 1:3-14). Our redemption by the blood of Christ, our regeneration, and the faith God has given us are all the result of God's faithfulness to his purpose of grace and love toward us in eternal election (Jeremiah 31:3; 1 John 1:9). Forgiveness, justification, acceptance, adoption, preservation, and glorification are all matters of God's covenant faithfulness to his people (2 Samuel 23:5).

Trust him

"God is faithful." We may safely rely upon him. No one has ever trusted him in vain. May he give us grace to believe him, to lean upon him completely and alone for everything. We often make the same mistake Jeremiah did. We judge God's faithfulness by our circumstances and experiences. We ought to judge our circumstances and experiences by his faithfulness, as the prophet learned to do (Lamentations 3:1-40). As he is faithful in all the operations of his grace in the fulfilment of his covenant and his promises, God is faithful in all the dispositions of his providence (Romans 8:28). Everything that comes to pass is brought to pass by his hand for the everlasting, spiritual good of our souls.

Yes, our great God, you have proved it to us, and we have proved it for ourselves in the sweet experience of your grace, "Great is thy faithfulness".

August 19
Today's Reading: Ezekiel 1-4
"The wheels and their work"
Ezekiel 1:16

Providence is the glorious, though mysterious, sovereign rule of the universe by our great and glorious, ever-gracious Lord God for the salvation of his people and the praise, honour, and glory of his own great name (Romans 8:28; 11:36; Ephesians 1:11). Ezekiel was inspired by God the Holy Ghost to write out the vision God gave him in which he saw God's providence set before him as wheels moving through the earth. Divine providence is like a wheel in at least three ways.

Changes
Firstly, that part of the wheel that is now on top will soon be on the bottom; and the bottom will soon be on the top. In other words, God brings about drastic, unexpected changes in the lives of men, in the affairs of nations, and in the affairs of this world, as it pleases him. He brings about all the changes we see and experience. It is our God, and he alone, who gives poverty and riches, sickness and health, tranquillity and turmoil, fame and ill-repute, peace and war (Isaiah 45:7).

No Change
Second, there is one part of the wheel that is always the same and never turns, the axle! We undergo many changes. All our lives are chequered with change. But the axle upon which the whole machinery of providence turns is always the same. That axle is God's everlasting, covenant love and grace (Ezekiel 11:16-20). Rejoice, O my soul, God never changes (Malachi. 3:6). His purpose never changes (Job 23:13). "He is of one mind, and who can turn him? And what his soul desireth, even that he doeth." God's love never changes (John 13:1). His grace never changes (Romans 11:29). And God's faithfulness never changes (2 Timothy 2:13, 19). "If we believe not, yet he abideth faithful: he cannot deny himself." "The foundation of God standeth sure, having this seal, The Lord knoweth them that are his."

Straight Path
Third, notice that when a wheel moves fast, the only thing you can see is the exterior circle. Instead of looking at parts of things, we need to look at the whole course of events in history, in our lives, in the affairs of God's church, and so on. When we look at things as a whole, we see one round circle of symmetry, teaching us that God is wise, and just, and good.

"When they went, they went upon their four sides: and they turned not when they went." God's providence, like the wheels Ezekiel saw, is universal, moving through all the earth. Yet, it moves in one direction, never turning to the right or to the left. All things are moved by our God in one direction. All things work together to accomplish the salvation of God's elect for the praise, honour, and glory of the Lord our Saviour.

Assurance
Nothing is more comforting, nothing inspires boldness, and nothing gives peace like a good understanding of and a confident faith in God's wise, adorable, and good providence. That is the subject of the vision we have read about in these opening chapters of Ezekiel.

God's prophet was assured, and we are assured that by means, "the wheels and their work", all God's elect remnant, scattered among the nations of the earth, all the Israel of God must and shall be saved; and Jerusalem, the New Jerusalem, the City of God, the Church of God's elect, shall be a city four square, perfect, complete, and fully inhabited by the ransomed of the Lord, to the praise of the glory of his grace (Ezekiel 11:22, 23).

Discovering Christ Day By Day

August 20
Today's Reading: Ezekiel 5-8
"Yet will I leave a remnant ... They shall lothe themselves ...
And they shall know that I am the LORD"
Ezekiel 6:8-10

What a wonderful display we have before us of the great mercy, love, and grace of our great God! In wrath, he remembers mercy, and promises to remember, preserve, and save his elect remnant.

Remnant
God the Spirit tells us that among the fallen, depraved, lost, condemned ruins of humanity "there is a remnant according to the election of grace" (Romans 11:5). And he assures us that the "remnant shall be saved" (Romans 9:27). In Isaiah 10 the Holy Ghost declares, "The remnant shall return, even the remnant of Jacob, unto the mighty God" (Isaiah 10:21).

With men, a remnant is something leftover, waste material, material for which there is no plan, purpose, or intended use. With God it is exactly opposite. God's remnant is the kernel; everything else is husk. God's remnant is that for which all things were planned and purposed. Without that elect remnant, everything else would be useless.

God inspired his prophets and apostles of old to speak of his people as a "remnant". God's people are a remnant, a "little flock" of God's choosing (Romans 9:27; Isaiah 10:21, 22; Luke 12:32). God has not chosen to save all men; but there is a remnant, chosen from among the ruins of Adam's fallen race, who must be saved (Ephesians 1:3-6; John 10:16).

Everything God does he does for his remnant. All men benefit from God's goodness to his remnant. Rain, sunshine, peace, and pestilence, drought, darkness, and war come upon all men alike. But they come for and belong to the remnant (1 Corinthians 3:21).

God is longsuffering with all men for the sake of the remnant (2 Peter 3:9). Were it not for God's elect remnant, he would have destroyed the world in his wrath long ago, as he did Sodom and Gomorrah. God's elect are truly the salt, the preservers of the earth. As God spared Adam for Abel's sake and Sodom for Lot's sake, God spares the world today for his elect's sake, that they all might be saved.

God will save his elect remnant (Romans 9:27, 11:26). Not one of that great remnant for whom God made, rules, and disposes of this world shall be lost. God the Father loved them. God the Son redeemed them. God the Spirit calls them. And God, by his great grace, will preserve them unto life everlasting.

Discovering Christ Day By Day

Repentance

That remnant, when they are returned to the Shepherd and Bishop of our souls, shall come to him in true repentance, just as Ezekiel was inspired of God the Holy Ghost to describe it in Ezekiel 7:16-18. There the prophet shows us the sweet properties of God's grace in the hearts of that remnant saved by the Lord. They remember the Lord. They loathe themselves. They mourn for their iniquity. The hands they once thought strong are feeble. The knees they once thought strong are feeble. They have no ability in themselves to do anything good; and they know it, because now they have been taught of God and know the Lord. Wherever God performs his wonders of grace in the heart, in Ezekiel's day and in ours, he causes saved sinners to loathe and abhor themselves and exalt and glorify the God of all grace. He makes the saved soul weak, that he might make us strong in our Saviour, finding all-sufficient grace in him.

August 21
Today's Reading: Ezekiel 9-12
"One man among them"
Ezekiel 9:2

The prophet of God saw the Lord Jesus standing beside the brazen altar as the Executioner of Divine justice upon the wicked. Beginning at the sanctuary of God, he shall pour out God's furious wrath upon all his enemies. His eye will spare none. He declares, "As for me also, mine eye shall not spare, neither will I have pity, but I will recompense their way upon their head" (Ezekiel 9:10). Then he said to his prophet, "And, behold, the man clothed with linen, which had the inkhorn by his side, reported the matter, saying, I have done as thou hast commanded me" (Ezekiel 9:11).

Sealed

This Man, this seventh Man, with the inkhorn by his side, is our dear Saviour, the Lord Jesus, the perfect Man, the Man of Grace, the God-man, our Mediator. He wrote the names of God's elect in the book of God, and put the mark of God upon their foreheads, preserving them from judgment (Ezekiel 9:3, 4). This man, the Lord Jesus, has marked the foreheads of God's chosen remnant. He commands his angels to hurt not the earth until the 144,000 (God's elect) have been sealed in their foreheads (Revelation 7; 2 Peter 3:9). Noah must be in the ark before the rain falls. Lot must be in Zoar before Sodom is burned. And God's elect must be called by grace before judgment falls upon the earth (2 Peter 3:9).

Linen

This seventh Man is the Man of Mercy. He "was clothed with linen". That is not the clothing of a warrior, or the clothing of an executioner, but the clothing of a priest

351

engaged in his priestly work in the holy of holies. The Man Ezekiel saw is Christ, our great High Priest, who has made atonement for the sins of his people, who has entered in once into the holy place, with his own blood, where he sat down, having obtained eternal redemption for us. There he sits on yonder throne in fine linen, clean and white, which is his perfect righteousness and our perfect righteousness, the righteousness of the saints.

Inkhorn
Our dear Redeemer is not here seen wearing a slaughter weapon at his side, as the others, but an inkhorn. In ancient times writers and secretaries, those who kept records, wore their inkhorns at their sides, so that they were always handy. Seeing this picture of my Saviour, I cannot help thinking that the inkhorn is intended to represent his wounded side. From that wounded side, his precious blood gushed out in a mighty stream, and washed away our sins forever!

Done
In the last day, when he has made all things new, when all his people are gathered in, and he delivers the kingdom up to the Father, presenting his ransomed holy, unblameable, and unreproveable before the presence of his glory, he will say with joy, "Lo, I and the children thou hast given me" (Isaiah 8:18). Then, the Man Christ Jesus, Jehovah's righteous Servant, who undertook our cause before the worlds were made (Ephesians 1:12; John 10:16-18), shall say, "I have done as thou hast commanded me" (Ezekiel 9:11).

August 22
Today's Reading: Ezekiel 13-15
"If the prophet be deceived, ...
I the LORD have deceived that prophet"
Ezekiel 14:9

What a solemn word this is from our God! Spirit of God, teach us this day what is here revealed and seal your Word to our souls for our everlasting consolation and safety in Christ. When men and women heap to themselves teachers having itching ears, and turn away from the truth and are turned unto fables, the Lord God sends them strong delusions to believe a lie, and gives them over to a reprobate mind in judgment (2 Thessalonians 2:11, 12). "The deceived and the deceiver are his" (Job 12:16).

Lying Prophets

Throughout the Word of God we are warned to beware of false prophets. Here the Lord God tells us plainly that they are lying prophets who "prophesy out of their own hearts ... prophets that follow their own spirit, and have seen nothing". In every age God's church has had to endure such men. They seduce the souls of men, saying, "Peace; and there was no peace" (Ezekiel 13:10). They make "pillows to all armholes", promising salvation and security to sinners by their own works. By their false doctrine, subverting the Gospel of God, they "hunt souls", "promising life" to sinners who refuse to submit themselves to the righteousness of God in Christ.

Unsent Prophets

There is another kind of false prophet. He may not speak lies; but he is not sent of God. Like Shemaiah, many preach in God's name whom God has not sent. They are volunteer prophets God has not called. They thrust themselves into the ministry. The ministry is to them a glamorous thing. For some, it yields a sense of power, importance, and honour. For others, it is lucrative. But all who put themselves into the work, not being called of God, do so by carnal motives. They will never be honoured of God or used of God.

Oh, that every man about to enter the service of the Sanctuary would pause at the threshold and ask himself, "Has God the Holy Ghost called me and gifted me for this work? Has God sent me into his Vineyard?" To all false shepherds the Lord God says, "I am against you" (Ezekiel 13:8). Oh, for grace to have a right understanding in this weighty matter!

Sweet Assurance

Sweet assurance is given to God's elect. The Lord God preserves his own from the vain delusions of false prophets. Indeed, he even uses the heresies they spew forth in his name to separate the elect from the reprobate (1 Corinthians 11:19). "I will deliver my people out of your hand" (Ezekiel 13:23). Christ's sheep hear his voice and follow him. A stranger they will not follow. While judgment is pronounced against false prophets, God's Israel is assured, that the Lord Jehovah will reveal himself to them. "And they shall know", he promises, "that I am the Lord their God" (Ezekiel 28:26).

In chapter 14 the Lord God closes the chapter of judgment with the assurance of mercy to God's chosen (Ezekiel 14:22, 23). The redeemed of the Lord will sing their songs of salvation on the sea of glass. They shall shout Jehovah's praise as they behold the everlasting destruction of God's enemies and theirs. When our blessed Christ has finally put all enemies under his feet and saved all his ransomed, we shall see and rejoice to declare, "He hath done all things well".

August 23
Today's Reading: Ezekiel 16
"Thy time was the time of love"
Ezekiel 16:8

For every chosen, redeemed sinner there is a set day appointed by the Lord God from everlasting called "the time of love", a specific, divinely ordained time when the God of all grace will make his everlasting love known to his elect, revealing Christ in his chosen, by the saving operations of his Holy Spirit. Meditate often, Oh my soul, on this, and find fresh reason every hour to praise, adore, love, and trust the Lord Jesus.

Ruined And Helpless
Ezekiel 16:4 and 5 give us a vivid display of our fallen, ruined, helpless condition by nature, the condition of all our race since the fall of our father Adam. Every son and daughter of Adam may be truly said to be cast out to the loathing of their person. All our race, if left to ourselves and left to men, is left to perish forever! How dreadful are the consequences of the fall! This is your state and mine by nature. Fallen, sinful, lost, ruined, helpless, dead in trespasses and in sin, we have no hope, except God do for us what we cannot and will not do for ourselves. Except God give us life, we could never have life!

Christ Passes By
Here is the wonderful, effectual cause of every chosen sinner's recovery from the fall. "I passed by". The Lord Jesus, the Divine Samaritan, passes by. Beholding our nature, polluted in our blood, he has compassion upon our poor souls. His grace, and not man's merit, is the sole source of all that follows in mercy. Though our dear Saviour takes occasion from our misery to magnify the riches of his grace, his love and mercy precede our misery. Wonderful grace!

Take note of this fact. For the comfort and assurance of our souls, because his grace seems too marvellous for us to believe, our blessed Saviour repeats himself. "Yea, I said unto thee when thou was in thy blood, Live." By his sovereign, effectual word, "Live", we are resurrected from the dead (Revelation 20:6). Then, he graciously confirms to our souls both his love for us and his operation of grace in and upon our souls by his almighty Spirit.

Washed, Decked, Perfect
When the Lord Jesus passed by, when he came into this world to seek and save that which was lost, he saw his church in the very state of this poor female child, cast out and loathsome in her person to every beholder but himself. It was Christ who spread his skirts of perfect righteousness and perfect atonement over us, took us into covenant with himself, and made us his own, one in union with himself. It was our dear Lord Jesus Christ who washed us in his blood and clothed us with the garment of his salvation. These, like fine linen and gold and silk, are the beautiful robes of our

covering. He is the Lord our Righteousness in whose righteousness we are made perfect through his comeliness, which he puts upon us!

Yes, O blessed Son of God, all the beauty and loveliness of perfection is ours in you, from you, and by you! In grace here and in glory to all eternity, it is in Christ and from Christ that we derive all righteousness, sanctification, and holiness; all perfect righteousness, perfect sanctification, and perfect holiness. "I will greatly rejoice in the Lord, my soul shall be joyful in my God; for he hath clothed me with the garments of salvation, he hath covered me with the robe of righteousness, as a bridegroom decketh himself with ornaments, and as a bride adorneth herself with her jewels" (Isaiah 61:10). Amen.

August 24
Today's Reading: Ezekiel 17-19
"The soul that sinneth, it shall die"
Ezekiel 18:20

There is nothing in all the Bible more clear than this fact: All men, women, and children are sinners. Every child of Adam is born in sin and spiritual death (Romans 5:12). And I know that God Almighty will punish sin. He must punish sin! The righteousness, holiness, truth, faithfulness, immutability, and justice of God demand that he punish sin. If sin could go unpunished, the Bible would prove to be a lie and God a myth. The infinitely holy and just God of heaven must demand an infinite satisfaction for sin.

Hell
Hell is a real place, a place of eternal, unlimited, unalterable woe for both body and soul, a place where God punishes sin relentlessly. Some who read these lines are, perhaps, running full speed to hell. You have made league with death. You are bent upon eternal damnation. You refuse to bow to Christ. You refuse to trust him. You despise his righteousness, and his substitutionary atonement, and his glorious exaltation. You will not have Christ the Lord. If you die in your rebellion and unbelief, hell will be your eternal portion. God will be perfectly just in sending every rebel to hell. As I think of this fact, it has a profound effect upon my heart and soul.

Emotions
There are certain emotions which arise in my heart, when I think of sinners suffering forever in hell. When I look upon the torments of the damned, I bow in submission to the will of God (1 Samuel. 3:18; Leviticus 10:3). I know God is just and righteous. No one will be found in hell but those who have well earned it.

A sight of the damned in hell fills my heart with gratitude for the grace of God (Ephesians 2:4, 5; Galatians 1:15). I deserve to go to hell. I did everything in my power to secure my place among the damned. But God intervened to save me! Considering the misery of those who are eternally lost, a deep feeling of humility comes upon my soul (2 Samuel 9:8). Who am I that God should have mercy upon me? I am but a brand plucked from the burning.

And a sense of solemn fear takes hold of me, when I think of the multitudes in hell who perished with a false peace. I fear lest, after all, I should come to that awful place of torment. I fear religious deception, the deception of my own heart, hypocrisy, and self-righteousness. I fear missing Christ! Dear Saviour, take me, hold me, keep me by your grace! I am sin. I can do nothing but sin. I have no righteousness of my own. I have nothing to bring to commend myself to my God. Precious Christ, you alone are my trust! You alone are my hope!

Facts
There are certain facts that grip my soul, as I think of the torments of the damned. Sin is an infinitely evil thing. Hell itself is not sufficient punishment for sin. The Lord God is infinitely and inflexibly just. He will not pass by sin. Yet, "He delighteth in mercy". God Almighty is willing to save sinners (Ezekiel 33:11). No man would ever go to hell were it not for his own wilful unbelief! And I find comfort here; all of God's elect have been effectually and fully redeemed from the pit of destruction by the precious blood of Christ (Job 33:24). "The soul that sinneth, it shall die." How sweet it is to look to Christ, and, trusting him, know that when he died, I died in him! "I am crucified with Christ: nevertheless I live; yet not I, but Christ liveth in me: and the life which I now live in the flesh I live by the faith of the Son of God, who loved me, and gave himself for me" (Galatians 2:20).

August 25
Today's Reading: Ezekiel 20, 21
"The bond of the covenant"
Ezekiel 20:37

How I delight to hear the omnipotent God of all grace, God who "delighteth in mercy", say, "I will". When God says, "I will", that means it is a done deal. When he says, "I will", nothing can hinder him. "You shall". God never says, "I might", and "maybe you shall". He never says, "I will, if you will". Oh, no! Not God! He says, "I will", and "you shall". That is a matter of certainty, because the cause is in him.

Cause You

"I will cause you". If we are the willing recipients of his grace, it is because he made us willing in the day of his power. If we come to Christ, trusting him alone as our Saviour and Lord, it is because he chose us and caused us to approach unto him. If we love him, it is because he first loved us. If we are alive unto God, it is because he gave us life. If we are redeemed, justified, saved, and sanctified, it is because he redeemed us, he justified us, he saved us, and he sanctified us!

"I will cause you to pass under the rod, and I will bring you into the bond of the covenant". This was God's word to Israel by his prophet, Ezekiel, at a time when the Israelites, scattered in every country, had forgotten who they were, had forgotten God, and had plunged themselves into gross idolatry.

Doctrine Of Balaam

Being scattered among the nations of the world, they adopted the doctrine Balaam. Living among pagans and idolaters, they behaved very pragmatically. They decided it would be wise and prudent, as much as possible, to pare off the rough edges of their doctrine, melt into the pagan society, mix the worship of God with the worship of idols, and become like the heathen around them.

The Lord God would not tolerate such compromise. He would not tolerate such idolatry. Neither would his purpose of grace be thwarted. He would not forsake his own. He would not let his chosen forsake him. Therefore, he graciously intervened. "And that which cometh into your mind shall not be at all, that ye say, we will be as the heathen, as the families of the countries, to serve wood and stone" (v. 32). Thank God for his omnipotent, intervening grace!

It is as though he said, "I have loved you with an everlasting love. I chose you to be my people. I redeemed you with the blood of my own darling Son. I will not lose you! I will not let you go." Whether they delighted in it or not, he would not let them go. He pronounced a solemn oath concerning them, "As I live, saith the Lord God, surely with a mighty hand, and with a stretched out arm, and with fury poured out, will I rule over you" (v. 33). They shall no more become Babylonians, than of old he would suffer them to become Egyptians.

At The Appointed Time

At the appointed time of love, all who were sanctified by God the Father, and are preserved in the Lord Jesus Christ shall be called by the irresistible, saving power, and omnipotent grace of God the Holy Spirit. All who are the objects of covenant grace shall be made to experience all the blessedness of covenant grace. Christ's sheep never perish. Goats they cannot become. His chosen shall never be made reprobate. Run as fast as we may to hell, the hardness of our hearts, the obstinacy of our wills, the corruption of our lives, and all the powers of hell combined cannot prevent the purpose of God and keep him from saving his own! If you are his, you shall be his. He will make you willing in the day of his power. Sooner or later, he will "cause you to pass under the rod" and "bring you into the bond of the covenant". He may drag you through hell along the way; but he will have you with him in heaven in the end.

August 26
Today's Reading: Ezekiel 22, 23
"Thou hast despised mine holy things"
Ezekiel 22:8

It is a sad fact that many to whom God has given the blessed privilege of having his worship established in their midst are guilty of despising his holy things.

The Charge
It is impossible for me to understand how men and women who claim to love Christ and the Gospel of his grace can willingly absent themselves from the ministry of the Word. It is one thing to despise the labours of a pastor who faithfully seeks a message from God and diligently preaches the gospel, that itself is horrible!, but a willing neglect of the Gospel is much, much more than despising the labours of a man. It is despising God's holy things: his Word, his ordinances, his praise, and his people. The Lord Jesus promised that wherever and whenever two or three gather together in his name, he will be with them, in the midst of them. To neglect that assembly is to despise Christ's company! That is the charge God laid against Israel of old; and that is the charge that must be laid against all who despise the worship of God today.

Gospel Cherished
I know many, many people who have no place of public worship and no faithful pastor to minister to their souls. Whenever a Gospel preacher comes within a hundred miles of them, they get excited and gladly drive the distance to hear the message of redeeming love and saving grace. They plan their vacations around Bible conferences, special meetings, and places of worship. They listen to and watch recorded messages every opportunity. When they get a chance to meet with God's saints and hear his Word, they are the first ones to arrive, and the last to leave. They simply cannot get enough of the Word. They soak it up like a dry sponge soaks up water. When the message is over, they talk about it enthusiastically. They cherish what many despise, who have a faithful Gospel church and a faithful Gospel preacher next door.

Gospel Despised
I know others, many others, to whom God has given faithful pastors, who have a regular place of worship nearby. There the Word of God is faithfully preached. The saints of God gather several times a week to worship Christ and enjoy the blessed fellowship of the Gospel. Yet, these people, though they profess to love Christ and the Gospel of his grace, seem to care little for the blessed privileges that surround them. If they attend a worship service once a week and give a little money to help with the light bill, they are more than content. In many places, where people claim to love the

message of God's free and sovereign grace in Christ, the Gospel goes begging for a hearing. The evening and mid-week worship services could be held in a closet with room to spare! Without question, it is to such people that God Almighty makes this charge. "Thou hast despised mine holy things."

Time To Wake Up
If that charge stings you, I am very thankful. I am thankful to know that you are not without sensitivity to these things. "It is high time to awake out of sleep: for now is our salvation nearer than when we believed. The night is far spent, the day is at hand: Let us therefore cast off the works of darkness ... and make not provision for the flesh" (Romans 13:11-14). If you are too busy to attend the worship of God, you are too busy! If you are too tired, you need to give something up, but not the worship of God! If you despise God's holy things, he will take them away from you and give them to someone else (Romans 11:21).

August 27
Today's Reading: Ezekiel 24-26
"Forbear to cry, make no mourning for the dead"
Ezekiel 24:17

In Ezekiel 25 and 26 the prophet of God was directed to set his face against the enemies of Jerusalem, the Ammonites, Moab, Seir, Edom, and the Philistines, and against Tyre. In the twenty-forth chapter, God's prophet was commanded to use the parable of a boiling pot to show his fury against Jerusalem. Then the Lord God issued that which appears to be a very strange command to his prophet. "Son of man, behold, I take away from thee the desire of thine eyes with a stroke: yet neither shalt thou mourn nor weep, neither shall thy tears run down. Forbear to cry, make no mourning for the dead" (Ezekiel 24:16, 17). Holy Spirit, show us your message to our souls.

Boiling Pot
This parable of a boiling pot, with the choice pieces, boiled over an open fire, was designed to represent the fiery indignation of the Lord God against Jerusalem. Her scum, her filth, had risen to an enormous height. The Lord tells us that her blood was in the midst of her. What a painful picture this is of the place that was called "the holy city", the Lord's Jerusalem. In the days of his flesh, our Saviour's soul was melted to tears when he beheld Jerusalem left desolate under the wrath of God (Luke 13:34, 35).

Faith in Christ brings deliverance from all curse and condemnation, but not from pain and sorrow. There are many things that bring tears to our eyes about which the world knows nothing. The world knows nothing of the warfare that rages in our souls between the flesh and the spirit. The world knows nothing of our struggles with and

359

weeping over inward sin, unbelief, hardness of heart toward God, and overmuch love of the world and of self. The world knows nothing of our nights of weeping and days filled with sorrow because of our lack of consecration to our God, our lack of devotion to our Saviour, and our lack of submission to the direction of the blessed Holy Spirit. And, as our tender Saviour wept over a perishing Jerusalem, believing hearts weep over perishing sinners, especially those dearest to them.

Tears Forbidden

The Lord God often deals with his faithful servants in wisdom and grace known only to himself. Here is a faithful prophet bereaved of one very near and dear to him. The Lord himself calls her the desire of Ezekiel's eyes, describing his great affection for her. But when she was suddenly taken from him by the hand of God, the prophet was forbidden to shed a tear for her loss. He was not allowed to show the slightest indication of grief or sorrow.

So it shall be in the last day. In heaven's glory our God will wipe all tears from our eyes. Impossible as it is for us to imagine, there is a time coming when we shall weep no more, when we shall have no cause to weep! Heaven is a place of sure, eternal, ever-increasing bliss; and the cause of that bliss is our God! Heaven is a place of joy without sorrow, laughter without weeping, pleasantness without pain! In heaven there are no regrets, no remorseful tears, no second thoughts, no lost causes, no sorrows of any kind! When we see all things clearly, there will be no pain felt and no tears shed among the redeemed because of the damned who suffer the wrath of God forever in hell.

Submission

Ezekiel was required to show complete and perfect submission to the will of God. Oh, may God give me grace day by day to submit to his will, never rebelling, but always approving of his providence! How I fail in this! My sin, my God, I confess. Your grace I beg. For the honour of Christ, the good of your people, and the benefit of my own soul, Spirit of God, teach me to "Rejoice in the Lord always".

August 28
Today's Reading: Ezekiel 27-29
No pricking brier, no grieving thorn
Ezekiel 28:24-26

When judgment is over and all the wicked are cast into hell, when the Israel of God has been saved and all the nations of them that opposed her have been destroyed, when our great God and Saviour appears in his glory and makes all things new, the Lord God promises ...

"There shall be no more a pricking brier unto the house of Israel, nor any grieving thorn of all that are round about them, that despised them; and they shall know that I am the Lord GOD. Thus saith the Lord GOD; When I shall have gathered the house of Israel from the people among whom they are scattered, and shall be sanctified in them in the sight of the heathen, then shall they dwell in their land that I have given to my servant Jacob. And they shall dwell safely therein, and shall build houses, and plant vineyards; yea, they shall dwell with confidence, when I have executed judgments upon all those that despise them round about them; and they shall know that I am the LORD their God".

Saved By Grace
Salvation involves all that is required to bring a sinner from the ruins of the fall into the glory of heaven. There is no aspect of salvation, no part of the package, neither on this side of eternity nor on the other, which depends upon, or is in any way, or to any degree determined by man.

God's election of some to salvation is the election of grace. Divine predestination is "to the praise of the glory of his grace". Our redemption by the precious blood of Christ, that redemption which purchased and secured for us the forgiveness of all sin forever, was effectually accomplished for us "according to the riches of his grace". We are "justified freely by his grace". We were born again by the power of God's grace. Our faith in Christ is the gift and operation of the grace of God. We are sanctified by that same free grace. If we persevere unto the end, it will be by that grace of God, which keeps us in grace and faith, being sealed by his Holy Spirit, "unto the redemption of the purchased possession", that is to say, until the day of our resurrection. When, at last, we stand before our God and Saviour in heaven, we shall possess all the glory of our heavenly inheritance forever, as "heirs of God and joint-heirs with Jesus Christ", by free grace alone.

When our great God and Saviour says, "Time shall be no more", when he makes all things new, when he presents us before the presence of the glory of God, holy, unblameable, and unreproveable, without any trace of sin upon us, when he who made all things for himself brings forth the headstone and puts it in the place of everlasting pre-eminence and glory before heaven, earth and hell, we will shout with Zerubbabel, "Not by might, nor by power, but by my Spirit, saith the Lord of hosts ... crying, Grace, grace unto it".

No Tears
So thorough, so complete, so full is God's salvation that when it is finished, there will be absolutely no regrets, no sorrows, and no tears in eternity for God's elect. "There shall be no more a pricking brier unto the house of Israel, nor any grieving thorn".

Difficult as that may be for us to grasp, it is plainly revealed in Holy Scripture. "And God shall wipe away all tears from their eyes; and there shall be no more death, neither sorrow, nor crying, neither shall there be any more pain: for the former things are passed away" (Revelation 21:4). Isaiah tells us the same thing. "He will swallow up death in victory; and the Lord God will wipe away tears from off all faces; and the rebuke of his people shall he take away from off all the earth: for the Lord hath spoken it" (Isaiah 25:8).

Notice the very slight, but very significant difference in the way the two texts (speaking of the same promise) are worded. Isaiah tells us that God will wipe away "tears from off all faces". He promises us that God will wipe tears from the faces of all who possess eternal life with Christ in everlasting glory. But in Revelation 21:4, the apostle John tells us that, "God shall wipe away all tears from their eyes". By Divine inspiration, he gives an added touch of grace. He tells us that our God is not only going to wipe tears from the eyes of all his people, but also that "God shall wipe away all tears from their eyes".

Put the two texts together and you have the glorious promise of God in the Gospel to every believing sinner. It is just this: when our great and glorious God is finished with all things, he will have so thoroughly and completely saved all his people from all sin and from all the evil consequences of sin forever that there will never be a tear in our eyes again!

August 29
Today's Reading: Ezekiel 30-32
"They shall tremble at every moment,
every man for his own life"
Ezekiel 32:10

In these three chapters (Ezekiel 30-32), everything is judgment. The Lord God strengthened the arms of Babylon to destroy Egypt and Pharaoh. These days of judgment are called "the time of the heathen". What more accurate name could be found to describe the day in which we live? Truly, this dark and cloudy day is "the time of the heathen". "Thus saith the Lord God; Howl ye, Woe worth the day". (Ezekiel 30:2)

Purpose Accomplished
By everything done in time, in every dispensation of providence, the Lord God our God is accomplishing his sovereign, eternal purpose. That which he purposed he does. All that he spoke in his eternal decree he will do in time. When we see the Lord Jehovah going forth to punish the nations of the world by famine, disease, pestilence, hurricanes, floods, tornadoes, and wars, we should always look upon these things as very solemn declarations of both God's justice and his sovereignty. In these chapters, the Lord God tells us that these judgments of providence fall upon the nations of the world because of their rebellion against God and their ill-treatment of his people.

By providential judgments, men are made to tremble; but believing men and women should bow and worship, not tremble. Oh, that God would teach me and give me grace more humbly to bow before the just and all-wise execution of his eternal purpose! It is God's jealousy for his people that brings judgment upon the nations of the world. "Shall not the Judge of all the earth do right?" All God's judgments upon the nations of the world (raising up one against another, strengthening Babylon to destroy Egypt, etc.) are performed for the everlasting good of his Israel, the "holy nation", the church of God's elect. Knowledge of this fact should be sufficient for us in all things to bow and worship with Eli of old, saying, "It is the Lord: let him do what seemeth him good".

Dwell Alone
God's church is well described as "the people (that) dwell alone, and shall not be reckoned among the nations" (Numbers 23:9). We cannot read of God's judgments upon the nations without being struck with astonishment at his tenderness to Israel. Israel, representing his elect, the Israel of God, we are repeatedly told, was as guilty as all the other nations. Yet, God spared Israel, protected Israel, preserved Israel, punished other nations for Israel, and saved Israel from the wrath of all nations. These things were done in history, and are recorded here in the Book of God to show us pictures of God's distinguishing mercy and sovereign goodness toward and upon us in Christ. God's Israel is a people who dwell alone, isolated by everlasting love and electing grace from all the nations of the earth in the eternal purpose of our God. We dwell alone, separated from all other people, being purchased out of every nation, kindred, tribe, and tongue, by the sin-atoning sacrifice of the Lord Jesus Christ. And we are a people who dwell alone, separated from the nations of the world by the grace and power of God the Holy Ghost in regeneration and effectual calling.

To you, our great God, Father, Son, and Holy Ghost, we bow this day and give you thanks. And we beg of you, give us grace to trust your wise, unerring providence at all times. Amen.

August 30
Today's Reading: Ezekiel 33, 34
"If you really want to get folks to open their wallets ..."
Ezekiel 34:2

"Woe be to the shepherds of Israel that do feed themselves! Should not the shepherds feed the flocks?" (Ezekiel 24:2).

While eating lunch at one of our favourite restaurants a few years ago, my wife and I could not help overhearing the conversation of two men sitting next to us. They were preachers. One was a young pastor. His guest was a middle-aged evangelist. I listened as the older man gave instructions to the younger. He talked about one trick and then another to get men and women to give their money, having special meetings to teach people to give, etc.. Every word they spoke to one another was about other people's money and how to get it. Finally, the older preacher said, "If you really want to get folks to open their wallets, you should", and proceeded to suggests another method of religious thievery as the young pastor sat spell-bound before his advisor. In the thirty or forty minutes it took us to eat, not one word was spoken about God, his Son, his glory, his grace, his salvation, or the souls of men. The whole conversation was about raising money!

Because it was a public place, and I was not a part of the conversation, I chose to say nothing; but I said to my wife, "I would like to say to that young man, 'If you will preach the free, saving grace of God in Christ three times a week to them, God's people will give generously because they want to. You will not have to get them to.'"

My abhorrence of such men is inexpressible. They are self-serving thieves! The Lord God declares that he is against them; and that he will require his flock at their hand in judgment (Ezekiel 34:10). God's people do not have to be tricked into opening their wallets, or talked into being generous; and they will not be threatened into tithing.

Givers, Not Tithers
God's people are givers, not tithers. Nowhere do I find in the New Testament that believing men are commanded to tithe. Such a commandment would be contrary to the Gospel of grace and the spirit of the new covenant. Legal commandments are good enough for children of bondage, like Ishmael. But the children of promise are motivated from a better principle. For them, it is enough to say, "Ye know the grace of our Lord Jesus Christ" (2 Corinthians 8:9). We do not niggardly divide out our tenth, like religious misers. We give ourselves and all that we have to Christ. Cheerfully we give all that we can for the cause of Christ and the support of the Gospel ministry. Why? Because we know his grace.

His Grace
Here is what Christ has done for us. This, according to 2 Corinthians 8:9, is his grace. "Though he was rich, yet for your sakes he became poor". The wealth of God, the treasures of the infinite, the riches of eternity are the possession of our blessed Saviour. From the highest throne of glory to the lowest pit in hell, the Lord Jesus Christ owns it all. It is true that Christ became the lowly man of Nazareth. But he is more. He is the eternal God, possessing all the riches of Divine wisdom, power, and glory.

"Yet he became poor" (Philippians 2:5-8). The eternal Son of God took manhood into union with himself. The God of glory robed himself in human flesh. Behold the depths of his poverty at Calvary! He was betrayed, mocked, and beaten. He was crucified. God made his Son to be sin for us! There he was robbed of all the joy of heaven and the comfort of his Father's presence. His dying bed was a malefactor's cross. His resting place was a borrowed tomb. What was the reason for such humiliation?

"That ye through his poverty might be rich." What riches are ours through the mediation of Christ! In him we have all, and abound. The riches of grace and redemption, time and eternity are ours. Do men who know such grace need to be tricked into giving or threatened by the law to make them tithe? No! The love of Christ constrains us. And in everything grace produces more than the law. Let us, poor sinners saved by the riches of his grace, give cheerfully and bountifully to the cause of our Redeemer, through whom and in whom we have been made "rich in faith".

August 31
Today's Reading: Ezekiel 35-37
"Can these bones live?"
Ezekiel 37:3

God's prophet was led by the Spirit into a valley full of bones, to show the universal state of all men by the fall. The lifeless state of the whole human race is vividly set before us in their dead and ruined circumstances. The resurrection of these bones to life by the Spirit of God (represented in the wind) and the preaching of God's prophet portrays the spiritual resurrection of God's elect in the new birth.

No Exaggeration
Death is a terrible picture of our natural condition before God; but it is by no means an exaggeration. The whole world lies before us as a valley of dry bones, according to Ezekiel's vision; and if ever these dry bones are to live, it will not be through some innate energy in the bones themselves, or through the influence of the most zealous prophet. Education cannot develop life out of death. Persuasion cannot excite a dead man to life. And reason cannot instil life in a corpse.

The arm of the Lord must be revealed or the case is beyond hope. Let men do all they can; weep, plead, preach, and prophesy; let all the "priests" of the world come with all their enchantments and drown the valley of dry bones in their "holy water" and let the most illustrious "soul winner" come with his latest bag of tricks to make the dry bones look alive; all will be vain. Unless the Lord himself breathes life, the dry bones cannot live.

Place Of Preaching
No, Ezekiel could not make the dry bones live; but he could prophesy to them. God commanded him to do so; and God gave him the ability to do so. Therefore, Ezekiel was responsible to prophesy to the dry bones. Spurgeon said, "We cannot turn the dry bones into living men, but we can prophesy upon them, and, blessed be God, we can also prophesy to the four winds, and by our means the dead may live".

Even so, we cannot give dead sinners life. Eternal life and faith in Christ are gifts of Divine grace created in the hearts of men by the sovereign power of God. But there are some things we can and must do for the souls of men. We can preach the Gospel of Christ to eternity bound sinners. We can make known the way of life to the lost.

We can instruct the ruined in Gospel truth. And that which we can do, under God, we must do.

"Necessity is laid upon me; yea, woe is unto me, if I preach not the gospel". If I know that a man is perishing under the wrath of God, and I know the way of eternal life by faith in the blood and righteousness of Christ, and if God gives me the ability and the opportunity to preach the Gospel to that perishing sinner, it becomes my responsibility to do it (Ezekiel 33). I preach the Gospel because I love Christ, I love his Gospel, and I am concerned for the souls of men. I do it willingly and cheerfully. Yet, I am under constraint to fulfil my responsibility. If I know that a man is under the just penalty of eternal death, and I refuse to tell that man the way of pardon and life in Christ, then I shall be under the penalty of death. God says, "His blood will I require at thine hand".

September 1
Today's Reading: Ezekiel 38, 39
"They shall dwell safely all of them"
Ezekiel 38:8

O God of all grace, what a great promise you have given us in this portion of your Word. In the midst of great judgment upon Gog and Magog, with all the assaults of the heathen "against the mountains of Israel", against your church, against your chosen, you have promised that your people, your chosen, your elect, your redeemed, your Israel "shall dwell safely all of them". He makes the same promise again in Ezekiel 38:14.

Gog And Magog
The Holy Spirit does not leave us to guess who Gog and Magog represent in these two chapters (Ezekiel 38, 39). In chapter 20 of Revelation, he tells us plainly that Gog and Magog represent all the nations of the world (under the delusion of Satan) set in opposition to Christ, his Gospel, and his church. But let us never imagine, not even for a moment, that this is something beyond God's control, or something not included in his sovereign purpose of grace in predestination. That is not the case. God says to these wicked ones, "I will bring thee upon the mountains of Israel" (Ezekiel 39:2).

Satan's Little Season
Our Lord Jesus Christ, by his death on the cross, defeated Satan and bound him with a great chain. The purpose of his binding was "that he should deceive the nations no more". As the result of Satan's binding, the glorious Gospel of Christ has been carried into the four corners of the earth. Our Lord has been gathering his elect out of the four corners of the earth for more than two thousand years.

Yet, he told us that when the time appointed (symbolized by the thousand years) is fulfilled, Satan must be loosed for a little season. In Revelation 20:7-10 the Holy Spirit teaches us four things about this "little season". (1.) At the end of this present Gospel age, just before the coming of Christ, Satan will once again be turned loose upon the nations of the world (Revelation 20:7). (2.) He will be allowed to deceive the nations of the world with false religion once more (Revelation 20:8). Gog and Magog, representing all the nations of the world, are set in opposition to Christ, his church, and the Gospel of his grace. God the Holy Spirit does not use "Gog and Magog" to represent Russia, China, or any other literal nation! He tells us plainly that Gog and Magog represent the nations of the world under the influence of satanic deception. (3.) Under the satanic delusion of false religion, all the nations of the world will rise up in opposition to Christ, his Gospel, and his church in the great battle of Armageddon (Revelation 20:9). This is the same battle described in Revelation 16:12-16 and 19:19-21. It is the final assault of Satan against the Lord Jesus Christ. The meaning of John's vision in Revelation 20 is clear. Toward the close of this Gospel age, before Christ comes in glory, Satan will deceive the world with a false gospel, a false Christ, a false god, a false spirit, and a false faith; and the world, in the name of Christ, will turn in violent persecution against Christ's kingdom. (4.) Satan's last assault, like all that have preceded it, will be foiled in the end (Revelation 20:10). The purpose of God will not be frustrated. The truth of God shall not be overturned. The saints of God shall not be deceived. The church of God shall not be harmed. The Christ of God shall thoroughly defeat his enemies. The punishment of the beast and the false prophet is described in Revelation 19:20. God the Holy Ghost assures us that Satan, the beast, and the false prophet will all be cast into the lake of fire in Revelation 20:10. In that horrible place of damnation they will be unceasingly tormented forever. This battle will end in swift and decisive victory for us when Christ comes in power and great glory (2 Thessalonians 2:8).

No Harm Done
Understand this, child of God, and rejoice. No harm shall be done to God's Israel; no harm shall be done to our souls by all Satan's devices. None of God's elect shall be lost to the devices of the wicked one. "They shall dwell safely all of them". And in the end, "they shall spoil those that spoiled them" (Ezekiel 39:10). "Then shall they know that I am the Lord their God" (Ezekiel 39:28).

<hr>

September 2
Today's Reading: Ezekiel 40, 41
"The visions of God"
Ezekiel 40:2

Beginning with chapter 40, and going to the end of his prophecy, Ezekiel gives us the "the visions of God", in which he describes the church, the City of God, the New Jerusalem. First, Ezekiel saw the Lord Jesus as a Man with a measuring reed in his hand. "Behold, there was a Man". Then he tells us about the City of God.

Ezekiel introduces this portion of his prophecy by saying, "The hand of the Lord was upon me". May the same be true of us, as we read the prophecy. Let us look up to God the Holy Spirit for understanding. None but he who gave the vision can explain it to the soul's joy. O Holy Spirit, be our Instructor!

The City
The place to which Ezekiel was brought by vision was Jerusalem. Nothing is said in these two chapters (Ezekiel 40, 41) about a temple. Yet, it is obvious that the whole of the city is considered as a temple. The visions of the New Jerusalem given to the beloved Apostle John on the Isle of Patmos were very much like "the visions of God" given to Ezekiel. John saw that there was no temple in that heavenly Jerusalem. "I saw no temple therein: for the Lord God Almighty and the Lamb are the temple of it" (Revelation 21:22).

The Man
The Man spoken of by Ezekiel is the Lord Jesus Christ, our Saviour. This is the Man John saw, too, whose feet were like fine brass (Revelation 1:15). This is the Man who is our God, the singular Object of every believer's faith. It is he alone who determines the measure and dimensions of the City of God. He is the Builder and Maker of his church, the New Jerusalem, his Holy Temple (Zechariah 6:13; Hebrews 11:10). That which God's prophet saw, he was commanded to declare to God's people. "Declare all that thou seest to the house of Israel". That is the responsibility and privilege of every Gospel preacher. God reveals and teaches nothing to his servants but that which is for his people.

The Imagery
Obviously, the imagery used by the Holy Spirit in these chapters is intended to be allegorical pictures of spiritual things. The steps of ascent tell us how redeemed sinners, saved by the grace of God, go up to God by faith in Christ, being taught and led by the Holy Spirit. The palm trees speak of God's saints, heaven-born souls, flourishing like palm trees in the house of God, "trees of righteousness, the planting of the Lord" (Psalm 92:12; Isaiah 61:3). The gates are made and opened for a specific people. They are the ones whose names are inscribed upon them, "the twelve tribes of the children of Israel", God's elect (Revelation 21:12-22:15). At every gate there is an angel, a messenger, calling for men to enter into the city. These messengers represent God's preachers. The gates are pearls, one pearl, even the Pearl of Great Price, Jesus Christ. He is the Door, the only door, by whom we enter the city. The gates to the City Beautiful are never shut. Christ is an open door by whom sinners draw near to and find acceptance with the eternal God. The tables, the porch, and the place of sacrifice in which the sons of Levi minister in God's holy things, speak of our Lord Jesus Christ who is the Table of offering, the Porch of access to the throne, the Sacrifice, the Sacrificer, and Altar by whom we come to God.

The doors and gates, in their breadth, and height, and length, described in Ezekiel 41 teach us that Christ is our way of entrance before God here in grace and into God's temple hereafter in glory. And when we read of the chambers of this house, we see our dear Lord Jesus bringing his spouse, the church, into his chambers, into the secrets of sweet and intimate communion and fellowship with him (Song of Solomon 1:4).

The Spiritual
These visions of God, like all other portions of Holy Scripture in the Old Testament, are to be read with the eye of faith in the light of the New Testament, always looking for their spiritual meaning, always looking for Christ, his Gospel, and his salvation. We cannot sufficiently bless God for the discovery he has been pleased to make of himself in and by the Person, work, grace, and salvation, of our Lord Jesus Christ. That which God's prophet saw in the City we now behold in the face of our crucified, risen, exalted Redeemer. He is the goodly Mountain of Lebanon, the Foundation Stone Jehovah has laid in Zion, on whom is built that City and Temple which is the church of the living God, the New Jerusalem. On him all his people rest secure and

eternally blessed. Blessed Saviour, hasten the glorious hour when all your church
shall fill the earth as the waters cover the sea. Amen!

September 3
Today's Reading: Ezekiel 42-44
"The man stood by me"
Ezekiel 43:6

The central figure in these visions of God is that Man with the measuring reed who
stood by the prophet as he beheld the visions. Ezekiel's Guide was none other than
our dear Saviour, the Lord Jesus, our Wonderful Counsellor (Isaiah 9:6), in whom are
held all the treasures of wisdom and knowledge (Colossians 2:3).

The Chambers
The many chambers described in chapter 41 beautifully portray the "many mansions"
prepared for us in our Father's house by our risen, exalted Redeemer (John 14:2). He
whom John saw he was in the midst of the golden candlesticks, declaring his presence in
the midst of his churches, is the only Object of adoration among God's saints on earth
and in heaven.

As we think of these chambers, we must not lose sight of him, who is himself the
Habitation of his saints and their portion forever. Ever adore the Lord Jesus in every
endearing character by which he reveals himself; and we shall find him to be our
Dwelling Place, our Temple, our Altar, our great High Priest, and our Sacrifice. All
his perfections suit our souls in every circumstance. His person, his blood, his
righteousness, and his grace are the security of all his redeemed. He brought us in; and
he will bring us home, clothed with his own garments of salvation. He feeds us with
his own body and blood, and communicates to us of his fulness and grace here and
glory forever. "I will greatly rejoice in the Lord, my soul shall be joyful in my God;
for he hath clothed me with the garments of salvation, he hath covered me with the
robe of righteousness, as a bridegroom decketh himself with ornaments, and as a bride
adorneth herself with her jewels" (Isaiah 61:10).

God's Glory God's Son
In Ezekiel 43 the prophet sees the Lord Jesus, God's Son, our Mediator, the Man who
is God in our flesh, coming from the way of the east, and calls him "the glory of the
God of Israel". Truly, the glory of God shines forth to our souls only in the face of our
Redeemer and his accomplishments on our behalf. Coming from the way of the east,
points to our Saviour as "the Bright and Morning Star" (Revelation 7:2; 22:16).

370

Most Holy
In one verse (Ezekiel 43:12) the Lord God twice declares this to be the law of the house: it "shall be most holy". So it shall be! Our God himself is the Builder and Maker of this City, the Mountain of God, his church. It is his Habitation. It "shall be most holy". The Son of God purchased it with his blood. He has cleansed it from all uncleanness. And as the bodies of God's children are the temple of the Holy Ghost who dwells in them, he will put away the unclean thing and the Canaanite out of the land of his habitation. The Lord Jesus shall present his church "to himself a glorious church, not having spot, or wrinkle, or any such thing; but that it should be holy and without blemish" (Ephesians 5:27). The Prince (Ezekiel 46:1-3), the Lord Jesus, entering into the heavenly sanctuary with his own blood, having obtained eternal redemption for us (Hebrews 9:11, 12) is the only Door to God. He shut the door of all Old Testament prophecy, fulfilling all by his accomplishments as our Substitute. All who enter into heaven must enter by him. To all who would enter by some other way the door is shut forever.

September 4
Today's Reading: Ezekiel 45-47
"A portion shall be for the prince"
Ezekiel 45:7

Our blessed Saviour, the Lord Jesus Christ is the glorious Prince spoken of here. He is the Sovereign of his church, his house, and his people. He the sum and substance of every oblation commanded by him and brought to him. He is the Alpha and the Omega of all things. He is our Prophet, our Priest, and our Prince. Through every dispensation and in all circumstances, he is over all God, blessed forever. Soon he will cause every man to know, every knee to bow before him, and every tongue to confess that he is Lord, the Prince and our Saviour, to the glory of God the Father.

Offerings And The Prince
Ezekiel 46 looks to the accomplishments of Christ as our Redeemer, when by the sacrifice of himself he forever put an end to the law, its commandments, its carnal ordinances, and all those offerings and sacrifices that could never put away sin. The offerings here point us to Christ's one offering by which he put away the sins of his elect forever.

The Prince is portrayed in the midst of his people, both at their going in and their going out. So our Christ is in all his churches. Without his presence, our assembling together would be in vain. This is the promise of God our Saviour by which he comforts his saints in all ages, "I am with you".

A Question
We have been led by the Prophet through the wonderful and the great city, the New Jerusalem, which he saw in "the visions of God" (Ezekiel 40-48). Well might we sing, "Glorious things are spoken of thee, O City of God" (Psalm 87:3). Admission here is life eternal in, with, and by Christ Jesus. The citizens of the heavenly Jerusalem are under the eye of God Almighty, and objects of the good will of the Triune Jehovah. But are we citizens of that city? Are we entitled to claim its privileges as our own? Do we speak the language of Canaan? Do we delight in the society of the chosen? Is the glorious Prince and King, Christ Jesus precious to us? Is his name as ointment poured forth to us? Are his people, his ordinances, and his worship cherished by us?

Let he who writes and those who read answer each for himself. Precious Saviour, give us this day sweet evidence that we are yours. Give us this day and every day and every hour the blessed gift of faith, trusting you alone as our Saviour, our Redeemer, our God. Give us the grace of your Holy Spirit that we may grow up in you to an holy temple in the Lord. Oh, the blessedness of belonging to the household and family of faith. If you, O Lord, have made us free, we shall forever be free indeed!

Sweet Waters
The forty-seventh chapter of Ezekiel's prophecy brings us in "the visions of God" to waters. If we compare Scripture with Scripture, as God the Holy Ghost commands (1 Corinthians 2:13), we will have no difficulty understanding the meaning of these waters. God the Holy Spirit is, in this Gospel age, poured out like water upon chosen sinners (Isaiah 44:3, 4; Joel 2:28). He is compared to living water in our souls (Zechariah 14:8; John 7:37-39). The sweet waters of life and grace flow like a river into our souls from the throne of God and of the Lamb (Revelation 22:1). God the Father is a Fountain (Jeremiah 2:13). God the Son is a Fountain (Song of Solomon 4:15). God the Spirit is a Fountain (John 7:37-39). The Triune God pours out his rich mercies like a river upon chosen, redeemed sinners, through the mediation of the God-man Christ Jesus (John 14:6), through whose pierced side blood and water poured forth for the cleansing of our souls (John 19:34). The swelling of these waters surely sets before us the glorious spreading of the Gospel to every nation, kindred, tribe and tongue, by which our great God gathers his elect from the four corners of the earth.

<hr>

September 5
Today's Reading: Ezekiel 48-Daniel 1
Jehovah-Shammah: "The LORD is there"
Ezekiel 48:35

Here we come to the end of "the visions of God" (Ezekiel 40-48) in which God the Holy Ghost gave Ezekiel pictures of his church, the New Jerusalem, the City of God.

This is the name given to God's church Jehovah-Shammah, "The LORD is there". While Ezekiel has in his mind's eye the church of God in its glorified state, this name is equally applicable to the church below. Wherever you find God's elect in this world individually, gathered as local churches, or considered as the whole church universal, "The LORD is there".

Our Blessedness
This name, Jehovah-Shammah, means that God dwells with us, "The LORD is there". It is the presence of God with her that is the blessedness, happiness, security and glory of God's church on earth and in heaven.

It is true that God is with all his creatures in a general way. He is everywhere at all times, because he is omnipresent. And the Lord is everywhere in a providential way, sovereignly performing his will and accomplishing his purpose in all things. But when the Holy Spirit calls the Church of God "Jehovah-Shammah", he means for us to understand "The LORD is there" in a special way to exercise his grace and power and make himself known. His presence with his people is our peculiar and distinguishing blessedness.

Special Presence
The Lord is in Zion as he is nowhere else. And the Lord does for Zion what he does for no one else. Therefore the Psalmist sang, "God shall help her, and that right early. The heathen raged, the kingdoms were moved: he uttered his voice: the earth melted. The Lord of hosts is with us; the God of Jacob is our refuge" (Psalm 46:5-7). The prophet Zephaniah said, "The Lord thy God in the midst of thee is mighty; he will save, he will rejoice over thee with joy; he will rest in his love, he will joy over thee with singing" (3:17). And the Lord himself declares, "I will be unto her a wall of fire round about, and will be the glory in the midst of her" (Zechariah 2:5).

To You
Child of God, your Lord and Redeemer has made all these blessed promises to you. Believe him. Wherever you are, whatever your trial, temptation, struggle, and trouble of heart is, "The LORD is there". He is present to support you, comfort you, help you, instruct you, guide you, and deliver you. Set your heart not upon your troubles, but upon your God. And "rejoice in the Lord alway, again, I say, rejoice. Let your moderation be known to all men, the Lord is at hand".

O my soul, this is God's promise to you. "Lo, I am with you alway". Spirit of God give me grace to believe my God! Our God is at hand. What shall we fear? Our God is at hand. Of whom shall we be afraid? Our God is at hand. What can make us sad, or cause our hearts to fail? Wherever you are, my brother, my sister, wherever I am, the name of that place is Jehovah-Shammah, "The LORD is there". Rejoice!

September 6
Today's Reading: Daniel 2, 3
"We will not serve thy gods"
Daniel 3:18

The book of Daniel is so manifestly a prophecy regarding the Person and work of our Lord Jesus Christ that the Jews declare that it is not a book of prophecy. The reason is obvious. Were they to acknowledge that the book of Daniel is a book of prophecy, they would be compelled to acknowledge that Jesus of Nazareth (whom they crucified) is the Christ, the Messiah.

Christ And Antichrist
The Book of Daniel deals with nations and wars, specifically identifying the rise and fall of kings and kingdoms, all opposing our God, all opposing Christ and his kingdom, the church of God. But all nations and their kings shall fall before Christ our King. Daniel declares, as does the Book of Revelation, the sure and certain triumph of Christ over antichrist, the sure and certain triumph of God's church over Babylon, the full redemption and salvation of God's elect, and the everlasting glory of Christ.

In chapter 2 Nebuchadnezzar had a dream. In his dream Nebuchadnezzar saw the image of a man. The head was made of gold, the chest and arms of silver, the stomach and thighs of brass, the legs of iron, and the feet and toes of iron mixed with clay. As Nebuchadnezzar looked, a stone was cut out, not by human hands, and thrown at the image, striking its feet. This stone then grew into a huge mountain that filled the earth. The meaning of this vision is given in verse 44. "And in the days of these kings shall the God of heaven set up a kingdom, which shall never be destroyed: and the kingdom shall not be left to other people, but it shall break in pieces and consume all these kingdoms, and it shall stand for ever". There must be a series of kingdoms in the earth, ruled according to man's ways, idolatrous and ungodly. But, ultimately, God's kingdom shall reduce them all to dust and fill the whole earth. The kingdoms of this world must crumble; but the kingdom of God shall endure forever (Revelation 11:15). The Stone "cut out without hands" is Christ. The mountain growing from that Stone and filling the whole earth is the church and kingdom of Christ (Matthew 16:18).

Daniel's Band
Daniel and his friends Shadrach, Meshach, and Abednego, lived in a time of Divine judgment upon their nation. The vast majority of the people of their land despised God and his commandments. Therefore God sent Israel into horrible bondage. Daniel and his band witnessed the conquest of their country, the rape of God's temple, and were themselves carried away into captivity.

In Babylon they were assigned to the service of the king. But everything in that heathen society blasphemed God. Idolatry was rampant. Immorality was promoted in the name of religion, enlightenment, and freedom. Because of their assigned position, they were assigned a luxurious diet of foods and drinks that had been offered to idols. Eating such food was clearly forbidden in the Scriptures. So Daniel quietly, but resolutely refused to do so. His three friends followed his lead. In the midst of a wicked, oppressive, perverse society, "Daniel purposed in his heart that he would not defile himself." He and his friends might have suffered greatly for their decision. But as they resolved to honour God, God began to display his favour toward and blessing upon them (1 Samuel 2:30).

We live in similar circumstances. In this society the house of God has been raped, the Gospel of God has been prostituted, and the name of God is everywhere blasphemed. We live in a generation under the judgment of God! Our government appears to have no purpose other than the promotion of sodomy, fornication, abortion, and the complete destruction of moral principle. In our schools the name of God cannot be mentioned, except to blaspheme it; but in the name of morality young children are taught how to commit fornication "safely"! In the media, in the schools, in the White House, in the congress, and in the churches of this country rebellion against God is promoted, often in the name of God!

As believers in this decadent society, we must draw the line, like Daniel, Shadrach, Meshach, and Abednego. We must resolve, by the grace of God, not to defile ourselves by yielding to the pressures of a heathen culture and the idolatry of freewill, works religion out of which it grows. As the children of God, we must constantly separate ourselves from the pagan influences around us (2 Corinthians 6:14-7:1). Spirit of God, give us grace to deny ungodliness and worldly lusts and say to this generation, "we will not serve thy gods".

Dare to be a Daniel, dare to stand alone!
Dare to have a purpose firm! Dare to make it known!

September 7
Today's Reading: Daniel 4, 5
"He is able"
Daniel 4:37

What could be a better, more delightful, more comforting thought for meditation after reading these two chapters of Daniel's prophecy than the great, omnipotent ability of our God? The Lord our God is the God of omnipotent ability. His ability is absolute. His power is unlimited. He can do anything he wills. Omnipotence knows no obstacles. Whatever is required to accomplish the purposes and promises of God, "he is able" to perform. Those three words are used seven times in the Sacred Volume of Holy Scripture with reference to God. All seven times they are used to declare God's ability to save his people.

Discovering Christ Day By Day

1. "Those that walk in pride he is able to abase" (Daniel 4:37). God is able to abase chosen sinners by the dispensations of his providence (Psalm 107), as he did the prodigal son, by the convictions of his Spirit (John 16:8-13), and by the revelation of Christ (Isaiah 6:1-6).

2. "What he has promised he is also able to perform" (Romans 4:21). Our great God is able to perform all his covenant promises (Jeremiah 31:31-34; 32:37-40; 2 Timothy 1:9; Titus 1:2), all his promises of redemption (Genesis 3:15), and all his promises of protection and provision. His name is Jehovah-Jireh. The Lord will provide!

3. "He is able even to subdue all things unto himself" (Philippians 3:21). He has subdued Satan. He is able to subdue chosen sinners by his grace. He will subdue all things to his purpose. Therefore, he is able to perform the resurrection of our bodies.

4. "He is able to keep that which I have committed unto him" (2 Timothy 1:12). He is able to keep my immortal soul in grace. He is able to keep me from temptation and in temptation. He is able to keep me from falling and to keep me when I fall. He is able to keep me in faith, in Christ, and in sanctification (1 Thessalonians 5:24).

5. "He is able to succour them that are tempted" (Hebrews 2:18). Being touched with the feeling of our infirmities, the Son of God is able to help his tempted people with a sympathetic heart and an omnipotent arm.

6. "He is able also to save them to the uttermost that come to God by him" (Hebrews 7:25). By effectual atonement, infallible grace, and prevailing intercession, Christ is able to save all who trust him.

7. "He is able to keep you from falling" (Jude 24). He is able to keep you from falling, though many do. He is able to present you faultless before the presence of his glory, though you are personally full of sin. And he is able to do so with exceeding joy, though it cost him great pain!

> He that formed me in the womb,
> He shall guide me to the tomb.
> All my times shall ever be,
> Ordered by his wise decree.
>
> O Thou gracious, wise and just,
> In Thy hands my life I trust.
> Thee, at all times, will I bless,
> Having Thee, I all possess.

September 8
Today's Reading: Daniel 6-8
"The king ... set his heart on Daniel to deliver him"
Daniel 6:14

Daniel 6 gives us a very clear picture of our Lord Jesus Christ, showing us the necessity of atonement by our great Saviour's sacrifice upon the cursed tree. Spirit of God, give us eyes to see the Lord Jesus here and hearts to trust him, rejoice in him, and devote ourselves to him who devoted himself to us from everlasting.

Darius' Dilemma
Why could not Darius deliver Daniel from the lions' den? He greatly desired to do so. He loved Daniel; but Daniel had broken the king's law. If he did not execute the sentence of the law upon Daniel, if he simply issued a pardon to the object of his love, King Darius would have had to disown his own decree, disgracing himself and promoting chaos throughout the realm. The law of the Medes and Persians would have become a charade; and the king could no longer have been trusted or feared. That was Darius' dilemma. The law had to be honoured. Justice had to be satisfied. The crime had to be punished. Thus, though "the king ... set his heart on Daniel to deliver him" he could not do so. Daniel must go to the lions' den.

Atonement Necessary
Darius' dilemma shows us the necessity of our blessed Saviour's sin-atoning sacrifice as our Substitute. It portrays the necessity of atonement by the shedding of his precious blood.

Did you ever ask yourself, "Why did the Lord Jesus have to die at Calvary?" If he died to show us his great love for us, surely he could have done so without going to the cross? My wife and family know my love for them. Love can be shown and known in many ways. Some will say, "Christ died for us to save us from our sins." That is certainly true. But why did the Lord Jesus have to die upon the cursed tree to save us from our sins? God the Holy Spirit tells us plainly. The Lord God sacrificed his darling Son upon the cursed tree to declare, "his righteousness: that he might be just, and the justifier of him which believeth in Jesus" (Romans 3:26).

We are the rightful subjects of an absolute Monarch "the living God", the mighty Monarch of the universe. He has issued good laws for the regulation of our hearts and lives, laws with a just, but a dreadful penalty. "The soul that sinneth, it shall die" (Ezekiel 18:20). We have broken God's holy law in every point. We have earned its penalty. "The wages of sin is death" (Romans 6:23). How can we be delivered? God cannot deny himself. He cannot disgrace himself. He cannot bring dishonour upon his holy law. He cannot and will not set aside his holy law. Is there no hope for fallen, sinful, guilty sinners like you and me?

Yes, blessed be his holy name forever, Jehovah found a way to save his people from their sins. In great wisdom and grace, he declares concerning his chosen,

"Deliver him from going down to the pit: I have found a ransom" (Job 33:24). What Darius could not do for Daniel, God has done for his elect. He has devised a way in which his holy law is honoured and its penalty is satisfied, while sin is completely forgiven. By the voluntary sufferings and death of his dear Son in our place, God's broken law has been fully honoured and satisfied, and every sinner who trusts the Lord Jesus is forgiven of all sin. He who is God our Saviour is "a just God and a Saviour" (Isaiah 45:21).

September 9
Today's Reading: Daniel 9, 10
"Messiah the Prince"
Daniel 9:25

The man Gabriel appeared to Daniel, assuring him of the coming of Christ and of our Saviour's great accomplishments as our Saviour at God's appointed time (Daniel 9:20-24). By the accomplishment of these six great feats of grace, "Messiah the Prince" is identified. He who accomplished these things is the Christ, the Son of God, our Saviour.

Transgression Finished
First, Gabriel told Daniel that when the Christ appeared, he would, by the sacrifice of himself, "finish the transgression". That is precisely what our blessed Saviour did when our transgressions were laid on him and borne by him, and he carried them all away in the stream of his precious blood when he made satisfaction for us. They shall never be seen or brought up again!

Sins End
Second, the Lord Jesus came here in our flesh to "make an end of sins". Yes, our blessed Saviour abolished the sins of his people forever when he paid to the full the price of our ransom, by the sacrifice of himself! He made an end of all the sins of all his redeemed forever (1 John 3:5; Psalm 32:1; Romans 4:8; Numbers 23:21, 23). No charge can be brought against us. No, the curse of the law cannot reach us. No sentence of the law can be executed upon us. No punishment can be inflicted upon us. We are entirely and completely saved from all our sins and all the evil consequences of them forever!

Reconciliation For Iniquity
Third, the Son of God came into the world to save his people from their sins by making "reconciliation for iniquity", by making blood atonement for it. By his precious blood, by the sacrifice of himself, by his sufferings and death, the law and

378

justice of God were fully satisfied; full reparation was made for the injury done by sin (2 Corinthians 5:17-21). For all our iniquities our dear Saviour has made complete reconciliation!

Everlasting Righteousness
Fourth, our dear Saviour came here "to bring in everlasting righteousness" for his people, righteousness by which he magnified the law and made it honourable. He brought in this perfect righteousness for us by his perfect life of obedience to the law and will of God as our Representative, even his obedience unto death as our covenant Surety and Substitute. This is the righteousness he bestows upon his redeemed, the righteousness we have received by faith in him, that everlasting righteousness in which we stand and shall forever stand before the holy Lord God in the perfection of beauty! This righteousness is a robe of righteousness that will never wear out. Its virtue to justify will continue forever. It is perfect righteousness, the very righteousness of God; and it is ours in Christ Jesus!

Seal Up The Vision
Fifth, by his obedience unto death and his resurrection from the dead, our Lord Jesus Christ "sealed up the vision and prophecy". That is to say, he fulfilled it all; all the Law, all the prophets, all the types, all the promises, all the Old Testament!

Anoint The Most Holy
Sixth, Christ came here "to anoint the most Holy". Christ's ransomed ones, God's elect, his Church; poor, ruined, wretched sinners like you and me, are here called "the most holy". Imagine that! Washed in the blood of Christ, clothed with his righteousness, and sanctified by his Spirit, we are in union with the Lamb of God, "the most Holy".

> With his spotless garments on,
> Holy as the Holy One!

Rejoice, O my soul, rejoice, and give praise to God forever!

September 10
Today's Reading: Daniel 11-Hosea 1
"Great shall be the day of Jezreel"
Hosea 1:11

Daniel 11 assures us of God's abiding, unfailing mercy, grace, love, and faithfulness to his chosen until "that that is determined shall be done" (Daniel 11:36). Even when his providence brings great sorrow, our heavenly Father's eye is ever watching over us for good. O Holy Spirit, let me never forget this! Give me grace ever to trust my God!

Daniel closes his prophecy with a picture of our Lord Jesus Christ, "Michael ... the great prince", as our great Mediator. Without question, this Michael is our Saviour (Revelation 12:7-11). It is he who stood up for us from everlasting, stands up for us now, and shall stand up for us forever (Proverbs 8:22, 23; Psalm 40:6-8; Hebrews 7:24, 25; 2 Thessalonians 1:10). This is our present and eternal safety and security.

Then Hosea begins his prophecy by describing God's undeserved love for his elect, and assuring us that it is, like our God himself, immutable love.

Yet the number of the children of Israel shall be as the sand of the sea, which cannot be measured nor numbered; and it shall come to pass, that in the place where it was said unto them, Ye are not my people, there it shall be said unto them, Ye are the sons of the living God. Then shall the children of Judah and the children of Israel be gathered together, and appoint themselves one head, and they shall come up out of the land: for great shall be the day of Jezreel. (Hosea 1:10, 11)

How sweetly we are reminded again and again, "He that scattered Israel will gather him, and keep him, as a shepherd doth his flock" (Jeremiah 31:10). Israel and Judah are here set before us as representing the whole "Israel of God", the Church of God's elect made up of Jew and Gentile, scattered among all the nations of the earth. Every sinner loved and chosen of God in eternal election and redeemed by the precious blood of Christ at Calvary shall be gathered to God by the omnipotent arm of his irresistible grace. In this Gospel age, with the calling of God's elect from among all nations, Hosea's prophecy is being fulfilled (Romans 9:26). And, soon, it shall be completely accomplished. "And so all Israel shall be saved" (Romans 11:26). "For great shall be the day of Jezreel."

September 11
Today's Reading: Hosea 2-7
"I will allure her"
Hosea 2:14

In Hosea 2:6-23 the Lord God himself is speaking. The subject about which he is speaking is the salvation of his own elect portrayed in the love of Hosea for Gomer and his goodness to her. In verse 14 our great God shows us five things about his saving grace.

The Wonder Of Grace
The wonder of grace is demonstrated in the words, "Therefore, behold". These words in the context refer to the horrible crimes we have committed against our God. Here is the wonder of grace: God finds a reason to be gracious when there is none! He overrules our sins, the reasons for his wrath, and makes our sinfulness a reason for his grace. Grace is for the guilty, the needy, the sinful!

The Will Of Grace
The will of grace is the "I will" of almighty God. In the Bible nothing is ever attributed to the will of man but sin. Salvation is by the will of God. Grace is caused, governed, directed, and exercised, not by the dictates of man's freewill, but by the dictates of God's sovereign will (Romans 9:15-18). Twenty times in this chapter God says, "I will". And the result of God's "I will" is the salvation of his elect.

The Wooing Of Grace
The wooing of grace is seen in the word "allure". I like that word. God does not say, "I will drag her" or "drive her". No. God will not have any until he has their hearts. He says, "I will allure her", court and woo her until I win her heart. He reveals himself in her heart by the revelation of Christ's glorious Person and work. And his wooing is effectual. It is the work of his Spirit.

The Work Of Grace
The work of grace is revealed in the words, "I will bring her into the wilderness". If he wills, he allures. If he allures, he brings his own into the wilderness. Like a bridegroom takes his bride away from family and friend to an isolated place to be with him alone, Christ Jesus separates his own elect from all others, and causes us to dwell with him alone by faith. In the wilderness he provides for, protects, guides, and instructs us.

The Word Of Grace
The word of grace is, "I will speak comfortably unto her". God says, when I allure her and bring her to myself, I will speak to the heart of my beloved. And my word to her will always be the word of comfort and grace, spoken to her heart. I will speak to my own of hope and joy (v. 15), of marriage and forgiveness (vv. 16, 17), and of covenant mercy (vv. 18-22) and blessed assurance (v. 23).

> Thank God for grace, his matchless grace,
> Amazing, free, eternal grace!
> Grace chose me and devised a way,
> To save me and put sin away!

September 12
Today's Reading: Hosea 8-14
"What shall I do unto thee?"
Hosea 6:4

"O Ephraim, what shall I do unto thee? O Judah, what shall I do unto thee? for your goodness is as a morning cloud, and as the early dew it goeth away". It is a fact that many, upon hearing the Gospel preached in the power of the Holy Spirit, experience deep religious convictions, which soon die away like the morning dew. Lot's wife (Genesis 19:15, 16), Israel at the Red Sea (Exodus 15:2, 22-24), the rich young ruler (Luke 18:18-23), Felix, the Roman governor (Acts 22:24, 25), and King Agrippa (Acts 26:28), all heard God speak and were moved toward repentance by the Word. But their convictions did not last long. Many others went further than these. Under deep conviction, Ananias and Sapphira, Simon Magus, and Demas professed faith in Christ, united with his people, and served his cause for a while. But in time their convictions died.

Moved, But Not Saved
Most people who sit under the sound of the Gospel are, at one time or another, moved by it. Few will read these lines who have not been convicted, in some measure, and moved toward repentance by the Word of God. God has spoken to you by his Word. Has he not? You have heard his voice in the Gospel. Yet, you harden your heart. You lay aside the claims of Christ in the Gospel, like Felix, saying, "At a more convenient season I will call for thee." But, like the morning dew before the rising sun, your convictions die away. Be warned, my friend. The road to hell is paved with good intentions. There are multitudes in hell who once wept and prayed over their souls, read Proverbs 29:1.

How many there are who once stood as pillars in the visible church of God whose convictions died away in time. They began well. But they are no longer among us. They did much, moved by conviction. They gave much, moved by conviction. But, where are they now? What happened? The convictions they once felt so strongly died altogether.

Dying Convictions
Are your convictions dying? Here are three symptoms of dying convictions. (1.) The neglect of private prayer (2.) The neglect of holy scripture (3.) The neglect of public worship. "Be watchful and strengthen the things which remain" (Revelation 3:2).

The Reasons
Why do the convictions of many die? I have preached to many who wept, but repented not. And I have preached to many who appeared to be truly penitent, who appeared to be men and women of strong, firm conviction, whose convictions faded away like the morning dew before the sun. How does this happen? Why do the convictions of many die? Here are four answers to those questions.

They never knew their own guilt, depravity, sin, and helplessness before God. You may see the doctrine of total depravity very clearly, without having any personal knowledge of inward corruption.

They never saw the beauty, glory, and fulness of Christ. Many know the doctrine of Christ who never embraced Christ. Many see his doctrine who never see him. Many love his doctrine who never love him.

They never bowed to the rule and dominion of Christ as their Lord. Many want a Saviour to keep them out of hell who refuse to bow to Christ as Lord to rule over them. But Christ will not be your Saviour if he is not your Lord.

They still love the world. If you love the world, the love of God is not in you. Nothing is more deadly than the cares and pleasures of the world and the deceitfulness of riches. Sooner or later, the love of the world will cause conviction to die. Materialism will destroy conviction.

Legal Convictions
Dying convictions are natural, legal convictions. Saving faith is the result of Holy Spirit conviction (John 16:8-11). True, saving, Holy Ghost conviction only grows and increases; but legal convictions are only dying convictions. And dying convictions are seldom corrected. God will not always speak to those who refuse to hear. He will not always call those who refuse to obey. There is such a thing as judicial reprobation. God will fix it so that those who will not obey the Gospel cannot obey. If you harden your heart, God will harden your heart (Proverbs 1:23-33; Luke 13:23-27). Take heed. In the Word of God I see no record of God ever crossing a sinner's path more than once! God has no method of saving sinners, but that which you have heard in the Gospel. If you reject the Gospel, you reject life. Convictions that are put off tend to make the heart harder. As iron is hardened by smelting and cooling, so is the heart of man.

September 13
Today's Reading: Joel 1-3
"The day of the LORD"
Joel 1:15

The theme of Joel's prophecy is "the day of the Lord". Joel speaks of "the day of the Lord" five times in these three short chapters. He tells us that history is moving constantly to an appointed end called, "the day of the Lord" (1:15; 2:1, 11, 31; 3:14). But Joel does not use this phrase, "the day of the Lord", to refer to a specific, single day or time. In chapter 1 (v. 15) "the day of the Lord" is immediate. It referred to the day in which the judgment of God was seen in the land. In chapter 2 (vv. 1, 11, 31) "the day of the Lord" is imminent, referring to judgment that may come at any time.

In chapter 3 (v. 14) "the day of the Lord" is future, referring to the final, consummate end of all things. As it is used by Joel, "the day of the Lord" refers to any day in which the Lord God displays his sovereignty as God. In other words, yesterday was "the day of the Lord". Today is "the day of the Lord". And tomorrow shall be "the day of the Lord". And there is a day coming when all creation shall acknowledge, this is "the day of the Lord". Joel declares that the Lord who is God shall accomplish his purpose.

Day Of Warning
First, Joel tells us that "the day of the Lord" is a day of warning, a day when the Lord God sends judgment to warn us of judgment. "Alas for the day! for the day of the Lord is at hand, and as a destruction from the Almighty shall it come" (1:15). When the Lord God visits a nation, a people, a generation, or an individual in providential judgment, it is a warning of judgment to come and a merciful call to repentance (1:13-16, 19). He is saying, "My Spirit shall not always strive with man". "Blow ye the trumpet in Zion, and sound an alarm in my holy mountain: let all the inhabitants of the land tremble: for the day of the Lord cometh, for it is nigh at hand" (2:1).

Hope Given
At the close of verse 11 in chapter 2, the question is raised "Who can abide the day of God's wrath?" (see Nahum 1:2-6). Yes, the Lord God will punish sin; he must. Judgment is sure. Hell is real. Eternity is forever. But "he delighteth in mercy". Even now, in the face of such horrible judgment, there is hope. In wrath, he does remember mercy. We know this because the Lord God calls us to repentance, declaring himself to be "gracious and merciful, slow to anger, and of great kindness" (2:12-14). In verses 15-17, God's prophet pleads with his people to heed the Lord's call and plead for his mercy, as Moses' did, for the glory of his own great name.

Grace Promised
Then, in the last part of chapter 2 (vv. 18, 19, 21, 23, 25-27), the Lord God promises us that as surely as we seek his mercy he will grant it (Hebrews 4:16). This promise of grace clearly involved the promise of Christ's coming as Mediator and his great, accomplished redemption (2:28-32; Acts 2:16-36; Galatians 3:13, 14). "Whosoever shall call upon the name of the Lord shall be delivered", saved by the grace of God. That means that anyone who trusts Christ has been chosen, redeemed, and called by the God of all grace. Joel 2:32 goes on to say, "for in mount Zion and in Jerusalem shall be deliverance, as the Lord hath said, and in the remnant whom the Lord shall call". That means that only a remnant of Adam's fallen race shall call upon Christ and worship him as their Saviour; and they call upon him only because they have been called by him; and all the called remnant shall call upon the name of the Lord. The remnant shall come to Christ, because Christ comes to the remnant in effectual, saving mercy.

Deliverance Assured
In chapter 3 the Lord God declares that he will save, that he will deliver all the hosts of his elect from the nations into which he has scattered them. The battle that takes

place "in the valley of decision" (vv. 2, 14) is never in doubt. That battle is not yours, but the Lord's (2 Chronicles 20:17, 20). Though they have forsaken him, he will never forsake them. But, before the great and terrible day of the Lord shall come, he will bring again the captivity of his Jerusalem. The Lord will cry out of Zion and gather his people, his heritage, his Israel out of the nations of the world. Then, his Spirit will cease to strive with man, and all Israel shall be saved. "So shall ye know that I am the Lord your God dwelling in Zion."

September 14
Today's Reading: Amos 1-5
"Yet have ye not returned unto me, saith the LORD"
Amos 4:11

Seven hundred and fifty years before our Lord's incarnation the nation of Israel was a rich, thriving, prosperous kingdom. During the reign of Jeroboam II, the nation was peaceful, stable, strong, and very, very religious (Amos 3:12, 15; 4:1, 4; 5:5, 21-23; 6:4-6; 8:3-10). Many enjoyed such wealth that they had winter houses and summer houses. Others were even more wealthy, living in ivory houses on great estates. But all was not well in Israel. The nation was morally degenerate. The land was filled with greed and corruption. Bethel, the house of God, had become Bethel, the house of transgression (4:4). Amos came storming into Samaria with a message of Divine judgment, a message of impending wrath upon a people who had abandoned God and his worship, crying, "Prepare to meet thy God, O Israel". Judgment had already begun; but it had no effect upon the hearts of the people. It would, therefore, increase and continue to increase until the nation was altogether destroyed. The Lord God swore by his prophet that because they repented not when he sent famine to their bodies, he would send a far worse, far more destructive famine, a famine of spiritual food (8:11, 12).

Divine Judgment
Amos began his message to Israel in a strange way. In chapters 1 and 2 Amos describes the judgments the Lord would bring upon the nations around Israel. These were the Gentiles among whom the Children of Israel lived. At the end of chapter 2 (vv. 6-16), he speaks to Israel, the Northern Kingdom, and declares that God will judge them for their corruption and for injustice, corruption and injustice greater than any of the other nations. The Lord God was pressed under them, as an over-loaded cart is pressed with its load (2:13). But the people of Israel were totally undisturbed, absolutely complacent. From verse 1 of chapter 3, Amos deals with these people exclusively, driving his message home to Israel. He begins by pointing out that they were a people who had a special, privileged position before God (3:1, 2). That is

exactly what they wanted to hear. You can picture them swelling with pride and arrogance. "We are God's elect, his chosen, favoured, special people. We have a great history and a great heritage." Then, the prophet hits them right between the eyes with a sledge-hammer. "Therefore I will punish you for all your iniquities."

Privilege And Responsibility

You see that which was their great pride was the very reason for their great judgment. Light despised brings great wrath. Privilege creates responsibility. And the greater our privileges are, the greater our responsibilities are. The nation of Israel had been given the greatest revelation, the greatest privileges of any nation. But they turned from them to walk in utter darkness and idolatry. Israel was the very house of God. But they had turned the house of God into a house of iniquity. They had the Gospel revealed to them; the passover, the feasts, the sacrifices, the priesthood, the temple, the altar, the mercy-seat, all spoke something of the Gospel. But they wilfully rejected God's revelation. Therefore, they were sentenced to the outpouring of God's wrath. This is exactly what Peter means when he says, "Judgment must begin at the house of God" (1 Peter 4:17). It always begins there. God always starts with his professed people, and then he moves out to those round about them. Israel despised God and his Word. For this reason, the prophet says, God is going to send judgment (3:3-8).

The Golden Calves

Do you remember the two golden calves that were erected by the first King Jeroboam in the cities of Bethel and Dan (1 Kings 12:28)? Israel was sent to worship there; and the people called those calves Jehovah. And they worshipped and bowed down before those golden images. Those two calves represented three basic evils in Israel, for which God was set in judgment against them, evils for which the judgment of God is manifest today. Those golden calves symbolized material greed, shameless pride, and sensuality. One might rightly conclude that the Holy Spirit intended Amos' prophecy for our own generation.

Call To Repentance

Yet, God ever remembers mercy, even in the midst of providential wrath and judgment. So Amos delivers a message of mercy. As God's ambassador, he calls Israel to repentance. He calls for them to turn from their idols to God. The sinner's only hope is reconciliation to God (5:4-8). But Israel continued to harden their hearts, taking refuge in their refuge of lies (5:18; 6:1). Sooner or later, either in grace or in judgment, the Lord God will destroy every sinner's refuge of lies.

God sees through us. He sees through our religion and our rituals. He sees our hearts. He demands truth in the inward parts, not a mere outward conformity to religious codes. God sees through all the sham and pretence, without the slightest difficulty. He is not impressed with the "bodily exercise" of religion. He requires "godliness". "Thou desirest truth in the inward part" (Psalm 51:6).

September 15
Today's Reading: Amos 6-9
"By whom shall Jacob arise?"
Amos 7:2

He by whom Jacob, that is, God's chosen people, shall arise from the ruins of Adam's fall is Jesus Christ our Lord. By the merits of his blood and righteousness, by the power of his grace, and by the efficacy of his intercession at the throne of grace, all God's elect shall arise to life eternal. Then, at his glorious second advent, we shall arise in resurrection glory! O blessed hope!

But Amos 6-9 is an assertion of Divine justice and of the certainty of Divine judgment. The prophet of God here calls sinners to flee for refuge and salvation to the Lord Jesus.

At Ease In Zion
In Amos 6:1 the prophet speaks a word of warning to sinners at ease, not in the world at large but at ease in Zion, under the roof of God's Church. What an awful picture! Here the Spirit of God is talking about people sitting under the preaching of the Gospel who are yet total strangers to a work of grace in their hearts, living among God's saints in ease, indolence, disregard, and utter contempt of God's salvation. They are not grieved for the affliction of Joseph, the agonies of the Lord Jesus (Lamentations 1:12 and Zechariah 12:10).

If the Lord God has delivered us from such carnal presumption, how we ought to unceasingly bow before him and bless his holy name! It is only by his grace that we are delivered.

Famine In The Land
Amos 8:11, 12 describe a time of horrible famine, "not a famine of bread, nor a thirst for water, but of hearing the words of the Lord". The prophet's words here describe this day of spiritual famine. We have churches everywhere; but the Gospel of Christ is found almost nowhere! God's messengers are, as Elihu stated, "one among a thousand" (Job 33:23), if that many! "And they shall wander from sea to sea, and from the north even to the east, they shall run to and fro to seek the word of the Lord, and shall not find it" (Amos 8:12).

What a terrible judgment this is upon any land or people! When God removes his Word, when he takes away his candlestick, all is darkness! When the Lord God removes his witness, when he takes the Gospel away, all hope is gone!

Blessed Lord Jesus, grant that our candlestick may never be removed out of its place, but let your sweet promise be our portion forever. Though the Lord give the bread of adversity and the water of affliction, yet shall not our teachers be removed into a corner anymore, but our eyes shall see our teachers, and our ears shall hear a word behind us, saying, "This is the way, walk ye in it, when ye turn to the right hand, and when ye turn to the left" (Isaiah 30:20, 21).

The Lord Judging

"I saw the Lord standing upon the altar" (Amos 9:1). Amos saw the Lord Jesus standing not between the cherubim upon the mercy-seat, but upon the altar. He stands not to be gracious, but to judge. Those before him run for refuge, climbing up to heaven and digging down to hell; but none can escape, except those who take refuge in Christ. "Behold, a King shall reign in righteousness, and princes shall rule in judgment. And a man shall be as an hiding place from the wind, and a covert from the tempest; as rivers of water in a dry place, as the shadow of a great rock in a weary land" (Isaiah 32:1, 2).

September 16
Today's Reading: Obadiah 1-Jonah 4
"Salvation is of the LORD"
Jonah 2:9

"Salvation" is a big word. It includes much more than a believer's initial experience of grace in regeneration and conversion. It includes everything required to bring fallen men from the pit of the damned into the eternal presence of God's glory in heaven. And, from first to last, it is the work of God's free grace alone. Man does nothing. Man contributes nothing. Nothing is determined by or dependent upon the will of man or the works or worth of man. "Salvation is of the Lord".

All True Doctrine

This is the essence of all true doctrine. Today, sinners are called upon to walk an aisle, say a prayer, or otherwise do something to obtain salvation. The prophet of God declares, "Stand still and see the salvation of the Lord" (Exodus 14:13). "Salvation is of the Lord" in its planning (Ephesians 1:3-6; 2 Timothy 1:9; Romans 8:28-30), in its purchase (Romans 3:24-26; Galatians 3:13; Hebrews 9:12; 1 Peter 1:18-20), in its execution (John 3:8; Ephesians 2:1-9) in its preservation (John 10:27-30; Jeremiah 32:38-40), and in its completion (Philippians 1:6; Ephesians 5:25-27; Jude 24, 25).

Christ's Work Alone

In old eternity, the Lord Jesus Christ assumed the responsibility of saving all God's elect as the Surety of the everlasting covenant. When Christ agreed to save us, he became responsible to save us (John 10:16-18). In his life of obedience to God as a man, our Saviour worked out a perfect righteousness for us, which is imputed to all who believe, making us worthy of God's acceptance (Romans 5:19; Colossians 1:12). When he died upon the cross, the Son of God fully satisfied the claims of Divine justice against us; and he made that satisfaction for a particular people (1 John 4:9, 10;

Isaiah 53:8; John 10:15, 26). Christ purchased for his redeemed people all the rights and privileges of salvation and eternal life. Then, having purchased eternal salvation for his elect, the Lord Jesus Christ was exalted to the throne of universal dominion, to sovereignly govern the universe for the purpose of giving eternal life to his elect, redeemed people (John 17:2). And in the last day, Christ our covenant Surety will present all the sheep, all God's elect, entrusted to his care, before the world began, holy, unblameable, unreproveable, and glorious, before the throne of the Triune God (Hebrews 2:13; Colossians 1:21, 22). Not one of God's elect shall ever perish, because "Salvation is of the Lord".

Damning Heresy
Jimmy Swaggart revealed his heretical theology in the plainest terms possible. He said: "Free-will is our passport to salvation. Free-will is our foundation in salvation. Free-will is our ticket out of salvation. Salvation is not up to God, it is up to you. It is not up to God, it is up to you." Such heresy none of God's elect can endure.

Let no one be deceived by the delusion of freewill. Salvation is not up to you. It is up to God. "It is not of him that willeth, nor of him that runneth, but of God that showeth mercy ... God has mercy on whom he will have mercy, and whom he will he hardeneth" (Romans 9:16-18). Free-will is not your passport to salvation. Our only passport to glory is the blood of Christ. Free-will is not your foundation in salvation. The only foundation of our souls is the Lord Jesus Christ himself, and the work he has performed as our Substitute (1 Corinthians 3:11). Free-will is not your ticket out of salvation. "Salvation is of the Lord". It is therefore eternal (Ecclesiastes 3:14; John 10:27-29).

Mercy's gate is God's gate. He alone holds the key. He opens the gate of mercy to whom he will; and he shuts the gate of mercy against whom he will. Not all the power of man's will can persuade God to open when he has shut; and all the power of hell cannot shut the gate of mercy when God opens it. It is God "that openeth, and no man shutteth; and shutteth, and no man openeth" (Revelation 3:7).

Others may overlook the blasphemous heresies of free-willism as "a minor error in doctrine", and embrace free-willers as brethren if they like. I assert that free-will, works religion is damning heresy. All who preach it are false prophets. All who believe it are lost in the darkness of Satanic delusion. "Salvation is of the Lord". All who know God, all who experience his salvation rejoice in that fact, giving the Triune Jehovah alone all praise, honour, and glory for his great salvation (Psalm 115:1)

September 17
Today's Reading: Micah 1-5
"The remnant of Jacob"
Micah 5:7

"The remnant of Jacob" is Christ's seed in the earth that shall serve him, the generation accounted to the Lord to serve him (Psalm 22:30), Abraham's seed and heirs according to the promise. "The remnant of Jacob" is God's elect, all those who must and shall be saved by his grace. "The remnant of Jacob" is the whole Church of God, the whole Israel of God, all who have been, all who are, and all who shall be saved in Christ. Blessed are they who are included in the number of "the remnant of Jacob"!

A Remnant
What is a remnant? A remnant is what is left over. A remnant is that which is useless, despised, and thrown away. A remnant is the last piece of cloth on a bolt, or roll. If it is not thrown away, it is sold at a discount, because it not worth much. That is a pretty good description of you and me. God's elect are looked upon as below the mark, not fit for society, as narrow, crude, crotchety, peculiar. Because of this, they are a nuisance and aggravation to all.

It was true in Micah's time, and it is true today, that the Church and people of the living God are a poor, needy remnant, a remnant scattered among the nations. An elect remnant, a redeemed remnant, a protected remnant, Micah tells us that we are God's remnant. Particularly and distinctly he tells us that we are God's remnant in Christ's hands, under Christ's care, given to Christ, our Prince, Priest, Provider, and Protector (Micah 5:4).

Remnant's Return
In the third verse of this chapter we read of this remnant, "Therefore will he give them up, until the time that she which travaileth hath brought forth: then the remnant of his brethren shall return unto the children of Israel." There is, without question, a prophecy here of the marvellous incarnation of the Son of God (v. 2). Yet, this is also a reference to the spiritual birth all God's elect experience in time, when Divine life is implanted in us and imparted to us by the Spirit of God, and the resurrection-power of our Lord Jesus Christ is experienced in the soul. "Then shall the remnant of his brethren return unto the children of Israel." Blessed be God, "to him shall the gathering of the people be". To him all the scattered remnant shall be gathered at God's appointed time of love. All the elect shall be born again. All the redeemed shall be made "partakers of the Divine nature". All the chosen shall be brought to Christ and brought to life in and with him in the blessed new creation of grace!

Shall Abide
Because Christ our Surety stands "in the majesty of his God they shall abide". The scattered ones who are gathered "shall abide". "They shall never perish." Then comes the glorious climax of this precious prophecy concerning Zion's King and Lord, "for now shall he be great unto the ends of the earth". In these words we have a glorious description of him whose goings forth have been from everlasting and shall be to everlasting in the salvation, glorification, and blessedness of his people.

What is the sure and certain result of the fact that the Lord Jesus Christ is our Prince, Priest, Provider, and Protector? "And they shall abide". O glorious security! Not one shall perish. None can pluck the weakest from his loving embrace. Not all the hosts of hell and earth combined shall separate us from the love of God which is in Christ Jesus our Lord.

Yes! It is gloriously true, "He shall stand and feed in the strength of the Lord, in the majesty of the name of the Lord his God, and they shall abide" on his loving heart, in his affectionate embrace, on his glorious throne, amidst the wreck of matter and the crush of worlds. "They shall abide", members of his body, never to be severed from him whom they love, because he first loved them. "They shall abide" as the bride of his heart never to be divorced by him, never allowed to leave him, and ever indulged with the sweet kisses of his mouth. "They shall abide". "They shall abide".

September 18
Today's Reading: Micah 6-Nahum 2
"Wicked balances, and ... deceitful weights"
Micah 6:11

Here the Lord God asserts in unequivocal terms that he abhors all injustice. If he saves, he will be "a just God and a Saviour" (Isaiah 45:21). If he damns, it will be upon the grounds of strict justice. He will never use wicked balances or deceitful weights. He has named himself God that will by no means clear the guilty (Exodus 34:7). "Behold, God will not cast away a perfect man, neither will he help the evil doers" (Job 8:20). "He that justifieth the wicked, and he that condemneth the just, even they both are abomination to the Lord" (Proverbs 17:15).

Christ Made Sin
Because the Lord God is holy, just, and true, he could not and would not impute sin to his dear Son and punish him for our sins, except he make him to be sin for us who knew no sin (2 Corinthians 5:21). No court on earth can impute guilt where there is none, unless the court itself is corrupt and unjust. The court of heaven is neither corrupt nor unjust. In fact, the Lord God specifically declares, "By mercy and truth iniquity is purged" (Proverbs 16:6).

When the Lord Jesus Christ bear our sins in his own body on the tree, he was made sin for us. When he was made sin for us, he became guilty as our Substitute; our sins were imputed to him. Then, the Lord God, the Triune Jehovah, cried, "Awake, O sword, against my shepherd, and against the man that is my fellow: smite the shepherd" (Zechariah 13:7). When Christ died at Calvary, he died because he was found worthy of death.

Justice could not punish an innocent man. Therefore Christ Jesus was made to be sin, that sin might be imputed to him, that he might be justly punished for our transgressions. By the just balances and honest weights of the court of heaven, the Son of God was justly executed upon Calvary's cursed tree as the sinner's Substitute. Wondrous mercy! Amazing grace! Incomprehensible love!

Sinners Made Meet

Just as the Lord Jesus Christ was so completely made to be sin for us that he fully deserved to die under the furious wrath of God, so all God's elect, all for whom Christ was made sin, all for whom he died are made the very righteousness of God in him (2 Corinthians 5:21). Our great and righteous God accepts his elect, he embraces us and assures us of everlasting blessedness in heaven righteously and justly.

He does not count us pure with wicked balances and a bag of deceitful weights. He does not bend his law and compromise his justice to save his chosen. Rather, by the wondrous works of his grace in Christ, he makes his chosen righteous. By the obedience of his Son as our Representative, we have fulfilled all righteousness. By the sin-atoning death of the Lord Jesus Christ as our Substitute, justice has been satisfied for us, for we were crucified with him (Romans 5:19; Galatians 2:20).

In the new birth God the Holy Spirit makes every chosen, redeemed sinner a new creature in Christ (2 Corinthians 5:17). All who believe on the Lord Jesus Christ have been made "partakers of the Divine nature" (2 Peter 1:4). That new man created in us is "Christ in you, the hope of glory" (Colossians 1:27), "created in righteousness and true holiness" (Ephesians 4:24). That new man is not going to be righteous and worthy of heaven some day. He is "created in righteousness and true holiness". He is born of God and "cannot sin because he is born of God" (1 John 3:9).

Because we have been made righteous by redemption and regeneration, all who believe on the Lord Jesus Christ are "meet to be partakers of the inheritance of the saints in light" (Colossians 1:12). If I am in Christ and Christ is in me, I am really and truly righteous, so perfectly righteous in him that I am worthy of God's approval, worthy of heavenly glory, worthy of eternal life! Yes, we who live in hope of eternal life have a good hope through grace, a confident "assurance of hope" because we are worthy of heaven in our Saviour!

Everlasting Damnation

Be assured, unrepentant sinner, be assured, the Lord God will not count you pure with wicked balances and deceitful weights! He will judge you in the last day according to the record of heaven. You shall receive wages according to your works, when you stand before the Great White Throne (Revelation 20:11-15). "The wages of sin is death" (Romans 6:23). Everlasting hell will be your just portion forever!

Flee away to Christ! Trust the Son of God. He is the only refuge for your soul. "Believe on the Lord Jesus Christ, and thou shalt be saved". Trust Christ, and the righteousness of God is yours forever. He has made you the very righteousness of God, just as he was made sin for you! God will, with the true balances of his strict justice and the honest weights of his holy law, count you pure in that great day!

Discovering Christ Day By Day

September 19
Today's Reading: Nahum 3-Habakkuk 3
Five stark contrasts
Habakkuk 1:11-3:6

Men and women love to make gods; but the gods men make are not at all like our God, the one true and living God. Of all the imaginary gods men have concocted, none is less God-like than the god of modern day Christianity. The god of this age no more resembles the God of the Bible than a gnat resembles an angel. The god of this age is no God at all. As Moses put it, "Their rock is not as our Rock" (Deuteronomy 32:31). The god of this age is impotent before the mighty will of man. The Jesus of this age tries to save everyone, but has no ability to save anyone, without the assistance of man. The Holy Spirit of this age is nothing but an influence for good. Like Aaron's golden calf, men call their god Jehovah; but the god of modern day, freewill, works religion no more resembles the God of the Bible than Allah, the ancient moon god worshipped at Mecca, or the various phallic symbols worshipped by our forefathers.

Habakkuk described the overthrow of Jerusalem and the temple of Divine worship by Nebuchadnezzar and the Chaldeans, and Israel's seventy years of Babylonian Captivity. God's prophet here told Israel that the Lord God would use base, pagan idolaters to chastise and correct his chosen. The whole thing is a picture of Babylon, the great whore, described in the Book of Revelation, who makes the earth drunk with the wine of her fornications, the intoxicating mixture of freewill and works righteousness, by which men and women around the world make shame their glory, expose their nakedness, and uncover their foreskins, showing that they are uncircumcised in their hearts. Like all idolaters, all will-worshippers impute their power (their will) to their god (Habakkuk 1:11). But, sooner or later, either in mercy or in judgment, all shall learn that the Triune Jehovah alone is God, just as Nebuchadnezzar did.

You will remember that when Nebuchadnezzar attributed his greatness and his power to his god in Babylon, the Lord God Almighty turned him into a lunatic and a grazing animal, until he learned to "praise and extol and honour the King of heaven, all whose works are truth, and his ways judgment" (Daniel 4:37). Here are five stark contrasts between the Lord our God and all the gods of men.

1. The Lord our God, the true God, makes his worshippers, whereas all worshippers of idols make their gods. He made us, and he made us his. He made us, and he makes us his worshippers (Psalm 100:3; James 1:18). The Lord God, the true and living God, makes his worshippers by a new creation of grace.

2. The true God is known only by self-revelation, only by the revelation of truth and grace in Christ, whereas all idols are dependent upon human teachers of lies (2 Corinthians 4:6; Galatians 1:15, 16). What multitudes have been conned into a profession of faith in a helpless Jesus by snake-oil religious hucksters walking them

down "the Romans' road" path into Babylon! "Woe unto him that giveth his neighbour drink, that puttest thy bottle to him, and makest him drunken also, that thou mayest look on their nakedness."

3. He who truly is God causes the work of all his servants, whereas all idols must be prompted by their worshippers. The will-worshipper prompts his god to act in response to his will. He moves him like the men of Ashdod moved Dagon. Our God, the true and living God, causes his chosen to live, causes them to trust him, and inspires our worship of him. In fact, we know that we cannot even worship him, except he give us grace to do so (1 Kings 18:21-40).

4. The true God commands his position by the might of his own power and grace, whereas breathless idols are manipulated by the hands of men. "Woe unto him that saith to the wood, Awake; to the dumb stone, Arise, it shall teach! Behold, it is laid over with gold and silver, and there is no breath at all in the midst of it." Read about Dagon's ups and downs in 1 Samuel 5:1-5, and laugh at the helpless gods men make.

5. The true God performs his own mighty deeds and commands his worshippers to be still, whereas the idols of men are still while their worshippers busy themselves with their religious commotion. The whole religious world around us is full of religious commotion: family nights, youth rallies, religious plays, ball teams, bake sales, hand waving, hip swaying praise nights, religious dialogue, religious debate, defending creeds, and ceremonies galore! "But the Lord is in his holy temple: let all the earth keep silence before him."

I say, with regard to all the will-worshipping pagans of our day, "Their rock is not as our Rock". Modern day religion makes the eternal God a pathetic failure! Preachers everywhere tell us that God is trying to save multitudes who are not saved. They tell us that God wants to do many things for us and with us that we will not let him do. We are told that Christ died for all the people of the world in an attempt to redeem and save all men, but that all are not saved. Modern religion tells us that the Holy Spirit of God calls all men alike to Christ; but some men resist the power of his grace, while others allow him to have his way. We are told that God has done all he can to save sinners, but some will not allow him to save them.

One of these modern prophets of deceit was my first theology professor when I was an eighteen-year-old college freshman. He put his blasphemous opinions about God into print. This is what he said "What is hell? It is an infinite negation. And it is more than that: hell is a ghastly monument to the failures of the Triune God to save the multitudes who are there ... Sinners go to hell because God Almighty himself could not save them! He did all he could, he failed."

Such a god, such a pathetic, miserable failure is to be pitied, or mocked, but never to be worshipped or thought of as God!

Discovering Christ Day By Day

September 20
Today's Reading: Zephaniah 1-Haggai 1
"Consider your ways"
Haggai 1:5

"Now therefore thus saith the LORD of hosts; Consider your ways. Ye have sown much, and bring in little; ye eat, but ye have not enough; ye drink, but ye are not filled with drink; ye clothe you, but there is none warm; and he that earneth wages earneth wages to put it into a bag with holes. Thus saith the Lord of hosts; Consider your ways."

The Lord Jesus has saved us by his amazing grace that we might be his witnesses unto all men. He has redeemed us with his precious blood that we might proclaim redemption everywhere. He has sent us forth into this world for the building of his house (the Church), the ingathering of his sheep, to build his kingdom. He has provided us with everything needful for the work. And we take what he puts in our hands (time, talent, money, and life) and devote it to our own pleasure! We are alive to everything else, excited about everything else, and devote ourselves to everything else, except the cause of Christ in our day! "Consider your ways."

Our Ways

"Consider your ways." What do we get for our love of the world, for our devotion to it? We eat like kings, and never have enough. We drink and gorge ourselves, and remain hungry and thirsty. We buy the finest clothes money can buy, and want more. We save our money and can never save enough, putting it "into a bag with holes" (Haggai 1:6). We run every man after his own things, looking for much, and it comes to little, because God blows it away. Why? Because God's house, God's cause, God's worship is despised and neglected (Haggai 1:9). We crave satisfaction, but seeking it in the things of the world, we find nothing but drought in our souls (Haggai 1:10, 11).

"Consider your ways." The Lord, our heavenly Father, dampens our enjoyments and tinges them with sorrow to expose our evil, to get our attention, to draw our hearts away from the world and remind us of the bounteous blessings of his grace upon us, to bring our hearts home to Christ. "Love not the world, neither the things that are in the world" (Hebrews 12:5-13; Colossians 3:1-3).

Pilgrims Here

O my brother, my sister, we are pilgrims here! We should use worldly things as wise pilgrims like staves to help us make our journey through this world. So long as they help us forward in our way, we should make use of them and value them accordingly. But when they become troublesome hindrances and cumbersome burdens, we would be wise to throw them away. Samuel Rutherford warned, "Do not build your nest in any of the trees of this forest. They are all marked to be burned."

395

Cherish Christ

We will have that upon which we set our hearts; but there is something better to set your heart on than this world. Christ is better! "Seek ye first the kingdom of God, and his righteousness; and all these things shall be added unto you." O Holy Spirit, set our hearts upon Christ (Colossians 3:1-3). Teach us to live for eternity!

September 21
Today's Reading: Haggai 2-Zechariah 4
"He that toucheth you toucheth the apple of his eye"
Zechariah 2:8

What an astounding statement! The first thing it tells me is that we, who are "the apple of his eye", are a terribly weak people who need our Lord's constant protection. The pupil of the eye is a very weak, tender, and sensitive part of our bodies. It is easily hurt with the least thing. This vividly displays the feeble state of God's people in this world. How soon and easily we are disturbed, distressed, and hurt by our enemies! But our safety does not depend on us and our strength.

> I am weak, but thou art mighty!
> Hold me with thy powerful hand!

God's Esteem

If we are "the apple of his eye", how highly esteemed we must be by our God and Saviour! He guards and cherishes his own as a man does his eyes, the very pupil of his eyes. He protects us as "the apple of his eye".

Whose eye is this? It is the eye of Christ, our God, who led his people through the wilderness, ever keeping them as "the apple of his eye" (Deuteronomy 32:10). As the pupil is a vital part of the eye, and a part of a man's self, highly honoured and tenderly protected; so are the Lord's people parts, as it were, of himself. We are members of his body, closely united to him; and whatever injury is done to us he reckons as done to himself. To one persecutor he spoke from heaven, saying, "Saul, Saul, why persecutest thou me?" (Acts 9:4). Being highly esteemed by him, and having the strongest affection for us, he personally resents every affront of our foes, and will punish all who seek to injure us. He so assuredly keeps us as the very apple of his eye that it is written, "There shall no evil happen to the just".

Real Union

The pupil of the eye is the most tender part of the most tender organ of our bodies. When our Saviour says by his prophet, "he that toucheth you toucheth the apple of his eye", he asserts that we are truly one with him, one with him in the truest, fullest, most real manner imaginable! As truly one with the Son of God as the pupil of your eye is one with your body!

No doubt this is one special reason why God is jealous over his people. He who touches you touches Christ himself. You and I are in the closest possible union with Christ, the glorious Head of the body. And it will be at the cost of eternal hazard that anyone touches Christ's mystical body. If you hurt his people wilfully, the Son of man will say, "Inasmuch as ye did it unto one of the least of these my brethren, ye have done it unto me", and the recompense shall follow.

Tender Affection
This word from our Saviour, "he that toucheth you toucheth the apple of his eye", also sets forth the inexpressible tenderness of God's love for us. As Calvin states, "There is nothing more delicate or more tender than the eye in the body of a man; for were one to bite my finger or prick my arm or my legs, or even severely to wound me, I should feel no such pain as by having the pupil of my eye injured".

Here is the lovingkindness and tender affection of God our Saviour for us. The Lord our God, who sits upon the circle of the earth, before whom the inhabitants thereof are as grasshoppers and the nations are as a drop of water in a bucket, and are counted as the small dust of the balance, declares, "he that toucheth you toucheth the apple of his eye".

How marvellous! His everlasting love is fixed upon such worthless worms as we are! That the Triune God should love such utterly worthless, insignificant, and sinful creatures as we are is utterly astounding! Even the heavens are not pure in his sight, and he charges his angels with folly. And how abominable is man, "who drinketh iniquity like water". Yet, he condescends to love us!

O great and glorious God! How is it that you could choose such debased, depraved, rebellious, hard-hearted creatures? Why should you look upon such and bring us into your favour? "What is man, that thou art mindful of him, or the son of man that thou visitest him?" This question we can never answer except in the words of our Saviour himself, "for so it seemed good in thy sight". It was of his grace, of his own will and good pleasure, that the Lord God has lifted us up from the dunghill and made us to sit among princes.

C. H. Spurgeon said, "God's love, which at first came to us freely, has so ennobled us in Christ that God's present esteem of us in Jesus is not without reason and justification. Love without cause has now imparted and imputed such loveliness to its objects, that in Christ they are fitting subjects for love's embrace."

We are "his workmanship", his masterpieces. God's wisdom is seen in the sun, the moon, and the stars. Infinite wisdom is seen in every flower and in every living thing. But the wisdom and the skill of the Almighty are far more clearly seen in the believer than in any other work of his hand. Man, as a creature of God, born the first time, is fearfully and wonderfully made. But when born again, created new in Christ and regenerated, he is far more fearfully and wonderfully made (2 Corinthians 5:17; Colossians 1:12; 2 Peter 1:4; 1 John 3:1, 9).

When we realize that our great God has made his people the objects of his eternal love, the trophies of his noblest skill, and vessels of honour fit even for the Master's use, it is but little wonder that he should guard them with a jealous care, even as a man does the apple of his eye.

September 22
Today's Reading: Zechariah 5-9
"They made their hearts as an adamant stone"
Zechariah 7:12

The Lord God declares that the heart of fallen man is as obstinate and hard "as an adamant stone". The adamant stone is a legendary stone of impenetrable hardness. It was thought to be harder than flint (Ezekiel 3:9). How hard, how impenetrable, how unbreakable the heart of man must be, if the Lord God compares it to an adamant stone!

Obdurate Hardness
The obdurate hardness of the heart of man is displayed throughout the Scriptures; but it is nowhere displayed more fully than in the Garden of Gethsemane on the night our dear Saviour was arrested and led away to the judgment hall. There were among those who "took Jesus, and bound him, and led him away" (John 18:12, 13) a great mixture of people. Some of them were Roman soldiers. Some were servants of the priests and Pharisees. Among them were Judas and the Pharisees.

But in one thing they were all alike. They all "made their hearts as an adamant stone". They all saw our Saviour's Divine power forcefully exhibited. The soldiers were compelled, by the mere force of our Saviour's name, "I AM", to fall backward as dead men to the ground. All saw the miracle our Lord performed when he touched Malchus' ear and healed him. Yet all remained unmoved, cold, indifferent, insensible, and hard.

Do you not find that astonishing? They all acted as if they had seen nothing out of the ordinary. "They made their hearts as an adamant stone." They saw these things and hardened their hearts, like Pharaoh, and went on coolly with their callous business. "They took Jesus, bound him, and led him away."

Goat's Blood
Oh, how hard the heart of man is! Nothing can break it! Nothing can penetrate it! Nothing but omnipotent grace! Bless God, there is hope for such hard hearts! The legendary adamant stone was thought the hardest of all stones, harder than flint (Ezekiel 3:9), harder than the nether millstone (Job 41:24). Fire could not burn it, or even cause it to be heated, except on it's very surface. The adamant stone could not be broken by a hammer. Yet, this legendary stone, the hardest of all stones, when soaked in a goat's blood was melted, dissolved, and broken, like an aspirin in water. So the

398

hardest heart of the most obstinate sinner is melted, dissolved, and broken when sprinkled with the precious blood of Christ, the sinner's Scapegoat.

Nothing can break the heart but the almighty, efficacious, irresistible grace of God. Nothing can soften the stony, adamant heart except the precious blood of Christ sprinkled upon it by the Spirit of God, declaring the forgiveness of sin.

Sinner's Hope
If God the Holy Spirit sprinkles our hearts with the blood of Christ, if he applies the blood, we look upon him we have pierced and mourn. Miracles will never penetrate our hard hearts. Judgments will never break our hearts. Tornadoes, hurricanes, floods, and earthquakes, though ever so frightening, will never penetrate the heart of a sinner. Affliction will never break it. The law, with all its threats and curses, will never break the heart of man. Hell itself cannot break the rebel heart of man. But the blood of Christ does!

The blood of Christ, sprinkled on stony hearts as hard and impenetrable as adamant, breaks the hard heart of man, humbles the sinner, and bows him as a contrite one before the throne of God's free grace, causing him to cry like the publican, "God be propitious to me, the sinner. Have mercy upon me through the sin-atoning blood of your dear Son."

September 23
Today's Reading: Zechariah 10-14
"At evening time it shall be light"
Zechariah 14:7

Zechariah is describing this day of grace and salvation, this day in which the Lord God is gathering his elect out of the nations. When he pours out upon his chosen the Spirit of grace and supplications (12:10), Christ is opened to the believing sinner as a Cleansing Fountain (13:1). Because the Shepherd was smitten, the scattered sheep shall be gathered (13:7-9). And in that day "at evening time it shall be light".

The Day Of Conversion
First and foremost, this word of grace refers to that wondrous, miraculous, irresistible work of God the Holy Spirit performed in the hearts of poor sinners, when he gives chosen, redeemed sinners faith in Christ. And when Christ is revealed in the heart of a sinner who has been engulfed in thick darkness, it is evening time in his soul; but it is a strange evening time, for it is an evening time of light.

Sunrise at sunset is contrary to nature; and the rising of the Sun of Righteousness is the wondrous work of God's free grace. Has such an event taken place in your soul? It is evening time in the soul, engulfed in midnight darkness, before first the Lord shines in the heart. Then, suddenly, when we have lost all hope and the darkness of guilt and sin and shame is so great that it is felt darkness in our hearts, the Lord God surprises his chosen with the light of his mercy, love, and grace in Christ. When the darkness is so great that we cry, "My way is hid from the Lord, and my judgment is passed over from my God" (Isaiah 40:27), God commands the light to shine out of darkness and shines in our hearts to give the light of the knowledge of the glory of God in the face of Christ (2 Corinthians 4:6).

Neither Clear Nor Dark
As it is in the beginning, so it is throughout this day of grace for God's people. God's prophet tells us that throughout our earthly pilgrimage the light shall be neither "clear, nor dark" (v. 6). We "walk in the light, as he is in the light" (1 John 1:7), trusting God our Saviour. Yet, we continually walk in darkness (Isaiah 50:10). Our soul's experience in this day of grace verifies Zechariah's prophecy. While we live in this world, it is neither "day, nor night". Ours is a mingled state of grace and corruption. When things seem to be utter darkness, when distresses come from within and from without, the Lord graciously divides light from darkness, causes "the light to shine upon it", and "discovereth deep things out of darkness, and bringeth out to light the shadow of death" (Job 3:4; 12:22). He graciously turns our darkness to light.

Yet, as long as we live in this body of flesh we must be led by our God "with weeping and supplications" (Jeremiah 31:9). It is in our weakness that Christ's strength is manifested and made perfect. We often cry with Jacob, "All these things are against me". But in the evening we find that all things have been for us. The Lord often brings darkness, that his light may be more strikingly brilliant in the evening. He hedges up our way with thorns, that the almighty hand that removes them may be more plainly seen. It is a blessed thing to be brought low, to be surrounded with difficulties, to see no way of escape, and have all human resources fail, that our extremity may be his opportunity, so that when we are most low, we may see Christ most high and exalted.

Are you stripped, humbled, convinced of your nothingness? Look away to our all-precious, all-suitable, all-glorious, all-gracious, all-compassionate Lord Jesus, and hear his sweet promise. "At evening time it shall be light."

The Evening Of Life
Certainly, this is a promise to God's saints in the evening time of life in this world. I have seen it verified on numerous occasions. Two in particular stand out in my memory. As a young pastor, back in 1976, I flew out to Washington, DC to visit a dying friend, Bro. Harold Martin. He was one of my deacons. I had the privilege of watching him die in Christ. These are the very last words my friend spoke before losing consciousness, "Preacher, it's good to come to this point and know that everything's under the blood."

In the spring of 1992 my wife, Shelby, and I drove up to Richwood, West Virginia to visit our dear, faithful friend, Bro. Darrell McClung. He was dying with cancer; but he was perfectly at ease. We had a blessed, blessed visit with Darrell and his wife, Betty. Darrell's last words to me were, "Brother, my hope is in that Man in heaven, whose blood has washed away all of my sins and given me perfect righteousness before God. Thank God for Christ. I thank God for the blood of Christ. I am thankful to know that there is a Man in glory who is my Substitute. My hope is in him." Yes, for the dying believer, "at evening time it shall be light".

Then, when this day of the Lord's grace is finished and the day of the Lord's glory is begun in heaven's wondrous blessedness, "at evening time it shall be light" forever (Revelation 21:1-5, 22, 23, 25; 22:1-5).

September 24
Today's Reading: Malachi 1-4
The messenger of the covenant
Malachi 3:1

In Isaiah 63:9, our Saviour is called "the angel of his presence". He is that One who constantly watches over and protects God's elect in this world. The Lord Jesus Christ, the eternal Son of God, is called "the messenger (Angel) of the covenant".

In the Old Testament, when we read of "the angel of the Lord" appearing to men, as he did to Abraham, Manoah and his wife, and others, the One appearing was the Son of God himself. Those pre-incarnate manifestations of Christ were preludes to the coming of our great Saviour to accomplish the redemption of his people. He is the Angel Abraham worshipped (Genesis 18), to whom Gideon built an altar (Judges 6:22, 23), and the Man of God who appeared to Manoah and his wife (Judges 13). That Man who stood before Joshua as "the captain of the Lord's host" (Joshua 5:13-15) is the Lord Jesus Christ, the Captain of our salvation.

No Contradiction
To say that Christ is "the angel of the Lord" does not in any way contradict the fact of his eternal Deity. He is both Jehovah and Jehovah's Messenger. In his eternal Deity, our Saviour is God himself, over all and blessed forever. In his mediatorial capacity, as our Surety and Substitute, he is "the angel of the Lord".

As the Angel of the Lord, "the messenger of the covenant", the Son of God comes to men to reveal and fulfil all the stipulations of the covenant of grace for us (Jeremiah 31:31-34; Hebrews 8:6-13), thereby securing our "eternal redemption" (Hebrews 9:12).

Enthroned Mediator
Having fulfilled all the requirements of the covenant as our Substitute, our Saviour now sits upon the throne of universal monarchy, ruling all things according to the purpose of God, as our God-man Mediator, to give eternal life to his people (John 17:2; Revelation 10:1-6). He, and he alone is able to open and fulfil the book of God's

decrees (Revelation 5:1-7). He who rules the universe is God in human flesh, our Saviour and Redeemer, the Angel of the covenant. Rejoice!

The Angel Of The Lord
Our Lord Jesus Christ is pre-eminently the Angel of the Lord. He is the Angel who came with a great chain of omnipotent power and bound Satan (Revelation 20:1-3). He is the Angel by whom all the earth shall be judged at last (Revelation 20:11-15). He is the Angel who sits upon the throne and will, at last, bring all the universe to its Divinely ordained completion (Revelation 21:6).

September 25
Today's Reading: Matthew 1-4
"Call his name JESUS"
Matthew 1:21

These were the words of the angel of the Lord to Joseph concerning the incarnation, birth, and work of the Son of God, our Lord Jesus Christ. "Thou shalt call his name JESUS: for he shall save his people from their sins." It seems to me that anyone who reads or hears that the Son of God assumed human flesh and came into the world as a man would want to know why he did so.

Why Did Jesus Come?
The angel of the Lord tells us plainly that God the Son came into this world for a specific purpose, to do a specific thing, on a specific mission. "Thou shalt call his name JESUS: for he shall save his people from their sins." The Lord of glory, the Son of God, assumed our nature and came into the world to save his people from their sins. This is the Father's will, which he came to perform (Hebrews 10:5-14; John 6:39). This is the stipulation of the covenant, which he came to fulfil (Hebrews 13:20; Isaiah 49:8). This is the commandment of God, which he came to obey (John 10:16-18).

My mind is lost in wonder and admiration when I think of the fact of Christ's coming into this world. Is it not astonishing to you that the Son of God would become the Son of Man? That he who created all things would become the woman's Seed? That he who is Lord of all would take upon himself the form of a servant to be despised and rejected of men, a man of sorrows and acquainted with grief? And that his purpose in doing so was that in the fulness of time he might die the painful, shameful, ignominious death of the cross in the place of guilty sinners? These things utterly astonish me! I say with Paul, "Great is the mystery of godliness; God was manifest in the flesh".

Discovering Christ Day By Day

Who Is This Jesus?

That may seem to be a strange question. You have heard about Jesus all your life. Perhaps you think, "Everyone knows who Jesus Christ is." You are mistaken. The fact is, very few people in this world know who the Lord Jesus Christ is. The Christ that is worshipped in the average church is nothing but an idolatrous figment of man's imagination. Our Lord himself warned us of these days, saying, "There shall arise false christs, and false prophets, and shall show great signs and wonders; insomuch that, if it were possible, they shall deceive the very elect (Matthew 24:24)". So when men come to you and say, "Lo, here is Christ, or there, believe it not" (Matthew 24:23).

That makes this question very important. Who is this Jesus? Who is the Christ of the Bible? We must know, trust, and worship this Christ, if we would know God and be accepted of him (John 17:3). If we trust a false Christ, no matter how sincere we are, we are lost and under the delusion of Satan. If you care for your soul, you will search the Scriptures, asking God the Holy Spirit to show you who this Jesus is, of whom it is written, "He shall save his people from their sins." This man, Jesus Christ of Nazareth, is God the Son, the second Person of the Holy Trinity.

Salvation is in him alone, completely and only in him. In fact, he is God's Salvation (Luke 2:30). You cannot be saved without him; and you cannot be saved if you try to mix your own works, feelings, emotions, or experiences with faith in him. The Lord Jesus Christ is able to save you from the guilt of sin, the power of sin, and all the consequences of sin (Hebrews 7:25). He is the all-sufficient Saviour.

He is the only one who has power in himself to forgive sin (Matthew 9:6). He is exalted "to give repentance and remission of sins" (Luke 24:47; Acts 5:31). By the sacrifice of himself, according to the will of God, the Lord Jesus Christ put away all the sins of his people, obtained eternal redemption for them, and established the only grounds upon which God can be both just and the Justifier of all who believe (Hebrews 1:3; 9:12, 26; 10:1-14; Romans 3:24-26).

Christ Is The Way

There is no other possible way of salvation. God's own beloved Son would never have been crucified to redeem and save us if salvation could have been obtained in any other way. Indeed, the apostle Paul reasons that if we could have been saved in some other way, "then Christ is dead in vain" (Galatians 2:21). Infinite wisdom found a way to save us. Infinite grace provided the great sacrifice. Infinite love brought the Son of God to lay down his life for his people. Why? Because there was no other way for God to both satisfy his justice in the punishment of sin and forgive his people of all their sins. Christ alone must be our Saviour. "Neither is there salvation in any other: for there is none other name under heaven given among men, whereby we must be saved" (Acts 4:12).

The only way sinners, like you and me, can obtain God's salvation is by faith in the Lord Jesus Christ. If you believe on Christ, you may be confident that your sins are forgiven by his blood and that God has made you perfectly righteous in him, because God appointed this way of salvation; and he has promised to save all who trust his dear Son (Romans 10:9-13). Indeed, if you now trust the Son of God, it is

403

because you are already born of God and you have everlasting life (John 3:36). You could not and would not believe, if he had not given you life.

September 26
Today's Reading: Matthew 5-7
"Except your righteousness ..."
Matthew 5:20

The scribes and Pharisees were in their day the most highly respected and admired religious leaders in the world. Everyone stood in awe of them. But our Lord Jesus said to his disciples, "Except your righteousness shall exceed the righteousness of the scribes and Pharisees, ye shall in no case enter into the kingdom of heaven." Those words must have been astounding to the people who first heard them. The scribes were the religious scholars of the day. They were the men who copied and expounded the scriptures. They gave their lives entirely to this one great work for God and his people. They consecrated themselves to this one noble work. The Pharisees were the strictest sect of the Jews. No one exceeded the Pharisee in outward morality, obedience to the law, saying of prayers, tithing, sabbath-keeping, Scripture memorization, personal righteousness, and public approval. Yet, our Lord declares, "Except your righteousness shall exceed the righteousness of the scribes and Pharisees," you cannot be saved.

No Righteousness
Is the Lord telling us that we must do more and be better than the scribes and Pharisees? Is he saying that we must gain a greater measure of personal holiness than those men had? Not at all. In fact, he is saying just the opposite. The Lord is telling us that it is utterly impossible for any man to gain favour with God on the basis of his own, personal righteousness.

There never has been a child of Adam upon this earth good enough, righteous enough, holy enough to inherit or inhabit the kingdom of heaven, and there never will be. You and I must get every thought of personal righteousness out of our minds, and the very word "good" out of our vocabulary, when we think or speak of any human being in God's sight. We have no righteousness of our own before God, and no ability to produce righteousness. If we would be saved, we must have the righteousness of God in Christ imputed and imparted to us. It is this righteousness that exceeds the righteousness of the scribes and Pharisees. Do what you may, without the righteousness of God in Christ, you cannot enter into the kingdom of heaven.

Perfect Righteousness
The fact is that without perfect righteousness no one can ever enter into heaven (Revelation 21:27; 22:11-14). The righteousness required by God is a perfect righteousness, a righteousness which no mere man can produce. In order to enter that perfect kingdom we must be made perfectly righteous by the righteousness of Christ (Romans 5:19; 2 Corinthians 5:21). All who believe are made the righteousness of God in Christ by two distinct acts of grace.

The righteousness of Christ is imputed to us in justification (Romans 4:3-8). Our sin was imputed to Christ at Calvary, when he was made sin for us. Though he never committed sin, he was made sin, and became responsible under the law for our sins as our Substitute. In exactly the same way, the righteousness of Christ has been imputed to us, though we never have performed a righteous deed. Just as the law punished Christ for our sin, which was made his, the law of God rewards every believer for the righteousness of Christ, which has been made ours.

The righteousness of Christ is imparted to us in regeneration (2 Peter 1:2-4; 1 John 3:4-9). "If any man be in Christ, he is a new creature: old things are passed away; behold, all things are become new" (2 Corinthians 5:17). If I am born again by the Spirit of God, I have a new nature created in my soul. A righteous nature is imparted to me, by which I reign as a king over the lusts and passions of my flesh. Yes, God's people do sin. Sin is mixed with all we do, so long as we live in this body of flesh. But sin no longer reigns over us. We are no longer under the dominion of sin (Romans 6:14-16; Galatians 5:22, 23). Sin now has no condemning power. Its tyrannical rule is over. It cannot threaten us with death and condemnation, because justice has been satisfied by our dear Substitute.

C. H. Spurgeon wrote, "Guilt must lose itself in imputed and imparted righteousness 'ere the soul can walk in fellowship with purity. Jesus must clothe his people in his own garments, or he cannot admit them into his palace of glory; and he must wash them in his own blood, or else they will be too defiled for the embrace of his fellowship."

September 27
Today's Reading: Matthew 8-10
"The very hairs of your head are all numbered"
Matthew 10:30

In this chapter the Lord Jesus called his Apostles and gave them their commission. As he sent them out to preach the Gospel to a hostile world, the Saviour warned them plainly of the opposition they would face. It is the same in every age; and we must expect no better. Yet, as soon as he gives the warning, our dear Lord assures us that we have nothing to fear, saying, "The very hairs of your head are all numbered".

With these words, our Lord Jesus Christ assures us that none of God's elect shall ever be in any real danger or suffer any real harm, for we are under the special care and protection of God himself. I see six things in this sentence, which are a constant source of peace and encouragement to me.

The Fact Of Divine Predestination
The text might be translated, "the very hairs of your head have all been numbered". Before the world began, our heavenly Father counted up and ordained the number of hairs that were to be upon your head at this very moment! This is meticulous predestination. What does it tell us? God's sovereign purpose of grace in predestination includes all that we do and experience.

An Assurance Of Divine Providence
The primary intent of the text is to show us our Father's constant rule of all things. The sparrow cannot fall to the ground, and a hair cannot fall from your head, without your Father's eternal decree in predestination and his direction in providence.

Our Father's Divine Knowledge
Our God, who predestinated all things and rules all things, knows all things. We are so well known by God that he has even numbered the hairs of our heads. "Your Father knoweth." We need no other comfort. The Lord's knowledge of us is constant and entire. His knowledge of us is the knowledge of a tender, sympathetic Father.

Our Father's Constant Care
He who takes the trouble to number the hairs of our heads must surely care for us. We are the apple of his eye. Cast all your care upon him. "He careth for you."

The Honour And Esteem God Has For Us
God has numbered our hairs because he values them. He holds us in honour and esteem above all the people of the world because of his gracious purpose toward us in Christ (Isaiah 43:3-5; 1 John 4:9-11).

Divine Protection
The hairs of our head are all numbered because our God intends that, "There shall not an hair of your head perish" (Luke 21:18). Trials are certain. Temptations are sure. Tribulations are constant in this world. But there is no cause for fear. "The very hairs of your head are all numbered."

September 28
Today's Reading: Matthew 11, 12
"Take my yoke upon you"
Matthew 11:29

This is something we must do. We must bow to and slip upon ourselves the yoke of Christ our Lord and Master. This is not something that is done once and forgotten. We must day by day put ourselves into the Master's yoke. There is no other way for believers to find peace. You will find rest for your soul, my brother, my sister, only as you voluntarily wear the Saviour's yoke. What is the yoke here spoken of?

His Profession
It is the yoke of his profession. We must confess Christ before men. The believer's confession of faith begins in baptism. Being buried with Christ in the watery grave, we identified ourselves with Christ and his people. Rising from the waters of baptism, we professed our allegiance to him, to walk with him in the newness of life (Romans 6:4-6). But our profession does not end in the ordinance of baptism. As we go through this world, we are to be his witnesses to all men.

His Precepts
This is also the yoke of his precepts. His Word alone is our rule of faith and practice. The believer is a person whose life is ruled by the Word of God. Our doctrine is the doctrine of Holy Scripture. The opinions of men, the theories of science, the "enlightenment" of the age has no influence upon our faith. "Thus saith the Lord" is our first and our final authority. Our lives are governed by the revealed will of God. Collectively, as the Church of God, we seek to govern all our practices, all our ordinances of worship, and all our deeds by Holy Scripture. Personally, every believer seeks to mould his life to the Scriptures.

His Providence
The yoke of Christ is the yoke of his providence. Trusting him, the believer submits to his wise and good dispositions of providence, saying with Eli, "It is the Lord: let him do what seemeth him good." We recognize that our Saviour is the sovereign Governor of the universe, and that he governs all things for the eternal, spiritual good of his people, and the glory of his own great name. He who loved us and gave himself for us will do us good. We trust him not because we are forced to, but because we want to. We have been made to realize that what he does is best. Simple as it sounds, it is true: Trust and obey, for there's no other way, to be happy in Jesus, but to trust and obey.

Easy Yoke
As the oxen have their master's yoke upon them, so that they are guided and directed by their master to do his will, so the believer has the yoke of his Master upon him. But our Master's yoke is easy. Every believing heart willingly takes it upon himself. Faith in Christ causes men and women to willingly become his slaves. It is our delight to

serve him. Our hearts ache, not because he is our Lord and we are his servants; but because we cannot serve him as we would. A person who is saved by the grace of God does not need to be told that he is under solemn obligations to serve Christ. The new life within tells you that! It is no burden to the believing heart to be under Christ's yoke. His yoke is easy and pleasant. He who believes gladly surrenders himself to Christ, his Master, instinctively. As soon as a sinner sees the glory and grace of Christ by faith, he willingly submits to him, saying:

> All to Jesus I surrender, humbly at his feet I bow;
> Worldly pleasures all forsaken, take me, Jesus, take me now.

September 29
Today's Reading: Matthew 13, 14
The parables of the kingdom
Matthew 13:1-50

Drawing his illustrations from the book of nature, our Lord Jesus Christ gave the multitudes who were gathered to hear him seven striking illustrations of gospel truth. Here is a great display of the tender heart of God our Saviour. He condescends to teach his redeemed in the most simple terms, so that none might miss his meaning.

The Parable Of The Sower (vv. 1-23)
The Gospel, the Word of God, is the seed of life. Many hear it without any benefit to their souls. But those whose hearts are prepared by grace receive the Word as seed sown in good ground. And it springs up in them unto everlasting life.

The Parable Of The Wheat And Tares (vv. 24-30)
In every local church, where God has planted his wheat, Satan sows his tares. And it is impossible to distinguish one from the other until harvest time. So we must let both grow together. In time of harvest God will do the separating.

The Parable Of The Mustard Seed (vv. 31, 32)
Faith begins in the heart as a small seed, and grows in a short time into a tree with far spreading branches. As the mustard seed is pungent, so faith even as a grain of mustard seed is powerful, overcoming the world.

The Parable Of The Leaven (v. 33)
The Gospel of the grace of God, like a small pinch of leaven, was sent forth into the world by the Spirit of God. Its power and influence will not cease until it has reached

every nation, kindred, tribe, and tongue, until "all Israel shall be saved". God's elect remnant scattered among all the nations of the world must and shall hear the Gospel and be converted to Christ.

The Parable Of The Treasure Hidden (v. 44)
The Church of God's elect is the treasure he has hidden in the earth. Christ, finding his treasure in the earth, has purchased the whole world (Psalm 2:8; John 17:2) that he might have his treasure. The price he paid was everything he had, even his own life!

The Parable Of The Pearl Of Great Price (vv. 45, 46)
This Pearl is our Saviour. If ever a sinner sees this great Pearl and rightly discerns his value, he will gladly part with everything to have him. Christ is the Pearl that makes men rich, truly rich, rich toward God, eternally rich!

The Parable Of The Great Net (vv. 47-50)
The preaching of the Gospel is like the casting of a great net into the sea. In the net both choice fish and useless carps are gathered. And Gospel preaching gathers both God's elect and the reprobate into the visible church. But, as the fishermen separate the good from the bad and throw the bad away, so at the end of the world, God will send his angels to sever the carnal professor from the true believer. And the reprobate he will cast into hell.

In every part of this blessed chapter, the Lord Jesus has drawn, as with a sunbeam, the striking difference between his elect and the reprobate of this world, assuring us of his faithful, tender care of his own. O Lord Jesus, give us grace to know that we are yours at all times and in all circumstances! And give us, blessed Saviour, grace to honour you at all times and in all circumstances!

September 30
Today's Reading: Matthew 15-18
Seven characteristics of true faith
Matthew 15:21-28

The purpose of God the Holy Spirit in revealing to us the story of the Syrophenician woman is to give us an object lesson about faith. What does this story show us about faith?

1. Faith is given to the most unlikely people (1 Corinthians 1:26-29). This woman was a Gentile, a godless pagan and a Canaanite, the child of a cursed race. But she was an object of God's eternal, electing love in Christ.

2. Faith is born in the heart by hearing the Gospel, by hearing of Christ (Romans 10:17; 1 Peter 1:23). I do not know how she heard, or how much she heard. But I do know what she heard. She "heard of him" (Mark 7:25). No one in this world can believe on Christ until he hears the Gospel of Christ.

3. Faith always seeks what only God can give, and that is, mercy. This woman never attempted to tell the Lord what to do. She simply cried, "have mercy on me". That prayer implied an acknowledgement of sin, hope of pardon, submission to the sovereign will and power of God, and confidence in Christ's ability to bestow mercy.

4. Faith cannot be silenced. Though the Lord seemed to ignore her cry, though the disciples treated her contemptuously, though she was confronted with God's sovereign election, though she knew and owned her own unworthiness, she would not give up her plea. Mercy! She must have mercy! Blessed be his name, every sinner who must have mercy finds mercy abundant and free in Christ Jesus (Hebrews 4:16).

5. Faith takes its proper place before God. This woman acknowledged the truthfulness of the Lord's description of her and the justice of his sovereignty in dispensing mercy. Faith does not argue with God. Faith submits to God.

6. Faith makes need an argument for mercy. This dear woman took the ground the Lord gave her. He called her a dog. And she not only owned the name, but made her base character an argument for his mercy. Dogs must be fed. Dogs under the table suggest that the Master has plenty. Dogs will settle for any morsel, be grateful and come back for more. And, being his dog, she was altogether dependent upon his care.

7. Faith always obtains what it seeks. Faith seeks nothing but mercy, and always gets it. Faith deals with and seeks necessities; healing, freedom, life, mercy. And the Lord Jesus always says to faith, "Be it unto thee, even as thou wilt". Faith honours Christ by believing; and Christ honours faith by giving.

Oh, let us come out of all the coasts of the Tyre and Sidon of this world and look to Christ for mercy this day! Beholding his mercy here, let us hope for mercy for all the Israel of God; for with him is "plenteous redemption". Dear Lord Jesus, have compassion, as you had in the days of your flesh upon this poor woman; and give us mercy this day! Mercy for ourselves! Mercy for the fruit of our children! Oh, God of all grace, show yourself gracious this day!

———————

Discovering Christ Day By Day

October 1
Today's Reading: Matthew 19-21
"A ransom for many"
Matthew 20:28

Here our Lord Jesus Christ tells us, in the plainest terms possible, that he did not die for everyone in general, but for many in particular. He says he gave his life a ransom "for many". In other words, he tells us that his sin-atoning death was an effectual atonement for a limited, chosen number of people.

How my soul rejoices in the great, glorious, soul-cheering Gospel doctrine of limited atonement. Our all glorious Christ, the Son of God, effectually accomplished the redemption of his people by the sacrifice of himself at Calvary. No doctrine of Holy Scripture is more vital; and none is more cheering to the needy soul. Yet, multitudes who profess to believe God denounce this sweet Gospel doctrine as heresy.

Heretical Doctrine
The fact is, all who claim to be Christians believe in and teach limited atonement to one degree or another. The will-worshipping Arminian; the free-will, works-monger, who asserts that Christ died for all men, for those who perish in hell as well as those who are saved, he limits the atonement of Christ contrary to Scripture. He limits the merit and efficacy of Christ's blood and the atonement made by his blood, asserting that the blood of Christ must be supplemented by man's decision, man's faith, man's obedience, man's baptism, etc.. The Arminian teaches it is man, by his obedience, who gives merit and efficacy to the blood of Christ. Such doctrine is utter blasphemy!

Gospel Doctrine
According to Holy Scripture, there is absolutely no limit to the merit and efficacy of Christ's precious blood and the atonement obtained and accomplished for God's elect by it. However, according to the Word of God, the atonement of Christ is limited in extent, scope, design, and purpose to God's elect. To suggest, imply, or teach, indeed, to believe, that there are some in hell for whom the Lord Jesus Christ shed his blood and made atonement is to betray an idolater's heart and blaspheme the Son of God, denying his very Godhead!

Such blasphemy, the blasphemy of universal redemption, makes the Son of God a failure. The doctrine of universal, ineffectual redemption, of universal, ineffectual atonement is just as damning to the souls of men as any other doctrine which necessarily denies our Saviour's divinity.

411

The Son of God very specifically tells us that he gave his life "a ransom for many". It is nowhere suggested or implied in the Word of God that Christ made atonement for, redeemed, or ransomed the entire human race, many of which were already in hell when he died. Those for whom Christ died are described as "many", not all, because these many are a distinct and peculiar people. They are the "many" who are ordained to eternal life (Acts 13:48), The "many" the Father has given to the Son (John 6:37-39), The "many" whose sins he bore on the cross (1 Peter 2:24), The "many" for whom his blood was shed for the remission of their sins (Matthew 26:28), The "many" who are made righteous by his obedience (Romans 5:19). The "many" sons he, the Captain of their salvation, brings to glory (Hebrews 2:10).

The Lord of Glory did not merely make redemption possible. He redeemed us with his blood! With his own blood, the Son of God actually obtained eternal redemption for all his people. For your great, eternally efficacious sacrifice, O Lamb of God, I give you my heartfelt praise and thanks.

October 2
Today's Reading: Matthew 22, 23
"Many are called"
Matthew 22:14

There is a personal, particular, irresistible call of grace, which goes forth from the Spirit of God to God's elect alone (John 10:3). This call of the Spirit always produces faith in Christ. It is always effectual. It always results in the salvation of the one who is called. Were it not for this effectual call of the Spirit, no one would ever be saved (John 6:44, 45). But when our Lord says, "Many are called", he is speaking of the earnest proclamation of the Gospel by his servants.

Gospel Call
Every time a true servant of God preaches the Gospel of God's electing love, redeeming mercy, and saving grace, sinners are called to faith in Christ (2 Corinthians 5:20). This call is universal in its scope. In Divine providence even this call is limited to those who are privileged to hear the Gospel. But we preach the Gospel indiscriminately to all men, urging all to come to Christ and be saved. This Gospel call is sincere and earnest (Romans 10:1-4). It is an unconditional call to salvation by Christ and peace with God. The Gospel preacher is God's ambassador, sent to proclaim the good news of redemption accomplished and salvation full and free in Christ Jesus. He calls sinners, by Divine authority, to be reconciled to God. Every sinner who obeys this call and trusts the Lord Jesus Christ is saved by God's free grace and possesses everlasting life in Christ (John 3:36; 5:24). Those who refuse to obey the Gospel call will perish without excuse.

412

Irresistible Grace
However, because man is spiritually dead, he has neither the will nor the ability in himself to obey the call of the Gospel. The preaching of the Gospel will never produce faith in Christ until the sinner is regenerated and called by the irresistible power and grace of the Holy Spirit. All reject the Gospel call as it comes forth from men; but none reject that call when it comes forth in the power of the Holy Spirit.

Why is it that many hear the Gospel and perish, while others hear the same Gospel from the lips of the same preacher, and are saved? The answer is very plain. "Many are called, but few are chosen." And those few who are chosen, having been redeemed by Christ, at God's appointed time are called by the effectual, irresistible power of God the Holy Spirit. Thank God! He has chosen some, and they shall be saved!

The Difference
The difference between those who believe and those who do not believe is the eternal purpose and choice of God's electing love. "Many are called, but few are chosen." Here are some men and women in this world whom God has chosen to save. The rest are left in their sins, to perish in their wilful unbelief. God has done them no injustice. He does not violate their will. He does not force them to do what they choose not to do. He simply leaves them to themselves! And if God leaves a man to himself, if God leaves a man to his own free-will, that man will never believe on Christ and be saved (John 6:37-40; 10:16, 26; Acts 13:46-48).

All who believe rejoice and give thanks to God that he did not leave us to ourselves. And there is yet a remnant according to the election of grace. God has chosen to save some. There is an elect people in this world, a people whom God has predestinated to eternal life, a people he has determined to save, a people of whom he says, "I will be their God and they shall be my people". How our souls rejoice in the fact that God the Holy Spirit would not take "no" for an answer from us! He would not allow us to resist his call. You sweetly drew us into your arms, blessed Lord Jesus, making us willing in the day of your power.

October 3
Today's Reading: Matthew 24, 25
Righteousness rewarded
"Well done, thou good and faithful servant ..."
Matthew 25:21

In the last day, every believer shall enter into heaven and obtain the inheritance of everlasting glory; and that will be righteousness rewarded. Immediately after the resurrection we must all be judged by God, according to the record of our works

(Revelation 20:12, 13). "It is appointed unto men once to die, but after this the judgment" (Hebrews 9:27). The Judge before whom we must stand is the God-man, whom we have crucified (John 5:22; Acts 17:31; 2 Corinthians 5:10). We will be judged out of the books, according to the record of God's strict justice.

The Books
In the Scriptures, God is often represented as writing and keeping books. And, according to these books, we all shall be judged. This is figurative language. God does not need books to remember man's sins. However, as John Gill wrote, "This judgment out of the books, and according to works, is designed to show with what accuracy and exactness, with what justice and equity, it will be executed, in allusion to statute-books in courts of judicature."

What are the books? The Book of Divine Omniscience (Malachi 3:5). The Book of Divine Remembrance (Malachi 3:16). The Book of Creation (Romans 1:18-20). The Book of God's Providence (Romans 2:4, 5). The Book of Conscience (Romans 2:15). The Book of God's Holy Law (Romans 2:12). The Book of the Gospel (Romans 2:16).

No Iniquity Found
But there are some against whom no crimes, no sins, no offences can be found, not even by the omniscient eye of God himself! "In those days, and in that time, saith the Lord, the iniquity of Israel shall be sought for, and there shall be none; and the sins of Judah, and they shall not be found: for I will pardon them whom I reserve" (Jeremiah 50:20). Their names are found in another book, a book which God himself wrote and sealed before the worlds were made. It is called, "The Book of Life". In this book there is a record of Divine election, the name of Christ our Divine Surety, a record of perfect righteousness (Jeremiah 23:6; cf. 33:16), a record of complete satisfaction, and the promise of eternal life.

The question is often raised, "Will God judge his elect for their sins and failures committed after they were saved, and expose them in the Day of Judgment?" The only reason that question is ever raised is because many retain a remnant of the Roman doctrine of purgatory, by which they hope to hold over God's saints the whip and terror of the law. There is absolutely no sense in which those who trust Christ shall ever be made to pay for their sins! Our sins were made Christ's and punished in him to the full satisfaction of God's infinite justice. They can never be charged to us again (Romans 4:8; 8:33, 34). Christ paid our debt to God's law and justice; and God will never require us to pay. God, who has blotted out our transgressions, will never write them again. He who covered our sins will never uncover them!

The perfect righteousness of Christ is ours in free justification. On the Day of Judgment, God's elect are never represented as having done any evil, but only good (Matthew 25:31-40). The Day of Judgment will be a day of glory and bliss for Christ and his people, not a day of mourning and sorrow. It will be a marriage supper. Christ will glory in his Church. God will display the glory of his grace in us. And we will glory in our God and Saviour.

Only The Worthy
Those who are found perfectly righteous, righteous according to the records of God himself, shall enter into eternal life and inherit everlasting glory with Christ. They that have done good, nothing but good, perfect good, good without any spot of sin, wrinkle of iniquity, or trace of transgression, shall enter into everlasting life (Revelation 22:11). Only those who are worthy to do so shall enter into heaven.

Who are these perfectly righteous ones? They are all who are saved by God's free and sovereign grace in Christ (1 Corinthians 6:9-11; Romans 8:1, 32-34). Though there shall be degrees of punishment for the wicked in hell, because there are degrees of wickedness, there shall be no degrees of reward and glory among the saints in heaven, because there are no degrees of redemption and righteousness. No degrees of worthiness!

Heaven was earned and purchased for all God's elect by Christ. We were predestined to obtain our inheritance from eternity (Ephesians 1:11). Christ has taken possession of heaven's glory as our Forerunner (Hebrews 6:20). We are heirs of God and joint-heirs with Jesus Christ (Romans 8:17). Our Saviour gave all the glory he earned as our Mediator to all his elect (John 17:5, 20). And in Christ every believer is worthy of heaven's glory (Colossians 1:12).

Glorification shall be the consummation of salvation; and salvation is by grace alone! That means no part of heaven's bliss and glory is the reward of our works, but all the reward of God's free grace in Christ! All spiritual blessings are ours from eternity in Christ (Ephesians 1:3), and all shall be ours forever in Christ, by Christ, and with Christ.

October 4
Today's Reading: Matthew 26
Peter's great fall
Matthew 26:69-75

Looking back upon the great mercy, love, and grace of God our Saviour in this magnificent chapter, how our hearts ought to erupt with praise and gratitude to God our Saviour! In tender mercy, our dear Redeemer established for us the perpetual ordinance of the Lord's Supper, that by eating the unleavened bread and drinking the wine, his Church might be moved to remember him and his great sacrifice week by week at the Lord's Table. O sweet communion feast, a feast for our souls in the presence of our crucified Lord!

Blessed Saviour, give me grace often to follow you into Gethsemane. Let me remember without ceasing your agony of soul as you anticipated being made sin for me, that I might be made the righteousness of God in you! O blessed Lord, let me never forget the cost of my salvation, paid entirely by you!

Peter's Denial
Then we come to this record of Peter's great fall. Peter was a true believer, a disciple of Christ, a righteous and godly man. But, in his hour of weakness, he fell into grievous sin, denying his Lord and Redeemer three times. Peter was not the infallible bishop of Rome, as the papists pretend. He was a fallible, sinful man, like the rest of us. The only thing that wicked man, the pope, has in common with Peter is his denial of Christ. Peter was tempted, and he fell; but he was not forsaken. The Lord graciously restored his erring child.

Sinners Still
Like Peter, we are all fickle, frail, sinful pieces of human flesh. Saved? Yes. Redeemed? Yes. Justified? Yes. Sanctified? Yes. In Christ all these blessings are ours, and more. But none of us are without sin (1 John 1:8-10). Far from it! Sin is mixed with everything we do. There is no evil in the world we would not readily commit, were not the evil passions of our hearts restrained by the grace of our God (Matthew 15:19). Let us not be proud, presumptuous, and self-confident (1 Corinthians 4:7; 10:12). Realizing our own sinfulness we should never be severe with our brethren (Galatians 6:1). All God's saints in this world are sinners still.

Grace Alone
Salvation is entirely by the grace of God. Surely, this record of Peter's fall should convince all that salvation is not in any measure whatsoever dependent upon good works (Ephesians 2:8, 9). From start to finish, salvation is by grace alone. Our standing and acceptance with God is not determined by what we do, but by what Christ has done for us.

Blessed Security
Peter also sets before us an undeniable proof that those who are saved by the grace of God can never be lost (John 10:27-29). Those who are in Christ are secure in him. We are kept and preserved by the grace and power of God. Nothing can ever sever one of the Lord's own from him. As our Lord prayed for Peter, he prays for us; and God will not charge any with sin for whom Christ undertakes to be an Advocate (1 John 2:1, 2; Romans 4:8). None of us have reason to boast of our faithfulness. Who would dare? But we all have every reason to boast of the faithfulness of God our Saviour, who will not let us perish!

416

October 5
Today's Reading: Matthew 27, 28
"My God, my God, why hast thou forsaken me?"
Matthew 27:46

Everything recorded in Psalm 22 was written prophetically, by Divine inspiration, as the very words spoken by our blessed Saviour when he hung upon the cursed tree, bearing our sins as our Substitute. Spurgeon wrote, with regard to Psalm 22 ...

> Before us we have a description both of the darkness and of the glory of the cross, the sufferings of Christ and the glory which shall follow. Oh for grace to draw near and see this great sight! We should read it reverently, putting off our shoes from off our feet, as Moses did at the burning bush, for if there be holy ground anywhere in Scripture it is in this psalm.

Christ Forsaken
The words of that psalm are the very words of our blessed Saviour when he hung upon the cursed tree as our Substitute, when he who knew no sin was made sin for us, that we might be made the righteousness of God in him. At the apex of his obedience, at the time of his greatest sorrow, in the hour of his greatest need the Lord Jesus cried out to his Father, "My God, my God, why hast thou forsaken me?" Speaking prophetically by the mouth of his servant David hundreds of years before he endured the agonies of Calvary, our dear Saviour, our all-glorious Redeemer told us how utterly forsaken he was, so utterly forsaken that the Father refused to hear the cries of his own darling Son in the hour of his greatest need. "Why art thou so far from helping me, and from the words of my roaring? O my God, I cry in the daytime, but Thou hearest not; and in the night season, and am not silent." I read those words with utter astonishment. I will not attempt to explain what I cannot imagine. But these things are written here for our learning, that we might, through patience and consolation of the Scriptures, have hope. I hang all the hope of my immortal soul upon this fact: when the Lord Jesus Christ was made sin for me, he was utterly forsaken of God and put to death as my Substitute; and by his one great, sin-atoning sacrifice, he has forever put away my sins. He not only bore our sins in his body on the tree, he carried them away!

The Reason
Yet, in Psalm 22:3 our holy Saviour, when he was made sin for us, answers the cry of his own soul's agony. He cried, "My God, my God, why hast thou forsaken me?" He declares, "But thou art holy, O thou that inhabitest the praises of Israel." Why was the Lord Jesus forsaken by his Father when he was made sin for us? Because the holy Lord God is of purer eyes than to behold iniquity. Our Saviour was forsaken by the Father when he was made sin for us, because justice demanded it. "Thou art of purer

eyes than to behold evil, and canst not look on iniquity" (Habakkuk 1:13). Here, when he was dying under the wrath of God, our blessed Saviour justified God in his own condemnation, because he was made sin for us. He proclaims the holiness of God in the midst of his agony. He is so pure, so holy, so righteous, so just that he will by no means clear the guilty (Exodus 34:7), even when the guilty One is his own darling Son! Rather than that his holy character be slighted, our Surety must suffer and die alone, because he was made sin for us.

Our Saviour had no sin of his own. He was born without original sin, being even from birth "that holy thing" (Luke 1:35). Throughout his life he "knew no sin" (2 Corinthians 5:21), "did no sin" (1 Peter 2:22), "and in him is no sin" (1 John 3:5). But on Calvary the holy Lord God "made him who knew no sin to be sin for us, that we might be made the righteousness of God in him" (2 Corinthians 5:21). Just as in the incarnation "the Word was made flesh and dwelt among us" (John 1:14), in substitution he who was made flesh "was made sin for us". I do not know how God could be made flesh, and never cease to be God; but he was. I do not know how God could die, and yet never die; but he did (Acts 20:28). And I do not know how Christ who knew no sin could be made sin, and yet never have sinned; but he was. These things are mysteries beyond the reach of human comprehension. But they are facts of Divine revelation, to which we bow with adoration.

Gethsemane
In dark Gethsemane, as he anticipated being made sin, our Saviour's holy soul shook within him; and his holy heart broke. Anticipating the pains of God's holy fury against sin, his unbending justice and unmitigated wrath were beyond calculation; and the Saviour's soul was so crushed within him that he was sore amazed, and very heavy, even unto a sweat of blood. His strength was gone; his spirit sank; he was in an agony.

Then, as he hung upon the cursed tree, bearing our sins in his own body, he cried, as we read in Psalm 22:6, 14, 15, "I am a worm, and no man; a reproach of men, and despised of the people ... I am poured out like water, and all my bones are out of joint: my heart is like wax; it is melted in the midst of my bowels. My strength is dried up like a potsherd; and my tongue cleaveth to my jaws; and thou hast brought me into the dust of death." It was the thought and anticipation of being made sin for us, not of simply paying the debt due to our sins, but of being made sin, that caused his bloody sweat in Gethsemane. It was this fact, the fact that he was made sin for us that caused him to be forsaken of his Father, as he hung upon the cursed tree on Golgotha's hill.

> Yes, my God bore all my guilt,
> This through grace can be believed;
> But the horrors which he felt
> Are too vast to be conceived!

October 6
Today's Reading: Mark 1
The Master's baptism
Mark 1:9-11

Baptism was not considered a light, insignificant thing by the Son of God. He walked all the way from Nazareth of Galilee to Jerusalem to be baptized by John. Why? I can give one very good reason, and only one. He knew it was his Father's will. It was not convenient; but it was his Father's will. It might not be understood by his family and friends; but it was his Father's will. He might be ridiculed as a fanatic; but none of that mattered to him. It was his Father's will for him to be baptized by John, so he came to John at Jerusalem to be baptized.

Humility
His baptism was an act of humility. This is no ordinary man coming to be baptized by John. This Man is the incarnate Son of God, the Lord of glory. He comes to be baptized in that same river that Naaman despised. Not only does he submit to the ordinance, but he comes to John to observe it. He does not call John to come to him.

Obedience
Our Saviour's baptism was an act of obedience. He came into this world to do his Father's will; and part of that will was this act by which, at the very outset of his public ministry, he identified himself with God's prophet, his message, and his people. There are many reasons for the practice of believer's baptism. It is the answer of a good conscience toward God. It is a picture of the Gospel. It identifies us with Christ, his people, and the Gospel of his grace. Yet there is no reason more noble than this: the Lord commands it. Baptism is the believer's first act of obedience to Christ as his Lord. Nothing is nobler in a servant than implicit obedience to his master.

Meaningful
Our Lord's baptism was a very meaningful act. Baptism is not an empty, meaningless religious ritual. It is now and has been from its inception a highly symbolic act. Though Mark does not give the details both Matthew and Luke tell us the meaning and significance of baptism. Our Master's baptism meant exactly the same thing that our baptism means.

Matthew tells us that our Saviour insisted on being baptized "to fulfil all righteousness" (3:13-15). Obviously, baptism did not make the Son of God righteous! But it did signify the means by which he must establish and bring in righteousness for his people. As our Substitute, the Lord Jesus brought in and fulfilled all righteousness as Man by his perfect obedience unto death (Philippians 2:5-11; Hebrews 10:5-14). Having perfectly obeyed the law of God, he was made to be sin for us, who knew no sin, that we might be made the righteousness of God in him. When he was made to be sin for us, he was slaughtered under the fury of God's unmitigated wrath. When he was slain as our Substitute, he was buried in the earth. After he had been in the earth for three days, to prove that he had indeed fulfilled all righteousness and had put away our sins, he was raised from the dead. That is exactly what was pictured in his baptism; and that is exactly what is pictured in believer's baptism today (Romans 6:3-6).

Luke records our Lord's later explanation of his baptism by John to have been an act by which he "justified God" (Luke 7:29, 30). Again, baptism does nothing to make God just; but it is the symbolic confession that our God is and must be just. His justice must be satisfied; and our Saviour, by his baptism, confessed that he would satisfy the justice of God by dying under the wrath of God as our Substitute. We come to the waters of baptism for exactly the same reason; to confess our sins and to confess our faith in him by whose blood God can be both "a just God and a Saviour".

October 7
Today's Reading: Mark 2, 3
The Lord of the sabbath
Mark 2:27, 28

As our Lord Jesus and his disciples walked through the cornfields, the disciples picked some corn and ate it. Of course, the Pharisees were watching. When they saw what they perceived as an act of great wickedness they accused the Lord's disciples of breaking the sabbath. By Divine arrangement those wicked religionists gave occasion for our Saviour to give us a sweet and rich word of instruction.

Gospel Feast
The Lord drew an allusion to David and his companions eating the showbread, "which was not lawful". Surely there is something intended in this for our souls. When our hungry souls seek him, the true showbread and the Bread of Life, we find in him a feast for our souls. On the Lord's Day and often through the week, we come to the House of God for this spiritual sustenance. The Lord Jesus, our Abiathar, our great High Priest, has made all his redeemed both kings and priests before God. So that, when our spiritual David and all who are with him come into the house of God, he sets a feast of fat things before us in the Gospel and in the blessed ordinances of Divine worship, and says, "Eat, O friends, drink, yea drink abundantly, Oh beloved".

Gospel Sabbath
There is a great depth of spiritual truth in Mark 2:27, 28, truths that simply must be understood and remembered by us. They are set before us in three crystal clear, simple statements. I do not doubt that neither the Pharisees nor the Lord's disciples understood them at the time. But there is no reason for confusion in these matters

today. The Holy Spirit has now taken the things of Christ and shown their meaning in the Apostolic Epistles.

Made For Man

"The sabbath was made for man." When our God established the sabbath day, he established it for the benefit of man. It was made to help, not to hurt, man. God instituted the sabbath observance of the Old Testament for exactly the same reason he instituted the temple, the priesthood, and the sacrifices of that typical age. He did it to portray to man the way of salvation and life by faith in Christ. Just as a man, in keeping the sabbath, ceased from his own works, trusting God to provide everything he needed, so we come to Christ, ceasing from our own works, trusting him alone for everything. Resting in him, we keep the sabbath of faith (Matthew 11:28-30; Hebrews 4:7-10).

Yet, when our Lord says the sabbath was made for man, we must never imagine that it was made for all men. The Scriptures are explicitly clear in telling us that the sabbath was made for the Jews of the Mosaic dispensation. It was never given to or required of Gentiles (Exodus 31:16, 17). Not only did the ancient Jews never require Gentiles to keep the sabbath, they positively forbade sabbath day observance by Gentiles.

Man was not made for the sabbath. Though the Lord God himself kept a sabbath of rest after creating the heavens and the earth, he never required it of anyone until the law was given to Moses and the Children of Israel at Sinai. Understand the meaning of this. Men and women worshipped and served God for hundreds, even thousands of years, without being under laws of sabbath keeping, or any other form of law for that matter. Enoch walked with God; but he never kept a sabbath day. Noah was a righteous man; but he never observed a sabbath. Abraham was the friend of God; but he never kept a sabbath day.

Typical Sabbath Fulfilled

Christ is the Lord of the sabbath. The simple, clear, and obvious meaning of this last sentence is that he who is the Christ of God instituted the sabbath, fulfilled the sabbath, dispensed with the sabbath, and abrogated the sabbath, in exactly the same way and to exactly the same degree as he did all the other carnal ordinances, rituals, and ceremonies of the legal dispensation. Therefore sabbath day observance is expressly and positively forbidden in the New Testament, just as much so as Passover observance (Galatians 4:10, 11; Colossians 2:16, 17). O blessed Sabbath, my Saviour, give me grace ever to rest in you! How sweet, how delightful, how comfortable it is to truly keep the Sabbath (Matthew 11:28-30), resting in Christ by faith!

October 8
Today's Reading: Mark 4, 5
"Jesus suffered him not"
Mark 5:19

A more pitiful sight can hardly be imagined than the sight of that wild, naked, filthy Gadarene demoniac living in a graveyard, running to and fro among the tombs, crying and cutting himself. Once the Saviour healed him by his grace, from the inside out, how things changed! A more delightful sight can hardly be imagined than the sight of that same man, after the Son of God saved him by his grace. We see him sitting at his Saviour's feet in adoring wonder, gratitude and love, "clothed and in his right mind".

Desire Denied
When the Lord Jesus is about to leave the coasts of Gadara, as he got into the ship, "he that had been possessed with the devil prayed him that he might be with him". I cannot imagine anything more reasonable. Can you? What a wonderful change grace had wrought in him. He, who but a few minutes before was a terror to everybody, is now so heavenly composed that he desires never to leave his great Saviour. His heart is fixed upon his Redeemer. He wants to be in his company permanently.

Is that not the case with every heaven-born soul? The sinner who has experienced the mighty transforming power of God's saving grace in Christ, being called of God and turned by omnipotent mercy "from darkness to light, and from the power of Satan unto God, that he may receive forgiveness of sins, and inheritance among them which are sanctified by faith" (Acts 26:18), desires "that he might be with" the Saviour. Having once tasted that the Lord is gracious, we cannot but long to be absent from the body and present with the Lord. But the Lord Jesus refused to grant this beloved soul the desire of his heart.

"Howbeit Jesus suffered him not, but saith unto him, Go home to thy friends, and tell them how great things the Lord hath done for thee, and hath had compassion on thee. And he departed, and began to publish in Decapolis how great things Jesus had done for him: and all men did marvel" (Mark 5:19, 20).

Blessed Reason
Soon, the Lord Jesus would bring him home to glory, but for the present he must remain among the Gadarenes, and tell his family and friends, all among whom he lived, what great things the Lord had done for him, how he had performed them by his omnipotent mercy, and how he had compassion upon him.

That is precisely the reason our Saviour has left us in this world. He has left us here to tell eternity bound sinners what great things he has done for us, how he has done them, and how he has had compassion upon our poor souls. I can think of no reason for God leaving us in this world except to use us as instruments in his hands for the salvation of other chosen, redeemed sinners. Every believer is completely fit for heaven (Colossians 1:12). We are completely forgiven of all sin, perfectly righteous, and approved of by God through the sin-atoning blood and perfect righteousness of the Lord Jesus Christ. And we have been given our Saviour's own righteous nature in regeneration. Righteousness has been imparted to us by the Spirit of God. Why then has God left us in this world to live in this body of flesh? It seems to me that the answer to that question is obvious. It is because he has chosen to use saved sinners to carry the Gospel to other sinners for the saving of his elect!

Our Work
Saved sinners are to go home to their unsaved friends, and show forth "the praises of him who hath called us out of darkness into his marvellous light" (1 Peter 2:9), until we have fulfilled the purpose for which our God put us in the world. Let us ever live with our eyes and our hearts in heaven with Christ, longing to depart and be with him who loved us and gave himself for us. Yet, we ought to be content to live on this earth for as long as our Saviour is pleased to use us for his glory and the calling of his elect.

The thought that the God of Glory might use such things as we are to build his house, his Church, his holy temple, that he should condescend to use us, putting into our hands the treasure of his Gospel, to save his elect is thrilling. Is it not? That ought to make us happy as we wait all the days of our appointed time until our change come (Job 14:14). That ought to inspire us to devote ourselves to this noble purpose and work. "Go home to thy friends, and tell them how great things the Lord hath done for thee, and hath had compassion on thee."

October 9
Today's Reading: Mark 6
"It is I; be not afraid"
Mark 6:50

The Lord's disciples were in the midst of a terrible storm, in the middle of a dark, dark night. They were toiling hard with trouble; but everything appeared to be contrary to them. In those circumstances, our all-glorious, ever-gracious Saviour came to his troubled friends, walking upon the sea that caused them so much trouble. As he approached their little, storm tossed boat, he said, "Be of good cheer: it is I; be not afraid". Then, "He went up unto them into the ship, and the wind ceased" (Mark 6:45-51).

This is written in the Book of God for you and me, "that we through patience and comfort of the Scriptures might have hope" (Romans 15:4). When the Lord Jesus graciously steps into our storm-tossed lives, he causes the winds that appear to be so contrary to us today to be calm.

423

Sent Into The Storm
Remember, it was the Lord Jesus who sent his friends into the storm, who sent them away from himself (Mark 6:45, 46). He seems to have done so specifically that he might come to them when they desperately needed him, speak these words to them, and make himself known to them in a way that was not otherwise possible. Surely, that is the case with us in all the storms into which he sends us? Listen, then, to the voice of our tender, omnipotent Saviour in the midst of every storm. "Be of good cheer: it is I; be not afraid."

"It is I"
"It is I" who raised the tempest in your soul, and will control it. "It is I" who sent your affliction, and will be with you in it. "It is I" who kindled the furnace, and will watch the flames, and bring you through it. "It is I" who formed your burden, who carved your cross, and who will strengthen you to bear it. "It is I" who mixed your cup of grief, and will enable you to drink it with meek submission to your Father's will. "It is I" who took from you your strength and health, your peace and tranquillity. "It is I" who made the light darkness about you and raised the contrary winds. "It is I" who have done all these things, not against you, but for you, not to hurt you, but to do you good.

I make the clouds my chariot, and clothe myself with the tempest as with a garment. The night hour is my time of coming to you. The dark, surging waves and billows are the pavement upon which I walk. Take courage! "It is I". Do not be afraid. "It is I", your Friend, your Brother, your God, your Saviour! I am causing all the circumstances of your life to work together for your good. "It is I" who brought the storm that assails you. Your affliction did not spring out of the ground, but came down from above, a heaven-sent blessing in disguise, an angel of light clad in a robe of darkness.

Divinely Ordered
Every trial, every affliction, every storm is Divinely ordered by our heavenly Father for our everlasting good. We need often to be reminded, as William Cowper put it:

God moves in a mysterious way his wonders to perform.
He plants his footsteps in the sea, and rides upon the storm.

Deep, in unfathomable mines of never failing skill,
He treasures up his bright designs, and works his sovereign will.

Ye fearful saints, fresh courage take, the clouds you so much dread
Are big with mercy and will break in blessings on your head.

Judge not the Lord by feeble sense, but trust him for his grace.
Behind the frowning providence he hides a smiling face.

His purposes will ripen fast, unfolding every hour.
The bud may have a bitter taste, but sweet will be the flower!

He who loves us with an everlasting love sends every storm in love for our souls, not in anger. Be assured, it is "that the Son of God might be glorified thereby". "Said I not unto thee, that, if thou wouldest believe, thou shouldest see the glory of God?" (John 11:4, 40) The trial will not be forever. It will not always cast you down. "It is I" who ordered, arranged, and controls it. In every stormy wind, in every dark night, in every lonely hour, in every rising fear, may God the Holy Spirit give us grace to hear our Saviour's voice, saying to us, "Be of good cheer: it is I; be not afraid."

October 10
Today's Reading: Mark 7, 8
"He hath done all things well"
Mark 7:37

If these men and women who had seen our Saviour's miracles were astonished and cried out, "He hath done all things well", how much more astonished we ought to be who have tasted and experienced his grace! How much more we ought to confess to God our Saviour, to the angels before his throne, to wondering worlds, and to one another, "He hath done all things well".

My Testimony
Looking over all the days of my life and everything I have experienced these 63 years, I lift my heart to heaven and say, "He hath done all things well". Like you, I've had a few trials and heartaches, a little pain and sorrow, a little hurt and bitterness. I am ashamed to confess, I have caused much more than I've experienced. But God my Saviour has been so kind and gracious to me, that were I to die this day, you can write these words on my gravestone. "'He hath done all things well!' Here lies a man who was for 63 years the benefactor of unceasing, special Divine care. And 'My Jesus hath done all things well.'"

A Question
Tell me, you who know my Saviour, can you not testify the same? "He hath done all things well." Does your own life's experience not verify this? I know it does.
     Yes, from first to last, from the day of our birth to this very hour, from the earliest pangs of sin's conviction to the blessed thrill of sin's forgiveness, from the cradle to the grave, from earth to heaven, this will be our testimony regarding all the way our ever-gracious God has led us through this wilderness and every experience along the way, "He hath done all things well".

Providence And Grace
In providence and in grace, in every truth revealed in his Word, in every token of his love, in every stroke of his rod, in every sunbeam of his goodness, in every cloud that has darkened our skies, in every sweet morsel he has put into our lives, in every bitter thing he has mixed into our cup, in all that has been mysterious, confusing, painful, and humiliating, in all that he has given, and in all that he has taken away, "He hath done all things well." This is, must be, and shall be our grateful acknowledgment through time and eternity. "He hath done all things well."

Our great God and Saviour who loved us, chose us, redeemed us, and saved us by his grace, who has kept us all our days and in all our ways, has done all things well! He who is our God is too wise to err, too strong to fail, and too good to do wrong.

Study his universe, all the history of it, study his creation, his providence, his judgments and his grace, view them in every light, examine them in their most minute detail, as you would the petals of a flower, or the wing of an insect, study all with the microscopic eye of faith, and this will be your glad testimony to his everlasting praise, "He hath done all things well."

October 11
Today's Reading: Mark 9, 10
"If thou canst believe ..."
Mark 9:23

Frequently, when pressing the claims of Christ upon sinners, I have had them respond, "I am trying to believe". How subtle Satan is! Once a sinner has moved from utter infidelity to being concerned for his soul, the old serpent convinces him that faith is a complex thing. It is not so. People think that faith in Christ has something to do with mysterious feelings, or that it comes as the result of deep emotions. The deceived soul vainly imagines that since he is trying to believe, the Lord looks favourably upon him. Nothing could be further from the truth.

Making God A Liar
Would your father be honoured if you said to him, "Dad, I want to believe you. I am really trying to believe you; but I have not yet come to the place that I can believe you."? I hardly think so! He would be insulted by your impudent rudeness. Your unbelief with regard to your father would be a declaration that in your opinion your father is a liar. That is exactly how God looks upon your unbelief. "He that believeth on the Son of God hath the witness in himself: he that believeth not God hath made him a liar; because he believeth not the record that God gave of his Son" (1 John 5:10). Faith in Christ is such a simple matter that when I try to explain it, I am always

fearful that my explanation will only confuse. Faith in Christ is simply believing God. Unbelief is declaring that, in your opinion, God is a liar.

Very Simple
Charles Spurgeon once told a story that beautifully illustrates the simplicity of faith. A Sunday-school teacher took out his pocket-watch and said to one of the boys in his class, "I will give this to you, John. Will you have it?" John began to think about the offer, wondering what the teacher meant, but made no response. So the teacher turned to another and said, "Here is my watch, Henry. Will you have it?" Henry, with modesty, replied, "No, thank you, sir". The teacher tried the same thing with several of the boys with the same result. One youngster had been eyeing the watch. Being much poorer than the others, he never dreamed of having one of his own; but he wanted it very much. When the teacher said to him, "Here is my watch, Billy. Will you have it", he said, "Thank you very much, sir", took the watch and put it in his pocket. One of the boys said, "Is it his to keep?" "Of course it is", the teacher replied. "I offered it to him. He accepted it. It is his." John said, "If I had thought you meant it, I would have taken the watch myself." Each one of the boys passed up the watch, because they did not believe the teacher. Billy went home with the watch in his pocket, because he believed.

If ...
If you can but believe God, you can lay this book down and go your way with Christ in your heart, with his righteousness laid to your account in heaven and in your own conscience, with the complete forgiveness of all your sins through his blood, and all the blessedness of eternal life and everlasting salvation in him. It is written, "Believe on the Lord Jesus Christ, and thou shalt be saved." Faith in Christ really is just that simple. It is believing God. If you believe on the Son of God, eternal life is yours. If you refuse to believe God, the wrath of God abides upon you. Oh, may God the Holy Spirit give you faith in the Lord Jesus Christ!

Believers
We who believe must never cease to remember and give thanks to our God for the precious gift of faith in Christ. Our faith in him is not the result of our choice. Like all others, we chose not to believe God. But God the Holy Ghost, by the mighty operations of his infinite mercy, wrought faith in us by irresistible grace, revealing Christ in us and causing us to come to him in the day of his power. And, as he first worked faith in us, he continues to give us faith, sustains us in faith, and keeps us coming to Christ, working faith in us by grace. "Thanks be unto God for his unspeakable gift!"

———————

October 12
Today's Reading: Mark 11, 12
"Nothing but leaves"
Mark 11:13

Nothing in all the world is so disgusting to the Son of God and so surely damning to our souls as fruitless religion. As our Lord and his disciples walked along, they saw a fig tree. It stood out from all the others because, though the time of figs had not yet come, this fig tree was in full foliage. The other trees were just beginning to shoot forth their buds; but this one was large, spreading its full foliage of leaves, and waving in the wind, as if to say, "Look at me". But when our Lord walked with his disciples over to the tree to gather some figs, he found "nothing but leaves", and immediately pronounced a curse upon the tree. By sun up the next morning, it had withered in death from its roots (v. 20). Without question, this event is full of spiritual meaning. It is a parable as full of instruction for our souls as any of our Lord's spoken parables.

Apostate Religion
This barren, cursed, withered fig tree certainly represents apostate Judaism. The Jews, the Scribes, the Pharisees, the Sadducees, all were rich in leaves. They possessed more leaves than anyone. Ceremony, creed, history, doctrine, show, tradition and reputation they had in great abundance. And they did not mind calling attention to their beautiful leaves. But they were utterly destitute of faith toward God. They had no fruit. Therefore, that nation and their religion has been specifically cursed of God and forever abandoned (Matthew 23:38)
    This barren fig tree represents every apostate church and religious denomination in the world. I am talking now about churches which claim to be Christian, which claim to believe in and defend the Book, the blood, and the blessed hope. Churches which wear the name of Christ but have departed from the doctrine of Christ. If I could get their attention, I would say to every man, woman, and child in such churches, "Escape for your life! Flee from Babylon. Get out of Sodom. The curse of God is in that place you think is the house of God." The greatest missionary field in the world today is the professed church of God. Where can you find a church today where the Word of God is faithfully preached, the glory of God is paramount, the will of God rules, and the Gospel of Christ is proclaimed? Robert Hawker rightly observed, "Deceiving by the appearance of large full leaves of a profession without fruit, in the end (they) will be found dried up from the roots, with the curse of a broken law falling everlastingly upon them, untaken away by Christ."

Hypocrisy
Above all else, this barren fig tree represents religious hypocrisy; carnal, half-hearted, hypocritical professors of Christianity. Let all who are content with a name that they live, though they are dead, see their faces in this mirror! Their fine, showy, impressive leaves, those things that impress them so much with themselves mean nothing to God Almighty. They stink in his nostrils! Their religion is their damning delusion! They

may have great experiences, but no experience of grace. They may have a rich history, but no holiness. They may enjoy religious excitement and displays of emotion; but they possess neither righteousness nor expiation. Their doctrine may be precise; but it is precisely dead. Their religion may be rich in ceremonial tradition; but it is poor in comfort and truth. It is useless religion, because it is fruitless religion. It does not produce faith in Christ, hope in Christ, or love for Christ.

Self-examination
In light of this barren fig tree let us make our calling and election sure. Baptism, church membership, religious ceremony, doctrinal orthodoxy, and deep religious emotions are not synonyms for Christianity! They are just leaves, nothing but leaves. They will no more cover the nakedness of our souls from God's all-seeing eye in the Day of Judgment than Adam's fig leaves covered his nakedness in the garden. Christianity is faith in Christ alone!

"Examine yourselves, whether ye be in the faith; prove your own selves. Know ye not your own selves, how that Jesus Christ is in you, except ye be reprobates?" (2 Corinthians 13:5) If Christ is in you, if Christ is in me, if he is dwelling in us by his Holy Spirit, if he is the life that is in us, he brings forth fruit, even the fruit of the Spirit in us (Galatians 5:22, 23).

I would rather stand before God in the Day of Judgment guilty of any crime known to man than stand before that bar of his august majesty guilty of self-righteousness and hypocrisy! If you die without Christ, your religion will sink your soul into the lowest hell! Your religion will be your greatest curse! The Son of God has pronounced his curse upon the barren fig tree and barren, fig-leaf religion!

October 13
Today's Reading: Mark 13, 14
"She hath wrought a good work on me"
Mark 14:6

Mark records the story of a woman coming into the house of Simon the leper and anointing the Lord Jesus for his burial. It is an event recorded in all four of the gospel narratives. Comparing Scripture with Scripture, I cannot avoid the conclusion that this woman was Mary, the sister of Martha and Lazarus, and that she is the same woman referred to as Mary Magdalene, out of whom the Lord Jesus had cast seven devils (Mark 16:9; Luke 8:2). Perhaps the reason Mark withheld her name was modesty. Some have suggested this woman was his mother.

An Example

She was a remarkable woman, modest and unassuming. She said very little. In fact, I have found only one sentence written in the Scriptures which was spoken by Mary. It is found in John 11:32. "Lord, if thou hadst been here, my brother had not died." Yet, God the Holy Spirit holds Mary before us on four occasions in Holy Scripture as an example of the love for, devotion to, and faith in Christ, that is inspired by and flows from the sweet experience of his saving grace.

In Luke 10:39 we see Mary sitting at the Lord's feet, absorbing every word that fell from his lips. John describes Mary falling at the Master's feet in humble, submissive faith (11:32). As a broken-hearted woman might run into the arms of her husband for comfort, Mary ran to the Lord Jesus, fell at his feet, and sought comfort in him in her time of great sorrow. Matthew tells us that early in the morning of the resurrection, Mary was at the tomb where our Lord's body had been buried (28:1-9). She was the first one to hear the good news of the resurrection. She was the first one to see the risen Christ. This woman was the first one to proclaim the resurrection. Here in Mark 14 we see Mary in the house of Simon the leper breaking "an alabaster box of ointment of spikenard very precious", anointing the Lord Jesus for his burial (Mark 14:3-9).

This picture of this dear woman is perhaps the most instructive of the four. Our Lord himself declares, "She hath wrought a good work on me ... She hath done what she could ... Verily I say unto you, Wheresoever this Gospel shall be preached throughout the whole world, this also that she hath done shall be spoken of for a memorial of her." Truly this woman sets before us a remarkable example to follow. She who had been forgiven much loved much and gave much. Blessed is that man or woman who is given grace to follow her example!

Her Work

Our Lord Jesus says of Mary's humble anointing of him, "She hath wrought a good work on me." This good work, which was performed by Mary, might be most reasonably expected from any believer. Like you and me, Mary had experienced the grace of God in Christ. This work which she performed was only the spontaneous response of gratitude and love for the grace of God she had experienced. It was but her reasonable service (1 Corinthians 6:19, 20). She had been given faith in Christ. The Lord Jesus revealed himself to her and gave her the gift of faith. He chose her and graciously caused her to choose him. The demons who tormented her and held her captive were driven from her and the Son of God established his throne in her heart. Her sins, which were many, were all forgiven her. The Lord graciously revealed to her the mysteries of the Gospel. Mary alone seems to have known and understood how the Lord Jesus would accomplish redemption by his death as our Substitute. With all these things in her heart, Mary came to Simon's house to anoint her Lord in anticipation of his death and resurrection.

Devotion Criticized

Yet, Mary's loving devotion and sacrificial zeal drew a very unexpected response from those who witnessed it (vv. 3-5). She must have been shocked by the comments she heard. She only wanted, in some modest way, to honour her Lord. The fact is, those who serve the Lord Jesus with the most ardent, self-sacrificing devotion are often ridiculed and criticized by those who ought to imitate their example.

For her good work, Mary was severely censored by Judas, the church treasurer (John 12:4-6). And all the disciples, following Judas' wicked lead, became indignant at what they considered was Mary's wastefulness. They said, "To what purpose is this waste?" (Matthew 26:8).

If you are committed to Christ, if you are inclined to do some unusual service for him, just for his honour and his glory, for the interests of his kingdom, for the furtherance of his Gospel, simply because you love him, simply out of a deep sense of overwhelming gratitude, do not expect the approval of either the world, religious hypocrites, or even true believers. Wholehearted devotion exposes and condemns half-hearted religion. It stirs up the wrath of those whose hearts are cold and indifferent. Real consecration to Christ is sure to be criticized and mocked by those who know nothing about it.

Highly Honoured
Though her actions were criticized and condemned by others, even by her friends, the Lord Jesus approved of, highly esteemed, and commended both Mary and her work (vv. 6-9). Nothing else mattered to her. No opinion was important to her but His. Because the Lord Jesus was pleased with Mary, she appears to have been oblivious to what anyone else had to say about the matter. She did it just for him. They really did not matter. Her faith in, love for, and devotion to the Son of God gave her courage and strength. May God be pleased to give me grace to follow the example of this blessed woman.

October 14
Today's Reading: Mark 15, 16
"My God, my God, why hast thou forsaken me?"
Mark 15:34

O my soul, be astonished and bow in humiliation, as you hear the Saviour's cry of untold agony and woe when he was made sin for me and abandoned of his Father because of my transgressions made his! Here are three things which I see in these words of lamentation which fell from the lips of the Son of God when he was made to be sin for us.

Infinite Evil
What an infinitely evil thing sin is! Sin is such a horrid thing that the holy Lord God cannot tolerate it even when it was found upon his own darling Son. Whenever God sees sin he will punish it without mercy. When the angels fell God cast them out of

heaven and holds them in chains of darkness until the Day of Judgment (2 Peter 2:4; Jude 6). When Adam sinned he was separated from God and driven from the presence of the Lord (Genesis 3). When God looked upon the wickedness of Noah's generation he destroyed the whole world in the flood of his wrath (Genesis 6). Upon the twin cities of perverseness, Sodom and Gomorrah, God poured out fire and brimstone (Genesis 19). And when God saw sin upon his darling Son, his only-begotten, well-beloved Son, he forsook him!

Be warned. If God finds sin on you, he will destroy you forever in hell, without mercy! Flee to Christ, who alone can cleanse you of all sin!

Complete Obedience
How thorough and complete was Christ's obedience to the Father as our Surety! We could never obey God perfectly. We could never fulfil the demands of the law or the Gospel. But Christ met and satisfied perfectly all the demands of God for his elect. This cry, "My God, my God", was made at the zenith of our Lord's obedience. Christ was obedient even unto death. Our salvation was accomplished both by his doing and by his dying. His doing is imputed to us for righteousness (Romans 5:19). His dying made atonement for our sins (Romans 5:11). Even when he was forsaken of God, our Surety remained obedient. This cry is an expression of Christ's perfect faith in God. As a man he believed God and showed us what it is to believe him. "Faith is believing the Word of God, not because we see it to be true, or feel it to be true, but because God said it" said Robert Murray M'Cheyne. We are often unbelieving. But our Surety never doubted God, even when he was forsaken of God. This cry is an expression of exemplary love and devotion. Here is love and devotion unrivalled. Hanging upon the cursed tree, without one drop of mercy, one smile from heaven, or one comfort for his soul, our great Christ loved the very God who forsook him!

Absolute Satisfaction
What unfathomable depth of hell our blessed Saviour endured! What is hell if it is not being abandoned totally by God? Why was Christ forsaken? Because there was no other way for us to be accepted. Justice had to be satisfied. When the Son of God was made sin for us and our sins were imputed to him, God forsook him and poured out upon him all the fulness of his holy wrath (Lamentations 1:12). God gave him everything our sins deserve. And now, the holy Lord God, accepts all who trust his dear Son, imputing to them his perfect righteousness. He rewards us with eternal glory for Christ's sake, giving us all that he deserves. And because, as he was made sin for us; chosen, redeemed sinners, all who trust the Lord Jesus Christ, are made the righteousness of God in him!

432

October 15
Today's Reading: Luke 1
"He shall be great"
Luke 1:32

When the angel of God announced to Mary that she had been chosen and favoured of God to be the woman through whose womb the Son of God would come into the world, he said, "Behold, thou shalt conceive in thy womb, and bring forth a Son, and shalt call his name JESUS. He shall be great, and shall be called the Son of the Highest: and the Lord God shall give unto him the throne of his Father David: And he shall reign over the house of Jacob forever; and of his kingdom there shall be no end." The angel's prophecy has come to pass. The Lord Jesus Christ, our Saviour, truly is great.

In His Person
Christ is great in his magnificent person. Here is God and man in one person, fully God and fully man, yet completely one! There is none like him. He is the great God, the great Man, the great King, the great Mediator between God and man, our Great High Priest, and our great Saviour. God took man into union with himself in the person of his dear Son, the Lord Jesus Christ, because there was no other way for God to save us from our sins. God could not suffer, and man could not satisfy; but the God-man both suffered and satisfied all that was required for the salvation of God's elect.

In His Propitiation
Our blessed Saviour is great in his propitiation. Having brought in an everlasting righteousness for us, the Son of God suffered the wrath of God as our Substitute. When he was made sin for us, God drew forth the sword of his holy justice and buried it in his Son! Now, there is no wrath left in God to be propitiated for us. He says, "Fury is not in me". Having punished our sins to the full satisfaction of his infinite and holy justice for us, God will never charge his elect with sin (Romans 4:8; 8:1, 34; 1 John 2:12).

In His Pre-eminence
Our mighty Redeemer is great in his pre-eminence. God has made his Son to be Head over all things and has given him pre-eminence over all things. Christ has all power, all dominion, all authority, and all honour. He is to have all the praise of all his people for all things. The Lamb upon the throne is worthy of praise from all who are about the throne. The Triune God has so arranged the affairs of the universe that Christ shall be praised forever by all things. All creation shall praise him as Creator (Revelation 4:11). All rational creatures shall praise him as their rightful Lord (Philippians 2:9-11). All angels and men, both righteous and wicked, shall render praise to Christ the Judge in the last day (Acts 17:31). And all God's elect shall praise Christ alone for the whole of their salvation forever (1 Corinthians 1:30, 31). Yes, Jesus Christ is the great

God and our great Saviour. Let us trust him, glory in him, and give praise to him this day, all the days of our lives, and then to all eternity!

October 16
Today's Reading: Luke 2, 3
"A prophetess"
Luke 2:36

Some will think it strange that a book of devotional readings includes matters of Gospel doctrine; but I make no apology for giving instruction in Divine truth. God's truth sets poor sinners free from the horrible bondage of religious tradition.

Never In A Bind
God Almighty is never put in a bind. He is never compelled by circumstances to change his mind, or alter his purpose. With regard to the salvation of his elect, God's purpose is crystal clear. There is a multitude of sinners in this world, scattered through all the nations of the world, whom God has chosen to save from eternity (Ephesians 1:3-6). The Lord Jesus Christ has redeemed that chosen multitude by the shedding of his precious blood and obtained eternal redemption for them (Galatians 3:13; Hebrews 9:12). At the appointed time of love, God the Holy Spirit will regenerate and call each of those chosen, redeemed sinners, by effectual, irresistible grace, creating life and faith in them (Psalm 65:4). The means by which he will do this is the preaching of the Gospel (1 Peter 1:23-25). And those by whom God is pleased to send the Gospel through the world are men; chosen, gifted, and called of God himself to the glorious work of the Gospel ministry (1 Timothy 3:1-7). None but men are called of God to this work. No woman has ever been called of God to that work.

Prophetesses In Scripture
Yet, we read in Luke 2:36 of a godly old woman by the name of Anna who was a prophetess. In this day of utter disregard for God's Word, in which women are being ordained and sent out by almost all religious denominations as deacons, preachers, missionaries, evangelists, pastors, and theologians, I must say something about the fact that Anna is here called a prophetess. Were it not for the universal confusion in the religious world about female preachers, I would pass over these words with little comment; but the fact that such confusion prevails compels me to speak.

There are a few instances of female prophets, prophetesses, in the Scriptures, both before and after the coming of Christ: Miriam, the sister of Moses and Aaron, Deborah the wife of Lapidoth, Huldah the wife of Shallum, and this woman Anna at the time of Christ's birth. Later, in the Book of Acts, we read about four daughters of Philip the Evangelist, who were prophetesses.

No Women Allowed

Does this mean that it is proper for God's Church to ordain women as deacons, missionaries, preachers, evangelists, and pastors today? No! The Word of God absolutely and clearly forbids such nonsense. The teachings of Holy Scripture in this regard are so plain that error here is without excuse. These are offices which, by God's order are for men only. This is not a matter of sexism, male chauvinism, or anything of the kind. It is a matter of reverence for God and obedience to his Word (1 Corinthians 14:34, 35; 1 Timothy 2:11, 12).

In all things godly women are modest, gladly living in subjection to their husbands. Believing women are not rebels to God, his order, or his Word. Just as men are to be in subjection to Christ and to all who are put in authority over them, just as deacons, elders, and churches are to be in subjection to their pastors, just as children are to be in subjection to their parents, women are to be in subjection to their husbands. In the house of God women serve in subjection to men. They are never to be placed in a position of dominance over men.

What then about these women who are called "prophetesses" in the Scriptures? Do we just ignore them? No. But neither do we build our doctrine on obscure statements. We build our doctrine on the plain instructions of Holy Scripture given in the place or places where the subject under consideration is taught. The fact that there were prophetesses in the Old Testament and through the Acts of the Apostles does not nullify the prohibitions given in the Epistles to female preachers. However, when the Word of God speaks of female prophets, and of women prophesying, that does not imply that they were preachers.

Worshippers

The word "prophetess" was used in ancient times much like we use the word "worshipper" today. We might say of such and such women, "they worshipped God". That would be the same thing as saying "they prophesied". The word "prophesy" does not necessarily mean "instruct", "foretell", or "preach" in any public way. The word is used commonly to speak simply of worship, praise, and witness (1 Samuel 10:10, 11; 18:10; 1 Kings 22:10-12; 1 Corinthians 11:5; and chapters 14 and 15). A prophetess was a woman who worshipped God, praised him, and bore witness to him. In fact one woman was called a prophetess simply because she was married to a prophet (Isaiah 8:3). The only female preacher ever spoken of in a church in the New Testament was that wicked woman at Thyatira, who called herself a prophetess, but whom our Lord calls "Jezebel" (Revelation 2:20). That is exactly what all self-appointed female preachers are properly called, because they are seducers and deceivers of men's souls. When God sets women up as rulers over men, in any capacity, it is an act of judgment, not an act of grace (Isaiah 3:12). In the Church and Kingdom of God there are no female preachers.

———

October 17
Today's Reading: Luke 4, 5
"Naaman the Syrian"
Luke 4:27

"Many lepers were in Israel in the time of Eliseus the prophet; and none of them was cleansed, saving Naaman the Syrian." The cleansing of Naaman was a famous story of the Old Testament Scriptures, with which the Jews of our Lord's day were very familiar. But, when our Lord Jesus recalled it to their attention, "they were filled with wrath". Those men understood perfectly well what the Lord Jesus was saying, and they greatly resented it. That which our Lord was teaching is just as violently opposed by modern religionists as it was by the Jews. But for those who are taught of the Holy Ghost this is a most delightful and comforting doctrine. Salvation is accomplished by the sovereign prerogative of God. This little story plainly and beautifully sets before us a picture of God's method of grace.

Divine Sovereignty
The sovereignty of God's grace was displayed in the cleansing of Naaman. It is evident that Naaman was the object of sovereign grace because he was the most unlikely candidate for mercy. Naaman was a heathen, a Gentile idolater. He was a sworn enemy of Israel, the people of God. Besides, Naaman lived a long way from the prophet's home. Yet, the grace of God passed by many lepers in Israel. Going far afield; it found this Syrian soldier. Blessed be God, he still operates in this same sovereign manner! Those whom men consider the least likely candidates for mercy are the objects of God's free-grace. Many others were passed by, more noble and excellent than he; but God chose Naaman.

Divine Means
But, mark this too. The grace of God always operates in a definite manner. God has not only ordained who will be saved. He has ordained the method by which they will be saved as well. First, Naaman had to hear the good news that healing was possible. Whenever God intends to save a sinner, he will send someone to tell him the Gospel. It may be a little Hebrew maid, or it may be an old man. But always, "Faith cometh by hearing". For another thing, it was imperative for Naaman to heed the message and obey the command. Even so, sinners must hear the Gospel and in humble faith be washed in the blood of Christ.

Great Faith
After giving us this picture of God's sovereignty and the use of Divinely ordained means to accomplish his purpose, in Luke 5 God the Holy Ghost gives us an example of the great usefulness of those who are used by God to accomplish his purpose of grace in his elect. Here are four men with a sick, impotent friend. They found out where the Lord Jesus was preaching and knowing that "the power of the Lord was present to heal", they picked up their friend on his bed and sought a way to bring him

into the presence of Christ. When the Son of God "saw their faith, he said unto him, Man, thy sins are forgiven thee". Those four men could not do a thing to change their crippled friend's condition. Yet they knew that Christ could. So they brought him to the Saviour, overcoming great obstacles and because of their faith in Christ, this poor sinner was both healed and saved! I sure would like to be such a friend. Would you?

Do you have such faith in Christ? Do I? Do we believe that the power of the Lord is present where the Gospel is preached to save lost men and women? If we do, there are some things we can do for them. I know we cannot change a sinner's condition. But we can do some things for lost people, and what we can do we are responsible to do. We can pray for those who believe not.

We can tell others what we know of our blessed Christ and his great grace (John 9:11). We can tell friends, neighbours, relatives and acquaintances what we have seen, heard, felt, and experienced by the Gospel. We can use what God has given us for the support of the Gospel ministry (3 John 5-8). You may not be able to go to Africa to preach, but you can help send a preacher. You may not be able to preach, but you can help feed and clothe the man who does.

We can distribute tracts, recordings, bulletins, and books to those who might profit from them. That which costs us so little may be of infinite value to another. We can work to prepare a place for sinners to hear the Gospel. Someone has to mow the lawn, shovel the snow, sweep the floor, replace the lights, wash the windows, and paint the walls at the church building. Angels would be honoured to do such work. Surely saved sinners should count such great service to Christ an honour!

We can bring sinners to hear the Gospel. If we want to, if we care, we will figure out a way to get people to hear the Gospel. We can exemplify the grace of God in our lives. We can adorn the doctrine of God, so that those who know us will want to hear the Gospel we believe.

O Spirit of God, fill us with grace; and make us useful to eternity bound sinners in our brief day for the glory of God!

October 18
Today's Reading: Luke 6, 7
"A woman ... which was a sinner"
Luke 7:37

The great mainspring and driving force of service to Christ is that love and gratitude which arises from a sense of great forgiveness. How I wish I could drive this point home to the hearts of all who attempt to rouse up men and women to live for and serve Christ. The driving force of true Christianity, the motive and inspiration for all devotion and service to Christ, which compels and constrains believers to live in this world for the glory of God is grace experienced, forgiveness known and their deep gratitude to and love felt for Christ. Believers are motivated by gratitude and love arising from the experience of God's free, sovereign, saving grace in our Saviour, not by the threat of law, the promise of reward, or the hope of recognition (2 Corinthians 5:14, 15; 8:9).

Who Was This Woman?

This woman, who was a sinner, is here held before us in the Book of God as an example for all who would honour Christ to follow. Yet, wisely and graciously, the Holy Spirit tells us nothing about this woman except these things. She was a sinner. She was a sinner who trusted Christ. She was a sinner forgiven of all her sins. She was a sinner who showed her gratitude, a sinner who loved Christ much.

What Did This Woman Do?

This saved sinner made it her business to know where the Saviour was, and came to him there. She brought with her an alabaster box of ointment. She came with a sacrifice of faith, with which she sought to honour her Redeemer. She stood in humiliation at the Saviour's feet, behind him. She wept because she was full of sorrow, knowing that the Lord Jesus must suffer and die upon the cursed tree to put away her sin. She wept with loving gratitude because of his great love for her soul. She washed his feet with her tears and wiped them with her hair. She tenderly kissed the Saviour's feet, with lips of love, devotion, and adoration. She anointed his feet in faith in anticipation of his death. In a word, as the Lord Jesus himself put it, she did what she could (Mark 14:3-9). Blessed are they to whom God the Holy Spirit gives such grace!

What Was Her Motive?

Why did this woman do what she did? How can such an act be explained? What would inspire a poor person to make such a great, and in the eyes of men, extravagant sacrifice? She had owed much. She had been forgiven much. And she loved much.

What Was The Result?

What was the result of this woman's love for Christ and her devotion and service to him? She was scorned by Simon the Pharisee, ridiculed by Judas, and misunderstood by her fellow disciples. Few there are who understand devotion, wholehearted devotion to Christ. But she had not come to Simon's house to be honoured. She had come there to honour God her Saviour; and honouring him, she was honoured by him (1 Samuel 2:30).

This one who honoured her Lord was highly honoured by her Lord. When she was ridiculed and scorned, the Son of God came to her defence (v. 47). He said, "Let her alone; why trouble ye her? she hath wrought a good work on me" (Mark 14:6). The Master assured her, before her judges and slanderers, that he had forgiven her of all her sins. "Thy sins are forgiven" (v. 48). Then her Saviour assured her of her faith and spoke peace to her heart (v. 50).

The only way to inspire consecration and devotion to Christ is to preach Christ. The only way to promote good works is to preach free grace (Titus 3:4-9). The soul that has experienced redemption, forgiveness, and saving grace is inspired by the knowledge of God's mercy, love, and grace in Christ to love him and seek his glory. "We love him, because he first loved us" (1 John 4:19).

Let all who read this portion of Holy Scripture, knowing him of whom it speaks, be reminded and tell sinners everywhere that the Lord Jesus Christ is a great Saviour, merciful, gracious, compassionate, and able and ready to save the very chief of sinners.

October 19
Today's Reading: Luke 8, 9
"The Christ of God"
Luke 9:20

At first glance, the careless reader might pass over these words, thinking there is nothing extraordinary in them; but such thoughts arise from great ignorance. Peter's confession here is truly remarkable. The more I study it, the more remarkable and blessed it appears. Consider it carefully.

An Oddity

This confession made Peter an oddity among his peers. It put him at odds with the rest of the world. Few were with Christ in those days. Many were against him. But Peter confessed him. When the rulers of his nation and all the religious people he knew, the Scribes, the Pharisees, the Sadducees, the priests and the people, all opposed Christ, Peter confessed him. Many would gladly acknowledge him to be a prophet, even a great prophet, even a resurrected prophet. But Peter confessed him to be "The Christ of God".

That put him at odds with the rest of the world; and that confession puts God's elect at odds with the world today, especially the religious world. Yes, all who call themselves Christians use the very words Peter used; but few, very few, know the meaning of this confession. To say that "Jesus is the Christ", is to confess that Jesus of Nazareth is God incarnate, and that he actually accomplished all that the Scriptures of the Old Testament said he would accomplish (Daniel 9:24; Isaiah 53). To confess that "Jesus is the Christ" is to assert that he brought in everlasting righteousness, made an end of transgression, and fully, effectually redeemed all God's elect.

Tremendous Faith

This confession of faith came from a man of tremendous faith, character, commitment, and zeal. Say what you will about Peter, he had his faults, I know, but do not underrate this man. His heart was under the rule of Christ. Grace is evident in him. Peter was a true-hearted, fervent, faithful servant of our God.

Matthew gives a more complete record of Peter's confession. Looking in the face of the Son of man, Peter said to that man, "Thou art the Christ, the Son of the living God" (Matthew 16:16). Peter confessed that the man Jesus is both the Christ of God and God the Son in our nature. He confessed that the despised Nazarene is the Christ, the promised Messiah, the One of whom all the prophets spoke. In a word, he confessed that the Man, Jesus, is God come to save his people from their sins (Matthew 1:21). I do not know what all Peter knew or did not know. But he knew Christ and confessed him. Do you?

Our Confession
"With the mouth confession is made unto salvation." Our confession does not save us; but it is a confession with reference to salvation accomplished by the Son of God. True, saving faith knows and confesses that the man Jesus of Nazareth is the Christ of God. "He said unto them, But whom say ye that I am? Peter answering said, The Christ of God".

Peter was, at times, erring and unstable, in some matters ignorant and unbelieving, far too proud, and far too quick to action. But when all is said and done, Peter was a remarkable man. In the midst of unbelieving religionists, when the overwhelming tide of religious opinion was rushing the other way, Peter was confident, loyal, willing to stand alone, and bold because he believed and loved his Saviour.

When he declared that the man standing before him was "the Christ of God", he asserted plainly that that man was and is the Incarnate God, the woman's Seed, Abraham's Seed, David's Son and David's Lord, the Saviour, that One of whom the Scriptures speak, the Divine Surety and Covenant Head, by whom alone all God's elect are and must be saved.

October 20
Today's Reading: Luke 10, 11
"One Thing"
Luke 10:42

May God the Holy Ghost rivet the attention of our hearts upon "one thing". Blessed are they who desire "one thing", live for "one thing", set their hearts on "one thing".

One Thing Desired
In Psalm 27:4 David said, "One thing have I desired of the Lord". The man after God's own heart desired but "one thing" and sought but "one thing" from the Lord God. "That I may dwell in the house of the Lord all the days of my life". David desired to dwell in the conscious awareness of Christ's manifest presence, in sweet communion on earth and perfect communion in heaven. "To behold the beauty of the

Lord" by faith here, and face to face hereafter. "And to inquire in his temple", to be taught and directed by his Spirit, and to be taught perfectly in his glorious presence.

One Thing Needful
In Luke 10:42 our Lord told Martha, "one thing is needful". It is true, we live in this world with many cares and responsibilities, which we must not neglect. Yet, even in this world, only "one thing is needful" and that one thing is Christ. "Martha was cumbered about much serving". Martha was "careful and troubled about many things". How sad! Mary chose one thing. Mary sought one thing. The one thing Mary sought is the one thing needful, Christ Jesus. Mary "sat at Jesus' feet, and heard his word". How blessed!

One Thing To Be Known
In John 9:25 the blind man, whose sight had been restored by the power of God, said, "one thing I know". He knew that once he was blind and he knew who caused him to see. That was enough! If you see the things of God, you know who caused you to see. Like the blind man, you lay all praise at the feet of Christ. If you know this one thing, you know enough.

> I am a poor sinner, and nothing at all;
> But Jesus Christ is my All in all.

One Thing To Be Done
In Philippians 3:13 the Apostle Paul said, "one thing I do". We have not yet attained perfection, or even come close. We have not yet won the prize we seek, perfect conformity to Christ. But this one thing we must do, "Forgetting those things which are behind, and reaching forth unto those things which are before", we must "press toward the mark for the prize of the high calling of God in Christ Jesus". We must persevere, expending every effort, using every means, seeking the Lord Jesus Christ, until at last we are found in him, righteous, perfectly holy, perfectly conformed to Christ in body, soul, and spirit by the grace and power of God.

October 21
Today's Reading: Luke 12
"Consider"
Luke 12:24-27

Our Saviour here calls us away from the care of the world to faith in our God, calling us to honour God by believing him. He does so by pointing out some things that ought

441

to be obvious to every kindergarten child. These things may seem to be simple, insignificant, even trivial lessons to carnal minds; but after studying this Book every day for the past 47 years, and reading hundreds of volumes of theology, I find the things mentioned in this passage to be matters of deepest importance. The more I ponder them, the weightier they become. The more I study them, the more profound they appear. Here is the "strong meat" of the Word of God.

Consider The Ravens
"Consider the ravens: for they neither sow nor reap; which neither have storehouse nor barn; and God feedeth them: how much more are ye better than the fowls?" If God Almighty condescends to provide for the needs of a bird, a raven at that, if he orders the affairs of providence to give the ravens their daily food, is it ever reasonable for us to imagine that he might fail to provide for us?

Consider Yourself
"And which of you with taking thought can add to his stature one cubit?" The word here translated "stature" can also be translated "life," or "age", as it is in John 9:21, 23 and Hebrews 11:11. What our Lord is saying here is that none of us can, by any means, add one bit to the height of our frames, the maturity of our years, or the days of our lives.

Consider The Lilies
"Consider the lilies how they grow: they toil not, they spin not; and yet I say unto you, that Solomon in all his glory was not arrayed like one of these. If then God so clothe the grass, which is to day in the field, and tomorrow is cast into the oven; how much more will he clothe you, O ye of little faith?" If the Lord God every year provides the lilies with fresh foliage and fresh blooms, how absurd it is for us to imagine that he might fail to clothe us today, or tomorrow.

Consider The Heathen
"For all these things do the nations of the world seek after: and your Father knoweth that ye have need of these things." What a shame it is for God's people to grovel like the heathen of this world after the things of the world. If God is my Father and Christ my Saviour and the Holy Spirit my Comforter, if heaven is my home and eternity is the span of my life, I ought not to find it difficult to live above the cares and anxieties of the heathen. Faith in Christ ought to make my heart light. The light of eternity ought to make the things of earth grow dim. Heavenly glory ought to make the baubles of earth utterly insignificant to me.

Consider Your Father
"Your Father knoweth that ye have need of these things." This fact alone ought to make us perfectly content. All our needs in this world are perfectly known to our Father, the Lord of heaven and earth. He can relieve our needs whenever he sees fit; and he will relieve our needs whenever it is best for us that they be relieved. He who spared not his own Son, but delivered him up to death to ransom our souls, he who gave us his darling Son will not fail to give us everything we need (Romans 8:32).

Oh, for fresh supplies of grace, day by day, hour by hour, and moment by moment to trust him implicitly!

October 22
Today's Reading: Luke 13, 14
"Blessed is he that shall eat bread in the kingdom of God"
Luke 14:15

Why did our Lord speak as he did at this dinner party? Why did he do the things he did? Our Master's purpose in his behaviour and in his speech, here and always, was to teach and instruct us in very important spiritual things, to set forth the Gospel of God's free grace in him. Let me call your attention to some of the obvious lessons our Lord would have us learn from this passage.

Sinners' Saviour
The first thing to be learned from our Master here is the fact that the Son of God came into this world to seek, serve, and save poor, needy sinners, from whom he could never receive any recompense. Our Lord Jesus is the Saviour of poor sinners like you and me. Needy sinners, like the man described in verse 2, who had the dropsy. You and I are poor, helpless, perishing sinners. We can do nothing for ourselves. We cannot help ourselves. When the Lord first begins his work of grace in us, it is not because we want him, or have sought him, or come to him, or have prayed for help. Not at all! This man apparently expected nothing from the Lord Jesus. There is no indication that he even looked at him. But the Master took up the rich Pharisee's invitation to dinner because that poor man with the dropsy was there, for whom the time of mercy had come.

Lowest Place
The second thing that is obvious here is the fact that in order to save such poor, needy sinners as we are, the Son of God took the lowest place among men. Humility is a gift of grace. The grace of God humbles men. But our Lord is not teaching this crowd to make themselves humble, that they might be exalted and recompensed in the Day of Judgment. Indeed, such self-serving humility is no humility at all, but a mere show of humility. Our Lord is describing true humility, his own (Philippians 2:1-11). His humility is exemplary. We ought to be of the same mind. But he is the pattern. His humility was voluntary. He humbled himself unto the very lowest, not that he might be exalted, but for the love he has to us and to the glory of God. For that he has been exalted and shall be recompensed in the Day of Judgment (2 Corinthians 8:9; Isaiah 45:20-25; 53:9-12).

Resurrection And Judgment
The third thing our Redeemer teaches us here is that there shall be a Resurrection Day and a Judgment Day. All our Saviour did in this world he did with eternity before his eyes. He lived in constant awareness of eternity. God give us grace to do the same! We are immortal souls. We are all dying creatures, moving rapidly to the grave (2 Corinthians 4:17-5:11). There shall be a resurrection of the dead, both of the just and of the unjust, a resurrection of life and a resurrection of damnation (John 5:28, 29). There shall be a Day of Judgment at which we shall all be forever recompensed for all that we have done (Acts 17:31; Revelation 20:11-15).

Let us live like those who believe in a resurrection and a life to come, and desire to be always ready for another world. Living thus, we shall look forward to death with calmness. Living thus, we shall take patiently all that we have to bear in this world. Trials, losses, disappointments, ingratitude will affect us little. We shall not look for our reward here. Knowing that all will be rectified in that great day, and that the Judge of all the earth will do right, we shall patiently await that day (Genesis 18:25).

But how can we bear the thought of a resurrection to judgment? What shall enable us to look forward to death, the resurrection, the judgment, and eternity without alarm? Faith in Christ! Believing him, we have nothing to fear. Our sins will not appear against us. The demands of God's law will be found completely satisfied. We shall stand firm in that great day, and none shall lay anything to our charge (Romans 8:33). All whose names are written in the Book of Life, who stand before God in Christ, washed in his blood, robed in his righteousness, shall be forever blessed. And the bliss and glory and blessedness heaped upon the saved in heaven shall be a just recompense, an exact recompense, and an everlasting recompense of Divine justice (Jeremiah 23:6; 33:16; 50:20).

There seems to have been one man in that crowd who heard and understood our Lord's words. Perhaps everything recorded in this passage came to pass specifically because the Lord Jesus had come to this place, to this Pharisee's house to seek and find this one sinner, whose time of love had come. Look at verse 15. "And when one of them that sat at meat with him heard these things, he said unto him, Blessed is he that shall eat bread in the kingdom of God." I have found it so. Have you? "Blessed is he that shall eat bread in the kingdom of God."

October 23
Today's Reading: Luke 15, 16
"Fell on his neck and kissed him"
Luke 15:20

In the parable of the prodigal son, our Lord Jesus Christ uses the simplest, most vivid language possible to show us how delightful it is to the God of Glory to bestow his superabundant grace upon sinners. We are told, "When" the poor prodigal "was yet a great way off, his father saw him, and had compassion, and ran, and fell on his neck, and kissed him." He kissed him earnestly. He kissed him eagerly. He kissed him ardently. He kissed him much. He kissed him continually. Meditate upon those kisses. I remind you that in this parable the father's actions toward his prodigal son beautifully display the boundless, overflowing love of God revealed to sinners who come to him by faith in the Lord Jesus Christ. What do these many kisses mean? What do they teach us? They teach us that when a sinner comes home to God by faith in Christ, God welcomes the sinner with all the fulness of his infinite love!

Kisses of Love
The Father's kisses signify love deeply felt and demonstrably expressed (Ephesians 3:17-19). These kisses express the great, everlasting and eternal love of our heavenly Father for his people that is felt in the very heart of God. These kisses speak of the great manifestations of God's love in the experience of believing sinners. True love cannot be dormant. Like fire, it must be active. Like water, it must break out. It must show itself in words, actions, deeds, and expressions. Look yonder to Calvary, and behold the love of God for sinners (John 3:16; 1 John 3:16; 4:9, 10). Our blessed Saviour did not have to die. We had no claims upon him. There was no appeal on our part for him to die. When he died for us the Lord Jesus knew that if he laid down his life for such sinners as we are, he would get no love in return from those for whom he died, except he create it. The Son of God died by the hands of men, as well as for the sake of men. He died for men who wished that he should be made to die, for men who counted him worthy of death. In dying for us, the Lord Jesus Christ, the Son of God, voluntarily took upon himself the awful mass of shame and dishonour which we deserve because of sin, and took unto himself an infinite, indescribable, ignominious relation to sin (2 Corinthians 5:21). Truly, "we love him because he first loved us". These kisses of grace are the means by which we perceive God's personal love for us.

Kisses Of Forgiveness
The Father's kisses mean full forgiveness, freely bestowed (1 John 1:9; Psalm 103:12; Isaiah 43:25). God has promised that he will forgive the sins of those who seek him (Isaiah 55:6, 7). The Lord Jesus Christ has, by his own precious blood, purchased complete forgiveness of all sin for his people (Ephesians 1:3-7; Hebrews 9:12). Now, by his warm embrace and tender kisses, our heavenly Father makes believing sinners to know that their many sins are all and forever forgiven. His kiss tells me that all my sins are gone (Hebrews 9:26). He gives another kiss, and tells me that he will never remember my transgressions (Hebrews 8:12). With another, he assures me that he sees no fault in me (Numbers 23:21; Jeremiah 50:20). With yet another, he tells me that he will never treat me any less graciously because of my sin (Romans 8:1; 17).

Kisses Of Restoration
The Father's repeated kisses mean complete restoration (Ephesians 2:11-13). With a kiss God owns me as his son again (1 John 3:1-3; Galatians 4:4-6). With the kiss of his grace God answers all my prayers and more. Not only am I accepted as a favoured servant, I am accepted as his Son! With the kiss of God upon my cheek, I am assured

that all my lost, forfeited privileges are completely restored. The Father's kisses mean intimate communion and complete reconciliation established by grace.

Kisses Of Joy

The Father's kisses are tokens of great, abundant joy (Luke 15:22-24). The angels of God rejoice because the prodigal, over whom they have watched with great care, whom they constantly protected (Hebrews 1:14), has now come home. The saints of God rejoice, because a lost brother has now come home. The Triune God rejoices, because the object of his eternal love has returned to his bosom. He has been returned by the grace of God. Yet, he gladly returns of his own accord (Psalm 65:4). The prodigal himself rejoices. He rejoices in his Father's great, indestructible love. He rejoices in the fatted calf slain for his soul, the crucified Christ, feasting upon him with an insatiable appetite. He rejoices in the Gospel of peace, by which reconciliation is proclaimed in the depths of his soul. He rejoices in the Holy Ghost, the seal of covenant grace, by which he is assured of his adoption. He rejoices in the robe of perfect righteousness, the righteousness of Christ, wherein he stands forever accepted.

Kisses Of Comfort

Surely, these kisses from the lips of our Father mean overflowing comfort for the hearts of redeemed sinners. They mean the past is all forgotten. The present is all peace. We are immutably "accepted in the Beloved". The future is all secure. At home, in our Father's house, there is no possibility of expulsion, or of us ever leaving on our own (Jeremiah 32:38-40).

Once in Christ, in Christ forever!
None from him my soul can sever.

The Father's kisses are strong assurance of grace most free. God's kisses assure us that his mercy, love, and grace are all real. His incessant kisses assure us that his love is immutable, unfailing, and everlasting. His kisses assure our hearts that we are indeed his! The kisses of God are kisses from the lips of our crucified Redeemer. "Let him kiss me with the kisses of his mouth: for thy love is better than wine."

October 24
Today's Reading: Luke 17, 18
"Where, Lord?"
Luke 17:37

The Lord Jesus has just declared that when he is revealed there will be a division among men, "the one shall be taken, and the other shall be left" (vv. 34-36). The disciples failed to understand what the Lord was saying, as they often did, and as we often do. They wanted to know where the division would take place, looking upon our Lord's words as a prediction of something that was to take place at a specific time and in a specific place. Our Lord's answer has puzzled many. "He said unto them, Wheresoever the body is, thither will the eagles be gathered together."

What is the meaning of our Lord's answer? Modern translations have not helped, but only compounded the confusion. Most translate the word "body" as "carcass", and the word "eagles" as "vultures". In both cases such translations are wrong. Our translation is exactly as it should be. "He said unto them, Wheresoever the body is, thither will the eagles be gathered together". The word "body" means the body of one who has been slain. Notice the definite article. Our Lord said, "Wheresoever the body is (not wheresoever bodies are), thither will the eagles be gathered together". Also, notice that he speaks of "eagles" in the plural.

Context
Remember the context. Our Lord is talking to us about the distinguishing grace of God. He is talking about faith in himself. The body of the One slain is our Lord Jesus Christ. "The eagles" are God's elect who are gathered to him in faith. God's elect are spoken of in the Scriptures as eagles (Deuteronomy 32:8-12; Job 9:25, 26). His Church is given "the wings of the eagle, that great eagle" (Revelation 12:14). "They that wait upon the Lord shall renew their strength; they shall mount up with wings as eagles" (Isaiah 40:31).

Our Lord's answer to his disciples' question, "Where, Lord?" is this "Wherever Christ crucified is set forth in the preaching of the Gospel, wherever the crucified Christ is revealed to men, by the power and grace of his Spirit, through the preaching of the Gospel, there will his elect be gathered unto him 'in the day when the Son of man is revealed'." Christ's eagles "gather" to him who is their food. He is the One upon whom we live. He is to us life eternal. The body of our slain Saviour, Christ crucified, is the meeting-point of his elect. He is the great magnet, drawing needy souls like eagles to the prey. He said, "I, if I be lifted up from the earth, will draw all men unto me." God our Creator, in the book of Job, says of the eagle, his creature, "she abideth upon the rock from thence she seeketh the prey; her eyes behold afar off ... where the slain are, there is she". God our Saviour adds his application. "As the eagles gather round the prey, so the souls of men, chosen, redeemed, and called by my grace, are gathered unto me."

Keen And Swift
Keen and swift as eagles for the prey are God's elect for Christ crucified. These are the words of our blessed Saviour. Let not one of them fall to the ground. "Wheresoever the body is, thither will the eagles be gathered together." The eagle is a bird of prey. In all birds of prey there is great, vast quickness of eye to find their proper food, even from a great distance. Added to its keen eye, the eagle has a ravenous appetite. Compelled by hunger, it flies quickly, at every opportunity to its feast.

Eagles, Not Vultures

But the eagle is not a vulture. It does not feed on dead things, but living. And the crucified Christ, upon whom our souls feed, though once slain as our Substitute, is alive for evermore. If he has given us life in himself, if he has made us alive by his grace, he gives us a continually increasing appetite and hunger for himself. Does he not? Do you not hunger, my friend, for him? For his grace? For his embrace? For his face? For his righteousness? For his blood? For his presence? Hungering for him, his eagles fly to the place where he is, as famished birds hastening to the prey: his house, his Word, his ordinances, his throne of grace.

As David longed for the waters of Bethlehem when he was thirsty, let my soul long for Christ. "As the hart panteth after the water brooks", so he longed for his God. May the same be true of us. Oh, for grace to have our souls hungering for Christ crucified day and night! As the eagles gather together unto the prey, so let us be found relentlessly feasting upon Christ crucified.

Crave Him

Crave him! Crave him, O my soul! Like birds of prey crave their food, Spirit of God, let me crave my Saviour! We have tasted that the Lord is gracious in times past. Let us feast upon him! O blessed Saviour, give me such an appetite for you! Create a hungering in me for you, a hungering that graciously forces me ever to fly to you, like an eagle to the prey! Give me an insatiable, constant, ever-increasing hunger for you. For everything you are! For everything you have given me! For everything you have done for me! For everything that belongs to you! For everything that touches you! For everything that smells of you! Let me so lose my life in you, my great God and Saviour, that I care nothing for my stuff in the house of this time-bound world! Oh, let this desire be so insatiable, so earnest, so unceasing, that nothing I have of you may so satisfy me that I long no more after you. Let all that I have of you, O blessed Christ, enflame my heart, causing me to hunger for more and more, until you bring me at last to feast upon you and with you forever in the Glory Land above.

October 25
Today's Reading: Luke 19, 20
"And he was rich"
Luke 19:2

It is always profitable for our souls to read about the conversion of a sinner by God's omnipotent grace. It is especially profitable to read and study the stories of God's converting grace given to us in the pages of Holy Scripture. We should read them often and study them with care, asking God the Holy Spirit to teach us the wonders of his grace. When we read about the conversion of the Samaritan woman in John 4, the conversion of Saul of Tarsus in Acts 9, and the conversion of Onesimus in the book of Philemon, we find our hearts saying, "That is what the Lord has done for me." Do we not? Today we have read the story of Zacchaeus' conversion by the Lord Jesus. He was saved by omnipotent grace, because the Lord Jesus came down here "to seek and to save that which was lost". And our blessed Saviour never changes. What he did for Zacchaeus, he still does for sinners today.

Context

As we read this story, we should read it in its context. Look back to Luke 18. In verses 18-25 we read about the rich young ruler, who refused to bow to Christ. As he walked away from the Master, we read in verses 24-26: "And when Jesus saw that he was very sorrowful, he said, How hardly shall they that have riches enter into the kingdom of God! For it is easier for a camel to go through a needle's eye, than for a rich man to enter into the kingdom of God." In verse 26 the disciples asked, "Who then can be saved?" Then, our Saviour said in verse 27, "The things which are impossible with men are possible with God." Beginning right there, he proceeds to demonstrate the fact that he is that God with whom alone salvation is possible. He and he alone is able to save unto the uttermost all who come to God by him, for he is himself God the Son, God who came to seek and to save that which was lost. In verse 30 he tells us that the salvation he brings is "in the world to come life everlasting". In verses 31-33 he tells us how this salvation, this life everlasting comes to our poor souls by his death upon the cursed tree as the sinner's Substitute. In verses 35-43, giving sight and salvation to the blind man as he approached Jericho, he shows us that the sure result of his finished work of redemption is the salvation of sinners by omnipotent grace.

Solemn Words

"And Jesus entered and passed through Jericho." What solemn words! The Lord Jesus entered into Jericho, and passed through it. As he was approaching Jericho, he saved Bartimaeus (Mark 10:46-52) and the blind man we read about in Luke 18. As he was going out of Jericho, he saved two blind men sitting by the wayside (Matthew 20:29-34). A short distance further out of Jericho, he saved Zacchaeus. But we read of no wonders of grace performed in Jericho. Rather, here we read, "And Jesus entered and passed through Jericho." Back in the days of Joshua, hundreds of years before, the Lord Jesus found a precious jewel for his crown there in a harlot named Rahab. Indeed, he found many jewels for his crown there over the years (1 Kings 16:34). But now he passes through Jericho. It appears that there were none within the walls of that great city he had come to save. Now he finds jewels for his crown among the poor, the blind, the publicans, and sinners, who were the castaways of Jericho. Luke seems to be saying to us, "Never cease to adore and give thanks to God our Saviour for his sovereign, distinguishing grace." He who has mercy on whom he will have mercy, has not left us to ourselves! Let us rejoice and worship him (Psalm 116:12, 13, 17).

Grace Omnipotent

Zacchaeus' conversion tells us that the grace of God that brings salvation is omnipotent and irresistible. None are too sinful, too base, too vile, or too far gone for Christ to save. His arm is not shortened that he cannot save. Oh, no! His mighty arm is omnipotent in the operations of his grace! None are beyond the reach of omnipotent mercy! Here is a notorious publican transformed into a saint. Here is a rich man made to pass through the needle's eye into the kingdom of God. Here is a covetous man transformed instantaneously into a self-sacrificing philanthropist! Our all-glorious, ever-gracious Christ is able to save to the uttermost! Here is a Physician before whom none are incurable! Yes, "all things are possible with God" and Jesus Christ is God our Saviour! He still breaks the power of cancelled sin and sets the captive free. He still makes the lame to walk again and causes the blind to see!

Sovereign Election
Salvation comes to chosen sinners because the purpose of God according to election is sure. Salvation came to Zacchaeus because Zacchaeus was a son of Abraham. He may or may not have been a Jew outwardly. We are not told. Many of the publicans were Jews. Others were Gentiles. But this publican was a child of promise (Galatians 4:28), one of Christ's, an heir of promise because he was numbered among Abraham's spiritual seed (Galatians 3:29). He was by nature a coarse, wicked man (Matthew 18:17). Like you and me, he was a sinner by birth, a sinner by nature, a sinner by choice, and a sinner by practice. But he was distinguished from all others in the crowd that day by God's distinguishing grace and called, because God had from the beginning chosen him to salvation.

Oh, my soul, roll these things over in your heart day by day. Never lose sight of them. The Son of God had his eye upon you from eternity, just as he had his eye upon Zacchaeus. You were chosen by him in everlasting love (Ephesians 1:3, 4). Your name was written in the Book of Life before the worlds were made (Revelation 13:8; Luke 10:20). You were one of those sheep given to the Good Shepherd by the Father from old eternity (John 10:27-29). And it is written, "The flocks shall pass again under the hands of him that telleth them, saith the Lord" (Jeremiah 33:13). He said, "I will cause you to pass under the rod, and I will bring you into the bond of the covenant" (Ezekiel 20:37). And so it came to pass!

October 26
Today's Reading: Luke 21, 22
"Being in an agony"
Luke 22:44

What was the cause of your agony, O blessed Saviour? What was the cause of this great heaviness and sorrow, this grief and agony that crushed your holy heart? What was the great heaviness of your tender soul that night? What so greatly disturbed you, my Redeemer? I know it was not the fear of physical pain, the fear of death, or even the fear of dying upon the cross.

It was not death on the cross that our Redeemer agonized over in Gethsemane. He stated very emphatically that he came for the purpose of dying as our Substitute upon the cursed tree. We should read the record of our Saviour's agony here in light of his earlier temptation in the wilderness. After that temptation, Satan left him for a season, awaiting another opportunity to assault him (Luke 4:13). In Gethsemane the prince of this world launched his final assault upon the Lord Jesus. Just as he assaulted Adam in the garden of Eden, he assaulted the last Adam in the garden of Gethsemane. In Gethsemane the serpent bruised the heel of the woman's Seed; and in Gethsemane the woman's Seed again overthrew his assault.

Agony Of Anticipating
That which crushed our Saviour's heart was the anticipation of being made sin for us. The heavy, heavy burden which crushed his very soul was the enormous load of sin and guilt, the sin and guilt of all God's elect, which was about to be made His. Our Saviour's sorrow was caused by his anticipation of being made sin for us. "It was", wrote J. C. Ryle, "a sense of the unutterable weight of our sins and transgressions which were then specially laid upon him." He who knew no sin was about to be made sin for us. He who is the only man who really knows what sin is, the only man who sees sin as God sees it was about to become sin. He who is the holy, harmless, undefiled Lamb of God was about to be made a curse for us. The holy Son of God was about to be forsaken by his Father.

Sore Amazed
Our Lord Jesus Christ, the Son of God, "began to be sore amazed", to be in great consternation and astonishment, at the sight of all the sins of his people coming upon him, at the black storm of Divine wrath that was gathering thick over him, at the sword of justice which was brandished against him, and at the curses of God's holy law and inflexible justice, which, like thunderbolts of vengeance from heaven, were directed at him. In consideration of these things, our Saviour began "to be very heavy". That which crushed our Saviour's heart and soul was the very thing for which he came into the world: the prospect of what he must endure as our Substitute.

Substitution
The message of the Word of God in its entirety is substitution. The Lord Jesus Christ, the incarnate God, our Mediator and Surety, died in our place, in the place of God's elect as our Substitute. By his own blood, when he was made sin for us, when he was slain in our stead, he satisfied the justice of God for us, magnified his holy law, made it honourable, and purchased for us the complete, everlasting forgiveness of all our sins. He died, the Just for the unjust, that he might bring us to God. Christ died at Calvary so that God might be both just and the Justifier of all who believe. It is written, "By mercy and truth iniquity is purged" (Proverbs 16:6; Romans 3:19-28; Ephesians 1:7). Since the Lord Jesus Christ died as the sinners' Substitute, since he has met and fully satisfied the justice of God for us, believing sinners have no reason ever to fear condemnation by God, accusation before God, or separation from God (Romans 8:1-4, 31-39).

It was the enormous load of our sin and guilt which crushed our Divine Substitute's heart in Gethsemane (Isaiah 53:4-6).

Sin's Ignominy

What a horrible, monstrous, ignominious thing sin must be! Nothing so displays the exceeding sinfulness of sin as the death of our Lord Jesus Christ at Calvary. When the holy Lord God found sin on his own darling Son, he killed him. God poured out all the unmitigated fury of his wrath upon his own darling Son when he found sin upon him, and forsook him. Those facts ought to startle every human being. They assure us that if God finds sin on us, he will do the very same thing to us forever. Let us never look lightly upon sin. At the very thought of being made sin for us, our dear Saviour's heart was broken and he sweat "great drops of blood falling to the ground". O Spirit of God, let me never look lightly upon that horrid evil in me for which my dear Saviour suffered such agony and died such a horrible death in my stead!

October 27
Today's Reading: Luke 23
"Barabbas"
Luke 23:18-25

"And they cried out all at once, saying, Away with this man, and release unto us Barabbas ... And Pilate gave sentence that it should be as they required. And he released unto them him that for sedition and murder was cast into prison, whom they had desired; but he delivered Jesus to their will."

What a beautiful picture we have here of the Gospel. Barabbas, the guilty man, was set free. The Lord Jesus Christ; the holy, innocent Lamb of God, died in his place. A great sinner went free because a great Substitute took his place. Barabbas was spared because Christ died in his place. That is, in its very essence and glory, the Gospel of God. It can be summed up in one word Substitution (Romans 3:21-26; 5:6-8; 8:1-4, 32-34; 2 Corinthians 5:20, 21).

Christ's Death

Luke 23 describes the slaying of "the Lamb of God, which taketh away the sin of the world". Whenever we think about the death of our Lord Jesus Christ upon the cross, we ought to always remember three things.

1. The death of Christ upon the cursed tree was a substitutionary sacrifice. The Lord Jesus Christ did not suffer for any crimes of his own. He did not die because of his own sins. He was not cut off from the land of the living for his own transgressions. The Lord of Glory died upon the cross for our sins, for the transgressions of his

people, for the iniquities of God's elect, which were made his and justly imputed to him. Yes, our all-glorious Christ was made sin for us that we might be made the righteousness of God in him. He "bare our sins in his own body" upon the cursed tree, and was made a curse for us, that the blessing of God's salvation might be ours in him (Isaiah 53:4-6, 8; Daniel 9:26; 2 Corinthians 5:21; Galatians 3:13, 14; 1 Peter 2:24; 3:18).

2. The substitutionary sacrifice and death of our Lord Jesus Christ is the focal point, the essence, and the message of all the Word of God. The law was given at Sinai to show us our need of a substitute. All the sacrifices, rites, rituals, and ceremonies of the Old Testament Scriptures, all the priests, priestly garments, and priestly functions, all the deliverances of Israel from the hands of their enemies, all the services of the tabernacle and the temple, all the psalms, all the prophets, and all the historical narratives, the manna, the rock, the brazen serpent, the pillars of fire and cloud, everything in the Old Testament and in the New was written by inspiration of God the Holy Ghost to reveal Christ, to show us our great, glorious, almighty Substitute (Luke 24:27, 44, 45; 1 Peter 1:23-25; John 20:30, 31).

3. The cross of Christ, the doctrine of substitution, is both the revelation of the glory of God and the glory of the Gospel (2 Corinthians 4:4-6; Galatians 6:14). The death of Christ upon the cross, the sacrifice of God's Lamb as our sin-atonement, is the life of our souls. Had the Lord Jesus Christ not died in our stead, the justice of God could never have been satisfied; and we would have perished in our sins forever.

God's Unspeakable Gift
When the apostle Paul thought of these things, he said, "Thanks be unto God for his unspeakable gift." May God the Holy Spirit so graciously flood our hearts and souls with the knowledge of our crucified Substitute that we may ever have our hearts and minds fixed upon our blessed Saviour and his great sacrifice of himself for us, and have the apostle's words reverberating in our souls. "Thanks be unto God for his unspeakable gift."

October 28
Today's Reading: Luke 24
"Ought not Christ to have suffered these things,
and to enter into his glory?"
Luke 24:26

Our Lord Jesus here asserts again what he had so often told his disciples, that there was an imperative, an absolute necessity that he suffer all that he suffered in

Gethsemane, Gabbatha, and Golgotha. And he tells them that one aspect of that necessity was the fact that he could never have entered into his glory had he not suffered all those things as our Surety, Substitute, and Saviour.

God's Greatest Work
Without question, the most wondrous of all God's works is the work of redemption. When we attempt to contemplate what that work involved we are lost in astonishment. When we think of the unutterable depths of shame and sorrow into which the Lord of Glory entered to save us, we are awed and staggered. That the eternal Son of God should lay aside the robes of his ineffable glory and take upon himself the form of a servant, that the Ruler of heaven and earth should be "made under the law", that the Creator of the universe should tabernacle in this world and "have not where to lay his head", is something no finite mind can comprehend. But where carnal reason fails, God-given faith believes and worships.

As we trace the path of our Saviour from the throne of life to the tomb of death and behold him who was rich, for our sakes, becoming poor, that we through his poverty might be made rich, we cannot fathom the depths of the wonders before us. We know that every step in the path of our Redeemer's humiliation was ordained in the eternal purpose of God. Yet, it was a path of immeasurable sorrow, unutterable anguish, ceaseless humiliation, bitter hatred, and relentless persecution that, at last, brought the beloved Son of God, the Darling of heaven, to suffer the painful, shameful death of the cross. Who could ever have imagined such things as these?

Standing at the foot of the cross, as I behold the Holy One nailed to the cursed tree, covered with his own blood and the spit of an enraged mob, made sin, forsaken, and cursed of God his Father, yet, realizing that this is the work of God's own hand, I am lost in astonishment. I am filled with reverence and awe (2 Corinthians 5:21; Galatians 3:13).

A Question
Awed as I am with amazement for my crucified Lord, still there is a question that I cannot suppress, a question that reason and sound judgment cannot fail to ask. The question is, Why? Why did the Son of God suffer such a death? Why did God so torment his beloved Son and kill him in such a horribly ignominious way? Why, O my Saviour, why were such sufferings heaped upon your holy soul?

Was it to save my soul? I know that he died so that I might live. He suffered, the Just for the unjust, that he might bring me to God. But was there no other way for the omnipotent God to save me? Was all this done to demonstrate the greatness of God's love to me? Indeed it was (Romans 5:8; 1 John 3:16; 4:9, 10). But, surely, God could have revealed his love to me in some other way. Why did he slay his Son? What necessity was there for the Son of God to suffer and die upon the cursed tree?

Only one answer can be found to that question. The justice of God had to be satisfied. There was no necessity for God to save anyone. Salvation is altogether the free gift of his grace. But, having determined to save his elect from the ruins of fallen humanity, the only way God could save his people and forgive their sins was by the death of his Son, the Lord Jesus Christ. "Without shedding of blood is no remission" (Hebrews 9:22). The justice of God had to be satisfied in order for God to save his people; and the only thing that could ever satisfy the justice of God is the blood of Christ. Justice demanded it (Proverbs 16:6; 17:15; Romans 3:24-26; 1 Peter 3:18).

Christ's Glory
There is something else suggested in Luke 24:26. Christ could not have entered into his glory except by his suffering and death as our Substitute. By this justice is satisfied, righteousness brought in, his work finished, and the people he came to save delivered. Let us ever admire and adore the perfections of our God (Psalm 85:10, 11). Admire his love. Adore his mercy. Rejoice in his grace. Stand in awe of his wisdom, holiness, justice, and truth. All shine forth gloriously in the satisfaction of Christ. "For it became him, for whom are all things, and by whom are all things, in bringing many sons to glory, to make the Captain of their salvation perfect through sufferings." Divine wisdom found a ransom for our souls in Christ. Holiness approved of it. Justice is satisfied with it. Truth proclaims it. "Ought not Christ to have suffered these things, and to enter into his glory?"

———

October 29
Today's Reading: John 1, 2
"Him of whom Moses in the law ... did write"
John 1:45

In John 1:43 we are told plainly that the Lord Jesus found Philip. Then, in verse 45, Philip told Nathanael, "We have found the Messiah". Which is true? Did the Saviour find Philip, or did Philip find him? Without question, all who get Christ seek him. Seeking him with all our hearts, we find him (Jeremiah 29:13, 14). Then, finding him, we discover that we began seeking him because he had first found us by his grace. Knowing where Philip was, the Shepherd and Bishop of his soul looked him up, found him out, and called him by his grace. When he was found of the Saviour, he found the Saviour.

> I sought the Lord, and afterward I knew
> He moved my soul to seek him, seeking me;
> It was not I that found, O Saviour true,
> No, I was found of Thee.

All who are saved are saved by the will of God our Saviour; and we gladly acknowledge that to be the case (Romans 9:16; John 15:16).

455

The Message
Today, I specifically want to call your attention and my own to the fact that the Holy Spirit here reminds us again that the message of the Old Testament is the same as that of the New Testament. Both are united in declaring Christ crucified. Many read the Bible as though it were two books: the old Bible and the new Bible. That is a serious mistake. The Word of God is one Book of Divine Revelation; and the message of the Book is one. It is the Gospel of Christ. When Philip described Christ to Nathanael, he said, "We have found him of whom Moses in the law, and the prophets did write, Jesus of Nazareth, the son of Joseph."

One "Him"
All the Old Testament speaks of just one "him". It speaks of just one Man. Moses and the prophets had nothing to say about anything or anyone else. Perhaps you think, "The Old Testament speaks about many people and many things: Adam, and Enoch, and Noah, and Abraham, creation, the nation of Israel, the Egyptian bondage, the plagues, the Red Sea, the giving of the law, the judges, the kings, the Babylonian captivity, etc.." Most people would agree with you. But here we are told that there is just one "him" of whom Moses and the prophets wrote. This is confirmed in many places (Luke 24:27, 44-47; Acts 10:43).

Christ is the sum and substance of the Old Testament. The Apostle Paul asserts that Christ crucified is "all the counsel of God" (compare Acts 20:27 and 1 Corinthians 2:2). To him the earliest promises pointed in the days of Adam, Enoch, and Noah, and Abraham, Isaac, and Jacob. To him every sacrifice pointed in the ceremonial worship appointed at Mount Sinai. Of him every high priest was a type, every part of the tabernacle a shadow, every judge and deliverer of Israel a picture.

The Pentateuch
If we read only what was written by Moses in the books of the law, the Pentateuch, we would see the Christ everywhere in the first five books of the Bible. He is set before us by Moses as the Seed of the woman, who must crush the serpent's head, the Seed of Abraham, in whom all nations would be blessed, Shiloh, to whom the gathering of the people would be, and the great Prophet, like Moses, whom God would raise up among the Children of Israel and whom God's chosen would obey.

The Prophets
Not only is Christ the message of Moses, he is the message of all the prophets, too. "We have found him of whom Moses in the law and the prophets did write." All the law and all the prophets spoke of him. They wrote of his birth of a virgin, the place of his birth; Bethlehem, his sufferings and the glory that should follow, his resurrection from the dead, his ascension to heaven, and his mediatorial reign at the right hand of God. They asserted many things relating to his person, office, and work.

The prophets described him as the King of the house of David, who came to be David's Lord as well as his son. He is the Lamb foretold by Isaiah, the righteous Branch mentioned by Jeremiah, the true Shepherd described by Ezekiel, the Messenger of the Covenant promised by Malachi, and the Messiah, who, according to Daniel, was to be cut off, not for himself, but for the people.

Faith's Object
If you want to know in whom those saints of old trusted, just read the Old Testament. When Philip said to Nathanael, "We have found him of whom Moses in the law and the prophets did write," Nathanael knew immediately that Philip was saying, "Nathanael, we have found the Christ." The Person they all saw afar off, on whom they all fixed their eyes was one and the same Christ we trust and worship. The Spirit which was in them testified of Christ (1 Peter 1:11).

Do you find it difficult to see Christ in the Old Testament? Do I? If we do, the fault is all our own. It is our spiritual blindness and ignorance that is to be blamed, not the imaginary ambiguity of the Book. The eyes of our understanding need to be enlightened. The veil needs to be taken away. Let us pray as we open the Scriptures, "O Spirit of God, open this Book to my heart and open my heart to this Book. Take the things of Christ written upon these pages and show them to me."

October 30
Today's Reading: John 3, 4
"Wearied with his journey"
John 4:6

The word "wearied" tells us that our Saviour was tired; but wearied is a much stronger word than "tired". This word, "wearied", means tired, sick, worn out, exhausted, beat down, burdened. Our Saviour was "wearied".

Voluntary Weariness
He was weary with fatigue from his journey, weary with care for the souls of men, and weary with the burden of his heart, the burden he carried throughout the days of his flesh, the fact that soon he must be made sin to put away sin. This weariness was real, more real than any of us can imagine. Yet, our Saviour's weariness was a voluntary weariness. This was a part of the curse he had come to remove, the curse that was due us, and seized upon him as a man, from the moment that he came forth from the womb, saying, "Lo! I come to do thy will, O my God."

Sympathizing Priest
When he took our nature into union with himself, our dear Saviour "took our infirmities and bare our sicknesses" (Matthew 8:17). He bore our griefs and carried our sorrows all the days of his humiliation (Isaiah 53:4). "For it became him, for whom are all things, and by whom are all things, in bringing many sons unto glory, to make the Captain of their salvation perfect through sufferings." "Wherefore in all things it behoved him to be made like unto his brethren, that he might be a merciful and faithful High Priest in things pertaining to God, to make reconciliation for the sins

of the people. For in that he himself hath suffered being tempted, he is able to succour them that are tempted" (Hebrews 2:10, 17, 18).

Faithful Still

Child of God, when weariness seems to overwhelm you, look up to Christ. What an example he has given us. Though wearied more than any man, his weariness did not prevent him from continuing in his journey. Weariness did not prevent him from pushing forward in his work. Weariness did not keep him from doing his Father's will. Weariness did not keep him from serving the needs of a poor, eternity-bound sinner. Weariness with his journey did not stop our Saviour from finishing his journey in the death he accomplished at Calvary for us.

Robert Hawker rightly asked, "And what can bring (such) relief to the pilgrimage tears of the redeemed, or so sweetly soothe the wearied frames of his people both in body and soul, as looking unto Jesus?"

Exemplary Weariness

Was he wearied with his journey through this world as Jehovah's Servant? He truly was. Yet, he turned not back. So let me be found faithful to the end, though often wearied in the journey. Was he wearied with his journey? He truly was, but never murmured because of it. So let me never grumble about mine. Was he wearied with his journey, having no place to rest his head? Yes, he truly was; but he never let it disturb his peace. So let me not repine if I find the world treating me as an outcast.

Was he wearied with his journey? Though rich, yet for my sake condescending to be poor; though the Lord of Life and Glory, yet "a man of sorrows, and acquainted with grief." He subjected himself to hunger and thirst, weariness and affliction, temptation and buffeting. He was despised; yea, "a worm, and no man, a reproach of men, and the outcast of the people". He truly was.

Spirit of God, grant me grace in every trying circumstance of life, as oft as I am weary of the journey appointed me in this world, to behold my blessed Lord "Jesus being wearied with his journey, (as) he sat thus on the well".

October 31
Today's Reading: John 5, 6
"Testify of me"
John 5:39

The Word of God is not a book about science, but the Book about Christ. It is not a book about morality, but the Book about Christ. It is not a book about history, politics, philosophy, or law. It is not even a book about prophecy, church dogma, or theology. The Scriptures, of course, address all these issues and many others; but that is not what they are about. The Book of God is a HIM-BOOK. It is all about him, the Lord Jesus Christ. The message of Holy Scripture, in its entirety, is the Lord Jesus Christ and him crucified. There is not a page in the Sacred Volume that does not speak of Christ, not a page!

One Message
The Son of God tells us plainly that he is the message and theme of Holy Scripture, that he is the living Word of whom the written Word speaks. This is not a matter of conjecture, speculation, or hermeneutical principal, but something plainly stated in Scripture (John 5:39; Luke 24:27, 44-47). The Apostle Paul, writing by Divine inspiration, makes the preaching of Christ to be synonymous with preaching all the counsel of God, for Christ is all the counsel of God! He said to the Ephesians, "Wherefore I take you to record this day, that I am pure from the blood of all men. For I have not shunned to declare unto you all the counsel of God" (Acts 20:26, 27). To the Corinthians he wrote, "I determined not to know anything among you, save Jesus Christ, and him crucified" (1 Corinthians 2:2). And Paul was not one of those men who preached one thing to one crowd and something else to another. He was not the servant of men, but the servant of God. Therefore, his message was always the same. The Bible, the Word of God, is a Book with one message, and that one message is redemption, righteousness, and eternal life in Christ.

Old Testament Prophecy
The Old Testament Scriptures speak of Christ, point us to Christ, and call us to faith in Christ. From the moment that God announced in the Garden of Eden that the Seed of the woman would crush the serpent's head (Genesis 3:15), Christ was the central fact and figure of Old Testament prophecy. Abraham, Jacob, Moses, David, Solomon, and all the prophets spoke of him. Here are a few of the many prophetic statements that pointed directly to the coming of Christ, his glorious Person, and his redemptive work (Genesis 22:13, 14; 49:10; Deuteronomy 18:15-18; Psalm 2:7, 8; 45:6, 7; 110:3; Proverbs 8:22, 23; Song of Solomon 1:2-4; Isaiah 53:8-11; Micah 5:2; Zechariah 12:10; Malachi 3:1).

Old Testament Types
In addition to the direct prophecies about the coming of Christ, God gave numerous types and pictures to foreshadow his coming. The types are so numerous that I cannot begin to name them all. Let us consider just a few. They may be divided into four different categories:

Typical people such as Adam (Romans 5:14), Noah (Hebrews 11:7), Melchisedec (Hebrews 7:1-3), Moses (Deuteronomy 18:15-18), Aaron (Hebrews 5:1-5), Joshua (Hebrews 4:1-9), Boaz (Ruth 2:1; 3:18), David (Acts 2:25-36), Solomon (1 Kings 10:1-24).

Typical things such as the ram caught in a thicket (Genesis 22:8-13), Jacob's ladder (John 1:51), the brazen serpent (John 3:14-16), the paschal lamb (1 Corinthians 5:7), the scapegoat (Leviticus 16:21), the manna (John 6:32, 33), the smitten rock (1 Corinthians 10:4), the altar of sacrifice (Hebrews 13:10), the mercy-seat (1 John 2:1, 2).

Typical events such as the coats made for Adam and Eve (Genesis 3:21), the deliverance of Israel out of Egypt across the Red Sea (Exodus 14, 15) The slaying of Goliath (1 Samuel 17:38-54), the deliverance of the Hebrew men from the fiery furnace (Daniel 13-30); Daniel's deliverance from the lions' den (Daniel 6:4-28).

Typical places such as the tabernacle (John 1:14), the temple (John 2:18-20), the cities of refuge (Hebrews 6:18).

The lists could go on and on. I have not even mentioned all the instituted, ceremonial types, the sabbath days, and the many other instituted types of the Old Testament, all of which pointed to the person and work of Christ as our Mediator. The reason we are forbidden to observe any of those carnal ordinances of Old Testament worship is that Christ has fulfilled them all (Colossians 2:16, 17).

New Testament
Likewise, the doctrine and message of the entire New Testament is the Lord Jesus Christ. As he was pre-eminent in all the types and prophecies of the Old Testament, so he is pre-eminent in all the New Testament. The Four Gospels give us four views of Christ. Matthew presents him as the promised King. Mark presents him as the Servant of God. Luke presents him as the Son of Man. John presents him as the Son of God. The Book of Acts demonstrates that our Lord Jesus Christ was the singular subject of preaching in the earliest days of Christianity. The words "preach", "preached", and "preaching", are used thirty-seven times in the Book of Acts. Every time they are used the subject preached was Jesus Christ and the resurrection! If the Book of Acts is to be taken for our standard, it must be concluded that unless Christ has been preached, no preaching has been done. That man who pretends to be a preacher but does not preach Christ, and him crucified, mocks the people who hear him; and rather than serving their souls he destroys them! The Epistles reveal and explain the mysteries of Christ and his Gospel: justification by his obedience (Romans 5:1-21), sanctification by his blood (Hebrews 10:1-14), the universality of God's mercy, love, and grace in Christ (Ephesians 3:1-21). Grace is for chosen sinners out of every nation, kindred, tribe, and tongue, not just for Jews. The Book of Revelation is a declaration of the sure triumph of Christ and his church by the Gospel (Revelation 1:7; 5:9-14; 19:1-6).

Gospel Ordinances
The only two ordinances of worship prescribed in the New Testament are designed to focus our hearts upon our dear Saviour, the Lord Jesus Christ. Baptism is a symbolic burial and resurrection with him (Romans 6:3-6). The Lord's Supper is a symbolic remembrance of Christ Jesus and his great work of redemption as our Substitute (1 Corinthians 11:24-26). Without reference to Christ, the ordinances are meaningless rituals.

O Spirit of God, ever give us grace, as we search the Scriptures you have given us, to understand that the Book of God is about our Saviour. Cause us to see him in everything you have written in the Sacred Volume.

November 1
Today's Reading: John 7, 8
"Where is he?"
John 7:11

Everyone knew that the Lord Jesus would be at Jerusalem during the feast of tabernacles. The whole city seems to have been buzzing with one question. "Where is he?" Some sought him to kill him, others to make him a king. Some were curious about him. Some wanted to see his miracles, some to hear his doctrine, and some to experience his grace. Are you interested in knowing where the Lord Jesus Christ is today? Are you concerned about finding him for yourself? The Word of God tells us plainly where he is.

On His Throne
The Lord Jesus Christ is in the bosom of the Father (John 1:18). He is the centre of heaven. He is the Glory of glory (Read Revelation 4 and 5). He is on the throne of universal dominion (John 17:2; Romans 14:9). There he sits in the serenity of total sovereignty. There he must reign until he has made all his foes his footstool. Jesus Christ is Lord of all forever! He is at the right hand of the majesty on high, in the place of representation and advocacy as our great High Priest (Romans 8:27, 34). The Lord Jesus Christ is on the throne of grace, dispensing mercy to helpless, guilty, needy sinners. The Son of God is within the reach of needy sinners like you and me. He is a God accessible to all who seek him (Hebrews 4:15, 16).

With His People
We have found by experience that the Lord Jesus will be found of all who seek him. How often I have rejoiced to find you, O blessed Saviour, at the mercy-seat when, in the closet of my heart, I have cried to you in secret prayer (Isaiah 65:24). Or, discovered you in your Word (John 5:39; Luke 24:44-47), in the assemblies of your people (Matthew 18:20), at the table of remembrance, in the bread and in the wine, and in the field of your service (Matthew 28:18-20).

As we serve the interests of his kingdom, his people, his Gospel, and his glory; as we seek to do his will and honour his name; as we endeavour to serve the souls of men; as we try to serve our generation by the will of God; our Saviour says, "I am with you always". He is with us in sympathy to guide us, strengthen us, protect us, and to make our way prosperous and successful, according to the will of God.

In The Furnace
I have found him in every fiery furnace of trial, lion's den of persecution, storm of difficulty, and river of woe to which I have been exposed. I have been a lot of places. I have experienced a lot of things. I have known a few troubles along the way. But I have never been in any place of need without him who is my Rock and my Salvation (Isaiah 43:1-5). I have always found my Redeemer to be a God at hand (Philippians 4:4-7). Is it not so with you, my brother, my sister? What shall we say to these things? "Oh how great is thy goodness" (Psalm 31:19).

November 2
Today's Reading: John 9, 10
"The good shepherd giveth his life for the sheep"
John 10:11

The Son of God laid down his life and died for those people who are specifically designated his sheep (John 10:11, 15, 26). The objects of redemption, those for whom Christ laid down his life as a ransom price, are described as "sheep". They are the sheep of Christ, his special property as the Good Shepherd. As such, they were given to him by his Father from eternity. These sheep are represented as being everlastingly distinct from others who are not his sheep. The whole human race is divided into two groups: sheep and goats. Sheep never become goats; and goats never become sheep. All of us are one or the other, either sheep or goats. Some of the sheep are saved. Some are lost. But all are safe. They are "his sheep". Some are folded. Some are straying. All are redeemed. They are "his sheep". The Word of God tells us certain, specific things about these sheep, things which distinguish the sheep from the goats.

Known By Christ
The sheep are known by Christ. He says, "I know my sheep", but not merely by his omniscience. In that sense he knows all men. The Lord Jesus knows his sheep distinctly as his own in a way that he does not know those who are not his sheep (Matthew 7:23). The Lord knows them that are his from others. That is just another way of saying Christ loves his sheep. He has knowledge of them, joined with special love and affection for them, as he has not for others, to whom he will say, "Depart from me: I never knew you."

Know Christ
The sheep know the Shepherd, too (John 10:4). Christ is "known" by those sheep of his for whom he laid down his life. They all know him in his person, offices, and grace. Whereas there are many who neither know the Father nor the Son. The sheep

know the voice of Christ; that is, the Gospel of Christ, the joyful sound. Whereas the Gospel is hid to them that are lost.

Called And Follow
Those sheep for whom the Good Shepherd laid down his life, once they are called, hearing his voice, "follow" the Shepherd who died for them (John 10:27). They follow his Word, his steps, his example, and his Spirit. They imitate him in the exercise of grace, love, patience, and faith, and in the performance of every duty, such as baptism, the Lord's supper, etc.. It is written, regarding all the redeemed from among men, that they "follow the Lamb whithersoever he goeth" (Revelation 14:4).

Never Perish
The sheep, being ransomed by the blood of Christ, "shall never perish" (John 10:28). The goats, set on Christ's left hand, he shall command to go, as cursed ones, into everlasting fire (Matthew 25:33, 34). The sheep shall be blessed forever. They are forgiven of all sin forever. They are perfectly justified from all things, from which they could never be justified by the law. They are perfectly holy, righteous before God, having the righteousness of Christ imputed to them in free justification, and imparted to them in the new creation. The sheep of Christ have that blessed "holiness without which no man shall see the Lord". They are sanctified unto the Lord by the purpose of God, the blood of Christ, and the indwelling of the Holy Spirit. They are sealed, kept, and preserved in grace and life in Christ forever! All praise and thanksgiving I give to you for your abounding, free, immutable grace, O blessed Shepherd of my soul!

November 3
Today's Reading: John 11, 12
"If thou wouldest believe"
John 11:40

"Jesus saith unto her, Said I not unto thee, that, if thou wouldest believe, thou shouldest see the glory of God?" He is saying, "Have faith in God. Only believe. Be not faithless, but believing. Trust God in everything and for everything. Even in the most trying circumstances, say, 'Is anything too hard for the Lord?'"
　　Faith honours God and God honours faith! He always has and he always will. Ask Job (Job 1:20-23; 2:9, 10; 42:10). Ask Noah (Genesis 7:23). Ask Abraham (Genesis 22:8, 13, 14; Romans 4:20-22). Ask Hannah (1 Samuel 2:1). Ask Naomi (Ruth 4:14, 15). Ask David (1 Samuel 17:45-51). Ask the Widow of Zarephath (1 Kings 17:14-16). Faith honours God and God honours faith!

Believe And See

If we would believe, we would see the glory of God. Martha and Mary were placed in hard, trying circumstances. Their beloved brother was dead. What could they hope might be done? Had the Lord arrived earlier they might have hoped that he would have healed Lazarus. But it appeared that he had arrived too late. Lazarus was dead. They comforted themselves with the hope of the great resurrection. But for the present, Martha was full of despair. Then the Lord spoke to Martha, saying, "Said I not unto thee, that, if thou wouldest believe, thou shouldest see the glory of God?" It is as much as if he had said, "Martha, Martha, if you would just trust me, I would do for you far greater things than you could ever think or ask. If you would but trust me, there is nothing I would not do for you, no length to which I would not go, no limit to the power I would exercise on your behalf to show you the glory of God."

He says the same thing to you and me. Child of God, you may be enduring some great trial right now. But your trial is no greater than Abraham's when he was called to offer up his son, Isaac. If he believed and staggered not, if he hoped against hope and was strong in faith, giving God the glory, why should we not do the same? Are we the children of Abraham, to whom the "God of glory" appeared? Is it not reasonable for our Lord, who is always faithful to us, to expect faith from us? After all he has done can we be hesitating, fearful, and distrustful? God forbid! This is his promise, "If thou wouldest believe, thou shouldest see the glory of God."

Seeing God's Glory

If we would believe, we would see the glory of God in salvation by Christ our Substitute (Exodus 33:18-23). The glory of God can be seen only by those who are standing upon the mount of sacrifice, looking through the blood of Christ slain upon the cursed tree (Romans 3:24-26). In the cross of Christ, in his death as the sinner's Substitute, I see the glory of God. There "mercy and truth have met together; righteousness and peace have kissed each other" (Psalm 85:10). We see the glory of God most fully in the substitutionary sacrifice and sin-atoning death of the Lord Jesus Christ, because in his death all the glorious attributes of God are plainly revealed; his sovereignty and his grace, his righteousness and his goodness, his inflexible justice and his pardoning mercy, his unmitigated wrath and his everlasting love (Exodus 33:19, 34:5-7). Believing on the Lord Jesus, we see the glory of God in the sacrifice of his Son. But those who believe not, never can. Reason may see the doctrine of the cross; but only faith can see the glory of the cross. Only faith can see the glory of God in the face of Jesus Christ.

If we would believe, we would see the glory of God in his wise and good providence (Romans 8:28; 11:36). If Martha had believed, she would have seen the glory of God in Lazarus' sickness and death, and in her own grief as well. All things are of God; but only faith can see the glory of God in all things. How adorable his providence is! But only faith sees the glory of God in providence.

If we would believe we would see the glory of God in the works he performs in our midst. God's glory is seen in his works. And faith perceives both his work and his glory in his work. God's glory is to be seen in what he has done, in what he is doing, and in what he shall do.

If we would believe we would see the glory of God in the fulfilling of his promise. "Put me in remembrance: let us plead together: declare thou, that thou mayest be justified" (Isaiah 43:26). I wonder how much spiritual blessedness we miss simply because we do not believe God. Because we insist upon having much goods laid up for many years, we miss the blessedness of seeing God raining manna from heaven, giving us each day our daily bread.

If we would believe, we would see the glory of God in his resurrection power (John 5:25-29). I know that God works in total sovereignty. He depends upon us for nothing. His work depends upon us for nothing. But I know this also, God works in his sovereignty by the faith of his people (Ezekiel 36:33-38). I take Ezekiel's prophecy to mean that if we would but believe God, we would see his glory in spiritual resurrections, we would see God save his elect. Yes, God will save all his elect, when and where it pleases him. But I am certain that in the Church of God we lack for conversions only because we lack faith. It is written, "When Zion travailed, she brought forth her children."

And if we believe, we shall see the glory of God in the resurrection of our bodies at the last day (Job 19:25, 26).

God's Gift
Faith to behold the glory of God is itself the gift of God's grace and a work in which his glory is to be seen (Ephesians 1:19; 2:8; Colossians 2:10-12). We believe only by the working of God's mighty power in us, only by the gift of his grace. If we now believe God, it is by that very same power that raised our Lord Jesus from the dead, it is by the creative, resurrection, omnipotent power of the omnipotent God! Yet, our Lord Jesus declares, "If thou wouldest believe thou shouldest see the glory of God." Believe God! Believe, O my soul, and you shall see the glory of God (Mark 9:23, 24).

November 4
Today's Reading: John 13, 14
"Thou shalt know hereafter"
John 13:7

How many times have you seen or known some terribly painful, traumatic, almost devastating thing, and thought to yourself, "What good can come of this? How can this work for good? How will this benefit anyone? Can this be honouring to God?" We know that our heavenly Father is too wise to err, too good to do wrong, and too strong to fail. Yet, when tragedies come close to home, we cannot help asking, "Why did this thing happen?" We may not openly say it but in frustration, perhaps even in anger and resentment, we ask, "God what are you doing?" This is God's gracious, merciful answer to our astonishment, confusion, and unbelief. "What I do thou knowest not now; but thou shalt know hereafter."

Mysterious
God's ways are always mysterious to our eyes. He never acts like we think he should. When Jacob awoke from his dream, he said, "Surely, the Lord is in this place; and I knew it not" (Genesis 28:16). When Samson's strength was gone, we are told, "he wist not that the Lord was departed from him" (Judges 16:20). What is said of our God's presence and absence, of his comings and goings, may also be said of his doings. "What I do", he says, "thou knowest not now."

Confusing
Jacob cried, "All these things are against me" (Genesis 42:36), because he did not know what God was doing. Joseph's path of experience never seemed to match God's promise of grace until he was on the throne in Egypt and his family was saved. I am sure Moses was confused when he announced that God had sent him to deliver Israel and Israel turned against him, when their sorrow was increased. "Thy way, O God, is in the sanctuary; thy way is in the seas, thy paths in the great waters, and thy footsteps are not known" (Psalm 77:13, 19). "Thy judgments are a great deep" (Psalm 36:6).

Contradictory
Do God's providences appear to contradict his promises? Do his acts of mercy and grace in providence look and feel like acts of wrath and judgment? Sometimes God appears to be favourable to the wicked and angry with the righteous. Many, many things in this world are confusing to God's saints. He often seems to lift with one hand while casting down with the other, to heal with one and wound with the other. This should not surprise us. He told us plainly, "What I do thou knowest not now." And there is a reason for it. Our God and Saviour will not let us walk by sight in this world. He demands and deserves we walk by faith. Yet, he gives us this promise to assure and comfort our troubled hearts, "But thou shalt know hereafter". In God's time, all will be cleared up; and we will know what God has done (Romans 11:33-36).

November 5
Today's Reading: John 15-17
"I have chosen you"
John 15:16

What could be more astounding, amazing, awe-inspiring, humbling, and glorious to a hell-deserving, sinful wretch than the assurance of his personal election to salvation by God?

Overwhelming Love
Do not talk to me about saved sinners who hate the doctrine of election! No such creatures exist! Find a sinner, I mean a person who knows something of the utter depravity of his heart, his complete spiritual impotence, and his just condemnation. Let that sinner be assured by Christ himself that he is the object of God's everlasting love, infallibly and unconditionally chosen to salvation before the world began, and immutably predestinated to obtain heavenly glory in Christ (Jeremiah 31:3; Ephesians2:4-6; 2 Thessalonians 2:13; Ephesians 1:11; Romans 8:29, 30). Find such a man and you will find a man full of love, gratitude, and praise to God, whose soul is overwhelmed by the realization of God's electing love. Saved sinners bow before God with adoring hearts and cry with David, "Who am I, O Lord God, that thou hast brought me hitherto?" (2 Samuel 7:18). Humbled at the knowledge of God's election, they cry with Mephibosheth, "What is thy servant that thou shouldest look upon such a dead dog as I am?" (2 Samuel 9:8).

Humbling Election
Only arrogant, self-righteous men and women, who vainly imagine that they deserve special recognition from God, reply against God's electing, distinguishing grace, declaring, "That's not right." Believers always thank God for election (2 Thessalonians 2:13, 14). God's election humbles his saints. Believers know that we would never have chosen Christ. We had no desire for him. Had we a desire for him we had no ability to come to him. We were dead in trespasses and in sins. Yet, he chose us! He chose us because he loved us. He loved us because he would. Nothing else can be said about it. God's election is a matter of free, unconditional grace.

Faith
When does the Son of God say to a sinner, "I have chosen you"? As soon as he believes! We make our calling and election sure by believing on the Lord Jesus Christ. Faith in Christ is both the fruit and the confirmation of election. The Lord Jesus asks, "Dost thou believe on the Son of God?" (John 9:35). If you do, it is because "God hath from the beginning chosen you unto salvation through sanctification of the Spirit and belief of the truth" (2 Thessalonians 2:13). Rejoice, my soul, in God's electing love and adore him forever!

'Tis not that I did choose Thee, for Lord, that could not be;
This heart would still refuse Thee, hadst Thou not chosen me.
Thou from the sin that stained me hast cleansed and set me free;
Of old Thou hast ordained me, that I should live to Thee.

'Twas sov'reign mercy called me and taught my op'ning mind;
The world had else enthralled me, to heav'nly glories blind.
My heart owns none before Thee, for Thy rich grace I thirst;
This knowing, if I love Thee, Thou must have loved me first.

November 6
Today's Reading: John 18, 19
"Let these go their way"
John 18:8

Our Lord Jesus Christ was in the Garden of Gethsemane; and the soldiers came to arrest him. When they came to take him away, our Saviour gave this commandment to the soldiers concerning his beloved disciples, "If therefore ye seek me, let these go their way: that the saying might be fulfilled, which he spake, of them which thou gavest me have I lost none."

Tender Love
Do you see the love and care which our Lord manifested toward his people, even in the hour of his trial? His love is strong as death. He voluntarily gave himself up to the enemy, but demands that his people be set free as a condition of his surrender. As a sheep before her shearers is dumb, he opens not his mouth for his own sake; but for the sake of his disciples, he gives a commandment of sovereign authority. This is love; constant, free, self-denying, unchanging love. But there is far more here than is to be found upon the surface.

Effectual Redemption
This is a beautiful picture of our great Substitute in his work of redemption. The Good Shepherd laid down his life for his sheep, but the condition was this; those sheep for whom he died must therefore go free, every one of them! Our Surety was bound and slain for us; and justice demands that those for whom he suffered and died as a Substitute must be set free to go their way.

Set Free
The Lord God says to his Son, our all-glorious Christ, our Divine Substitute, "As for thee also, by the blood of thy covenant I have sent forth thy prisoners out of the pit wherein is no water" (Zechariah 9:11). In the midst of our worse-than-Egyptian bondage, that voice rings out as a word of power, "Let these go their way." Out of the slavery of sin, out of the bondage of Satan, out from under the curse of the law the redeemed of the Lord must come.

Justice Demands
The Lord Jesus says, upon the merits of his own infinite sacrifice, "Let these go their way." With the eye of his justice upon the blood of his Son, the Lord God says of all his elect, "Let these go their way." "Deliver them from going down to the pit: I have found a ransom." Satisfied justice demands it!

The thunder-cloud of Divine wrath burst upon our Saviour's head as he hung upon the cross of Calvary. Now God's elect, his chosen sheep, those sinners who,

being called by his grace, believe on Christ, they shall never be smitten by the bolts of the law's justice and vengeance. They must go free!

November 7
Today's Reading: John 20-Acts 1
"It is not for you to know"
Acts 1:7

Language could not be more emphatically clear. The Lord Jesus tells us, "It is not for you to know the times or the seasons, which the Father hath put in his own power".

Foolish Questions

All men are curious about the future. One aspect of man's universal fascination with the future is the fact that it allows him to momentarily escape the realities and responsibilities of the present. Another reason for this curiosity about future things is that all men want to avoid any present sense of guilt, condemnation, and judgment. Certainly, this curiosity also arises from the fact that all human beings have both a God consciousness and a sense of immortality, from which they cannot escape. But the fact remains God does not intend for us to know the times and seasons. He has given no man the ability to map out the future. He has given no man the key to discover the timetable of predestination. And he never will (Deuteronomy 29:29; 1 Thessalonians 5:1, 2).

God the Holy Ghost plainly warns us in Holy Scripture not to give "heed to fables and endless genealogies, which minister questions, rather than godly edifying which is in faith" (1 Timothy 1:4). We are expressly told to "avoid foolish questions" because "they are unprofitable and vain" (Titus 3:9). The attempts of men to pry into secret things belonging only to God reveals horrible pride and utter contempt for the revelation of God in Holy Scripture.

Revealed Things

There are some great events of the future clearly revealed in Holy Scripture; and those things that are revealed belong to God's elect. These are the things we are to look into, meditate upon, study, preach, and adore. The more clearly they are understood and appreciated by us, the better. It is by being instructed in these things that are revealed that God's saints are edified.

Here are some precious examples. All God's elect shall be saved (John 10:16; Romans 11:26). Christ is coming in power and glory (Revelation 1:7). There will be a resurrection of the dead (John 5:28, 29). All will stand in judgment before God (2 Corinthians 5:10).

The Lord Jesus Christ will create a new heavens and a new earth, wherein dwelleth righteousness (2 Peter 3:11-13). All the righteous will live in an eternal state of bliss and glory with Christ in heaven; and all unbelievers will exist forever in a state of undying death, misery, and woe, under the wrath of God in hell (Revelation 22:11). And, the Lord our God, in the Trinity of his sacred Persons, will be exalted, praised, glorified, and forever honoured by all things that are, have been, and shall be (Revelation 19:5-7).

Looking For Christ
God has told us plainly that these things will happen. But he has given us absolutely no information as to when these things shall take place. God does not tell us when the end of the world is coming. He does not even give us a single shred of evidence indicating the general course of events leading up to the time of the end. Those passages of Scripture that refer to "signs of the times" are referring to signs of events that have already taken place, by which these last days, which began two thousand years ago, were announced.

We are never told to be looking for signs of our Saviour's second coming. Look not for signs, my brother. Look not, my sister, for indications of the end of time. Ours is to live in the immediate hope and expectation of Christ's glorious appearing. Let us busy ourselves every day, serving him on the tiptoe of faith, in anticipation of his coming, "Looking for that blessed hope, and the glorious appearing of the great God and our Saviour Jesus Christ" (Titus 2:13).

November 8
Today's Reading: Acts 2, 3
"All that believed were together"
Acts 2:44

In the New Testament, three things always characterized and identified the people of God. There were three ordinances maintained in the early Church by which believers identified themselves with one another and with Christ.

Believers' Baptism
If you want to understand what the Bible teaches about any specific doctrine, you must go to the place in the Bible where that doctrine is taught and explained. Romans 6:1-11 explains the meaning of believers' baptism. Baptism, the burial of our bodies in water by immersion, is the believer's public, symbolic confession of faith in Christ. It is the answer of a good conscience toward God and a picture of salvation by Christ our Substitute, picturing the fulfilment of all righteousness by his obedience unto

death for us (Acts 22:16; 1 Peter 3:21; Matthew 3:15). Believers' baptism is the believer's public avowal of commitment to Christ and his people.

Church Membership
Many think little of church membership. Many who profess to be believers today are not identified with or committed to any local church. Whatever their reason they are wrong. In the New Testament, those who followed Christ, by one means or another, applied for and obtained membership in a local church (Acts 9:26; Romans 16:1).

The fellowship of believers in a local church is vital to their spiritual welfare. Our spiritual growth in the grace and knowledge of our Lord Jesus Christ is, in great measure, dependent upon our relationship to and fellowship with the body of Christ. Believers need the fellowship, encouragement, and strength of one another. The first sign of apostasy is usually seen in the neglect of public worship in the assembly of the saints (Hebrews 10:24-29).

The Lord's Supper
One of the most blessed privileges we have in this world is the privilege of coming together at the Lord's Table to celebrate redemption by eating the bread and drinking the wine that symbolize the body and blood of Christ. This is not an ordinance shrouded in mystery. It is a very simple, but very precious picture of our redemption by Christ (1 Corinthians 11:23-30). Like baptism and church membership, this ordinance is for believers only. Those who discern the Lord's body and realize their need of and interest in Christ as their Substitute, are worthy to receive the ordinance. They are worthy because they are in Christ. Those who do not trust Christ are not to intrude upon it.

How blessed are those saints of God in this world who, "continuing together with one accord ... eat their meat with gladness and singleness of heart."

November 9
Today's Reading: Acts 4, 5
"Salvation"
Acts 4:12

Salvation. What a blessed word! It is perhaps the greatest word in the language of man. I know it is the most blessed word there is to a lost, condemned sinner. Salvation is a very inclusive term. It takes in all the blessings of grace and all the bliss of glory. Salvation is the cleansing of our consciences from all guilt, the redemption of our souls from the curse of the law, the renewing of our hearts by the Spirit of God, and the deliverance of our spirits from the reigning power and dominion of sin. To be saved is to be loved and chosen of God, justified in Christ, born again by the Holy

Spirit, forgiven of all sin, adopted into the family of God, and accepted in the Beloved. If I am saved, I am an heir of God and joint heir with Jesus Christ! If I have salvation, I have wisdom, righteousness, sanctification, and redemption in Christ. Salvation is the undoing of all that Adam did, and more. Salvation is the total restoration of man from his fallen state. Salvation in Christ fixes our standing more secure than it was before we fell. Grace finds us broken in pieces by the sin and fall of our father Adam; defiled, stained, corrupt, and condemned. Salvation heals our wounds, takes away our curse, washes us clean, and sets our feet on the Rock Christ Jesus. And in its final end, salvation lifts us up above all principality and power, and crowns us with eternal glory in Christ, the King of heaven.

That which Paul states with regard to his deliverance from physical death by the hands of wicked men is a very good declaration of God's great work of grace in the salvation of our souls by Christ. "We had the sentence of death in ourselves that we should not trust in ourselves, but in God which raiseth the dead: Who delivered us from so great a death, and doth deliver: in whom we trust that he will yet deliver us" (2 Corinthians 1:9, 10). Salvation is the deliverance of our souls from the sentence of death by the grace of God.

My Experience
Allow me to tell you my own experience of grace. There was a time when I was "pressed out of measure, above strength, insomuch that I despaired even of life." There was a time when the Lord God caused me to see that I was a lost sinner, cursed, condemned under the just sentence of eternal death in hell. When I had the sentence of death in my soul, I was made to see that I should not, must not, and could not trust in myself. When the law of God had done its work, I was altogether shut up to Christ, graciously, sweetly forced to trust "in God which raiseth the dead". Yes, "salvation" is a big, big word. It includes all that is involved in delivering our souls from the sentence of death into "the glorious liberty of the sons of God". If you will search the Scriptures, you will find that salvation is described throughout the Book of God in various tenses. In fact, when we speak of "salvation" in Bible terms, we must recognize that it is God's work alone, and that it is a work with four tenses.

The Eternal Past
Salvation is a work of the eternal past. The Holy Spirit tells us in Hebrews 4:3 that all the works of God involved in this thing called salvation "were finished from the foundation of the world". God's elect were chosen in eternal love (Jeremiah 31:3), redeemed by the blood of the Lamb slain from the foundation of the world (Revelation 13:8), accepted in the Beloved and blessed with all spiritual blessings in him before the world began (Ephesians 1:3-6), justified, sanctified, preserved, and glorified in Christ by God's decree in old eternity (Romans 8:29, 30; 2 Timothy 1:9, 10; Jude 1).

The Historic Past
The Spirit of God also declares that our salvation was finished by the obedience of Christ as our Substitute in the historic past. When our Saviour cried, "It is finished", our salvation was finished (John 19:30; Hebrews 9:12). Redemption and

righteousness were finished by Christ when he died as our Substitute upon the cursed tree. He brought in everlasting righteousness for us, put away our sins by the sacrifice of himself, and made us the righteousness of God. When he arose from the dead, we rose with him. When he sat down in heaven, we sat down with him.

The experience of grace in salvation is also spoken of as something accomplished in the historic past. The experience of salvation involves that which we come to experience personally in time. It is the experience of the new birth, the experience of receiving Christ. There came a time when we were born again by God's omnipotent mercy and grace, being called from death to life by irresistible mercy, given faith in Christ and sealed in him by the Spirit of God (Ephesians 1:13, 14; 2:1-9; Psalm 34:6). Now we stand in grace experimentally (Romans 4:25-5:11).

The Present Tense
This thing called salvation is frequently spoken of in the present tense. We who trust Christ are being saved. Paul tells us in 1 Corinthians 1:18 that the preaching of the gospel is "unto us who are being saved" the power of God. In Romans 13:11 we read, "now is our salvation nearer than when we believed". Yes, I have been saved; and I am being saved. I have come to Christ; and I am coming to Christ (1 Peter 2:4). I am being saving in this sense, I am "kept by the power of God through faith unto salvation ready to be revealed in the last time" (1 Peter 1:5), being continually forgiven of all my sins by God's faithfulness, justice and grace in our Lord and Saviour, Jesus Christ (1 John 1:9-2:2).

The Future Tense
The Scriptures speak often of our salvation in the future tense, too. Truly, with regard to this matter of our salvation, "the best is yet to come". There is a very real sense in which the salvation of our souls is a salvation yet to be revealed (1 Peter 1:3-9). What a glorious revelation that shall be!

November 10
Today's Reading: Acts 6, 7
"They stoned Stephen, calling upon God"
Acts 7:59

The first martyr in the history of the New Testament Church was Stephen, a faithful deacon. The death of this faithful man is recorded more fully than the death of anyone else in the New Testament, except that of our Lord Jesus Christ. Here is a man dying for the testimony of Christ, dying by the hands of wicked men, but dying in grace and dying graciously for the glory of God.

The Spirit of God directed Luke to identify just one of Stephen's murderers. Those who stoned Stephen "laid down their clothes at a young man's feet, whose name was Saul". Saul was probably the man who examined Stephen and had been baffled by his speech when he stood before the Sanhedrin (Acts 6:8-10).

Striking Contrast

Here is a striking contrast. Stephen and Saul are in glory now. One cannot help wondering how Saul felt when Stephen's smile met him at the throne! What a joyous meeting they must have had, Stephen and Saul embracing one another! But in this world these two men are poles apart. They had nothing in common. Stephen was about to die. Saul was holding the clothes of those who stoned him. Saul was a proud, self-righteous Pharisee. He was proud of his pedigree, his learning, his works, his religious position, and his great reputation. Stephen was a broken, humbled sinner, saved by the grace of God, whose only hope was in Christ. Saul was wrapped up in himself. Stephen was wrapped up in Christ. His heart was elated not by looking into a mirror, but by looking to Christ, his exalted Lord. He drew his comfort not from what he had done, but from what Christ had done for him. Saul was a religious ritualist. He placed great weight and importance on the externals of religion. To him the law, the temple, the priesthood, and the ceremonies were everything. Stephen's religion was a matter of the heart, a living, spiritual union with God in Christ (Philippians 3:3; Acts 7:48-50). He knew that religious ceremony without faith in Christ is useless (Isaiah 1:10-15). Saul thought God was impressed with rituals and ceremonies. Stephen knew what few know "The Lord looketh on the heart" (1 Samuel 16:7; Luke 16:15). Saul defended his religion. For the defence of his religion he was willingly cunning, cruel, and callous. Stephen defended the cause of Christ, even at the cost of his own life. The cause of Christ, his Church, his truth, and his glory were of greater value to Stephen than life itself. Stephen was gracious to the end, ever truthful, gentle, forgiving, and self-sacrificing.

Overruling Providence

Our great God graciously overrules all things for the good of his elect and the glory of his name. The stoning of Stephen though a terrible act of barbaric cruelty and sin, was best, the very best thing that could have happened on that day. God was in total control of the situation. If Saul had not been there, Stephen would not have prayed for him. If Stephen had not prayed, Saul would have never preached. Even the evil performed by men and devils is good for God's elect, and shall bring praise to his name (Psalm 76:10; Proverbs 12:21; 16:7; Romans 8:28; 1 Peter 3:12, 13).

Dying Grace

When the time comes, the Lord God gives his people grace to die well. Those who die in the arms of Christ, who die in faith, die well. What God did for Stephen, he will do essentially for all who trust Christ. Stephen died, being full of the Holy Spirit, with his heart fixed on Christ, looking up steadfastly into heaven. He died without a care in the world, trusting his sovereign Substitute, calling on the name of God. He saw heaven opened! He saw the glory of God! He saw the Lord Jesus standing in the place of power to receive him! He died without any malice in his heart! Really, he did not die at all (John 11:25, 26). He simply dropped the body of death. He fell asleep in the arms of Christ and woke up in glory, in life! Blessed Saviour, give me grace so to live and so to die!

November 11
Today's Reading: Acts 8, 9
"Walking in the fear of the Lord"
Acts 9:31

Believers are people who walk in the fear of the Lord. God's people do not have a slavish dread of God. We are not afraid to speak to him and about him. We are not afraid that he will become angry with us, disinherit us or punish us for sin. Faith in Christ removes that kind of terrifying fear. Yet, the believer does not think, talk about, or speak to God carelessly, flippantly, or without reverence for his infinite, glorious, righteous Being. A true knowledge of the Triune God will produce godly fear in the heart.

Reverence
The fear of the Lord is simply reverence for him. It is much like the reverence a son has for his father, involving both love and respect. God has won the admiration of his children's hearts, causing us to reverence him. We revere his name, his Being, his Word, and his works. All that God is, all that has to do with him, all that he says, and all that he does is held in high esteem by those who know him.

Hate Evil
This fear of the Lord shows itself in many ways. To fear God is to hate evil. The man who knows God hates the evil of his own heart and life, hates the evil performed by others, hates the evil of false doctrine, which robs God of his glory, and hates those who perpetrate such evil. "Do not I hate them, O Lord, that hate thee? ... I hate them with perfect hatred: I count them mine enemies" (Psalm 139:21, 22).

Quench Not
We are urged to jealously guard the blessed joy of our communion with God, "walking in the fear of the Lord", when the Apostle admonishes us to "quench not" and "grieve not the Holy Spirit of God". Fearing the Lord, we take great care not to offend him. We cherish our fellowship with the eternal God; Father, Son, and Holy Ghost. Therefore we take care not to grieve and offend him. We want nothing to hinder the fellowship we enjoy with God our Saviour.

Withhold Nothing
The heart that fears the Lord withholds nothing from him, no matter how dear and valuable, when he calls for it. To fear the Lord is to worship him. It is to worship God, as he is revealed in Scripture, in our hearts. Such fear of the Lord is a continual and progressive thing. Believers walk in the fear of the Lord. The more we know him, the more we fear him.

Blessed Holy Spirit, give me grace day by day, that I may be found "walking in the fear of the Lord". Amen.

November 12
Today's Reading: Acts 10-12
"To him give all the prophets witness"
Acts 10:43

The chapters we have read today tell us about the way the Lord God taught Cornelius the Gospel, employing the use of both an angel of God and a preacher. How marvellous and delightful it is to be reminded of God's great goodness to our souls, as we read about his gracious dealings with this Gentile. He makes his angels to be ministering spirits to the souls of his elect, those he has ordained to be the heirs of his great salvation in Christ (Hebrews 1:14). And at the appointed time of love, when the chosen, redeemed sinner must be called to life and faith in Christ, the God of all grace sends a Gospel preacher to preach the good news of redemption accomplished by Christ Jesus, creating life and faith in him (Romans 10:17; 1 Peter 1:23-25).

Singular Message
In Acts 10:43 we are reminded again, as we are so often in the Sacred Volume, that the Book of God is all about his dear Son, our great Saviour, the Lord Jesus Christ. "To him give all the prophets witness".

The whole message of the Bible is Jesus Christ and him crucified. I would never say anything to lower your reverence for Holy Scripture. Indeed, what I am about to say, if you have a heart to receive it, will give you the highest possible reverence for the Word of God. If you removed Christ from the pages of Holy Scripture, you would have nothing left but processed wood in leather bindings. If you could squeeze the whole Volume of Inspiration down to its very essence and substance, you would find Christ, only Christ, and nothing but Christ. Our Lord said, concerning the whole of the Scriptures, "They testify of Me" (John 5:39). The purpose of God the Holy Spirit in moving men to write the Bible was to reveal Christ. That is the only purpose for which the Inspired Volume was given (John 16:14). To use the Scriptures for any other purpose is to misuse and abuse them.

Look For Him
I cannot find better words to express what I so earnestly want you to see than these of C. H. Spurgeon, "Brethren, we should always read Scripture in this light; we should consider the Word of God to be as a mirror into which Christ looks down from heaven; and, then, we looking into it see his face reflected as in a glass; darkly, it is true, but still in such a way as to be a blessed preparation for seeing him as we shall see him face to face. This Volume contains Jesus Christ's letters to us, perfumed by love. These pages are the garments of our King and they all smell of myrrh, and aloes, and cassia. Scripture is the golden chariot in which Jesus rides, and it is paved with love for the daughters of Jerusalem. The Scriptures are the swaddling bands of the holy child, Jesus; unroll them, and you find your Saviour."

When we read the Word, may God the Holy Ghost cause us to look for Christ and give us eyes to behold him. When we study the Word, let us study Christ. When we talk about the Word, let us talk of Christ. When we live by the Word, let us live Christ. And we who are sent of God to preach the Word, let us preach Christ.

November 13
Today's Reading: Acts 13, 14
"By him all that believe are justified from all things"
Acts 13:39

God the Holy Spirit sent out Paul and Barnabas by the Church at Antioch to preach the Gospel. Two key features of their ministry are revealed in Acts 13 and 14. First we see their faithful service, labouring in the Gospel, enduring trouble at the hand of a lost religious world set in opposition to God. Second we see the success of their labours by the blessing of God. Wherever they went preaching the Gospel, "as many as were ordained to eternal life believed" (Acts 13:48). In every placed, these faithful men preached Christ crucified, expounding "the Word of his grace" (Acts 14:3), declaring one glorious message to poor, needy sinners. "By him all that believe are justified from all things, from which ye could not be justified by the law of Moses." O bless his holy name forever, "God according to his promise raised unto Israel a Saviour, Jesus" (Acts 13:23).

Pause, my soul, and meditate upon this wondrous gift of God in the Lord Jesus. Your Saviour freely bestowed upon poor needy sinners by his immaculate mercy, complete justification! What can be more blessed?

Our Saviour
Poor, guilty sinners need a rich and holy Saviour. We cannot justify ourselves in the sight of God. With Job we cry, "If I justify myself, mine own mouth shall condemn me: if I say I am perfect, it shall also prove me perverse" (Job 9:20). None can be

justified by the deeds of the law; for by the law is the knowledge of sin. By the law we learn that we have sinned and come short of God's glory. The law identifies, exposes, and condemns sin; but the law cannot remove sin. We cannot be justified by the offerings and sacrifices made under the law of Moses; for the blood of bulls and of goats can never take away sin. How then, by what means can a sinner be justified? Who can perform this great work? "It is God that justifieth", and God alone; and even God himself can perform this great work only by the doing and dying of his darling Son as our God-man Mediator and Substitute; the Saviour he raised up according to his promise. "By him (the Lord Jesus Christ) all that believe are justified from all things."

Soul Satisfying
Oh, how completely satisfying to the conscience is redemption by the Christ of God, "whom God hath set forth as a propitiation, through faith in his blood". This blessing of grace reaches to all who believe. It is justification from all things! It is a present, and a gift. It is full, free, irreversible justification. "The blood of Jesus Christ his (God's) Son cleanseth us from all sin." The righteousness of Christ is to all and upon all that believe.

Rejoice as you remember that free, full, absolute justification means that all who believe are equally justified. Yes, some believers are strong and some weak, some are very knowledgeable and some not very knowledgeable, some are very experienced in grace and some are newborn babes in grace; but all who believe on the Lord Jesus Christ "are justified from all things". All are equally justified because all are fully justified. This is truly a soul-satisfying justification. Our justification does not hinge or depend upon our apprehension of it, but upon Christ alone. Who dares lay anything to the charge of God's elect? "It is Christ that died".

Everlasting Security
This complete justification of our souls is the everlasting safety and security of our souls. There is not in any believer a single spot or speck of sin before God, but only perfection and holiness; the perfection and holiness of Christ. There is nothing lacking in any believer. In union with Christ, being justified by his blood, "by him all that believe are justified from all things, from which they could not be justified by the law of Moses". Trusting him, we have "peace with God through Jesus Christ our Lord" and are assured by God himself that we shall never come into condemnation!

November 14
Today's Reading: Acts 15, 16
"Believe on the Lord Jesus Christ, and thou shalt be saved"
Acts 16:31

Faith in Christ is the gift of God. Faith in Christ is not hereditary. Faith in Christ cannot be produced by human logic or religious atmosphere. Faith in Christ is not the result of providential judgment, or even the terror of eternal damnation. Saving faith, true faith in Christ is produced in the hearts of sinners by the gracious operation of God the Holy Spirit (Ephesians 1:19; 2:8, 9; Colossians 2:12).

A Revelation Of Grace
In order for a sinner to trust the Lord Jesus Christ three things have got to happen: (1.) You must hear the gospel. No one will ever trust Christ until he hears the gospel preached in the power of the Holy Spirit (Romans 10:13-17). (2.) You must be born again. No man will ever trust the Lord Jesus Christ until he is regenerated, born again by the Spirit of God (John 3:3-8). (3.) Christ must be revealed in you. No sinner will ever trust the Son of God until he is revealed in his heart by God the Holy Ghost (2 Corinthians 4:6; Galatians 1:15, 16). Faith in Christ is produced by the revelation of Christ in the heart. As soon as a man sees Christ he will trust Christ.

Believe
Some, when seized by terror under a sense of God's wrath, thinking they can and must do something to appease God's wrath and save themselves, ask, "What must I do to be saved?" To such people we must respond, "Do?" You can do nothing to be saved! Salvation is by grace! The Philippian jailor, however, was not of this mould. His cry, "What must I do to be saved?" was the cry of a helplessly lost soul. He was so filled with despair that he was about to take his own life! When God's servants heard his hopeless, helpless cry, they answered, "Believe on the Lord Jesus Christ, and thou shalt be saved!"

Salvation is by grace alone and there is nothing you can do to earn or merit God's favour. Yet, you must believe on the Lord Jesus Christ. You must trust Christ as your Lord and Saviour. It is promised, "Believe on the Lord Jesus Christ, and thou shalt be saved." I urge you to do so now. Oh, may God give you faith in his dear Son!

Three Things
Faith in Christ involves three things. (1.) To believe on Christ is to bow to and surrender your life to the rule and dominion of Christ as your Lord. It is losing your life to Christ. No one will ever be saved until he raises the white flag of surrender to Christ in his heart (Mark 8:34-38; Luke 14:25-33). (2.) Faith in Christ is trust. You must trust the blood of Christ as your only atonement for sin. You must trust the righteousness of Christ as your only righteousness before God. You cannot be forgiven of sin, but by his blood. You cannot be accepted of God unless you are robed in righteousness. All who trust him are freely forgiven and fully accepted as justified

479

in God's sight (Romans 3:24-26). (3.) The proof of faith is confession (Matthew 10:32, 33; Romans 10:9, 10). And the believer's first act of confessing Christ is baptism. Baptism will not save you. But without baptism, faith is not complete. Baptism is the answer of a good conscience toward God. Until it is done, your conscience will give you no peace. If you believe, be baptized (Mark 16:15, 16).

November 15
Today's Reading: Acts 17-19
"This day's uproar"
Acts 19:40

The uproar of the multitudes against the saints of God at Ephesus was no accident. It was not the result of men being beyond God's control. Rather, it was one event among many by which the Lord our God sovereignly accomplished and is accomplishing his purpose of grace. The uproar came to pass because wicked men, with wicked hearts, for wicked purposes set themselves in opposition to the preaching of the gospel of God's free and sovereign grace in Christ. But God overruled their wickedness for the accomplishment of his good designs.

God Rules
God our Father rules everything in providence to accomplish the salvation of his elect and the glory of his own great name (Romans 8:28; 11:36). Nothing in creation is left to luck, chance, fate, or the will of man. Everything is directed by God so that in the end all his people shall be with Christ and like Christ (Romans 8:29, 30), and everything that has been shall praise him (Revelation 5:13). It was no accident that brought Rebecca to the well to meet Abraham's servant. It was not a streak of luck that brought Joseph to Egypt "to save much people alive". It was not by chance that Pharaoh's daughter found Moses in the ark and preserved him alive. It was not blind fate that directed the millstone which crushed Abimelech's head. Every event in history is directed by the hand of God. He even charges the lightning bolt to strike its mark (Job 28:26; 37:3; 38:25, 35). Study the events recorded in Acts 19:21-41 seeking to see how the hand of God sovereignly ruled, even amid the uproar at Ephesus; and understand that the unseen hand of Divine providence rules all things today for the good of God's elect and the glory of his name.

Led Of God
First, we see here that all who are born of God are led of God (vv. 21, 22). As it was the Spirit of God who led Simeon to the temple to see Christ (Luke 2:27), so it was the Spirit of God who led Paul from place to place preaching the gospel of Christ (Acts 20:22), and so it is to this day. The steps of God's people are ordered by God

the Holy Ghost: ordered by Divine providence and ordered by the guiding hand of God's Spirit in us (Psalm 37:23; Romans 8:14). Timothy and Erastus ministered to Paul and ministered to God's saints under Paul's direction (v. 22). They subjected themselves to the Lord's Apostle, being themselves filled with the Spirit (Ephesians 4:18, 21; Hebrews 13:7, 17). Those who are led of the Spirit submit themselves to those whom God has placed in authority over them.

Wrath Stirred
Second, the gospel of Christ always stirs up the wrath of men (vv. 23-28). Men are never indifferent to the message or the messengers of God's free grace. Anytime the gospel of Christ is preached in the power of the Holy Spirit, those who hear it will either bow to the claims of Christ or rise up in opposition against his ambassador (Matthew 10:22, 34). "There arose no small stir about that way." The gospel of Christ is distinct from the religions of men. The way of grace, the way of Christ, is not one way among many, but the way, "that way" that is altogether different from the ways of men. All the religions of men make the way to God and salvation dependent in some way upon man. But the way of freewill, works religion is the way of death (Proverbs 14:12; 16:25). The gospel of Christ makes the way to God and salvation to be Christ alone (John 10:9; 14:6). Notice two things in this portion of today's reading: (1.) The business of religion has always been, as it is today, a popular, profitable business (vv. 24, 25). These men made and sold religious trinkets, icons, images, etc. just as many today sell crosses, images, religious pictures, etc.. (2.) The gods which men make and cherish are puny, helpless things, worthy of contempt rather than praise (vv. 26-28; Isaiah 46:5-7; 1 Kings 18:27-29).

Trials And Persecutions
Third, trials and persecutions are for the good of God's people (vv. 29-34). Yes, even the wrath of wicked men is used by God for the good of his elect (Psalm 76:10). By means of this uproar and persecution, God's church was refined. The chaff was separated from the wheat. In the midst of the trial, Gaius and Aristarchus stood firm. Alexander the Coppersmith withered before the fire (1 Timothy 1:19, 20; 2 Timothy 4:15, 16). Yet, God stopped his mouth (vv. 33, 34).

Deliverance Sure
Fourth, the Lord knows how to deliver his people out of their troubles (vv. 35-41; Psalm 18:1-7, 43-50). The Lord God used the priests of the temple of Diana (v. 31) and a frightened town clerk to preserve his people from a raging mob. "Thus God, one way or other, sometimes by friends, and sometimes by foes, kept his church and people from being ruined; and his hand is not shortened now" wrote Matthew Poole. If the Lord our God will give us grace to trust his wisdom, love, and grace toward us in Christ and to understand that all things are under his absolute control, we will worship and trust him at all times, and give thanks to him at all times, in all things, and for all things (1 Thessalonians 5:16-18). O Spirit of God, give me such grace!

November 16
Today's Reading: Acts 20, 21
"Purchased with his own blood"
Acts 20:28

The Church of God is that which God purchased with his own blood. Yes, he who died upon the cursed tree is himself our God.

Atonement And Deity
Atonement for sin stands or falls with the deity of Christ. All who deny our Saviour's deity deny the atonement. What value or merit can there be in the blood of a mere man? And all who deny the efficacy of his atonement, that is to say, all who deny that all for whom the Saviour died shall be saved by the grace and power of his Spirit, deny his deity. They make his most important work, his most stupendous task, and that upon which the Triune God hangs his glory as God, a failure, asserting that he failed to accomplish his purpose in dying, that he shall never, with satisfaction, see of the travail of his soul. Such doctrine denies atonement altogether. Such doctrine leaves sinners with no atoning sacrifice for sin, and no hope.

Glory Revealed
The Gospel of God is the revelation of the glory of God in the face of his crucified Son, the Lord Jesus. When, with the eye of faith, we see the doing and dying of the Son of God, when we see Immanuel obeying the law, rendering by his obedience and death complete satisfaction to the violated justice of the Most High, offering a sin-atoning sacrifice to God for sin, then we see how the holy God can be "a just God and a Saviour". In the face of the crucified Lamb of God we see such glory, merit, and efficacy breathing through every thought, word, and action of our all-glorious Christ, that we embrace him with every desire and affection of our heaven-born souls, embrace all that he is, all he has done, all that he has.

All Our Hope
Christ crucified is all our hope and the whole of our religion. All God given faith, hope, and love flow to, and are fixed and concentrated upon Jesus Christ and him crucified. Nothing else can save and sanctify. Nothing else can clear the conscience of guilt, speak pardon to the soul, support us in life, comfort us in death, and make us fit for eternity. When the Lord Jesus Christ is thus revealed to us and in us by the omnipotent mercy of God the Holy Spirit, when he is brought near, we see, with the eye of faith, his pure and perfect humanity and his eternal deity. And these two distinct natures we see combined, but not intermingled, in one glorious Person; Immanuel, God with us. Until thus favoured of God, a person may see the deity of Christ taught in the Scriptures and believe it as a point of doctrine; but he does not

have that faith that appropriates the doing and dying of the God-man to himself, saying with Thomas, "My Lord and my God".

November 17
Today's Reading: Acts 22-24
"So worship I the God of my fathers"
Acts 24:14

The god of this apostate generation no more resembles the God of the Bible than a gnat resembles an angel. The puny, pigmy, frustrated god of our earthly fathers is an idol carved from the trees which grow wild in the dark forests of their depraved minds. The God of our spiritual fathers, the God of the Bible, is infinitely and indescribably above the gods of man's imagination.

The God of the Bible makes his worshippers (Isaiah 43:7, 14, 15, 21); whereas the worshipers of idols make their gods.

The God of the Bible is known by his self-revelation of the truth in his Word by the power of his Spirit (Matthew 11:25-27); whereas all the gods of men are known by teachers of lies, and their character changes from age to age, place to place, and circumstance to circumstance.

The God of the Bible inspires and causes chosen sinners to worship him "From me is thy fruit found" (Hosea 14:8; Philippians 2:13); whereas all worshippers of idols inspire and cause themselves to worship their gods.

The God of the Bible commands his position of sovereign supremacy and universal dominion by the might of his own power; whereas the breathless idols of men are manipulated by the hands and wills of men (Habakkuk 2:18-20).

The God of the Bible performs all his mighty deeds by his own mighty hands, and commands his worshippers to be still (Exodus 14:13, 14); whereas the gods of men sit still while their worshippers busy themselves with religious commotion.

Do you see the difference? The God I worship, "the God of my fathers", the Lord who is "the God" cannot even be compared to the gods of Arminian, freewill-works religion (Isaiah 46:9-11). That God who truly is God has distinct attributes which set him apart from all the gods of men, four distinct attributes which specifically set him apart from the imaginary god of this apostate generation.

Sovereignty

Our God truly is God. He rules all things, everywhere, at all times absolutely. A god who wants or desires or wills what he does not have, or what does not come to pass is no God at all (Isaiah 45:7; 46:9-11; Psalm 115:3; 135:6).

Holiness
"Holy and reverend is his name." When Isaiah saw the Lord God in his holiness, sitting upon his throne, high and lifted up, when he heard the seraphim cry, "Holy, holy, holy, is the Lord of hosts: the whole earth is full of his glory", he fell on his face and confessed his sin before the thrice holy God (Isaiah 6:1-8).

Justice
The God of the Bible is, unlike all the gods of men, just and true. He always deals with all his creatures upon the basis of strict justice. He will by no means clear the guilty (Exodus 34:7). Yet, this great sovereign, holy, and just God is infinitely and indescribably gracious.

Gracious
He says, "I will be gracious to whom I will be gracious". He found a way to deliver his chosen from going down to the pit (Job 33:24). That way is the satisfaction of justice by the substitutionary sacrifice of his own dear Son, our great Saviour, the Lord Jesus Christ (Isaiah. 53:4-6, 8, 9-11; 2 Corinthians 5:21).

November 18
Today's Reading: Acts 25, 26
"One Jesus, which was dead, whom Paul affirmed to be alive"
Acts 25:19

Paul was just the man to affirm it. After his resurrection, the Lord Jesus spoke to Paul from heaven. But Paul was by no means alone in this affirmation. John, the beloved apostle, gave the church his repeated testimony to it. The Lord Jesus not only made his appearance to John, in common with the other apostles, but appeared to him alone on Patmos and proclaimed, "Fear not; I am he that liveth, and was dead; and behold, I am alive for evermore" (Revelation 1:17, 18). Peter testified to the Saviour's resurrection before Cornelius and his household. All the apostles, being the Saviour's chosen witnesses, testified that they saw him and ate and drank with the Lord Jesus after his resurrection (Acts 10:41).

Resurrection Affirmed
How can I prove the resurrection of Christ in my own experience, so that, like Paul, I can with confidence say of this "One Jesus", this only One, this blessed One, who was once dead, I affirm him to be alive? Can that be confidently affirmed by me? Can you affirm it?

Remember, my soul, what the Saviour promised his chosen just before he died. He said, when redemption's work is done, "the Comforter, which is the Holy Ghost, whom the Father will send in my name, he shall teach you all things, and bring all things to your remembrance, whatsoever I have said unto you" (John 14:26). If God the Holy Spirit is come, then Christ is risen from the dead and ascended on high. God the Father has confirmed his perfect approbation of, delight in, and satisfaction with the righteousness and death of the Lord Jesus as the Surety of his people by raising him from the dead, setting him on his own right hand, and sending down the Holy Ghost, as the Saviour promised.

My Affirmation
But can I affirm the Saviour's resurrection in my own experience? Can you? If we are born of God and taught of God, we can. Is he my resurrection and life? Has he recovered me by the life-giving power and grace of his Holy Spirit? Has he brought me from death to life by his omnipotent grace? Is the Lord Jesus Christ the daily life-giving, life-imparting, life-strengthening source of all my faith, and life, and hope, and joy? Is Christ Jesus to my soul as the morning dew, reviving and refreshing me? Does He, by his Holy Spirit, convince me of sin, and righteousness, and judgment, causing me ever to confess my sin, trust his righteousness, and rejoice to know that there is no condemnation for my soul and no possibility of condemnation?

This "One Jesus" lived and died for me. Yes, I affirm by the sweet, daily experience of his life in me that he is alive! Do you so affirm his resurrection, not merely as a historic fact and a doctrinal truth, but as a matter of day by day life experience of his grace, his salvation, and his life? Let us then proclaim him to all, far and near, as his witnesses. Wherever we go, to all people, let us affirm that Jesus, the Christ of God, once died in the accomplishment of redemption and is now alive, saving those poor sinners for whom he died, "the Just for the unjust, that he might bring us to God".

November 19
Today's Reading: Acts 27, 28
"Broken pieces"
Acts 27:44

The Lord our God takes pleasure in using "broken pieces". In fact, it might be right to say, with regard to the people the Lord uses as instruments of good to his elect, he only uses "broken pieces".

Rare
A broken heart, a contrite spirit, and a subdued will are rare things, especially in this age in which men everywhere are taught to demand their rights; and the church house has become a place where man is exalted and enshrined as though he were God. Self-

485

esteem, self-worth, and self-promotion is the cry of the day. Every man does that which is right in his own eyes. All men by nature are very proud, selfish people.

Preachers today, knowing man's natural pride, have capitalized upon it. They have developed a flesh-pleasing theology of pride. Our forefathers exalted the dignity, majesty, and supremacy of the eternal God. Now smooth-tongued prophets of deceit in our day have set themselves to exalt the dignity, majesty, and supremacy of man. It seems that religion today is dedicated not to the honour of God, but to the honour of man. Its purpose is to make man feel good about himself. Therefore we hear little about brokenness of heart, contrition of the soul, and the subduing of man's will.

Yet, of this one thing you may be sure: "The sacrifices of God are (still) a broken spirit: a broken and contrite heart, O God, thou wilt not despise" (Psalm 51:17). The Lord God declares, "To this man will I look, even to him that is poor and of a contrite spirit, and trembleth at my word" (Isaiah 66:2). God will have broken material with which to build his kingdom. Sooner or later, the Lord God will bring us to nothing before his presence, or we will never experience his salvation. God's people, all of God's people, are a broken people.

Christ Revealed
No man has ever known the grace of God in salvation until his heart is broken before the holy Lord God, revealed in the crucified Saviour, the Lord Jesus Christ. If ever a man finds out who he is, who God is, who the Lord Jesus Christ is and what he has done for sinners, if a man ever really learns these things, he will be a broken man.

When Job saw himself in the presence of his three miserable friends, he vindicated himself, and even cursed his day. He said, "Why did I not perish from the womb? Why did I not give up the ghost when I came out of the belly?" But when he stood in the presence of God, he was a broken man; and he spoke as a broken man. He saw himself in all the hideousness of his sin; and he saw God, in all the holiness of his glorious majesty. Then he said, "Behold I am vile! I have heard of Thee by the hearing of the ear: but now mine eye seeth thee. Therefore I abhor myself, and repent in dust and ashes" (Job 40:4; 42:5, 6). There is no pride and egotism here, no haughtiness, no self-vindication. Once Job had seen the Lord, he was broken. He loathed himself and blamed himself. Once Job saw the Lord, he honoured God and vindicated him. The truly broken heart will always vindicate God, no matter the cost.

Found At The Cross
This brokenness can be produced in proud, stubborn, sinful men and women only by the saving revelation of Christ in our hearts. Brokenness is found at the cross, only at the cross. The Lord God declares that when he pours upon the hearts of his elect the Spirit of grace, then "they shall look upon me whom they have pierced, and they shall mourn for him, as one mourneth for his only son, and shall be in bitterness for him, as one that is in bitterness for his firstborn" (Zechariah 12:10). Have you been to the cross? Have you had the crucified Christ revealed in your heart? Has your heart been broken by the knowledge of the Lord? O Lord, evermore break our hearts before thee.

Discovering Christ Day By Day

November 20
Today's Reading: Romans 1, 2
"The name of God is blasphemed"
Romans 2:24

If ever a generation existed to which Paul's stern words of condemnation apply, it is the generation in which we now live. Ours is a generation under the judgment of God, because ours is a generation that has "changed the truth of God into a lie". Here are five fatal errors commonly taught by all forms of false religion, by which Satan destroys the souls of men, giving them a refuge of lies.

The basis of belief in the religious world today is not the Word of God but emotion, experience, and tradition. While appealing to the Scriptures and quoting them, men make void the Word of God by interpreting the Scriptures according to their feelings, experiences, and the traditions of men (Matthew 15:6, 9; Colossians 2:20-23). The basis of our faith is and must be the Word of God alone (2 Timothy 3:15-17). Any preacher, church, doctrine, or belief that is not according to the Word of God is not of God, but of the devil (Isaiah 8:20). It arises not from light, but from darkness.

Modern religion makes God's sovereign operations of grace to be nothing more than opportunities to be saved. Grace is God's almighty, effectual, irresistible work and operation by which salvation is wrought in us (Ephesians 1:18, 19; 2:8, 9; Colossians 2:12; Titus 3:5-7). Salvation is not God giving everyone a chance to be saved. He has never done that (Matthew 11:20-26). "Salvation is of the Lord". It is altogether the operation and performance of God (Romans 9:16).

All false, antichrist religion makes the cross of Christ of none effect. The heart of the gospel is the doctrine of the cross. And the heart of all false religion is its attempt to make the cross irrelevant and meaningless. Those who teach that Christ died for all men without exception make the cross irrelevant and meaningless in the affair of salvation. If Christ died for all men and some are not saved, then not only did he die in vain for those who perish but his death is evidently not the determining factor in salvation for any. The only relevant, meaningful thing must be the will of man. This is blasphemy!

The Word of God declares that the cross of Christ effectually accomplished the redemption of God's elect and infallibly secured their everlasting salvation (Isaiah 53:8-11; Hebrews 9:12; Galatians 3:13). To say that Christ died for everyone is to say that he died in vain. To say that Christ died for any who perish is to assert that his death did nothing for anyone, but only made salvation possible by removing the obstacles between God and man. The Word of God constantly speaks of Christ's sin-atoning death as a limited atonement. In the types of the Old Testament, sacrifices were provided and atonement was made for Israel alone. The rest of the world had no atoning priest, no sacrifice, no altar, and no mercy-seat. Even in Old Testament types the atonement was limited. It is limited to those who are loved of God (Psalm 5:5;

487

Romans 9:13), to those for whom Christ makes intercession (John 17:9, 20), to the Lord's sheep (John 10:11, 26), to the "us all" from whom God will withhold no good thing (Romans 8:32-35), and to those who are actually saved by it (Ephesians 5:25-27; Revelation 5:9, 10). Universal atonement is universal blasphemy, trampling underfoot the blood of our Lord Jesus Christ (Hebrews 10:29).

Modern, freewill religion reduces the work of the Holy Spirit in conversion to a moral persuasion that depends entirely upon the will of man if salvation is to be the result. We are told that the Holy Spirit calls all sinners to repentance and faith in Christ, and that those who are saved are those who by their freewill decision yield to the Spirit's call. Hence, preaching is reduced to one man trying to influence another man's will. Preaching becomes a sales job. Any means is justified, if the preacher can only get the sinner to "decide for Jesus". But according to the Word of God, salvation is the mysterious, miraculous work of God the Holy Spirit in the exercise of his sovereign, irresistible grace and power, by which sinners are raised from spiritual death to spiritual life and given faith in Christ (Psalm 110:3; John 1:13; 3:8; Romans 9:16; Ephesians 2:8, 9).

Modern religion also perverts the doctrine of the final perseverance of the saints, making it a matter either of carnal security or of spiritual probation. Some say, "Once saved always saved", giving unregenerate souls a false assurance based upon a false, empty profession of faith. Others say, "No, that is not right. Though you are saved, if you sin, you may fall from grace and lose your salvation." But God's Word declares that all true believers are saved forever. Being preserved and kept by the grace of God, true believers persevere in the way of faith and holiness until they leave this world and enter into glory (Job 17:9; Matthew 10:22; John 10:27-30; Philippians 1:6; 2:12; Jude 24, 25). Those who forsake Christ, his gospel, and his church have never been saved (1 John 2:19).

November 21
Today's Reading: Romans 3-5
"Propitiation"
Romans 3:25

What a sweet, sweet word this word "propitiation" is! Propitiation is the appeasement of God's wrath by the blood of Christ. The word "propitiation" is used three times in the New Testament. In all three places we are told that Christ is our propitiation. The very same Greek word translated "propitiation" in the New Testament is translated "mercy seat" in the Greek version of Exodus 25:21 and in Hebrews 9:5. The mercy seat which covered the Ark of the Covenant and covered God's broken law, upon which the cherubim were fixed, upon which they constantly looked, was the place where the atonement blood of the paschal lamb was sprinkled. The mercy seat was the seat of Divine Majesty where God promised to meet his people in mercy. To the mercy seat men were bidden to look in the hope of obtaining mercy from and communing with God following the appeasement of his wrath. Now we are bidden to come to the Throne of Grace that we may obtain mercy and find grace to help in time of need, because there Christ has sprinkled his blood.

The publican mentioned by our Lord in Luke's gospel had an eye of faith to Christ as the one represented in the mercy seat. He cried, God be merciful (be propitious) to me a sinner" (Luke 18:13). He sought mercy through the propitiatory sacrifice of the Lord Jesus Christ, the Messiah. The Lord Jesus Christ is our Propitiation.

Set Forth
"Whom God hath set forth to be a propitiation through faith in his blood, to declare his righteousness for the remission of sins that are past, through the forbearance of God" (Romans 3:25). The Lord Jesus Christ was set forth by God the Father to be our propitiation. He is the One who has made propitiation for us, the One in whom propitiation is found, the One for whose sake God is propitious to sinners, and the One who is himself our Propitiation. Christ is our Mercy Seat. He alone is the place where God meets with sinners, receives us, and blesses us. He is the One by whom justice has been appeased. He is the One who is our Peace. He is the propitiatory Sacrifice for our sins. Just as God, in the Old Testament types smelled the sweet savour of the typical, legal sacrifices, and was ceremonially content with them, so Christ's precious blood is a sweet smelling savour to him.

John Gill rightly tells us, "His sacrifice was an offering of a sweet smelling savour to (the Father). He was well pleased with it. It gave him contentment and satisfaction, because his justice was appeased by it and the demands of his law were answered. Yea, it was magnified and made honourable."

How has God the Father set forth his dear Son as our Mediator to be the propitiation for our sins? Obviously, Paul does not suggest that the Son was compelled to be subservient to the Father. Not at all. This thing was agreed upon by both the Father and the Son. The Son was just as willing to be our Propitiation as the Father is willing to receive his propitiatory sacrifice. Yet, the Holy Spirit here tells us that it was God the Father who set forth his Son to be a propitiation. How has he done this?

Christ was set forth to be the propitiation for our sins in the eternal purposes and decrees of God. He is the Lamb of God who, verily, was foreordained, before the foundation of the world, to be slain as the ransom price and propitiatory sacrifice for his people. His sufferings and death as such were according to the determinate counsel and foreknowledge of God (1 Peter 1:19; Acts 2:23; 4:28).

He was set forth to be our Propitiation in all the promises, prophecies, and pictures of the Old Testament Scriptures. He is the Seed of the woman promised to Adam and Eve in the Garden who must come to crush the serpent's head. He is the paschal lamb, the brazen serpent, the morning and evening sacrifice, and the promised Substitute of whom the prophets wrote.

Discovering Christ Day By Day

In the fulness of time, the Son of God was set forth as our Propitiation in human flesh. He was actually made of a woman, made under the law, that he might redeem his people who were under the law.

Christ is still set forth in the gospel to be the Propitiation for our sins, and shall be until time shall be no more. As God's servants faithfully expound the Book of God, preaching the gospel in the power of his Spirit, Christ is set forth as the only and all-sufficient, effectual Propitiation for our sins.

For Our Sins
"And he is the propitiation for our sins: and not for ours only, but also for the sins of the whole world" (1 John 2:2). The Lord Jesus Christ is the propitiatory sacrifice for the sins of God's elect, Jews and Gentiles, throughout all the world. He is the sacrifice upon which God is merciful to us, being pacified towards us for all that we have done (Hebrews 8:12; Ezekiel 16:6). Because Christ is our Propitiation, the propitiation for our sins, though we sin, we are not cast off and can never be in danger of being cast off! Because Christ is our Propitiation we joyfully sing with the sweet psalmist of Israel, "Blessed is the man to whom the Lord will not impute sin" (Romans 4:8).

Love Revealed
"Herein is love, not that we loved God, but that he loved us, and sent his Son to be the propitiation for our sins" (1 John 4:10). Because of his great love for us, God the Father sent his darling Son into the world to be the propitiation for our sins by offering up his soul and body as a sacrifice to Divine justice to make atonement for us.

When the Apostle John, guided by the Holy Spirit of God and writing by Divine inspiration, looked for a display of love, he looked not to the love of heavenly angels to God's elect, or the love of God's elect for him, or the love of God's saints for one another, or his own heart's love for God and his saints, but to the Lord God himself. Looking back to Calvary, looking up to God the Father in heaven, in all the wondrous splendour of his condescending grace and eternal mercy in sending his only begotten, dearly beloved Son into the world to die in the place of poor sinners like us, John wrote with joyful praise, "Herein is love!" He seems to be saying, all love is here, love at its utmost height, love at its climax, love outdoing itself. "Herein is love, not that we loved God, but that he loved us, and sent his Son to be the propitiation for our sins."

"Propitiation!" Sweet, sweet word from God with which to fill our thoughts this day!

490

November 22
Today's Reading: Romans 6-8
"Likewise reckon ye also"
Romans 6:11

Are you a believer? Do you trust the Lord Jesus Christ? If you do, because of your relationship to and union with Christ, who died unto sin once but is now alive unto God, you ought to reckon yourself in him, and reckon yourself dead indeed unto sin and alive indeed unto God. "Likewise", as Christ is, "reckon ye also yourselves to be dead indeed unto sin, but alive unto God through Jesus Christ our Lord".

O my soul, did you hear that? Is that God's word to me? Indeed it is. God the Holy Spirit here tells every poor sinner who looks to Christ alone for eternal salvation to reckon himself as God reckons him in Christ, "because as he is so are we in this world" (1 John 4:17), "dead indeed unto sin, but alive unto God".

Dead To Sin
Believers should always consider themselves to be dead indeed unto sin. Because we have been completely discharged from sin by the blood of Christ, we should not fear condemnation and death on account of it. Sin shall never be imputed to us, or have any power to condemn us. Christ, dying under the penalty of our sins, has satisfied the justice of God and put away our sins. Being dead to sin through the sacrifice of Christ, we should have no fellowship with it. "How shall we that are dead to sin live any longer therein?" Always look upon yourself as one who is dead to sin. And have nothing to do with it.

Alive Unto God
We should always look upon ourselves as being alive unto God. We are justified! The law of God has no cause against us. Having laid hold of Christ by faith, looking to him as our Saviour, we have received righteousness from him. And God declares that we are alive, spiritually alive and eternally alive. The perfect righteousness of Christ, freely imputed to us and imparted to us, gives us the right and title to eternal life to live with God forever. He "hath made us meet to be partakers of the inheritance of the saints in light" (Colossians 1:12).

Through Christ
The basis of this blessed assurance is Christ. We are to reckon ourselves dead unto sin, but alive unto God "through Jesus Christ our Lord". Being justified by his blood and born again by his Spirit, we live through Christ, by virtue of our union with him. And we shall live to God and with God forever. As Christ died, rose again, and lives unto God and with God in eternal glory, so shall we!

Being dead unto sin by his death and quickened together with him by his Spirit, the second death shall have no power over us (Revelation 20:6). We shall live forever! As we have experienced the first resurrection, the resurrection of our souls from spiritual death, we shall experience the second resurrection, the resurrection of our bodies from physical death. This is eternal life.

November 23
Today's Reading: Romans 9-11
"So then"
Romans 9:16

In Romans 8 God the Holy Ghost declares that all who are saved by grace in time were saved by grace from eternity, and that God rules the world to accomplish his purpose of grace toward us in Christ Jesus (Romans 8:28-30). In Romans 9 he compares the salvation of our souls to the work of a potter with clay, making one vessel unto honour and another to dishonour. In this indescribably sweet portion of his Word, God tells us that salvation is his work alone. How believing hearts rejoice to hear him declare, "So then it is not of him that willeth, nor of him that runneth, but of God that showeth mercy."

The language of Holy Scripture is so plain and clear regarding the matter of salvation by grace alone that only the wilfully ignorant and those who wrest the scriptures to their own destruction can fail to see it. Paul tells us here most plainly that salvation is neither by the will of man, nor by the works of man, "but of God that showeth mercy".

Not Our Will
Salvation is not accomplished by the sinner's free-will. It is true that no man is saved against his will, or without his will. All who trust Christ bow to Christ and worship Christ, and do so willingly. They are made willing in the day of his saving power (Psalm 110:3). But no one is saved because of his own will. The will of man is not the determining factor in salvation, but the will of God (John 1:12, 13). It is God's will that determined to save, elected a people, provided a Redeemer, and gives dead sinners life in Christ. The fact is man has no free will. His will is bound by his nature. His will is governed by the nature of his heart. Man by nature is corrupt, sinful, rebellious, and totally depraved. He has no will to be righteous, to come to God, to honour God, or to trust Christ and submit to his dominion, unless God gives him such a will by his Holy Spirit in regeneration. Salvation is not by our will. How thankful we ought to be that God's salvation does not wait on our will!

Not Our Works
And salvation is not in any way determined by or dependent upon the works of men. What monstrous pride and self-righteousness must that man be possessed of who supposes that his works have merit with God! Our best deeds are motivated by self-

492

love, at least in some measure. Our purest thoughts are vile. Our noblest ambitions are corrupt. God demands and accepts nothing short of absolute perfection, perfect righteousness, and perfect holiness. And these things no man can produce. We are saved by grace alone through the perfect righteousness of Christ. Christ's blood made atonement for our sins, satisfying the demands of justice (Romans 3:24-26). Christ's righteousness is bestowed upon us by an act of God's free grace (Romans 5:19-21).

But Of God
God is in no way obliged by the will or works of men to bestow his mercy. Man's will does not govern God's will; and man's works do not determine God's works. God is absolutely sovereign. It is his right entirely to give his mercy to whom he will, or withhold it from whom he will; and he can never be called to give an account of his actions to anyone.

God willed to be gracious for the glory of his own great name. Having determined to create a world with a race of angels and a race of men, he chose to save some angels in their original holiness and leave others to fall; and he determined to allow all men to fall into sin representatively in our father Adam, choosing to save some for the glory of his grace and to pass by others. God determined who he would save, choosing his own elect in Christ, and predestinating all things to bring them into their heavenly inheritance as the sons of God. God willed to give his Son to die as a sin-atoning substitute for his elect.

In his eternal purpose of grace, God looked upon his Son as the Lamb slain from the foundation of the world, and accepted his people in him. And in the fulness of time, God sent his Son into the world to magnify his law and make it honourable, so that he might be just and yet justify the ungodly. At the time appointed, God sends his Spirit to regenerate his elect and call them to faith in Christ by the gospel. This call of God the Holy Spirit is a sovereign, irresistible, distinguishing, effectual call. It goes only to God's elect, only to the redeemed; and it always results in salvation. And it is God who preserves his elect in life. His saved ones cannot perish. All of them will endure unto the end and be glorified at last. If even one of God's elect were to perish, his purpose would fall to the ground, the blood of Christ would be of none effect, the Spirit's power would be broken, and God's name would be mocked in hell forever. These things can never be. We are sure that God will be glorified in the salvation of all his elect, because nothing depends upon man, but all depends upon "God who showeth mercy".

Discovering Christ Day By Day

November 24
Today's Reading: Romans 12-15
"Now is our salvation nearer than when we believed"
Romans 13:11

What a blessed portion of Holy Scripture we have before us today! Romans 12 begins by calling us to the most reasonable thing in the world complete devotion to our ever-gracious Lord Jesus! Romans 13 assures us that our heavenly Father, the sovereign of the universe, rules all the rulers of this world. In chapters 14 and 15 God the Holy Spirit teaches us to love our brethren and bear one another's infirmities. All of this is written in the light of the glorious, blessed hope that is ours in Christ. "Knowing the time, that now it is high time to awake out of sleep: for now is our salvation nearer than when we believed."

God's Salvation
It is a common mistake among many to think of salvation only in terms of the experience of faith. But the Word of God never limits salvation to a time, a place, or an experience. When Paul writes, "Now is our salvation nearer than when we believed", he is clearly speaking of salvation as an ongoing process of grace. It is a process of grace that began in eternity past before the beginning of time, is experienced by faith in Christ in time, and shall be consummated in eternity to come when time shall be no more.

This great work of salvation is the work of God alone. It was planned by God, purchased by God, produced by God, is preserved by God, and shall be perfected by God. From start to finish, "Salvation is of the Lord." Therefore God alone shall have the praise for it. God's work of grace that is called "salvation" must be understood as a work consisting of three things.

Salvation Past
Salvation is what God has done for us in Christ. In eternity, before the worlds were made, the Lord God loved us, chose us, predestinated us to be his own, adopted us, accepted us, and blessed us; justified us, sanctified us, and glorified us in and with Christ (Ephesians 1:3-6; Romans 8:29, 30; Jude 1). Our salvation was arranged and accomplished in that covenant of grace ordered in all things and sure made between the three Persons of the Holy Trinity before the world began. In that everlasting covenant, God the Father became our Father, God the Son became our Surety, and God the Spirit became our Sanctifier. In time, our salvation was obtained by the obedience of Christ as our Substitute. We have been forgiven, justified, and sanctified by the merits of his righteousness and shed blood.

Salvation Now
Salvation is also what God has done and is doing in us. We were dead. He made us alive (Ephesians 2:1-4). He made us new creatures in Christ. He gave us a new heart, a new will, and a new nature in sovereign regeneration. He produced repentance and

494

faith in us (Ephesians 2:8-10). He is working in us to will and to do of his good pleasure (Philippians 2:13), and preserving us in life and grace by his almighty power (1 Peter 1:5).

The Lord God will save us through all the days of our earthly pilgrimage (Isaiah 41:10, 11; 43:1-7). I do not know what troubles we may face tomorrow; but God will not forsake us now. He will finish his work in us. He who has kept us and is keeping us will keep us still by his infallible, unfailing grace (Malachi 3:6). In the hour of temptation, God will save us. When Satan assaults, God will save us. Though trials come, one upon the heels of another, God will save us.

Salvation Near
As we have been saved by the decree of God, the blood of Christ, and the power of his Spirit, and are being saved by his almighty grace, so we hope that we shall yet be saved. In this sense our salvation is yet future. When the Lord God is finished with us, when our salvation is complete, we will be exactly conformed to the image of Christ (Romans 8:29). And he shall at last present us faultless before his throne, and in the ages to come shall "show the exceeding riches of his grace in his kindness toward us through Christ Jesus" (Ephesians 2:7).

We have good reason to anticipate the completion of our salvation by the grace of God. Our salvation will not be complete until the final restoration of all things under the dominion of King Jesus. But at God's appointed time, that shall come (1 Corinthians 15:24, 25). All Christ's enemies shall lick the dust before him and acknowledge his rightful dominion. He will rid the earth of all rebels against his throne, either by grace or by wrath. And sin shall be purged from God's creation. The glory of Christ shall be established everywhere and in all things. In heaven, earth, and hell everybody and everything shall glorify our Lord Jesus Christ. In that day we shall be conformed to the exact likeness of Christ our Saviour. Then, but not until then, our salvation will be complete (Romans 8:17-23). God will bring our bodies into union with our souls in perfect glorification. Then we shall be saved from all sin, all the consequences of sin, and all the sorrow that follows sin. We have been saved. We are being saved. And, soon, we shall be saved!

November 25
Today's Reading: Romans 16-1 Corinthians 3
"The God of peace shall bruise Satan under your feet shortly"
Romans 16:20

At a time in my life when I was weaker physically, mentally, and emotionally than I ever imagined I could be, a friend sent me a card with only a Scripture reference on it. When I looked up the text and read the words, I thought, "Oh, what a promise". Being blessed of God to my heart, it did more for me, and gave me greater strength, comfort, and peace than all the cards, letters, and visits of well-meaning friends. The text was Romans 16:20 "And the God of peace shall bruise Satan under your feet shortly. The grace of our Lord Jesus Christ be with you. Amen."

God Of Peace
Here is a most suitable title for our God. "The God of Peace." This is a title ascribed to him only by the apostle Paul (Romans 15:33; Philippians 4:9; 1 Thessalonians 5:23; Hebrews 13:20). He is called "The God of Peace" because he alone is the author, cause, and giver of all peace: temporal peace, spiritual peace, and eternal peace. God alone can say, "I make peace" (Isaiah 45:7). That "peace which passeth understanding" is God's gift to his people. His thoughts toward us were "thoughts of peace" from everlasting (Jeremiah 29:11). The covenant of grace is a "covenant of peace" made between God the Father, God the Son, and God the Holy Spirit before the world began (Isaiah 54:10; Ezekiel 34:25; 37:26). God the Father appointed his dear Son to be the Peacemaker between God and men. It pleased God to reconcile all things to himself by Christ (Colossians 1:19-22). The Lord God laid upon his Son the chastisement of our peace (Isaiah 53:5). God the Holy Spirit speaks peace to the consciences of chosen, redeemed sinners in effectual calling, when he applies the merit of Christ's blood to them (Hebrews 9:14). We find happiness and satisfaction in this world only to the extent that the peace of God rules our hearts and minds (Colossians 3:15).

A Sure Promise
Here is a sure promise for the tried. "The God of peace shall bruise Satan under your feet shortly." This is not a promise to everyone that is tried. But it is a promise for every child of God who is tried. Tempted, troubled, tried believer, read the promise and rejoice. Victory is sure. It will come speedily! Yet a little while, and he that shall come will come. When Satan seems to have prevailed, and you are ready to give up, he will come. And when he comes to your aid, "The God of peace shall bruise Satan under your feet." As Christ bruised Satan under his feet, so, too, shall he bruise Satan under your feet. Paul does not say that we shall bruise Satan under our feet, but that he shall. We are now out of the old serpent's reach. Soon we shall not even hear his hiss! Hold on a while longer. Be patient a little while more. "The God of peace shall bruise Satan under your feet shortly."

Amen
Until that time comes, here is a blessed benediction for your soul. "The grace of our Lord Jesus Christ be with you. Amen." All grace comes to us from Christ. And all grace is ours in Christ. His grace is sufficient to meet our every need in this world, even when Satan buffets us. And his grace will bring us to glory at last. The grace of Christ is sure to God's elect! Amen.

Discovering Christ Day By Day

November 26
Today's Reading: 1 Corinthians 4-7
"The mysteries of God"
1 Corinthians 4:1

The word "mystery", as it is used in the New Testament, refers to something once hidden but now revealed. That which was hidden under the types and shadows of the law is now revealed in the gospel. That which is hidden from natural, unregenerate, unbelieving people is revealed to believers by the Holy Spirit. The word is used twenty-two times in the New Testament. But the mysteries revealed are seven.

1. The Mystery of Godliness (1 Timothy 3:16) is the whole body of revealed truth regarding the Person and work of the Lord Jesus Christ the incarnate, crucified, risen, exalted, saving Son of God (Ephesians 6:19; Colossians 2:2; 4:3).

2. The Mystery of Faith (1 Timothy 3:9) is the message of salvation by the grace of God, through faith in the Lord Jesus Christ. It is the message of the gospel (1 Corinthians 2:7).

3. The Mystery of Spiritual Union (Ephesians 5:32; Colossians 1:27) is the blessed union of God's elect with Christ. We are in Christ and Christ is in us. Believers are so thoroughly one with Christ that all that he is and has as the God-man, we are and have in him. His doing is our doing. His acceptance is our acceptance. And his reward is our reward.

4. The Mystery of Providence (Romans 11:25-27; Ephesians 3:3-9) is the fact that God has always intended to save chosen sinners out of every nation. To that end he sovereignly rules all things. Even the fall and casting away of the Jews was used by God to be a means of bringing the gospel to the Gentiles.

5. The Mystery of the Stars and Candlesticks (Revelation 1:20) is the assurance given to faithful pastors (stars) and gospel churches (candlesticks) that they are in the hands of Christ, established, provided for, and preserved by him.

6. The Mystery of Iniquity (2 Thessalonians 2:7) and of Babylon (Revelation 17:5) is the wicked influence of freewill, works religion, as it is used by God to be an instrument of judgment upon those who receive not the love of the truth.

7. The Mystery of the Resurrection (1 Corinthians 15:51-58) is the wonder of how Christ will both raise the dead and reconcile all things to God (Ephesians 1:9, 10) at his glorious second advent.

O my soul, give thanks to God for his rich grace heaped upon you by his Holy Spirit, for "Unto you it is given to know the mysteries of the kingdom of God" (Luke 8:10). I am compelled to cry with my Saviour in gratitude and praise, "I thank thee, O Father, Lord of heaven and earth, because thou hast hid these things from the wise and prudent, and hast revealed them unto babes. Even so, Father: for so it seemed good in thy sight" (Matthew 11:25, 26).

November 27
Today's Reading: 1 Corinthians 8-10
"The Lord's table"
1 Corinthians 10:21

Let us take a few moments today to reflect upon and prepare our hearts for the Lord's Supper. May God the Holy Ghost ever make the observance of this blessed gospel ordinance sweet to our souls.

Every Lord's Day evening we gather around the Lord's Table to celebrate our redemption by Christ exactly as he commanded us, eating the unleavened bread that represents his holy humanity and drinking the cup of wine which represents his precious blood. This is a highly symbolic ordinance, full of instruction for all who behold it, delightful to all who participate in it properly, and honouring to our Redeemer. It has absolutely no saving merit or efficacy. It has no mystical power. It is not a sacrament (a means of grace), but an ordinance to be observed by those who have experienced grace. The table is an ordinary wooden table, not an altar. The bread is ordinary unleavened bread, not the body of Christ, except in symbol. The wine is ordinary grape wine, not the blood of Christ, except in symbol. Yet, the ordinance is highly significant.

Christ's Death
It symbolizes our Saviour's death as our Substitute (1 Corinthians 11:26). The broken bread portrays his body, crushed to death under the wrath of God for us. The cup of wine represents his blood, poured out unto death at Calvary for the remission of our sins, securing for God's elect all the blessings of the covenant of grace forever.

Faith In Christ
This ordinance is a declaration of our faith (1 Corinthians 10:16). Eating the bread and drinking the wine, we profess to all our faith in and dependence upon Christ's finished work for the pardon of our sins and righteousness with God.

Grateful Remembrance
Observing the ordinance is an act of grateful remembrance (1 Corinthians 11:25). It is an ordinance that can only be properly observed when it is observed in remembrance of Christ. It is meaningful only as it reminds us of who he is and what he has done.

Spiritual Union
The Lord's Table is a symbol of our union with one another in Christ (1 Corinthians 10:17). As the bread is one loaf, so all true believers are one body in Christ, because all are partakers of him.

Prophetic Picture
The Lord's Table is also a prophetic ordinance. It is the showing forth of the Lord's death "till he come" (1 Corinthians 11:26). As the Jews of old ate the Passover with their staff in their hands, their shoes on their feet, and their coats on their backs, so we must ever keep this ordinance in anticipation of that great day when Christ shall come again and feast with us in his Father's kingdom (Matthew 26:29).

November 28
Today's Reading: 1 Corinthians 11-13
"Not discerning the Lord's body"
1 Corinthians 11:29

Take a few minutes again today to prepare your heart for the Lord's Supper. I do not doubt that the verses 1 Corinthians 11:27-29 have been more troubling to sensitive souls than any others in the New Testament, simply because of the terribly poor teaching of men who do not understand the Scriptures. Many of the Lord's people read these three verses and think, "Surely, if anyone is unworthy to receive the Lord's Supper it is me." Satan roars against the weak, untaught, and poorly taught believer, accuses him of sin and guilt, and tries to put him upon a legal footing before God. The old serpent is hellishly subtle and clever. Under the guise of humility and holiness, he would have us turn our eyes of faith away from Christ to ourselves. He seeks to make us look to ourselves, rather than to Christ for our worthiness and acceptance before God. Who is and who is not worthy to receive the Lord's Supper? Let me answer that question clearly and distinctly.

Context
It is not possible to understand Paul's comments in 1 Corinthians 11:27-29 until we understand the entire context in which it is found (verses 20-34). For that matter, it is not possible to understand any text of Scripture isolated from its immediate context, and from the larger context of the entire Volume of Inspiration. In this part of 1

Corinthians Paul, by divine inspiration, sets before us the proper order of public worship in all gospel churches. The Holy Spirit tells us exactly what we should and should not do in the observance of the Lord's Supper.

Not Taught

Without question, there is a sense in which it may be said that we eat and drink the bread and wine unworthily, if we use the wrong elements, observe the ordinance without proper reverence, fail to properly think of and remember Christ our Lord, or do not clearly understand the meaning of the ordinance. All of those things are unworthy of men and women who claim to worship our God and unworthy of our great and glorious Christ. But none of those things can be found in this text.

Commonly, this verse is interpreted to mean that a person is unworthy to receive the Lord's Supper who has a certain amount of unconfessed sin in his life, has not prayed as he should, read the Bible enough, or lived as he should. Again, I grant, there is certainly a sense in which we are all unworthy to observe this ordinance, or any other ordinance of divine service, because we are sinners! But that certainly is not the meaning of the Holy Spirit's words in 1 Corinthians 11.

It is certain that the unworthiness spoken of here has absolutely nothing to do with the manner in which we keep the ordinance, or the depravity, sinfulness, and corruption of our hearts, or even the sins and evil behaviour of our lives, for one simple reason: that person who eats and drinks unworthily is guilty of the body and blood of the Lord Jesus. Therefore, according to verse 29, he eats and drinks damnation unto himself. Those things simply cannot be said of any true believer. No true believer can ever become reprobate and be damned (John 10:27-30; Philippians 1:6; 1 Peter 1:5; 1 Thessalonians 5:24; Romans 8:28-39; Malachi 3:6; Psalm 23:1-6).

Not Discerning

In verse 29 the Holy Spirit tells us exactly what it is to eat and drink unworthily. Those who eat and drink unworthily are those who do not discern the Lord's body. They are religious, but lost. They may know their church creed forwards and backwards; but they do not know God. They may be very smart and have much discernment about many things; but they have no spiritual discernment. They profess faith, but do not possess faith. They do not discern the Lord's body. That means they do not understand the sin and depravity of their own hearts, the law and justice of God, the necessity of Christ's incarnation, or the accomplishments of Christ in his flesh. That is to say, they do not know the gospel of the grace of God. Believers discern these things, unbelievers do not.

Not discerning the Lord's body, lost religionists practise religion and go through the bodily exercise of it, presuming that they are righteous. And this presumption of redemption, righteousness, regeneration, and acceptance with God without the knowledge of and a God given faith in the Lord Jesus Christ is damning. Therefore, the judgment of God falls upon many (v. 30), who like Uzzah of old, lift their hands to assist God in the work of salvation (1 Chronicles 13-15).

Discerning

Believers, discerning the Lord's body, judge themselves and are not judged with the world (v. 31; Psalm 51:1-5; Isaiah 6:1-6). And those who genuinely acknowledge and confess their sin before God are recipients of and have experienced the grace of God in Christ (1 John 1:7-10). They shall never come into condemnation. All who thus discern the Lord's body, all who knowing their need of Christ trust him, every true believer, every sinner who trusts Christ alone as his wisdom, righteousness, sanctification, and redemption is worthy of receiving, and is obliged to receive the Lord's Supper.

November 29
Today's Reading: 1 Corinthians 14, 15
"Then cometh the end"
1 Corinthians 15:24

When everything has run its predestined course, when time shall be no more, when this earth is dissolved in a ball of fire, the resurrection is past, and the judgment is over, we read, "Then cometh the end".

Though creation has revolted against God and sin has marred his handiwork, though it appears that everything here is in utter chaos, though antichrist seems to reign among men without rival, though Babylon, the great whore of free-will, works religion, has made all the earth drunk with the wine of her fornications, there is a day coming called "the times of the restitution of all things, which God hath spoken by the mouth of all his holy prophets since the world began" (Acts 3:21).

Though today all the world, all men, and all events appear to be set in direct opposition to Christ, there is a day coming called "the dispensation of the fulness of times", in which the Lord God will "gather together in one all things in Christ, both which are in heaven and which are on earth, even in him" (Ephesians 1:10).

Though all men by nature despise his rule, there is a day appointed by God, in which "at the name of Jesus every knee shall bow, of things in heaven, and things in earth, and things under the earth; and every tongue shall confess that Jesus Christ is Lord, to the glory of God the Father" (Philippians 2:10, 11).

Though all men by nature are the enemies of God, though Satan and all the demons of hell oppose his purpose, though men and devils unite as one in thought, word, and deed to rob the Triune God of his glory, in the end, through the blood of his cross, by our Lord Jesus Christ, almighty God shall "reconcile all things unto himself, whether they be things in earth or things in heaven" (Colossians 1:20).

Read what the Lord God himself has to say about the way things shall be in the end, and hearken unto the gracious counsel he gives (Isaiah 45:20-25). "Look unto me, and be ye saved, all the ends of the earth: for I am God, and there is none else."

501

In the end, every creature in heaven, earth, and hell, every deed performed in God's creation by men, angels, devils, and Satan himself; every deed great and small, good and evil, and every event of providence shall magnify, honour, exalt, and praise our great and glorious God. Then, when the end comes, the Lord Jesus Christ shall deliver up the kingdom unto God the Father (1 Corinthians 15:24-28). What do those verses mean?

Do Not Mean
First, let me tell you what they most certainly do not mean. When the Scriptures here declare that the Son shall deliver up the kingdom unto the Father, they do not teach, suggest, or in any way imply that Christ is not God (1 Timothy 3:16), that the Son of God is in any way inferior to the Father (1 John 5:7), or that Christ will cease to be Prophet, Priest, and King over his Church and Kingdom (Hebrews 1:8).

Christ's Final Work
What does Paul mean when he tells us that Christ shall deliver up the kingdom unto God, even the Father, and shall be subject to him? When the resurrection is over, when the great white throne judgment is done, and all things are created new, when all God's elect are saved, there will be one final work to be done by our Lord Jesus Christ as Jehovah's Servant, as the Surety and Mediator of the covenant. The Shepherd will present his sheep to the Father, who entrusted them to him. The Saviour will present his Church in glory. The Son will present his brethren, all of them, to their Father. The King will present his Kingdom to God, even the Father (John 10:16; Ephesians 5:25-27; Hebrews 2:13).

Augustus Toplady was exactly right when he wrote, "I take the kingdom to consist of that innumerable company whose names were written in heaven; and which, when their numerical fulness is completed, the Son of God, who graciously consented to become the Son of Man for their sakes, will present in one, entire, and glorified body to the Father."

In that great day, in the end, Christ will stand before his Father and our Father, with all his elect by his side in the perfection of his holiness, and say, "Lo, I and the children which thou hast given me. All are here. Not one is lost! All, my Father, you chose and gave to me, all you trusted me to redeem, here they are, just as I promised; holy, unblameable, unreproveable, washed in my blood, robed in my righteousness. All that I redeemed, every blood-bought soul is here. All those who have been regenerated, called, and sealed by the blessed Holy Spirit are here."

He will, no doubt, go on to say, "Now, my Father, all the purpose of grace is fulfilled. All the counsel of peace is accomplished. All that we agreed upon in the covenant is done. In all things our great purpose in predestination is now fully accomplished. Now grace reigns through righteousness unto eternal life."

God All In All
This shall be the end of all things, "That God may be all in all". God Almighty has from eternity ordained everything that comes to pass in time to make himself an everlasting and a glorious name (Isaiah 63:12, 14), that in all things Christ might have the pre-eminence (Colossians 1:18). And in the end, God, the Triune God, Father,

Son, and Holy Spirit, as he is revealed, known, loved, and worshipped in the Person and work of Christ, our God-man Mediator, shall be "ALL IN ALL".

November 30
Today's Reading: 1 Corinthians 16-2 Corinthians 3
"Where the Spirit of the Lord is, there is liberty"
2 Corinthians 3:17

What liberty is this? Being brought into the family of God, we are brought into the sweet liberty of grace here and shall be brought into "the glorious liberty of the children of God" in the world to come. But what is that liberty that is ours in Christ?

Acknowledged Facts
Honesty compels us to acknowledge certain facts. We are not here freed from the raging lusts of our sinful hearts; for we still carry about a body of sin under which we groan. We are not freed from Satan's temptations; for he still roars against us and hurls his fiery darts at our souls. We are not freed from temptations, trials, and troubles; for we still live in this world of sin and woe. It must be confessed, too, that we are not freed from inward fears; for our shameful unbelief begets many. Blessed be his name, we are not here freed from the chastisement of our wise, kind, and ever-gracious heavenly Father; for then we would never know many sweet visits of his love under the rod, by which he causes us to know and love him. And we are not yet freed from sickness and death; for the stroke of death we must feel, often preceded by painful and long illness. Our blessed Saviour has promised to make even our sicknesses good by his grace and has taken death's sting away by his blood and righteousness.

Blessed Liberty
From these things we are not yet at liberty, though chosen in eternal love, redeemed by Christ's precious blood, and saved by almighty grace. What, then, is that liberty that is given to our souls in and with Christ Jesus by the Spirit of the Lord?
God the Spirit, discovering to our souls the glory of the Lord Jesus and our interest in him, has brought us into liberty. Sweet and blessed liberty it is! Who can apprehend, let alone describe, the vastness of this liberty? We have access to the Throne of Grace at all times and upon all occasions. Having received the Spirit of adoption, we cry "Abba, Father!" We lift our hearts to heaven and confidently call the Lord God himself our Father! The Spirit bears witness with our spirits, that we are children of God. We are freed from the burden of sin's guilt and the fear of its punishment. O sweet, sweet liberty!

503

"Where the Spirit of the Lord is there is liberty!" God's law, being magnified and made honourable by Christ, justice is satisfied and everlasting righteousness is ours. Justice no longer terrifies. The accusations of Satan are all answered. Conscience is appeased. This is liberty; is it not? Having passed from death to life, we have peace with God through the blood of the cross. "There is therefore now no condemnation to them which are in Christ Jesus, who walk not after the flesh, but after the Spirit!"

This liberty is ours, child of God, because of our oneness with Christ. We can no more be brought into the bondage of sin, and guilt, and death, and law than he can. This blessed liberty ought to sustain our souls and cheer our hearts in the face of every temptation, every sorrow, every trial, and every affliction!

Shout, my soul, and echo to the apostle's words, "Where the Spirit of the Lord is there is liberty!" All the liberty of grace and all the liberty of glory too! Liberty to adore, worship, love, trust, and live forever with God our Saviour; Father, Son, and Holy Ghost, who opened our prison doors and brought us out of the deep pit wherein was no water and no light!

Change Made

When God the Spirit reveals Christ in the chosen, redeemed sinner, causing the heaven-born soul to behold with open face, as in a mirror, "the glory of the Lord" a marvellous change takes place. Looking to our dear Saviour by faith, we are changed into his image. Beholding Christ in his glory, admiring him, being ravished with his love, we imitate the One we love. Constrained by his love for us and the love he has created in us for him, saved sinners seek to be made like the Saviour, and are made like him. O wondrous liberty!

Blessed Lord Jesus, be it my portion here to behold your face in righteousness, until I awake in your likeness in glory in complete and everlasting satisfaction (Psalm 17:15). Truly, this is "the glorious liberty of the children of God!"

Discovering Christ Day By Day

December 1
Today's Reading: 2 Corinthians 4-7
"He hath made him to be sin for us"
2 Corinthians 5:21

In order to save me, the Lord Jesus Christ was made to be sin for me. The Son of God voluntarily took upon himself that horrible, ugly, vile, ignominious thing which he most hates: sin. O my soul, be forever astonished! The God-man became sin for me, that I might be made the righteousness of God in him!

A Door Opened For Sinners
When he was made to be sin for me, my sins were imputed to him; he was treated as the obnoxious thing itself, and suffered all the wrath of God due to me for my sin. The Father forsook him. Justice was executed upon him. And when the infinite justice of God had spent itself upon the sinners' Substitute, a door was opened in heaven for sinners, whereby we may draw near to God (Hebrews 10:19-23).

"For Us"
Christ was made to be sin "for us". That little word "us" is very important. Every time the Bible sets forth the glorious, gospel doctrine of substitutionary redemption, every time the Word of God explains the meaning of Christ's death and the atonement he made for sinners at Calvary, it speaks of his work as something done for a specific people, by which he accomplished the eternal redemption and secured the everlasting salvation of a specific people called "us". The Son of God was made to be sin for, and redeemed, "us". "Us" whom he came to save (Matthew 1:21). "Us" his church and espoused bride (Ephesians 5:25-27). "Us" for whom he prays (John 17:9, 20). "Us" who are the elect of God (Ephesians 1:3-6). "Us" who come to God by him (Hebrews 7:25). "Us" who, walking in the light of the gospel, believe on him (1 John 1:7, 9).

Like all the other blessings of grace, redemption is for God's elect alone. If Christ were Surety and Substitute for all men, then all men must be saved. Had he paid the debt of all men, then none could ever suffer the wrath of God for sin. Justice would not allow it. But that he did not do. Jesus Christ died for us. He died for me and paid my debt in full. How I rejoice to know that I shall, therefore, never be called to account for myself.

Security In Christ
I know that Christ died for me because I trust him. My faith in him which is the gift of his Spirit, is the result of his death for me (Galatians 3:13, 14). Oh, how the Son of God must love me (1 John 4:9, 10). Oh, how I ought to love him! Now, in him I am absolutely safe and secure. Christ has magnified the law and made it honourable for

me. He has put away my sin. This sinner, for whom the Son of God was made to be sin, can never be charged with sin again (Romans 4:8; 8:34).

> He bore that I might never bear
> His Father's righteous ire!

In him, God is both just and the justifier of this sinner, who believes on his Son (Romans 3:24-26).

December 2
Today's Reading: 2 Corinthians 8-11
"The simplicity that is in Christ"
2 Corinthians 11:3

"I fear, lest by any means, as the serpent beguiled Eve through his subtilty, so your minds should be corrupted from the simplicity that is in Christ" (2 Corinthians 11:3). Satan is a crafty, subtle deceiver. He does not care what the issue is by which men and women are beguiled so long as they are beguiled. He does not care what he gets you to embrace so long as he gets you to turn away from Christ. When the fiend of hell turns anyone away from Christ he has won the day. Here are four dangers we are all naturally susceptible to, four snares of Satan multitudes have been deceived by. Many who were once so promising, so encouraging, so impressive have been turned away from Christ by one of these four satanic snares. Mark them and be warned.

Worldliness
Worldliness is a very great danger. The care of this world and the deceitfulness of riches, the love of the world; its riches, its power, its acceptance, its pleasures, have slain many. Usually, these weeds do their work slowly, but they do it effectively. Beware of worldliness (Matthew 13:22; 1 John 2:15-17).

Arminianism
Arminianism is a great danger, because we are all proud Arminians by nature. No matter how thoroughly convinced we are of free grace, our proud, sinful nature still cries up, "Freewill". We all want to build the altar at which we worship by our own hands (Exodus 20:24, 25). We all want to think that salvation, at least some part of salvation, at least in some measure, is of our own doing. Arminianism is a monster with many heads. Every time it raises one of its ugly heads, cut it off quickly. Do not endure for a moment any thought that promotes man's dignity, or any thought that robs God of his glory (Romans 9:16).

Intellectualism

Being proud, arrogant worms, we all have to face the danger of intellectualism, too. Satan knows how proud we all are of our puny brains. Because we are so very proud of our mental abilities, we vainly imagine that by much study and diligent research we can find out all things. We foolishly imagine that we can by searching find out God! So we give ourselves to answering one question, then another, and then another. Those who give in to this lust of the flesh soon make the gospel of Christ a sideline, because there is no end to foolish questions. And when the gospel of Christ becomes a sideline in any church or ministry, or any individual, Satan has won the day (1 Timothy1:4; 2 Timothy 2:23; Titus 3:9).

Legalism

The spirit of bondage and legality is more frequently and more forcefully dealt with in the New Testament than any other error. To one degree or another, worldliness, Arminianism, and intellectualism all have their roots in the spirit of legality. Let me be crystal clear.

Legalism is any doctrine which teaches that man can be justified before God by something he does. Legalism is any doctrine which makes sanctification and holiness something a man does for himself. Legalism is any doctrine which teaches that man can put God under obligation to him, that man can, by something he does, merit God's favour. Legalism is any attempt to bring the people of God back under the bondage of the law.

This demon of legality must be exposed and eradicated. The Holy Spirit says, "Cast out the bondwoman and her child." Nothing is more harmful, or more deadly than this foolish attachment of sinful men to the law. It promotes pride and self-righteousness. It turns a man's eyes away from Christ to himself. It causes strife and division among God's people, causing sinful man to think he is something when he is nothing. It destroys every foundation of true peace and assurance before God. It is in direct opposition to the plainest statements of Holy Scripture.

Legalism, in any form, to any degree is totally contrary to the gospel of Christ. Law and grace simply will not mix. We who believe on Christ, being saved by the free grace of God in Christ, are not under the law in any sense, to any degree, for any reason. We will not, we must not allow anyone to bring us under the yoke of bondage to the law. (Romans 6:15; 7:4; 10:4; Galatians 3:1-3, 13, 24, 25; 5:1-4; 6:12, 13; Colossians 2:16, 17; 1 Timothy 1:5-10).

I use great plainness of speech, because I want to be understood. Let men call me a foul, base antinomian and promoter of licentiousness as often and as loudly as they please. I will not be moved. There is no room for Hagar in Sarah's house! You cannot rest on Zion's hill of grace until you quit trying to climb Sinai's dark, high mountain. Ishmael shall never be heir with Isaac. We can have either grace or works, but not both. We can have either Moses or Christ, but not both. We can either work or rest, but we cannot do both! Any mixture of law with grace is a total denial of grace. If we cling to the one, we cannot hold the other (Romans 11:6).

December 3
Today's Reading: 2 Corinthians 12-Galatians 1
"The grace of the Lord Jesus Christ"
2 Corinthians 13:14

I cannot imagine a better way to mark the day than by meditating upon, "The grace of the Lord Jesus Christ, and the love of God, and the communion of the Holy Ghost."

The Grace Of Christ
"The grace of our Lord Jesus Christ" is the ground and foundation of all he has done and suffered for us. It was his grace that caused him to become our Surety in the covenant, caused him to assume our nature in his incarnation, caused him to live in obedience to God as our Representative, bringing in everlasting righteousness for us. Grace caused him to set his face like a flint from old eternity and made him willing to suffer the painful, shameful, ignominious death of the cross as our Substitute at Calvary. It is that same grace of Christ that inspires his advocacy and intercession for us in heaven, and directs the rule of his throne in daily providence for our good.

"Be with you all." Yes, his grace is always with us; but we do not always have an awareness of his grace, do we? O blessed Saviour, grant us an abiding awareness of your boundless, free grace! Spirit of God, cause us to walk in the sunshine of our Saviour's grace, ever aware of his smiling face, knowing the security of his embrace!

The Love Of God
"The love of God" our Father; eternal, everlasting, free, underserved, and sovereign, the distinguishing love of God, immutable and indestructible, is forever ours! It is his love that chose us, his love that gave his Son for us, his love that called us, and his love that keeps us.

Could we with ink the oceans fill, and were the skies of parchment made,
Were every stalk on earth a quill, and every man a scribe by trade,
To write the love of God above would drain the oceans dry!
Nor could the scroll contain the whole, though stretched from sky to sky.

"Be with you all." May it please our great God, whose infinite love is ever ours in Christ, to cause us to live in the blessed awareness of his love; may it be shed abroad in our hearts by his Holy Spirit that we may be rooted and grounded in love, comprehending its length and breadth, and depth and height, that we might be "filled with all the fulness of God".

The Communion Of The Holy Ghost
"The grace of our Lord Jesus Christ and the Love of God" our Father will be ours continually only as we enjoy "the communion of the Holy Ghost". It is God the Holy Spirit who takes the things of Christ and shows them to us, giving us communion with our Father in our blessed Saviour and causing us to enjoy sweet communion with one another.
"Be with you all." O Holy Spirit, divine Comforter and Teacher, come, abide upon your people and grant us grace to walk together in sweet communion with our great, eternal, Triune God in Christ and with one another all the days of our lives. Let nothing deprive us of the boundless blessedness of this benediction here pronounced by you upon us! Blessed as we have been and are in the united mercies of the Triune God, let this blessedness evermore be ours in the constantly increasing experience of grace. Perfect that which you have begun in us, for Christ's sake.

A Reasonable Hope
Is it reasonable for you and me to expect our God to do such a great thing as this? Can we reasonably hope, upon good ground, to constantly enjoy "The grace of the Lord Jesus Christ, and the love of God, and the communion of the Holy Ghost?" Can we rightly expect such precious, abiding tokens of goodness and good will from the Three-in-One God? As surely as the Book of God is true, we may.
God our Father so loved us in Christ as to give him for us and to us. "He that spared not his own Son, but delivered him up for us all, How shall he not with him, also, freely give us all things?" God the Son, our blessed Saviour, so loved us that he gave himself for us. It was the zeal of his holy heart for his Father's honour and the longing of his holy soul for our salvation that led him through all the work of redemption and now engages his very Being in heaven. He will not be satisfied until he has brought all his redeemed home to glory; and there "He shall see of the travail of his soul and shall be satisfied". God the Holy Ghost is unceasingly engaged to make the whole work effectual, by taking of the things of Christ, and showing them to us. Yes, our God will give us such tokens of boundless good in the grace of Christ, in the love of God, and in the communion of the Holy Ghost here, and "in the world to come life everlasting". "The Lord will give grace and glory." Open and close, O Lord, according to your own word, every day of our lives with "the grace of the Lord Jesus Christ, and the love of God, and the communion of the Holy Ghost" until grace is consummated in everlasting glory. Amen and Amen.

December 4
Today's Reading: Galatians 2-4
"I am crucified with Christ"
Galatians 2:20

"I am crucified with Christ: nevertheless I live; yet not I, but Christ liveth in me: and the life which I now live in the flesh I live by the faith of the Son of God, who loved me, and gave himself for me" (Galatians 2:20). What a wondrous declaration for any sinner to make! Yet, here is a declaration made under divine inspiration, by a believing sinner just like me, just like you. That means it is a declaration that any sinner, and every sinner, who trusts Christ, can and should confidently make.

Crucified With Christ
"I am crucified with Christ". A equally acceptable translation is, "I have been crucified with Christ". When he died as my Substitute, I died in and with him. My union with Christ is so real, so complete, so thorough that anything that is true of him as my Mediator is true of me. When he died, I died (Romans 6:6; Galatians 6:14; Colossians 2:20). When he was buried, I was buried (Romans 6:3, 4). When he arose, I arose (Ephesians 2:5, 6). When he sat down in glory, I sat down with him in glory (Ephesians 2:6)!

Nevertheless
"Nevertheless I live." Being crucified with Christ, I am dead to the law. Yet, being born again by his Spirit, I live, live by him, with him, and for him.
"Yet not I, but Christ liveth in me." When God the Holy Spirit regenerated me, he made me a partaker of the divine nature (2 Peter 1:4), put Christ in me (Colossians 1:27), imparted to me his righteous nature (1 John 3:9); and now Christ lives in me. He is Life. I have no life but him. And it is this gift of new life, Christ in me, that Paul declares is the hope of glory. The only basis of that hope is the fact that I have been crucified with Christ. But the hope of faith, the confident hope of eternal life is "Christ liveth in me." I had no hope until I had Christ.

By Faith
"And the life which I now live in the flesh I live by the faith of the Son of God." This life that I possess and live in this mortal body, I live by the merit, virtue, and efficacy of the faith and faithfulness of the Son of God, my God-man Mediator, who lived in perfect obedience to God in my room and stead, and was faithful even unto death for me. O holy Saviour, give me grace to live, day by day, looking to you alone for pardon, righteousness, peace, joy, comfort, every supply of grace in this world, and for eternal salvation in the world to come!

Loved Me
"The Son of God, who loved me." The Son of God loved me! He loved me, a sinner, lost and undone. He loved me eternally. He loved me freely. He loved me, knowing

all the evil that I would become and all the evil I would do. I did not love him; but he loved me. I did not want his love; but he loved me. He loved me, knowing full well that he would get no love from me in return, except he create it in me by his grace. I am amazed that anyone could love me, and count the love of any toward me a thing of great value. But this is amazing and wonderful beyond imagination. "The Son of God loved me."

Gave himself
"The Son of God, who loved me, and gave himself for me." How do I know that he loved me? He "gave himself for me." Gave himself? Yes, himself. He gave me his gifts. He gave me his grace. He gave me his salvation. Indeed, he has given me all things! But all cannot be compared to this. He "gave himself for me." I deserved his wrath, but he "gave himself for me." I deserved hell, but he "gave himself for me."

He gave his body and his soul, his perfect humanity in union with his eternal deity, into the hands of divine justice. He gave himself up unto death upon the cursed tree in my room and stead as a Sacrifice for sin that he might have me! He gave himself a ransom for many. He gave himself for his Church, to redeem it as his holy bride. He gave himself for his elect, to satisfy divine justice for them and save them. Yet, he "loved me and gave himself for me", to redeem me, to atone for my sin, to save me!

O my soul, look up! Be encouraged to hope, to believe, to hang upon the Son of God, "who loved me, and gave himself for me." Oh, for faith to believe him! Oh, for grace to love him and give myself to him, "who loved me, and gave himself for me." Precious Saviour, blessed Author and Finisher of our faith, eternal Lover of my soul, grant me this mercy!

December 5
Today's Reading: Galatians 5-Ephesians 2
"By the will of God"
Ephesians 1:1

As Paul was made an apostle "by the will of God", he tells us that all who are saved are saved "by the will of God" and that all things come to pass in time "by the will of God", the Triune Jehovah, our great God; Father, Son, and Holy Ghost. We worship the Triune God (1 John 5:7); and we are saved by the work of the Triune God. All three Persons in the Godhead are equally gracious; and all three are involved in the salvation of our souls. This is what Paul shows us in Ephesians 1. As the three Persons of the Godhead are equal in divinity, but distinct in personality, so all three Persons in the Godhead are equal in grace, but distinct in the operations of grace.

The Father's Work
God the Father is set before us as the Fountain of all grace (Ephesians 1:3-6). It was God the Father who in the covenant of grace proposed redemption, devised the method, and chose the people whom he would save by his almighty grace. He found a way whereby his banished ones must be brought home. Then, in the fulness of time he sent his Son into the world to be the Medium, or Mediator of grace (Galatians 4:4-6).

The Son's Work
God the Son, the Lord Jesus Christ, is the Channel of all grace (Ephesians 1:7-12). All grace comes to sinners through Christ the Mediator. Everything God does for sinners and gives to sinners is "in Christ". Apart from Christ there is no grace. Am I chosen of God? I am chosen in Christ. Am I blessed of God? I am blessed in Christ. Am I predestinated by God? I am predestinated to be like Christ. Am I adopted of God? I am adopted in Christ. Am I accepted of God? I am accepted in Christ. Am I redeemed by God? I am redeemed in Christ. Am I forgiven by God? I am forgiven in Christ. Do I know God? I know him in Christ. Do I have an inheritance with God? I have it in Christ. Am I called of God? I am called in Christ.

All grace comes to us through Christ! There is no other way the grace of God can reach a sinner. Let no rejecter of God's Son imagine that he shall be the beneficiary of God's grace. It is the work of Christ upon the cross that brought grace and justice together in the salvation of sinners. Through his blood, "mercy and truth are met together; righteousness and peace have kissed each other" (Psalm 85:10).

The Spirit's Work
The Fountain of all grace is God the Father. The Channel of all grace is God the Son. And God the Holy Spirit is the Administrator of all grace (Ephesians 1:13, 14). It is God the Holy Spirit who effectually applies the blood of Christ to God's elect. He regenerates the dead by omnipotent power. He calls the redeemed with irresistible grace. He gives faith by almighty operations of grace. He forms Christ in us, giving us a new and righteous nature, which is "Christ in you, the hope of glory". He seals to God's elect all the blessings and benefits of the covenant of grace, and seals us in the covenant, preserving all the chosen, redeemed, called ones of God unto everlasting glory.

Without the gracious operations of God the Holy Spirit in conversion, no sinner would ever become the beneficiary of grace. He takes the things of Christ and shows them to his people. He quickens those the Father chose, reclaims those the Son redeemed, and leads to the Good Shepherd all the sheep for whom he laid down his life (John 10:11).

We were saved by the purpose of God the Father in election (Romans 8:29, 30; 2 Timothy 1:9). We were saved by the purchase of God the Son at Calvary (Romans 4:25; Hebrews 10:10-14). And we are saved by the power of God the Holy Spirit in the new birth (John 6:63; Ephesians 1:18-20; 2:1-4). All three Persons in the Godhead are equally gracious; and all three must be praised. The work of the Father is no less and no more vital than the work of the Son and the Spirit; and the works of the Son and the Spirit are no less and no more vital than the work of the Father.

We worship and adore God the Father for his free, electing love. We worship and adore God the Son for his accomplished redemption, by which we have the forgiveness of all sin. And we worship and adore God the Spirit for his mighty operations of grace in regeneration, by which he has made us "partakers of the divine nature". Therefore, we sing ...

> Praise God from whom all blessings flow!
> Praise Him all creatures here below!
> Praise Him above, ye heavenly hosts!
> Praise Father, Son, and Holy Ghost!

December 6
Today's Reading: Ephesians 3-5
"Created in righteousness and true holiness"
Ephesians 4:24

In Hebrews 12:14 the Spirit of God tells us that there is a "holiness without which no man shall see the Lord." In Ephesians 4:24 he declares that all who are born of God are born new creatures in Christ Jesus, "created in righteousness and true holiness". That holiness without which none can enter into heaven is the righteousness of God imparted to the heaven-born soul in regeneration, the divine nature of which we are partakers by grace (2 Peter 1:4). This is the experience of the new birth; and it is just as necessary to the salvation of our souls as the righteousness of Christ imparted to us in justification.

The new birth is the certain result of our Saviour's accomplishments in his death as our Substitute; but if we have no living, vital union with Christ, his mediatorial accomplishments at Calvary cannot effect our deliverance from the wrath to come.

Born Of The Spirit
Though the obedience of Christ unto death met all the claims of the law and satisfied divine justice for all the chosen seed, that obedience does not impart to the redeemed a title for the enjoyment of heaven. For that we must be born again. "Except a man be born of water and of the Spirit, he cannot enter into the kingdom of God. That which is born of the flesh is flesh; and that which is born of the Spirit is spirit" (John 3:5, 6).

Here we are presented with two distinct births from two distinct elements, necessarily producing two distinct beings. The flesh produces beings incapable of entering into the kingdom of God. The flesh cannot enter into, understand, or enjoy that which is spiritual, let alone that which is heavenly. But the Spirit produces beings capable of entering into the kingdom of God, capable of entering, understanding, and enjoying that which is spiritual, making all who are born of the Spirit "meet to be partakers of the inheritance of the saints in light" (Colossians 1:12). By the new birth, being given faith in Christ, God's elect are brought into an open and manifest union with Christ; but our experience of it is not the beginning of this union.

An Everlasting Union
The believer's vital union with Christ the Mediator is an everlasting union of grace. This union between Christ and our souls is the nearest, dearest, closest, most intense, and most enduring relationship that can be imagined. We live because Christ lives, and our lives are hid with Christ in God. This is a relationship that is closer than that of a husband and wife, or children and their parents.

This union of Christ and his people is one of the greatest mysteries revealed in the Book of God. "We are members of his body, of his flesh, and of his bones" (Ephesians 5:30). We are members of Christ. We form his mystical body. This is the closest relationship imaginable. It is such a close relationship, such a close union, that the Lord Jesus Christ would be as incomplete without us as we would be without him (Ephesians 1:23; Colossians 2:9, 10). We are identified with him; and he is identified with us. He has made us essential to himself, just as he has made himself essential to us! He is the head of the body and we are the members of that body. That is a truly vital union! "We are members of his body."

Partakers Of Christ
As Eve derived life from Adam (Genesis 2:18-25), so we derive life from Christ. As Eve was made partaker of Adam's nature, so we are made partakers of Christ's nature. As Eve's life was but an extension of Adam's life, so our life is but an extension of Christ's life. He is eternal life; and we have eternal life by the gift of God. That eternal life is "Christ in you" (Colossians 1:27). We are partakers of his life. Our spiritual life proceeds from and is sustained by Christ. He is the source of our present spiritual life, and of our eternal life in glory with him.

Let us never diminish one aspect of our Saviour's work to make another appear more glorious. All that Christ is made to us and all that he does for us is vital. We cannot be saved without his work for us; and we cannot be saved without his work in us. Both are vital.

Astonishing But Real
There are three great mystical unions revealed in Holy Scripture. The union of the three persons of the Godhead, being one God, is the doctrine of the Trinity (1 John 5:7). The Scriptures also reveal the union of divinity and humanity in the person of our Lord Jesus Christ. "The Word was made flesh" (John 1:14). And the Book of God reveals this vital union of God's elect with Christ. Nothing can be more astonishing; but nothing is more real than our union with Christ.

Be astonished, O my soul! I and my Saviour are one! Child of God, you are one with the Christ of God! You were "buried with him in baptism into death", wherein also you have risen with him. You were crucified with him upon the cursed tree. You have gone up into heaven with him. God has raised us up together and made us to sit together in the heavenly places in Christ Jesus. You are one with Christ! I am one with Christ!

514

Be astonished, O my soul! Being one with him, the Lord Jesus himself assures us that the Lord God our Father loves us as he loves him! He loves me to the same degree, with the same love, and for the same reason he loves his Son as my Mediator. He loves me and his Son with an everlasting love (John 17:23).

Since we are members of his body, he will one day present us to himself without spot or wrinkle or blemish or any such thing. We will be perfect, even as he is perfect. We will enter into the eternal joy in the Lord. We are joint heirs with Christ; therefore whatever he has we shall have.

December 7
Today's Reading: Ephesians 6-Philippians 2
"Jesus Christ is Lord"
Philippians 2:11

Rejoice, O my soul! "Jesus Christ is Lord." This is the result of our Saviour's finished work of righteousness and redemption on the earth as our Substitute. God the Holy Ghost here tells us that all the vast empire of God's creation has been placed under the dominion of the God-man, our Saviour. He assures us that there is no limit to the realm and sphere of our Redeemer's total sovereignty. He is Lord of all! Christ is Lord of all people, Lord of all things, and Lord of all events. The Lord God has given to his Son "A name which is above every name", and the name he has given him is "Lord". Jesus Christ our Redeemer is Lord Supreme over all God's creation!

All People
Jesus Christ is Lord over all people upon this earth. He is Lord over the righteous and the wicked, the living and the dead, the believing and the unbelieving (Romans 14:9). Believers recognize, acknowledge, and willingly surrender to his Lordship. Unbelievers deny it and rebel against it. But he is nonetheless Lord. All are under his control, do his bidding, perform his will, and accomplish his purpose, always and in all things.

Powers Of Darkness
Jesus Christ is Lord over all the powers of darkness (Colossians 2:15). Those souls damned forever in hell, the demons of hell, and Satan himself are all under the dominion of King Jesus. Not one of our Lord's enemies can breathe or move, except by his permission; and even then their moves are governed by him to accomplish nothing but good for his people and the eternal purpose of God (Job 1:12; 2:6).

All Providence
Jesus Christ is Lord over all the affairs of providence (Isaiah 53:10-12; Romans 8:28; Hebrews 1:1-3). Rejoice, O my soul, rejoice forever! Jesus Christ my Saviour is Lord everywhere, over everything, all the time! There is no place in this universe, from the throne of God in the highest glory to the lowest pit of the deepest hell, where Jesus Christ does not rule in total, absolute, sovereign power. God's creation is not out of control. Nothing is thrown into confusion. Jesus Christ is Lord. His purpose is being accomplished. And his purpose is good.

Heaven
Jesus Christ is Lord over all the vast regions of heaven (Revelation 12:10). The King of the City Beautiful is Immanuel, God in our nature. The Light of that city is Christ himself. The Reward of heaven is Christ. All the songs of the redeemed in heaven shall be praises to the Lord the Lamb forever.

December 8
Today's Reading: Philippians 3-Colossians 1
"That I may know him"
Philippians 3:10

I know that Christ is mine and I am his. Yet, I count all things but loss and dung that I might win him, that I might be found in him, that I might know him.

I know him; but, oh, how I want to know him! I want constantly renewed, ever increasing knowledge of and communion with the Son of God. This is the ambition of my heart. I want to know him, my God and my Saviour, my Redeemer and my Lord!

I want to know him who is the great Benefactor of my soul. I want to know the mysteries and glories of his person, the riches of his grace, the greatness of his salvation, the benefits of his mercies, and the depth of his love. May the God of all grace give us grace never to take our eyes off of Christ! My soul, let Christ be the all-consuming Object of your being! "That I may know him."

The Power Of His Resurrection
I want to "know him in the power of his resurrection". It is the power of his resurrection that declares that we are justified (Romans 4:25). The power of his resurrection gives us spiritual and eternal life in him (Ephesians 1:19). The power of his resurrection guarantees our resurrection (1 Corinthians 15:47-49). I want to live every day, experimentally walking in the knowledge of the power of his resurrection. Walking with Christ in the newness of life, I want the power of his resurrection to dominate, control, and direct my life in all things. I want to be continually made new by him.

The Fellowship Of His Sufferings
I want "to know him in the fellowship of his sufferings". I want to know my personal interest in his sufferings. And I want to know what he accomplished in his sufferings. We know that our blessed Saviour accomplished our forgiveness, justification, and sanctification, and obtained eternal redemption for us by his suffering and death as our Substitute. As his sufferings are his glory, I want his sufferings to be my glory (Galatians 6:14).

Conformed To His Death
I want to know Christ and the fellowship of his sufferings to such an extent that I am ever "being made conformable unto his death". This is what that means. I want to be conformed to Christ in his death, to be entirely consecrated to the glory of God, perfectly submissive to the will of God, and motivated by nothing but love for my God and his people.

That I Might Attain
"If by any means I might attain unto the resurrection of the dead. Not as though I had already attained, either were already perfect: but I follow after, if that I may apprehend that for which also I am apprehended of Christ Jesus. Brethren, I count not myself to have apprehended: but this one thing I do, forgetting those things which are behind, and reaching forth unto those things which are before, I press toward the mark for the prize of the high calling of God in Christ Jesus" (vv. 11-14).

Certainly, this includes a great desire for the resurrection of my body at the last day. But primarily, the yearning spoken of here is a yearning for that moral, spiritual resurrection of grace that lifts us out of the death and darkness of sin. The world, the flesh, and all human life are death. In Christ there is life, real life, eternal life, a life of righteousness, peace, and joy in communion with God. This is what I want. I have not yet attained it; but I am reaching for it.

In a word, I want all that God purposed for me in eternity and Christ purchased for me at Calvary (Ephesians 1:3-6). I want to be like Christ! These are the ambitions of my heart, the goals I seek, the things for which I live. I pray that God will make them more and more real to me. And I pray that he will make them your heart's ambitions as well.

"That I may win him". "And be found in him". "That I may know him". "If by any means I might attain unto the resurrection of the dead".

Let us set our hearts upon these things, and by the grace of God we shall have them. "For our conversation is in heaven; from whence also we look for the Saviour, the Lord Jesus Christ: Who shall change our vile body, that it may be fashioned like unto his glorious body, according to the working whereby he is able even to subdue all things unto himself" (vv. 20, 21).

———————

517

December 9
Today's Reading: Colossians 2-4
"Ye are complete in him"
Colossians 2:10

"Ye are complete in him." There is no middle ground. Either you are complete in Christ, lacking nothing, or you are altogether without hope before God. We either have everything God requires of man, everything God gives to men, everything Christ has and is as the Mediator between God and man, or we have nothing. "Ye are complete in him." Precious sentence! Sweeter than honey to my soul! If you believe on the Lord Jesus Christ, though utter emptiness in yourself, "Ye are complete in him." Weak, poor, helpless, unworthy though you are in yourself, in him, your Lord, your Redeemer, your Saviour, you are complete in the fullest, broadest, and most varied sense of that mighty word "complete". What wonders of grace we have before us! May God the Holy Spirit be our Teacher and Guide as we dive into this deep sea and contemplate the mystery of the perfection that is ours in Christ.

The Spirit of God seems to have but one object in view in giving us this sweet sentence. His purpose is to cause every believing soul to look to Christ with the confident "joy of faith", seeing clearly that as all the fulness of the godhead dwells in him, so all the fulness of Christ is yours and mine, "and ye are complete in him".

Ye
You who believe on the Lord Jesus Christ, you, all of you, and only you, "are complete in him." You, who were "dead in trespasses and sins", are complete in him! You, who "in time past walked according to the course of this world, according to the prince of the power of the air", are complete in him! You, who "were by nature children of wrath, even as others", are complete in him! You, who were once "without Christ, being aliens from the commonwealth of Israel, and strangers from the covenants of promise, having no hope, and without God in the world", are complete in him! You, who labour and toil, vex and perplex your hearts continually because of the indwelling sin you hate, are complete in him! You, who are groaning under a conscious sense of the body of sin and death that is in you, are complete in him! You, who are loved and chosen of God, redeemed by the precious blood of Christ, justified and sanctified by his grace, born of his Spirit, and robed in his righteousness, being clothed with the garments of salvation, are complete in him!

Are
The Scriptures plainly declare that God's elect have been complete in Christ from eternity (Romans 8:28-30; Ephesians 1:3-6). Our completeness is in Christ. We have been complete in him for as long as we have been in him; and there never has been a time when we were not in him. It is a blessed thing to live in the sweet assurance that we shall be complete in Christ in heaven's everlasting glory and bliss. "When we see him we shall be like him, for we shall see him as he is." What a sweet hope that is! But here Paul is talking about that which is the present blessedness of every sinner

who believes on the Son of God. He does not say you shall be complete some day, when your faith is stronger, or when your love is more mature, or your works are better, or you see more clearly. There are no conditions or qualifications for us to meet that we might be complete in Christ. "Ye are complete in him." Right now, at this present moment, "Ye are complete in him." Do not imagine that there is something lacking, some deficiency you must make up, something you must complete. He is saying, "Know this and rejoice: you are full, complete, and perfect in Christ. Being one with him, in union with him, his fulness, completion, and perfection is your fulness, completion, and perfection."

Complete
What does the word "complete" mean? How far are we to carry this statement "Ye are complete in him"? Is it possible to carry it too far? Must we be careful not to go overboard here? Never! Whatever we are in Christ, we are completely. Whatever we have in Christ, we have completely. In all matters regarding our spiritual welfare and our soul's salvation, we are complete in Christ, complete without any supplement of any kind. Rejoice, O my heart, to hear God the Holy Ghost declare, "Ye are complete in him." Blessedly, absolutely complete! Just as complete in him as "all the fulness (completion) of the godhead dwelleth in him bodily." O my soul, believe this and rejoice! Be ashamed, my heart, of every reluctance to believe that which God has declared! Let our admiration be fixed upon this delightful privilege. Arise, my brother! Arise, my sister! Shake off the fears and doubts with which Satan would bind you! Behold yourself as God declares you to be, as you really are, "perfect in Christ Jesus". Do not let your sins shake your faith in him and cause you to question his all-sufficiency and his all-sufficient grace.

In Him
"Ye are complete in him." Pause over those two little words, "in him". Everything is in Christ! If we are "in him", we are complete. We are complete because we are "in him". Complete because of our union with him. "Ye are complete in him." Amen.

December 10
Today's Reading: 1 Thessalonians 1-5
"Knowing, brethren beloved, your election of God"
1 Thessalonians 1:4

Everyone who reads the Bible, even casually, knows that it teaches the doctrine of election. All God's saints rejoice in that blessed gospel doctrine. Nothing sounds sweeter in the believer's ear than the voice of the Son of God saying, "Ye have not chosen me, but I have chosen you." Yet, no mere man can open and read the Lamb's

Book of Life. No mortal can ever know who the elect are until they are regenerated and called by God the Holy Spirit. However, each of us can prove our own selves. We can make our calling and election sure.

In 1 Thessalonians, the Apostle Paul, writing by Divine inspiration, tells us that he knew those men and women in the Church at Thessalonica were elect, chosen of God, and precious by five distinct marks of grace upon them. If you are numbered among God's elect, these five marks are upon you. If I am one of the elect, these marks are upon me. There is no need for guess work about this matter. God the Holy Spirit shows us five evidences of God's election in 1 Thessalonians chapter one.

First, God's elect are people who hear the gospel preached and receive the gospel as it is preached in the power of God the Holy Spirit (v. 5). The elect are those who are called by the effectual, irresistible power and grace of God the Holy Spirit. They are called by the Spirit through the preaching of the gospel (Romans 1:15-17; 10:13-17; 1 Corinthians 1:21-23; 15:1-3; Hebrews 4:12; James 1:18; 1 Peter 1:23-25). God does not save sinners by the sound of chirping birds, or by the babbling heresies of Arminian, free-will, works religion. God saves his chosen through the preaching of the gospel of his free and sovereign grace in Christ.

Second, God's elect are those who follow Christ (vv. 3, 6). Chosen sinners, when saved by the grace of God, are made disciples, followers of Christ, voluntary servants of King Jesus. Believers are not perfect, and never pretend to be. They know something of the corruption of their own hearts. Yet, in the tenor of their lives, those who are born of God follow Christ. We follow his doctrine, his example, his Word, his Spirit, and his will, as it is revealed to us by his Word and the direction of his Spirit. We follow our Saviour by faith, constrained by love, and motivated by gratitude.

Third, God's elect are a people who are committed to Christ and the gospel of his grace (v. 8). As the saints at Thessalonica sounded out the gospel to perishing sinners in their generation, so God's saints today make it their business to make the gospel known for the glory of God.

Fourth, God's elect experience repentance and conversion by the power of his grace. When called of God, they turn from their idols to serve the living God (v. 9). Believers forsake their idols and the idolatrous religious practices of their former manner of life. They are not found worshipping a false god. You do not find God's children kneeling before a pagan deity, kissing a crucifix, or professing faith in a helpless, frustrated god; whose purpose, will, and work are prevented by man's imaginary free-will!

Fifth, God's elect are waiting for Christ (v. 10). Believers live upon the tiptoe of faith, looking for that blessed hope, the glorious appearing of the great God, our Saviour, the Lord Jesus Christ. Believing his Word, we live in hope and expectation of the resurrection. Every child of God rejoices in God's electing love. We rejoice, like the hymn writer of old, to say ...

> Hail, sovereign love, that first began,
> The scheme to rescue fallen man!
> Hail, matchless, free, eternal grace,
> That gave my soul a hiding-place!

On him almighty vengeance fell,
That must have sunk a world to hell;
Christ bore it for the chosen race,
And thus became their hiding-place.

A few more rolling suns, at most,
Will land me on fair Canaan's coast;
Where I shall sing the song of grace,
And see my glorious hiding-place!

December 11
Today's Reading: 2 Thessalonians 1-1 Timothy 1
"God hath from the beginning chosen you"
2 Thessalonians 2:13

According to Holy Scripture, the very first work of God's grace in saving his people was that of election. No doctrine in the Bible is more delightful and comforting than the doctrine of election. This is not a doctrine taught in a few isolated passages of Scripture. It is taught prominently throughout the Word of God.

The doctrine of election, simply stated, is the teaching that God chose some of Adam's race to be the objects of his grace and predestinated them unto eternal salvation in Christ before the world began.

Does the Bible teach this doctrine? Yes, it does. You cannot read the Book of God and miss the doctrine of election (Psalm 65:4; Matthew 20:28; John 15:16; Romans 8:28-30; 9:11-13; 11:5; Ephesians 1:3-6; 1 Thessalonians 1:4; 2 Thessalonians 2:13, 14; 1 Peter 1:2). What do these passages of Scripture teach about God's electing grace? At least these five things ...

1. Election is in Christ. We were chosen in him, chosen to be like him, and accepted in him before the world began. All grace is in Christ. All that God does for sinners is in Christ.

2. Election is unconditional. God did not choose us because he "foreknew" that we would do good! He chose us because he loved us with an everlasting love (Jeremiah 31:3), even though he "knew" what sinners we would be!

3. Election is unto salvation. Election is not salvation, but there could be no salvation without it. We could never be saved had God not chosen to save us.

4. Election took place before the worlds were made. The Lamb's Book of Life is not being written in time. Every name that shall be found in that book when the world has been destroyed was written there before God created the universe.

5. Election is the fountain-head of all grace. Read the first chapter of Ephesians carefully. Every blessing of grace from adoption to redemption, to forgiveness, to regeneration, to the resurrection of the body, to the inheritance of the saints in glory flows freely to chosen sinners "according as" God has chosen them in Christ!

The doctrine of election declares, "Salvation is of the Lord." It is not the will of man in time that is the determining factor in salvation, but the will of God in eternity. He declares, "I will have mercy on whom I will have mercy."

<hr>

December 12
Today's Reading: 1 Timothy 2-6
"The man Christ Jesus"
1 Timothy 2:5

This Man is no ordinary man. This Man is himself God. He is the God-man. He became a man that he might redeem men. He lived in this world as the Representative Man, the Representative of God's elect. He lived the full age of a man in perfect obedience to the will and law of God to establish righteousness for men, even the righteousness of God, by magnifying the law and making it honourable. Then, when his hour had fully come, this Man, the God-man, our Lord Jesus Christ, died upon the cursed tree as our Substitute, "the just for the unjust, that he might bring us to God". Now, this Man, who as a man put away sin by the sacrifice of himself, is seated upon the very throne of God in glory, accepted as a man, with God. Hear the good news of that fact. Since there is a Man in glory, accepted of God, there may be another, and another, and another! Because this Man, the God-man, is in glory, "He is able also to save them to the uttermost that come unto God by him."

Who Is He?
This man, the Lord Jesus Christ, is "the brightness of God's glory and the express image of his person." Christ is both God himself and the singular revelation and expression of the glory of God. The Father and the Son are the same as the sun and its rays. One is not before the other; and they cannot be divided or separated. He is the perfect revelation and the exact image and character of the Father (Isaiah 9:6; John 1:1-3; 10:30; 14:8-10; Matthew 1:21-23).

What Has He Done?
Much needs to be said in answer to this question; but allow me to simply declare that which is the essence of all our Saviour did as the God-man, our Mediator. The Lord Jesus Christ has "by himself purged our sins". The Lord Jesus, of himself, by himself alone, and by the sacrifice of himself, made atonement for all the sins of God's elect. He took our sins upon himself, bore them, and died under the penalty of them, thereby abolishing them completely and forever (2 Corinthians 5:21; Hebrews 9:26; Colossians 1:19-22; Isaiah 53:4-6).

Where Is He Now?
He is yonder in glory, where more than two thousand years ago, "He sat down on the right hand of the Majesty on High". The "Majesty on High" is God the Father to whom majesty belongs and who is clothed with majesty. His right hand is the place of power, greatness, acceptance, and glory. There sits the Man, Christ Jesus, and all his elect in him. We have been made to sit down with him in heavenly places!

> There, like a man, the Saviour sits; the God, how bright he shines;
> And scatters infinite delight on all the happy minds.

Do You See Him?

> The head that once was crowned with thorns, is crowned with glory now;
> A royal diadem adorns that mighty Victor's brow.
> No more the bloody crown, the cross and nails no more:
> For hell itself shakes at his frown, and all the heavens adore.

December 13
Today's Reading: 2 Timothy 1-4
"Turned unto fables"
2 Timothy 4:4

The prophecy made by the Apostle Paul in 2 Timothy 4 has come to pass in our day. Throughout the world, religious people gather every week in solemn assemblies in the name of Christ to worship God. They read the Bible, say their prayers, invoke God's blessing, and give their money. They may be devoted to their religious cause; but they are lost! They have faith; but theirs is a false faith. They have hope; but their hope is a delusion. Having been led and taught by blind and ignorant men, "They will not endure sought doctrine; but after their own lusts ... they heap to themselves teachers, having itching ears ... They turn away their ears from the truth and have been turned unto fables."

A fable is a brief story, dreamed up by a man to teach a moral, ethical lesson; but factually it is not true, it is a lie. Here are four common religious fables, dreamed up by men to teach moral principles. They are universally embraced, proclaimed, and defended. These four fables are presented throughout the world as the very truth of God; but they are lies, damning to the souls of all who believe them.

1. "God loves all people, without exception". That simply is not so. If God loved all, all would be saved. Nowhere does the Bible say or imply that he does. The proof text most commonly used to "prove" this assertion is John 3:16; but neither John 3:16 nor any other passage of Holy Scripture teaches that God's love is universal. In the Word of God the word "world" seldom means everyone in the world without exception; and the word "all" seldom means all without exception. Luke 2:1 and Romans 5:18, 19 are two clear examples of this fact. The fact is the Word of God plainly tells us that God does not love everyone (Psalm 7:11; 11:5; Romans 9:13; Isaiah 43:1-5). "God is love." We rejoice in that blessed revelation of grace. But God's love is in Christ. The Scriptures never give assurance of God's love to anyone apart from faith in Christ.

2. "God wills the salvation of all men." If God willed the salvation of all, he would save all. "What his soul desireth, even that he doeth" (Job 23:13). The proof text by which blaspheming will-worshippers attempt to prove that God wills the salvation of all is 2 Peter 3:9. "The Lord is not slack concerning his promise, as some men count slackness; but is longsuffering to us-ward, not willing that any should perish, but that all should come to repentance." Peter here declares that the reason God has not yet destroyed this world is that he is not willing that any of his elect perish. Therefore, he is long suffering to "us ward" (his elect). We are assured of this in 2 Peter 3:15, where the Holy Spirit tells us plainly that, "the long suffering of our God is salvation".

3. "The Lord Jesus Christ died to redeem and save all people." Nowhere does the Word of God teach, or in any way imply that Christ laid down his life for and redeemed anyone, but his sheep, his elect. Men attempt to prove that Christ died for all, those who perish in hell as well as those who are saved, by referring to four texts, which, we are told, prove universal redemption (John 3:16; Hebrews 2:9; 2 Peter 2:1; 1 John 2:1, 2). But none of those passages (or any others) teach such blasphemy. The word "world" in John 3:16 obviously refers to God's elect scattered throughout the world, Gentiles as well as Jews.

The words "every man" in Hebrews 2:9 should read simply "every", referring to every "son" he brings to glory (v. 10), every person "sanctified" by union with him (v. 11), every one of his "brethren" (v. 12), every child given to him by the Father (v. 13), every one of Abraham's seed (v. 16), and every one of "the people" for whom he accomplished reconciliation (v. 17). The word "bought" in 2 Peter 2:1 simply refers to the fact that the Lord Jesus Christ, by his obedience unto death, bought the right to rule over all flesh, even over his enemies, as the God-man Mediator (John 17:2-5). The passage has nothing to do with the accomplishment of redemption. As in John

3:16, in 1 John 2:1, 2 the word "world" refers to the world of his elect, or his elect scattered throughout the whole world.

The Son of God did not shed his blood for every person in the world. He did not die for all without exception! The Bible nowhere teaches or implies that Christ died for, redeemed, or came to save those multitudes who are at last lost in hell. Those for whom Christ died shall never die! The Son of God redeemed all whom he came to redeem, and he shall save all whom he came to save.

4. "The Holy Spirit strives with all to persuade all to trust Christ." Nothing could be further from the truth. There are multitudes to whom the Spirit of God has never even sent his Word. The Bible says nothing of the Spirit trying to reprove, convince, or regenerate anyone. He does not try to do anything! He does what he will. "It is the Spirit that quickeneth; the flesh profiteth nothing." But those who wrest the Scriptures to their own destruction point to Genesis 6:3 as a proof text for the Holy Spirit's impotence in grace. Let us be honest with God's Word. Every word, every phrase, every verse of Holy Scripture must be interpreted in its context, both its immediate context and the whole context of Divine Revelation. Genesis 6:3 says nothing about God's saving operations, but speaks of Noah's generation and the wrath of God upon that generation.

The whole religious world, to one degree or another, declares that salvation is accomplished by the will of man, the worth of man, and the work of man. But the Word of God declares that salvation is by the will of God alone, the worth of Christ alone, and the work of the Holy Spirit alone.

December 14
Today's Reading: Titus 1-Philemon
"The faith of God's elect"
Titus 1:1

There are many who have faith who do not have "the faith of God's elect". Theirs' is a faith like what James describes as the faith of devils, a mere factual, mental faith, a faith which will only increase their guilt at the bar of God. In the light of that fact, we ought to constantly bring our faith to the touchstone of Holy Scripture and prove it. We ought to ask ourselves, as we read the Book of God, "Do I have the faith of God's elect?"

The Gift Of God
True faith is the gift of God. It is not merely a logical or emotional decision, though it is both logical and emotional. It is much more. Saving faith is created in the heart by the power of God the Holy Spirit. It is the gift of almighty grace. We "believe

according to the working of his mighty power" (Ephesians 1: 19). We are united to Christ "through the faith of the operation of God" (Colossians 2:12). God alone can create faith in the heart of a sinner. God alone gives men faith. And he does it through the preaching of the gospel, by which Christ is revealed in the heart (Romans 10:17; James 1:18; 1 Peter 1:23-25).

One Object

True saving faith is concerned with but one thing; the person and work of the Lord Jesus Christ. Do you believe on the Son of God? That is the one issue which is of eternal importance. "What think ye of Christ?" Nothing else really matters. True faith is taking God at his Word. It is believing what God says about his Son. It is submitting to the revelation of God in the Scriptures. It is trusting, believing, receiving Christ as he is revealed in Holy Scripture. "Whosoever believeth that Jesus is the Christ is born of God ... He that hath the Son hath life; and he that hath not the Son of God hath not life" (1 John 5:1, 12). Yet, saving faith is much more than mental assent to the truth of divine revelation. The Puritan, John Owen, wrote, "Of all the poison which at this day is diffused in the minds of men, corrupting them from the mystery of the gospel, there is no part that is more pernicious than this one perverse imagination, that to believe in Christ is nothing at all but to believe the doctrine of the gospel".

Heart Work

Saving faith is a work of the heart (Romans 10:9, 10). True faith is the wilful, deliberate, voluntary confidence of my heart in the power and grace of the Lord Jesus Christ. It is trusting the merits of his blood and righteousness as my only basis of acceptance before God. This faith in Christ involves the surrender of my heart to him as my Lord. True faith is the bowing and submission of my very life to the Son of God as my Lord (Luke 14:25-33).

Persevering

True faith, the faith of God's elect is persevering faith (Hebrews 3:6, 14). That is to say, if a person truly believes on Christ, he will continue to believe on Christ. Faith is not an event in life. It is the believer's way of life. "The just shall live by faith" (Galatians 3:11). The true believer never ceases to live by faith in Christ. God's elect begin in faith, live in faith, and die in faith (Hebrews 11:13). True faith never quits. It is not the man who begins the race who wins the prize, but the one who finishes the race.

Discovering Christ Day By Day

December 15
Today's Reading: Hebrews 1-5
Justice satisfied
Hebrews 2:9, 10

Let us meditate this day on both the necessity and the blessedness of Christ's satisfaction of Divine justice by his death on the cross as our almighty, saving Substitute. O Spirit of God, give us clear understanding concerning this matter of great importance and inspire within us a deep, abiding gratitude for our Saviour's accomplishments at Calvary on our behalf. Is this not the glory of the gospel and the glory of the Christian faith? It is the satisfaction of Divine justice by the death of Christ that distinguishes Christianity from all other religions. Take the cross out of Christianity, take away the satisfaction of Christ by his death upon the cross, and Christianity is of no more value and benefit to our souls than Judaism, Islam, or Hinduism. It is of paramount importance, because without satisfaction for sin, there could be no salvation from it.

The Necessity
It was necessary for Christ to suffer and die on the cross under the wrath of God to save his people. He did not have to save us. But if he would save us, he could not save in any other way. Justice demanded it (Proverbs 16:6; 17:15; Romans 4:5; 1 Peter 3:18). This is what the Spirit of God teaches us in Hebrews 2:9, 10.

Since it was the design, purpose, and pleasure of the Almighty to bring some of the sons of men into eternal glory and happiness as the sons of God by Christ, it was necessary for Christ, the Son of God, to suffer all that the law and justice of God required for the punishment of sin, dying under the wrath of God as our Substitute.

I am not suggesting that the satisfaction of Christ procured the love of God for us. It does not. The death of Christ is the fruit of God's love, not the cause of it. But I am saying that it is the death of Christ and the satisfaction of justice by his death that opens the way for sinners to enjoy the glorious, saving embraces of God's almighty, gracious arms. We could never have been reconciled to God without the shedding of Christ's blood.

Every Believer
Every sinner who is reconciled to God by faith in Christ is included in the number of those for whom satisfaction was made at Calvary. John Gill wrote, "Have you any reason to believe that you have, at any time, had communion with God, in private or in public, in your closet, or in the family, or in the house of God, under any ordinance, either the ministry of the Word, or prayer, or the Supper of the Lord? Then you may be assured Christ has made satisfaction for you; or you would never have enjoyed such communion." If you believe on the Son of God, he made satisfaction for you. I trust Christ. Trusting him, I am assured of my redemption by him. That is the peace and joy of my soul.

527

What a horrible evil sin is! Nothing but the blood of Christ could make satisfaction for it. God almighty will punish sin. The death of Christ as the sinner's Substitute demonstrates the strictness of God's holy law. Yet, there is a way open for sinners to come to God. Christ is the Way. He has made satisfaction for sin. If you trust him, if you come to God by faith in him, he made satisfaction for your sin!

Perfections Revealed
Let us ever and increasingly admire and adore the perfections of our God revealed in the gospel (Psalm 85:10, 11). Admire his love! Adore his mercy! Rejoice in his grace! Stand in awe of his wisdom, holiness, justice, and truth! All shine forth gloriously in the satisfaction of Christ. "For it became him, for whom are all things, and by whom are all things, in bringing many sons to glory, to make the Captain of their salvation perfect through sufferings." Wisdom found a ransom. Holiness approved of it. Justice is satisfied with it. The gospel proclaims it!

December 16
Today's Reading: Hebrews 6-8
"A surety of a better testament"
Hebrews 7:22

The Lord Jesus Christ, our great, all glorious Surety, died for and redeemed those for whom he assumed all responsibility as a surety in the covenant of grace before the world began. Bow, O my soul, and worship him who is your eternal, infallible, saving Surety, the Lord Jesus Christ. Rejoice, O my heart, in this great Surety of that better covenant, by which salvation comes to God's Israel!

Though very few in this reprobate age understand it, this is as blessed a truth of the gospel as it is vital. Our great Saviour's sacrificial work as our sin-atoning Substitute, as our great High Priest, was made for those for whom he undertook to be a Surety in the covenant of grace before the world began. Those for whom Christ died, those who have been redeemed by his blood are the people for whom he became a covenant Surety.

He is the Surety of the better testament, the covenant of grace. He became a Surety for those, and for none other than those for whom that covenant was made. In that great covenant the Son of God engaged himself to be our Surety and Redeemer.

Foundation Of Redemption
It is Christ's suretyship which is the ground and foundation of redemption. This is the reason why our sins were made his, and the punishment of our sins was laid upon him, the reason why he bore and endured the wrath of God for our sins, and paid all our debts as his people, and the reason why he redeemed us out of the hands of divine

justice. The Son of God pledged himself to God the Father as a Surety, and laid himself under obligation to do all these things for us. He became totally responsible for his elect in all matters. But he was not obliged to pay the debts of those for whom he did not become a Surety, or to suffer and die in their room and stead. Christ's suretyship and redemption are of equal extent, and reach to the same objects. They are the Lord's Benjamins, the sons of his right hand, his beloved sons, for whom Christ, the antitype of Judah, became a surety. As our Surety, the Lord Jesus laid himself under obligation to bring all God's elect safe to glory, and present them to his Father.

Absolute Surety
When we think of a surety, we usually think of a mere guarantor, one who co-signs a mortgage or a bank loan. If the original debtor fails to pay the note for any reason, both he and the co-signer are responsible for the debt and all the interest accumulated by it. What the lending institution cannot collect from one party, it will attempt to collect from the other. That is not the kind of Surety Christ is. Our most glorious Christ is an absolute Surety. When he struck hands with the Father as our Surety, he voluntarily became totally responsible for all the debts and obligations of all his people forever!

Shifted Responsibility
This is one place where I love and seek to promote shifted responsibility. All the responsibilities of God's elect were shifted from us to our Surety. As our covenant Surety, the Lord Jesus Christ promised to fulfil all righteousness for us, satisfy divine justice for us, give us a new (holy) nature by his Spirit, preserve us unto the end, raise us up at the last day, and present us in eternity before his Father's throne holy, unblameable, and unreproveable. Upon this pledge to redeem and save his people, the Father trusted his Son as the Surety of his people, and placed us in his hands (Ephesians 1:12; John 6:38, 39). And upon the revelation of him in our hearts by the gospel, being chosen, redeemed, and called by grace, we trust Christ as our Surety before God (Ephesians 1:13). If you can trust him, Christ is your Surety, too! God help you now to trust him, for Christ's sake.

December 17
Today's Reading: Hebrews 9, 10
"He taketh away the first that he may establish the second"
Hebrews 10:9

This is a pattern of God's work among the sons of men. He takes away the first that he may establish the second. That which is first, once its purpose has been fulfilled, has to be taken away, so that that which is second may be brought in and established.

Both in this world and in the world to come, the Lord Jesus Christ, our God and Saviour, gives the best things last. That is what we are taught in Hebrews 10:9.

Examples
There are many, many examples of this mentioned in the Book of God. Let me just call your attention to four of them. (1.) The earthly paradise has been taken away by sin; but the Lord God has given us salvation in Christ and heavenly glory with him (Psalm 69:4). (2.) The first man, Adam, failed miserably as our representative; but Christ, the last Adam, has represented us perfectly, and still does (Romans 5:12-19; 1 Corinthians 15:22, 47, 49). (3.) The first covenant, that legal covenant of works, has been broken and is forever cast aside; but the second covenant, the everlasting covenant of grace, has been brought in and gloriously replaces the first (Galatians 4:22-31; 2 Samuel 23:5; Jeremiah 31:31-34; Jeremiah 32:38-40). (4.) The first temple, with all its symbolic glory and splendour, has been thoroughly destroyed; but there is a spiritual house being built by God our Saviour, which can never be destroyed (Zechariah 4:6-10).

God's Grace
This is also the pattern of God's work in the blessed experience of his saving grace. "He taketh away the first that he may establish the second." It is a painful thing to experience, but it is necessary. If God did not take away the first, he would never establish the second. Our first righteousness has been taken away by the conviction of the Spirit; but the righteousness of Christ is established by the same grace and the same Holy Spirit conviction (Romans 7:7-9). Our first peace has been dashed in pieces like a broken vessel; but we have found real peace in the Rock of Ages. Our natural, carnal joy he turned into bitterness; but now our dear Saviour has given us the blessed joy of faith. This is joy indeed! What a joy it is to trust Christ; his blood, his righteousness, his providence, and his promises! Christ took away our endless, meaningless wandering and vain conversation; but he brought us into the way of life, gives us the direction of his Spirit, and holds us in the path of faith. Blessed be the name of God, our Saviour! "He taketh away the first that he may establish the second."

Our Hope
And this is our hope of better things to come. "He taketh away the first that he may establish the second." This body of flesh is decaying and dying now. God is taking it away. But it shall be renewed in the image and likeness of Christ. "As we have borne the image of the earthy, we shall also bear the image of the heavenly" (1 Corinthians 15:49). This tabernacle of clay must be dissolved, that we may "have a building of God, an house not made with hands, eternal in the heavens" (2 Corinthians 5:1). "He taketh away the first that he may establish the second."

December 18
Today's Reading: Hebrews 11, 12
"Holiness without which no man shall see the Lord"
Hebrews 12:14

There is a holiness to be pursued, without which no man shall see the Lord. God is holy. Being perfectly holy, he demands perfect holiness. He requires perfect righteousness. Anyone who is not perfectly holy will be consumed by the fire of his glorious holiness. He declares, "I am Almighty God; walk before me, and be thou perfect." "It shall be perfect to be accepted; there shall be no blemish therein." "Be ye holy; for I am holy."

God's Requirement
God demands character holiness. We are required to be holy on the inside, in heart, at the very core of our being. "The Lord looketh on the heart" (1 Samuel 16:7). He demands conduct holiness. We must be holy on the outside, in behaviour. "Be ye holy in all manner of conversation" (1 Peter 1:15). In a word, God demands complete holiness. We must be entirely without sin. "The soul that sinneth, it shall die" (Ezekiel 18:20).

Our Inability
God demands holiness; but we cannot produce holiness. Not one of us can do one good thing before God. It is written, "There is none that doeth good, no not one" (Romans 3:12). Purity cannot come from our corrupt nature. We cannot even seek the Lord on our own, much less correct our past record, change our present wretchedness (Psalm 51:1-5), or control our future thoughts and deeds (Galatians 3:10).

The whole purpose of God's law is to show us our utter inability to keep it and to convince us of our need of a Substitute (Galatians 3:24). And the first work of God the Holy Spirit in a sinner's heart is to convince him of sin, of his need of a Substitute (John 16:9).

God's Character
A person's definition of righteousness depends entirely upon his understanding of who God is. The problem with this religious generation is that they have never seen the holy, righteous, just character of God Almighty. They have never seen the absolute holiness of God. And no one will ever see the holy character of God until he sees what happened at Calvary (Isaiah 6:1-6).

God's Gift
How good does a person have to be to get to heaven? He must be as good as God. "It must be perfect to be accepted." God cannot and will not accept anything short of perfection. "Who shall ascend into the hill of the Lord? or who shall stand in his holy place? He that hath clean hands, and a pure heart; who hath not lifted up his soul unto vanity, nor sworn deceitfully" (Psalm 24:3, 4), and no one else. Yet, it is written,

"They that are in the flesh cannot please God." "Cursed is everyone that continueth not in all things written in the book of the law to do them" (Galatians 3:10). But the fact that we cannot produce perfect holiness does not mean that it cannot be produced. God can do it. Man cannot please God; but God can please God. Man cannot produce righteousness and holiness; but God can produce them for us, and he has done so by the incarnation, life, and death of his own dear Son, and by the gift of his Son in the new birth making us "partakers of the divine nature", creating us in "righteousness and true holiness" in the new creation of grace.

December 19
Today's Reading: Hebrews 13-James 2
"I will never leave thee, nor forsake thee"
Hebrews 13:5

Here is a word of promise from our great God. "I will never leave thee, nor forsake thee." Here is a word from God that is full of spiritual meaning and instruction. This is bread for the Father's children. This is a staff upon which weary pilgrims may lean. It will give us strength for our journey, comfort for our souls, and vigour for our hearts. This sentence is a chest full of rich treasure. May God the Holy Spirit graciously open it and cause our souls to be enriched by it. "I will never leave thee, nor forsake thee." The Lord our God promises his perpetual presence and care to every believer forever.

This is a quotation from the Old Testament Scriptures. How many times have you heard someone deny the application of a promise, a warning, or a doctrine by saying, "That is in the Old Bible", or "That is in the Old Testament"? Many are of the opinion that only a very small portion of the Bible was really intended for us in this day. They say, "The Old Testament was for the Jews. The four Gospels are for the tribulation saints. The Book of Revelation is for the Millennial saints. The epistles of Peter, James, and John were for Jewish believers in the first century. And Paul's epistles alone are really intended for the Gentile believers of this age." Rubbish!

God the Holy Ghost caused the inspired writer here to quote a promise from the Old Testament. In doing so, he teaches us to honour the Old Testament Scriptures as the Word of God, just as we do the New Testament. And he tells us that the promises of God made to his ancient people are the promises of God made to his people today (2 Corinthians 1:20).

Five Times
We find this promise given five times in the Old Testament. (1.) It was given to Jacob at Bethel when he was on his way to Laban's house and fourteen years of great trial (Genesis 28:15). (2.) It was given to Moses just before the Lord took him up into the

mountain to kill him, a promise by which God assured Moses that everything would be well with Israel after he was gone (Deuteronomy 31:6-8). (3.) It was given to Joshua when he was commissioned to lead the people of God in Moses' place, and again just as he began the work to which God had called him (Deuteronomy 31:7, 8; Joshua 1:5). (4.) It was given to Solomon when he was about to assume the throne of Israel, and was commissioned to build the house of the Lord (1 Chronicles 28:20). And (5.) it was given to God's afflicted people when they had to face their mighty enemies (Isaiah 41:10-14; 43:1-5).

Lessons
What are we to learn from the fact that the inspired writer here gives us the same promise that God gave to Moses, Jacob, Joshua, Solomon, and Israel? You will notice that he gives us the sense of the promise, not the very words of the promise, teaching us that the sense of Scripture, the spiritual message of Scripture, is the meaning of Scripture. Many know the Scriptures "by heart" who do not know the heart of the Scriptures!

I know there is a danger here. We believe in the verbal, plenary inspiration of Holy Scripture. But we do not interpret the Scriptures in a strictly literal way. The Spirit of God gives us spiritual understanding to discern the message of Scripture. And the message is always a spiritual, Christ centred, Christ honouring message (Luke 24:27, 44-47).

It is also evident that every word from God to any believer is the Word of God to every believer. God who made the promise never changes (Malachi 3:6; Hebrews 13:8). All the promises of God in Christ Jesus are yea and amen (2 Corinthians 1:20), conditioned on Christ alone! The promises made to one are made to all, for all believers in Christ are one body (Ephesians 4:4).

The Bible a Book written for me. It is a word from the Lord to me. Robert Murray M'Cheyne put it, "Every word of divine love and tenderness that he has written in this book belongs to me." So this promise from the Lord is God's promise to me particularly. "I will never leave thee, nor forsake thee." And this, my brother, my sister, is the promise of God to you. "I will never leave thee, nor forsake thee."

December 20
Today's Reading: James 3-1 Peter 1
"Imputed unto him for righteousness"
James 2:23

The Holy Spirit declares, "Abraham believed God, and it was imputed unto him for righteousness: and he was called the Friend of God". He could never have been the friend of God without righteousness; neither can we.

The Lord Jesus Christ came into this world for the purpose of fulfilling all righteousness as the Representative of God's elect. And he did it! He brought in, established, and finished the work of righteousness for all his people by his obedience to the Father as our Federal Head and Covenant Surety. It is this righteousness, the righteousness of God in Christ, that is proclaimed to sinners in the preaching of the gospel (Romans 3:24-28). Until the righteousness of God, which was accomplished by the faithful obedience of Christ, is plainly declared, the gospel has not been preached. And any gospel that offers sinners any other righteousness than that which Christ has accomplished is a false gospel. It is this righteousness, accomplished by Christ, which is imputed to us for justification and acceptance with God. The Word of God speaks of a threefold imputation.

Adam's Sin Imputed To All
Adam's sin has been imputed to all men when we all sinned in Adam's fall (Romans 5:12, 18, 19). By God's appointment, Adam was the head and representative of all our race. When he sinned, we all sinned in him; and, sinning, we all became sinners. God laid the charge and guilt of Adam's sin (our sin in Adam) upon us. Adam's sin was imputed to all the human race, because we all sinned in our father, Adam. We became sinners not by what we do personally, but by what Adam, our representative, did, by what we did in him.

Our Sin Imputed To Christ
All the sins of God's elect were imputed to Christ when he was made sin for us (Isaiah 53:6, 8; 2 Corinthians 5:21). Our Lord Jesus never committed any act of sin. But when he was made sin as our Substitute, our sins were imputed to him, charged to his account. When he was made sin, he was justly punished for sin as our Substitute, suffering all the just consequences of sin for us, being made a curse for us (Galatians 3:13). Sin could never have been imputed to him had he not been made sin for us. O wondrous grace! O wondrous Saviour! He who knew no sin was made sin for us, that we might be made the righteousness of God in him!

Christ's Righteousness Imputed To Us
And the righteousness of Christ is imputed to every believer, because we have been made the righteousness of God in him (Romans 3:23, 24; 2 Corinthians 5:21; Romans 5:19). We are not made righteous by something we do, any more than Christ was made to be sin by something he did. Christ's obedience has been charged to the account of all God's elect, those represented by him, those for whom he lived and died, those who trust him. God looks upon us in Christ as men and women who are perfectly righteous. He reckons us to be righteous in his sight. And you can be sure of this: if God looks upon us as being righteous, reckons us righteous, and declares that we are righteous, we are righteous! And just as he justly rewarded Christ for our sins, when he was made sin for us, he justly rewards us with eternal life for that perfect righteousness which is ours in Christ.

534

Discovering Christ Day By Day

December 21
Today's Reading: 1 Peter 2-5
"Unto you therefore which believe he is precious"
1 Peter 2:7

This is not some far-fetched, fanatical notion. It is a fact. God the Holy Ghost has caused it to be written in the volume of inspiration as the truth of God. It is confirmed by the history of the Church from Abel to Malachi, from John the Baptist to John the Beloved. It is confirmed by those martyrs who suffered imprisonment and death from Stephen to Polycarp, from Latimer and Ridley to Bunyan. The blood of God's saints cries out from the ground, from the dungeons of Rome, and from the torture chambers of the Pope's inquisition, "Christ is precious." And it is confirmed by the experience of all who believe. From their inmost soul, God's elect all agree, "He is precious." This is faith's estimation of the Lord Jesus Christ.

Precious In Himself
When we think of our Saviour's glorious person, we say, "He is precious." He is the God-man. Jesus Christ is himself God Almighty, the eternal Son of the eternal Father. The brightness of the Father's glory and the express image of his Person is Christ our Saviour. And he is man, the perfect man, "holy, harmless, undefiled, and separate from sinners." He is precious in himself, intrinsically precious. He is the Rose of Sharon, the Lily of the Valley, the Fairest among Ten Thousand. He is Altogether Lovely. Who can compare with this glorious Person? He is precious.

Precious To Me
And when I recall what he has done for my soul, I am overwhelmed with his love and grace. Beholding Christ as my redeeming Substitute, my heart is constrained to say, "He is precious." In love he chose me and became my Surety in the covenant of grace. He lived upon the earth, in conformity to the law of God, to accomplish righteousness for me. And he died in my stead upon the cursed tree, putting away all my sin. Being made sin for me, that I might be made the righteousness of God in him, the Son of God bore all the fury of God's infinite wrath unto the full satisfaction of divine justice on my behalf. For me he arose and assumed the throne of universal dominion. Behold, O my soul, Jesus Christ your crucified, risen, exalted, reigning Redeemer, and know this, "He is precious."

Precious To You
Is Christ precious to you? If he is, you are a true believer. If he is not, you do not have the faith of God's elect. Do you believe in Jesus for life and salvation? If you do, he is precious to you. He is precious in himself; and God's gift of faith working in you makes him precious to you. Is the Lord Jesus precious in his person, precious in his work, precious in his offices, precious in his relations, precious in his whole

535

character? Do you know him, so as to love him, to live to him, to rejoice in him, and to cast your whole soul upon him, for life and salvation? Do you accept him as the Father's gift, the Sent, the Sealed, the Anointed, the Christ, of the Father? Is he so precious, that there is nothing in him but what you love, nothing you would change? His cross is precious, as well as his crown! Afflictions with him are sweeter than prosperity without him.

No Other
Pause, my soul, to think about these things. There is nothing outside of Christ that can be truly satisfying. Your dearest earthly relation, however sweet, has some tinge, some alloy, something impure, something bitter. But there is no mixture of impurity or bitterness in Christ. All he is is pure, and lovely, and transcendently glorious. He is, as one of old described him, "a sea of sweetness, without a single drop of gall". "Unto you therefore which believe he is precious."

December 22
Today's Reading: 2 Peter 1-3
"Partakers of the divine nature"
2 Peter 1:4

As all men were created in and simultaneously with the first Adam, all God's elect were created new and simultaneously with the last Adam, the Lord Jesus Christ. As we had being in Adam from the beginning of creation, all God's elect have had being with Christ from eternity. Being born of Adam in natural generation, we necessarily partake of Adam's nature. And being "born of God" in regeneration, we are made "partakers of the divine nature". As the seed of the first Adam partake of his nature, the seed of the last Adam partake of his nature.

Two Natures
The children of the first Adam are born of the flesh and are earthy in all their thoughts, feelings, and affections. The children of the last Adam are born of the Spirit, and are spiritual and heavenly in all their thoughts, feelings, and affections. The children of the first Adam are born for the earth. The children of the last Adam are born for heaven.

These two men, the old and the new, Adam and Christ, flesh and spirit, dwell in every child of God in this world; but they do not dwell together. They are in a state of perpetual warfare (Romans 7:14; Galatians 5:16-25). The flesh, the old man, is altogether sinful and corrupt. It can do nothing but sin. The spirit, the new man, that which is born of God, is altogether righteousness and cannot sin (1 John 3:5-10).

536

Real Union
Our existence in Adam was a representative existence, yes; but it was more. It was a real, vital existence. We had being in our father Adam from the beginning, being created in him and with him. Our union with him in the Garden was real. When he sinned, we sinned in him. When he died, we died in him. It is not merely that we were reckoned to have sinned and reckoned to have died. We sinned in Adam and we died in Adam, because we were one with Adam from the beginning.

Now, here's the good news. Our existence in Christ from the beginning, before the foundation of the world, our eternal union with Christ was and is a real, vital existence with the God-man, our Mediator, Surety, and Saviour. When he stood forth as our Surety before time began and was accepted of God as "the Lamb slain from the foundation of the world" (Revelation 13:8), we were accepted in him and blessed with all spiritual blessings in him (Ephesians 1:3-6).

Made Fit
Yet, before we could enter heaven as heirs of God and joint-heirs with Christ, something more must be done. Justice satisfied does not make anyone fit for heaven. Righteousness imputed does not make the ransomed sinner worthy of heavenly glory. It is only when redeemed sinners are made "partakers of the divine nature" in the new birth that the righteousness of Christ is imparted to them and they are, by the grace and gracious operations of God, made "meet to be partakers of the inheritance of the saints in light" (Colossians 1:12). The imputed righteousness of Christ in redemption makes us worthy of heaven. The imparted righteousness of Christ in regeneration makes us fit for heaven.

December 23
Today's Reading: 1 John 1-5
"In him is no sin"
1 John 3:5

The Lord Jesus Christ was manifested to take away our sins; and in him there is no sin. Though he was made sin for us, our Lord Jesus Christ had no sin of his own. "He knew no sin, neither was any guile found in his mouth." "He was holy, harmless, undefiled, and separate from sinners." In order for him to be a suitable sacrifice for sin, it was necessary that our Saviour be without sin. The sinner's Substitute must himself be innocent, righteous, and holy.

Made Sin
Yet, in order to redeem us from our sins and to justify us before God, the Son of God had to be made sin for us. When the Lord Jesus was made sin for us, our guilt was

made his guilt, and our curse was made his curse. Being made sin for us, our sin and our guilt was imputed to the Lord Jesus Christ; and God's holy law exacted from him the just penalty of our sins. "He hath made him to be sin for us, who knew no sin, that we might be made the righteousness of God in him." "Christ hath redeemed us from the curse of the law, being made a curse for us: for it is written, cursed is everyone that hangeth on a tree."

No Sin
Now, having taken our sins upon himself, suffering for us the just penalty of our sins, our glorious Mediator in heaven once again has no sin. That One who sits in heaven and makes intercession for us has no sin. We know and are assured that God will accept him and will accept his intercession for us, because he is perfect. He is holy. He has no sin. This is the basis of our assurance and confidence with God. We have a perfect Substitute and Sacrifice whom the Father will accept.

No Sin In Him
But here, as he was infallibly inspired by God the Holy Ghost, the Apostle John is speaking of those who are in Christ. He is telling us that in Christ we have no sin. In ourselves we are sinners. The old nature of sin is with us, and will be with us so long as we are in this world. Anyone who denies this is a liar, and makes God a liar. But before God, in the sight of God, those who are in Christ by a living faith have no sin. "He was manifested to take away our sins." And he has done it, "And in him is no sin." The all-seeing eye of God's holy law sees no sin in his elect (Numbers 23:21), because in Christ we have no sin.

In the covenant of grace God promised that he would forgive us of our sins and remember them no more (Jeremiah 31:33, 34; Hebrews 8:10-12; 10:16-18). The means whereby he has accomplished this blessed forgiveness of sin is the substitutionary sacrifice of his dear Son. Our Lord Jesus Christ has, by his one atoning sacrifice, put away our sins; and they are no more (Romans 8:3; Colossians 2:14). "Now once in the end of the world hath he appeared to put away sin by the sacrifice of himself."

> My sin, O the bliss of this glorious thought,
> My sin, not in part, but the whole,
> Is nailed to his cross, and I bear it no more,
> Praise the Lord, It is well with my soul.

Because the Lord Jesus Christ has put away our sins by his great atonement, God will never charge with sin, in anyway whatsoever, those for whom Christ suffered and died. "Blessed is the man to whom the Lord will not impute sin."

Now, believing on the Lord Jesus Christ, we are freed from sin. Being united to him by faith, we have no sin in him (Romans 6:7, 8; 1 Peter 4:1, 2). Trusting Christ as our Representative and Substitute, we fulfil the law of God perfectly and completely, because he fulfilled the law for us, as our Representative (Romans 8:4).

Child of the living God, get hold of this blessed revelation of the gospel and rejoice in it, "In him is no sin."

> Did you hear what Jesus said to me?
> "They're all taken away:
> Your sins are pardoned, and you are free:
> They're all taken away."

If we are in Christ, we are no longer under the dominion of sin; we are no longer subject to condemnation because of sin; in the eyes of the law we are no longer guilty of, or accountable for, sin; and we will never be charged with or punished for sin. Sin cannot be justly punished where sin is not found. Blessed be God for his great grace which put us "in Christ". "And in him is no sin."

December 24
Today's Reading: 2 John-Jude
"Him that is able"
Jude 24

As Jude comes to the close of his Epistle, having warned us of the incessant assaults of hell, showing us the terrible apostasy of many, he urges us to "keep ourselves in the love of God". And he tells us that we must do so, "building ourselves up in our most holy faith, praying in the Holy Ghost, looking for the mercy of our Lord Jesus Christ unto eternal life."

When I read that admonition, immediately my thought is, "But I can't do that. I'm too weak, too sinful. I cannot keep myself in the love of God. It is my responsibility. I must do it. There the commandment stands. 'Keep yourselves in the love of God.' But I can't do it." Then, I read verses 24 and 25, and my heart dances with joy. I cannot keep myself; but God my Saviour, the Lord Jesus Christ can and will keep me. And keeping me, he will cause me to keep myself.

Having told us what we must do, Jude commends us to the grace and power of God our Saviour, teaching us to trust him, from whom alone we expect eternal life. Oh, for grace to trust him who alone is able to keep us from falling. Except he keep us, we can never keep ourselves.

Who?
When Jude speaks of "him that is able to keep you", I have to ask, of whom does he speak? Without question, God the Father, our heavenly Father, is able to keep us. With God all things are possible. Nothing is too hard for the Lord. Jude here assures

us that our God's omnipotent power and ability is engaged by promise and by covenant office as our Father.

God the Holy Spirit, the Comforter, by whom we are sealed unto the day of redemption, is able to keep us, and is engaged to do so. He who is the Earnest of our inheritance will make certain that we come into the full possession of our inheritance.

And God the Son, our Lord Jesus Christ, who is the Guardian of our souls, the Shepherd of the sheep, and the King of Zion, is able to keep us, and is engaged to do so as our covenant Surety. In a word, the eternal, Triune God is our Keeper.

We fall not, because God will not let go his hold upon us. Our necessities and difficulties are so great that nothing less than divine power can keep us. We are "kept by the power of God through faith unto salvation." "Behold, he that keepeth Israel shall neither slumber nor sleep. The LORD is thy keeper: the LORD is thy shade upon thy right hand" (Psalm 121:4, 5).

Our weak flesh says, "I will fail." The world says, "I will choke out the influence of the Word of God upon them." False religion says, "I will deceive them." The devil says, "I will take them." But he who is God our Saviour, the Custodian of our souls, says, "I will keep them. I will never fail them, nor forsake them." That is our safety and security!

Our Relief

What a great relief it is to my feeble faith to read of "him that is able to keep you". It is "him that is able to keep you", who said, "I give unto them eternal life; and they shall never perish, neither shall any man pluck them out of my hand. My Father, which gave them me, is greater than all; and no man is able to pluck them out of my Father's hand" (John 10:28, 29). He declares in his Word that all his own shall stand firm in his grace on this earth until they stand in the fulness of his glory in heaven. "Yea, he shall be holden up: for God is able to make him stand" (Romans 14:4).

Boaz And Jachin

At Solomon's command, we are told that Hiram set two pillars in the porch of the temple and named them "Boaz" and "Jachin". "Boaz" means "Strength". And "Jachin" means "He will establish" (1 Kings 7:21). Boaz, as you know, typified Christ our Kinsman-Redeemer. Jachin was a priest in Israel. As such, he was also typical of our Saviour. And Christ our Redeemer and Priest is our Strength, and he will establish. The power of God and the grace of God in him are the two pillars upon which our confidence stands.

God's Power

Here is the power of God our Saviour. He who is our omnipotent Saviour is "him that is able". What a great thought that is! He who is our God and Saviour is a God with whom all things are possible. "He is able." Those three words mean that nothing is too hard for the Lord. No problem is too great for him. "With God nothing shall be impossible."

December 25
Today's Reading: Revelation 1-3
"The Revelation of Jesus Christ"
Revelation 1:1

Today all the world is reminded of the fact that God the Son came into the world in human flesh to redeem and save his people from their sins. How fitting it is that today we have begun to read the book of our Saviour's conquests "The Revelation of Jesus Christ". The Book of Revelation gives us seven visions of the Person and work of our great God and Saviour, the Lord Jesus Christ. In these seven visions the Lord revealed to John what he had done, is doing, and shall hereafter do for his Church, in his Church, and with his Church.

The whole purpose of the closing book of Holy Scripture is to assure God's children in this world of our ultimate conquest over the world, the flesh, and the devil. Our translators call the last book of the Bible "The Revelation of Saint John the Divine" and many refer to it as "The Book of Revelations" (plural). Both are incorrect. The final book of Holy Scripture is the revelation (singular) of our blessed Saviour. God the Holy Spirit specifically gives it this title: "The Revelation of Jesus Christ".

By revealing to us who he is and what he does, our Lord calls for us to ever look to him with confident faith, and assures us that we are "more than conquerors through him that loved us".

Seven Visions
The seven visions John saw and recorded by divine inspiration are set before us in consecutive order in the twenty-two chapters of this Book. He saw ...

1. The Lord Jesus Christ in the midst of his churches, the seven golden candlesticks, in this world (chapters 1-3).
2. The Lamb of God opening and fulfilling the seven-sealed book of God's sovereign, eternal purpose (chapters 4-7).
3. The Lord Jesus answering the prayers of his people, protecting them from their enemies and vindicating them by executing the seven trumpets of judgment in his providential rule of the universe (chapters 8-11). God's judgments upon the world are but God's vindication of his elect.
4. The Son of God and his Church persecuted by Satan, world government, and false religion, the war between Christ and Satan (chapters 12-14).
5. The Lord Jesus sending forth his angels to pour out the seven vials of his wrath upon the earth (chapters 15, 16).
6. Christ's conquest over Babylon; all false, freewill, works religion, the beast, and the false prophet (chapters 17-19).

7. Christ's glorious dominion over and destruction of Satan, and the glory of the New Jerusalem (chapters 20-22).

These seven visions each cover the whole gospel age from the first to the second coming of Christ. They do not represent different ages, dispensations, or prophetic events. They all tell the same story. They all tell us what our Lord has done, is doing, and shall do for the salvation of his people, assuring us of the ultimate triumph of Christ and his Church by the gospel.

The Number Seven
The use of the number "seven" in the Book of Revelation is striking. There are "Seven Golden Candlesticks", "Seven Churches", "Seven Stars", "Seven Seals", "Seven Trumpets", "Seven Angels", "Seven Vials".
Seven is the number of perfection, completion, and satisfaction. And in each of these seven visions, the Holy Spirit assures us of the perfect rule of Christ as the Monarch of the universe for the complete victory and eternal salvation of his Church. What a blessed assurance that is. Christ has prevailed! Christ is prevailing! Christ shall prevail!
The number of the beast, we are told, is 666 (Revelation 13:18). Six is the number of man, the number of frustration, failure, and defeat. God's elect have nothing to fear from him whose number is six!

Our Comfort
When your soul is heavy, when your life is filled with chaos, when darkness blackens your sky, when everything in your life seems to be turning upside down, and confusion seizes your very soul, lift up your eyes unto the hills and hope in God our Saviour, who closes his Book with "The Revelation of Jesus Christ", "the Lion of the tribe of Juda", who has prevailed to fulfil all the good will and purpose of God for your soul. Behold the Lamb upon his throne and rejoice. Be easy, O my soul! The Lamb of God who loved me and gave himself for me sits upon the throne of heaven! "The Lord God omnipotent reigneth." Let us be glad and rejoice!

December 26
Today's Reading: Revelation 4-7
"Worthy is the Lamb"
Revelation 5:12

God our Saviour, the Lord Jesus Christ and he alone is worthy of honour, worship, praise, love, trust, and glory. I have read it in God's Book. I have heard it in the preaching of the gospel. I have experienced it in my soul. "Worthy is the Lamb." The apostle Paul said, "This man was counted worthy of more glory." The angels are not worthy, but Christ is. No man is worthy, but Christ is. The church is not worthy, but Christ is. The preacher is not worthy, but Christ is. In heaven, all the saints and angels unite in this glorious eternal song, "Worthy is the Lamb."

Divine Creator
Christ is worthy of all honour because he is the divine Creator (Revelation 4:11). In heaven, everyone delights to worship Jesus Christ as God. And if ever a man gets to glory, he will have had to worship Jesus Christ upon the earth as God the eternal Son, the Creator of all things, who created the world in the beginning by infinite power. He creates men anew by sovereign power. And he creates all the events of providence according to his own wise decree. In the end, all things will prove to be for his pleasure, his honour, and his glory (Proverbs 16:4).

Merciful Redeemer
Christ is worthy of all worship because he is our merciful redeemer (Revelation 5:9, 10). The Triune Jehovah, "who first trusted in Christ" (Ephesians 1:12), counted him worthy to be the Substitute, Surety, and Redeemer of his people, committing the salvation of our souls into his hands as "the Lamb slain from the foundation of the world". His righteousness is worthy to clothe us. His sufferings are worthy to satisfy divine justice for us. His blood is worthy to make us clean. His power is worthy to preserve us. His love is worthy to win our hearts. Christ proved himself worthy. As the Lion of Judah he prevailed with God. As the Lamb of God He redeemed us to God, making us a generation of priests and kings. And now, with our hearts, we say Christ is worthy! He is worthy of our implicit faith, worthy of our steadfast obedience, worthy of our unwavering love, and worthy of our hearts' utter devotion and humble worship!

Exalted King
Christ is worthy of eternal praise because he is God's exalted King (Revelation 5:11-14). As God's exalted King every creature of God, in heaven, in the earth, and under the earth shall say, "Worthy is the Lamb that was slain." In the end, in "the times of the restitution of all things", all that is, has been, and shall hereafter be shall say with a loud voice, "Worthy is the Lamb that was slain to receive power, and riches, and wisdom, and strength, and honour, and glory, and blessing. And every creature which is in heaven, and on the earth, and under the earth, and such as are in the sea, and all that are in them, heard I saying, Blessing, and honour, and glory, and power, be unto him that sitteth upon the throne, and unto the Lamb for ever and ever. And the four beasts said, Amen. And the four and twenty elders fell down and worshipped him that liveth for ever and ever."

_____

December 27
Today's Reading: Revelation 8-10
"I saw another mighty angel come down from heaven"
Revelation 10:1

As we come to Revelation 10, six trumpets have sounded and the seventh, final trumpet is about to sound. Just before John sees the final, consummate judgment of God fall upon the earth, the Lord Jesus Christ appears with one last word of warning. He stood "upon the sea and upon the earth (and) lifted up his hand to heaven, and sware by him that liveth for ever and ever." Because he could sware by no greater, he swore by himself, "that there should be time no longer". It is as though the Lord is saying, "No more delay! Prepare to meet thy God." If you read chapters 8-11 at one sitting, you cannot fail to see that chapter 10 is an abrupt interruption of events. It is almost parenthetical. It stands as both a word of warning to God's enemies of the certainty of divine judgment, and a word of comfort to God's elect for it portrays and assures us of the providential rule of our Lord Jesus Christ, the Angel of the Covenant. What could be more comforting than the fact that he who loved us from eternity, died to redeem us at Calvary, and saves us by his almighty grace, sovereignly rules all things according to God's eternal purpose for us? This is the picture we have before us in this wondrous chapter.

A Mighty Angel
Here, John sees the Lord Jesus as "a mighty angel". Our Lord Jesus Christ is the mighty God, our Saviour, the mighty Mediator, and the mighty King. He is able to protect, defend, and save his own. Chapter 9 describes the terrible woe that must come upon the earth. Then, Christ, the mighty Angel, appears. This appearance seems to say, "Let not your heart be troubled. The ark of God is safe." This mighty Angel is Christ our Saviour, who sovereignly rules all things.

Come Down
Next, we are told that John saw Christ, as a mighty Angel "come down from heaven". This does not refer to our Lord's incarnation, or to his coming down to judge the world in the last day. These words refer to our Lord's appearance in providence to protect, defend, and comfort his people. Though the Lord Jesus is in heaven, seated upon the throne of glory, he has not forsaken his Church. His body has been taken from us, but not his heart. Christ is always with his people. As often as we need him, he comes to us in special grace, revealing his presence and power to us (Daniel 3:25).

Clothed With A Cloud
When Christ appeared to John, he was "clothed with a cloud". Remember, John has just seen days of terrible spiritual darkness, apostasy, and false religion, which devour men's souls as locusts devour vegetation (Revelation 9:3, 4). In such times, the Lord Jesus hides himself from men. They cannot see his glory. It is as though he has hidden himself in a cloud. They know his name, but not his power. They know the facts of

his death, burial, and resurrection, but not the accomplishments of his redemptive work. They know that Christ is in heaven, but know nothing of the majesty of his heavenly throne. They know that he makes intercession, but know nothing of the efficacy of his intercession. They know that Jesus saves, but not how he saves. They know the words "redeeming blood", "saving grace", and "matchless love". But they know nothing of the blood's atonement, grace's power, or love's immutability. This world is in a fog insofar as the things of Christ are concerned. If we see the glory of his Person and the efficacy of his saving grace, we have great reason to pause and give thanks. "Flesh and blood hath not revealed it unto thee, but my Father which is in heaven" (See Matthew 11:25-27).

A Rainbow

The rainbow upon our Redeemer's head tells us that the covenant of grace is fulfilled in him and by him. He is ever mindful of his covenant. Even in the worst of times, our dear Saviour rules this world according to the stipulations of the covenant. He will not allow his people to be overwhelmed by the flood of antichrist's religion. The gates of hell shall not prevail against his Church. The Messenger of the covenant appears to bring us peace, to let us know that better days are coming. Soon we shall have times of refreshing, either from the presence of the Lord, or in the presence of the Lord. No matter how dark the storms of life may be, if we can see that rainbow upon that head, our hearts will find peace and satisfaction (2 Samuel 23:5).

Like The Sun

Next, our Saviour's face is "as it were the sun". This is how the disciples saw him on the mount of transfiguration (Matthew 17:1-8). This expression speaks of the purity and glory of Christ, both as God and as man. Being God, Jesus Christ our Saviour is the brightness of the Father's glory and the express image of his Person. He lived as a man in this world in perfect righteousness. In all things he was and is; holy, harmless, undefiled, and separate from sinners. And the God-man in heaven is clothed with all the ineffable glory of the eternal God, for he is God. As God, he is light (1 John 1:5). As the Mediator between God and men, he imparts the light of grace and glory to the sons of men.

Pillars Of Fire

His feet are "as pillars of fire". Our Lord's feet are like fire. In all his ways of providence, he is a consuming fire to his enemies. He will destroy them in a moment, like raging fire consumes dried grass. But he is a wall of fire about his Church to defend and protect us. His feet are pillars, unshaken, immovable pillars to uphold all who trust him. Lean upon him. Christ is a mighty Saviour. All his ways of grace, providence, mercy, and judgment are righteous altogether. He is too wise to err and too good to do wrong. His throne, his work, and his purposes are both righteous and sure. His feet are "as pillars of fire".

December 28
Today's Reading: Revelation 11-13
"The book of life"
Revelation 13:8

In Revelation 13:8 God the Holy Spirit, our divine Comforter, reminds us of three comforting, assuring, soul-cheering truths taught throughout the Word of God. In the midst of a vision of darkness and woe, we are given three bright, shining lights of joy.

Eternal Election
First, this sweet text sets before us the eternal election of grace. It speaks of "the book of life" and those whose names are written in it, as well as those whose names are not written in it. We are here assured that there is a book in which all the names of God's elect are registered and have been registered "from the foundation of the world". It is called "the Lamb's book of life" in Revelation 21:27. It is mentioned here to remind us that as long as the world stands there will be "a remnant according to the election of grace" (Romans 11:5). Even in the darkest days of apostasy, though the world is engulfed in the religion of anti-christ, God has an elect people whom he will save, a people who will not perish with the world (Matthew 24:22-24). God's eternal election secures his people from the delusion of false religion (2 Thessalonians 2:11-14).

Eternal Redemption
Second, the Spirit of God assures us of the eternal redemption of God's elect. John describes our Saviour as "the Lamb slain from the foundation of the world". In doing so, he is telling us, by the inspiration of God the Holy Spirit, that redemption was accomplished for God's elect before the world began, because our Lord Jesus Christ was slain before the world was made. Had it not been for the eternal accomplishment of redemption in the covenant of grace before the world began (2 Timothy 1:9; Romans 8:29, 30), God would have immediately destroyed the race as soon as Adam sinned in the garden. God's longsuffering with men in general is for the salvation of his elect, the result of his eternal grace toward his elect (2 Peter 3:9, 15). God preserves the reprobate for the sake of his elect; those for whom the Lamb was slain from the foundation of the world, who must and shall be saved.

Eternal Security
Thirdly, eternal election and eternal redemption assure us of the eternal security of God's elect. Those whose names were written in the book of life, for whom the Lamb was slain, cannot perish. If even one believing sinner should fail to attain heavenly glory with Christ, the purpose and grace of God would fall to the ground defeated, the blood of Christ would mean nothing, and the glory of God would be gone!

December 29
Today's Reading: Revelation 14-16
"Blessed are the dead which die in the Lord"
Revelation14:13

Death for the believer is not a thing to be dreaded. The grave is but a bed for his body. By death "the righteous is taken away from the evil to come" (Isaiah 57:1, 2). As soon as he dies, the child of God enters into a state of blessedness in heaven, even while he awaits the glorious resurrection of his body.

Blessed In Dying
The believer is blessed in his dying. It does not matter when, where, or by what means the child of God dies. Those who die in the Lord are blessed in the expectation of death (2 Timothy 1:12; 4:6-8; Job 19:25-27), in the experience of death (2 Samuel 23:5; Acts 7:56), and in the event of death.

Blessed After Dying
God's saints are forever blessed after they die (2 Corinthians 5:1-9). "Blessed are the dead which die in the Lord from henceforth." That is to say, after death nothing awaits us but blessedness, forever! "God shall wipe away all tears from their eyes." After death, for the believer, there will be no more sorrow, no more weeping, no more pain, no more trouble, no more sickness, no more suffering, no more sin!

Blessed Rest
Once we have dropped this robe of flesh, we shall rest from our labours. Do not imagine the saints of God in heaven have no more service to render to Christ. Heaven is a place of unending, perfect service. But we shall rest from the labour of our service. In heaven there will be no ignorant ones to teach, no erring ones to rebuke, no despondency to comfort, no weakness to strengthen, no error to oppose, no needy ones to supply, no enemies to engage, no fences to mend, no strife to heal, no sick ones to visit, no bereaved ones to console, no straying ones to correct, no sinners to convert, no tears to dry. We shall rest from our labours; labours of the body, labours of the soul, labours of the heart, labours for Christ, labours in the gospel.

The word "labours" has in it the idea of woe. In heaven we shall rest from the woe of our labours. In this world all that we do for Christ has a certain measure of woe connected with it. You cannot serve Christ here without cost. But there we shall rest from the toils, sorrows, faults, failures, discouragement, disappointments, and strife of our labours. Nothing of sorrow will defile the blessedness of heavenly glory! "Blessed are the dead which die in the Lord from henceforth: Yea, saith the Spirit, that they may rest from their labours."

December 30
Today's Reading: Revelation 17-19
"His name is called the Word of God"
Revelation 19:13

Our Lord Jesus Christ is the Word of God incarnate (John 1:1-14). "In the beginning was the Word." This is a term used in the New Testament almost exclusively by John, identifying Christ as one who is God, and yet a distinct Person from the Father. I can think of only two places in which other inspired writers used this term in the New Testament with reference to our Saviour. In Hebrews 4:12, 13 we read "For the word of God is quick, and powerful, and sharper than any twoedged sword, piercing even to the dividing asunder of soul and spirit, and of the joints and marrow, and is a discerner of the thoughts and intents of the heart. Neither is there any creature that is not manifest in his sight: but all things are naked and opened unto the eyes of him with whom we have to do." In 2 Peter 3:5 we read, "that by the word of God the heavens were of old".

Deity Expressed
A word is an expression, a means of manifestation, communication, and revelation. Christ manifests the invisible God, communicates the love, mercy, and grace of God, and reveals the attributes and perfections of God. The Word of God, then, is Deity expressing itself. Therefore Christ is called the Word of God (Hebrews 1:1-3). Our dear Saviour is the true and complete expression of the eternal, Triune God. He is the living Word of whom the written Word speaks and in whom the written Word is fulfilled. When he comes in judgment, he will reveal the righteousness, justice and truth of God.

Alpha And Omega
In Revelation 1:8 our Saviour declares himself to be God's alphabet. "I am Alpha and Omega, the beginning and the ending, saith the Lord, which is, and which was, and which is to come, the Almighty." Christ is the Word in and by whom the Triune God makes himself known to men, the personal enunciation of Jehovah (John 1:18).

Record In Heaven
Christ, the Word, is one of the Holy Three-in-One that bear record in heaven. "There are three that bear record in heaven" (1 John 5:7). Bear record of what? That Jesus is the Son of God? No. Heaven needs no evidence of that! These three bear record in heaven that God has given us eternal life, in strict accordance with his just and righteous law, by the merits of Christ's obedience and death as our Substitute. The three persons of the holy Trinity bear record in heaven that Christ has accomplished redemption for God's elect by his blood atonement. "There are three that bear record in heaven, the Father, the Word, and the Holy Ghost: and these three are one."

God the Father bears record that redemption is accomplished by his acceptance of Christ as our Representative and Surety (Hebrews 1:1-9; 6:19, 20; 10:11-14). When the Father raised Christ from the dead and received him back into heaven as our Mediator, he accepted all his elect in Christ and bare record that redemption's work was done (Ephesians 1:6; John 17:1-5).

God the Son, the living, eternal Word, the second person of the blessed Trinity, bears record of his people's right to eternal life by his perpetual advocacy and intercession at the Father's right hand (Romans 8:34; 1 John 2:1, 2; Hebrews 6:20; 7:24, 25). The record he bears, which secures the eternal salvation of God's elect, by which we merit heaven and eternal life, is twofold; his righteousness as our Representative and his satisfaction as our Substitute.

God the Holy Spirit, the third person of the holy Trinity, bears record of the accomplishment of redemption, by effectually applying the blood of Christ to the hearts of God's elect in effectual calling (John 16:14; Hebrews 9:13, 14). The Spirit of God takes the merit of Christ's blood and righteousness and reveals our acceptance with God to us by the gospel. In effectual calling chosen, redeemed sinners hear the gospel. But they hear more than the bare word of the gospel. We hear the Spirit of God speak in our hearts! Each one hears God speak pardon to his own soul by the gospel of his salvation (Ephesians 1:13; 2 Corinthians 5:16). This is the record of heaven. The Father, the Word, and the Holy Spirit point to the blood and righteousness of Christ and say, "It is finished! Redemption is accomplished!"

One God
"And these three are one." The three Divine Persons are one God. But more, the record of the Father, the record of the Word, and the record of the Spirit are one. What is that record? Redemption is accomplished by Christ alone! Every chosen sinner has the right to enter into heaven by the blood-gate, by the merits of Christ. "God hath given us eternal life, and this life is in his Son."

Christ, The Word
"His name is called The Word of God." That is a statement so full of meaning that it cannot be adequately declared. Christ is called The Word because he is the Wisdom of God. He is called The Word because he is the Person spoken of in all the Old Testament prophecies and the sum of all the promises. Our Redeemer is called The Word because he is the Speaker, the Revealer, and the Interpreter of the Father's will. And he is called The Word because he is the Image of the invisible God, the Offspring of the Father's mind, the Express Image of his Person, just as our words (if honestly spoken) are the express image of our minds.

All grace comes to chosen sinners through Christ, The Word, who is from everlasting "with God". There is no other way the grace of God can reach a sinner. It is the work of Christ upon the cross which has brought grace and justice together in the salvation of sinners. It is through his blood, only through the blood of the cross, that "mercy and truth are met together; righteousness and peace have kissed each other" (Psalm 85:10). Blissfully lost in the contemplation of God's matchless grace in Christ, John Bunyan expressed the sentiments of my soul this day in these rapturous words;

O Thou Son of the Blessed! Grace stripped Thee of Thy glory. Grace brought Thee down from heaven. Grace made Thee bear such burdens of sin, such burdens of curse as are unspeakable. Grace was in Thy heart. Grace came bubbling up from Thy bleeding side. Grace was in Thy tears. Grace was in Thy prayers. Grace streamed from Thy thorn-crowned brow! Grace came forth with the nails that pierced Thee, with the thorns that pricked Thee! Oh, here are unsearchable riches of grace! Grace to make sinners happy! Grace to make angels wonder! Grace to make devils astonished!

December 31
Today's Reading: Revelation 20-22
"Behold, I make all things new"
Revelation 21:5

What a blessed word with which to conclude the year and anticipate the dawn of the New Year! He who is God our Creator and God our Saviour makes all things new.

Grace
Has he who sits upon the throne of grace made you a new creature in grace? Has he reconciled you to God by his obedience on your behalf? Has he caused your old record of sin to pass away forever by his atoning sacrifice? Has he given you a new record of righteousness, imputing to you his perfect righteousness? Has he given you a new nature by his omnipotent mercy in the new birth? It is written, "If any man be in Christ he is a new creature." Settle these questions for yourself. Believe on the Son of God, and they are settled forever. Your faith in Christ is the evidence of all these things not seen.

Glory
Believing on the Son of God, let us live in the constant and confident expectation of this glorious work of God our Saviour yet to come (Isaiah 65:17-19). What a great and glorious prospect this is! Our God declares that when he has finished with us, when he has created new heavens and a new earth, when our salvation is complete and consummate, we will enter into an everlasting joy that will eclipse all the joys we have known in this world. He bids us rejoice now in the anticipation of the joy awaiting us in eternity. He declares, "the former things shall not be remembered or come to mind." Our sins will not be remembered against us, for Christ has totally purged them away (Hebrews 1:3). They will cause us no sadness in heaven. In that

great and glorious day, our God will make us perfectly joyful. And the Triune God will, in all his holy Being, "rejoice over thee with joy". He will rejoice over us "as a bridegroom rejoiceth over the bride". Imagine that!

No Tears
In that great and glorious new creation, God will wipe all tears from the eyes of his people forever! Listen to the apostle John. "And God shall wipe away all tears from their eyes; and there shall be no more death, neither sorrow, nor crying, neither shall there be any more pain: for the former things are passed away." There will be no tears in heaven to mar God's new creation. No tears over past sins. No tears over failures, losses, bad experiences, or even lost loved ones. Why not? Because "God himself" will be with us; and Christ will be our husband and our joy forever. Who can grasp the fulness of this promise? It is too great, too broad, too incomprehensible for our mortal brains. Yet, it is gloriously true! Our great God shall, in heaven's glory, remove us from all sin, remove all sin from us, and remove us from all the evil consequences of sin. He will remove us from every cause of grief. He will bring us at last into the perfection of complete salvation. Every desire of our hearts will be completely gratified. God's salvation is so perfect and complete that when he is finished, we will not even have the slightest tinge of sorrow for anything! He who is God our Saviour has promised it; and he will do it. "Behold, I make all things new."

Amen.